T0122405

Security and Privacy in Biometrics

Patrizio Campisi

Editor

Security
and Privacy
in Biometrics

 Springer

Editor
Patrizio Campisi
Section of Applied Electronics
Department of Engineering
University of Roma Tre
Rome, Italy

ISBN 978-1-4471-6201-8   ISBN 978-1-4471-5230-9 (eBook)
DOI 10.1007/978-1-4471-5230-9
Springer London Heidelberg New York Dordrecht

Printed on acid-free paper

Springer is part of Springer Science+Business Media (www.springer.com)

Preface

In the last decade biometrics has emerged as a valuable means to automatically recognize people, on the base is of their either physiological or behavioral characteristics, due to several inherent advantages they offer over conventional methods. In fact biometrics-based recognition relies on who a person is or what a person does in contrast with traditional authentication approaches, based on what a person knows, e.g. a password, or what a person has, e.g., ID card, token, etc. Therefore, biometrics-based recognition systems, being based on personal traits, either biological or behavioral, it is much harder for biometric data to be lost, forgotten, stolen, copied or forged than traditional identifiers. The recent technological developments have made possible the deployment of biometrics-based systems deploying mature biometrics, like face, iris, and fingerprints, in a wide range of applications ranging from criminal investigation to civilian registration, border control, national identity document verification, e-commerce, e-banking, on-line payment, physical and logical access control.

In the design of a biometrics-based authentication system, different issues, strictly related to the specific application under analysis, must be taken into account. As established in literature, from an ideal point of view, biometrics should be universal, unique, permanent, collectable, and acceptable. Moreover, besides the choice of the biometrics to employ, many other issues must be considered in the design stage. Specifically, the system accuracy, the computational speed and cost are also important design parameter, especially for those systems intended for large populations.

Biometrics-based people recognition poses new challenges related to personal data protection, not raised by traditional recognition methods. If biometric data are captured or stolen by an attacker, they may be replicated and misused. Users' biometrics cannot be changed if compromised, different from a PIN or a password which can be reissued if needed. Moreover, the use of biometrics poses additional privacy concerns since biometric data may reveal sensitive information about a person's personality and health, which can be stored, processed, and distributed without the users' authorization. This information can be used to discriminate against people for instance by denying insurance to people with latent health problems. Moreover the uniqueness of biometrics across individuals allows cross-matching to biometric databases thus performing unauthorized tracking of the subjects' activities. Also, in a scenario where either governmental agencies or private companies can collect huge databases of citizens' biometrics, some risks for the person's privacy and human dignity could be foreseen. In fact, in the aforementioned scenario, *function creep*, that is a situation where the data, collected for some specific purposes, are used for different ones, is likely to happen in the long run. All this would lead to users' privacy loss.

Therefore the need to protect both privacy and security from a procedural, legal, and a technological point of view arises. This book examines the up to date solutions for protecting both security and privacy in a holistic way tackling also ethical, legal, and procedural aspects. Specifically, this book deals with both theoretical and practical implementations of secure and privacy compliant solutions to the problem of automatic people recognition. It focuses on new approaches and new architectures for unimodal and multimodal template protection, signal processing techniques in the encrypted domain, security and privacy leakage assessment, and standardization aspects. Some practical applications of secure and privacy compliant systems are also presented with specific focus on biometrics-based electronic documents, face and fingerprint based automatic user recognition, and biometric systems employing smart cards for enhancing security and privacy. Moreover, the ethical implications of a spread use of biometrics in everyday life and its effect on human dignity are addressed. Best practices for the processing of biometric data are indicated and a legal framework is eventually given.

The book is organized as follows. In Chap. 1 a general introduction to both the privacy and security issues affecting biometric systems are given along with some state of the art mitigation approaches. Chapter 2 introduces the main security requirements for the biometric processing pipeline and summarizes general design principles and approaches. General security principles in information technology and selected paradigms such as template protection by biometric hashing and biometric cryptosystems are reviewed. Moreover a brief introduction on the design principles of biometric matching algorithms operating in the encrypted domain is given. In Chap. 3 the limitations of public key infrastructure (PKI) for key management are pointed out and a novel paradigm making use of biometrics for mitigating the PKI related trust problems at both the user and certificate authority level is proposed. An innovative infrastructure, namely biocryptographic key infrastructure (BKI), able to guarantee a high level of privacy while establishing trust, is thus proposed. Chapter 4 deals with the issue of biometric template protection and a categorization of the state of the art approaches is given. A theoretical analysis is provided and practical implementations for real world biometrics are discussed. In Chap. 5, privacy and secrecy aspects of biometric key-binding systems are analyzed within an information theoretic framework. Specifically, the fundamental trade-off between secret-key rate and privacy-leakage rate is determined for independent and identically distributed Gaussian biometric sources. The effect of code selection and binary quantization in the fuzzy commitment cryptographic protocol is also reported. In Chap. 6 the issue of template protection for multi-biometric systems is addressed. Specifically, a multi-biometric cryptosystem based on the fuzzy commitment scheme, in which a crypto-biometric key is derived from multi-biometric data is presented. The scheme, in principle applicable to different modalities, is detailed for a multi-unit system based on the use of two-irises and for a multi-modal system using a combination of iris and face. It is shown that in addition to generation of strong keys, the proposed systems address the issues of revocability, template diversity, and protection of user's privacy. In Chap. 7 some approaches to process the biometric data in encrypted form stemming from the "Secure Two Party Computation" theory are described. Specifically, homomorphic encryption and garbled circuits are discussed and the ways such techniques can be used to develop a full biometric matching protocol are detailed. The significant advantage of the illustrated techniques is that any risk that private biometric information is leaked during an identification process is eliminated whereas they surely require a better efficiency to be deployed in real life applications. Chapter 8 deals with a practical application of template protection techniques to recognition systems relying on fingerprints. Specifically, practical challenges related to the use of fingerprints, like the need of registration without any information leakage about the deployed features, and the extraction of highly characterizing yet stable features are addressed. An analysis of how the design choices affect the trade-off between the security and matching accuracy is also provided. In Chap. 9 biometric cryptosystems are used as a Privacy-Enhancing Technology in a face biometrics-based watch list scenario that has been successfully employed in the Ontario Lottery and Gaming Corporation's self-exclusion program. The proposed architecture treats the biometric cryptosystem module as an important component in a multi-layered approach to privacy and security of the overall system. Chapter 10 shows how smart card technology can be beneficial to biometric systems. Special emphasis is given to the security mechanisms included in most smart cards and how these mechanisms can be employed to protect biometric data and processes. Different architectures for the integration of biometrics and smart cards are presented and two major deployments making joint use of smart cards and biometrics, specifically the ePassports and the Electronic Spanish National ID Card, are described. In Chap. 11, two secure and privacy compliant systems, one devoted to local access control and the other one to remote identification, to be deployed in real life applications are described. A synergic use of biometric cryptosystems, match on card, and advanced cryptographic protocols is made in order to guarantee security, performance, and accuracy. Chapter 12 discusses biometric data protection from the standardization perspective. It covers technical standards developed at ISO (e.g., SC27, SC37, and TC68) and at other standards development organizations as well as technical reports developed by these groups. In addition to those that address the confidentiality and integrity of biometric/identity data directly, other standards covering security of biometric systems in general are discussed. Chapter 13 considers the impact on and ethical implications for society of widening biometric applications to daily life. Moreover it explores the contradictions between the claims that biometrics will boost security and prevent identity theft, and the growing evidence of increased, with introduction of more biometric documents, e-crime that threatens personal identity and security, and collective security in the cyber space and in the personal life. Chapter 14 discusses best practices which can be put in place for the processing of biometric data, taking privacy and data protection into account, particularly for the private sector. More specifically, it is pointed out that the revocability, irreversibility, and unlinkability of biometric identities, obtained by specific methods and technologies, are essential for the use of biometric data in the private sector from a privacy and data protection point of view. In Chap. 15 a comprehensive analysis of the legal principles governing personal data are given and the European data protection framework for biometrics is detailed. A deep understanding of the privacy and data protection challenges brought by the use of biometric data is gained. The impact of the choices like the use of different system architectures, voluntary or compulsory enrolment, raw data or templates, and the use of different kinds of biometrics is analyzed in a holistic way from the legal perspective and eventually some recommendations are given. In Chap. 16, based on two cases of biometric application, which have been assessed by the Danish Data Protecting Agency, a set of recommendations is presented to legislators, regulators, corporations, and individuals on the appropriate use of biometric technologies put forward by the Danish Board of Technology. The recommendations are discussed and compared to the similar proposal put forward by the European Article 29 Data Protection Working Party.

June 2013   Patrizio Campisi

Contents

Chapter 1
Security and Privacy in Biometrics: Towards a Holistic Approach

Patrizio Campisi

Abstract Security and privacy in biometric systems have been traditionally seen as two requirements hindering each other. Only in the recent past researchers have started investigating it as a joint optimization problem which needs to be tackled from both a legal, procedural, and a technological point of view. Therefore in this chapter we take a holistic approach and we introduce some basics about the privacy and the security issues which can affect a biometric system and some possible mitigation approaches, both procedural and technological, that can help in designing secure and privacy compliant biometric based recognition systems.

1.1 Foreword

In the last few years biometric technologies have been employed for automatic people recognition at an increasing rate due to several inherent advantages they offer over conventional methods. In fact biometrics-based recognition systems rely on who a person is or what a person does, in contrast with traditional authentication approaches, based on what a person knows (password) or what a person has (e.g., ID card, token). Being based on personal, either physiological or behavioral traits, it is much harder for biometric data to be lost, forgotten, stolen, copied or forged than traditional identifiers. Loosely speaking, biometric systems are essentially pattern-recognition-based systems, performing verification or identification using features derived from either physiological biometric data like fingerprint, face, iris, retina, hand geometry, thermogram, vein patterns, ear shape, body odor, or behavioral traits like voice, signature, handwriting, key stroke, gait, to cite a few.

In the design of a biometrics-based recognition system, different issues, strictly related to the specific application under analysis, must be taken into account. As well established in literature, from an ideal point of view, the employed biometrics should be universal, unique, permanent, collectable, robust to attacks, and acceptable. Moreover, besides the choice of the biometrics to employ, other issues must

P. Campisi (✉)
Section of Applied Electronics, Department of Engineering, University of Roma Tre, Via Vito Volterra 62, 00146 Rome, Italy
e-mail: patrizio.campisi@uniroma3.it

P. Campisi (ed.), *Security and Privacy in Biometrics*,
DOI 10.1007/978-1-4471-5230-9_1, © Springer-Verlag London 2013

be considered in the design stage. Specifically, the system accuracy, the computational speed, the cost of the systems and its maintenance are also important design parameters, especially for those systems intended for large populations.

Besides all the aforementioned requirements, the use of biometric data raises many security issues which are peculiar of biometrics-based recognition systems not affecting other approaches employed for automatic people recognition. In fact, some biometrics such as voice, face, fingerprints, and many others are exposed traits, they are not secret and therefore they can be covertly acquired or stolen by an attacker and misused. This can lead for example to identity theft. Moreover, raw biometrics cannot be revoked, canceled, or reissued if compromised, since they are user's intrinsic characteristics and they are in limited number. Therefore, if a biometrics is compromised, all the applications making use of that biometrics are compromised, and since biometric identifiers are permanent an issue is raised when it is needed to change them. The use of biometrics poses also many privacy concerns, in fact, when an individual gives out his biometrics, either willingly or unwillingly, he discloses unique information about himself. It has also been demonstrated that biometric data can contain relevant information regarding people health. This information can be used, for example, to discriminate people for hiring or to deny insurance to those with latent health problems. The use of biometrics can also raise cultural, religious as well as ethnicity related concerns. To some extent, the loss of anonymity can be directly perceived by users as a loss of autonomy.

Therefore the need to protect both privacy and security from both a legal, procedural, and a technological point of view arises.

In the following we provide some basic notions about the privacy and security issues which can affect a biometric system and the possible mitigation approaches that can help in designing secure and privacy compliant biometrics-based recognition systems. Specifically the privacy and security issues affecting a biometric system are introduced in Sects. 1.2 and 1.3 respectively, whereas the relationship between privacy and security within the biometric scenario is briefly addressed in Sect. 1.4. An historical perspective of the privacy enhancing technologies is given in Sect. 1.5. The major international projects related to privacy and security are briefly sketched in Sect. 1.6. Eventually, some possible research directions are highlighted in Sect. 1.7.

1.2 Privacy in Biometric Systems

In this Section the different connotations of the term "privacy" are illustrated as long as with some basic principles and procedures that can provide directions towards the development of privacy compliant applications. Moreover the specific privacy risks related to the use of biometric data are illustrated.

Fig. 1.1 Privacy
connotations

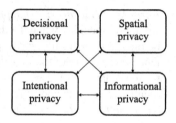

1.2.1 Privacy Conceptualization

The word privacy is a general term which encompasses both different areas of study
and real life situations. It is commonly accepted [1, 2] that the general term privacy
can assume slightly different connotations as depicted in Fig. 1.1 and specified in
the following. In detail, we talk about:

- *decisional privacy* when we refer to the right of the individual to make decisions
  regarding his life without any undue interference;
- *spatial privacy* when we refer to the right of the individual to have his own personal physical spaces which cannot be violated without his explicit consent;
- *intentional privacy* when we refer to the right of the individual to forbid/prevent
  further communication of observable events (e.g., conversations held in public)
  or exposed features (e.g., publishing photos);
- *informational privacy* when we refer to the right of the individual to limit access
  to personal information which represents any information that could be used in
  any way to identify an individual. It is worth pointing out that some data which
  do not appear to be personal information could be used in the future to identify
  an individual.

Of course there are no clear boundaries among the given connotations as sketched
in Fig. 1.1. According to the application, a particular privacy conceptualization may
be chosen as prevalent, the other aspects still being worth of consideration in the privacy assessment. However, because of the dramatic advances of information technology in the last decades, informational privacy has gained a predominant role
within the considered scenario.

1.2.2 Fair Information Practices

In 1980, a formalization of the guidelines governing the protection of privacy and
transnational flow of personal data, which represents a milestone for privacy, was introduced by the Organisation for Economic Co-operation and Development (OECD)
in [3]. The OECD privacy guideline relies on a set of eight principles, often referred
to as Fair Information Practices, namely:

- *Purpose specification principle*: the purpose for which the data are collected should be specified when the data are collected. Moreover, the data usage should be limited to the fulfillment of the specified purposes and should not be changed.
- *Openness principle*: the objectives of research, the main purposes of the use of personal data and the policies and practices related to their protection, and the identity of the data controller should be open to the public.
- *Collection limitation principle*: the collection of personal data should be obtained by lawful and fair means and, whenever applicable, with the knowledge and consent of the individual.
- *Data quality principle*: personal data should be relevant, accurate, complete, and up to date for the intended purposes.
- *Accountability principle*: a data controller should be accountable for complying with measures which give effect to the stated principles.
- *Use limitation principle*: personal data should be not be made available for other purposes than the ones agreed with the individual in the Purpose Specification Principle except with the consent of the data subject or by the authority of the law.
- *Individual participation principle*: the individual should have the right to:
  - know from the data controller if some data regarding him are stored;
  - to have communicated to him, if there are data relating to him, within a reasonable time, at a charge, if any, that is not excessive, in a reasonable manner, and in a form that it is intelligible to him;
  - to be given reasons if a request made under this principle is denied, and to be able to challenge such denial;
  - to challenge data relating to him and, if the challenge is successful to have the data erased, rectified, completed or amended.
- *Security safeguards principle*: personal data should be protected against security risks like unauthorized disclosure, use, modification, destruction, and loss.

These are the basic principles which need to be translated into procedures and legislation to prevent violations of privacy.

1.2.3 Privacy Compliance Lifecycle

A privacy compliance lifecycle [4] is aimed at integrating privacy protection into systems which collect, process, or produce personal information. It has to be performed at the earliest stages of the system design in order to embed into the system the answers to the privacy concerns which have been identified and to limit the potential costs resulting from negligent information management. It is worth pointing out that the privacy compliance assessment must be continuously carried out throughout the life of the system.

An example of privacy compliance assessment procedure is sketched in Fig. 1.2 and it comprises the following steps:

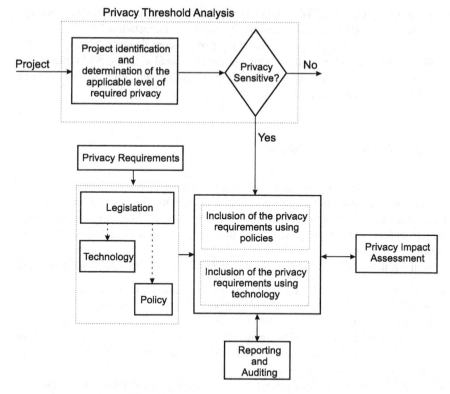

Fig. 1.2 Privacy compliance lifecycle: an example

- Project identification and determination of the applicable level of required privacy. This analysis aims at identifying privacy sensitive applications and for the identified projects further steps, described in the following, need to be performed.
- Inclusion of the privacy requirements in the design and development of the system. In this step, legislation, procedural approaches, and technology concur together in order to embed the identified privacy requirements into the system design.
- The privacy impact assessment is a bidirectional process which is intended to identify and overcome both procedural and technological issues arisen from the inclusion of privacy requirements in the system using both procedural and technological means. In fact the privacy assessment should verify that the system purposes declared by the authority in control of the system are complaint with the actual system. Moreover, the data must be used appropriately, that is, their use should allow achieving the stated purpose of the data collection, and not more. If there is a shift between the declared use and the actual use of the system, a privacy risk is occurring. The privacy assessment should also include an analysis of the control a user has on the way his data are used, if the data are used for the original purpose they were intended for, and if not, if there is an informed user's

agreement. The individual should have the authority to get access to his data and to check if the data are used according to the user's expectations.

- Production of reports on the status of the privacy compliance analysis to be deployment to the proper entities which might include also public deployment.
- Audit procedures to be periodically run to reveal any unauthorized use of both the data and the system.

1.2.4 Privacy vs. Biometrics

Privacy compliance analysis of an automatic biometrics-based recognition system is a key issue both during the system design process and for its deployment in real life applications. Within this respect, both the perception by the user of the potential threats and the real risks to privacy have to be carefully considered when designing a biometric system.

In the following, the main concerns related to the use of biometrics are described.

- Biometrics can be collected or shared without specific user's permission, adequate knowledge, or without specific purpose.
- Biometrics, which has been collected for some specific purposes, can be later used for another unintended or unauthorized purpose. This is known as "function creep", and it can have dramatic consequence since it leads to the loss of the public trust in a given system.
- Biometrics can be used for purposes other than the officially declared purpose or biometrics can be misused to generate extra information.
- Biometrics can be copied or removed from the user and used for secondary purposes.
- Biometrics use can violate the "principle of proportionality" [5], which states that biometric data may only be used if adequate, relevant and not excessive with respect to the system's goal. If this principle is violated, the users may feel that the benefit coming from revealing their biometrics is much less than what they get in exchange.
- Biometrics can be used to reveal gender and ethnicity. Moreover, details on the medical history of the individual can be elicited. Medical conditions can be deduced by comparing biometrics acquired at the time of the enrollment and biometrics acquired later for recognition. Moreover, biometrics can give directly information on health conditions [6]. As a consequence, biometrics can be used to profile people according to their health status.
- Biometrics can be used to pinpoint or track individuals. Since biometric data are considered unique, they have the potential to locate and track people physically as they try to access some facilities or their biometric traits are recorded by some surveillance system. Also associating people's biometrics to their identifiers, such as name, address, passport number, can represent a risk, being then possible to access, gather, and compare a wide range of information starting from a single biometric trait. Moreover the use of biometrics as a universal identifier can allow

user tracking across different databases. All this can lead to covert surveillance, profiling, and social control.

- Biometric use can be associated by the individual to forensic purposes. Therefore the use of biometric traits, such as fingerprints, which are associated, for historical reasons, to criminal investigations and forensic activities, can have a low acceptability rate.
- Biometrics can be improperly stored and/or transmitted. This would expose biometrics to external attacks. Moreover biometrics may also be exposed to administrator or operator abuses, since they could misuse their privileges for accessing a biometric database.

It is worth pointing out that the evaluation of the "real" risk of privacy invasiveness must be performed considering both the final application and the employed biometric trait. For example biometric overt applications are less privacy-invasive than covert ones. Mandatory biometrics-based recognition systems bear more privacy risks than optional ones. Privacy is considered to be more at risk when physiological data are used since they are more stable in time and allow a higher accuracy than behavioral biometrics. If the biometrics-based recognition system is used in the verification mode, less privacy concerns are implied than those involved in a system operating in the identification mode. This is due to the fact that in the identification mode, one-to-many comparisons have to be performed through a database search. This action introduces more privacy threats than the ones introduced when one-to-one comparison is performed as in the verification mode. The privacy risks increase when the biometric data are stored for an unlimited amount of time. In fact, if the system deployment is indefinite in time, threats such as function creep may arise. If the database is violated, biometric traits related to several users are compromised. Biometric systems where identifiable biometrics, such as faces, voice patterns, and so on, are retained are more prone to privacy risks than those which store templates. Moreover, if the biometric data are stored in a centralized database, serious privacy concerns arise since data are stored out of user's control, whereas if the user can maintain the ownership of the biometric data, less privacy risks can occur since the user can control the collection, usage, etc. of biometric information. The use of biometrics can have secondary purposes when both either governmental institutions or private companies are involved. In different societies, one or the other can be perceived more threatening to privacy. Also the role of the individual in the biometric system, employee, citizen or customer, impacts on the privacy assessment.

1.3 Biometric System Security

Although the definition of the notion of security for a biometric based system is a very challenging task, a significant effort has been done by the scientific community to highlight the main security concerns related to a biometrics-based recognition system (see for example [7–11]).

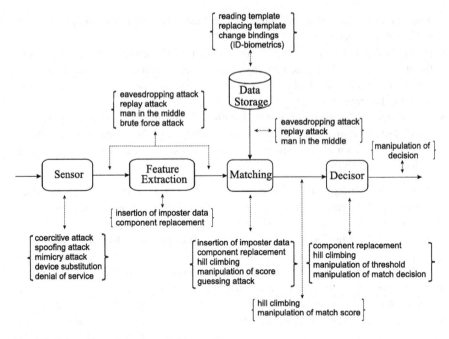

Fig. 1.3 Points of attack in a generic biometric system

Roughly speaking a biometric system can be vulnerable either because of intrinsic failure or because of intentional attacks.

A system characterized by a high False Acceptance Rate is very prone to be violated since it is likely that an arbitrary biometric feature presented to the system will match. This can happen also if there is no adversary willing to attack the system, case usually referred to as *zero-effort attack*.

In Fig. 1.3 a biometric system is sketched as the cascade of the acquisition sensor, the feature extractor module, the module that performs matching between the output of the feature extractor and the templates stored in the database, and finally the decisor that drives the application device. As discussed in [8–12] and also illustrated in Fig. 1.3 the major potential intentional attacks that can be perpetrated against the different blocks of a biometric system can be summarized as follows:

- *Sensor*

    - *coercive attack*: the true biometric is presented but in some unauthorized manner, e.g. when an impostor forces a legitimate user to grant him access to the system;
    - *spoofing attack* and *mimicry attack* related to physiological and behavioral biometrics respectively. These attacks consist in copying, by means of different strategies, the biometric feature of the enrolled user, and to transfer it to an impostor in order to fool the system;

- *device substitution*: substitution of a legitimate biometric capture device with a simulated, modified or replacement unit;
- *denial of service*: massive attacks on the system cause the system failure.

- *Feature extractor* that could be forced by an attacker to produce pre-selected features by inserting impostor data or component replacement.
- *Matcher* that can be attacked to produce fake scores. This task can be achieved in different ways:

  - *manipulation of the match scores*: capturing and changing the value of a match score before it affects the decision;
  - *reply attack*: a recorded version of the true data is injected in the channel;
  - *component replacement*: substitution of one of the software/hardware components in order to control its behavior:
  - *hill climbing attack*: iterative attack [13] that can be performed when access is granted to the match scores. Specifically, given an input, a slight modification of the input is performed. If the match score is increased the modification is kept, otherwise the modification is discarded. The procedure is iterated until the matching score is greater than the threshold.

- *Channels* interconnecting the different parts of a biometric system, like the channel between the sensor and the feature extractor, between the feature extractor and the matcher, between the database and the matcher, and between the matcher and the application device, can be intercepted and controlled by unauthorized people. Among the possible attacks we can mention the:

  - *eavesdropping attack*: the act of surreptitiously listening to biometric data transmission;
  - *man in the middle attack*: an attacker is able to manipulate the messages exchanged between two parties without the parties knowing that the link has been compromised;
  - *brute force attack*: exhaustive presentation of a large set of biometrics inputs to the recognition system to find one that works;
  - *replay attack*;
  - *hill climbing attack*;
  - *manipulation of match score*;
  - *manipulation of the decision*: capturing and changing the value of the decision.

- *Database*: reading templates, modification of one or more records in the database, replacing templates, changing links between ID and biometrics, are very threatening attacks.

It is also worth pointing out that automatic biometrics-based recognition systems are also prone to enrollment threats related to identity proofing, since forged ID cards could be used in the enrollment stage. This could lead to having a valid enrolled biometric but bound to a false identity. On the other hand a valid identity could be bound to fake biometrics.

Different kind of attacks or vulnerabilities require different kind of countermeasures. For example liveness detection techniques could be used as countermeasure

Table 1.1 Most feasible system architectures for a biometrics-based recognition system

Storing \ Matching	Server	Client	Device	Token
Server	YES	–	–	YES
Client	–	YES	–	–
Device	–	–	YES	YES
Token	–	–	–	YES

against spoofing, the hill climbing can be counteracted using encrypted channels or matching scores coarsely quantized, eavesdropping using secure channels, and so forth.

Furthermore some threats may be eliminated by the actual implementation of the system. In fact, different security requirements need to be considered according to the location where storage and matching are performed. Specifically, in [12] the different threats of the general architecture of a biometrics-based recognition system shown in Fig. 1.3 are particularized to the most feasible system architectures summarized in Table 1.1. Each of these architectures presents its own pros and cons. For example the one based on the template storage on a physical token has the advantage not to have any central storage to protect. On the contrary the architecture where the storage is made on the server poses many security and privacy concerns for the central database storage, although the use of centralized storage allows simplified administration.

The use of multibiometric systems [14] can be also foreseen to increase the level of security of biometrics-based recognition systems. In fact the increase of the number of credentials required for proper recognition can deter the spoofing attack, improving the matching accuracy and increasing the population coverage. On the other end multibiometric systems also increase the cost and the complexity of the system.

1.4 Privacy and Security

Within the biometric framework, the term "security" refers to making the data available for authorized users and protected from non-authorized users, whereas the term "privacy" is used to limit the use of shared biometrics only to those individuals who need to know the data and to limit it to the original purposes for which the data have been collected in the first place in agreement with the OECD purpose specification, use limitation, and collection limitation principles. Moreover, within the security framework the ultimate control over the data is made by the system owner/administrator, whereas within the biometric framework, the ultimate control over the data is made by the individual in agreement with the OECD Individual participation principle. Therefore privacy means something more than keeping biometric data secret. Most biometric characteristics like face images, voice, iris images, fingerprints, gait, to cite a few, are exposed and therefore not secret, and technology is available to covertly capture with different degrees of difficulty. As stated in [15], privacy and security have been treated in the recent past as requirements hindering each other, which imply that when more emphasis is given to security, less emphasis will be given to privacy. Moreover, since in general the public concern for security is very high, privacy has been often penalized. However, in the recent past an always increasing level of attention towards the problems of privacy protection has lead to the development of techniques that allow both to enhance security and minimize privacy invasiveness.

1.5 Privacy Enhancing Technologies: An Historical Perspective

The unauthorized access to biometric templates is among the most dangerous threats to users' privacy and security [16]. In fact, although it was commonly believed that it is not possible to reconstruct the original biometric characteristics from the corresponding extracted template, some concrete counter examples, which contradict this assumption, have been provided in the recent literature as in [13] where it is shown that the knowledge of the face biometric template and of the match score can lead to face reconstruction and in [17] where an efficient algorithm has been proposed to generate a fingerprint from its matching minutiae points.

Therefore, storing biometric templates would not be secure enough and in case the template is compromised it is highly desirable to revoke or to renew it, and also to obtain from the same biometrics different keys to access different locations, either physical or logical, in order to avoid unauthorized tracking.

To summarize, a template protection scheme should satisfy the following properties [10]:

- *Renewability*: it should be possible to revoke a compromised template and reissue a new one based on the same biometric data.
- *Diversity*: each template generated from a biometrics should not match with the others previously generated from the same data. This property is needed to ensure the user's privacy.
- *Security*: it must be impossible or computationally hard to obtain the original biometric template from the stored and secured one. This property is needed to prevent an adversary from creating fake biometric traits from stolen templates.
- *Performance*: the biometric recognition error rates in terms of False Rejection Rate or False Acceptance Rate should not degrade significantly with the introduction of a template protection scheme, with respect to an unprotected approach.

The design of a template protection scheme able to properly satisfy each of the aforementioned properties is not a trivial task, mainly due to the unavoidable intra-user variability shown by every biometric trait. In the recent years, many different solutions have already been proposed for the generation of secure and renewable templates. A variety of possible classifications for template protection algorithms have been proposed so far and some attempts to harmonize the vocabulary have already been done [18] although a common vocabulary has not been established yet

Fig. 1.4 Scheme of principle of a transform-based approach

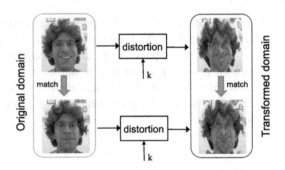

in the scientific community. In the following, among the possible classifications of template protection algorithms, we will refer to two categories [10], namely *biometric cryptosystems* and *feature transformation* approaches.

1.5.1 Features Transformations for Template Protection

In a feature transformation approach, a function dependent on some parameters, which can be used as key, is applied either in the original biometric domain or in the feature domain to generate either transformed biometrics or transformed feature vectors. The matching is then performed in the transformed domain (see Fig. 1.4 for a simple schematization). The employed function can be either *invertible*, resulting in a *salting* approach, whose security is based on the protection of the function parameters, or *non-invertible*, when a one-way function is applied to the template and it is computationally hard to invert the function even if the transformation parameters are known. The use of the methods belonging to the first category typically results in low false acceptance rates, but if a user-specific key is compromised, the user template is no longer secure due to the invertibility of the transformation. On the contrary, when non-invertible transforms are used, even if the key is known by an adversary, no significant information can be acquired on the template, thus obtaining better security than the one achievable when using a salting approach. Specifically, the security of the non-invertible transform-based schemes relies on the difficulty of *inverting* the transformation to obtain the original biometric data. Moreover, differently from the cryptosystem approaches, the transformed templates can remain in the same feature space of the original ones, being then possible to employ standard matchers to perform recognition in the transformed domain. This allows achieving performances similar to those of an unprotected approach. In addition to the benefits on the performance deriving from using standard matchers in the transformed domain, transformation-based approaches typically result in matchings scores which can be fused in multi-biometric approaches. Therefore, the use of transform based approaches for template protection in multi-biometrics systems allows using either score level fusion techniques or decision level fusion techniques [14], whereas only the latter, less effective than the former, can be employed when biometric cryptosystems are considered.

The transformation function should be designed in order to keep the intra-class and inter-class distances in the transformed domain similar to the corresponding ones in the original domain in such a way to preserve the features discriminability. Moreover the transformation should be non-invertible. Unfortunately, it is difficult to design transformation functions which preserve both the template discriminability and the non-invertibility properties simultaneously. Furthermore, a rigorous security analysis concerning the non-invertibility of the scheme is very difficult especially when the transformation algorithm and related keys/parameters are also compromised. Therefore, extra care should be taken when designing and analyzing this type of schemes.

The concept of achieving template security through the application of non-invertible transformations has been first presented in [8], where it has been referred to as *cancelable biometrics* although this expression has been later used in a more general sense. Since then many approaches have been proposed with application to different biometric modalities. Without any claim of completeness, some examples follow. In [19] cancelable face biometrics are obtained by convolving the face image with a two-dimensional array of random numbers, generated via a password, and a cancelable correlation filter is designed from such "randomized" biometric signature. In [20] a geometric transform has been employed to protect minutiae templates but obtaining a significant performance degradation. More general geometric transforms, specifically, Cartesian, polar, and functional, have been later studied in [21], where better recognition performances have been achieved, but with a very limited amount of non-invertible data in practice. Moreover, the approaches presented in [20] and [21] are vulnerable to a record multiplicity attack: having access to two or more different transformed versions of the same minutiae pattern, it is possible to identify the original position of the considered minutiae [22]. A registration free construction of cancelable fingerprint templates has also been proposed in [23]. From each detected minutia, a square patch is extracted and transformed using an orthogonal transformation matrix. The approach presented in [23] is more robust than the one proposed in [21], being able to withstand also a record multiplicity attack, but it exhibits lower verification performances than the one obtained in [21]. A voice based cancelable template method has been proposed in [24], where a non invertible transformed version of the originally acquired voiceprint is generated. The original biometrics cannot be obtained from the template stored in the server during enrollment, even if the keys employed for transformations are disclosed. In [25, 26], a set of non-invertible transformations, based on the convolution operator, has been introduced in order to generate multiple transformed versions of a template. The framework in [25, 26], applicable in principle to any biometrics whose template can be represented by a set of sequences, has been there applied as proof of concept to an on-line signature recognition system, where a Hidden Markov Model based matching strategy is employed.

It is worth pointing out that, when using templates distortions techniques, with either invertible or non-invertible transforms, only the distorted data are stored in the database. This implies that even if the database is compromised, in principle, that is if the keys are unaccessible and the transformation perfectly non invertible, the biometric data cannot be retrieved. Moreover, different templates can be generated from the original data, simply by changing the parameters of the employed transforms.

1.5.2 Biometric Cryptosystems for Template Protection

Biometric cryptosystems provide the means to adapt cryptographic protocols to biometric data which are inherently noisy data. They can be classified into *key generation* schemes, where binary keys are directly created from the acquired biometrics, and *key binding* schemes, which store information obtained by combining biometric data with randomly generated keys.

The main issue affecting key generation approaches regards the possibility of creating multiple keys from the same biometrics without using any external data, and the stability of the resulting cryptographic key. Moreover, due to the difficulties in managing the intra-class variability of biometric data, the recognition performance of such schemes are typically significantly lower than those of their unprotected counterparts [27].

A key binding system can be twofold: it can be used to protect a biometric template by means of a binary key, thus securing a biometric recognition system, or to release a cryptographic key only when its owner presents a specific biometric trait. In both cases a secret key, independent of the considered biometrics, is combined during enrollment with a reference template to generate some publicly available data, the so-called *helper data*, from which it should be impossible, or at least computationally hard, to retrieve information about the original biometric trait or the key. The helper data is then used in conjunction with a query biometrics during recognition to retrieve the secret. Typically, these approaches are able to manage the intra-user variations in biometric data by exploiting the capabilities of error correcting codes. However, it is generally not possible to use sophisticated and dedicated matchers, thus reducing the system matching accuracy.

In a key generation scenario the major design problem is related to the variability of the biometric traits. Therefore many efforts have been devoted to obtain robust keys from noisy biometric data. In [28] and in [29] cryptographic keys have been generated from voice and faces respectively. Significant activity has been devoted to the generation of keys from signature. As proposed in [30] and further detailed in [31] a set of parametric features has been extracted from each dynamic signature and an interval matrix has been used to store the upper and lower admitted thresholds for correct recognition. A similar approach has been proposed in [32]. Both methods provide protection for the signature templates. However, the variability of each feature has to be made explicitly available, and both methods do not provide template renewability. In [33] biometric secrecy preservation and renewability have been obtained by applying random tokens, together with multiple-bit discretization and permutation, to the function features extracted from the signatures. In [34] biometric keys have been generated using a genetic selection algorithm and applied to on–line dynamic signature. In [35] a technique to increase the level of entropy offered by a generic biometric modality has been presented. In [36] key generation for iris biometrics has been investigated by selecting the most reliable feature of each subject.

In a key binding scenario, among the cryptographic protocols most commonly employed, we can mention the fuzzy commitment [37] where a secret key is chosen by the user, encoded, and the result is XORed with the biometric template to ensure the security and privacy of the template. More in detail the approach proposed in [37] stems from the one described in [38], where the role of error correction codes used within the framework of secure biometric recognition is investigated and provides better resilience to noisy biometrics. In order to cope with set of unordered data in [39] the fuzzy vault protocol based on polynomial-based secret sharing has been introduced. Both the fuzzy commitment and the fuzzy vault have been widely used for biometric systems relying on different identifiers. The fuzzy commitment scheme has been applied to ear biometrics [40], fingerprint [41, 42], 2D face [43], 3D face [44], iris [45, 46], and online signatures [47, 48] among the others. The fuzzy vault scheme has been applied to fingerprint [49–51], signature [52], face [53], iris [54], and palmprint [55], to cite just a few.

In [56] two primitives, namely the *fuzzy extractor* and the *secure sketch*, have been introduced. The first extracts a uniformly random string from an input in a error tolerant way, that is, in such a way that even if the actual input differs from the original one, still remaining close, the string can be exactly recovered. The second allows an exact reconstruction of the input by using some public information extracted from it, namely the *sketch*, which does not reveal significant information about the input itself, and a noisy replica of the input close enough to the original one. Constructions and rigorous analysis have been given for three metrics: Hamming distance, set difference, and edit distance. In [57] the practical issues related to the design of a secure sketch system have been analyzed with specific application to face biometrics. In [58] fuzzy extractors have been employed in a setting where data obtained in enrollment and verification are stored in different representations. A proof of concept has been given with application to fingerprints. In [59] fuzzy extractors for continuous source data have been considered and in [60] fuzzy extractors for continuous domain with application to faces have been proposed.

In the recent years many efforts have been devoted to the analysis of the applicability of biometric cryptosystems in real life applications with respect to the level of security and privacy that can be actually achieved. Specifically in [61] the secrecy and privacy leakage properties in fuzzy commitment schemes have been investigated. In [62] an empirical analysis on the security and privacy of the fuzzy commitment scheme with application to an existing system for 3D face recognition has been given. In [63] the cross-matching attack within the framework of the fuzzy commitment scheme has been theoretically analyzed, the analysis has been applied to real world datasets, and some possible countermeasures have been proposed. In [64] the security of the fuzzy commitment has been analyzed from a practical point of view with application to iris biometrics. Also the vulnerabilities of the fuzzy vault have been investigated. Specifically in [65] some criteria to distinguish chaff points of a fuzzy vault scheme from minutiae in a fingerprint based recognition system have been given and experimentally validated. Moreover, it has been proven that the fuzzy vault is vulnerable to the cross-matching attack [66]: if an adversary has access to two different vaults obtained from the same data, he can easily identify the genuine points in the two vaults. A practical implementation of the cross-matching attack for the fuzzy vault scheme for fingerprints has been presented in [67].

In [68] it has been shown that some implementations of the fuzzy extractor and of the fuzzy sketch are not adequate when the same secret is employed for multiple uses and some models and conditions that allow reusable secrets are given. Some improved solutions are presented in [69]. In [70] it has been demonstrated that fuzzy sketches always leak some information about their inputs and in [71] the analysis of weather an attacker can determine whether two documents are encrypted using the same biometrics is addressed. In [72] a theoretical framework for the analysis of privacy and security trade-offs in secure biometric recognition systems has been given. Specifically a comparative information-theoretic analysis of both fuzzy commitment and secure sketch-based protection schemes has been provided.

In the last few years some efforts have been also devoted to the design of template protection mechanisms for multi-biometric systems. Although the development of the topic is still in its infancy some interesting contributions have already been proposed. In [73] face and fingerprints templates have been fused at a feature level and secured using the fuzzy commitment scheme. In [74] a multi-biometric system based on the fusion at the feature level of fingerprints and iris and secured by using the fuzzy vault scheme has been proposed. In [75] different forms of fusion, specifically feature, score, and decision level fusion have been investigated within the framework of the fuzzy commitment construct. In [76] a multibiometric system combining iris and face to obtain a long cryptographic key having high entropy has been proposed. In [77] a feature level fusion approach for the implementation of multibiometric cryptosystems based on the use of both the fuzzy commitment and the fuzzy vault has been proposed. Specifically fingerprint, iris, and face have been simultaneously employed.

1.6 Research Projects on Privacy and Security in Biometrics

The privacy and security aspects of emerging biometric identification technologies have been object of research in several funded projects worldwide. Specifically, within the framework of the European Union Framework Programs, the BITE (Biometric Identification Technology Ethics) project [78], which ended in February 2007, and the HIDE (Homeland Security, Biometric Identification & Personal Detection Ethics) project [79], which ended in 2011, focused on the ethical and privacy issues of biometrics and personal detection technologies with specific reference to those applications which require cooperation among National and International agencies is crucial. Moreover the project PRIME (Privacy and Identity Management in Europe), which ended in February 2008, focused on solutions for privacy-enhancing identity management that supports end-users' sovereignty over their private sphere and enterprises' privacy-compliant data processing. The IRISS (Increasing Resilience in Surveillance Societies) project [80], a two year project which started in October 2011, is aimed at investigating the development and deployment of surveillance technologies and their impact on the citizen's democratic rights and their social and economic costs. The SurPRISE (Surveillance, Privacy and Security) project [81], a three year project which started in February 2012, is aimed at identifying those factors which contribute to the shaping of security technologies as effective, non-privacy-infringing and socially legitimate security devices. European projects with the objective of implementing some of the discussed privacy enhancing technology are the 3DFace [82] and the TURBINE (TrUsted Revocable Biometric IdeNtitiEs) [83] projects. The 3DFace project is a three-year project which started in April 2006. The objective of the 3DFace project was to develop a prototype of an automated border control biometric system incorporating privacy enhancing technology based on 2D and 3D face images. The TURBINE project is a three-year project which started in February 2008. Its aim was to develop innovative digital identity solutions by combining secure, automatic user identification based on electronic fingerprint authentication and reliable protection of the biometrics data through privacy enhancing technology. The BEAT (Biometrics Evaluation and Testing) project [84], a four year project which started in March 2012, aims at proposing a framework of standard operational evaluations for biometric technologies with emphasis on the analysis of the performance of the underlying biometric system, of the robustness to vulnerabilities such as direct (spoofing) or indirect attacks, and of the strength of privacy preservation techniques. The TABULA RASA (Trusted Biometrics under Spoofing Attacks) project [85], a 42 month project which started in November 2011, aims at addressing some of the issues of spoofing attacks to trusted biometric systems.

However, despite the efforts devoted in these projects, privacy and security within biometrics still pose a wide range of challenging problems that need to be further investigated.

1.7 Research Agenda on Privacy and Security

The design of secure and privacy compliant biometric based systems is a challenging problem which involves several disciplines ranging from legislation and ethics to signal processing, pattern recognition, information theory and cryptography. Therefore, although on one side the aforementioned goal is a very demanding one, on the other side it can offer several research opportunities in heterogeneous fields of research in which scientists necessarily need to act synergically in order to achieve tangible results. Some examples follow.

As for the security, a system is usually referred to as a *strong* system when the cost of attacks is greater than the potential advantage to the adversary. On the contrary, a *weak* system is a system for which the cost of attacks is lower than the corresponding potential advantage. The definition of the level of security in biometric systems has been performed so far through the identification of possible attacks, vulnerabilities, possible countermeasures, and a global cost analysis. It is not straightforward to define the security which is ensured by a specific system and in particular by a biometric system in a quantitative rather than in a qualitative way. Therefore, major efforts need to be done towards the definition of metrics to be employed for assessing the performance of a system in terms of the level of security achieved.

With specific reference to biometric template protection schemes, different taxonomies have been proposed so far, with the risk to potentially generate confusion. Therefore a vocabulary harmonization is really needed by the scientific community. Currently, some activities are being carried out in standardization bodies to achieve this goal. Moreover, although several biometric template protection approaches have been proposed in literature, still a systematization on the benchmark metrics need to be done. It is worth pointing out that some metrics tailored to characterize specific biometric template protection systems have already been proposed. However, their applicability is limited to those approaches which share the same basic principles. For example, within the *fuzzy extractor* and *secure sketch* framework introduced in [56], the concepts of *min-entropy* and *entropy loss* related to the length of the extracted biometric key and to the information leakage given by the public data respectively are given. On the other hand, when transformation based template protection approaches are considered, different performance evaluation metrics need to be defined. Therefore the definition of a holistic approach able to cope with the performance assessment of a generic template protection approach would be a significant achievement. Some preliminary attempts within this regard have been performed, see for example [86], but a significant amount of research effort needs to be still put in place.

In the recent past, multi-biometric systems are witnessing an always increasing interest from the scientific community due to their intrinsic capabilities of addressing the universality issue better than uni-modal systems and to the increasing level of security they can potentially achieve. However, a comprehensive analysis on the possible additional threats, attacks, vulnerabilities, and countermeasures, specific to multi-biometric systems still needs to be systematically carried out. Moreover, the issue of designing template protection approaches tailored to multi-biometric systems, still in its infancy, is a fertile field of research. Also, the assessment of the effectiveness of the aforementioned systems requires proper procedures and metrics, yet to be designed.

It is worth pointing out that in the past it has been given more emphasis to ensure security rather than designing privacy compliant systems. Only recently privacy and security have been treated as two factors to be jointly optimized and not as two requirements hindering each other. This has lead to the need to include the privacy requirements in the early stage design of a biometric system. Appealing research topics include analyzing the privacy risks, defining the needed requirements to guarantee individual's privacy, developing proper best practices, architectures, and systems with the purpose to implement the needed privacy constraints. Finally a testing stage to assess whether the privacy requirements have been fulfilled is required. The modeling and quantification of privacy properties such as anonymity, unlinkability, etc. are essential steps towards the deep understanding of what is intended for privacy and towards the definition of metrics which are needed to assess the level of privacy protection provided by different biometric systems. However privacy preservation is a multidisciplinary area of research which has relevant legal, social, economic, political, and cultural aspects which must be understood in depth and developed in order to design effective approaches for the protection of individual's privacy. Therefore research expertise beyond engineering is needed in order to tackle the privacy protection problem in biometric systems effectively.

References

1. Privacy & biometrics building a conceptual foundation. NSTC, Committee on Technology, Committee on Homeland and National Security, Subcommittee on Biometrics. Tech rep, September 2006
2. Woodward JJD (2008) The law and use of biometrics. In: Jain AK, Flynn P, Ross AA (eds) Handbook of Biometrics. Springer, New York
3. Guidelines on the protection of privacy and transborder flows of personal data. OECD (Organisation for Economic Co-operation and Development), Paris, France. Tech rep, 1980 (accessed in December 2012). [Online]. Available: www.oecd.org/document/18/0,2340,en_2649_34255_1815186_1_1_1_1,00.html
4. Privacy technology implementation guide. Homeland security. Tech rep, 16 August 2007 (accessed in December 2012). [Online]. Available: http://www.dhs.gov/xlibrary/assets/privacy/privacy/guide/ptig.pdf
5. Article 29—data protection working party 2003, working document on biometrics 12168/02/en. Tech rep
6. Mordini E (2008) Biometrics, human body and medicine: a controversial history. In: Duquenoy P, George C, Kimppa K (eds) Ethical, Legal and Social Issues in Medical Informatics. Idea Group Inc, Hershey
7. Biometric security concerns. UK biometric working group. Tech rep, September 2003
8. Ratha N, Connell J, Bolle R (2001) Enhancing security and privacy in biometrics-based authentication systems. IBM Systems Journal 40(3):614–634
9. Uludag U, Jain A (2003) Attacks on biometric systems: a case study in fingerprints. In: Proc SPIE-EI 2004, Security, Steganography and Watermarking of Multimedia Contents VI, 18–22 January 2003, pp 622–633
10. Jain AK, Nandakumar K, Nagar A (2008) Biometric template security. EURASIP Journal on Advances in Signal Processing 2008
11. Roberts C (2006) Biometric attack vectors and defences. Computers & Security 26(1)
12. INCITS-M1/07-0185rev, Study report on biometrics in e-authentication. InterNational Committee for Information Technology Standards, INCITS Secretariat, Information Technology Industry Council (ITI). Tech rep, 30 March 2007 (accessed in December 2012). [Online]. Available: http://standards.incits.org/apps/group_public/download.php/24528/m1070185rev.pdf
13. Adler A (2003) Can images be regenerated from biometric templates? In: Proc Biometrics Consortium Conference, September 2003
14. Ross A, Nandakumar K, Jain AK (2006) Handbook of Multibiometrics. Springer, Berlin
15. Cavoukian BA, Stoianov A (2007) Biometric encryption: a positive-sum technology that achieves strong authentication, security and privacy, Toronto, Canada. Tech rep, 2007 (accessed in December 2012). [Online]. Available: www.ipc.on.ca

16. Tuyls P, Skoric B, Kevenaar T (2007) Security with Noisy Data. Privacy Biometrics, Secure Key Storage and Anti-counterfeiting. Springer, Berlin
17. Ross A, Shah J, Jain AK (2007) From template to image: reconstructing fingerprints from minutiae points. IEEE Transactions on Pattern Analysis and Machine Intelligence 29(4):544–560
18. Breebaart J, Busch C, Grave J, Kindt E (2008) A reference architecture for biometric template protection based on pseudo identities. In: BIOSIG, Darmstadt, Germany, September 2008
19. Savvides M, Vijaya Kumar BVK, Khosla PK (2004) Cancelable biometric filters for face recognition. In: Proceedings of the 17th International Conference on Pattern Recognition, ICPR 2004, vol 3, Cambridge, UK, August 2004, pp 922–925
20. Ang R, Safavi-Naini R, McAven L (2005) Cancelable key-based fingerprint templates. In: ACISP. Lecture Notes on Computer Science, vol 3574, pp 242–252
21. Ratha NK, Chikkerur S, Connell JH, Bolle RM (2007) Generating cancelable fingerprint templates. IEEE Transactions on Pattern Analysis and Machine Intelligence 29(4):561–572
22. Quan F, Fei S, Anni C, Feifei Z (2008) Cracking cancelable fingerprint template of Ratha. In: International Symposium on Computer Science and Computational Technology, ISCSCT'08, Shanghai, China, December 2008, pp 572–575
23. Chikkerur S, Ratha N, Connell J, Bolle R (2008) Generating registration-free cancelable fingerprint templates. In: IEEE Second International Conference on Biometrics: Theory, Applications and Systems, BTAS'08, Washington, DC, USA, 28 September–1 October 2008
24. Xu W, He Q, Li Y, Li T (2008) Cancelable voiceprint templates based on knowledge signatures. In: Proceedings of the 2008 International Symposium on Electronic Commerce and Security, ISECS'08, Guangzhou, China, August 2008
25. Maiorana E, Martinez-Diaz M, Campisi P, Ortega-Garcia J, Neri A (2008) Template protection for hmm-based on-line signature authentication. In: IEEE Intl Conf on Computer Vision and Pattern Recognition, Anchorage, Alaska, USA, 23–28 June 2008
26. Maiorana E, Campisi P, Fierrez J, Ortega-Garcia J, Neri A (2010) Cancelable templates for sequence based biometrics with application to on-line signature recognition. IEEE Transactions on Systems, Man and Cybernetics. Part A 40(3):525–538
27. Ballard L, Kamara S, Reiter M (2008) The practical subtleties of biometric key generation. In: 17th Annual USENIX Security Symposium, San Jose, CA, USA, 28 July–1 August 2008
28. Monrose F, Reiter M, Li Q, Wetzel S (2001) Cryptographic key generation from voice. In: IEEE Symp on Security and Privacy, Oakland, CA, USA, May 2001
29. Goh A, Ngo D (2003) Computation of cryptographic keys from face biometrics. In: International Federation for Information Processing. Lecture Notes on Computer Science, vol 2828
30. Vielhauer C, Steinmetz R, Mayerhoefer A (2002) Biometric hash based on statistical features of online signatures. In: 21st International Conference on Pattern Recognition, ICPR 2012, Tsukuba Science City, Japan, November 2012
31. Vielhauer C, Steinmetz R (2004) Handwriting: feature correlation analysis for biometric hashes. EURASIP Journal on Applied Signal Processing 4:542–558. Special issue on biometric signal processing
32. Feng H, Chan C (2002) Private key generation from on-line handwritten signatures. In: Information Management and Computer Security, pp 159–164
33. Kuan Y, Goh A, Ngo D, Teoh A (2005) Cryptographic keys from dynamic hand-signatures with biometric secrecy preservation and replaceability. In: Proc Fourth IEEE Workshop on Automatic Identification Advanced Technologies, AUTO ID 2005, Buffalo, New York, USA, October 2005, pp 27–32
34. Freire M, Fierrez J, Galbally J, Ortega-Garcia J (2007) Biometric hashing based on genetic selection and its application to on-line signatures. In: Lecture Notes on Computer Science, vol 4642, pp 1134–1143
35. Ballard L, Kamara S, Monrose F, Reiter MK (2008) Towards practical biometric key generation with randomized biometric templates. In: Proceedings of the 15th ACM Conference on Computer and Communications Security, CCS'08, Alexandria, VA, USA, October 2008

36. Rathgeb C, Uhl A (2010) Privacy preserving key generation for iris biometrics. In: Proceedings of the 11th IFIP TC 6/TC 11 International Conference on Communications and Multimedia Security, CMS'10, Linz, Austria, 31 May–2 June 2010
37. Juels A, Wattenberg M (1999) A fuzzy commitment scheme. In: Proc ACM Conf on Computer and Communications Security, CCS99, Singapore, November 1999, pp 28–36
38. Davida G, Frankel Y, Matt B, Peralta R (1999) On the relation of error correction and cryptography to an off line biometric based identification scheme. In: Proceedings of WCC99, Workshop on coding and cryptography, Paris, France, January 1999
39. Juels A, Sudan M (2002) A fuzzy vault scheme. In: IEEE Intl Symp on Information Theory, ISIT 2002, Lausanne, Switzerland, 30 June–5 July 2002
40. Tuyls P, Verbitsky E, Ignatenko T, Schobben D, Akkermans A (2004) Privacy protected biometric templates: acoustic ear identification. In: Proceedings SPIE, Biometric Technology for Human Identification, vol 5404, Orlando, FL, USA, April 2004, pp 176–182
41. Tuyls P, Akkermans A, Kevenaar T, Schrijen G, Bazen A, Veldhuis R (2005) Practical biometric authentication with template protection. In: AVBPA, Rye Brook, NY, USA, pp 436–446
42. Nandakumar K (2010) A fingerprint cryptosystem based on minutiae phase spectrum. In: IEEE International Workshop on Information Forensics and Security, WIFS10, Seattle, USA, December 2010
43. Van der Veen M, Kevenaar T, Schrijen G-J, Akkermans T, Zuo F (2006) Face biometrics Brazil, with renewable templates. In: SPIE Proc on Security, Steganography, and Watermarking of Multimedia Contents, vol 6072, San Jose, CA, USA, January 2005
44. Kelkboom E, Gökberk B, Kevenaar T, Akkermans AHM, Van der Veen M (2007) 3d face: biometrics template protection for 3d face recognition. In: Lecture Notes on Computer Science, vol 4642, pp 566–573
45. Hao F, Anderson R, Daugman J (2006) Combining crypto with biometrics effectively. IEEE Transactions on Computers 55:1081–1088
46. Rathgeb C, Uhl A (2009) Systematic construction of iris-based fuzzy commitment schemes. In: Proceedings of the Third International Conference on Advances in Biometrics, ICB'09, Alghero, Italy, June 2009
47. Maiorana E, Campisi P, Neri A (2008) User adaptive fuzzy commitment for signature templates protection and renewability. SPIE Journal of Electronic Imaging 17(1), January–March. Special section on biometrics: advances in security, usability and interoperability
48. Maiorana E, Campisi P (2010) Fuzzy commitment for function based signature template protection. IEEE Signal Processing Letters 17(3):249–252
49. Uludag U, Jain A (2004) Fuzzy fingerprint vault. In: Workshop on Biometrics: Challenges Arising from Theory to Practice, August 2004, pp 13–16
50. Yang S, Verbauwhede I (2005) Automatic secure fingerprint verification system based on fuzzy vault scheme. In: IEEE Intl Conf on Acoustics, Speech, and Signal Processing, ICASSP 2005, Philadelphia, PA, USA, March 2005, pp 609–612
51. Nandakumar K, Jain A, Pankati S (2007) Fingerprint-based fuzzy vault: implementation and performance. IEEE Transactions on Information Forensics and Security 2(4):744–757
52. Freire M, Fierrez J, Martinez-Diaz M, Ortega-Garcia J (2007) On the applicability of off-line signatures to the fuzzy vault construction. In: Proc Intl Conf on Document Analysis and Recognition, ICDAR 2007, Brazil, September 2007
53. Nyang D, Lee KH (2007) Fuzzy face vault: how to implement fuzzy vault with weighted features. In: Proceedings of the 4th International Conference on Universal Access in Human Computer Interaction: Coping with Diversity, UAHCI'07, Beijing, China
54. Lee Y, Bae K, Lee S, Park K, Kim J (2007) Biometric key binding: fuzzy vault based on iris images. In: Lecture Notes on Computer Science, vol 4642. Springer, Berlin, pp 800–808
55. Kumar A, Kumar A (2009) Development of a new cryptographic construct using palmprint-based fuzzy vault. EURASIP Journal on Advances in Signal Processing 2009
56. Dodis Y, Reyzin L, Smith A (2004) Fuzzy extractors: how to generate strong keys from biometrics and other noisy data. In: Eurocrypt. Lecture Notes on Computer Science, vol 3027. Springer, Berlin, pp 523–540

57. Sutcu Y, Li Q, Memon N (2007) Protecting biometric templates with sketch: theory and practice. IEEE Transactions on Information Forensics and Security 2(3):503–512
58. Li Q, Guo M, Chang E-C (2008) Fuzzy extractors for asymmetric biometric representations. In: IEEE Computer Society Conference on Computer Vision and Pattern Recognition Workshops, CVPRW'08, Anchorage, AK, USA, June 2008
59. Buhan I, Doumen J, Hartel P, Veldhuis R (2007) Fuzzy extractors for continuous distributions. In: 2nd ACM Symposium on Information, Computer and Communications Security (ASIACCS), Singapore, March 2007, pp 353–355
60. Sutcu Y, Li Q, Memon N (2009) Design and analysis of fuzzy extractors for faces. In: Proc SPIE Optics and Photonics in Global Homeland Security V and Biometric Technology for Human Identification VI, vol 7306, Orlando, Florida, USA, April 2009
61. Ignatenko T, Willems F (2010) Information leakage in fuzzy commitment schemes. IEEE Transactions on Information Forensics and Security 5(2):337–348
62. Zhou X, Kuijper A, Veldhuis R, Busch C (2011) Quantifying privacy and security of biometric fuzzy commitment. In: International Joint Conference on Biometrics, IJCB 11, Washington, DC, USA, October 2011
63. Kelkboom E, Breebaart J, Kevenaar T, Buhan I, Veldhuis R (2011) Preventing the decodability attack based cross-matching in a fuzzy commitment scheme. IEEE Transactions on Information Forensics and Security 6(1):107–121
64. Zhou X, Kuijper A, Busch C (2012) Retrieving secrets from iris fuzzy commitment. In: International Conference on Biometrics, ICB 12, New Delhi, India, 29 March–1 April 2012
65. Chang E-C, Shen R, Teo FW (2006) Finding the original point set hidden among chaff. In: Proceedings of the 2006 ACM Symposium on Information, Computer and Communications Security, ASIACCS'06, Taipei, Taiwan, March 2006, pp 182–188
66. Scheirer W, Boult T (2007) Cracking fuzzy vaults and biometric encryption. In: Biometrics Symposium, Baltimore, MD, USA, September 2007
67. Kholmatov A, Yanikoglu B (2008) Realization of correlation attack against the fuzzy vault scheme. In: SPIE Symp Security, Forensics, Steganography, and Watermarking of Multimedia Contents X, vol 6819, San Jose, CA, USA, January 2008
68. Boyen X (2004) Reusable cryptographic fuzzy extractors. In: Proceedings of the 11th ACM Conference on Computer and Communications Security, CCS 2004, Washington, DC, USA, October 2004, pp 82–91
69. Boyen X, Dodis Y, Katz J, Ostrovsky R, Smith A (2005) Secure remote authentication using biometric data. In: Advances in Cryptology—EUROCRYPT 2005. Lecture Notes in Computer Science, vol 3494
70. Dodis Y, Smith A (2005) Correcting errors without leaking partial information. In: STOC'05: Proceedings of the 37th Annual ACM Symposium on Theory of Computing, Baltimore, MD, USA, May 2005, pp 654–663
71. Simoens K, Tuyls P, Preneel B (2009) Privacy weaknesses in biometric sketches. In: Proc IEEE Symp Security and Privacy, pp 188–203
72. Wang Y, Rane S, Draper SC, Ishwar P (2012) A theoretical analysis of authentication, privacy, and reusability across secure biometric systems. IEEE Transactions on Information Forensics and Security 7(6):1825–1840
73. Sutcu Y, Li Q, Memon N (2007) Secure biometric templates from fingerprint-face features. In: IEEE Computer Society Conference on Computer Vision and Pattern Recognition. Workshop on biometrics, Minneapolis, MN, USA, June 2007
74. Nandakumar K, Jain AK (2008) Multibiometric template security using fuzzy vault. In: 2nd IEEE International Conference on Biometrics: Theory, Applications and Systems, BTAS'08, Washington, DC, USA
75. Kelkboom E, Zhou X, Breebaart J, Veldhuis R, Busch C (2009) Multi-algorithm fusion with template protection. In: 3rd IEEE International Conference on Biometrics: Theory, Applications and Systems, BTAS'09, Washington, DC, USA
76. Kanade S, Petrovska-Delacretaz D, Dorizzi B (2010) Obtaining cryptographic keys using feature level fusion of iris and face biometrics for secure user authentication. In: IEEE Computer

Society Conference on Computer Vision and Pattern Recognition. Workshop on biometrics, San Francisco, USA, June 2010

77. Nagar A, Nandakumar K, Jain AK (2012) Multibiometric cryptosystems based on feature level fusion. IEEE Transactions on Information Forensics and Security 7(1):255–268

78. Biometric identification technology ethics (BITE). Tech rep (accessed in December 2012). [Online]. Available: http://www.biteproject.org

79. Homeland security, biometric identification & personal detection ethics (HIDE). Tech rep (accessed in December 2012). [Online]. Available: http://www.hideproject.org

80. IRISS (Increasing Resilience in Surveillance Societies) EU Project. [Online]. Available: http://irissproject.eu/

81. SURPRISE (Surveillance, Privacy and Security) EU Project. [Online]. Available: surprise-project.eu/

82. 3DFace, 3DFace EU Project. [Online]. Available: http://www.3dface.org/home/welcome

83. TURBINE (TrUsted Revocable Biometric IdeNtitiEs) EU Project. [Online]. Available: http://www.turbine-project.eu/

84. BEAT (Biometrics Evaluation and Testing) EU Project. [Online]. Available: http://www.beat-eu.org/

85. TABULA RASA EU Project. [Online]. Available: http://www.tabularasa-euproject.org/project

86. Simoens K, Yang B, Zhou X, Beato F, Busch C, Newton E, Preneel B (2012) Criteria towards metrics for benchmarking template protection algorithms. In: 5th IAPR International Conference on Biometrics, ICB 12, New Delhi, India, 29 March–1 April 2012

Chapter 2
Design Aspects of Secure Biometric Systems and Biometrics in the Encrypted Domain

Claus Vielhauer, Jana Dittmann, and Stefan Katzenbeisser

Abstract This chapter introduces the main security requirements for the biometric processing pipeline and summarizes general design principles and approaches. General IT security principles are reflected and selected paradigms such as template protection by biometric hashing, fuzzy commitment schemes, and fuzzy extractors are reviewed. Further, we discuss the design principles of biometric matching algorithms that operate in the encrypted domain. The overall algorithm design, implementation, and configuration issues are summarized and discussed in an exemplary manner for the case of face biometrics.

2.1 Security Requirements for the Biometric Processing Pipeline

Recently security has become one of the most significant and challenging problems during the introduction of new information technology. It therefore plays an important role for biometric systems and applications. Since digital biometric data can easily be copied without information loss, manipulated at will or forged without noticeable traces, security solutions are required to counter these threats. In order to judge and evaluate the overall trustworthiness, security criteria need to be defined, e.g. taken from the Europe-wide valid ITSEC catalogue of criteria [16], and applied to biometrics.

In general we can notice a rising awareness of security for biometric solutions. In which way security mechanisms can be applied to biometric data and their applica-

C. Vielhauer (✉)
Brandenburg University of Applied Sciences, Potsdam, Germany
e-mail: claus.vielhauer@fh-brandenburg.de

C. Vielhauer · J. Dittmann
Otto-von-Guericke University Magdeburg, Magdeburg, Germany

J. Dittmann
e-mail: jana.dittmann@iti.cs.uni-magdeburg.de

S. Katzenbeisser
Technische Universität Darmstadt, Darmstadt, Germany
e-mail: skatzenbeisser@acm.org

P. Campisi (ed.), *Security and Privacy in Biometrics*,
DOI 10.1007/978-1-4471-5230-9_2, © Springer-Verlag London 2013

tions needs to be analyzed individually for each application and biometric modality. This is mainly due to the structure and complexity of biometric data as well as the privacy requirements derived from the right of all individuals to protect person-related data and information, as codified in data protection laws. Based on the central issues of IT-security, this chapter introduces the most important security requirements, which must be fulfilled by today's biometric systems. We first provide an overview of the basic security requirements (also called security aspects) in general by enumerating five generally known security aspects (confidentiality, integrity, authenticity, non-repudiation, and availability) and proceed with a discussion of privacy issues (unlinkability, unobservability, anonymity, and pseudonymity) that are commonly linked to biometric applications.

The security requirements of confidentiality, integrity, authenticity, non-repudiation, and availability are essential for computer and network systems (see for example [3] and [7, 27] or [20]). In the case of biometrics we consider as security target under investigation the involved resources such as humans (subjects), entities (such as components or processes) and biometric data (information).

Confidentiality refers to the secrecy or prohibition of unauthorized disclosure of resources. In cases of a biometric system it mainly refers to biometric and related authentication information, which needs to be kept secret from unauthorized entities. Confidentiality may ensure secrecy of user's biometric data when it is captured, transferred or stored. Particularly biometric information should only be accessible in full quality to the person it belongs. Beside this issue, during biometric verification or identification the accessing party needs to be restricted with appropriate security measures. This ensures that nobody apart from the allowed parties can use the measurement. An attack goal could be the unauthorized access to and copying of reference data, such as fingerprints. Biometric data is highly sensitive and personal, because any illegitimate possession and use of stolen data may lead to uncontrollable subsequent illicit use. For example, a stolen fingerprint reference can be used to construct artificial silicon fingerprints [24] for identity theft or even to lay fake fingerprint traces by printing the fingerprint patterns with amino acids as described in [21]. Some biometric modalities even reveal medical patterns that potentially indicate diseases [15].

Integrity of a biometric system refers to the overall integrity of all resources such as biometric and related authentication information and all software and hardware components involved in the biometric processing pipeline. Integrity is the quality or condition of being whole and unaltered (resource is not altered or manipulated) and refers to its consistency, accuracy, and correctness. Security measures offering integrity usually ensure that modifications are detectable. Different integrity degrees such as *low, middle, high* can be defined, see for example the International Electrotechnical Commission safety standard IEC-Standard 61508 (see the website http://www.iec.ch, 2011). Appropriate levels need to be defined and integrity policies for the overall system design, implementation, and configurations need to be imposed. For a biometric system the integrity should be defined as "high" for all components, which means that any malicious manipulations during operation and storage should be avoided or at least detected including its notification and correction.

Authenticity: two aspects of authenticity play an important role in a biometric system, namely entity authenticity and data origin authenticity:

- *Entity authenticity* ensures that all entities involved in the overall processing are the ones they claim to be. For example, humans need to be correctly identified as originator or system entities such as sensors or processes need to be identified as sender or receiver. Here for example the following threat occurs: an attacker can try to gain unauthorized access, without possessing copies of biometric reference data. Obviously, the security risk in this case is entity authenticity of legitimate users of a biometric system. This category has apparently attracted most scientific and non-scientific work recently, with numerous publications addressing techniques to attack biometric authentication systems without any or with little knowledge about the original biometric trait of the subject under attack. Recent works in this domain include, for example, reverse engineering and hill-climbing attacks to handwriting modality attacks, see for example [13] and [22].
- *Data origin authenticity* ensures the origin, genuineness, originality, truth, and realness of data. For example, for biometric data captured with sensor devices, data origin authenticity ensures that the captured data comes from a genuine sensor and is not spoofed from a previous recording.

Non-repudiation involves an identification of involved parties such as entities and used components, and binds all actions to these parties. It either proves that the involved parties performed a certain action or that an event occurred. Furthermore, this fact can be proven to third parties. For example an event or action can be the biometric identification or verification of humans including the used system entities and components, the capturing and sampling of biometric traits, the creation or generation and sending of a derived message, the receipt of this message and the submission or transport of this message. Non-repudiation also can refer to so-called accountability ensuring that, for example, a sender of biometric information and recipients of this information cannot successfully deny having sent or received biometric information. With respect to third parties, legal enforceability can be achieved, ensuring that a user can be held liable to fulfill his or her legal responsibilities.

Availability: a resource has the property of availability with respect to a set of entities if all members of the set can access the resource. A further aspect is the so-called reachability to ensure that an entity such as a human or a system process either can or cannot be contacted, depending on user interests. Attackers might be interested to set the system in an inoperable state for rightful users, thus preventing them from using authenticated applications and services. Such attacks clearly target the availability and represent a Denial-of-Service (DoS) attack variant to biometric systems, in analogy to DoS attacks to other IT systems such as Web applications.

Due to the private nature of biometrics, besides the classical five security aspects from common IT security definitions discussed before, additional *privacy* requirements become important especially if the biometric data is associated to a certain situation, place, belief, action, and so on. Privacy summarizes the ability of a human to determine and control her- or himself which personal information is revealed during data collection, usage, storage, modification, transfer, and deletion. The classification into personal relevant information depends often on society, culture and individual preferences and is subject to change. Therefore subjects have the right to request corrections, locking or deletion. Sometimes privacy is related to confidentiality and anonymity to describe that the information is personally sensitive and should not be attributed to a specific person. However, privacy itself is much broader than confidentiality and anonymity and covers all security aspects mentioned including the concepts of appropriate usage with transparent rules for each individual, minimal principle, and appropriation as well as protection and deletion strategies.

With respect to user privacy, confidentiality, and entity authenticity of the user (human) during his or her actions, further security requirements (such as anonymity, unobservability, unlinkability, and pseudonymity) can be defined, see also the terminology in [17] and [29]: Here we understand anonymity as the state of being not identifiable and therefore indistinguishable within a set of subjects, the so-called anonymity set. It can also be seen as unknown authorship or origin, lacking individuality, distinction, or recognizability within the anonymity set by reducing the likelihood to be identified as originator. The definition can, of course, be also applied to the recipients and the overall communication. Anonymity does not mean that a person cannot be identified, rather that he is indistinguishable within some particular group. In the literature [31], so-called degrees of anonymity are defined such as *provably exposed, exposed, possible innocence, probable innocence, beyond suspicion*, and *absolute privacy*. Applied to biometric systems these different degrees can be used to describe and provide anonymity properties to the users involved and further to select appropriate security mechanisms.

Unobservability covers the infeasibility of observation of a resource and service usage by humans or entities (parties). Parties not involved should not be able to observe the participation, such as the act of sending or receiving of messages (state of being indistinguishable). From the summary of [29] and [30], unobservability covers undetectability against all subjects uninvolved and anonymity even against the other subject(s) involved.

Unlinkability addresses the relation between two or more humans and entities (e.g., subjects, messages, events, actions). In an unlinkable biometric system it should not be possible to derive any further information on the relation between two entities than is available through a-priori knowledge, see further discussions in [29].

Pseudonyms (also called Nyms in its shortened form) are identifiers that cannot with confidence be associated with any particular human or entity. This is achieved by a mapping between real identities and fictitious identities. Re-identification is only possible by knowing the mapping function. More details about pseudonymity with respect to accountability and authorization can be found in [29].

In the following we sketch which of the five security aspects and the discussed privacy issues are particularly important in the biometric processing pipeline. Here

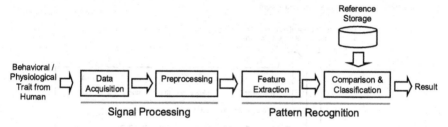

Fig. 2.1 Biometric authentication pipeline as a signal processing and pattern recognition model [37]

we consider the biometric systems as a generalized chain of signal processing and pattern recognition primitives, as suggested by [37]. This idea is motivated by the fact that the origin of any biometric recognition process is the collection of physical phenomena by means of a sensor (*data acquisition*), resulting in some form of electronic measurement. This initial process is followed by analog-digital (A/D) conversion and subsequent digital signal processing steps for conditioning (*preprocessing*) of the raw data. From the pre-processed data, characteristics are determined by *feature extraction* and finally, the authentication is performed by *comparison* of the extracted features to stored *references* through some *classification* method. Figure 2.1 from [37] illustrates this model for biometric authentication.

The following figures briefly illustrate, based this the model-oriented view, the impact of the above mentioned security and privacy aspects on the biometric processing pipeline.

As seen in Fig. 2.2, in each step itself and in the communication between the steps of the biometric pipeline, authenticity of all entities such as the subject and all processing parties including all running processes, data authenticity and data integrity needs to be ensured. Furthermore for the reference storage, it needs to be ensured that the reference storage in its hardware and software itself and all related application processes are authentic and integer (e.g. not spoofed or manipulated entities) as well as the stored data has authenticity and integrity (e.g. is not spoofed or manipulated). Two examples should illustrate the protection goals:

(a) During acquisition it needs to be ensured that the data comes from a human and is captured by a sensor with genuine hardware and software (otherwise a replay of recorded human traits cannot be prevented).
(b) Furthermore after data acquisition, all subsequent processing steps need to be checked for entity authenticity, data authenticity and integrity to avoid that e.g. malicious software is injected and can manipulate the overall processing steps.

The security aspect of confidentiality (see Fig. 2.3) plays an important role when data is acquired and further processed; it needs to be ensured in each step of the processing pipeline, for the communication of all processes (inter-process communication) and in the reference storage. As person related data is usually involved, privacy requirements such as anonymity or pseudonymity, unobservability, and unlinkability become important (see also Fig. 2.3). Privacy is hereby a mandatory aspect derived

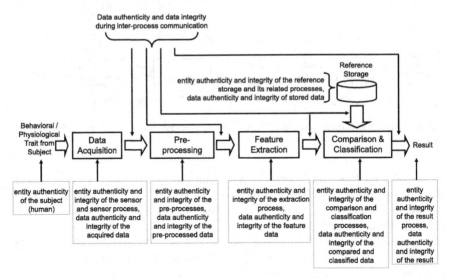

Fig. 2.2 Entity authenticity, data authenticity and integrity for the biometric authentication pipeline

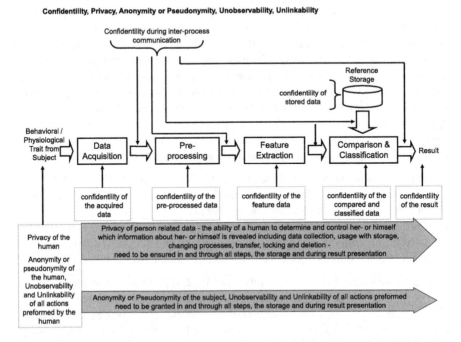

Fig. 2.3 Confidentility, privacy, anonymity or pseudonymity, unobservability, unlinkability for the biometric authentication pipeline

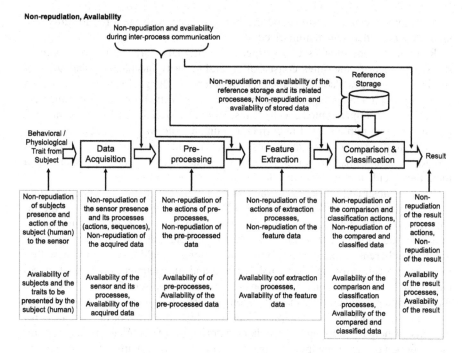

Fig. 2.4 Non-repudiation and availability for the biometric authentication pipeline

from related privacy laws of the. For an anonymous, unobserved or unlikable communication, specific protocols needs to be used in all actions performed in each step and between steps of the pipeline.

If biometric systems are used to ensure a certain provable service or action, then usually non-repudiation plays an important role and needs to be ensured from the subject of investigation (non-repudiation of the subject presence and actions itself) through and between all steps (with non-repudiations of sensor presence and all related processes, as well as of all actions and processes of and between pre-processing, feature extraction, comparison and classification, storage) in the biometric pipeline including the reference storage (see Fig. 2.4). Availability aspects include the availability of the subjects and the required traits, the corresponding sensor technology, and the availability of all processes and building blocks of the biometric pipeline, including the storage of references (see also Fig. 2.4).

2.2 Summary of General Design Principles and Approaches

In this section we start with a brief summary of terminology and a definition of risk as well as basic design principles known for example from discussions in [2] for a biometric system derived from overall IT security principles. We further briefly introduce exemplary organizational and technical security measures and mechanisms.

Furthermore selected measures and mechanisms specifically tailored towards biometric measurements are summarized.

Regarding terminology, security aspects (requirements) are met by security measures, and security measures consist of several security mechanisms and security services (sometimes also called methods of defense). The goal is to prevent, detect or recover from a malicious incident that violates security. From [2], prevention involves that the implemented mechanisms cannot be overridden by users and can be trusted to be implemented in correct and unalterable ways. In particular, detection tries to determine that a malicious incident is under way (or has occurred) and provides mechanisms to report it. Recovery resumes correct operation either after a malicious incident or even while a malicious incident is under way.

From an abstract point of view, the risk of a malicious incident depends mainly on the expected loss (vulnerabilities) and the probability of occurrence of the incidents. For a biometric system it is therefore important to reduce the number of vulnerabilities and potential threats by performing an adequate risk management. To avoid inherent vulnerabilities, biometric systems should be designed based on the common rules of simplicity (make design and interactions easy so that its security can be evaluated) and restrictions (minimize the power of entities, "Need To Know" principle and compartmentalization). Further design principles can be found in [3] and [33] such as the principle of least privilege, principle of fail-safe (secure) defaults, principle of economy of mechanism, principle of complete mediation, principle of open design, principle of separation of privilege, principle of least common mechanism, and principle of psychological acceptability.

We distinguish between organizational and technical measures and mechanisms. For a biometric system, organizational aspects should be defined a priori in terms of security policies, i.e., statements of what is, and is not, allowed. Policies can be expressed mathematically or in natural language as a list of allowed and non-allowed actions, also including the required non-technical or technical security mechanisms of enforcing the described security policy. If several policies exist, the policies need to be combined by composition. Attention needs to be paid to policy conflicts, as discrepancies may create subtle security vulnerabilities. Therefore policy composition requires checking and resolving for inconsistencies among policies.

In the following we give examples of technical security measures [7], which can be divided further in active and passive approaches, transforming the overall security target with or without changes. For example, general methods for data authentication to ensure data origin authenticity and/or data integrity can be applied a priori by actively introducing authenticity or integrity labels, e.g. by watermarking. This label changes the original target and allows tracing and verifying either or both security properties integrity or authenticity. Different design strategies such as robust and fragile watermark patterns are know today to describe the level of authenticity or integrity of multimedia data, which can be potentially applied to biometric data as well. These concepts are based on the assumption that (at least) two parties are involved in the authentication process: at the origin, an entity who performs the transformation of the data and communicates it to a set of receivers. At the recipient side, (at least) one verifier inspects the received data and checks its authenticity and/or integrity.

For example, by embedding a label, known to the verifier and a secret symmetric key, mutually shared between the origin entity and the verifier, data origin authenticity verification can be achieved in the following way:

- The origin entity embeds a label in a key-dependent manner using some watermarking algorithm and the shared key into the biometric data and subsequently communicates it,
- The verifier receives the biometric data and attempts to retrieve the known label using the shared key. If retrieved successfully, the verifier can assume origin authenticity; if not, authenticity is not ensured.

Additional aspects for the application of watermarking to biometric data are robustness, i.e. the possibility to perform authentication even after transformations such as image processing (e.g. cropping/scaling/compression), and/or integrity verification by so-called fragile watermarks. The latter kind of watermarks is designed in such way that even minor modifications of the cover media lead to dissolving of the embedded label, indicating any kind of modification to the verifier. For further details on the concept of using watermarking for authentication and integrity verification, see for example [7] or [6].

In comparison to active changes of the target, *passive cryptography* transforms the target without changing the target at the recipient side itself (encryption functions ensure confidentiality) or transforms and compresses the target from arbitrary length to a fixed length as one way function (hashing). *Cryptography* can be used to ensure the security aspects summarized in Fig. 2.2 for integrity and authenticity and Fig. 2.3 for confidentiality in this chapter. As commonly known, see for example in [2], encryption is in general the process of transforming data to conceal content without concealing the existence of data, i.e. the transformed data is visible but cannot be understood. It is implemented by use of cryptosystems consisting of a set of (keyed) invertible functions. Private-key cryptosystems use shared secret keys, whereas public-key cryptosystems make use of pairs of a public and private key, where the public key is used for encryption and the secret key for decryption. An authentic link between the public key and its owner with the corresponding secret key is needed to achieve the overall security goals. Such a link is provided by so-called public-key certificates issued by a so-called Trust Center (TC), as summarized for example in [7]. Thereby trust centers authenticate the link of users (also our users of the biometric system) to their public keys by means of certificates and provide further services like non-repudiation (such as summarized in Fig. 2.4 in this chapter), revocation handling, timestamping, auditing, and directory service.

Besides ensuring confidentiality with symmetric or asymmetric encryption schemes, *cryptography* as *a priori passive protection* helps to ensure *integrity* by means of *cryptographic hash functions* (as verifiable code). As stated before, hash functions are functions that transform input data of arbitrary length into output data of fixed length, preserving the following properties as commonly known, see also for example in [2]:

- Reproducibility: for any two identical input data, the hash functions outputs identical values.

- Collision Resistance: for any two different input data, it is very unlikely for the function to produce identical values.
- Irreversibility: it is computationally very hard to reproduce original input to any given output.
- Bit-Sensitivity: Minor changes in input data (e.g. single bit flipping) cause severe changes in the output.

Given these properties, hash functions provide building blocks for preservation of integrity in systems, by attaching reference hash value to targets as known and widely applied, see also in [2]. Any malicious or non-malicious change during processing or communication can then be detected by re-calculating the hash values at the end of the process pipeline and comparing it to the reference values. Further, hash functions can be applied to achieve authenticity by introducing the knowledge of keys and binding of hash function to keys (then called Message Authentication Codes, MAC) or symmetric ciphers with symmetric keys or asymmetric ciphers as digital signatures with private and corresponding public keys.

Finally, as widely known, cryptographic hash functions can be useful to preserve confidentiality of reference data in authentication applications. Password-based authentication, for example, requires the comparison of a reference password with an actual one during every login. For security reasons, it is unwise to store such reference passwords in clear text (as a potential intruder could get hold of all passwords of all users). To overcome this problem, passwords (extended by other data) are generally transformed by hash functions prior to storage and comparison during login takes place in the transformed, hash domain.

In summary, cryptographic methods can be used for the following purposes in system design:

- Data Confidentiality: symmetric/asymmetric encryption
- Data Integrity and Reference Data Confidentiality: hash functions
- Data origin authenticity: symmetric key encryption
- Data origin authenticity and Data integrity: MAC (hash functions using symmetric keys), Digital Signatures (hash functions plus asymmetric keys)

However, as we discuss further on in this chapter, there are specific requirements to biometric systems, which may limit the usefulness of cryptographic schemes. For example, cryptographic hash functions commonly cannot be used for reference data protection, due to the intra-class variability of biometric data (which obviously stands in conflict to the property of bit-sensitivity).

In the biometric domain, the need for specific methods and designs towards increased security of biometric systems has been recognized and addressed by several new concepts. Specific key problems here address all security aspects of biometric reference data, as discussed in this section. Generally, as can be seen from the variety of approaches found in the literature, the methods can be categorized in two classes: *Template Protection* methods focus on securing biometric reference data and often suggest transformations of biometric data in such way that it is made unusable in case of theft by potential intruders. This includes aspects such as non-reversibility, cancelation, and renewal of template information. *Crypto-Biometrics* aspires to integrate biometric data and cryptographic functions, for example by derivation of cryptographic keys from biometrics. In the following, we briefly outline some concepts; in the subsequent section, we focus on one additional concept (Biometrics in the encrypted domain) in more detail and give a description based on a practical example.

Template Protection by Transformation: the goal here is to maintain confidentiality of biometric references (templates), by applying techniques to avoid the necessity of keeping original biometric in the Reference Storage (see Fig. 2.1). Rather than original biometric data, only selected features from the reference samples are stored during enrollment. These features need to be selected in such way that reconstruction of original data from them is next to impossible. For example, a signature verification system could store significant statistical properties of reference signatures, such as writing duration and velocity, number of pen lifts, aspect ratio etc. during enrollment. Provided that these features possess sufficient discriminatory power, it will be sufficient, for a later verification, to calculate the same features from every newly acquired sample and compare them to the stored values. However, it will be hard for an attacker to reconstruct the original data given the template. Generally speaking, this protection scheme is based on *non-reversible transformations* of biometric raw data during enrollment and authentication. Selected early examples for such transformations are Biometric key generation from speech [25], Biometric Hashes for handwriting [38] and [37], Fuzzy Commitments [18] and Secure Sketches [8] and [34]; meanwhile numerous additional approaches for literally all biometric modalities have been suggested. A review of additional related concepts from the literature is provided in [19].

Note that typically, these concepts are purely transformations by means of transform function and optionally some additional public information (for example denoted as helper data). They do not consider any dependency on additional credentials such as keys or other secrets. Typically, these protection schemes assume that transformation takes place within a protected process of the biometrics processing chain (e.g. as part of feature extraction) prior to reference storage or comparison, but also concepts for on-device transformations have been suggested [23]. The analysis of the non-reversibility property of the transformation function, i.e. attempts of generating sets artificial biometric raw data raw from transformed templates, leading to close matches these templates, is a relatively recent area of interest related to Transformation techniques, see for example [14, 22] and [26].

Cancelable Biometrics: the goal of cancelable biometrics is to provide means to make biometric references unusable, even after data theft occurred. Cancelation can be performed either alone by the owner or system operator, respectively, or as a joint operation. Most concepts suggested for Cancelable Biometrics are based on the principle to link fuzzy biometric data, sometimes along with some public helper data, to secret information, in order to from some authentication information. Only if both secret knowledge and biometric information are present, the biometric matching can be performed. For cancelation, principals need to withdraw, i.e. "forget" their secret knowledge parts. Such concepts are also often referred to as *Revocable Biometrics*, for the case when cancelation is initiated solely by the users. Examples of methods from the variety include Fuzzy Extractors [8], anonymous, and cancelable fingerprint biometrics [4] and application of BioHash for cancelable biometrics [35].

Renewable Biometrics: there are two main reasons for the necessity of Renewable Biometrics: Firstly, since biometric properties are subject to biological and mechanical changes (e.g. aging, injuries), the accuracy of biometric authentication may decrease over time. Particularly for behavioral biometrics such as speech or handwriting, it is quite obvious that aging impacts the way people speak or write. Similar observations can be made for physiological traits such as face. From the perspective of biometric systems, this observation leads to the tendency of potential increase of false non-matches, i.e. legitimate users of biometric systems are more frequently rejected. This effect is commonly referred and has been addressed in research, see for example [5] and [12]. Secondly, compromised or stolen Biometric data are problems for biometric systems. Once any original biometric raw data has been compromised, it may be potentially used for replay attacks. For example, it has been shown that gummy fingerprints can be produced from digital fingerprint images and used gain illegitimate authentication by fingerprint systems [24].

For both reasons, it may be desirable to renew biometric reference data: one goal is to maintain the recognition performance for individual subjects over time of operation of biometric systems, by frequently updating reference data. The second aim is to be able to replace compromised biometric data in such ways that after renewal any attacker in possession of stolen biometric references is unable to achieve illegitimate access, while the owner of the stolen data (victim) can still be authenticated. In this sense, Renewable Biometrics can be seen as a derivative of Cancelable Biometrics with an additional requirement for re-enrollment. In order to renew biometric references for any given user, the biometric system will cancel the previous reference and, in a second step, acquire a new biometric reference from the user. This concept obviously implies that the newly acquired sample needs to be considerably different from the previously canceled one in such way that the compromised data cannot be misused for false authentication. This can be achieved for example by using a different finger in physiological biometrics, different writing or speech content in behavioral systems or by simply involving a new secret in systems that combine secret knowledge and biometric information. Consequently, potentially all concepts for cancelable biometrics, which are based on withdrawal of secret information, appear particularly appropriate for renewable biometrics.

Encrypted Biometrics: in this scenario, protection of biometric data is ensured by encryption of sensitive data using cryptographic encryption and decryption functions and keys. Access to biometric information thus is only possible for entities in possession of the appropriate key. In general, protection can be applied straightforward to biometric systems, e.g. by cryptographically protecting all communication channels and storage components of the biometric pipeline, as suggested earlier in this chapter. However, usually any data processing (such as feature extraction or comparison) is performed in clear text domain, requiring decryption of data at run time; an alternative solution is described in the next section.

Table 2.1 Summary of main security concepts and their properties towards security of biometric systems with respect to reference data

Security concept	Key properties
Template protection by transformation	Non-reversible transformations on original data
	Optionally additional public helper data for the transforms
	Maintaining some similarity or identity property in the transformed domain
	Authentication by comparison in transformed domain, without necessity of processing sensitive biometric raw data
Cancelable biometrics	Means to make biometric references unusable after data theft
	Cancelation alone by the owner, system operator or jointly
	Mostly based on link fuzzy biometric data in combination with secret information
	Special case: *Revocable* Biometrics, when cancelation process is initiated solely by users
Renewable biometrics	See Cancelable Biometrics
	In addition: replacement of compromised biometric data, i.e. attacker is unable to achieve access, while owner can still be authenticated after replacement
Encrypted biometrics	Use of using cryptographic encryption and decryption for protection of biometric data
	Biometric data/signal processing requires prior decryption
Biometric key management	Controlled access to a key management system by means of biometrics
	User-related keys are released upon successful biometric authentication from trusted systems
	No intrinsic binding between keys and biometrics

Biometric Key Management: methods in the domain of biometric key management are based on controlled access to a key management system by means of biometric user authentication, as discussed for example in [36]. User-related keys are stored in protected and trusted system environments and keys are only released after successful biometric authentication. This concept can be categorized as Crypto-Biometrics, although in a narrow sense, it is not related to the security of biometric systems themselves, as no intrinsic binding between the keys and biometric data exists.

To summarize common security principles specific for biometrics, Table 2.1 provides an selected overview of the security concepts discussed in this section, along with their key properties. In summary, it can be stated that cryptographic methods are important building blocks to secure biometric systems and should be implemented throughout the biometric processing pipeline. However, the methods discussed above come to a limit whenever the processing of biometric data requires availability of the original biometric data in the clear. To overcome this problem, biometric matching "in the encrypted domain" can be applied.

2.3 Biometrics in the Encrypted Domain

All approaches that match a newly measured biometry against a protected template are only able to provide security of templates while they are stored in a database or on a server, and make the assumption that the matching process itself is performed in a secure environment (such as on a trusted server or directly on a smart card). This is important since the device that performs the matching operation has access to the newly collected biometrics in the clear. In some applications this assumption is questionable. Consider, for example, an authentication scenario, where a biometric measurement is obtained by a client device, which submits the measurement (or a template derived thereof) to an authentication server that performs matching against a large set of templates in a database. In case the server is compromised (for example through malware), it can collect biometric templates of all clients who request an authentication. In order to avoid this leak, biometric verification can be performed in such a way that a protected template is matched against an encrypted biometric measurement—we speak of matching in the encrypted domain.

The overall design of a system that performs matching in the encrypted domain consists of a client and a server; the client has access to a new biometric measurement, and the server wants to match this measurement against a set of templates. Depending on the application scenario, these templates can either be stored in the clear or in protected/encrypted form. The former case is, for instance, applicable to surveillance scenarios, where a large number of people are matched against a small list of known suspects, and where the privacy of all checked people should be protected. The latter case is relevant for authentication scenarios, where biometric templates stored at the server need to be protected against misuse, such as identity theft or cross-matching. We can also distinguish between scenarios where the matching result is available to the server or the client. The former is relevant in authentication scenarios, whereas the latter can be of interest in applications that use biometric services on a large scale and where cross-matching between individual service requests should be prohibited (such as a service that matches surveillance images against a small set of "suspects").

In both cases techniques of *signal processing in the encrypted domain* [9] can be applied, which provides methods to manipulate signals that are encrypted through semantically secure homomorphic encryption schemes. Using this specific class of encryption schemes, algebraic operations can be performed on ciphertexts without decryption: more precisely, for additively homomorphic encryption schemes, an encryption $[x + y]$ of a sum can be computed from encryptions $[x]$ and $[y]$ of the individual terms (we use square brackets to denote encryptions), without knowledge of the secret cryptographic key in use and without learning the result or the two factors in the clear. Since multiplication with a constant can be seen as a repeated addition, an encryption $[x]$ can also be multiplied by a constant a available in the clear to obtain an encryption of $[ax]$, again without learning the value of x. Thus, linear operations can directly be performed on ciphertexts without decryption. More complex operations (such as multiplications of two encrypted values or equality tests) can be implemented by adopting concepts from secure-two-party computation, which provides interactive protocols between a party that performs the computations and a party that has access to the secret key. Still, the protocols are designed in such a way that both parties do not gain information on the data they operate on; details on the utilized protocols can be found in [9].

Note again that most protocols used to compute with encrypted values require interaction. Due to the employed homomorphic encryption scheme, the communication overhead can be substantial: if instantiated with the common Paillier encryption scheme, every ciphertext will require 2048 bits or more to obtain security comparable to state-of-the-art RSA. Thus, there may be a significant communication overhead compared to a biometric matching process implementation in the plain; this is particularly pronounced in case a biometric signal (such as an image or a time series of measurements) needs to be encrypted sample by sample: each encrypted sample may then take thousands of bits instead of just a few. This drawback can be mitigated by "packing" several samples into one encryption [1].

We illustrate the concept of matching biometrics in the encrypted domain by the example of a face recognition service [10]. Suppose that a client (Alice) and a server (Bob) jointly want to execute a standard biometric face recognition algorithm in a privacy-friendly manner. In this scenario, Alice owns a face image, while Bob owns a database containing a collection of face images (or corresponding feature vectors) from individuals. Both parties are interested in running a face recognition algorithm in order to determine whether the picture owned by Alice shows a person whose biometric data is in Bob's database. While it is acceptable that Alice learns the basic setup of the face recognition algorithm (i.e., the algorithm employed as well as some parameters of the matching process), the content of Bob's database is considered private data that he is not willing to reveal. Alice trusts Bob to execute the face recognition algorithm correctly, but is neither willing to share the image nor the detection result with Bob. This ensures that Bob, who does the biometric matching, cannot relate subsequent matching results, as he cannot see which person was identified on the image. After termination of the protocol, Alice will only learn if a match occurred or, alternatively, the identity of the matched person. The full protocol can be found in [9]. Subsequent research considered optimizations of both cryptographic protocols in use in "private face recognition" as well as the basic face recognition algorithm [28, 32].

As example, we provide some details on [9], which considered private face recognition based on the Eigenface recognition algorithm, where face images are represented as vectors in a subspace, which is determined by Principal Component Analysis of training images. Before the protocol starts, Alice generates a public/private key pair of a homomorphic encryption algorithm (such as Paillier); the public key is distributed between both parties, while the private key is kept secret by Alice. Alice furthermore possesses an input image as private data, which shows a face that she wants to identify with help of Bob. On the other hand, Bob knows all data computed during the enrollment process: the basis vectors of the face space and biometric templates of all enrolled people (images projected onto the face space).

When describing the protocol we make the design decision of not publishing the face space basis vectors. This is due to the fact that these vectors inevitably leak some information on the training or enrollment images used to derive them. Since it

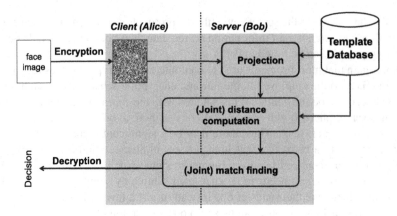

Fig. 2.5 Schematic description of face recognition in the encrypted domain

is difficult to quantify this potential information leak, we consider the basis vectors private to the server; this ensures that *no* information on the training data is leaked to the client. If the basis vectors are computed from a public source of face images (and are independent of enrollment data), the protocol can be simplified by publishing the basis vectors, see below.

In order to jointly run the algorithm, all steps of the face recognition system must be performed securely "under encryption" (see Fig. 2.5):

- *Projection*: In a first step, the input image is encrypted pixel-by-pixel by Alice and sent over to Bob, who has to project the image onto the face space. Since Bob has access to the basis vectors of the face space in the clear, and projection is a linear operation, he can directly compute (by use of the homomorphic properties of the encryption scheme) an encryption of the biometric template of the face to be recognized.

  If we assume that the basis vectors of the face space are independent of the enrollment data, we can drastically simplify this step: Alice herself can project the face image onto the publicly available basis vectors, encrypt the result and send it to Bob. This saves both computation (since each operation on encrypted values corresponds to an operation in a finite ring) and communication (transmitting the encrypted face image pixel-by-pixel is rather costly compared to the transmission of the encrypted template).

- *Distance computation*: Subsequently, Alice and Bob jointly compute encrypted distances between the encrypted face template obtained in the first step and all templates stored in the database by Bob. Since computing the (squared) Euclidean distance between two vectors is not a linear operation, this step requires interaction between Alice and Bob. In particular, one requires to compute the square of an encrypted number, which cannot be done by homomorphic encryption alone. For this purpose, they can run a small two-party protocol.

- *Match finding*: After the second step is finished, Bob has access to encryptions containing distances between the newly obtained biometrics and all templates of the database. As a third step, both parties have to pick the encryption that contains the smallest distance, and compare this against the threshold. If the smallest encrypted distance is smaller than the threshold, a match is achieved.

Technically, this step can be performed by repeatedly running cryptographic protocols for solving Yao's millionaire's problem (see Sect. 5 of [9]), which allows picking the minimum of two encrypted values. Given the set of encrypted distances, the protocol is run iteratively: during each iteration two distances are compared and the smaller distance is retained (in a way that the server does not "see" which encryption is kept, this can be realized by re-randomizing the encryption). This process is iterated until only one distance is left. Finally, this distance is (again using the protocol to solve Yao's Millionaire problem) compared to the threshold, and the encrypted binary answer is sent to the client, who can decrypt and interpret the result.

This way, the client learns the result of the matching process, while the server is completely oblivious about the computations: he does not obtain the input values, the output values or intermediate values during computation. The price to pay is a higher computation and communication effort.

The solution sketched above works in a scenario where the server (Bob) has access to all templates in the clear. However, in situations where the actual templates should be hidden from the server, signal processing in the encrypted domain can be applied as well. To this end, template protection can be combined with encrypted processing in a way that the server matches an encrypted newly measured biometric against a set of encrypted templates in an interactive fashion. Details of the construction can be found in [11].

2.4 Conclusions

In this chapter we discussed the basic security requirements of biometric identification. We showed that security considerations must be an integral part of the entire biometric processing pipeline, starting from the acquisition of the biometric through a sensor down to the comparison with stored templates. Furthermore we showed that biometric matching "under encryption" is possible so that the party that does the computation does not learn the biometrics or the matching result. This enables implementation of biometric technologies even on hostile or untrusted devices.

References

1. Bianchi T, Piva A, Barni M (2010) Composite signal representation for fast and storage-efficient processing of encrypted signals. IEEE Transactions on Information Forensics and Security 5(1):180–187
2. Bishop M (2002) Computer Security: Art and Science. Addison–Wesley, Reading
3. Bishop M (2005) Introduction to Computer Security. Addison–Wesley, Reading

4. Bringer J, Chabanne H, Kindarji B (2009) Anonymous identification with cancelable biometrics. In: Proceedings of the 6th International Symposium on Image and Signal Processing and Analysis, Salzburg, Austria, pp 494–499
5. Carls JW (2011) A Framework for Analyzing Biometric Template Aging and Renewal Prediction. ProQuest, UMI Dissertation Publishing, Cambridge
6. Cox I, Miller M, Bloom J, Fridrich J, Kalker T (2008) Digital Watermarking and Steganography, 2nd edn. Morgan Kaufmann, San Mateo
7. Dittmann J, Wohlmacher P, Nahrstedt K (2001) Multimedia and security—using cryptographic and watermarking algorithms. IEEE Multimedia 8(4):54–65
8. Dodis Y, Reyzin L, Smith A (2004) Fuzzy extractors: how to generate strong keys from biometrics and other noisy data. In: Cachin C, Camenisch J (eds) Advances in Cryptology—Eurocrypt 2004. Lecture Notes in Computer Science, vol 3027. Springer, Berlin, pp 523–540
9. Erkin Z, Piva A, Katzenbeisser S, Lagendijk R, Shokrollahi J, Neven G (2007) Protection and retrieval of encrypted multimedia content: when cryptography meets signal processing. EURASIP Journal on Information Security
10. Erkin Z, Franz M, Guajardo J, Katzenbeisser S, Lagendijk I, Toft T (2009) Privacy-preserving face recognition. In: Privacy Enhancing Technologies Symposium (PET 2009). Lecture Notes in Computer Science, vol 5672, pp 235–253. Springer, Berlin
11. Failla P, Sutcu Y, Barni M (2010) ESketch: a privacy-preserving fuzzy commitment scheme for authentication using encrypted biometrics In: ACM Workshop on Multimedia Security, MMSect 2010. ACM, New York
12. Fenker SP, Bowyer KW (2012) Analysis of template aging in iris biometrics. In: Proceedings of IEEE Computer Vision and Pattern Recognition Workshops (CVPRW), pp 45–51
13. Galbally J, Fiérrez-Aguilar J, Ortega-Garcia J (2007) Bayesian hill-climbing attack and its application to signature verification. ICB 386–395.
14. Galbally J, Cappelli R, Lumini A, Maltoni D, Fierrez J (2008) Fake fingertip generation from a minutiae template. In: Proc Intl Conf on Pattern Recognition, ICPR, Tampa, USA
15. Gupta UK, Prakash S (2003) Dermatoglyphics: a study of finger tip patterns in bronchial asthma and its genetic disposition. Kathmandu University Medical Journal 1(4):267–271
16. Information Technology Security Evaluation Criteria (ITSEC): provisional harmonised criteria. V 1.2, Jun 1991
17. ISO99 ISO/IEC IS 15408 (1999). http://www.iso.org/iso/home/store/catalogue_tc/catalogue_detail.htm?csnumber=50341. Website request 24.5.2013
18. Juels A, Wattenberg M (1999) A fuzzy commitment scheme. In: Proceedings of the 6th ACM Conference on Computer and Communications Security, CCS'99. ACM, New York, pp 28–36
19. Kanade SG, Petrovska-Delacrétaz D, Dorizzi B (2012) Enhancing Information Security and Privacy by Combining Biometrics with Cryptography. Morgan & Claypool Publishers, San Rafael
20. Kiltz S, Lang A, Dittmann J (2007) Taxonomy for computer security incidents. In: Janczewski LJ, Colarik AM (eds) Cyber Warfare and Cyber Terrorism. Information Science Reference (IGI Global), Hershey. ISBN 978-1-59140-991-5
21. Kiltz S, Hildebrandt M, Dittmann J, Vielhauer C, Kraetzer C (2011) Printed fingerprints: a framework and first results towards detection of artificially printed latent fingerprints for forensics. In: Proc of SPIE: Image Quality and System Performance VIII, San Francisco, USA. doi:10.1117/12.872329
22. Kümmel K, Vielhauer C (2010) Reverse-engineering methods on a biometric hash algorithm for dynamic handwriting. In: Proceedings of the 12th ACM Workshop on Multimedia and Security. ACM, New York, pp 62–72
23. Kümmel K, Vielhauer C (2011) Biometric Hash algorithm for dynamic handwriting embedded on a Java card. In: Biometrics and ID Managements. Lecture Notes in Computer Science, vol 6583. Springer, Heidelberg, pp 61–72
24. Matsumoto T, Matsumoto H, Yamada K, Hoshino S (2002) Impact of artificial "Gummy" fingers on fingerprint systems. In: Proceedings of SPIE Conference on Optical Security and Counterfeit Deterrence Techniques IV, vol 4677

25. Monrose F, Reiter MK, Li Q, Wetzel S (2001) Using voice to generate cryptographic keys. In: Proceedings of Odyssey 2001. Proceedings of the Speaker Verification Workshop
26. Nagar A, Nandakumar K, Jain AK (2010) Biometric template transformation: a security analysis. In: Proceedigns of SPIE Conference on Media Forensics and Security II, vol 7541. doi:10.1117/12.839976
27. Oermann A, Dittmann J (2006) Trust in e-technologies. In: Khosrow-Pour M (ed) Encyclopedia of E-Commerce, E-Government and Mobile Commerce, vol 2. Idea Group Reference, Hershey, pp 1101–1108
28. Osadchy M, Pinkas B, Jarrous A, Moskovich B (2010) SCiFI—a system for secure face identification. In: IEEE Symposium on Security and Privacy 2010. IEEE Press, New York, pp 239–254
29. Pfitzmann A, Hansen M A terminology for talking about privacy by data minimization: anonymity, unlinkability, undetectability, unobservability, pseudonymity, and identity management. (Version v0.34, 10 Aug 2010). http://dud.inf.tu-dresden.de/literatur/Anon_Terminology_v0.34.pdf. Web request from 15th February 2011
30. Pfitzmann A, Waidner M (1986) Networks without user observability—design options. In: Pichler F (ed) Advances in Cryptology—EUROCRYPT'85. Lecture Notes in Computer Science, vol 219, pp 245–253
31. Reiter MK, Rubin AD (1998) Crowds: anonymity for web transactions. ACM Transactions on Information and System Security 1(1):66–92
32. Sadeghi A, Schneider T, Wehrenberg I (2009) Efficient privacy-preserving face recognition. In: Information, Security and Cryptology—ICISC 2009. Lecture Notes in Computer Science, vol 5984. Springer, Berlin, pp 229–244
33. Saltzer JH, Schroeder MD (1975) The protection of information in computer systems. Proceedings of the IEEE 63(9):1278–1308
34. Sutcu Y, Li Q, Memon N (2007) Protecting biometric templates with sketch: theory and practice. IEEE Transactions on Information Forensics and Security 2(3):503–512
35. Teoh A, Kuan Y, Lee S (2007) Cancelable biometrics and annotations on BioHash. Pattern Recognition 41(6):2034–2044
36. Uludag U, Pankanti S, Prabhakar S, Jain AK (2004) Biometric cryptosystems: issues and challenges. Proceedings of the IEEE 948–960
37. Vielhauer C (2006) Biometric User Authentication for IT Security: From Fundamentals to Handwriting. Springer, New York
38. Vielhauer C, Steinmetz R, Mayerhöfer A (2002) Biometric Hash based on statistical features of online signatures. In: Proceedings of the IEEE International Conference on Pattern Recognition (ICPR), Quebec City, Canada, vol 1, pp 123–126

Chapter 3
Beyond PKI: The Biocryptographic Key Infrastructure

Walter J. Scheirer, William Bishop, and Terrance E. Boult

Abstract Public Key Infrastructure is a widely deployed security technology for handling key distribution and validation in computer security. Despite PKI's popularity as a security solution, Phishing and other Man-in-the-Middle related attacks are accomplished with ease throughout our computer networks. The major problems with PKI come down to trust, and largely, how much faith we must place in cryptographic keys alone to establish authenticity and identity. In this chapter, we look at a novel biometric solution that mitigates this problem at both the user and certificate authority levels. More importantly, we analyze the problem of applying unprotected biometric features directly into PKI, and propose the integration of a secure, revocable biometric template protection technology that supports transactional key release. A detailed explanation of this new *Biocryptographic Key Infrastructure* is provided, including composition, enrollment, authentication, and revocation details. The BKI provides a new paradigm for blending elements of physical and virtual security to address network attacks that more conventional approaches have not been able to stop.

3.1 Introduction

To motivate the contribution of this paper, we first turn to the technology that underpins the problem. Public Key Infrastructure (PKI) [1, 10, 11, 31] has been a popular, yet often maligned technology since its widespread adoption in the 1990s. PKI (Fig. 3.1) is the infrastructure for handling the complete management of digital

W.J. Scheirer (✉) · T.E. Boult
Vision and Security Technology Lab, Department of Computer Science, University of Colorado, Colorado Springs, CO 80918-7150, USA
e-mail: wjs3@vast.uccs.edu

T.E. Boult
e-mail: tboult@vast.uccs.edu

W. Bishop
Securics, Inc., Colorado Springs, CO 80918-7150, USA
e-mail: bill.bishop@levault.net

P. Campisi (ed.), *Security and Privacy in Biometrics*,
DOI 10.1007/978-1-4471-5230-9_3, © Springer-Verlag London 2013

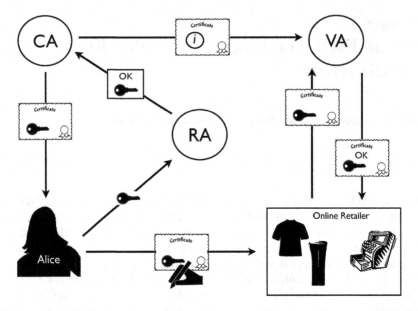

Fig. 3.1 An overview of Public Key Infrastructure. A website owner, Alice, wants to obtain a digital certificate for her web store. She applies to a Registration Authority (RA) with her public key for the certificate. The RA confirms Alice's identity, and then contacts the Certificate Authority (CA), which issues the certificate. With a valid certificate, Alice can now digitally sign off on contracts involving her web store. Alice's identity can be confirmed when visitors to her web store present her certificate to a Validation Authority (VA), which receives information about issued certificates from the CA

certificates (x.509 compliant), which contain a piece of trusted information: a public key. PKI attempts to solve an important problem in key management—namely, how can Alice verify that Bob's public key is really Bob's? Addressing this problem remains a paramount concern, as the Internet has experienced an explosion of successful Phishing and other Man-in-the-Middle attacks in recent years. Users of networks, both those well-informed and those blissfully ignorant of security protocols, routinely ignore security provisions put into place by PKI to guard them against such attacks (how often have *you* blindly clicked through a browser certificate warning?). Sadly, providers of information security services are also to blame, by providing PKI as a catch-all security solution, and ignoring its limitations.

The problems with PKI [16, 17] are well-known, and have remained mostly unsolved thus far. Ellison and Schneier [15] specifically highlight a series of identity related PKI risks by asking the following questions:

1. Who do we trust, and what for?
2. Who is using my key?
3. Is a name a unique identifier?
4. Is the user part of the security design?
5. How did the CA identify the certificate holder?

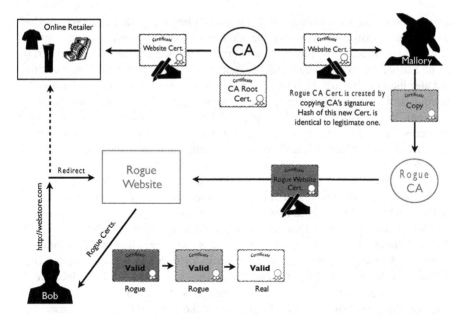

Fig. 3.2 The chosen-prefix collision attack of [37]. A malicious attacker, Mallory, wishes to deploy a rogue website that after a redirect attack will look identical to a legitimate online retailer, with valid certificates. To accomplish this, she requests a legitimate website certificate from a real CA (cert. in *upper right* of the diagram). Mallory crafts a rogue CA certificate (*light gray* cert. in the diagram) by copying the signature from her legitimate website certificate to an illegitimate CA certificate. She is able to do this by creating a CA certificate that will collide with the legitimate signature when the same hash function is applied. Mallory can now create a rogue website certificate (*dark gray* cert. in the diagram) that bears the online retailer's identity, but contains a different public key and is signed by the rogue CA. When Bob is redirected to the rogue website, he can successfully validate in sequence the rogue website's certificate, the rogue CA's certificate and the real CA's root certificate. The transaction will appear to be legitimate

The overarching criticism stems back to the notion of trust in a PKI system—why would we place any trust in a system with entities (both certificate authorities and users) signifying their identities with only randomly generated keys? A practical and recent attack [36, 37] highlights the ease with which a rogue certificate authority can be established, using an MD5 hash collision attack against the digital signatures used for certificate validation (illustrated in Fig. 3.2). With all trust being placed in digital signatures, presumedly derived from *legitimate* keys, there is no way to tell the difference between a Man-in-the-Middle and a legitimate site—if a collision has been located that matches the legitimate certificate's signature. While MD5 enables the attack in this instance, the entire infrastructure will always be susceptible to trust related attacks if any cryptographic component is flawed. What if we extend the notion of trust beyond keys to include identity specific information?

By adding a second factor, we can mitigate these inherent identity related trust problems with PKI. Biometrics, those methods of uniquely recognizing humans based on physiognomy or behavior have become ubiquitous in many areas of technology and society, and are mature to the point of being generally accepted as valid and useful security tools. For PKI, the addition of biometric data has a very attractive feature—if a user or certificate authority presents a key and biometric during some action, we have more confidence that this action is legitimate (but this does not absolutely prove that the owner of the key and biometric actually performed the action—stolen keys and spoofing attacks are not prevented by two-factor authentication). With biometrics, we have improved *non-repudiation*. A series of related concerns follow the trust problem: the security of the verifying computer, certificate authority establishment, and general certificate issue. With the proper protocols including a biometric component, we can address each of these.

But to solve these problems correctly, we cannot simply use standard biometric templates (the data representation of the collected biometric feature) embedded within x.509 certificates, because a *revocation* of raw biometric data can only happen for a limited number of times (we have one face, two irises, 10 fingers). ISO/IEC 19794-2 standard templates, while being an abstract representation of the original biometric features, are still effectively invertible [9]. Moreover, unprotected biometric data that is even under the control of "trusted" entities is still vulnerable to attack. To understand why, we first must take a look at Fig. 3.3, which depicts what we term the *Biometric Dilemma*. In essence, as the use of biometrics increases, so does the chance for compromise. If a malicious attacker, Mallory, wishes to impersonate Alice at an area of high security, she can obtain the exact biometric data she needs from a different, much lower security area. How well might Alice's gym be protecting her biometric data that she uses to access her locker? Low-hanging fruit is plentiful, and can often be obtained legitimately. In 2001, the state of Colorado tried to sell its DMV face and fingerprint databases [23] to anyone who wanted to buy them. The resulting protests moved the data back off the market, but the state still offers them to any requesting law enforcement agency.

A second, and equally dangerous attack is what we term the *doppelganger threat* (Fig. 3.4), which takes advantage of the operational security performance characteristics of the underlying biometric matching algorithm. If the False Accept Rate (FAR) of a system is 1 in X attempts, then a doppelganger attack consists of trying more than X different biometric samples. This attack is the biometric equivalent of a dictionary attack. Once again, one need not break the law to gather the data necessary for a successful attack. The hundreds of thousands of fingerprints that are publicly available (including four well known algorithm challenges [5], testing data from NIST [28], and even 100,000+ prints being offered by a private company [14]) provide at least a basic doppelganger dictionary for anyone willing to spend a small amount of money.

Previous work on the integration of biometrics into PKI has not considered the biometric dilemma or doppelganger attack, favoring a simplistic unsecured application of biometrics. Proposed standards for PKI with biometrics go back to the mid 1990s, with recommendations from the defense space [30], commercial Internet related interests [40], and NIST [24]. Both Benavente [3] and Martinez-Silva et al. [26] suggest augmenting x.509 certificates with BioAPI [4], which provides the templates and matching capability needed to use the biometric data. Dawson

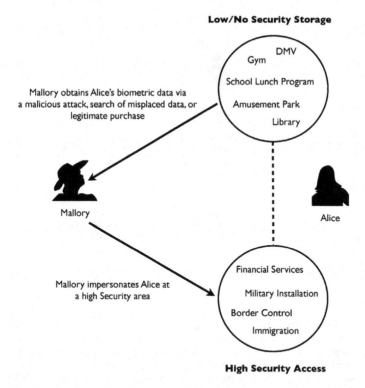

Fig. 3.3 The biometric dilemma: as the usage and storage of biometric data increases, so does the vulnerability. A malicious attacker, Mallory, may obtain Alice's biometric data with relative ease from a low/no security source (possibly through a legitimate transaction) to attack a high security target. The indiscriminate use of biometrics makes this threat possible, and if not addressed, limits the integration of biometrics into existing security infrastructure like PKI

et al. [12] also recommend augmenting x.509 certificates with biometric data, as part of a much larger defense-in-depth approach to authentication. Finally, Kwon and Moon [25] suggest the use of a biometric PKI scheme for border control applications. These previous standards recommendations and research works do not place adequate safeguards around biometric data. All store and match unprotected templates, and have no facility for biometric template revocation and re-issue.

In response to the threat of permanent biometric feature compromise, very recent research [19] has emerged from both the pattern recognition and cryptography communities to address the problem of *biometric template security*. Solutions to this problem create a transformation of original biometric features that can be matched in an encoded space, and revoked and re-issued if a compromise is detected, in much the same manner as a traditional password or PIN. For unattended network authentication, the risk of spoofing is greatly reduced by secure templates. Unique templates can be generated for different domains and applications, making a template harvested by an attacker at one domain useless when applied to a different domain. This addresses the biometric dilemma described above. A wide variety of

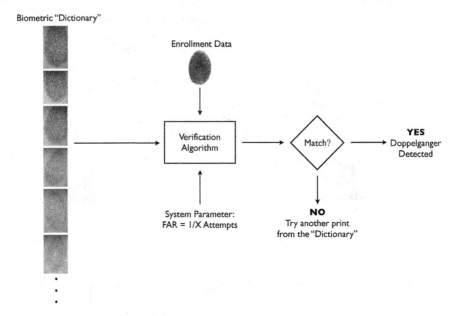

Biometric "Dictionary"

Enrollment Data

Verification Algorithm

Match?

YES
Doppelganger Detected

System Parameter:
FAR = 1/X Attempts

NO
Try another print
from the "Dictionary"

Fig. 3.4 The Doppelganger Threat. What happens when a large database of biometric data is stolen, hacked, or sold? For example, consider a database containing unique records for 4 million individuals. If the matching system is operating at a False Accept Rate (FAR) of 1 in 1,000, a malicious attacker in possession of the database may, on average, be given a choice of approximately 4,000 identities to use to compromise the matching system. Even at a FAR of 1 in 1,000,000, the attacker still gets four choices, on average, to compromise the matching system

approaches have been proposed in the literature, including non-invertible transforms [29], fuzzy commitment [21], fuzzy vaults [20], fuzzy extractors [13], BioHashing [38], and revocable biotokens [7]. Even more interesting for trusted data transfer is that certain classes of these schemes support key release upon successful matching. *Key-binding* biometric cryptosystems bind key data with the biometric data. *Key-generating* biometric cryptosystems derive the key data from the biometric data. Both classes support a key release that may be used for cryptographic applications, including standard symmetric key cryptography, where key storage is problematic.

Secure templates enable completely new ways to transfer secret information. Consider a key-binding biometric cryptosystem where the key can be bound even after enrollment and which also provides public secure templates that can be used in the same manner as a public key. With these components, we have the building blocks for a *Biocryptographic Key Infrastructure*. The primary benefit (Fig. 3.5) of such an infrastructure is the ability to store public templates (referred to in this article as *biotokens*) in x.509 compliant digital certificates. Through a transformation of a public template with an embedded secret (the transformed template is referred to in this article as a *bipartite biotoken*) by an entity that wants to convey information to the template's owner, secure key exchange and unique transactions can be supported. Only the owner of the public biotoken can unlock the secret. By adding this

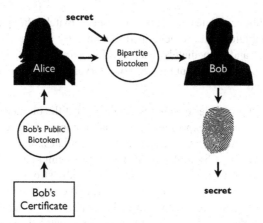

Fig. 3.5 The primary benefit of a Biocryptographic Key Infrastructure: the ability to store *public* biotokens in digital certificates. Any entity in the infrastructure can send secret data that only the owner of the biotoken can unlock. In this example, Alice wants to convey a secret message to Bob. Bob's public biotoken can be retrieved from his certificate, allowing Alice to transform it into a bipartite biotoken, which conveys an embedded secret. Alice has assurance that an identity must be present to unlock the secret—not just a key

biometrically derived data to a certificate, an additional component must validated (with the help of a validation authority in possession of enrollment data), making attacks such as the one described above much more difficult to perpetrate.

The rest of this chapter introduces the details for the Biocryptographic Key Infrastructure. In Sect. 3.2, the fundamental biometric requirements are defined, including the properties necessary for protecting the biometric data, secure key release, and revocation support. In Sect. 3.3 our full infrastructure is described, including a description of the overall composition, the enrollment process for both biometric certificate authorities and users, the certificate validation process, authentication protocols, and revocation and re-issue procedures. Section 3.4 takes these ideas into the real world with suggestions on how BKI can be applied in place of PKI with stronger security. In the concluding remarks of Sect. 3.5, we make the case for standards consideration of revocable biometric template technologies and BKI.

3.2 Fundamental Biometric Requirements for BKI

Many different secure template technologies exist, but not all are appropriate for use in a PKI-like framework. To be useful for PKI, a secure template technology must possess the following properties:

1. Cryptographically strong protection of the underlying biometric features.
2. The ability to revoke and re-issue the template.
3. Nested re-encoding, allowing a hierarchy of templates to be generated from a single base template.

4. Support for public templates that cannot be used to match other public templates, and private templates that are generated dynamically from a biometric sample during matching and immediately discarded following.
5. Key-binding capability without the need of intervention by the person associated with the template.

The first and second properties ensure resilience against the biometric dilemma and doppelganger attacks by not exposing the original biometric features during matching, allowing the creation of application specific templates, and rendering a compromised template useless by replacing it with a new template via different cryptographic keys and/or transformations. Cryptographically strong protection implies that it should not be feasible for an attacker to retrieve the original biometric features from a compromised secure template without knowledge of relevant transformation information (such as keys used to protect the biometric data). The third, fourth, and fifth properties guarantee the PKI-like operations we'd like our secure templates to possess to be useful for protocols common to PKI.

Throughout the rest of this chapter, we will use *revocable biotokens* [7, 33, 34] as a case study for the BKI described herein, though any secure template technology supporting the five aforementioned properties could be used. To date, only revocable biotokens support all five. Some secure template technologies are appropriate for authentication protocols [39, 41] but lack support for key transfer, while others support key transfer [8] but lack the flexibility for unique transactions. A scheme such as the one presented in [22] could be used to support some of the functionality of BKI (namely requirement 5), though it does not support nested re-encoding and is susceptible to attack.[1] We briefly introduce the fundamentals for revocable biotokens in the remainder of this section as an illustration of the biometric requirements. Interested readers should refer back to the prior published work on revocable biotokens [7, 33, 34] for modality specific algorithm details and security analysis, though that level of depth is not necessary to understand the higher level concepts that enable BKI.

The notion of data splitting to support revocable biotokens was introduced by Boult et al. [7]. In general, encrypted biometric data cannot be matched, because of the unstable nature of the data, which can vary as a function of environment, age, and acquisition circumstances. However, many biometric modalities yield features that can be split into stable and unstable (or residual) components. By encrypting the stable component, matching can occur in the encrypted space because this portion of the data is not impacted by any instability at the bit level. Additional residual matching adds accuracy [7]. Using this knowledge, and the concept of public key cryptography, we can develop the re-encoding methodology for revocable biotokens. The re-encoding property, introduced by Scheirer and Boult [33], is essential

---

[1]The template described in [22] consists of a secret key + error correction θ_{ps} XOR*ed* with shuffled biometric data θ_{canc}, yielding θ_{lock}. If an attacker knows θ_{ps}, they can simply XOR it with θ_{lock}, yielding θ_{canc}, which can be used by the attacker to match from that point forward. This is a straightforward application of the SKI attack [32].

for supporting a viable transactional framework—tokens with unique data must be generated quickly and automatically to support cryptographic transactions (such as session key exchange). The *bipartite biotoken* form of a revocable biotoken supports data-binding (key-binding) at the transactional level. Bipartite biotoken generation from a stored biotoken allows the required data release when only matching against tokens generated from data derived from original biometric features during the course of the transaction.

Assuming the biometric produces a value v that is obfuscated via scaling and translation to $v' = (v - t) * s$, the resulting v' is split into the stable component q, and the residual component r. The amount of stable and unstable data is a function of the biometric modality being considered. In a basic scheme, for a user j, their residual $r_j(v')$ is left un-encoded. For the initial *transformation* $w_{j,1}(q_j(v'), T_1)$ some transformation function T (which may be a strong hash function like SHA-256 that is minimally impacted by collision attacks, or another application of public key cryptography) is applied. For nested re-encodings, w_j is re-encoded using further transformations, creating a unique new encoding for each hash or key that is applied:

$$w_{j,1}(q_j(v'), T_1), \ w_{j,2}(w_{j,1}, T_2), \ldots, w_{j,n}(w_{j,n-1}, T_n)$$

If public key cryptography is used for every transformation, the nesting process can be securely invertible if the private keys all the way back to the first stage (the root) of encoding are available. Partially inverting the nesting facilitates revocation and automatic re-issue of the biotoken, which is an attractive feature for the BKI system. A tree introducing our standard hierarchy of biotokens with descriptions for each is shown in Fig. 3.6. We note that any public keys used for encoding here are strictly for this biotoken generation process, and are different from the keys contained in the user's certificate. With this nesting in mind, we can define three properties for the bipartite biotoken:

1. Let B be a secure biotoken, as described in [7]. A bipartite biotoken B_B is a transformation $bb_{j,k}$ of user j's kth transformation of B. This transformation supports matching in encoded space of any bipartite biotoken instance $B_{B,k}$ with any secure biotoken instance B_k for the biometric features of a user j and a common series of transforms $T_1, T_2, \ldots, T_k$.
2. The transformation $bb_{j,k}$ must allow the embedding of some data d into B_B, represented as: $bb_{j,k}(w_{j,k}, T_k, d)$.
3. The matching of B_k and $B_{B,k}$ must release d if successful.

The design of bipartite biotokens that satisfies the above properties is an extension of the fuzzy vault [20] concept, where a polynomial embedding hides the data d. The bipartite representation implements Reed–Solomon (RS) for error correction, and does not store the points at which the embedded polynomial is evaluated. For efficiency, we choose to work over a Galois Field of size 2^8, where the coefficients and evaluation points are all 8 bit quantities. We represent the data d to be stored as a K-byte block, with E bytes of error correction, yielding a total payload block $N = K + E$. The polynomial encodes the N bytes of data. The Reed–Solomon polynomial representing the N byte payload body is then evaluated at a set of points, with the value of the resulting polynomial stored in the template.

Fig. 3.6 The biotoken
issue/re-issue tree. Biotokens
can be re-encoded, starting
from the root token generated
at enrollment time, through
subsequent applications of
public key encryption
(supporting automatic
revocation and re-issue),
or a hash function

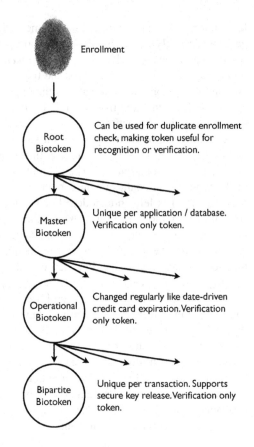

For illustrative purposes, assume that a biometric sample produces three features a_1, a_2, a_3 that must be protected. Let sa_1, sa_2, sa_3 be the stable components of these features, and let ra_1, ra_2, ra_3 be the residuals. For polynomial evaluation, the 24 bits of sa_1, sa_2, sa_3 are hashed into i, an 8 bit quantity that is stored in the template. The value i is then hashed, per transaction, a second time to define the point at which the polynomial is evaluated. To support multiple embedded data "columns," this second hash h is evaluated for different polynomials yielding values $rs_1, \ldots, rs_4$. Note the evaluation point/hash value h is not stored.

The result is an "encoded bipartite row" that contains the unprotected fields and six protected fields (the encoded stable field w used for matching, index i and four columns of evaluated polynomials). For data d that is less than 512 bits we spread the data over columns in 16 rows; above 512 bits, we spread equally over the columns taking as many rows as needed. We require at least 14 rows, and pad d if it does not require four columns to represent it. The location of w is randomized per row. The evaluated Reed–Solomon polynomials for the four key columns, $rs_1, \ldots, rs_4$, follow w using a circular mapping of the six slots. For example, if the random index was 3, then the sequence would be $[rs_3, rs_4, w, rs_1, rs_2, i]$.

When matching a probe, the system creates all the fields for each of its rows, including the "un-stored" hash value h for polynomial evaluation. A probe row potentially matches a gallery row if it finds a matching w among the encoded fields and the residuals (ra_1, ra_2, ra_3) are within some threshold. This test is necessary, but not sufficient, for a correct match. With w identified, the algorithm can then extract the evaluated polynomial values, $rs_1, \ldots, rs_4$. If w is incorrectly identified, if the row is an accidental match, or if the underlying hash value h is incorrect (because of a random collision in generating/matching w), some values labeled $rs_1, \ldots, rs_4$ will be extracted, but will be incorrect. We extract the k values for each of the j embedded data columns and obtain a set of hash evaluation points h_j and their Reed–Solomon polynomial evaluations $rs_{j,k}$ at the associated points.

Now comes one of the important implementation details, addressing both security and efficiency. One could effectively improve robustness by increasing the level of ECC, but doing so increases the ease with which an attacker can compromise d. Instead we use a two level hashing to improve robustness. Our two level hashing will, in general, map multiple sa_1, sa_2, sa_3 sets to the same index. Next, a procedure is followed to collect the multiple values during the mapping, check for consistency and use that consistency to help resolve any conflicts that arise when noisy data is mapped. The consistency check accounts for noise in the matching process, and the many-to-one mapping that permits non-unique mapping results. The result of the mapping and consistency check is a vector of length N polynomial values (some of which may be missing) that holds the values of the evaluated Reed–Solomon polynomial for each location. The vector of length N, with gaps marked, is used as input to the Reed–Solomon decode function, which allows us to recover d with up to g gaps and e errors, as long as $2g + e < E$, where E is the number of ECC bytes used. Each key column is recovered separately, with larger keys being the concatenation of multiple columns. For added security, a checksum is computed over the six unprotected columns of the enrollment biotoken. The data d are XORed with a checksum before embedding, and again after decoding, which prevents any tampering with the biotoken.

When implemented, the above design for bipartite biotokens lays the foundation for the protocols of BKI. The primary benefit of BKI is the ability to store public biotokens that any user in a particular infrastructure can retrieve and use to generate a bipartite biotoken to send some secret back to the owner of the biotoken, with the assurance that the certificate containing the biotoken is valid (a validation process is described in Sect. 3.3.1). The security of such a scheme to publicly distribute biotokens derived from biometrics is of course a concern. It has been shown [7, 34] that revocable biotokens are cryptographically secure and guard against the secure template attacks of Scheirer and Boult [32]. Considering the doppelganger attack of Sect. 3.1, prior work [34] shows a test of over 500 *million* impostor trials, with no false accepts—possibly the largest trial to date for this sort of test.

The amount of information leaked by the residual component of the biotoken, in an information theoretical sense, has yet to be analyzed. However, while unencoded, this information is still protected via the obfuscation scheme of folding the residual data back into the encrypted stable data, thus hiding its original position (described in Sect. 2 of [7]). Thus, an attacker would have to resolve the positional ambiguity of the residual data, before beginning to mount some sort of correlational attack with the collected residuals from multiple biotokens. The variational and very limited nature of the residual data (4 bytes per row component of the Bozorth fingerprint implementation [7]) makes their value as a unique identifier questionable. We also note that the residuals can be discarded, leading to a small reduction in accuracy when just the stable components of the features are matched, thus completely alleviating this concern. From these considerations, we have confidence that revocable biotokens can be used in a public setting.

3.3 A Biocryptographic Key Infrastructure

A Biocryptographic Key Infrastructure must incorporate elements from several different domains, including biometrics, cryptography and network security. Network entities (including clients and servers), enrollment procedures, validation procedures, data structures, authentication protocols and revocation protocols are all necessary for a fully functional infrastructure. Here we examine those details.

3.3.1 Composition, Enrollment and Validation

An overview of the Biocryptographic Key Infrastructure is shown in Fig. 3.7. Several distinct entities are shown in the BKI graph. *Biometric Certificate Authorities* (BCAs) are certificate authorities that support both public keys and revocable biotokens, and are biometrically verified by higher-level authorities, in a process described in detail below. As in PKI, a central root authority exists to authorize all BCAs below it. Enrollment and key management follows from each BCA up to the root. Auth Stations exist at the outermost regions of the graph, and are the places where users submit their biometric samples to generate enrollment biotokens or biotokens for a particular session. Report Engines can also be deployed throughout the BKI graph to propagate registration and transaction reports to other authorities.

In order to support the biotoken, we add some additional fields to the base x.509 v3 certificate via its extensions provision, similar to the approach of Martinez-Silva et al. [26]. This is shown in Fig. 3.8. We can use certificates in both an online and offline setting, as is shown in Fig. 3.7. If we are operating in an offline setting, such as a standalone computer or private network, we are not able to connect to BCAs on outside networks, including the root. In order to indicate the operating mode to the underlying BKI software, the certificate contains an "Online Only" flag and an "Offline Only" flag. For the user's biotoken, we first note the type of biotoken included. Recall from Fig. 3.6 that a tree of different biotokens exists for a particular user, with the possibility of a Root Biotoken, Master Biotoken, or Operational Biotoken being included in a certificate. Following the "Biotoken type" flag, the biotoken itself is included.

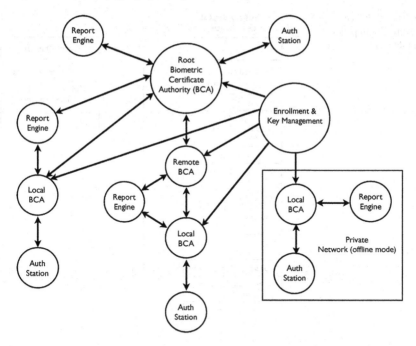

Fig. 3.7 Overview of Biocryptographic Key Infrastructure flow. The BKI can be viewed as a graph of interconnected nodes, each with a specific role. In a particular BKI, we find a root Biometric Certificate Authority (BCA), as we would have a root authority in PKI. The BCA trust path follows back centrally to the root, with individual local BCAs managing their own end-user enrollees. Offline BKI components (standalone computers or private networks) can also be supported

We need BCAs to trust each other, and we need to be able to place some trust in our end-users. To do this, we need an enrollment process where we require that someone biometrically register with the root BCA, which can search for this person in the existing records. To introduce an increased level of trust with biometrics, the standard Certificate Signing Request (CSR) [31] is augmented as per Fig. 3.9. The CSR is the message sent to a CA by a user requesting a new certificate. The augmentation takes advantage of the open nature of registration information detail for new text fields, and the open extensions in the certificate template, as defined by [31].

Specifically for enrollment, BKI requires that a representative of an organization making a request generate an *enrollment biotoken*, which is passed up to the root authority for a *duplicate enrollment check* (which can tell us if this person been flagged as a malicious user, or if they are impersonating someone else). The enrollment biotoken is always generated as a Root Biotoken (Fig. 3.6) using the root authority's public key, to enable matching across all enrollees (if keys differ between enrollments at this stage, it will not be possible to match any of them). The enrollment token is stored at the root BCA for use in all future enrollment checks. While this does not protect the privacy of the organizational representative at the database level, it does maintain the integrity of the BCA establishment, and still pro-

W.J. Scheirer et al.

Fig. 3.8 Digital certificate supporting both public keys and biotokens

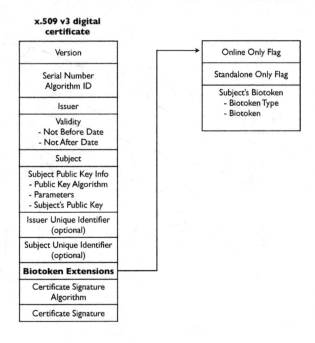

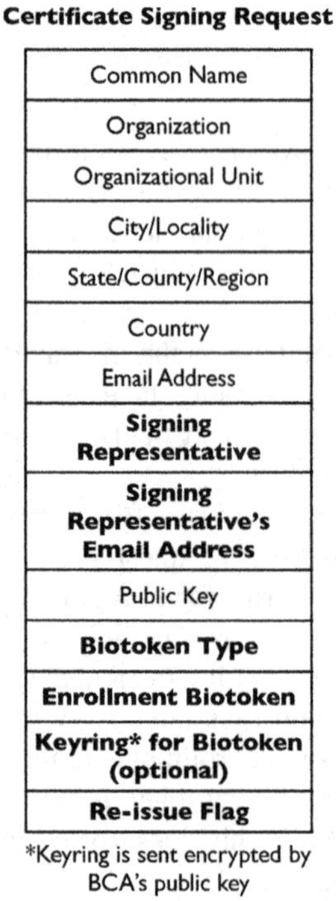

Fig. 3.9 A modification of the typical CSR message, including biotoken enrollment information

Certificate Signing Request

Common Name
Organization
Organizational Unit
City/Locality
State/County/Region
Country
Email Address
Signing Representative
Signing Representative's Email Address
Public Key
Biotoken Type
Enrollment Biotoken
Keyring* for Biotoken (optional)
Re-issue Flag

*Keyring is sent encrypted by BCA's public key

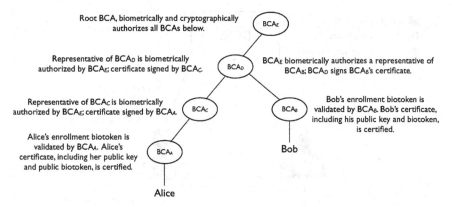

Fig. 3.10 The path from Alice, who wants to obtain Bob's certificate, to BCA_B, which certifies Bob's certificate, and ultimately Bob, who possess a certificate with his public key and biotoken

tects the security of the representative's biometric data. This process is illustrated in Fig. 3.10.

The same process follows for end users, except the enrollment token need not be passed up all the way back to the root from the user's Auth Station; more local BCAs can manage it. This is also illustrated in Fig. 3.10. For both BCA and end user certificates, the validation process includes an analysis of the certificate with a BCA that is established as a VA. This is similar to the standard process for PKI, with a further step of biotoken validation to ensure a Man-in-the-Middle has not replaced the public biotoken in the certificate with his own. From a stored operational biotoken at the BCA, a local biotoken can be generated and matched against a bipartite biotoken generated from the public biotoken in question [33]. If the match is successful, then the certificate can be validated. This reduces the threat of the collision attack described in Sect. 3.1 in both the BCA and user scenarios, since an attacker would have to find a hash collision that validates the rogue certificate and compromise biometric data that will correctly match against the biotoken of the authorized representative of the BCA or end user.

3.3.2 Authentication Framework

For authentication, we must first understand how certificates are retrieved by parties wishing to communicate with some properly certified entity in the BKI structure. This procedure follows from PKI [35]. In Fig. 3.10, an example of certificate retrieval is depicted, whereby a user Alice traverses an infrastructure composed of five different BCAs ($\text{BCA}_A, \ldots, \text{BCA}_E$) to retrieve another user Bob's certificate. Alice's certificate containing her public key and biotoken is certified by BCA_A; Bob's is certified by BCA_B. BCA_C has a certificate signed by BCA_A, so Alice can begin following the path through the graph to Bob. BCA_D has a certificate signed by BCA_C, and BCA_B has a certificate signed by BCA_D. By moving through the

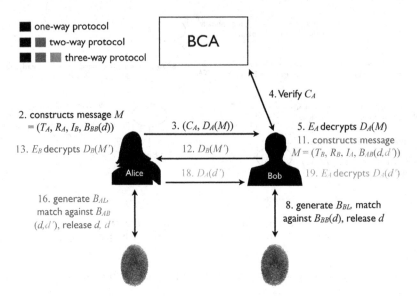

Fig. 3.11 The data-transfer steps for the one-way, two-way, and three-way protocols described in Sect. 3.3.2. It is assumed that Alice has Bob's certificate C_B at the beginning of the one-way protocol

graph to BCA_D, and then down to Bob, Alice can validate Bob's certificate, and retrieve his public key and biotoken for use in some protocol/transaction. BCA_E is the root BCA, signing every BCA's certificate below it and biometrically authorizing all BCA representatives, and having its certificate signed by the same BCAs.

Extending the protocols defined in Sect. 24.9 of Schneier [35], we can support authentication with stronger non-repudiation. For the following three protocols (illustrated in Fig. 3.11), presume Alice has established a certification path to Bob, as described above, and Bob's certificate, containing his public key and biotoken. The numbering of the protocols is sequential, with each protocol after the first relying on the protocol(s) before it.

3.3.2.1 The One-Way Protocol

1. Alice generates a random number, R_A.
2. Alice constructs a message, $M = (T_A, R_A, I_B, B_{BB}(d))$, where T_A is Alice's timestamp, I_B is Bob's identity, and d is a small piece of arbitrary data. d is embedded into a bipartite biotoken $B_{BB}(d)$ that is generated from Bob's biotoken.
3. Alice sends $(C_A, D_A(M))$ to Bob. (C_A is Alice's certificate; D_A is Alice's private key.)
4. Bob verifies C_A and obtains E_A. He makes sure these keys have not expired. (E_A is Alice's public key).

5. Bob uses E_A to decrypt $D_A(M)$. This verifies both Alice's signature and the integrity of the signed information.
6. Bob checks the I_B in M for accuracy.
7. Bob checks the T_A in M and confirms that the message is current.
8. Bob submits a biometric sample to a sensor; a local biotoken B_{BL} is then generated from the sample. B_{BL} is then matched against $B_{BB}(d)$, releasing d.
9. As an option, Bob can check R_A in M against a database of old random numbers to ensure the message is not an old one being replayed.

This protocol is an improvement over the "signature server" protocol previously introduced by Scheirer and Boult [33] for several reasons. Most obviously, it consists of a single message, as opposed to a 4-way transaction, and establishes the identities of both Alice and Bob and the integrity of any information sent from Alice to Bob, especially if d is a shared secret. This protocol also works by encrypting d with Bob's public key—but with the biometric version, Bob does not need to have his private key handy. Further security is provided if Alice has access to a private BCA that holds Bob's certificate, which would make Bob's biotoken a shared secret. Thus, a successful Man-in-the-Middle would need to know not only Alice's private key, but Bob's secret stored biotoken and secret d, as well.

3.3.2.2 The Two-Way Protocol

10. Bob generates another random number, R_B.
11. Bob constructs a message $M' = (T_B, R_B, I_A, B_{AB}(d))$, where T_B is Bob's timestamp, I_A is the identity of Alice, and d is the same data as in step 2. d is embedded into a bipartite biotoken $B_{AB}(d)$ that is generated from Alice's biotoken, obtained from C_A.
12. Bob sends $D_B(M')$ to Alice.
13. Alice uses E_B to decrypt $D_B(M')$. This verifies both Bob's signature and the integrity of the signed information.
14. Alice checks the I_A in M' for accuracy.
15. Alice checks the T_B in M' and confirms that the message is current.
16. Alice submits a biometric sample to a sensor; a local biotoken B_{AL} is then generated from the sample. B_{AL} is then matched against $B_{AB}(d)$, releasing d. If this d matches the d sent in the first transmission, Alice can be ensured that Bob's biometric was used to unlock $B_{BB}(d)$.
17. As an option, Alice can check R_B in M' to ensure the message is not an old one being replayed.

Now Alice has further assurance Bob is actually Bob, and not an impostor. But Bob still has no assurance of Alice's identity beyond her certificate. This can be solved by a three-way protocol, where in addition to the original d, Bob also sends a d' in the same token (step 16). Alice can verify d (step 17), and send d' back to Bob for validation.

3.3.2.3 The Three-Way Protocol

18. Alice takes the recovered d' from step 16, and sends $D_A(d')$ back to Bob.
19. Bob uses E_A to decrypt $D_A(d')$, unlocking d'. Bob can be ensured that Alice's biometric was used to unlock $B_{AB}(d)$ in step 17.

3.3.3 Revocation and Reissue

Unlike standard PKI, we cannot just revoke a certificate, generate a new random key and re-issue—we must address the biometric re-issue as well. While many works in the research literature describe revocation as a property of a particular template protection scheme, only one work [2] has gone as far as describing the revocation procedure, albeit on a per template basis. Below we detail three different scenarios for BKI protocol driven revocation and re-issue. When we describe compromise here, we mean a compromise of the biotoken itself, and not the original biometric features.

3.3.3.1 Scenario 1: Manual Re-issue

The BCA that issued the certificate must maintain a certificate revocation list (CRL). This list only contains revoked certificates, and not expired certificates. If the user's key has been compromised, or the user's biotoken has been compromised, or the BCA's key has been compromised, or because the BCA no longer wants to certify the user, the user's certificate can be revoked. In this scenario, it is presumed that the BCA has not retained any transformation information necessary to invert the biotoken it stores.

To begin the revocation process with re-enrollment, the BCA places the certificate in question on its CRL, and notifies the owner with a Certificate Re-issue Notification (Fig. 3.12) (CRN) via the contact information provided in the CSR. This CRN is a new notice introduced in this work. If the owner is allowed to re-issue, a new public-private key pair and a new biotoken are generated at the Auth Station. This information is sent back to the BCA in the form of a new CSR. If this CSR is accepted, a new certificate is issued.

In an alternate, yet valid, scenario for manual re-issue, re-enrollment is not required. If the user's biotoken, or biotoken and key pair, has been compromised, and the BCA possesses a stored uncompromised base biotoken that was used to generate the compromised biotoken, the owner can re-issue their certificate by varying the transformations used for encoding on their end, while not needing to submit another biometric sample. To begin this revocation process, the BCA places the certificate in question on its CRL, and notifies the owner with a CRN via the contact information provided in the CSR. This CRN contains the owner's base biotoken. The owner will generate new keys for biotoken re-encoding, and use them to generate a new biotoken. This new biotoken, and optionally a new public key, is sent back to the BCA in a new CSR.

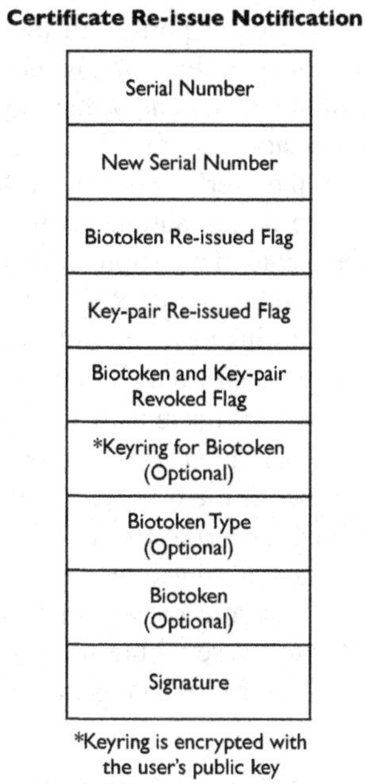

Fig. 3.12 The newly defined
CRN message for certificate
revocation and re-issue

Certificate Re-issue Notification

Serial Number
New Serial Number
Biotoken Re-issued Flag
Key-pair Re-issued Flag
Biotoken and Key-pair Revoked Flag
*Keyring for Biotoken (Optional)
Biotoken Type (Optional)
Biotoken (Optional)
Signature

*Keyring is encrypted with
the user's public key

While two scenarios for automatic re-issue are discussed below, if a public key and biotoken are compromised for a particular certificate, then manual re-issue with re-enrollment will always be forced. Manual re-issue with re-enrollment is also forced if the BCA's key has been compromised, where trust can no longer be placed in the existing data stored at the BCA.

3.3.3.2 Scenario 2: Automatic Re-issue of Biotoken

In cases where the BCA detects a compromise (especially in its own infrastructure) of a stored biotoken, it is very desirable to revoke and re-issue certificates in some automated fashion. To support this, the BCA must possess the necessary keys to invert the token, and subsequently generate a new token based on stored information. This stored information *need not be* the original biometric features. Referring back to the biotoken issue/re-issue tree of Fig. 3.6, any level of token can be generated by an Auth Station, and transmitted on to the BCA. Thus, if the biotoken exists at the 2nd–nth level of encoding, any BCA (except possibly the root, as described in Sect. 3.2) performing the inversion will not be able to recover the original biometric features.

The initial enrollment process is modified in this scenario to transmit the transformation key information used to create the enrollment biotoken to the BCA. The CSR contains an optional field (shown in Fig. 3.9) to include a keyring with all of the necessary keys/passwords/identifiers used to encrypt the stable (that is, some encoding $w_{j,n}(w_{j,n-1}, T_n)$, where $n > 1$, if the original biometric features are to be protected) portion of the biotoken, during the transform. The requesting entity will include this keyring, encrypted by the BCA's public key, in its CSR. The BCA will store this encrypted keyring for later use if revocation and re-issue becomes necessary.

If the user's biotoken has been compromised, the user's certificate can be revoked and re-issued automatically. To begin the revocation process, the BCA places the certificate in question on its CRL, and notifies the owner via the contact information provided in the CSR. If the owner is allowed to re-issue, the BCA will take it upon itself to invert the biotoken back a level (to $w_{j,n-1}$, where $n > 1$), generate a new set of transformation key information, and re-encode the biotoken (producing $w'_{j,n}$). A new certificate is then created with the new biotoken, and the original public key. The BCA then sends the owner of the certificate a CRN, which indicates the serial number of the revoked certificate, the serial number of the re-issued certificate, and the new keyring for the new biotoken (encrypted with the user's public key). This message is signed by the BCA.

Automatic re-issue may happen transparently to the user, with the underlying BKI software taking note of the CRN, and updating the transformation key information for biotoken generation at the user's Auth Station.

3.3.3.3 Scenario 3: Automatic Re-issue of Key-Pair

Similar to Scenario 2, it is very desirable to revoke and re-issue certificates in some automated fashion when the public/private key-pair becomes compromised. To support this, the BCA can use a bipartite biotoken generated from the uncompromised biotoken stored in the user's certificate to convey a secret back to the user.

If the user's key-pair has been compromised, the user's certificate can be revoked and re-issued automatically. To begin the revocation process, the BCA places the certificate in question on its CRL, and notifies the owner via the contact information provided in the CSR. If the owner is allowed to re-issue, the BCA will take it upon itself to generate a new key-pair. A new certificate is then created with the new public key, and the original biotoken. The BCA then embeds the new private key into a bipartite biotoken generated from the user's biotoken. The BCA then sends the owner of the certificate a Certificate Re-issue Notification (CRN), which indicates the serial number of the revoked certificate, the serial number of the re-issued certificate, and the bipartite biotoken containing the embedded private key. This message is signed by the BCA.

The automatic re-issue process will require some intervention by the user here. Namely, the user must submit his/her biometric at the Auth Station to release their new private key from the bipartite biotoken in the CRN.

3.4 Applications

Now that we have seen the underlying infrastructure and protocols, we can begin to think about the utility of BKI for different applications. Internet tools are of primary interest, because they are at the front-line of the security battleground. Enforcing server validation is a must, if we want to defeat Phishing and Man-in-the-Middle attacks. In Sect. 3.3.2.1 we introduced a one-way protocol that is suitable for server validation, and forces the user to take action by presenting a biometric sample when receiving any certificate. For server validation, d can be a "welcome message" that Bob enters during enrollment. The biometric component of this scheme forces Bob to validate the integrity of the server, even if the certificate check has occurred, and has been ignored. If Bob can unlock $B_{BB}(d)$ and get his "welcome message" back, the server is indeed valid. If Bob's biotoken is a shared secret, he has further confidence the server is legitimate. This protocol can be integrated into common Internet tools, such as web browsers, email clients, and instant messaging clients that already support PKI. The only difference for the users is that they are required to submit a biometric sample upon receiving a certificate from a server.

In terms of network services, BKI enabled services can allow for robust authentication, giving the user more confidence in the server, and the server more confidence that it is dealing with a legitimate user. The work of [33] suggested the use of bipartite biotokens with Kerberos [27], but in a standalone configuration without certificates certifying biotokens. One can also envision an S/Key-like [18] one-time password scheme using bipartite biotokens. In this scheme, once receiving the request, the authentication server generates a one-time password, and creates a bipartite biotoken containing this password. If the client matches the bipartite biotoken sent from the authentication server, it will release the password, and complete the authentication. In order to solve the biotoken distribution problem for network authentication, PKI-enabled LDAP [6] can be used in the same manner for BKI applications. Thus, a wide variety of authentication schemes can take advantage of a common certificate repository, including user records, keys, and biotokens.

Digital documents represent another important application area for BKI. Many sensitive documents, including medical records, financial records, and government records are protected using PKI and digital signatures, but we cannot tell who exactly is accessing these documents beyond knowing that a particular key unlocks or verifies them. Using bipartite biotokens, the key used to encrypt a document that belongs to Bob can be embedded into Bob's bipartite biotoken. Thus, only Bob can release the key, and access the document. For digital signatures, a signature server protocol [33] can add a biometric authorization component to the standard signature process. Again, with BKI providing the certificate distribution mechanism, a full security solution for document management is realized.

In all of these applications, usability is, of course, a legitimate concern. By adding a second physical factor, we also add more work for the user, and a small cost for the additional sensor hardware. However, not much more work is required to submit a biometric sample—it can be as simple as placing a finger down on a sensor for just a few seconds. Thanks to the recent prevalence of biometric systems, many corporate, government, and even home users are already used to this. Many laptops are already equipped with inexpensive fingerprint sensors, and many PC vendors offer low-cost fingerprint enabled mice. A good compromise is the judicious use of the biometric component; if the user is very concerned about the security of their financial activities, they may choose to only use BKI for particular sites related to financial services, and take their chances with more conventional PKI provisions for everything else.

3.5 Conclusions

In this chapter, we have taken a look at security issues with both PKI and biometrics, and introduced a Biocryptographic Key Infrastructure incorporating a secure template technology that solves problems with both. In summary, PKI suffers from problems related to the trust that is presumed for all entities in the infrastructure. By incorporating a secure biometric template technology such as revocable biotokens into digital certificate signing requests, we can achieve improved non-repudiation, and thus increase the trust placed in both certificate authorities and users, while addressing the biometric dilemma and biometric doppelganger attack. Moreover, with a second factor that allows the secure transfer of embedded data, we can support automatic certificate revocation and re-issue. Ultimately, the goal here is to prevent common Phishing and Man-in-the-Middle attacks, which can be accomplished using the protocols we have defined for secure authentication between two parties using keys and biotokens. With the base protocols, we can go on to enhance common applications such as LDAP, Internet tools (browsers, email clients, IM clients), and digital document signing.

Proposed standards for PKI including biometrics have been constrained to the direct application of traditional biometric templates into certificates. Secure template technologies, including revocable biotokens, have matured to the point of being useful for systems integration. To date, no formal document exists outlining requirements or specifications for secure template technology, let alone a combination of secure templates and PKI. This hampers the widespread adoption of a good two-factor solution to the shortcomings of PKI. Thus, we propose moving this emerging paradigm out of the realm of pure research and into the hands of a standards body, such as IETF, for serious consideration. It is our hope that the sketch of BKI presented here will provide a solid foundation to the first round of a standards process.

Acknowledgements   This work was supported in part by NSF STTR Award Number 0750485 and NSF PFI Award Number 065025.

References

1. Adams C, Farrell S (1999) Internet X.509 public key infrastructure certificate management protocols. RFC 2510 (proposed standard). http://www.ietf.org/rfc/rfc2510.txt. Accessed 18 May 2011
2. Arndt C (2004) Biometric template revocation. In: Jain A, Ratha N (eds) Biometric Technology for Human Identification. Proceedings of the SPIE, vol 5404. SPIE, Bellingham, pp 164–175

3. Benavente O (2005) Authentication services and biometrics: network security issues. In: Proc of the 39th Annual International Carnahan Conference on Security Technology (CCST 2005), pp 333–336
4. BioAPI (2010) Business objectives and values. BioAPI consortium. http://www.bioapi.org/objectives.asp. Accessed 18 May 2011
5. BioLab (2006) FVC 2006: fingerprint verification competition. University of Bologna. http://bias.csr.unibo.it/fvc2006/databases.asp. Accessed 18 May 2011
6. Boeyen S, Hallam-Baker P (2006) Internet X.509 public key infrastructure repository locator service. RFC 4386 (proposed standard). http://www.ietf.org/rfc/rfc4386.txt. Accessed 18 May 2011
7. Boult T, Scheirer W, Woodworth R (2007) Secure revocable finger biotokens. In: Proc of the IEEE Conference on Computer Vision and Pattern Recognition (CVPR 2007)
8. Boyen X, Dodis Y, Katz J, Ostrovsky R, Smith A (2005) Secure remote authentication using biometric data. In: Proc of EUROCRYPT, pp 147–163
9. Cappelli R, Lumini A, Maio D, Maltoni D (2007) Fingerprint image reconstruction from standard templates. IEEE Transactions on Pattern Analysis and Machine Intelligence 29(9):1489–1503
10. Chokhani S, Ford W, Sabett R, Merrill C, Wu S (2003) Internet X.509 public key infrastructure certificate policy and certification practices framework. RFC 3647 (proposed standard). http://www.ietf.org/rfc/rfc3647.txt. Accessed 18 May 2011
11. Cooper D, Santesson S, Farrell S, Boeyen S, Housley R, Polk W (2008) Internet X.509 public key infrastructure certificate and certificate revocation list (CRL) profile. RFC 5280 (proposed standard). http://www.ietf.org/rfc/rfc5280.txt. Accessed 18 May 2011
12. Dawson E, Lopez J, Montenegro J, Okamoto EB (2003) Biometric authentication and authorization infrastructure. In: Proc of the International Conference on Information Technology: Research and Education (ITRE 2003), pp 274–278
13. Dodis Y, Reyzin L, Smith A (2007) Fuzzy extractors. In: Tuyls P, Skoric B, Kevenaar T (eds) Security with Noisy Data: Private Biometrics, Secure Key Storage and Anti-counterfeiting. Springer, Berlin, pp 79–99. Chapter 5
14. East-Shore (2007) Fingerprint image database. East shore technologies. http://www.east-shore.com/data.html. Accessed 18 May 2011
15. Ellison C, Schneier B (2000) Ten risks of PKI: what you're not being told about public key infrastructure. Journal of Computer Security 16(1):1–7
16. Gerck E (2000) Overview of certification systems: X.509, PKIX, CA, PGP and SKIP. Bell 1(3):8
17. Gutmann PPK (2002) It's not dead, just resting. IEEE Computer 35(8):41–49
18. Haller N (1995) The S/KEY one-time password system. RFC 1760 (proposed standard). http://www.ietf.org/rfc/rfc1760.txt. Accessed 18 May 2011
19. Jain A, Nandakumar K, Nagar A (2008) Biometric template security. EURASIP Journal on Advances in Signal Processing
20. Juels A, Sudan M (2002) A fuzzy vault scheme. In: Proc of the IEEE International Symposium on Information Theory, p 408
21. Juels A, Wattenberg M (1999) A fuzzy commitment scheme. In: Proc of the 6th ACM Conference on Computer and Communications Security, pp 28–36
22. Kanade S, Petrovska-Delacrétaz D, Dorizzi B (2010) Generating and sharing biometrics based session keys for secure cryptographic applications. In: Proc of the IEEE Fourth International Conference on Biometrics: Theory, Applications, and Systems (BTAS 2010)
23. Krause M (2001) The expanding surveillance state: why Colorado should scrap the plan to map every driver's face and should ban facial recognition in public. The Independence Institute. http://www.i2i.org/articles/8-2001.PDF. Accessed 18 May 2011
24. Kuhn D, Hu V, Polk W, Chang S (2001) Introduction to public key technology and the federal PKI infrastructure. National Institute of Standards and Technology, SP 800-32
25. Kwon T, Moon H (2005) Multi-modal biometrics with PKI technologies for border control applications. In: Intelligence and Security Informations. Lecture Notes in Computer Science,

vol 3495, pp 99–114. Springer, Berlin

26. Martinez-Silva G, Henriquez F, Cortes N, Ertaul L (2007) On the generation of X.509v3 certificates with biometric information. In: Proc of the 2007 International Conference on Security and Management (SAM'07)

27. Neuman C, Yu T, Hartman S, Raeburn K (2005) The kerberos network authentication service (V5). RFC 4120 (proposed standard). http://www.ietf.org/rfc/rfc4120.txt. Accessed 18 May 2011

28. NIST (2011) National Institute of Standards and Technology NIST special database 29. Standard reference data. http://www.nist.gov/srd/nistsd29.cfm. Accessed 18 May 2011

29. Ratha N, Chikkerur S, Connell J, Bolle R (2007) Generating cancelable fingerprint templates. IEEE Transactions on Pattern Analysis and Machine Intelligence 29(4):561–572

30. Reinert L, Luther S (1997) User authentication techniques using using public key certificates, National Security Agency, Central Security Service

31. Schaad J (2005) Internet X.509 public key infrastructure certificate request message format (CRMF). RFC 4211 (proposed standard). http://www.ietf.org/rfc/rfc4211.txt. Accessed 18 May 2011

32. Scheirer W, Boult T (2007) Cracking fuzzy vaults and biometric encryption. In: Proc of the 2007 Biometrics Symposium, Held in Conjunction with the Biometrics Consortium Conference (BCC 2007), Baltimore, MD

33. Scheirer W, Boult T (2008) Bio-cryptographic protocols with bipartite biotokens. In: Proc of the IEEE 2008 Biometrics Symposium, Held in Conjunction with the Biometrics Consortium Conference

34. Scheirer W, Boult T (2009) Bipartite biotokens: definition, implementation, and analysis. In: Proc of the IEEE/IAPR International Conference on Biometrics, pp 775–785

35. Schneier B (1996) Applied Cryptography, 2nd edn. Wiley, New York

36. Sotirov A, Stevens M, Appelbaum J, Lenstra A, Molnar D, Osvik DA, de Weger B (2008) MD5 considered harmful today. HashClash project. http://www.win.tue.nl/hashclash/rogue-ca/. Accessed 18 May 2011

37. Stevens M, Sotirov A, Appelbaum J, Lenstra A, Molnar D, Osvik DA, de Weger B (2009) Short chosen-prefix collisions for MD5 and the creation of a rogue CA certificate. In: Proc of the International Cryptology Conference on Advances in Cryptology

38. Sutcu Y, Sencar T, Memon N (2005) A secure biometric authentication scheme based on robust hashing. In: Proc of the 7th ACM Workshop on Multimedia and Security (MM-Sect 2005)

39. Tang Q, Bringer J, Chabanne H, Pointcheval D (2008) A formal study of the privacy concerns in biometric-based remote authentication schemes. In: Proc of the Information Security Practice and Experience Conference

40. The Open Group (1999) Architecture for public-key infrastructure (APKI)

41. Ueshige Y, Sakurai K (2006) A proposal of one-time biometric authentication. In: Arabnia H, Aissi S (eds) Proc of the International Conference on Security and Management (SAM 2006)

Chapter 4
Secure Sketches for Protecting Biometric Templates

Yagiz Sutcu, Qiming Li, and Nasir Memon

Abstract As biometric technologies are becoming pervasive, it is imperative to protect the users of these technologies from misuse of their biometric data. However, unlike user credentials in traditional security systems, such as passwords or tokens, biometric features cannot be consistently sampled, and the matching process can be complex. Furthermore, the consequences of losing biometric data can be far more severe than passwords or tokens. Secure sketches, a recently developed cryptographic primitive, allow noisy data to be restored using some helper-data, while providing bounds on how much sensitive information such helper-data would reveal when obtained by malicious parties. In this chapter, we discuss security threats on the use of biometric templates in security systems, and how secure sketches can be used to address these threats under various circumstances.

4.1 Introduction

Increasing use of biometric technology raised many concerns related to user privacy in biometric deployments. In fact, when an individual gives out his biometrics, either willingly or unwillingly, he discloses unique information about himself [36]. This implies that his biometrics could be easily replicated and misused. More specifically, once some biometric data are compromised, they remain compromised forever and the privacy concerns arise from the fact that biometric data are tightly bound to a person's identity such that they can be used to violate their privacy. This is clearly a serious problem, made worse by the fact that an individual cannot generate new

Y. Sutcu (✉) · N. Memon
Polytechnic Institute of New York University, Brooklyn, NY, USA
e-mail: yagiz@isis.poly.edu

N. Memon
e-mail: memon@nyu.edu

Q. Li
Clault Pte. Ltd., Singapore, Singapore
e-mail: liqiming@gmail.com

P. Campisi (ed.), *Security and Privacy in Biometrics*,
DOI 10.1007/978-1-4471-5230-9_4, © Springer-Verlag London 2013

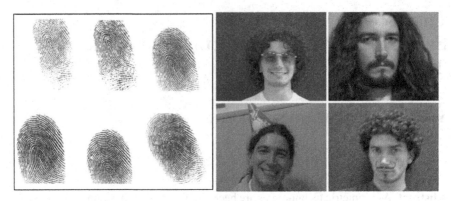

Fig. 4.1 Every time a biometric is measured, the observation differs slightly (Sample fingerprints (*left*) and face images (*right*) of the same person)

biometrics if the system is compromised. Therefore, storing biometric templates in a secure way is crucial.

Secure storage of user credentials is not a new problem. In many UNIX-like systems, user credentials are stored in a shadow password file, where the passwords are hashed (using cryptographically secure hashing algorithms such as SHA-1) and only the hash values are stored [41]. When a user enters a password, it is hashed and matched against the stored hash value, and the user is considered as authentic if the hash values are exactly the same. In this way, if the hashed passwords are compromised, it would still be difficult for any attacker to guess the passwords, even if the hashing function is publicly known. Legitimate users, after detecting the compromise, can change their passwords, which makes old passwords useless to attackers.

Unfortunately, while passwords or ID numbers can be securely stored via a cryptographic hash, such techniques cannot be easily adapted to protect biometric templates. This is because of the noisy nature of personal biometrics. Every time a biometric is measured, the observation differs slightly. For example, a fingerprint reading might change because of elastic deformations in the skin when placed on the sensor surface, dust or oil between finger and sensor, or a cut to the finger. That difference may be usually more dramatic when face images are considered (Fig. 4.1). Therefore, biometric authentication systems must be robust to such variations, which are not encountered in traditional password-based authentication systems.

In a typical biometric system, a template is generated from some discriminative features extracted from the raw biometric data and this template is stored instead. Since different biometric modalities have different signal representations, they usually require different feature selection/extraction algorithms. Even for the same type of biometric data, different types of feature extraction strategies may be employed depending on the application. For example, ridge map and minutiae points (Fig. 4.2 (left)), which are the endpoints and bifurcations of fingerprint ridges, are two different types of representation used for fingerprints. Similarly, locations of some fa-

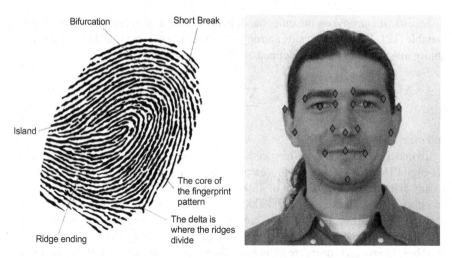

Fig. 4.2 In a typical biometric system, a template is generated from some discriminative features extracted from the raw biometric data and this template is stored instead

cial points (Fig. 4.2 (right)) such as, eye corners, nose, lips, etc. and their relative positions can be used as a template as well as the feature vectors calculated from complete face images via principal component analysis (PCA) or some other feature selection method.

Although most of the feature extraction algorithms employed in biometric systems are complex and seem hard to invert, it is often not clear exactly how difficult it is to forge some biometric data such that similar features can be extracted from them. As an example, consider minutiae point representation as a fingerprint template. In fact, an efficient algorithm is recently proposed that can generate a fingerprint from its matching minutiae points [39] (see also [20]). Therefore, storing the biometric features directly as templates would not be secure enough. Furthermore, biometric templates must be generated in a way that makes it very difficult to re-create or even estimate the original biometrics data, and their compromise should not introduce major risks.

4.1.1 Metrics for Template Security

In order to be able to measure how secure the templates are, defining some metrics and deriving some mathematical formulation would be necessary.

Consider a traditional password/key-based authentication mechanism, for instance. *Keyspace*, for this case, is defined as the size of the set that contains all possible values that can be chosen as a password/key. For example, if a password/key should have exactly n characters, where each of those characters can have c different values, the keyspace will be

$$k_{\text{password}} = c^n. \tag{4.1}$$

Statistical entropy, on the other hand, is the measure of uncertainty in a random variable [12]. More specifically, entropy of a discrete random variable X with probability mass function $p(x)$ is defined as

$$H(X) = -\sum_{i=1}^{n} p(x_i) \log_2\big(p(x_i)\big) \tag{4.2}$$

and measured in bits.

To understand the basic difference between keyspace and entropy, let us consider six-digit PINs, for example. In this case, the keyspace size is $10^6 = 1000000$, which means that there is a maximum of 1000000 different PIN choices. In other words, an attacker would have a 1 in 1000000 chance that any single guess would match a given PIN. This is true if PINs were selected/generated randomly with uniform probability over the entire keyspace. In this case, the entropy is $\log_2(1000000) = 19.9$ bits. However, if users are allowed to choose their own six-digit PINs, although the keyspace remains the same, the entropy can be much lower. That is mainly due to the fact that most of the users would choose a PIN that is more memorable than a random one (e.g., a calendar date in "ddmmyy" format). Therefore, a PIN chosen in this way would have only about 365 possible values per each year with 100 possibilities for years. Assuming these dates are chosen uniformly, the entropy, in this case is $\log_2(365 \times 100) = 15.2$ bits, which is almost 5 bits fewer than maximum for the keyspace.

A biometric, on the other hand, does not have a fixed number of possible values. However, for comparison purposes, it is still possible to define the *effective keyspace* of a biometric [34]. For instance, if the passwords are distributed uniformly over the keyspace, the probability of correctly guessing any single password sample is one over the keyspace

$$P(\text{correct guess}) = 1/k_{\text{password}}. \tag{4.3}$$

The probability of falsely matching a biometric is analogous to the probability of succeeding in a password guessing attack. Since the probability of matching a given biometric to any other biometric sample in a database is the false accept rate for a single verification attempt, the effective keyspace of a biometric can be defined as[1]

$$k_{\text{biometric}} = 1/\text{FAR}(\tau). \tag{4.4}$$

In fact, the use of FAR (with a fixed FRR) as the measure of security in a biometric authentication system is the correct measure when the storage of template is secure and the attacker only uses the biometric data of a random user. However, when discussing security, one is often interested in the probability that the adversary

---

[1]It is worth mentioning the fact that the $k_{\text{biometric}}$ is based on an experimentally determined value of $\text{FAR}(\tau)$. Therefore, the k_{password} and $k_{\text{biometric}}$ will be comparable only if the password character selection is uniformly random [34].

predicts a random value (e.g., guesses a secret key). The adversary's best strategy, of course, is to guess the most likely value. Therefore, the *min-entropy*, defined as

$$H_\infty(X) = -\log\left(\max_a \left(\Pr[X = a]\right)\right) \tag{4.5}$$

can thus be viewed as the "worst-case" entropy and would be a better measure when smart attackers are considered.

Let us consider a simple example for illustration. Assume that the random variable X can take values from the set $A = \{0, 1, 2, 3, 4\}$ according to the probability distribution defined as: $\Pr[X = 0] = 0.5$ and $\Pr[X = i] = 1/8$ for $i > 0$. In this case, the entropy of X will be $H(X) = 0.5 * 1 + 4 * 1/8 * 3 = 2$. However, if attacker always guesses the value 0, he will succeed with probability 0.5 for random X. Therefore, the "correct" security measure should report 1 bit of security instead of 2 bits. In this case, the min-entropy of the random variable X is 1 bit, which correctly reflects the fact that a smart attacker who knows the distribution can succeed with probability at least 0.5.

However, it is not possible to *choose* a biometric as is the case for passwords. Furthermore, although it is not possible to determine the entropy of biometrics exactly due to the lack of exact knowledge of their distributions, biometrics are usually of lower *estimated* entropy compared with modern standard of cryptographic keys [13, 14, 35]. Therefore, extra care should be taken when designing/analyzing biometric systems.

4.1.2 How to Secure Biometric Templates

There has been intensive study on how to secure the templates such that (1) they can still be used for matching with reasonable performance, and (2) it is hard to forge "original" biometric data that would match a given template. In recent years, many different ideas/approaches have been proposed to overcome this problem. A comprehensive coverage of many proposed solutions can also be found in [23, 52].

The first group of techniques is associated with the notion of *cancelable biometrics* which was first introduced by Ratha et al. [37]. The underlying idea is to apply a similarity-preserving, noninvertible (or hard-to-invert) transformation to biometric templates before they are stored. New biometric samples are transformed in the same way before they are matched with the templates. In the literature, one can found significant number of applications/variants of this idea. Some examples can be found in [1, 2, 30, 38, 40, 42, 47].This idea is illustrated in Fig. 4.3.

In many feature transformation-based approaches, transformation functions are typically governed by some random parameters. One of the advantages of these approaches is the fact that the templates can be easily revoked by applying other (random) transformations or by simply using other random parameters for the same transformation. Moreover, if the representation of the biometric data stay the same after the transformation, this makes it possible to use off-the-shelf matching algorithms/devices which are already available.

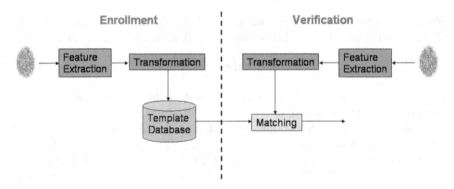

Fig. 4.3 Enrollment and authentication stages of transformation based approaches

However, the security and/or performance of these approaches mostly rely on the secure storage of the transform parameters. Moreover, it is not only difficult to design such transformations that satisfy necessary requirements, but also different biometric modalities require different types of transforms. Furthermore, the security of these schemes relies on the difficulty of *inverting* the transformation to obtain the original biometric data. Some of the works give analysis on the entropy of the biometrics, and approximated amount of efforts required by a brute-force attacker. Although it is believed that such transformations are difficult to invert, a rigorous security analysis (concerning the one-wayness) of the scheme is very difficult especially when the transformation algorithm and related keys/parameters are also compromised. Therefore, extra care should be taken designing and analyzing those type of schemes.

Besides transformation-based cancelable techniques, another class of approaches, which makes information-theoretic security analysis possible, is based on use of some *helper-data*[2], as illustrated in Fig. 4.4. In this group of techniques, main idea is to create/extract some user-specific auxiliary information from the original biometric data in a way that does not reveal *much* information about the biometric data. Later, this auxiliary information is used to recover/estimate the original biometric data from a noisy instance of itself. This information can be in the form of a *helper-data* [26, 49], a *syndrome* [17, 18, 31] or a *secure sketch* [16].

One of the basic tools that is used in this group of techniques is error correcting codes (ECC). On the one hand, the error correction capability of a code can accommodate the slight variation between multiple measurements of the same biometric. On the other hand, the check bits of the ECC can be used as *helper-data*, which only contains a limited amount of information about the original biometric itself, and can perform much the same function as a cryptographic hash of a password on conven-

---

[2]Although the term *helper-data* is used as the name of the techniques proposed in [26, 49], in this chapter we use the term *helper-data* for categorizing the template protection methods without referring to any specific technique/method.

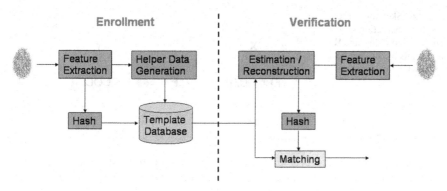

Fig. 4.4 Enrollment and authentication stages of helper-data based approaches

Fig. 4.5 In fuzzy commitment scheme, if the noisy biometric (x') is close enough to the template (x), decoder successfully corrects the error. The only information stored are δ and hash(K)

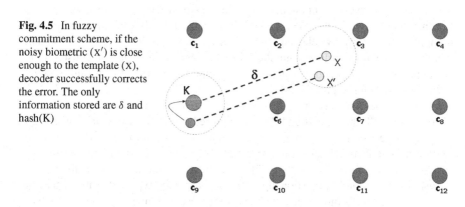

tional access control systems. Just as a hacker cannot invert the hash and steal the password, he cannot just use the check bits to recover and steal the biometric.

There have been a number of studies that make use of ECC to deal with the joint problem of providing security against attackers while accounting for the inevitable variability of biometrics. Davida et al. [15] were among the first to propose an off-line biometric authentication scheme based on error correcting codes for iris. They suggested storing a signed form of biometric template in a portable storage device, like smartcard, instead of a database and matching the biometric data locally.

Juels and Wattenberg [25] proposed a fuzzy commitment scheme which is also based on ECC. The basic idea in [25] is that a secret key is chosen by the user and then encoded using a standard ECC. This encoded secret key is xored with the biometric template to ensure the security of the template and then stored in the database. During verification, the biometric data is xored with the values stored in the database. If the biometric data is close to the one presented at the enrollment stage, the decoder will be able to correct some of the errors/differences (present in the newly measured biometric data) and secret key will be retrieved correctly and revealed to the user. This idea is simply illustrated in Fig. 4.5. (For detailed analysis of the information leakage in Fuzzy Commitment schemes, see [22].)

Fig. 4.6 Sketch Generation and Reconstruction in Discrete Domain (here **R** represents the randomness invested in the sketch)

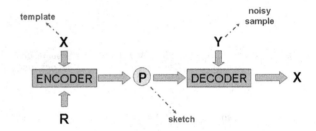

Later, to address the problem of unordered feature representations (e.g., the minutiae representation of fingerprints), Juels and Sudan [24] proposed the "fuzzy vault" scheme which combines the polynomial reconstruction problem with ECC. In this method, an appropriately chosen secret polynomial with degree k is evaluated at each and every component of an n-dimensional feature vector (with $n > k$) to construct a set of points. Then, a number of fake (randomly generated) points that do not lie on the initially selected polynomial are mixed with the real points so that genuine users with a sufficient number of real points will be able to reconstruct the secret polynomial. For some examples of the application of the fuzzy vault scheme to fingerprints refer to [11, 33, 50, 53].

Although the construction of ECC and their associated encoding/decoding procedures are well-understood and deeply explored topics, it is not straightforward to apply these techniques to real biometric data. First of all, many biometric data require a quantization/binarization step in order to be able to efficiently use the ECC-based techniques [7, 10, 44, 45]. In addition to the difficulty in finding an *optimal* quantization/binarization algorithm for a specific type of biometric data at hand [10], even if the biometric templates are represented in discrete forms (such as iris patterns), existing theoretical results may still be not applicable due to the high error correcting capability requirement for coding part to handle the inherent high variability of biometric data.

Recently proposed cryptographic primitive called *secure sketch* is another approach that aims to solve the very same problem [16]. Similarly, in this approach, some public information which does not reveal too much information about the original biometric data, is extracted/created and used to recover the original biometric data given a noisy sample of the same biometric data that is sufficiently *similar* to the original one. This is depicted in Fig. 4.6. Such schemes include [8, 27]. Actually, from the implementation point of view, fuzzy commitment [25] and fuzzy vault [24] schemes may also be analyzed under the secure sketch framework where fuzzy commitment scheme (which is based on binary error-correcting codes) considers binary strings where the similarity is measured by Hamming distance and the fuzzy vault scheme considers sets of elements in a finite field with set difference as the distance function.

There are few reasons why their framework does not only allow more rigorous security analysis compared to many other approaches, but also helps generalizing the much of the prior helper-data based work. First of all, a sketch allows exact recovery of the biometric template. Therefore, a *strong extractor* (such as pair-wise

independent hash functions) can be further applied on the template to obtain a key
that is robust, in the sense that it can be consistently reproduced given any noisy
measurement that is similar to the template. This key can then be used in the same
way as passwords. Furthermore, in this framework, it is possible to demonstrate
some general results that do not depend on any particular notion of closeness between two measurements of the same biometric data as long as this closeness is
defined in a metric space. This is very important since different biometric modalities have different representations and error patterns.

Constructions and rigorous analysis of secure sketch are given in [16] for three
metrics: Hamming distance, set difference and edit distance. Secure sketch schemes
for point sets in [8] are motivated by the typical similarity measure used for
minutiae-based fingerprint templates, where each template consists of a set of points
in 2-D space, and the similarity measure does not define a metric space.

Linnartz and Tuyls [29] consider a similar problem for biometric authentication
applications. They consider zero mean i.i.d. jointly Gaussian random vectors as biometric templates, and use mutual information as the measure of security against
dishonest verifiers. Tuyls and Goseling [48] consider a similar notion of security,
and develop some general results when the distribution of the original is known and
the verifier can be trusted. Some practical results along this line also appear in [49].

Boyen [3] shows that a sketch scheme that is provably secure may be insecure
when multiple sketches of the same biometric data are obtained. Same issue is
further discussed in [28]. Boyen et al. further study the security of secure sketch
schemes under more general attacker models in [4], and techniques to achieve mutual authentication are proposed.

However, there are a few difficulties in extending these techniques to biometric
templates in practice. Most importantly, many biometric templates are not discrete,
but are instead points in continuous domains (e.g., real numbers resulted from some
signal processing techniques). In such a case, it is hard to define what the *minimum
entropy* of the original biometric template should be. Furthermore, extracting a discrete key from such a template would require some form of quantization [27]. In
this case, since the entropy of the original data can be very large, and the length of
the extracted key is typically quite limited, the "entropy loss" as defined in [16] can
be arbitrarily high, which can be misleading [43]. While designing secure sketches
for continuous data with Gaussian assumption is investigated in [6], key extraction
from general nondiscrete signals is investigated in [51]. Moreover, randomized and
cancelable secure sketches are introduced in [5, 46].

Although secure sketches may have some nice properties that would allow us to
handle all attackers and all biometric distributions, using min-entropy and entropy
loss alone may not be sufficient to measure the security. In many cases, although
the entropy loss can be bounded, the min-entropy of the original biometric data
cannot be easily determined, hence making it difficult to conclude the key strength
of the resulting system. Even the min-entropy of the original biometric data can
be fixed in some way, the entropy loss may be too large to be useful and it can
be misleading. Therefore, cautions have to be taken when analyzing the security of
biometric authentication schemes that employs secure sketches.

4.2 Secure-Sketch as a Cryptographic Primitive

The main challenge in using biometric data in cryptography is that they cannot be reproduced exactly. Some noise will be inevitably introduced into biometric samples during acquisition and processing. There have been active discussions on how to extract a reliable cryptographic key from such noisy data. Some recent techniques attempt to correct the noise in the data by using some public information P_X derived from the original biometric template X. In this chapter, we follow Dodis et al. [16] and call such public information P a *sketch*.

Typically, there are two main components in a secure sketch scheme. The first is the sketch generation algorithm, which we will refer to as the *encoder*. It takes the original biometric template X as the input, and outputs a sketch P_X. The second algorithm is the biometric template reconstruction algorithm, or the *decoder*, which takes another biometric template Y and the sketch P_X as the input and outputs X'. If Y and X are sufficiently similar according to some similarity measure, we will have $X = X'$. An important requirement for such a scheme is that the sketch P_X should not reveal too much information about the biometric template X. Dodis et al. [16] gives a notion of *entropy loss*, which (informally speaking) measures the advantage that P_X gives to any adversary in guessing X, when X is discrete in nature (Sect. 4.2.1 provides the details).

4.2.1 Preliminaries

4.2.1.1 Entropy and Entropy Loss in Discrete Domain

In the case where X is discrete, we follow the definitions by Dodis et al. [16]. They consider a variant of the *average min-entropy* of X given P, which is essentially the minimum strength of the key that can be consistently extracted from X when P is made public.

In particular, the min-entropy $\mathbf{H}_\infty(A)$ of a discrete random variable A is defined as

$$\mathbf{H}_\infty(A) = -\log\left(\max_a \Pr[A = a]\right). \tag{4.6}$$

For two discrete random variables A and B, the average min-entropy of A given B is defined as

$$\widetilde{\mathbf{H}}_\infty(A \mid B) = -\log\left(\mathbb{E}_{b \leftarrow B}\left[2^{-\mathbf{H}_\infty(A|B=b)}\right]\right). \tag{4.7}$$

For discrete X, the entropy loss of the sketch P_X is defined as

$$\mathscr{L} = \mathbf{H}_\infty(X) - \widetilde{\mathbf{H}}_\infty(X|P). \tag{4.8}$$

This definition is useful in the analysis, since for any ℓ-bit string B, we have $\tilde{\mathbf{H}}_\infty(A \mid B) \geq \mathbf{H}_\infty(A) - \ell$. For any secure sketch scheme for discrete X, let R be the randomness invested in constructing the sketch, it is not difficult to show that when R can be computed from X and P, we have

$$\mathscr{L} = \mathbf{H}_\infty(X) - \tilde{\mathbf{H}}_\infty(X \mid P) \leq |P| - \mathbf{H}_\infty(R). \tag{4.9}$$

In other words, the entropy loss can be bounded from above by the difference between the size of P and the amount of randomness we invested in computing P. This allows us to conveniently find an upper bound of $\mathscr{L}$ for any distribution of X, since it is independent of X.

4.2.1.2 Secure Sketch in Discrete Domain

Our definitions of secure sketch and entropy loss in the discrete domain follow that in [16]. Let $\mathscr{M}$ be a finite set of points with a *similarity* relation $\mathsf{S} \subseteq \mathscr{M} \times \mathscr{M}$. When $(X, Y) \in \mathsf{S}$, we say the Y is similar to X, or the pair (X, Y) is similar.

Definition 4.2.1 A sketch scheme in discrete domain is a tuple $(\mathscr{M}, \mathsf{S}, \mathsf{Enc}, \mathsf{Dec})$, where $\mathsf{Enc} : \mathscr{M} \to \{0, 1\}^*$ is an encoder and $\mathsf{Dec} : \mathscr{M} \times \{0, 1\}^* \to \mathscr{M}$ is a decoder such that for all $X, Y \in \mathscr{M}$, $\mathsf{Dec}(Y, \mathsf{Enc}(X)) = X$ if $(X, Y) \in \mathsf{S}$. The string $P_X = \mathsf{Enc}(X)$ is the sketch, and is to be made public. We say that the scheme is $\mathscr{L}$-secure if for all random variables X over $\mathscr{M}$, the entropy loss of the sketch P_X is at most $\mathscr{L}$. That is, $\mathbf{H}_\infty(X) - \tilde{\mathbf{H}}_\infty(X \mid \mathsf{Enc}(X)) \leq \mathscr{L}$.

We call $\tilde{\mathbf{H}}_\infty(X \mid P_X)$ the *left-over entropy*, which in essence measures the "strength" of the key that can be extracted from X given that P_X is made public. Note that in most cases, the ultimate goal is to maximize the left-over entropy for some particular distribution of X. However, in the discrete case, the min-entropy of X is fixed but can be difficult to analyze. Hence, entropy loss becomes an equivalent measure which is easier to quantify.

4.2.1.3 Issues and Challenges

There are several difficulties in applying many known secure sketch techniques to known types of biometric templates directly. Firstly, many biometric templates are represented by sequences of n points in a continuous domain (say, $\mathbb{R}$), or equivalently, points in an n-dimensional space (say, $\mathbb{R}^n$). In this case, since the entropy of the original data can be very large, and the length of the extracted key is typically quite limited, the "entropy loss" as defined in [16] can be very high for any possible scheme. For example, X is often a discrete approximation of some points in a continuous domain (e.g., decimal fractions obtained by rounding real numbers). As the precision of X gets higher, both the entropy of X and the entropy loss from

P become larger, but the extracted key can become stronger. Hence, this notion of entropy loss alone is insufficient, and the seemingly high entropy loss for this type of biometric data would be misleading. We will discuss this issue in detail in Sect. 4.2.2, and give a complementary definition of *relative entropy loss* for noisy data in the continuous domain. Informally speaking, the relative entropy loss of a sketch measures the imperfectness of the rounding, which is the maximum amount of additional entropy we can obtain by the "optimal" rounding. At the same time, the entropy loss from P serves as a measure of the security of the sketch in the discrete domain.

Secondly, even if the biometric templates are represented in discrete form, there are practical problems when the entropy of the original template is high. For example, the iris pattern of an eye can be represented by a 2048 bit binary string called *iris code*, and up to 20 % of the bits could be changed under noise [21]. The fuzzy commitment scheme based on binary error-correcting codes [25] seems to be applicable at the first glance. However, it would be impractical to apply a binary error-correcting code on such a long string with such a large error-correcting capability. A two-level error-correcting technique is proposed in [21], which essentially changes the similarity measure. As a result, the space is no longer a metric space.

Thirdly, the similarity measures for many known biometric templates can be quite different from those considered in many theoretical works (such as Hamming distance, set difference and edit distance in [16]). This can happen as a result of technical considerations (e.g., in the case of iris codes). However, in many cases this is due to the nature of biometric templates. For instance, a fingerprint template usually consists of a set of minutiae (feature points in 2-D/3-D space), and two templates are considered as similar if more than a certain number of minutiae in one template are near distinct minutiae in the other. In this case, the similarity measure has to consider both Euclidean distance and set difference at the same time.

We observe that many biometric templates can be represented in a general form: The original X can be considered as a list of n points, where each point x of X is in a bounded continuous domain. Under noise, each point can be perturbed by a distance less than δ. This formulation is different from that in [8] in two ways: (1) The points are in a continuous domain, and (2) the points are always ordered.

To handle points in continuous domain, a general two step approach is to (1) quantize (i.e., discretize) the points in X to a discrete domain with a scalar quantizer $\mathcal{Q}_\lambda$, where λ is the step size, and (2) apply secure sketch techniques on the quantized points $\widehat{X} = \mathcal{Q}_\lambda(X)$ in the quantized domain, which is discrete. For example, if points in X are real numbers between 0 and 1, assume that we have a scalar quantizer $\mathcal{Q}_\lambda$ with step size $\lambda = 0.1$, such that $\mathcal{Q}_\lambda(x) = \widehat{x}$ if and only if $\widehat{x}\lambda \leq x < (\widehat{x}+1)\lambda$, then every point in X would be mapped to an integer in $[0, 9]$. After that, we can apply a secure sketch for discrete points in the domain $[0, 9]^n$ to achieve error-tolerance. This idea is illustrated in Fig. 4.7.

However, there are two difficulties when this approach is applied. Firstly, if we follow the notion of secure sketch and entropy loss as in [16], the quantization error

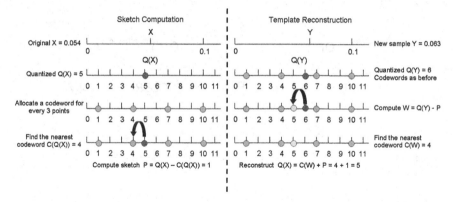

Fig. 4.7 A simple example for sketch computation and template reconstruction in quantized domain

$X - \widehat{X}$ in the first step has to be kept in the sketch, since exact reconstruction of X is required by definition. However, it can be difficult to give an upper bound on the entropy loss from the quantization errors. Even if we can, it can be very large.

Furthermore, as the quantization step λ becomes very small, the bound on the entropy loss in the quantized domain during the second step can be very high. For instance, for $x \in [0, 1)$ and $\delta = 0.01$, when $\lambda = 0.01$, the entropy loss in Step (2) will be $\log 3$, and the bound is tight. When $\lambda = 0.001$, the entropy loss will be $\log 21$. However, the big difference in entropy loss in the quantized domain can be misleading. We will revisit this example in Sect. 4.2.2, and will show that the second case actually results in a stronger key if X is uniformly distributed.

Instead of trying to answer the question of how much entropy is lost during quantization, we study how different quantizers affect the strength of the key that we can finally extract from the noisy data. In particular, given a secure sketch scheme in the discrete domain and a quantizer $\mathcal{Q}_1$ with step size λ_1, we consider any quantizer $\mathcal{Q}_2$ with step size λ_2. Assuming that m_1 and m_2 are the strengths of the keys under these two quantizers, respectively, we found that it is possible to give an upper bound on the difference between m_1 and m_2, for any distribution of X, and any choices of λ_2 (hence $\mathcal{Q}_2$) within a certain range. This bound can be expressed as a function of λ_1. In other words, although we do not know what is the exact entropy loss due to the quantizer $\mathcal{Q}_1$, we do know that at most how far away $\mathcal{Q}_1$ can be from the "optimal" one. Based on this, we give a notion of *relative entropy loss* for data in continuous domain. Furthermore, we show that if X is uniformly distributed, the relative entropy loss can be bounded by a constant for any choice of λ_1.

We note that our proposed schemes and analysis can be applied for two parties to extract secret keys given correlated random variables (e.g., [32]), where the random variables take values in a continuous domain (e.g. $\mathbb{R}$). The entropy loss in the quantized domain measures how much information can be leaked to an eavesdropper, while the relative entropy loss measures how many additional bits that we might be able to extract.

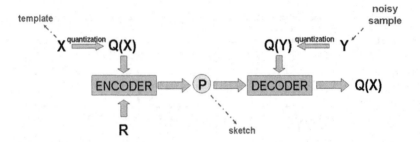

Fig. 4.8 Sketch Generation and Reconstruction in Continuous Domain (Here **R** represents the randomness invested in the sketch)

4.2.2 Secure Sketch in Continuous Domain

In this section we propose a general approach to handle noisy data in a continuous domain. We consider points in a universe $\mathscr{U}$, which is a set that may be uncountable. Let S be a similarity relation on $\mathscr{U}$, i.e., $S \subseteq \mathscr{U} \times \mathscr{U}$. Let $\mathscr{M}$ be a finite set of points, and let $\mathscr{Q} : \mathscr{U} \to \mathscr{M}$ be a function that maps points in $\mathscr{U}$ to points in $\mathscr{M}$. We will refer to such a function $\mathscr{Q}$ as a *quantizer*.

Definition 4.2.2 A quantization-based sketch scheme is a tuple $(\mathscr{U}, S, \mathscr{Q}, \mathscr{M}, \mathsf{Enc}, \mathsf{Dec})$, where $\mathsf{Enc} : \mathscr{M} \to \{0, 1\}^*$ is an encoder and $\mathsf{Dec} : \mathscr{M} \times \{0, 1\}^* \to \mathscr{M}$ is an decoder such that for all $X, Y \in \mathscr{U}$, $\mathsf{Dec}(\mathscr{Q}(Y), \mathsf{Enc}(\mathscr{Q}(X))) = \mathscr{Q}(X)$ if $(X, Y) \in S$. The string $P = \mathsf{Enc}(\mathscr{Q}(X))$ is the sketch. We say that the scheme is $\mathscr{L}$-secure in the quantized domain if for all random variable X over $\mathscr{U}$, the entropy loss of P is at most $\mathscr{L}$, i.e., $\mathbf{H}_\infty(\mathscr{Q}(X)) - \widetilde{\mathbf{H}}_\infty(\mathscr{Q}(X) \mid \mathsf{Enc}(\mathscr{Q}(X))) \leq \mathscr{L}$

In other words, a quantization is applied to transform the points in the continuous domain to a discrete domain, and a sketch scheme for discrete domain is applied to obtain the sketch P. During reconstruction, we require the exact reconstruction of the quantization $\mathscr{Q}(X)$ instead of the original X in the continuous domain. This is illustrated in Fig. 4.8. If required, a strong extractor can be further applied to $\mathscr{Q}(X)$ to extract a key (as the fuzzy extractor in [16]). That is, we treat $\mathscr{Q}(X)$ as the "discrete original". Similarly, we call $\widetilde{\mathbf{H}}_\infty(\mathscr{Q}(X) \mid P)$ the left-over entropy.

When $\mathscr{Q}$ is fixed, we can use the entropy loss on $\mathscr{Q}(X)$ to analyze the security of the scheme, and bound the entropy loss of P. However, using this entropy loss alone may be misleading, since there are many ways to quantize X, and different quantizer would make a difference in both the min-entropy of $\mathscr{Q}(X)$ and the entropy loss. Since our ultimate goal is to maximize the left-over entropy (i.e., the average min-entropy $\widetilde{\mathbf{H}}_\infty(\mathscr{Q}(X) \mid P)$), the entropy loss alone is not sufficient to compare different quantization strategies.

To illustrate the subtleties, we consider the following example. Let x be a point uniformly distributed in the interval $[0, 1)$, and under noise, it can be shifted but still within the range $[x - 0.01, x + 0.01)$. We can use a scalar quantizer $\mathscr{Q}_1$ with step size 0.01, such that all points in the interval $[0, 1)$ are mapped to integers $[0, 99]$. In this case, the min-entropy $\mathbf{H}_\infty(\mathcal{Q}_1(x)) = \log 100$. As we can see later, there is an easy way to construct a secure sketch for such $\mathcal{Q}_1(x)$ with entropy loss of $\log 3$. Hence, the left-over entropy is $\log(100/3) \approx 5.06$. Now we consider another scalar quantizer $\mathcal{Q}_2$ with step size 0.001, such that the range of $\mathcal{Q}_2(x)$ is $[0, 999]$. A similar scheme on $\mathcal{Q}_2(x)$ would give entropy loss of $\log 21$, which seems much larger than the previous $\log 3$. However, the min-entropy of $\mathcal{Q}_2(x)$ is also increased to $\log 1000$, and the left-over entropy would be $\log(1000/21) \approx 5.57$, which is slightly higher than the case where $\mathcal{Q}_1$ is used.

Intuitively, for a given class of methods of handling noisy data in the quantized domain, it is important to examine how different precisions of the quantization process affect the strength of the extracted key. For this purpose, we propose to consider not just one, but a family of quantizers $\mathbf{Q}$, where each quantizer $\mathcal{Q}$ drawn from $\mathbf{Q}$ defines a mapping from $\mathcal{U}$ to a finite set $\mathcal{M}_{\mathcal{Q}}$. Let $\mathbf{M}$ be the set of such $\mathcal{M}_{\mathcal{Q}}$ for all $\mathcal{Q} \in \mathbf{Q}$. We also define a family of encoders $\mathbf{E}$ and decoders $\mathbf{D}$, such that for each $\mathcal{Q}$ and $\mathcal{M}_{\mathcal{Q}}$, there exist uniquely defined $\mathsf{Enc}_{\mathcal{Q}} \in \mathbf{E}$ and $\mathsf{Dec}_{\mathcal{Q}} \in \mathbf{D}$ that can handle $\mathcal{Q}(X)$ in $\mathcal{M}_{\mathcal{Q}}$.

Definition 4.2.3 A quantization-based sketch family is a tuple $(\mathcal{U}, \mathsf{S}, \mathbf{Q}, \mathbf{M}, \mathbf{E}, \mathbf{D})$, such that for each quantizer $\mathcal{Q} \in \mathbf{Q}$, there exist $\mathcal{M} \in \mathbf{M}$, $\mathsf{Enc} \in \mathbf{E}$ and $\mathsf{Dec} \in \mathbf{D}$, and $(\mathcal{U}, \mathsf{S}, \mathcal{Q}, \mathcal{M}, \mathsf{Enc}, \mathsf{Dec})$ is a quantization-based sketch scheme. We say that such a scheme is a member of the family, and is identified by $\mathcal{Q}$.

Definition 4.2.4 A quantization-based sketch family $(\mathcal{U}, \mathsf{S}, \mathbf{Q}, \mathbf{M}, \mathbf{E}, \mathbf{D})$ is $(\mathbf{L}, \mathbf{R})$-secure for functions $\mathbf{L}, \mathbf{R} : \mathbf{Q} \to \mathbb{R}$ if for any member identified by $\mathcal{Q}_1$ (with encoder Enc_1) we have

1. This member is $\mathbf{L}(\mathcal{Q}_1)$-secure in the quantized domain; and
2. For any random variable X, and any member identified by $\mathcal{Q}_2$ (with encoder Enc_2), we have

$$\tilde{\mathbf{H}}_\infty(\mathcal{Q}_2(X) \mid \mathsf{Enc}_2(\mathcal{Q}_2(X))) - \tilde{\mathbf{H}}_\infty(\mathcal{Q}_1(X) \mid \mathsf{Enc}_1(\mathcal{Q}_1(X))) \le \mathbf{R}(\mathcal{Q}_1).$$

In other words, to measure the security of the family of schemes, we examine two aspects of the family. Firstly, we consider the entropy loss in the quantized domain for each member of the family. This is represented by the function $\mathbf{L}$, which serves as a measure of security when the quantizer is fixed. Secondly, given any quantizer in the family, we consider the question: If we use another quantizer, how many more bits can be extracted? We call this the *relative entropy loss*, which is represented by the function $\mathbf{R}$.

We observe that for some sketch families, the relative entropy loss for any given member can be conveniently bounded by the size of the sketch generated by that member. We say that such sketch families are *well-formed*. More precisely, we have

Definition 4.2.5 A quantization-based sketch family $(\mathcal{U}, \mathsf{S}, \mathbf{Q}, \mathbf{M}, \mathbf{E}, \mathbf{D})$ is well-formed if for any two members $(\mathcal{U}, \mathsf{S}, \mathcal{Q}_1, \mathcal{M}_1, \mathsf{Enc}_1, \mathsf{Dec}_1)$ and $(\mathcal{U}, \mathsf{S}, \mathcal{Q}_2, \mathcal{M}_2,$

Enc$_2$, Dec$_2$), it holds for any random variable X that

$$\tilde{\mathbf{H}}_\infty\big(\mathscr{Q}_1(X) \,\big|\, (P_1, P_2)\big) = \tilde{\mathbf{H}}_\infty\big(\mathscr{Q}_2(X) \,\big|\, (P_1, P_2)\big), \tag{4.10}$$

where $P_1 = \mathsf{Enc}_1(\mathscr{Q}_1(X))$ and $P_2 = \mathsf{Enc}_2(\mathscr{Q}_2(X))$.

Theorem 4.2.1 *For any well-formed quantization-based sketch family, given any two members $(\mathscr{U}, \mathsf{S}, \mathscr{Q}_1, \mathscr{M}_1, \mathsf{Enc}_1, \mathsf{Dec}_1)$ and $(\mathscr{U}, \mathsf{S}, \mathscr{Q}_2, \mathscr{M}_2, \mathsf{Enc}_2, \mathsf{Dec}_2)$, we have for any random variable X*

$$\tilde{\mathbf{H}}_\infty\big(\mathscr{Q}_2(X) \,\big|\, P_2\big) - \tilde{\mathbf{H}}_\infty\big(\mathscr{Q}_1(X) \,\big|\, P_1\big) \le |P_1|,$$

where $P_1 = \mathsf{Enc}_1(\mathscr{Q}_1(X))$ and $P_2 = \mathsf{Enc}_2(\mathscr{Q}_2(X))$.

Proof First, it is not difficult to show that for any random variables A, B and C, we have

$$\tilde{\mathbf{H}}_\infty(A \mid B) - |C| \le \tilde{\mathbf{H}}_\infty\big(A \mid (B, C)\big) \le \tilde{\mathbf{H}}_\infty(A \mid B). \tag{4.11}$$

Let $\widehat{X}_1 = \mathscr{Q}_1(X)$ and $\widehat{X}_2 = \mathscr{Q}_2(X)$. Since the sketch family is well-formed,

$$\tilde{\mathbf{H}}_\infty\big(\widehat{X}_1 \,\big|\, (P_1, P_2)\big) = \tilde{\mathbf{H}}_\infty\big(\widehat{X}_2 \,\big|\, (P_1, P_2)\big). \tag{4.12}$$

Substituting B by P_1, C by P_2, and A by $\widehat{X}_1$ and $\widehat{X}_2$, respectively, in (4.11), we have

$$\tilde{\mathbf{H}}_\infty\big(\widehat{X}_2 \mid P_2\big) - |P_1| \le \tilde{\mathbf{H}}_\infty\big(\widehat{X}_2 \,\big|\, (P_1, P_2)\big)$$
$$= \tilde{\mathbf{H}}_\infty\big(\widehat{X}_1 \,\big|\, (P_1, P_2)\big) \le \tilde{\mathbf{H}}_\infty\big(\widehat{X}_1 \mid P_1\big). \tag{4.13}$$

$\square$

4.3 A General Scheme for Biometric Templates

We observe that many biometric templates can be represented as a sequence of points in some bounded continuous domain. There are two types of noise that can occur. The first noise, *white noise*, perturbs each points by a small distance, and the second noise, *replacement noise*, replaces some points by different points.

Without loss of generality, we assume that each biometric template X can be written as a sequence $X = \langle x_1, x_2, \ldots, x_n \rangle$, where each $x_i \in \mathbb{R}$ and $0 \le x_i < 1$. In other words, $X \in \mathscr{U} = [0, 1)^n$. For each pair of biometric templates X and Y, we say that $(X, Y) \in \mathsf{S}$ if there exists a subset C of $\{1, \ldots, n\}$, such that $|C| \ge n - t$ for some threshold t, and for every $i \in C$, $|x_i - y_i| < \delta$, for some threshold δ.

Similar to the two-part approach in [8], we construct the sketch in two parts. The first part, the *white noise sketch*, handles the white noise in the noisy data, and the second part, the *replacement noise sketch*, corrects the replacement noise. We will concentrate on the white noise sketch in this chapter, and the replacement noise sketch can be implemented using a known secure sketch scheme for set difference (e.g., that in [9, 16]).

4.3.1 Quantization-Based Sketch Family

Each member of the family is parameterized by a λ such that $\lambda \in \mathbb{R}$ and $0 < \lambda \le \delta$.

Quantizer $\mathcal{Q}_\lambda$ Each quantizer $\mathcal{Q}_\lambda$ in $\mathbf{Q}$ is a scalar quantizer with step size $\lambda \in \mathbb{R}$. For each $x \in \mathcal{U}$, $\mathcal{Q}_\lambda(x) = \widehat{x}$ if and only if $\lambda \widehat{x} \le x < \lambda(\widehat{x} + 1)$, and the quantization of X is defined as $\widehat{X} = \mathcal{Q}_\lambda(X) \triangleq \langle \mathcal{Q}_\lambda(x_1), \ldots, \mathcal{Q}_\lambda(x_n)\rangle$. The corresponding quantized domain is thus $\mathcal{M}_\lambda = [0, \lceil \frac{1}{\lambda} \rceil]^n$. The encoders and the decoders work only on the quantized domain. The white noise appeared in the quantized domain is of level $\widehat{\delta}_\lambda = \lceil \delta/\lambda \rceil$. In other words, under white noise, a point $\widehat{x}$ in the quantized domain can be shifted by a distance of at most $\widehat{\delta}_\lambda$. Let us denote $\Delta_\lambda \triangleq 2\widehat{\delta}_\lambda + 1$.

Codebook $\mathscr{C}_\lambda$ Furthermore, for each quantized domain $\mathcal{M}_\lambda$ we consider a *codebook* $\mathscr{C}_\lambda$, where every codeword $c \in \mathscr{C}_\lambda$ has the form $c = k\Delta_\lambda$ for some non-negative integer k. We use $\mathscr{C}_\lambda(\cdot)$ to denote the function such that given a quantized point $\widehat{x}$, it returns a value $c = \mathscr{C}_\lambda(\widehat{x})$ such that $|\widehat{x} - c| \le \widehat{\delta}_\lambda$. That is, the function finds the unique codeword c that is nearest to $\widehat{x}$ in the codebook.

Encoder Enc_λ   Given a quantized $\widehat{X} \in \mathcal{M}_\lambda$, the encoder Enc_λ does the following.

1. For each $\widehat{x}_i \in \widehat{X}$, compute $c_i = \mathscr{C}_\lambda(\widehat{x}_i)$;
2. Output $P = \mathsf{Enc}_\lambda(\widehat{X}) = \langle d_1, \ldots, d_n \rangle$, where $d_i = \widehat{x}_i - c_i$ for $1 \le i \le n$.

In other words, for every $\widehat{x}_i$, the encoder outputs the distance of $\widehat{x}_i$ from its nearest codeword in the codebook $\mathscr{C}_\lambda$.

Decoder Dec_λ   For a corrupted template Y, it is first quantized by $\widehat{Y} = \mathcal{Q}_\lambda(Y)$. Given $P = \langle d_1, \ldots, d_n \rangle$ and $\widehat{Y} = \langle \widehat{y}_1, \ldots, \widehat{y}_n \rangle$, and the decoder Dec_λ does the following.

1. For each $\widehat{y}_i \in \widehat{Y}$, compute $c_i = \mathscr{C}_\lambda(\widehat{y}_i - d_i)$;
2. Output $\widehat{X} = \mathsf{Dec}_\lambda(\widehat{Y}) = \langle c_1 + d_1, \ldots, c_n + d_n \rangle$.

In other words, the decoder shifts every $\widehat{y}_i$ by d_i, maps it to the nearest codeword in $\mathscr{C}_\lambda$, and shifts it back by the same distance.

4.3.1.1 Security Analysis

For each member of the sketch family with parameter λ, the difference d_i between $\widehat{x}_i$ and p_i ranges from $-\widehat{\delta}_\lambda$ to $\widehat{\delta}_\lambda$. Intuitively, $\log \Delta_\lambda$ bits are sufficient and necessary to describe the white noise in the quantized domain (recall that $\Delta_\lambda = 2\widehat{\delta}_\lambda + 1 = 2\lceil \frac{\delta}{\lambda} \rceil + 1$). Hence, we have

Lemma 4.3.1 *The quantization-based sketch scheme* $(\mathcal{U}, \mathsf{S}, \mathcal{Q}_\lambda, \mathcal{M}_\lambda, \mathsf{Enc}_\lambda, \mathsf{Dec}_\lambda)$ *is* $(n \log \Delta_\lambda)$*-secure in the quantized domain.*

Proof Note that the size of each d_i generated in the second step of the encoder is $\log \Delta_\lambda$. Hence the total size of the sketch is $n \log \Delta_\lambda$. Therefore, the entropy loss of the sketch P is at most $n \log \Delta_\lambda$ by (4.9). □

It is not difficult to see that the above bound is tight. For example, when each $\widehat{x}$ is uniformly distributed in the quantized domain, the min-entropy of each $\widehat{x}$ after quantization would be $\log \lceil \frac{1}{\lambda} \rceil$, and the average min-entropy of $\widehat{x}$ given P would be at most $\log |\mathcal{C}_\lambda| = \log \lceil \frac{1}{\lambda} \rceil - \log \Delta_\lambda$.

Now we consider the relative entropy loss. First of all, we observe that the proposed sketch family is well-formed according to Definition 4.2.5.

Lemma 4.3.2 *The quantization-based sketch family defined in Sect.* 4.3.1 *is well-formed.*

Proof We consider any two members in the sketch family. The first is identified by $\mathcal{Q}_{\lambda_1}$ with step size λ_1, and the second is identified by $\mathcal{Q}_{\lambda_2}$ with step size λ_2.

For any point $x \in X$, let $\widehat{x}_1 = \mathcal{Q}_{\lambda_1}(x)$. Recall that during encoding, a codeword is computed as $c_1 = \mathcal{C}_{\lambda_1}(\widehat{x}_1)$, and the difference $d_1 = \widehat{x}_1 - c_1$ is put into the sketch. Similarly, let $\widehat{x}_2 = \mathcal{Q}_{\lambda_2}(x)$, $c_2 = \mathcal{C}_{\lambda_2}(\widehat{x}_2)$ and $d_2 = \widehat{x}_2 - c_2$.

Since $\lambda_1 \le \delta$ and $\lambda_2 \le \delta$, it is easy to see that if d_1, d_2 and $\widehat{x}_1$ is known, we can compute $\widehat{x}_2$ deterministically. Similarly, given d_1, d_2 and $\widehat{x}_2$, $\widehat{x}_1$ can also be determined. Thus, we have

$$\widetilde{\mathbf{H}}_\infty\big(\widehat{x}_1 \mid (d_1, d_2)\big) = \widetilde{\mathbf{H}}_\infty\big((\widehat{x}_1, \widehat{x}_2) \mid (d_1, d_2)\big) = \widetilde{\mathbf{H}}_\infty\big(\widehat{x}_2 \mid (d_1, d_2)\big). \qquad (4.14)$$

The same arguments can be applied to all the points in X. Hence, let $P_1 = \mathsf{Enc}_{\lambda_1}(X)$ and $P_2 = \mathsf{Enc}_{\lambda_2}(X)$, we have

$$\widetilde{\mathbf{H}}_\infty\big(\widehat{X}_1 \mid (P_1, P_2)\big) = \widetilde{\mathbf{H}}_\infty\big((\widehat{X}_1, \widehat{X}_2) \mid (P_1, P_2)\big) = \widetilde{\mathbf{H}}_\infty\big(\widehat{X}_2 \mid (P_1, P_2)\big). \qquad (4.15)$$

That is, the proposed sketch family is well-formed. □

By combining Theorem 4.2.1 and Lemma 4.3.2, and considering that for the member of the sketch family identified by $\mathcal{Q}_{\lambda_1}$ with step size λ_1, the size of the sketch $|P_1| = n(\log \Delta_{\lambda_1})$, we have the following lemma.

Lemma 4.3.3 *For the quantization-based sketch family defined in Sect.* 4.3.1, *given any member identified by* $\mathcal{Q}_{\lambda_1}$ *with step size* λ_1 *and encoder* Enc_{λ_1} *we see that, for every random variable* $X \in \mathcal{U}$ *and any member identified by* $\mathcal{Q}_{\lambda_2}$ *with step size* λ_2 *and encoder* Enc_{λ_2}, *we have*

$$\widetilde{\mathbf{H}}_\infty\big(\mathcal{Q}_{\lambda_2}(X) \mid \mathsf{Enc}_{\lambda_2}(\mathcal{Q}_{\lambda_2}(X))\big) - \widetilde{\mathbf{H}}_\infty\big(\mathcal{Q}_{\lambda_1}(X) \mid \mathsf{Enc}_{\lambda_1}(\mathcal{Q}_{\lambda_1}(X))\big) \le n(\log \Delta_{\lambda_1}).$$

In other words, the relative entropy loss is at most $n(\log \Delta_{\lambda_1})$ *for* $\mathcal{Q}_{\lambda_1}$.

Not only the above is a worst case bound, we can show that the worst case can indeed happen.

Lemma 4.3.4 *The relative entropy loss in Lemma* 4.3.3 *is tight for sufficiently small* δ.

Proof For any given λ_1, we find a λ_2 such that it is possible to find $\Delta_{\lambda_1} \triangleq (2\lceil \delta/\lambda_1 \rceil + 1)$ points $W = \{w_0, \ldots, w_{\Delta_{\lambda_1}-1}\}$ such that $\mathcal{Q}_{\lambda_1}(w_i) - \mathcal{C}_{\lambda_1}(\mathcal{Q}_{\lambda_1}(w_1)) = i - \lceil \delta/\lambda_1 \rceil$, and $\mathcal{C}_{\lambda_2}(w_i) = c_i$ for some codeword $c_i \in \mathcal{C}_{\lambda_2}$. In other words, we want to find points such that each of them would generate a different d_i in the final sketch with $\mathcal{Q}_{\lambda_1}$, but would generate exactly the same number (i.e., 0) in the sketch when $\mathcal{Q}_{\lambda_2}$ is used. Note that when δ is sufficiently small, there would be sufficiently many codewords in $\mathcal{C}_{\lambda_1}$, and it is always possible to find such λ_2 (e.g., $\lambda_2 = \lambda_1/2$).

When each $x \in X$ is uniformly distributed over W, we can see that the sketch from the scheme identified by $\mathcal{Q}_{\lambda_1}$ would reveal all information about X, but in the case of $\mathcal{Q}_{\lambda_2}$, the left-over entropy would be exactly $\log \Delta_{\lambda_1}$.   □

Therefore, combining Lemmas 4.3.1, 4.3.3 and 4.3.4 we have

Theorem 4.3.5 *The quantization-based sketch family defined in Sect.* 4.3.1 *is* $(\mathbf{L}, \mathbf{R})$-*secure where for each member in the family identified by* $\mathcal{Q}_\lambda$ *with step size* λ, *where* $\mathbf{L}(\mathcal{Q}_\lambda) = \mathbf{R}(\mathcal{Q}_\lambda) = n \log \Delta_\lambda$. *Furthermore, the bounds are tight.*

For example, if $\lambda = \delta$, we would have $\mathbf{L}(\mathcal{Q}_\lambda) = \mathbf{R}(\mathcal{Q}_\lambda) = n(\log 3)$. Note that although decreasing λ *might* give a larger left-over entropy, this is not guaranteed. In fact, if we use a $\lambda' < \lambda$, by applying the above theorem on $\mathcal{Q}_{\lambda'}$, we can see that it may result in a smaller left-over entropy than using $\mathcal{Q}_\lambda$ (e.g., consider the example in the proof of Lemma 4.3.4).

4.3.1.2 A Special Case

We further study a special case when each point $x \in X$ is independently and uniformly distributed over $[0, 1)$. We further assume that $1/\delta$ is an integer, and the family of schemes only consists of members with step size λ such that $1/\lambda$ is an integer that is a multiple of Δ_λ. This additional assumption is only for the convenience of the analysis, and would not make too much difference in practice.

In this case, the entropy loss in the quantized domain for the member identified by $\mathcal{Q}_\lambda$ with step size λ would be exactly $n(\log \Delta_\lambda)$, which shows that Lemma 4.3.1 is tight. Moreover, it is interesting that the relative entropy loss in this case can be bounded by a constant.

Corollary 4.3.6 *When each* $x \in X$ *is independently and uniformly distributed, the quantization-based sketch family defined in Sect.* 4.3.1 *is* $(\mathbf{L}, \mathbf{R})$-*secure where for each member in the family identified by* $\mathcal{Q}_\lambda$ *with step size* λ, *where* $\mathbf{L}(\mathcal{Q}_\lambda) = n(\log \Delta_\lambda)$, *and* $\mathbf{R}(\mathcal{Q}_\lambda) = n \log(1 + \frac{\lambda}{2\delta}) \leq n \log(3/2)$.

Proof The claim $\mathbf{L}(\mathcal{Q}_\lambda) = n(\log \Delta_\lambda)$ follows directly from Lemma 4.3.1, so we only focus on **R**. Consider two members of the family identified by $\mathcal{Q}_{\lambda_1}$ and $\mathcal{Q}_{\lambda_2}$, respectively. Without loss of generality, we assume $\lambda_1 > \lambda_2$. Consider any $x \in X$, let $\widehat{x}_1 = \mathcal{Q}_{\lambda_1}(x)$, $c_1 = \mathcal{C}_{\lambda_1}(\widehat{x}_1)$. Similarly we define $\widehat{x}_2 = \mathcal{Q}_{\lambda_2}(x)$ and $c_2 = \mathcal{C}_{\lambda_2}(\widehat{x}_2)$. Hence, the min-entropy in the quantized domain would be $\log(1/\lambda_1)$ and $\log(1/\lambda_2)$, respectively.

Clearly, c_1 and c_2 are also uniformly distributed over $\mathcal{C}_{\lambda_1}$ and $\mathcal{C}_{\lambda_2}$, respectively, and do not depend on d_1 and d_2. Hence, the left-over entropy for these two members would be $\log(|\mathcal{C}_{\lambda_1}|) = \log \frac{1}{\lambda_1 + 2\delta}$ and $\log(|\mathcal{C}_{\lambda_2}|) = \log \frac{1}{\lambda_2 + 2\delta}$, respectively. Furthermore, recall that $0 < \lambda_2 < \lambda_1 \leq \delta$, and the difference between these two quantities can be bounded as

$$\log(|\mathcal{C}_{\lambda_2}|) - \log(|\mathcal{C}_{\lambda_1}|) = \log \frac{\lambda_1 + 2\delta}{\lambda_2 + 2\delta} < \log\left(1 + \frac{\lambda_1}{2\delta}\right) \leq \log \frac{3}{2}.$$

Therefore, the relative entropy loss is bounded by $n \log(3/2)$ as claimed. □

4.3.2 Quantization-Based Secure Sketch with Randomization

There are few reasons of using such a randomization in our scheme. First of all, randomization provides a better noise tolerance. In particular, the noise on the original components seems to be smoothed out by the random mapping, which makes the scheme more robust for the same FAR. Secondly, randomization provides cancelability and diversity simultaneously. More specifically, users will be able to use the same biometric data with newly generated random mapping in case of any data compromise. Furthermore, the cross-matching across different databases will not be feasible since different applications will use different random mapping. The randomized quantization-based secure sketch implementation is illustrated in Fig. 4.9.

4.3.2.1 Template Representation

We assume that we can extract a feature vector of size n from each biometric sample. Therefore,

$$B_i = [b_{i1} \quad b_{i2} \quad \cdots \quad b_{in}]^T \tag{4.16}$$

represents the n-dimensional feature vector of ith user of the system where each coefficient $b_{ij} \in R$ is a real number.

In addition, we also assume that the value of each coefficient b_{ij} can vary within a certain *range*, which is going to be determined through experiments on the data set. In other words, we consider the jth coefficient for the ith user to be always associated with a range, which is defined by a *mid-point* and a *range* ρ_{ij}. Here, the mean-point $\overline{b}_{ij}$ for the jth component of the ith user is determined as the mid-point value of the jth component of the feature vector observed in the training data

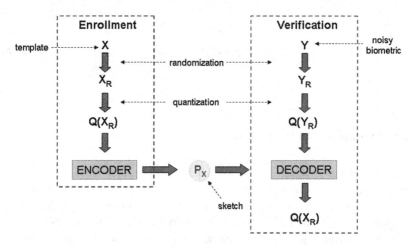

Fig. 4.9 Randomized sketch generation and reconstruction in continuous domain

set of user i. Similarly, the range size ρ_{ij} for the jth component of the ith user is determined as $\rho_{ij} = (\mathrm{mx}_{ij} - \mathrm{mn}_{ij})/2$ where mn_{ij} (resp. mx_{ij}) is the minimum (resp. the maximum) value of the jth component of the feature vector observed in the training data set of user i.

Therefore, the template for the ith user consists of two vectors. The first is the list of n mid-points $\bar{b}_{i1}, \ldots, \bar{b}_{in}$, and the other is the list of range sizes for each coefficients $\rho_{i1}, \ldots, \rho_{in}$.

In the simplest case, for the ith user in the system, we can consider a sample $B_i = [b_{i1} \ b_{i2} \ \cdots \ b_{in}]^T$ as authentic if

$$\bar{b}_{ij} - \rho_{ij} \leq b_{ij} \leq \bar{b}_{ij} + \rho_{ij} \tag{4.17}$$

for all $j = 1, \ldots, n$.

4.3.2.2 Randomization

Before generating a sketch from the coefficients extracted from raw samples of biometric data, we can further apply user-specific random mapping on these feature vectors. In particular, we generate k-by-n matrices whose elements are uniformly distributed random numbers between $-\theta$ and θ, where θ is a parameter. We call such matrices *randomization matrices*.

Let R_i be the randomization matrix for user i and by multiplying the feature vector with this random matrix, an n dimensional feature vector can be mapped into another k dimensional feature vector. That is, for user i and a raw sample $B_i = [b_{i1} \ \cdots \ b_{in}]^T$, we compute $V_i = R_i B_i = [v_{i1} \ v_{i2} \ \cdots \ v_{ik}]^T$.

Similar to the simple case in Sect. 4.3.2.1, mid-points $\bar{v}_{ij}$'s and range sizes δ_{ij}'s are recalculated and for any $V_i = R_i B_i = [v_{i1} \ v_{i2} \ \cdots \ v_{ik}]^T$, we consider it as authentic if

$$\overline{v}_{ij} - \delta_{ij} \leq v_{ij} \leq \overline{v}_{ij} + \delta_{ij} \tag{4.18}$$

for all $j = 1, \ldots, k$.

4.3.2.3 Quantization and Codebook

In order to generate a sketch for the biometric template, first step is to discretize every component of the feature vector such that we can apply a sketch scheme for discrete domains. Therefore, we employ a straightforward method, which uses a scalar quantizer for each of the coefficients to map it to a discrete domain.

First, we determine global ranges of each and every component of the feature vectors from the training data set obtained during enrollment phase. Let these values be $\text{MN}_j = \min_i(v_{ij})$ and $\text{MX}_j = \max_i(v_{ij})$. Next, the discrete domain $\mathscr{C}_j$ for the jth component is computed by quantizing the overall user range by the quantization step δ_j. That is,

$$\mathscr{C}_j = \{\text{MN}_j - r_j, \text{MN}_j - r_j + \delta_j, \text{MN}_j - r_j + 2\delta_j, \ldots, \text{MN}_j - r_j + L_j\delta_j\}, \tag{4.19}$$

where L_j is appropriately chosen integer which satisfies $\text{MN}_j - r_j + L_j\delta_j \geq \text{MX}_j$ and r_j is a positive random number.

In this way, for the jth component of the ith user, a range of mid-point $\overline{v}_{ij}$ and size δ_{ij} can be translated to a discrete range where the discrete mid-point is quantization of $\overline{v}_{ij}$ in $\mathscr{C}_j$, and the discrete range size d_{ij} is given by

$$d_{ij} = \left\lceil \frac{\delta_{ij}}{\delta_j} \right\rceil. \tag{4.20}$$

Finally, the codebook C_j^i for the jth component of the ith user is a subset of $\mathscr{C}_j$, and can be determined by choosing one point out of every $2d_{ij} + 1$ consecutive points in $\mathscr{C}_j$.

In this setup, δ_j's are simply determined as a function of the minimum range size of each component of the feature vector observed in overall user space. That is,

$$\delta_j = \alpha \min_i(\delta_{ij}), \tag{4.21}$$

where α is a parameter which can take different values.

It is worth noting that, in the above formulation, the quantization step δ_j can be determined in many different ways. However, it is reasonable to assume that δ_j should be related to some statistics of the range of the feature components, namely δ_{ij}'s.

4.3.2.4 Sketch Generation and Template Reconstruction

During enrollment, the biometric data of each user are acquired and feature vectors
are extracted several times as a part of training process. Then the variation (i.e,.
the mid-point and range size) of each feature vector component is estimated by
analyzing the training data set. Next, we construct a codebook for each component
of each user as in Sect. 4.3.2.3.

Therefore, the sketch P_i for user i is a vector

$$P_i = [p_{i1} \quad p_{i2} \quad \cdots \quad p_{ik}]^T, \tag{4.22}$$

where

$$p_{ij} = Q^i_j(\overline{v}_{ij}) - \overline{v}_{ij} \tag{4.23}$$

and $Q^i_j(\overline{v}_{ij})$ is the codeword in C^i_j that is closest to $\overline{v}_{ij}$.

During authentication, biometric data of the ith user is taken and corresponding feature vector is computed. Let us denote this noisy feature vector as $\widetilde{V}_i =
[\widetilde{v}_{i1} \, \widetilde{v}_{i2} \, \cdots \, \widetilde{v}_{in}]^T$. Then the decoder takes $\widetilde{V}_i$ and P_i and calculates $Q^i_j(\widetilde{v}_{ij}) - p_{ij}$
for $j = 1, \ldots, n$. Reconstruction of the original biometric will be successful if

$$-d_{ij} \le Q^i_j(\widetilde{v}_{ij}) - Q^i_j(\overline{v}_{ij}) < d_{ij}, \tag{4.24}$$

where d_{ij} is the user specific error tolerance bound for the jth component. It is not
difficult to see that $Q^i_j(\widetilde{v}_{ij}) - p_{ij} = Q^i_j(\widetilde{v}_{ij}) - Q^i_j(\overline{v}_{ij}) + \overline{v}_{ij}$ and the errors up to
the some preset threshold value will be corrected successfully.

4.4 Secure Sketch for Multiple Secrets

We have seen that secure sketch and secure extractor schemes are very helpful in
protecting biometric data because we can bound the entropy loss in case the sketches
are compromised. However, this bound alone is not sufficient to protect the confidentiality of the biometric templates, nor the data that is protected by them. The
reason is simple: The strengths of the keys that can be extracted from the biometric
data, taking into consideration of possible information leakage due to the sketches,
are typically weak for commonly used biometric features such as fingerprints and
facial features. This is similar to the problem of weak passwords. Although we can
protect passwords by applying one-way hash functions on them, weak passwords
can still be broken by brute-force. As a result, it would not be a good idea to use
the keys extracted from biometric data directly to protect other data (e.g., to encrypt
sensitive documents).

A common way to utilize biometric data in a security system is to use multiple
secrets together. Some of these secrets can be "fuzzy", such as biometric data, and
some of them can be passwords or cryptographic keys. For example, in a multi-
factor authentication system, a user may be asked to present both a valid fingerprint

and a matching password or a smartcard before certain resource is accessible. In some multi-modal biometric authentication systems, a user may have to present multiple valid biometric features, such as retina patterns and fingerprints.

A straightforward way of using multiple secrets is to use them independently. For example, we can simply put the key extracted from a fingerprint and that from a password together to form a new key. In this way we can obtain a strong key from two or more weak keys, which solves part of the problem. However, we can also easily see that different types of secrets may have different characteristics. The likelihood of being lost, stolen or forgotten, and the ease of revocation and replacement can be quite different for different secrets. For example, a key stored in a smartcard can be easily made very strong, but such a key has to be stored in the memory, which makes it easier to be compromised. Passwords, on the other hand, can be remembered by human beings, but they typically have lower entropy. Both smartcards and passwords have the advantage that they can be easily replaced and/or revoked. Biometrics, on the other hand, would yield keys with reasonable entropy, which are often difficult to revoke or replace.

Therefore, to cater for different characteristics of different secrets, they have to be mixed together in a smart way.

4.4.1 Two-Factor Authentication: An Example

Here we describe a simple multi-factor authentication scheme using biometrics and smartcards. Suppose a user has biometric data X and a smart card with a key K of length n. We further assume that there is a cryptographic pseudo-random number generator G that takes a short seed S and outputs pseudo-random bits that cannot be efficiently distinguished from random bits. During registration, the user computes the hash of X and uses it as the seed S (i.e., $S = h(X)$ for some cryptographic hash function h), then applies $G(S)$ to generate n pseudo-random bits. Let $K_p = G(S)$ be the output. Next, the user computes a sketch P_X from X, and chooses a random string Q, where $|Q| = |P_X|$. The string Q is stored in the authentication server, and the result of $Q \oplus P_X$ is stored in the smartcard, where $\oplus$ denotes bit-wise xor operation. Also, the result of $K \oplus K_p$ is also stored in the authentication database. The use of pseudo-random number generator allows the string K_p to be of any polynomial length, so that it can be easily xored with K.

During authentication, the server retrieves $Q \oplus P_X$ from the smartcard, and uses it to recover P_X, which is then returned to the user. Next the user reconstructs X using P_X and a fresh scan of the biometrics, and applies the same function $G(h(X))$ to recover K_p. After that the user would be able to generate the key $K \oplus K_p$ for authentication. (See Fig. 4.10 for the illustration of the proposed protocol.)

In this way, if the authentication database is compromised, only Q and $K \oplus K_p$ is revealed. Since K are completely random, so is $K \oplus K_p$. Hence the data stored at the server does not reveal any information about X. On the other hand, if the smartcard is stolen or lost, what an attacker would be able to find out is $Q \oplus P_X$

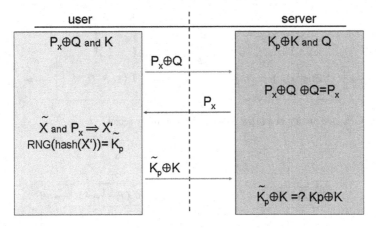

Fig. 4.10 A simple secure sketch-based multi-factor scheme that uses biometrics and smartcards

and K, which are just random strings. Since K and Q are independent from the user biometrics, they can be easily revoked and replaced.

In the worst case, the attacker is able to steal the smartcard and compromise the server at the same time. In that case, P_X and K_p would be revealed. However, P_X reveals only limited information about X, and it can be computationally infeasible to compute X from K_p, if the min-entropy of X is high enough. Other secrets (e.g., passwords) can be used in combination with X to make it harder to compute X from K_p. Therefore, we can achieve unconditional security when one of the storage (database and smartcard) is compromised, and some extent of computational security when both storage devices are compromised.

4.4.2 Cascaded Mixing

The example given in Sect. 4.4.1 is a special case of a mixing strategy called *cascaded mixing* given by Fang et al. [19].

The idea of cascaded mixing is intuitive. As can be seen in the example, some secrets (biometrics) are more *important*, because they are tightly linked to identities and hard to revoke or replace, and some secrets (K and Q) are less important because they are only loosely linked to identities and easily revocable and replaceable. Naturally, it makes good sense to use less important secrets to protect more important ones, as what happens in the example: Both the sketch of the biometric data P_X and the extracted key K_P are further xored (encrypted) using Q and K, respectively.

At this point we must note that although there are other cryptographic operations happening in this example, such as hashing and encryption of the extracted key, these operations are actually independent from the protection of the biometric data. We include these in our example to make it a complete authentication system. However, to analyze the security of such mixing, we need a more abstract model.

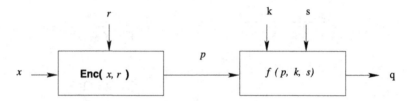

Fig. 4.11 Cascaded mixing of a fuzzy secret with a non-fuzzy secret

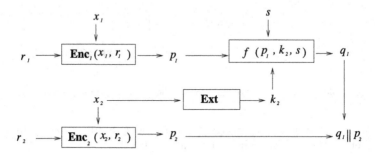

Fig. 4.12 Cascaded mixing of two fuzzy secrets

In general, the process of using a non-fuzzy key to protect another more important fuzzy secret is illustrated in Fig. 4.11. In this figure, Enc is the encoder, f is a mixing function, x is the fuzzy secret, r is the randomness used by the encoder, p is the sketch of x, k is the non-fuzzy secret, s is the randomness used by the mixing function f, and q is the final sketch.

During reconstruction, given a key k and some x', which is a noisy version of x, we first use q and k to recover the sketch p, and use p to recover x from x'.

Similarly, when both secrets are fuzzy, the mixing process is depicted in Fig. 4.12, where Ext represents an extractor. In essence, given two secrets x_1 and x_2, where x_1 is more important, we can compute the sketches p_1 and p_2, respectively, and use the key k_2 extracted from x_2 to mix with the sketch p_1 to produced the mixed sketch q_1, and the final sketch is constructed by simply putting q_1 and p_2 together.

When a user presents y_1 and y_2 that are close to x_1 and x_2, respectively, x_2 is first reconstructed using y_2 and p_2, and a key k_2 is extracted from x_2, which in turn is used to retrieve p_1 if f is invertible. After that, x_1 is reconstructed using y_1 and p_1. The final cryptographic key can be obtained by applying an extractor on the concatenation $x_1 \parallel x_2$.

Intuitively, the cascaded mixing approach in Fig. 4.12 gives more protection to the first secret x_1. If the mixing function is chosen properly, the mixed q_1 contains little or no information about x_1. In this case, if an attacker wants to exploit the information in the final sketch $q_1 \parallel p_2$ in attempts to find out x_1, it would require the attacker to guess x_2 using p_2 before any useful information can be obtained from the final sketch by computing p_1 from q_1 and x_2.

Now, let us consider the mixing function

$$f : \{0, 1\}^{|P|} \times \{0, 1\}^{|K|} \times \{0, 1\}^{|S|} \to \{0, 1\}^{|Q|}$$

and random variables Q, P, K and S such that $Q = f(P, K, S)$. We assume that $|Q| \le |P| + |S|$. We further require f to have certain properties (as in [19]). First, f must be invertible.

Definition 4.4.1 (Invertibility) A mixing function f is invertible if there exists a function $g(\cdot, \cdot)$ such that for all $p \in \{0, 1\}^{|P|}$, $k \in \{0, 1\}^{|K|}$ and $s \in \{0, 1\}^{|S|}$, we have $g(f(p, k, s), k) = p$.

In addition, in our analysis we consider mixing functions with the following properties on recoverability of the randomness invested.

Definition 4.4.2 (Recoverable Randomness) For a mixing function f, the randomness S is called recoverable if for any $p \in \{0, 1\}^{|P|}$, $k \in \{0, 1\}^{|K|}$ and $s, s' \in \{0, 1\}^{|S|}$, if $f(p, k, s) = f(p, k, s')$, we have $s = s'$.

Definition 4.4.3 (β-Recoverable Key) For a mixing function f, the key K is called β-recoverable if for any $p \in \{0, 1\}^{|P|}$, $q \in \{0, 1\}^{|Q|}$, the cardinality of the set $\mathcal{K}_{p,q} = \{k \in \{0, 1\}^{|K|} | \exists s \in \{0, 1\}^{\beta}, f(p, k, s) = q\}$ is at most 2^{β}.

For example, we can construct an invertible mixing function with recoverable randomness from a stream cipher E where the mixing is done by encrypting the concatenation of the sketch and the randomness using the key (i.e., $f(p, k, r) = E_k(p \parallel r)$). In this case, both the inversion and the randomness recovery can be done at once by simply decrypting a given q.

4.4.3 Security Analysis of Two-Secret Sketch

The idea of mixing may look intuitive at first. The real challenge, however, is to mix the secrets in the correct way. In fact, the security of the resulting scheme can be worse than without mixing if it is not done carefully.

To analyze the security of a cascaded mixing scheme, let us examine the simplest case, where one secret is fuzzy and more important (say, a fingerprint) and the other secret is not fuzzy and independent from the fuzzy secret. Let $x \in \mathcal{M}$ and $k \in \{0, 1\}^{|K|}$ be the fuzzy and non-fuzzy secrets, respectively. Consider a secure sketch scheme described by the tuple $(\mathcal{M}, \mathsf{S}, \mathsf{Enc}, \mathsf{Dec})$, where S is a similarity function on $\mathcal{M}$ and Enc and Dec are the encoder and decoder, respectively. Let p be the sketch computed from fuzzy secret x and randomness s, i.e., $p = \mathsf{Enc}(x, r)$. We consider two scenarios with different lengths of the non-fuzzy secret key k with respect to the size of the sketch p.

In our analysis, we use small letters such as x, k, p, q, r and s to represent instances of secrets, sketches and randomness, and use the capital letters X, K, P, Q, R and S to represent the corresponding random variables.

If the key K that is uniformly distributed and the length of K is no shorter than the sketch, we can use the key to hide the sketch P completely by simply using the one-time pad as the mixing function and K as the key. However, from the mixed sketch Q, some information about the key may be revealed. This is due to the fact that P is unlikely to be uniformly random in practice, and knowledge about the sketch will reveal information about the key.

If K is shorter than P, it is not possible to hide P completely. This scenario is more interesting in some scenarios because it is well-known that the entropy of user chosen PIN numbers and passwords is typically low. Hence, it is important to determine how much information of the secret X remains when the mixed sketch is revealed, and whether the mixing may reveal more information than the simple method that encodes the secrets independently. In other words, for random variables X, K, R, S, P and Q, we need to investigate the remaining entropies $\widetilde{\mathbf{H}}_\infty(X|Q)$ and $\widetilde{\mathbf{H}}_\infty(K|Q)$, and compare $\widetilde{\mathbf{H}}_\infty(X, K|Q)$ and $\widetilde{\mathbf{H}}_\infty(X|P) + \mathbf{H}_\infty(K)$.

For the overall remaining entropy $\widetilde{\mathbf{H}}_\infty(X, K|Q)$, we have the following lemma.

Lemma 4.4.1 [19] *Given random variables X, K, R, S and mixing function f such that $|Q| \le |P| + |S|$, We have $\widetilde{\mathbf{H}}_\infty(X, K|Q) \ge \mathbf{H}_\infty(X) + \mathbf{H}_\infty(K) + \mathbf{H}_\infty(R) - |P|$.*

Proof Since S is recoverable, we can consider Enc and f together as the encoding algorithm for the final sketch Q. Similarly we can group R and S together as the recoverable randomness. The inequality (4.9) in Sect. 4.2.1 applies. Note that $|Q| \le |P| + |S|$, and we have

$$\widetilde{\mathbf{H}}_\infty(X, K|Q) \ge \mathbf{H}_\infty(X, K) + \mathbf{H}_\infty(R) + \mathbf{H}_\infty(S) - |Q|$$
$$\ge \mathbf{H}_\infty(X) + \mathbf{H}_\infty(K) + \mathbf{H}_\infty(R) - |P|. \qquad \square$$

It is worth to note that the requirement that $|Q| \le |P| + |S|$ can always be easily met. For example, the equality holds if we construct f by using a stream cipher as mentioned earlier.

Lemma 4.4.1 gives a lower bound of the remaining entropy of the secrets X and K. In general, if both secrets are fuzzy, we can similar obtain the bound:

$$\widetilde{\mathbf{H}}_\infty(X_1, X_2|Q) \ge \mathbf{H}_\infty(X_1) + \mathbf{H}_\infty(X_2) + \mathbf{H}_\infty(R_1) + \mathbf{H}_\infty(R_2) - |P_1| - |P_2|,$$

where X_1 and X_2 are both fuzzy secrets, R_1 and R_2 are the randomness invested in constructing the sketch P_1 and P_2 for the two secrets, respectively. We note that this bound is the same as in the case where simply encode the two secrets independently.

Now that we have the bound on the overall entropy loss, let us further investigate the entropy loss for individual secrets (i.e., $\widetilde{\mathbf{H}}_\infty(X|Q)$ and $\widetilde{\mathbf{H}}_\infty(K|Q)$), so that we know if the more important secret X is indeed given more protection.

When the non-fuzzy secret K is sufficiently long, the mixing function f can be simply one-time pad, and Q would not reveal any information about P. In other words, for X, the remaining entropy is the same as the min-entropy of X (i.e., $\widetilde{\mathbf{H}}_\infty(X|Q) = \mathbf{H}_\infty(X)$).

The entropy loss for K, however, requires more careful analysis. In Theorem 4.4.3, we are going to show that $\widetilde{\mathbf{H}}_\infty(K|Q) = \mathbf{H}_\infty(K) + \mathbf{H}_\infty(P) - |P|$. We can see that if the sketch is sufficiently random, and $\mathbf{H}_\infty(P) = |P|$, the remaining entropy of K given Q would be the same as the min-entropy of K (i.e., $\widetilde{\mathbf{H}}_\infty(K|Q) = \mathbf{H}_\infty(K)$). It is also worth to note that, for some distributions of X, the sum of the remaining entropies for each individual secret given the final sketch can be greater than the overall remaining entropy.

As we mentioned earlier, when the key K is extracted from a PIN, a password or another biometrics, the length of K can be small (say, 30 bits) compared to typical cryptographic keys. In this scenario, we may not be able to use a one-time pad to protect the sketch completely, and the final mixed Q may leak some information about the key K. Nevertheless, partial leakage of K is acceptable as long as it can provide more protection to X. Indeed, the next theorem shows that entropy loss of X from the sketch P can be diverted to K.

Theorem 4.4.2 [19] *Given three independent random variables X, K and R distributed over $\mathscr{M}$, $\{0, 1\}^{|K|}$ and $\{0, 1\}^{|R|}$, respectively, and an $(\mathscr{M}, \mathsf{S}, \mathsf{Enc}, \mathsf{Dec})$-sketch scheme. Let P be the sketch of X, i.e., $P = \mathsf{Enc}(X, R)$, where R is recoverable, and let $f : \{0, 1\}^{|P|} \times \{0, 1\}^{|K|} \to \{0, 1\}^{|Q|}$ be an mixing function and $Q = f(P, K, S)$, where S is $|S|$ bits of recoverable randomness. If f is invertible and the key K is $|S|$-recoverable. Then*

$$\widetilde{\mathbf{H}}_\infty(X|Q) \geq \mathbf{H}_\infty(X) + \mathbf{H}_\infty(K) - |Q|. \tag{4.25}$$

Proof First, let $\mathscr{K}_{x,q} \subset \{0, 1\}^{|K|}$ be the set of secret $k \in \{0, 1\}^{|K|}$ such that there exists an $r \in \{0, 1\}^{|R|}$ and $s \in \{0, 1\}^{|S|}$ so that q can be computed from x, r, k and s. That is,

$$\mathscr{K}_{x,q} = \left\{ k \in \{0, 1\}^{|K|} | \exists r, s, f\big(\mathsf{Enc}(x, r), k, s\big) = q \right\}.$$

Since the key of the mixing function f is $|S|$-recoverable, it is clear that the cardinality $|\mathscr{K}_{x,q}|$ is no more than the number of all possible r's multiplied by $2^{|S|}$, where $|S| = |Q| - |P|$. That is, $|\mathscr{K}_{x,q}| \leq 2^{|R|+|S|}$ for any x and q. Now, consider

$$A = 2^{-\widetilde{\mathbf{H}}_\infty(X|Q)-|R|-|S|}$$

$$= \sum_q \Pr[Q = q] \max_x \Pr[X = x | Q = q] 2^{-|R|-|S|}$$

$$= \sum_q \max_x \Pr[X = x, Q = q] 2^{-|R|-|S|}.$$

On the other hand, we have

$$B = 2^{-\tilde{\mathbf{H}}_\infty(X,K|Q)}$$

$$= \sum_q \max_{x,k} \Pr[X = x, K = k | Q = q].$$

For any $q_0 \in \{0, 1\}^{|Q|}$, let us consider

$$\max_x \Pr[X = x, Q = q_0] 2^{-|R|-|S|}$$

$$= \max_x \sum_k \Pr[X = x, Q = q_0, K = k] 2^{-|R|-|S|}$$

$$\leq \max_x \left(\max_k \Pr[X = x, Q = q_0, K = k] 2^{|R|+|S|} \right) 2^{-|R|-|S|}$$

$$= \max_{x,k} \Pr[X = x, Q = q_0, K = k].$$

The inequality holds because for any x, there will be at most $|\mathcal{K}_{x,q_0}| \leq 2^{|R|+|S|}$ non-zero terms in the summation, hence the sum will be at most $2^{|R|+|S|}$ times the largest term in the summation. As a result, we have

$$A \leq \sum_q \max_{x,k} \Pr[X = x, Q = q, K = k] = B.$$

This is equivalent to

$$\tilde{\mathbf{H}}_\infty(X|Q) + |R| + |S| \geq \tilde{\mathbf{H}}_\infty(X, K|Q).$$

By applying the bound on overall entropy loss (Lemma 4.4.1), and considering that the recoverable randomness includes the $|R|$ bit R and $|S|$ bit S, we have

$$\tilde{\mathbf{H}}_\infty(X|Q) \geq \tilde{\mathbf{H}}_\infty(X, K|Q) - |R| - |S|$$

$$\geq \mathbf{H}_\infty(X) + \mathbf{H}_\infty(K) - |Q|.$$

Therefore the theorem holds as claimed.   □

Note that the above theorem holds for any distributions of X and for uniformly distributed K. This theorem also implies that $\tilde{\mathbf{H}}_\infty(X|Q) \geq \mathbf{H}_\infty(X) + |K| - |Q|$.

To compare with the straightforward approach that treats the two secrets independently, we can consider the remaining entropy of X given the sketch P.

$$\tilde{\mathbf{H}}_\infty(X|P) \geq \mathbf{H}_\infty(X) + |R| - |P|. \tag{4.26}$$

We can see from Theorem 4.4.2 and inequality (4.26) that when $\mathbf{H}_\infty(K) - |Q| \geq |R| - |P|$, or equivalently, when $\mathbf{H}_\infty(K) \geq |R| + |S|$, the entropy bound when using a cascaded mixing function is no worse than not using it.

As a special case, we can consider a deterministic sketch scheme where no randomness is used during sketch construction (i.e. $|R| = 0$), and a length preserving mixing function with respect to the sketch P (i.e., $|P| = |Q|$), the difference between the right hand side of the inequality (4.25) and that of (4.26) is $\mathbf{H}_\infty(K)$. In other words, the remaining entropy of X given Q can be increased by $\mathbf{H}_\infty(K)$. This clearly shows that the information leakage on X can be "diverted" to K, hence X receives more protection.

Now, we consider only the non-fuzzy secret k and analyze the entropy loss.

Theorem 4.4.3 [19] *Given an* $(\mathcal{M}, \mathsf{S}, \mathsf{Enc}, \mathsf{Dec})$*-sketch scheme, and let* X, K, R, P, Q, f, S *be as defined in Theorem* 4.4.2, *we have*

$$\widetilde{\mathbf{H}}_\infty(K|Q) \geq \mathbf{H}_\infty(K) + \mathbf{H}_\infty(R) - |P|. \tag{4.27}$$

Proof Since $Q = f(P, K, S)$, we can regard Q as a sketch of K where the mixing function f is an encoder, and $P = \mathsf{Enc}(X, R)$ and S are the "randomness" invested in computing Q, which are recoverable. Clearly, we can apply the general bound (4.9) on K and Q. Since R is recoverable, we have

$$\mathbf{H}_\infty(X) + \mathbf{H}_\infty(P) \geq \widetilde{\mathbf{H}}_\infty(X, P) \geq \mathbf{H}_\infty(X) + \mathbf{H}_\infty(R),$$

which means that $\mathbf{H}_\infty(P) \geq \mathbf{H}_\infty(R)$, hence the theorem holds. $\qquad\square$

Note that the bound in Theorem 4.4.3 is tight. In other words, there exists random variables and functions such that the equality in (4.27) holds. As a result, if $|P|$ is large but the min-entropy $\mathbf{H}_\infty(P)$ is low, the bound $\mathbf{H}_\infty(K) + \mathbf{H}_\infty(P) - |P|$ may be reduced to 0 or even less than 0. When this happens, the bound becomes not very meaningful and Q may reveal all information about K.

Now that we have analyzed the case where one secret is fuzzy and the other is not, we can easily extend the results to the case of two fuzzy secrets as illustrated in Fig. 4.12.

Suppose there are two independent secrets $x_1 \in \mathcal{M}_1$ and $x_2 \in \mathcal{M}_2$, and two sketch schemes with encoders Enc_1 and Enc_2, respectively. Like the previous case, we assume that x_1 is more important and needs better protection. Given x_1, x_2 and randomness r_1 and r_2, the final sketch q is computed in the following steps.

1. Compute $p_1 = \mathsf{Enc}_1(x_1, r_1)$ and $p_2 = \mathsf{Enc}_2(x_2, r_2)$.
2. Extract a key k_2 from x_2 using an extractor Ext.
3. Compute $q_1 = f(p_1, k_2, S)$ using a mixing function f.
4. Output the final sketch $q = q_1 \| p_2$.

It is possible to design Ext such that K_2 and P_2 are independent, and $\mathbf{H}_\infty(K_2)$ is only slightly smaller than $\widetilde{\mathbf{H}}_\infty(X_2|P_2)$ [16]. Let δ be the parameter determined by the extractor used to extract K_2 from X_2, that is, $\mathbf{H}_\infty(K_2) \geq \widetilde{\mathbf{H}}_\infty(X_2|P_2) - \delta$ for some small δ, where the actual value of δ is determined by how close the distribution of K_2 is to the uniform distribution.

As a result, the bound in Theorem 4.4.2 still applies to x_1 and k_2. Consider random variables X_1 and K_2, and corresponding sketches P_1 and P_2, mixed sketch Q_1, and final sketch Q, we have

$$
\begin{aligned}
\widetilde{\mathbf{H}}_\infty(X_1|Q) = \widetilde{\mathbf{H}}_\infty(X_1|Q_1) &\geq \mathbf{H}_\infty(X_1) + \mathbf{H}_\infty(K_2) - |Q| \\
&\geq \mathbf{H}_\infty(X_1) + \mathbf{H}_\infty(X_2|P_2) - \delta - |Q| \\
&\geq \mathbf{H}_\infty(X_1) + \mathbf{H}_\infty(X_2) + \mathbf{H}_\infty(R_2) - |P_2| - \delta - |Q|,
\end{aligned}
$$

where R_2 is the recoverable randomness used in computing P_2. In this case, the small δ can be considered as the overhead of using the extractor Ext.

As a comparison, if we treat the two secrets independently, and consider $P = P_1 \parallel P_2$, we have

$$
\widetilde{\mathbf{H}}_\infty(X_1|P) = \widetilde{\mathbf{H}}_\infty(X_1|P_1) \geq \mathbf{H}_\infty(X_1) + |R_1| - |P_1|.
$$

We can conclude that if $\mathbf{H}_\infty(K_2) \geq |R_1| + |S|$, we can obtain a better bound on the entropies when we choose to mix k_2 with p_1. Otherwise, doing so may reveal more information about X_1.

The entropy loss on the second secret X_2 can be obtained using the bound in Theorem 4.4.3. That is,

$$
\begin{aligned}
\widetilde{\mathbf{H}}_\infty(X_2|Q) \geq \widetilde{\mathbf{H}}_\infty(K_2|Q_1) &\geq \mathbf{H}_\infty(K_2) + \mathbf{H}_\infty(P_1) + \mathbf{H}_\infty(S) - |Q| \\
&\geq \mathbf{H}_\infty(X_2|P_2) + \mathbf{H}_\infty(P_1) - |P_1| - \delta \\
&\geq \mathbf{H}_\infty(X_2) + \mathbf{H}_\infty(R_2) + \mathbf{H}_\infty(R_1) - |P_1| - |P_2| - \delta.
\end{aligned}
$$

The overall entropy loss in Lemma 4.4.1 applies to the general case. That is,

$$
\widetilde{\mathbf{H}}_\infty(X_1, X_2|Q) \geq \mathbf{H}_\infty(X_1) + \mathbf{H}_\infty(X_2) + \mathbf{H}_\infty(R_1) + \mathbf{H}_\infty(R_2) - |P_1| - |P_2|.
$$

Cascaded mixing functions provide an opportunity to give more protection to more important secrets, but on the other hand, there may be scenarios where the cascaded mixing approach is not desirable. Here we give some guidelines for the application of such cascaded mixing functions to two secrets. Same principles can be applied to multiple secrets.

1. If the importance of the secrets cannot be determined or is the same for both secrets, mixing is not recommended.
2. For the more important secret, if there are two secure sketch schemes that differ only in the amount of randomness used in the construction; choose the one that uses less randomness.
3. If the randomness invested cannot be decoupled from the sketch, cascaded mixing is not advisable unless the length of consistent key is longer than the length of the sketch.

4.4.4 *Mixing Strategy of Multiple Secrets*

In some systems, it may be desirable to use more than two secrets. For example, in a multi-factor system, a user credential may include a fingerprint, a smartcard and a PIN, or two fingerprints and a password.

Similar to the case of two secrets, we can simply encode each secret independently, but in many scenarios it would be desirable to mix them. Unlike the two secret case, there are many different cascaded strategies as to how to mix the secrets.

Given secrets $x_1, x_2, \ldots, x_s$ and the corresponding sketches $p_1, p_2, \ldots, p_s$, the following are the main strategies to mix them, assuming we have mixing functions $f_1, \ldots, f_{s-1}$.

1. (Fanning) Apply mixing functions f_i on x_1 and p_{i+1} for all $1 \leq 1 \leq s - 1$.
2. (Chaining) Apply mixing function f_i on x_i and p_{i+1} for all $1 \leq 1 \leq s - 1$.
3. (Hybrid) Use a combination of fanning, chaining and independent encoding. For example, we can mix x_1 with p_2 and p_3, and further mix x_2 with p_4, but x_5 is encoded independently.

We can construct a graph of s nodes $n_1, \ldots, n_s$, and there is an edge from n_i to n_j if and only if x_i is mixed with p_j. In this case, the fanning approach will give a tree of two levels, with x_1 as the root, the chaining approach will give a path, and the most general hybrid approach gives a forest.

With the fanning approach, the entropy loss would be mostly diverted to the first secret. Hence, there is a chance that all other secrets can be well protected by reducing the security on one secret, which may be the one that is most easily revoked and replaced. However, this approach requires that the first secret has sufficiently high entropy, since otherwise it may be relatively easy to obtain the first secret from the mixed sketch. In practice, this approach can be used when a long revocable key is available, such as in the case where a smartcard with sufficient storage is used.

On the other hand, using the chaining approach only requires that the entropy of the ith secret is sufficient to mix with the $(i + 1)$th sketch. In this case, the secrets should be mixed in the order of their "importance", which could be, for example, the ease of revocation and replacement, or the likelihood of being lost or stolen. This method applies to scenarios where all secrets are relatively short, but it is not difficult to determine their relative importance. For example, in a system where users are authenticated using their both index fingers and a password, the password may be regarded as least important because it is most likely to be lost or stolen, and for right-handed people, the fingerprint of the left index finger may be considered as most important because it is less likely to be accidentally left behind compared.

Note that when the chaining approach is employed, it is crucial to determine the exact order of importance of the secrets. If a secret x_2 thought of as important in the sense that it is less likely to be stolen than x_1, and later it turned out that it is the most likely, an adversary may be able to easily obtain x_2, compute p_2 and find the secret x_1 mixed with the sketch p_2.

If no single secret is of sufficient entropy, and the order of importance among secrets is not always clear, a hybrid approach may become more appropriate. As a special case, when all secrets are short and no secret is more important than others, it would not be advisable to use the mixing approach and a straightforward method can be better.

References

1. Ang R, Safavi-Naini R, McAven L (2005) Cancelable key-based fingerprint templates. In: ACISP. LNCS, vol 3574, pp 242–252
2. Boult T, Scheirer W, Woodwork R (2007) Revocable fingerprint biotokens: accuracy and security analysis. In: IEEE Conf Computer Vison and Pattern Recognition (CVPR)
3. Boyen X (2004) Reusable cryptographic fuzzy extractors. In: Proceedings of the 11th ACM Conference on Computer and Communications Security. ACM, New York, pp 82–91. doi:10.1145/1030083.1030096
4. Boyen X, Dodis Y, Katz J, Ostrovsky R, Smith A (2005) Secure remote authentication using biometric data. In: Eurocrypt
5. Bringer J, Chabanne H, Kindarji B (2008) The best of both worlds: applying secure sketches to cancelable biometrics. Science of Computer Programming 74(1–2):43–51. Special issue on security and trust
6. Buhan I, Doumen J, Hartel P, Veldhuis R (2007) Fuzzy extractors for continuous distributions. In: 2nd ACM Symposium on Information, Computer and Communications Security (ASIACCS), Singapore, 20–22 March 2007, pp 353–355
7. Bui F, Martin K, Lu H, Plataniotis K, Hatzinakos D, (2010) Fuzzy key binding strategies based on quantization index modulation (qim) for biometric encryption (be) applications. IEEE Transactions on Information Forensics and Security 5(1):118–132
8. Chang EC, Li Q (2006) Hiding secret points amidst chaff. In: Eurocrypt, pp 59–72
9. Chang EC, Fedyukovych V, Li Q (2006) Secure sketch for multi-set difference. Cryptology ePrint archive, report 2006/090. http://eprint.iacr.org/
10. Chen C, Veldhuis R, Kevenaar T, Akkermans A (2008) Biometric binary string generation with detection rate optimized bit allocation. In: IEEE Computer Society Conference on Computer Vision and Pattern Recognition Workshops (CVPRW). IEEE Press, New York, pp 1–7
11. Clancy T, Kiyavash N, Lin D (2003) Secure smartcard-based fingerprint authentication. In: ACM Workshop on Biometric Methods and Applications, Berkeley, CA, USA, pp 45–52
12. Cover TM, Thomas JA (1991) Elements of Information Theory. Wiley, New York
13. Dass SC, Zhu Y, Jain AK (2005) Statistical models for assessing the individuality of fingerprints. In: AUTOID'05: Proceedings of the Fourth IEEE Workshop on Automatic Identification Advanced Technologies, pp 3–9
14. Daugman J (2003) The importance of being random: statistical principles of iris recognition. Pattern Recognition 36(2)
15. Davida G, Frankel Y, Matt B (1998) On enabling secure applications through off-line biometric identification. In: Proc IEEE Symp on Security and Privacy, pp 148–157
16. Dodis Y, Reyzin L, Smith A (2004) Fuzzy extractors: how to generate strong keys from biometrics and other noisy data. In: Eurocrypt. LNCS, vol 3027. Springer, Berlin, pp 523–540
17. Draper S, Khisti A, Martinian E, Vetro A, Yedidia J (2007) Secure storage of fingerprint biometrics using Slepian-Wolf codes. In: Information Theory and Applications Workshop, San Diego, CA
18. Draper S, Khisti A, Martinian E, Vetro A, Yedidia J (2007) Using distributed source coding to secure fingerprint biometrics. In: IEEE Conf on Acoustics, Speech and Signal Processing (ICASSP), pp 129–132

19. Fang C, Li Q, Chang EC (2010) Secure sketch for multiple secrets. In: International Conference on Applied Cryptography and Network Security. LNCS, vol 6123. Springer, Berlin, pp 367–383
20. Galbally J, Cappelli R, Lumini A, de Rivera GG, Maltoni D, Fiérrez J, Ortega-Garcia J, Maio D (2010) An evaluation of direct attacks using fake fingers generated from ISO templates. Pattern Recognition Letters 31:725–732
21. Hao F, Anderson R, Daugman J (2006) Combining crypto with biometrics effectively. IEEE Transactions on Computers 55(9):1081–1088
22. Ignatenko T, Willems F (2010) Information leakage in fuzzy commitment schemes. IEEE Transactions on Information Forensics and Security 5(2):337–348
23. Jain AK, Nandakumar K, Nagar A (2008) Biometric template security. EURASIP Journal on Advances in Signal Processing. Special issue on pattern recognition methods for biometrics
24. Juels A, Sudan M (2002) A fuzzy vault scheme. In: IEEE Intl Symp on Information Theory
25. Juels A, Wattenberg M (1999) A fuzzy commitment scheme. In: Proc ACM Conf on Computer and Communications Security, pp 28–36
26. Kevenaar T, Schrijen G, der Veen MV, Akkermans A, Zuo F (2005) Face recognition with renewable and privacy preserving binary templates. In: Fourth IEEE Workshop on Automatic Identification Advanced Technologies, pp 21–26
27. Li Q, Sutcu Y, Memon N (2006) Secure sketch for biometric templates. In: Asiacrypt. LNCS, Shanghai, China, pp 99–113
28. Li Q, Guo M, Chang EC (2008) Fuzzy extractors for asymmetric biometric representations. In: IEEE Computer Society Workshop on Biometrics, June 2008
29. Linnartz JPMG, Tuyls P (2003) New shielding functions to enhance privacy and prevent misuse of biometric templates. In: AVBPA 2003, pp 393–402
30. Maiorana E, Campisi P, Ortega-Garcia J, Neri A (2008) Cancelable biometrics for hmm based signature recognition. In: Proceedings of the IEEE Second International Conference on Biometrics: Theory, Applications and Systems (BTAS 2008), Crystal City, VA, USA
31. Martinian E, Yekhanin S, Yedidia JS (2005) Secure biometrics via syndromes. In: 43rd Annual Allerton Conference on Communications, Control, and Computing, Monticello, IL, pp 45–52
32. Maurer U, Wolf S (2000) Information-theoretic key agreement: from weak to strong secrecy for free. In: Eurocrypt
33. Nandakumar K, Jain AK, Pankanti S (2007) Fingerprint-based fuzzy vault: implementation and performance. IEEE Transactions on Information Forensics and Security 2(4):744–757
34. O'Gorman L (2003) Comparing passwords, tokens, and biometrics for user authentication. Proceedings of the IEEE 91(12):2021–2040
35. Pankanti S, Prabhakar S, Jain AK (2002) On the individuality of fingerprints. IEEE Transactions on Pattern Analysis and Machine Intelligence 24:1010–1025
36. Prabhakar S, Pankanti S, Jain AK (2003) Biometric recognition: security and privacy concerns. IEEE Security and Privacy 1(2):33–42. doi:10.1109/MSECP.2003.1193209
37. Ratha N, Connell J, Bolle R (2001) Enhancing security and privacy in biometrics-based authentication systems. IBM Systems Journal 40(3):614–634
38. Ratha NK, Chikkerur S, Connell JH, Bolle RM (2007) Generating cancelable fingerprint templates. IEEE Transactions on Pattern Analysis and Machine Intelligence 29(4):561–572
39. Ross A, Shah J, Jain AK (2007) From template to image: reconstructing fingerprints from minutiae points. IEEE Transactions on Pattern Analysis and Machine Intelligence 29(4):544–560
40. Savvides M, Kumar BV, Khosla P (2004) Cancelable biometric filters for face recognition. In: Proceedings of the 17th International Conference on Pattern Recognition, ICPR 2004, vol 3, pp 922–925
41. Schneier B (1996) Applied Cryptography, 2nd edn. Wiley, New York
42. Soutar C, Roberge D, Stojanov S, Gilroy R, Kumar BV (1998) Biometric encryption using image processing. In: SPIE, Optical Security and Counterfeit Deterrence Techniques II, San Jose, CA, USA, vol 3314

43. Sutcu Y, Li Q, Memon N (2007) Protecting biometric templates with sketch: theory and practice. IEEE Transactions on Information Forensics and Security 2(3):503–512
44. Sutcu Y, Rane S, Yedidia J, Draper S, Vetro A (2008) Feature extraction for a Slepian-Wolf biometric system using LDPC codes. In: 2007 IEEE International Symposium on Information Theory, Toronto, Ontario, CA, 6–11 July 2008
45. Sutcu Y, Rane S, Yedidia J, Draper S, Vetro A (2008) Feature transformation of biometric templates for secure biometric systems based on error correcting codes. In: 2007 IEEE Computer Society Conference on Computer Vision and Pattern Recognition (CVPR 2008), Anchorage, AK, USA, 23–28 June 2008
46. Sutcu Y, Li Q, Memon N (2009) Design and analysis of fuzzy extractors for faces. In: SPIE International Defense and Security Symposium, Orlando, FL
47. Teoh A, Gho A, Ngo D (2006) Random multispace quantization as an analytic mechanism for biohashing of biometric and random identity inputs. IEEE Transactions on Pattern Analysis and Machine Intelligence 28(12):1892–1901
48. Tuyls P, Goseling J (2004) Capacity and examples of template-protecting biometric authentication systems. In: ECCV Workshop BioAW, pp 158–170
49. Tuyls P, Akkermans A, Kevenaar T, Schrijen G, Bazen A, Veldhuis R (2005) Practical biometric authentication with template protection. In: AVBPA, pp 436–446
50. Uludag U, Jain A (2004) Fuzzy fingerprint vault. In: Workshop on Biometrics: Challenges Arising from Theory to Practice, pp 13–16
51. Verbitskiy E, Tuyls P, Obi C, Schoenmakers B, Skoric B (2010) Key extraction from general nondiscrete signals. IEEE Transactions on Information Forensics and Security 5(2):269–279
52. Vetro A, Memon N (2008) Biometric system security. In: Tutorial Presented at IEEE International Conference on Acoustics, Speech and Signal Processing, Las Vegas, NV, USA, April 2008
53. Yang S, Verbauwhede I (2005) Automatic secure fingerprint verification system based on fuzzy vault scheme. In: IEEE Intl Conf on Acoustics, Speech, and Signal Processing (ICASSP), pp 609–612

Chapter 5
Privacy Leakage in Binary Biometric Systems: From Gaussian to Binary Data

Tanya Ignatenko and Frans M.J. Willems

Abstract In this chapter we investigate biometric key-binding systems for i.i.d. Gaussian biometric sources. In these systems two terminals observe two correlated biometric sequences. Moreover, a secret key, which is independent of the biometric sequences, is selected at the first terminal. The first terminal binds this secret key to the observed biometric sequence and communicates it to the second terminal by sending a public message. This message should only contain a negligible amount of information about the secret key. Here, in addition, we require it to leak as little as possible about the biometric data. For this setting the fundamental trade-off between secret-key rate and privacy-leakage rate is determined. Moreover, we investigate the effect of binary quantization on the system performance. We further discuss the popular fuzzy commitment scheme. It is shown that from the perspective of privacy leakage, there are better options for fuzzy commitment than its typical implementation based on BCH codes.

5.1 Introduction

Considerable interest in the topic of biometric secrecy systems resulted in the proposal of various techniques over the past decade. In this chapter we concentrate on the biometric authentication systems which are based on secret key transmission, also called key-binding. The approach to the problem of transmitting a secret key is closely related to the concept of secret sharing, which was introduced by Maurer [16] and slightly later by Ahlswede and Csiszár [1]. In the source model of Ahlswede and Csiszár [1] two terminals observe two correlated sequences $\underline{X}$ and $\underline{Y}$ and aim at producing an as large as possible common secret S by interchanging a public message M. This message, to which

T. Ignatenko (✉) · F.M.J. Willems
Eindhoven University of Technology, Den Dolech 2, 5612 AZ Eindhoven, The Netherlands
e-mail: t.ignatenko@tue.nl

F.M.J. Willems
e-mail: f.m.j.willems@tue.nl

P. Campisi (ed.), *Security and Privacy in Biometrics*,
DOI 10.1007/978-1-4471-5230-9_5, © Springer-Verlag London 2013

we refer as helper data, should only provide a negligible amount of information on the secret. It was shown that the maximum secret-key rate in this model is equal to the mutual information $I(X; Y)$ between the observed sequences. The secret sharing concept is also closely related to the concept of common randomness generation that was studied by Ahlswede and Csiszár [2] and later extended with helper terminals by Csiszár and Narayan [7]. Venkatesan and Anantharam [23] studied the idea to use channel noise for generation of common randomness. In common randomness setting the requirement that the helper data should provide only a negligible amount of information on the generated randomness is dropped.

Consider a secret transmission biometric system. This technique is typically called key-binding in the review paper by Jain et al. [10]. In this setting an independently chosen secret key should be transmitted by the first terminal via a public message to the second terminal. The two terminals observe two dependent biometric sequences $\underline{X}$ and $\underline{Y}$. Here the public helper data should be uninformative about the transmitted secret key. Moreover, in a biometric setting, where the X-sequence corresponds to the enrollment data and the Y-sequence to the authentication data, it is crucial that the public message M leaks as little information as possible about the biometric data, since compromised biometric data cannot be replaced. Smith [19] has investigated this leakage (privacy leakage) and came to the conclusion that it cannot be avoided. Moreover, recently the fundamental trade-off between secret-key rate and privacy-leakage rate for the i.i.d. discrete case in the key-binding setting was determined by the authors [9], and independently and at the same time, by Lai et al. [14].

While in [9] and [14] the discrete case is considered, in this chapter we study the case where the biometric sequences are assumed to be generated by a Gaussian correlated source. For such a Gaussian source we determine the fundamental balance between the secret-key rate and the privacy-leakage rate. Moreover we focus on the fundamental issues that occur when Gaussian biometric sequences are binary (two-level) quantized. Binary quantization of biometric data was first proposed by Daugman [8] for iris recognition. Later Tuyls et al. [22] considered binary quantization in practical secret-key generation systems, with an emphasis on generating reliable components. Kelkboom et al. [12] focused specifically on binary quantized Gaussian biometrics and found an expression for the corresponding cross-over probability in the binary domain. Quantization in quantum key distribution protocols is discussed by Van Assche et al. [3]. Standard (natural and Gray coded) multi-level quantizers for biometrics combined with LDPC codes were studied by Ye at al. [28]. Sutcu et al. [20] considered biometric-specific quantizers, also focusing on LDPC codes. A multi-level quantizer based on likelihood ratios was proposed by Chen et al. [5]. In Li et al. [15] biometrical quantizers were analyzed. It is observed by these authors that the quantizer has a large impact on the so-called entropy loss.

It should be noted that the references above did not actually focus on privacy leakage in their research. It is our objective to demonstrate that quantization not only has a significant effect on the secret-key rate as we know from classical communication theory, but also on the trade-off between the secret-key rate and the privacy-leakage rate.

Finally we consider the fuzzy commitment scheme by Juels and Wattenberg [11], which is a realization of key-binding biometric systems. We demonstrate that popular fuzzy commitment constructions which are based on BCH codes, see e.g. [13] and [27], result in high privacy leakage and are far from optimum. We also give an example of the fuzzy commitment based on the convolutional code. This example demonstrates that it is possible to achieve better performance in fuzzy commitment if capacity achieving codes are used, but also if no quantization is performed at the decoder side.

Before we start with the presentation of our results we want to make the reservation that we do not discuss the validity of the Gaussian assumption here. It is well-known that most transmission channels can be modeled as additive white Gaussian noise channels, however whether such models can be used for a wide range of biometrics will probably remain a point of discussion for the next years.

5.2 Gaussian Biometric Systems with Key-Binding

5.2.1 Definitions

5.2.1.1 A Gaussian Biometric Source

A Gaussian biometric system is based on a *Gaussian biometric source* $\{G_\rho(x, y),$ $x \in \mathbf{R}, y \in \mathbf{R}\}$ that produces an X-sequence $\underline{x} = (x_1, x_2, \ldots, x_N)$ with N real-valued symbols and a Y-sequence $\underline{y} = (y_1, y_2, \ldots, y_N)$ also having N real-valued components. The density corresponding to sequence pair $(\underline{X}, \underline{Y})$ is given by

$$p_{\underline{X},\underline{Y}}(\underline{x}, \underline{y}) = \prod_{n=1}^{N} G_\rho(x_n, y_n), \tag{5.1}$$

where

$$G_\rho(x, y) = \frac{1}{2\pi\sqrt{1-\rho^2}} \exp\left(-\frac{x^2 + y^2 - 2\rho xy}{2(1-\rho^2)}\right), \tag{5.2}$$

for $x \in \mathbf{R}$, $y \in \mathbf{R}$, and correlation coefficient $|\rho| < 1$. Thus, the source pairs $\{(X_n, Y_n), n = 1, \ldots, N\}$ are independent of each other and identically distributed (i.i.d.) according to $G_\rho(\cdot, \cdot)$. Also note that scaling can always be applied to obtain unit X-variance and unit Y-variance.

The enrollment and authentication biometric sequences $\underline{x}$ and $\underline{y}$ are observed by an encoder and decoder, respectively. One of the outputs that the encoder produces is an index $m \in \{1, 2, \ldots, M_H\}$, which is referred to as helper data. The helper data are made public and are used by the decoder.

Fig. 5.1 Model for biometric
authentication based on
key-binding

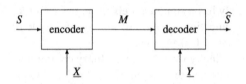

In biometric authentication systems with key-binding, the first terminal has to
bind and *transmit* a secret key to the second terminal. This secret key s assumes
values in $\{1, 2, \ldots, M_S\}$. The decoder's estimate $\widehat{s}$ of the secret key s also assumes
values from $\{1, 2, \ldots, M_S\}$. Moreover, the secret key s is a uniformly distributed
index, hence

$$\Pr\{S = s\} = 1/M_S \quad \text{for all } s \in \{1, 2, \ldots, M_S\}. \tag{5.3}$$

Since helper data are assumed to be public, we require the helper data to leak
only negligible information about the secret key and to leak as small as possible
information about the biometric enrollment sequence $\underline{x}$.

5.2.1.2 Encoding and Decoding

In a biometric key-binding system, see Fig. 5.1, a secret S that is to be transmitted
from the encoder to the decoder is uniformly distributed, see (5.3). The encoder
observes the source sequence $\underline{X}$ and the secret S and produces the integer helper
data M, hence

$$M = e(S, \underline{X}), \tag{5.4}$$

where $e(\cdot, \cdot)$ is the encoder mapping. The public helper data M are sent to the decoder.

The decoder observes the authentication biometric source sequence $\underline{Y}$ together
with helper data. It forms an estimate $\widehat{S}$ of the secret that was transmitted, hence

$$\widehat{S} = d(M, \underline{Y}), \tag{5.5}$$

and $d(\cdot, \cdot)$ is the decoder mapping.

5.2.1.3 Achievability

Now we are interested in finding out what *secret-key rates and privacy-leakage rates*
can be jointly realized by an authentication system based on key-binding with negligible *error probability* and negligible *leakage about the secret*. We are interested in
secret-key rates as large as possible and privacy-leakage rates as small as possible.
All this leads to the following definition of achievability.

Definition 5.1 In a Gaussian biometric key-binding authentication system, a secret-key and privacy-leakage rate pair (R, L) with $R \geq 0$ is achievable if for all $\delta > 0$ for all N large enough there exist encoders and decoders such that[1]

$$\Pr\{\widehat{S} \neq S\} \leq \delta,$$

$$\frac{1}{N} \log M_S \geq R - \delta,$$

$$\frac{1}{N} I(S; M) \leq \delta, \qquad (5.6)$$

$$\frac{1}{N} I(\underline{X}; M) \leq L + \delta.$$

Moreover, we define $\mathcal{R}_\rho$ to be the region of all achievable secret-key rate and privacy-leakage rate pairs for a key-binding authentication system based on Gaussian source density $G_\rho(\cdot, \cdot)$.

5.2.2 Statement of the Result

We first state our result. Then in the next section we discuss properties of the achievable region $\mathcal{R}_\rho$ and then we present the proof of our theorem.

Theorem 5.1 (Gaussian Biometric Authentication System with Key Binding) *For the Gaussian biometric source as defined by* (5.1) *and* (5.2)

$$\mathcal{R}_\rho = \left\{ (R, L) : 0 \leq R \leq \frac{1}{2} \log\left(\frac{1}{\alpha\rho^2 + 1 - \rho^2}\right), \right.$$

$$\left. L \geq \frac{1}{2} \log\left(\frac{\alpha\rho^2 + 1 - \rho^2}{\alpha}\right), \text{ for } 0 < \alpha \leq 1 \right\}. \qquad (5.7)$$

5.2.3 Properties of the Region $\mathcal{R}_\rho$

5.2.3.1 Convexity

To prove the convexity of $\mathcal{R}_\rho$ we define the rate-leakage function

$$R_\rho(L) \triangleq \max_{(R,L)\in\mathcal{R}_\rho} R, \qquad (5.8)$$

for which we can write

$$R_\rho(L) = \frac{1}{2} \log\left(\frac{1 - \rho^2/2^{2L}}{1 - \rho^2}\right). \qquad (5.9)$$

Now it can be shown that the second derivative $d^2 R_\rho(L)/dL^2 \leq 0$. Therefore $R_\rho(L)$ is $\cap$-convex in $L \geq 0$ and, consequently, region $\mathcal{R}_\rho$ is convex.

---

[1] We take 2 as base of the log throughout this chapter.

5.2.3.2 Asymptotic Secret-Key Rate

Note that asymptotically for increasing privacy-leakage rate

$$
\begin{aligned}
\lim_{L\to\infty} R_\rho(L) &= \lim_{L\to\infty} \frac{1}{2}\log\left(\frac{1-\rho^2/2^{2L}}{1-\rho^2}\right) \\
&= \frac{1}{2}\log\left(\frac{1}{1-\rho^2}\right) \\
&= I(X;Y).
\end{aligned}
\tag{5.10}
$$

It is important to notice that the privacy-leakage rate has to increase to infinity to achieve this limit.

5.2.3.3 Slopes

If one is interested in achieving a small privacy-leakage rate L, the ratio between the secret-key rate and the privacy-leakage rate becomes important. For the "rate-zero slope" γ_0 of the tangent to $R_\rho(L)$ at $L=0$ we find

$$
\gamma_0 \triangleq \left.\frac{dR_\rho(L)}{dL}\right|_{L=0} = \frac{\rho^2}{1-\rho^2}.
\tag{5.11}
$$

Inspection shows that this slope is equal to the signal-to-noise ratio (SNR) for the "channel" from X to Y.

Another interesting parameter is the "rate-one slope" defined as

$$
\gamma_1 \triangleq \max_{(R,R-1)\in\mathcal{R}_\rho} \frac{R}{1-R}.
\tag{5.12}
$$

It is not difficult to see that in the Gaussian case

$$
\gamma_1 = \frac{2-\log(4-3\rho^2)}{\log(4-3\rho^2)}.
\tag{5.13}
$$

5.2.3.4 Example

In Fig. 5.2 we have depicted the boundary of the region $\mathcal{R}_\rho$, i.e. $R_\rho(L)$, as a function of the privacy-leakage rate L for three values of the square of the correlation coefficient ρ, i.e. for $\rho^2 = 1/2, 3/4$, and $15/16$. Observe that the correlation coefficient characterizes the quality of biometric data generated by the Gaussian biometric sources. Note that the corresponding asymptotic secret-key rates $I(X;Y)$ are $1/2, 1$, and 2 bit, respectively. We can also determine the rate-zero slopes for these three values of ρ^2. It turns out that the slopes are $1, 3$, and 15, respectively. We may conclude from this behavior that biometric data of better quality have a better rate-zero slope. Therefore it is important to put enough effort in pre-processing the biometric data, such that as little extra noise as possible is introduced.

Fig. 5.2 Boundary of the achievable region $\mathcal{R}_\rho$ for three values of ρ

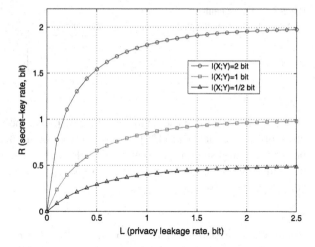

5.2.4 Proof of the Result

The proof of our theorem consists of two parts. The first part, i.e. the converse will be treated in detail. The second part concerns the achievability of which we will only provide an outline.

5.2.4.1 The Converse

First we consider the entropy of the secret. We use $\widehat{S} = d(M, \underline{Y})$ and Fano's inequality, see e.g. [6], $H(S|\widehat{S}) \leq F$, where $F \triangleq 1 + \Pr\{\widehat{S} \neq S\} \log M_S$. We have

$$
\begin{aligned}
\log M_S = H(S) &= I(S; M, \underline{Y}) + H(S|M, \underline{Y}, \widehat{S}) \\
&\leq I(S; M, \underline{Y}) + H(S|\widehat{S}) \\
&\leq I(S; M) + I(S; \underline{Y}|M) + F \\
&\leq I(S; M) + I(S, M; \underline{Y}) + F \\
&= I(S; M) + h(\underline{Y}) - h(\underline{Y}|S, M) + F.
\end{aligned}
\tag{5.14}
$$

Now we continue with privacy leakage:

$$
\begin{aligned}
I(\underline{X}; M) &= H(M) - H(M|\underline{X}) \\
&\geq H(M|\underline{Y}) - H(M|\underline{X}) \\
&= H(S, M|\underline{Y}) - H(S|M, \underline{Y}, \widehat{S}) - H(S, M|\underline{X}) + H(S|M, \underline{X}) \\
&\geq H(S, M|\underline{Y}) - H(S|\widehat{S}) - H(S, M|\underline{X}) \\
&\geq H(S, M|\underline{Y}) - F - H(S, M|\underline{X}) \\
&= I(S, M; \underline{X}) - I(S, M; \underline{Y}) - F \\
&= h(\underline{X}) - h(\underline{X}|S, M) - h(\underline{Y}) + h(\underline{Y}|S, M) - F.
\end{aligned}
\tag{5.15}
$$

Fig. 5.3 Additive equivalent
relation between two unit
variance correlated variables
X and Y

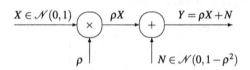

We are now ready to use Shannon's entropy power inequality [18]. For a simple
proof of this inequality see [24]. We use here a conditional version of the entropy
power inequality similar to Lemma II in [4]. First, however, we have to transform
the statistical relation between X and Y as described by the density in (5.2) into an
additive version. Note that

$$Y = \rho X + N, \tag{5.16}$$

where N is Gaussian with mean zero and variance $1 - \rho^2$, and is independent of X,
see Fig. 5.3.

From the (conditional version of the) entropy power inequality we may conclude
that if $\frac{1}{N}h(\underline{X}|S, M) = \frac{1}{2}\log(2\pi e\alpha)$ then $\frac{1}{N}h(\underline{Y}|S, M) \geq \frac{1}{2}\log(2\pi e(\alpha\rho^2 + 1 - \rho^2))$.
Note that we may assume that $0 < \alpha \leq 1$, since X has unit variance, and $\alpha = 0$
would imply that $H(S, M) = \infty$, which is impossible for finite ranges M_S and M_H.

Now for achievable (R, L) for all $\delta > 0$ and N large enough, we obtain

$$\frac{1}{N}\log M_S = \frac{1}{N}H(S) \leq \frac{1}{N}\left(I(S; M) + h(\underline{Y}) - h(\underline{Y}|S, M) + F\right)$$

$$\leq \delta + \frac{1}{2}\log\left(\frac{1}{\alpha\rho^2 + 1 - \rho^2}\right) + \frac{1}{N} + \frac{1}{N}\delta\log M_S, \tag{5.17}$$

for some $0 < \alpha \leq 1$. Here in the last inequality we used the fact that Y has unit variance and then we obtain for differential entropy $h(\underline{Y}) = \frac{N}{2}\log(2\pi e)$. From (5.17)
we may conclude that

$$R - \delta \leq \frac{1}{N}\log M_S \leq \frac{1}{1 - \delta}\left(\delta + \frac{1}{2}\log\left(\frac{1}{\alpha\rho^2 + 1 - \rho^2}\right) + \frac{1}{N}\right). \tag{5.18}$$

Moreover, for achievable (R, L) for all $\delta > 0$ and N large enough, we get

$$L + \delta \geq \frac{1}{N}I(\underline{X}; M)$$

$$\geq \frac{1}{N}\left(h(\underline{X}) - h(\underline{X}|S, M) - h(\underline{Y}) + h(\underline{Y}|S, M) - F\right)$$

$$\geq \frac{1}{2}\log\left(\frac{\alpha\rho^2 + 1 - \rho^2}{\alpha}\right) - \frac{1}{N} - \frac{1}{N}\delta\log M_S, \tag{5.19}$$

for some $0 < \alpha \leq 1$. Here in the last inequality we used that the differential entropies
$h(\underline{X}) = h(\underline{Y})$, since X and Y both have unit variance.

If we let $\delta \downarrow 0$ and $N \to \infty$, then we obtain the converse from both (5.19) and
(5.18). As an intermediate step it follows from (5.18) and $|\rho| < 1$ that $1/N \log M_S$
is finite.

Fig. 5.4 Additive noise V transforming U into X

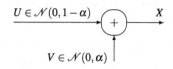

Fig. 5.5 The masking layer. Addition modulo M_S is denoted by $\oplus$, and subtraction modulo M_S is denoted by $\ominus$

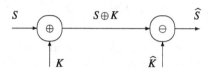

5.2.4.2 Outline of the Achievability Proof

Let $0 < \alpha \leq 1$. We start by fixing the joint density of U, X, and Y such that the Markov condition $U - X - Y$ holds. Let U be Gaussian with mean zero and variance $1 - \alpha$. Moreover, assume that

$$X = U + V, \tag{5.20}$$

where V is independent of U and is Gaussian with mean zero and variance α, see Fig. 5.4. Finally, Y is statistically related to X as in Fig. 5.3. Note that now $I(U; Y) = \frac{1}{2} \log(\frac{1}{\alpha\rho^2 + 1 - \rho^2})$ and $I(U; X) = \frac{1}{2} \log(\frac{1}{\alpha})$.

Next we randomly generate roughly $2^{NI(U;X)}$ sequences $\underline{u}$, Gaussian, with mean zero and variance $1 - \alpha$. Each of those sequences gets a random k-label and a random m-label. These labels are uniformly chosen. The k-labels can assume roughly $2^{NI(U;Y)}$ values, the m-label roughly $2^{N(I(U;X) - I(U;Y))}$ values.

The encoder, upon observing the source sequence $\underline{x}$, first finds a sequence $\underline{u}$ that is jointly typical with $\underline{x}$. It is understood that we use Gaussian typicality here, see Cover and Thomas [6], Chap. 9, and also [26]. Since there are roughly $2^{NI(U;X)}$ such sequences, this is possible with vanishing error probability. The encoder produces the k-label and m-label corresponding to this sequence. The encoder also chooses uniformly at random a secret key s from $2^{NI(U;Y)}$ indices and uses k in a one-time pad system to conceal this secret key s, see Fig. 5.5. The m-label and the masked secret key $s \oplus k$ are send to the decoder as helper data.

The decoder observes the authentication source sequence $\underline{y}$ and determines the auxiliary source sequence $\widehat{\underline{u}}$ with an m-label matching with the first part of the helper data, such that $\widehat{\underline{u}}$ and $\underline{y}$ are jointly typical. It can be shown that the decoder can reliably recover $\underline{u}$, the corresponding secret-key label $k(\underline{u})$, and, consequently, using the second part of the helper data, i.e. $s \oplus k$, the secret key s now.

It is easy to check that the privacy leakage $I(\underline{X}; M)$ is not larger than $I(U; X) - I(U; Y)$. An important additional property of the proof is that the auxiliary sequence $\underline{u}$ can be recovered reliably from both the k-label and the m-label. Using this property we can prove that $I(K; M)$ is negligible, and that the secret K is close to uniform. Using these results it is straightforward to show that also $I(\underline{X}; M, K \oplus S)$ is not larger than $I(U; X) - I(U; Y)$ and $I(S; M, K \oplus S)$ is negligible.

5.3 Binary Biometric Systems

5.3.1 Binary Symmetric Biometric Systems

A binary symmetric biometric system is based on a *binary symmetric double source* $\{Q(x, y), x \in \{0, 1\}, y \in \{0, 1\}\}$. This source produces a sequence $\underline{x} = (x_1, x_2, \dots, x_N)$ with N symbols from $\{0, 1\}$ and a sequence $\underline{y} = (y_1, y_2, \dots, y_N)$ also having N components in $\{0, 1\}$. Sequence pair $(\underline{x}, \underline{y})$ occurs with probability

$$\Pr\{(\underline{X}, \underline{Y}) = (\underline{x}, \underline{y})\} = \prod_{n=1}^{N} Q(x_n, y_n). \tag{5.21}$$

We consider a binary symmetric double source with cross-over probability $0 \le q \le 1/2$, hence $Q(x, y) = (1 - q)/2$ for $y = x$ and $q/2$ for $y \ne x$. For such a source the rate-leakage function, for key-binding system, is equal to

$$R_q(L) = 1 - h(p * q), \tag{5.22}$$

for p satisfying $h(p * q) - h(p) = L$, where $h(\cdot)$ is the binary entropy function in bits, and $p * q = p(1 - q) + q(1 - p)$. This result was proved by the authors in [9].

The first problem now is to find what the rate-zero slope for a binary system is, as a function of the cross-over probability q of the binary symmetric double source. Therefore we consider the behavior of $1 - h(p)$ for $\varepsilon = \frac{1}{2} - p$ close to zero. Note that in this case

$$\frac{1 - h(\frac{1}{2} - \varepsilon)}{\log(e)} = \ln(2) + \left(\frac{1}{2} - \varepsilon\right) \ln\left(\frac{1}{2} - \varepsilon\right) + \left(\frac{1}{2} + \varepsilon\right) \ln\left(\frac{1}{2} + \varepsilon\right)$$

$$= \left(\frac{1}{2} - \varepsilon\right) \ln(1 - 2\varepsilon) + \left(\frac{1}{2} + \varepsilon\right) \ln(1 + 2\varepsilon)$$

$$= \frac{1}{2} \ln\left(1 - 4\varepsilon^2\right) - \varepsilon \ln(1 - 2\varepsilon) + \varepsilon \ln(1 + 2\varepsilon)$$

$$\approx 2\varepsilon^2. \tag{5.23}$$

Next observe that

$$p * q = \left(\frac{1}{2} - \varepsilon\right)(1 - q) + \left(\frac{1}{2} + \varepsilon\right) q$$

$$= \frac{1}{2} - \varepsilon(1 - 2q). \tag{5.24}$$

Therefore we can make the following approximations:

Fig. 5.6 Secret-key rate
versus privacy-leakage rate
functions for three values of
the cross-over probability q

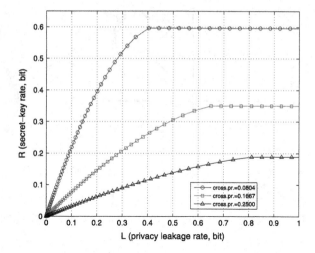

$$1 - h(p*q) \approx \log(e)2\varepsilon^2(1-2q)^2,$$

$$h(p*q) - h(p) = 1 - h(p) - 1 + h(p*q) \tag{5.25}$$

$$\approx \log(e)2\varepsilon^2\big(1 - (1-2q)^2\big),$$

and, finally, we may conclude that

$$\gamma_0 \triangleq \left.\frac{dR_q(L)}{dL}\right|_{L=0} = \frac{(1-2q)^2}{1-(1-2q)^2}. \tag{5.26}$$

For cross-over probabilities $q = 0.2500, 0.1667$, and 0.0804 we have computed
the rate-leakage function using (5.22). The resulting curves are plotted in Fig. 5.6.
Check that the rate-zero slopes for L close to 0, are 0.3333, 0.8000, and 2.3801,
respectively.

5.3.2 Binary Quantization

In this section we study the effect of binary quantization of the Gaussian biometric sequences. We assume that after quantization processing on the resulting binary sequences is performed. It will be clear that the resulting binary statistic is binary symmetric as in the previous section. The main problem is now to find how the cross-over probability q relates to the correlation coefficient ρ of the Gaussian statistic.

Suppose that the cigar in Fig. 5.7 corresponds to coordinates (x, y) where the Gaussian density $G_\rho(x, y)$ equals some constant. Now the variance in the $Y = X$ direction is $(1+\rho)/2$ and in the $Y = -X$ direction is $(1-\rho)/2$. Note that the cross-over probability q corresponds to the mass of the cigar in the second or fourth quadrant. Instead of manipulating with the integral, we can compress the cigar in the $Y = X$ direction, by a factor $\sqrt{(1+\rho)/(1-\rho)}$, to transform it into a ball, see

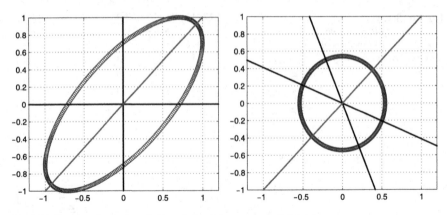

Fig. 5.7 Compressing a cigar (*left*) such that it becomes a ball (*right*)

Fig. 5.7. Then the cross-over probability is the angle between the two black lines, divided by π. Compression brings the tangent of half the angle between the black lines from one down to $\sqrt{(1-\rho)/(1+\rho)}$. Therefore

$$q = \frac{2}{\pi} \arctan\left(\sqrt{\frac{1-\rho}{1+\rho}}\right). \tag{5.27}$$

This formula, together with (5.26) allows us to determine the zero-rate slope of a binary quantized system.

In Fig. 5.6 we have chosen the cross-over probabilities q according to (5.27) for squared correlation-coefficients 1/2, 3/4, and 15/16. It can be checked that the resulting zero-rate slopes (0.3333, 0.8000, and 2.3801, respectively) are significantly smaller than the corresponding zero-rate slopes (1, 3, and 15, respectively) from Fig. 5.2.

For small values of the squared correlation coefficient ρ^2 we can quantify the loss that is caused by binary quantization. In that case we can approximate q by

$$q \approx \frac{1}{2} - \frac{\rho}{\pi}, \tag{5.28}$$

and formula (5.26) results in the rate-zero slope

$$\gamma_0 = \frac{(2\rho/\pi)^2}{1 - (2\rho/\pi)^2}. \tag{5.29}$$

We can conclude from this and (5.11) that the squared correlation coefficient ρ^2 must be increased by a factor of $\pi^2/4$ to compensate for the binary quantization actions, if we are interested in maintaining the rate-zero slope constant.

Representing this loss in decibels gives 3.92 dB, which is twice the loss in signal-to-noise ratio that we get in transmission over an AWGN channel when we do binary signaling at the transmitter and hard decision at the receiver, and focus on capacity (see Proakis [17], p. 460) at small signal-to-noise ratios. The factor of two could be explained from the fact that in a biometric system we quantize at both sides.

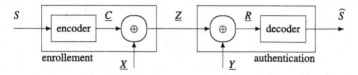

Fig. 5.8 A fuzzy commitment scheme

5.4 Practical Constructions for Biometric Systems: Fuzzy Commitment

In this section we discuss the privacy-leakage properties of key-binding schemes that are described in the literature. The schemes are based on the popular fuzzy commitment scheme introduced by Juels and Wattenberg [11]. It should be noted that here we consider the operational rates.

5.4.1 Fuzzy Commitment

Consider a particular realization of key-binding systems, the fuzzy commitment scheme, introduced by Juels and Wattenberg [11]. In this scheme, see Fig. 5.8, a uniformly distributed secret key s from alphabet $\{1, 2, \ldots, M_S\}$, see (5.3), is chosen at random independently of biometric data. This secret key s is observed at the enrollment side together with a biometric enrollment sequence $\underline{x}$. Key binding is performed as follows. The secret key s is encoded into a binary codeword $\underline{c} = (c_1, c_2, \ldots, c_N)$ with $c_n \in \{0, 1\}$ for $n = 1, 2, \ldots, N$, then

$$\underline{c} = e(s), \tag{5.30}$$

where $e(\cdot)$ is the encoding function. Then the biometric enrollment sequence is added modulo 2 to the codeword. This results in the sequence $\underline{z} = (z_1, z_2, \ldots, z_N)$ with $z_n \in \{0, 1\}$ for $n = 1, 2, \ldots, N$, hence

$$\underline{z} = \underline{c} \oplus \underline{x} = e(s) \oplus \underline{x}. \tag{5.31}$$

This sequence is referred to as helper data and is public. The helper data are released to the authentication side.

During authentication, a biometric authentication sequence $\underline{y}$ is observed and added modulo 2 to the received helper data $\underline{z}$, resulting in a binary sum

$$\underline{r} = \underline{z} \oplus \underline{y} = e(s) \oplus \underline{x} \oplus \underline{y}. \tag{5.32}$$

This sum $\underline{r} = \{r_1, r_2, \ldots, r_N\}$ with $r_n \in \{0, 1\}$ for $n = 1, 2, \ldots, N$ can be seen as the codeword $\underline{c}$ to which a noise sequence $\underline{x} \oplus \underline{y}$ is added. This codeword $\underline{r}$ is then decoded, hence the estimate $\hat{s}$ of the secret key s is determined as

$$\hat{s} = d(\underline{r}) = d\big(e(s) \oplus (\underline{x} \oplus \underline{y})\big), \tag{5.33}$$

where $d(\cdot)$ is the decoding function.

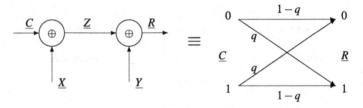

Fig. 5.9 For binary symmetric double biometric source, the channel between $\underline{C}$ and $\underline{R}$ is a BSC with cross-over probability $q = Q(0, 1) + Q(1, 0)$

Observe that for binary symmetric double biometric source, the "channel" between $\underline{C}$ and $\underline{R}$ is a binary symmetric channel (BSC) with cross-over probability $Q(1, 0) + Q(0, 1) = q$, see Fig. 5.9.

It is easy to see that if the rate of the code used in fuzzy commitment is R, then the secret-key rate is R too, and the privacy-leakage rate L is equal to $1 - R$ if the enrollment sequence is uniform and identically distributed, see [21]. If the observed biometric is symmetric with cross-over probability q and $R = 1 - h(q)$, the secret-key and privacy-leakage rate pair $(R, 1 - R)$ is optimal, i.e. it satisfies (5.22), with $p = 0$. When the rate is taken smaller than $1 - h(q)$, however, the leakage increases and the resulting pair (R, L) becomes suboptimal.

5.4.2 Coding for Fuzzy Commitment

Now we investigate coding techniques that are used for fuzzy commitment implementation and their influence on the privacy leakage. Note that a typical implementation of fuzzy commitment involves enrollment and authentication biometric sequences that are binary. Therefore we first consider a situation when Gaussian continuous biometric input sequences are first binary quantized and the result is fed as an input to fuzzy commitment, see e.g. [22]. In the second setting we look at the case where we only quantize biometric data at the encoder and use soft information at the decoder.

Consider a practical example[2] when we have to implement a biometric fuzzy commitment system based on the biometric source with the following characteristics. The target biometric source is Gaussian with SNR roughly equal to 3 (or 4.7 dB), note that SNR $= \frac{\rho^2}{1-\rho^2}$. This source produces biometric sequences of length $N = 512$. Now the question is what codes we have to use if we need to realize a system with a word error probability (WER) of roughly 0.01 (1 %).

Note that for such a biometric source ideally we can achieve 1 bit per source symbol secret-key rate at infinite privacy leakage, which follows from the asymptotic secret-key rate result discussed before and the example in Fig. 5.2.

---

[2]This example is based on the parameters of fingerprint feature vectors. The data used in this example are synthetic though.

Fig. 5.10 Performance of
(511, 31, 109) BCH code

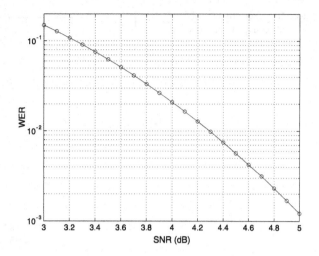

5.4.2.1 Two-Side Binary Quantization, BCH Codes

One of the most popular implementations of fuzzy commitment uses BCH codes, see e.g. [13, 27]. Therefore we first analyze the performance of the system realized with BCH codes. First we apply binary quantization for both the X- and the Y- biometric sequences. Then the resulting binary sequences are used in a fuzzy commitment scheme with a BCH code of length $N = 511$ and dimension (secret-key length) 31. This code can correct up to $t = 109$ errors.

Now in Fig. 5.10 we plot WER performance for this BCH codes at different SNR. Thus we see that our BCH code achieves the target performance of 0.01 at an SNR of 4.3 dB. If we look at the biometric system characterization in terms of secret-key rate and privacy leakage, then we see that for this code the (code and) secret-key rate is $R = 31/511 = 0.0607$ and the privacy leakage is $L = 480/511 = 0.9393$, note that $L = 1 - R$.

In order to characterize the loss caused by applying a certain method, let us look at the minimal SNR corresponding to the biometric system with given secret-key and privacy-leakage characteristics. From (5.9) it follows, after some algebraic steps, that

$$\text{SNR}_{\min}(R, L) = \left(2^{2R} - 1\right)\frac{2^{2L}}{2^{2L} - 1}. \tag{5.34}$$

It turns out that $\text{SNR}_{\min}$ corresponding to the above secret-key and privacy-leakage pair is -9.2 dB. Thus fuzzy commitment combined with our BCH code is 13.5 dB from optimal. The reason for this poor behavior can be explain by two factors. First, binary quantization at two-sides is not optimal, and, second, the BCH code with low rate is far from optimal.

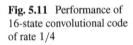**Fig. 5.11** Performance of
16-state convolutional code
of rate 1/4

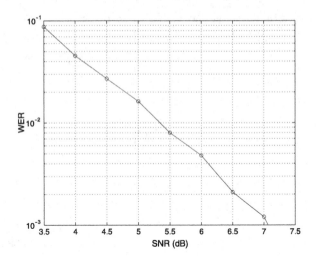

5.4.2.2 Quantization at the Encoder, Convolutional Codes

Let us try to improve the performance of fuzzy commitment. In order to do this
instead of a BCH code we apply convolutional code and perform quantization only
at the encoder. We decide to use a 16-state convolutional code of rate 1/4. For
this code, the trellis length is 128, and therefore the codeword length is $N = 512$.
Decoding is performed using soft information from Y-sequence by Viterbi decoding
algorithm [25]. The performance of this code is shown in Fig. 5.11.

We see that now WER of 0.01 is achieved at SNR = 5.3 dB. If we look at the
characteristic of the resulting biometric system, then we see that the secret-key rate
is $R = 124/512 = 0.2422$, while the privacy leakage is $L = 388/512 = 0.7578$.
Therefore in this case we can achieve secret-key length four times larger than the
one that can be achieved with BCH codes. Moreover, the corresponding SNR_{min}
becomes -2.1 dB, thus showing that fuzzy commitment with a convolutional code
is only 7.4 dB from optimal and 6 dB better than the one with the BCH code.

5.5 Concluding Remarks

In this chapter we studied biometric authentication systems with key-binding. We
have determined the fundamental trade-off for i.i.d. Gaussian sources. Moreover, we
looked at the loss in the system performance due to binary quantization. We would
like to mention that, in practice, biometric sequences consist of components having
correlation values within a smaller or larger range. It should be possible to find the
rate-leakage function for such sources based on the basic trade-off for the i.i.d. case
that was found here.

We also studied the effect of the code selection and binary quantization in fuzzy
commitment. In order to characterize the loss of a chosen coding method we use

minimal SNR for biometric source for a given secret-key rate and privacy-leakage rate. It turns out that popular constructions based on BCH codes operate at 13.5 dB from the fundamental limit in our practical example. We also showed that by selecting a better code, i.e. a convolutional code, and by using soft information at the decoder, we could drastically, by 6 dB, improve the performance of fuzzy commitment.

References

1. Ahlswede R, Csiszár I (1993) Common randomness in information theory and cryptography—part I: secret sharing. IEEE Transactions on Information Theory 39:1121–1132
2. Ahlswede R, Csiszár I (1998) Common randomness in information theory and cryptography—part II: CR capacity. IEEE Transactions on Information Theory 44:225–240
3. Assche GV, Cardinal J, Cerf N (2004) Reconciliation of a quantum-distributed Gaussian key. IEEE Transactions on Information Theory 50(2):394–400
4. Bergmans P (1974) A simple converse for broadcast channels with additive white Gaussian noise (corresp). IEEE Transactions on Information Theory 20(2):279–280
5. Chen C, Veldhuis R, Kevenaar T, Akkermans A (2008) Multi-bits biometric string generation based on the likelihood ratio. In: IEEE Computer Society Conference on Computer Vision and Pattern Recognition, Workshop on Biometrics, Anchorage, Alaska, US, 24–28 June 2008, vol 24, pp 1–7
6. Cover TM, Thomas JA (1991) Elements of Information Theory. Wiley, New York
7. Csiszár I, Narayan P (2000) Common randomness and secret key generation with a helper. IEEE Transactions on Information Theory 46(2):344–366
8. Daugman J (1993) High confidence visual recognition of persons by a test of statistical independence. IEEE Transactions on Pattern Analysis and Machine Intelligence 15(11):1148–1161
9. Ignatenko T, Willems F (2008) Privacy leakage in biometric secrecy systems. In: Proc of Forty-Sixth Annual Allerton Conf on Communication, Control, and Computing, Monticello, IL, USA, 23–26 September 2008, pp 850–857
10. Jain AK, Nandakumar K, Nagar A (2008) Biometric template security. EURASIP Journal on Advances in Signal Processing
11. Juels A, Wattenberg M (1999) A fuzzy commitment scheme. In: 6th ACM Conf on Computer and Communications Security, pp 28–36
12. Kelkboom E, Molina GG, Kevenaar T, Veldhuis R, Jonker W (2008) Binary biomterics: an analytic framework to estimate the bit error probability under Gaussian assumption. In: 2nd IEEE International Conference on Biometrics: Theory Applications and Systems (BTAS), Sep–Oct 2008, pp 1–6
13. Kevenaar TAM, Schrijen GJ, van der Veen M, Akkermans AHM, Zuo F (2005) Face recognition with renewable and privacy preserving binary templates. In: AutoID, pp 21–26
14. Lai L, Ho S-W, Poor HV (2008) Privacy-security tradeoffs in biometric security systems. In: Proc of 46th Ann Allerton Conf on Comm, Control, and Computing, Monticello, IL, USA, 23–26 Sept 2008, pp 23–26
15. Li Q, Sutcu Y, Memon N (2006) Secure sketch for biometric templates. In: Asiacrypt, Shanghai, China, Dec 2006. LNCS, vol 4284.
16. Maurer U (1993) Secret key agreement by public discussion from common information. IEEE Transactions on Information Theory 39:733–742
17. Proakis J (2001) Digital Communications, 4th edn. McGraw–Hill, New York
18. Shannon CE (1948) A mathematical theory of communication. The Bell System Technical Journal 27:623–656

19. Smith A (2004) Maintaining secrecy when information leakage is unavoidable. PhD dissertation, MIT
20. Sutcu Y, Rane S, Yedidia J, Draper S, Vetro A (2008) Feature extraction for a Slepian-Wolf biometric system using ldpc codes. In: IEEE Int Symp Inf Theory (ISIT), Toronto, Canada, 6–11 July 2008, pp 2297–2301
21. Ignatenko T, Willems F (2010) Information leakage in fuzzy commitment schemes. IEEE Transactions on Information Forensics and Security 5(2):337–348
22. Tuyls P, Akkermans A, Kevenaar T, Schrijen G-J, Bazen AM, Veldhuis R (2005) Practical biometric authentication with template protection. In: 5th Int Conf on Audio- and Video-Based Personal Authentication (AVBPA), pp 436–446
23. Venkatesan S, Anantharam V (1998) The common randomness capacity of a pair of independent discrete memoryless channels. IEEE Transactions on Information Theory 44:215–224
24. Verdu S, Guo D (2006) A simple proof of the entropy power inequality. IEEE Transactions on Information Theory 52(5):2165–2166
25. Viterbi AJ (1967) Error bounds for convolutional codes and an asymptotically optimum decoding algorithm. IEEE Transactions on Information Theory 13:260–269
26. Willems F (1989) Coding theorem for the awgn channel in terms of jointly typical sequences. In: 10th Symp Inf Theory in the Benelux, Houthalen, Belgium, 25 & 26 May 1989, pp 13–18
27. Yang S, Verbauwhede I (2007) Secure iris verification. In: IEEE Int Conf on Acoustics, Speech and Signal Processing (ICASSP), vol 2, pp 133–136
28. Ye C, Reznik A, Shah Y (2006) Extracting secrecy from Gaussian random variables. In: IEEE Int Symp Inf Theory (ISIT), Seattle, USA, 9–14 July 2006, pp 2593–2597

Chapter 6
Obtaining Cryptographic Keys Using Multi-biometrics

Sanjay Kanade, Dijana Petrovska-Delacrétaz, and Bernadette Dorizzi

Abstract Multi-biometric systems have several advantages over uni-biometrics based systems, such as, better verification accuracy, larger feature space to accommodate more subjects, and higher security against spoofing. Unfortunately, as in case of uni-biometric systems, multi-biometric systems also face the problems of nonrevocability, lack of template diversity, and possibility of privacy compromise. A combination of biometrics and cryptography is a good solution to eliminate these limitations. In this chapter we present a multi-biometric cryptosystem based on the fuzzy commitment scheme, in which, a crypto-biometric key is derived from multi-biometric data. An idea (recently proposed by the authors) denoted as *FeaLingECc* (*Fea*ture *L*evel Fus*i*on through Weighted *E*rror *C*orrection) is used for the multi-biometric fusion. The *FeaLingECc* allows fusion of different biometric modalities having different performances (e.g., face + iris). This scheme is adapted for a multi-unit system based on two-irises and a multi-modal system using a combination of iris and face. The difficulty in obtaining the crypto-biometric key locked in the system (and in turn the reference biometric data) is 189 bits for the two-iris system while 183 bits for the iris-face system using brute force attack. In addition to strong keys, these systems possess revocability and template diversity and protect user privacy.

6.1 Introduction

An important development in the field of biometrics is to combine information from multiple biometric sources (i.e., cues). A system that consolidates the evidence pre-

S. Kanade · D. Petrovska-Delacrétaz (✉) · B. Dorizzi
TELECOM SudParis, CNRS SAMOVAR UMR 5157, Départment Electronique et Physique,
MINES TELECOM, 9 Rue Charles Fourier, 91011 Evry, France
e-mail: Dijana.Petrovska@telecom-sudparis.eu

S. Kanade
e-mail: Sanjay.Kanade@telecom-sudparis.eu

B. Dorizzi
e-mail: Bernadette.Dorizzi@telecom-sudparis.eu

P. Campisi (ed.), *Security and Privacy in Biometrics*,
DOI 10.1007/978-1-4471-5230-9_6, © Springer-Verlag London 2013

sented by multiple biometric cues is known as a multi-biometric system. Such systems offer several advantages over uni-biometric systems, some of which are discussed below.

- Multi-biometric systems can substantially improve the matching accuracy of the system.
- Having multiple information sources increases the size of the feature space available to individual users, thus making it possible to accommodate more individuals in a system.
- Multi-biometrics may address the problem of nonuniversality, e.g., in a speaker recognition system, the individuals who cannot speak cannot be enrolled. But inclusion of another biometric such as iris may enable that person to enroll.
- When multiple biometric traits are involved, it becomes more difficult for an impostor to spoof the system.

However, the main disadvantage of multi-biometric systems is their increased complexity.

Depending on the sources of information combined in it, the multi-biometric system can be called multi-sensor, multi-sample, multi-algorithm, multi-unit (or multi-instance), and multi-modal. The information fusion can be carried out at different levels of the biometric system, such as sensor, feature, score, decision, or rank level [30].

Unfortunately, despite all these advantages over uni-biometric systems, their limitations such as nonrevocability, lack of template diversity, and possibility of privacy compromise are also inherited by the multi-biometric systems. In recent years, a lot of efforts have been made to overcome these issues in uni-biometric systems by using various template protection mechanisms. Some of these mechanisms transform the biometric data in a non-recoverable manner so that the comparison is carried out in the transformed domain. In some other schemes, a stable key is obtained from biometric data and such systems are denoted as biometric cryptosystems [10]. However, the main aim of the biometric cryptosystems is to obtain a key for cryptographic purposes and many of these systems do not possess the property of revocability.

Despite these efforts in case of uni-biometrics, there are very few works in literature that deal with these issues in multi-biometric systems. Multi-biometrics-based cryptosystems, which obtain cryptographic keys using multi-biometrics are a promising solution to this problem. In this chapter, first a review of such multi-biometric cryptosystems is presented. The review is followed by a detailed description of the multi-biometric key regeneration schemes recently proposed by the authors.

This chapter is organized as follows: the state of the art related to multi-biometric cryptosystems is discussed in Sect. 6.2. A generic scheme for multi-biometric template protection based on the fuzzy commitment scheme [12] is described in Sect. 6.3. This is in fact a multi-biometrics-based key regeneration scheme which also provides template protection. Two adaptations of this scheme, a multi-unit type system using two irises and a multi-modal type system using iris and face, along with their experimental evaluation, are then described in Sects. 6.4 and 6.5, respectively. These two systems were recently published in [15] and [16], respectively. Finally, conclusions and perspectives are given in Sect. 6.6.

6.2 Obtaining Cryptographic Keys Using Multi-biometrics: State of the Art

The key regeneration systems described in this chapter combine techniques from biometrics and cryptography. In literature, such systems are generally denoted *biometric template protection schemes* and are classified into two main categories [10]: feature transformation and biometric cryptosystems. In feature transformation type systems, a user specific transformation is applied on the biometric features [14, 20, 29]. The goal of the systems in this category is to induce revocability, template diversity, and privacy protection into biometric systems. The comparison between two biometric samples is carried out in the transformed domain using some distance metric similar to the classical biometric systems. Therefore, using multi-biometrics in these kind of systems is straightforward. Classical fusion techniques, such as feature level and score level fusion, can be applied directly to these systems.

On the other hand, the main aim of the systems from the biometric cryptosystems category is to obtain a stable multi-bit string from biometrics [9, 11, 12]. Such crypto-bio keys are strongly linked to the user's identity and therefore can enhance the security of the system. In fact, many systems in this category were originally designed for obtaining cryptographic keys and did not possess revocability. However, if properly designed, revocability, template diversity, and privacy protection properties can be induced in these systems.

For example, the fuzzy commitment-based key regeneration system [12], which is the most widely studied approach for template protection (and key generation), treats biometric data matching as an error correction issue by considering it as a problem of data transmission through a noisy communication channel. First, a randomly generated key $\mathbf{K}$ is encoded using Error Correcting Codes (ECC) and the variations in the biometric data are transferred onto the encoded key. These variations, treated as errors, are corrected by the ECC to regenerate the random key $\mathbf{K'}$ at the verification step. This system does not store the biometric features or templates as in classical biometric systems. The biometric features are stored in a protected form in the crypto-biometric template. Since there is no stored biometric template, nor are there features, classical biometric comparison cannot be performed in this system and no match score can be obtained. In fact, such systems directly output the regenerated key. The user verification success or failure decision, unlike classical biometric systems, depends on the exact comparison between the crypto-bio keys obtained with the system. Since there is no score, score level fusion cannot be applied for multi-biometric information fusion in key regeneration systems.

The decision level fusion is possible in these systems, but the increase in the key entropy can be a maximum of one bit. The key entropy indicates the difficulty in obtaining the key without having the genuine biometric data which is, in turn, the security of the stored template. In decision level fusion, depending on the verification results of two individual biometric systems, a combined key can be released. If the length and entropy of each of these keys is N and H bits, respectively, the combined key will have a length equal to $2N$ bits but the entropy will increase by only one bit to $H + 1$. The reason behind this is the entropy is measured on logarithmic scale. If an attacker needs 2^H attempts to guess the key, then the entropy is H bits. When two such keys are present, the number of attempts increases to 2×2^H resulting in an entropy of $H + 1$ bits. Thus, the entropy increase in such a case is only one bit.

Therefore, if multi-biometric techniques are to be used for template protection, specific methods for information fusion need to be developed. There are very few systems found in literature that address the issue of multi-biometric template protection which are summarized below.

One of the first systems to use multi-biometrics with template protection is by Sutcu et al. [32] (in 2007). They proposed a method to combine fingerprint and face features in a fuzzy sketch scheme. But they did not carry out experiments with the fused biometric information but rather predicted the results for the multi-biometric system from the two uni-biometric system results.

Nandakumar and Jain [23, 24] (in 2008) proposed a fuzzy vault scheme which combines fingerprints with iris. A significant improvement in verification performance over the uni-biometric systems is observed (e.g., from a Genuine Acceptance Rate (GAR) of 88 % and 78.8 % for individual iris and fingerprint systems, respectively, to 98.2 % for the multi-biometric system). However, despite these improvements in the verification performance, the entropy of the key increases from 40 bits (for uni-biometric system) to 49 bits (in the multi-biometric case) which is still low from a security point of view.

Cimato et al. [5] (in 2008) proposed a multi-modal biometrics-based cryptosystem. Similar to that of Nandakumar and Jain [24], the two modalities employed in their system are iris and fingerprints. Their proposed system is based on the fuzzy extractor concept [3, 7]. They experimentally showed that the performance of the multi-modal system is as good as the best performing single modality system. However, they did not provide security analysis of the system in terms of key entropy.

Kelkboom et al. [17] (in 2009) proposed various ways of combining multi-biometrics with fuzzy commitment-based schemes. Their proposed systems involve multi-algorithmic fusion at feature-, score-, and decision-level. However, their performance evaluation suggests that the improvement due to multi-biometrics occurs only in terms of verification performance. The security of the system does not improve significantly.

Fu et al. [8] (in 2009) proposed theoretical models describing multi-biometric cryptosystems. They proposed fusion at the biometric and cryptographic levels and then derived four models adopted at these two levels. However, this work is theoretical and no actual evaluation of verification performance as well as key entropy is carried out.

In this chapter, a new technique recently proposed by the authors, called *FeaLingECc* (*Fea*ture *L*evel Fus*i*on through Weighted *E*rror *C*orrection), is described. With this technique, the biometric information obtained from different cues can be combined into a fuzzy commitment-based template protection system. We explore the possibilities of using multi-biometrics in a fuzzy commitment-based scheme [12] using two different methodologies:

1. multi-unit (also called multi-instance) type system combining information from left and right irises of a person, and
2. multi-modal type system which combines information from iris and face biometrics.

For both these systems, the information fusion is carried out at feature level, which increases the key entropy. The *FeaLingECc* technique allows to apply different weights to different modalities (or different information sources). The general description of this proposed scheme is presented in the next section.

6.3 Multi-biometrics Based Key Regeneration

The basic structure of our scheme is shown in Fig. 6.1. It is based on the fuzzy commitment scheme [12]. In this scheme, the biometric data variability is treated with error correcting codes. There are two levels of error correction: Level-1, also called inner level, and Level-2, which is the outer level. A randomly generated key **K** is assigned to a user and is then encoded using Level-2 encoder. The output of the Level-2 encoder is then randomized with a shuffling key by applying the shuffling scheme proposed by Kanade et al. [13]. The shuffled output is further encoded by Level-1 encoder. The output of the encoder is called *pseudo code* θ_{ps}. The reference biometric data is XORed with this *pseudo code* to obtain the *locked code* θ_{lock}. The reference biometric data cannot be recovered from the locked code unless the pseudo code or another biometric data sample from the same user is provided.

In the proposed scheme, the biometric data is a combined data from two biometric cues. The biometric information fusion is carried out in the feature domain. The proposed system is based on the fuzzy commitment scheme and therefore requires the feature vectors in binary form. Assuming that the binary feature vector corresponding to the first biometric source is denoted as θ_1 and that to the second biometric source as θ_2, the reference feature code is obtained by concatenating these two feature vectors as, $\theta_{\mathrm{ref}} = \theta_1 \| \theta_2$. This reference feature code θ_{ref} is XORed with the pseudo code θ_{ps} to obtain a locked code θ_{lock},

$$\theta_{\mathrm{lock}} = \theta_{\mathrm{ps}} \oplus \theta_{\mathrm{ref}}. \tag{6.1}$$

This locked code along with the hash value $H(\mathbf{K})$ of the key **K** is the crypto-biometric template. The locked code is required for regeneration of the key **K**, whereas the hash value is required to check the correctness of the regenerated key.

At the time of key regeneration/verification, a multi-biometric test feature vector θ_{test} is obtained by following a procedure similar to that at the enrollment step.

Fig. 6.1 Schematic diagram showing the structure of the proposed multi-biometrics-based cryptographic key regeneration scheme

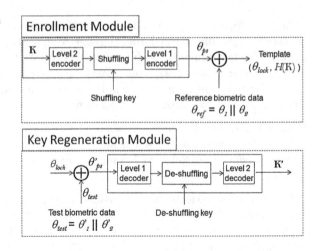

This test feature vector is XORed with the locked code θ_{lock} to obtain a modified version θ'_{ps} of the pseudo code. This modified version consists of the pseudo code θ_{ps} contaminated with the errors e between reference and test biometric vectors. The Error Correcting Codes (ECC) decoding scheme corrects these errors and retrieves a trial value $\mathbf{K}'$ of the random key $\mathbf{K}$. A comparison between the hash values of the original and the regenerated key is carried out and a positive result indicates key regeneration success;

$$\theta'_{\text{ps}} = \theta_{\text{lock}} \oplus \theta_{\text{test}}$$
$$= \theta_{\text{ps}} \oplus \theta_{\text{ref}} \oplus \theta_{\text{test}}$$
$$= \theta_{\text{ps}} \oplus e, \tag{6.2}$$
$$\mathbf{K}' = \text{ECC}^{-1}\left(\theta'_{\text{ps}}\right). \tag{6.3}$$

The Level-1 error correcting codes perform majority of the error correction. These ECC correct bit-level errors occurring in blocks. If the number of errors in a block is more than the error correction capacity of the Level-1 ECC, that block is decoded incorrectly. Such incorrectly decoded blocks are further treated by the Level-2 codes. Thus, the Level-2 ECC work on block level. In order to cope with the cascading structure of the two ECC, the number of bits in each symbol of the Level-2 ECC must be the same as (or possibly an integer multiple of) the number of bits in Level-1 ECC input block.

6.3.1 FeaLingECc (Feature Level Fusion Through Weighted Error Correction)

When feature vectors corresponding to two biometric sources are combined, it is required that the two vectors have a common representation which is not always the case. For example, fingerprint minutiae set consists of minutiae locations and orientation information, while the iris feature vector is a binary string. The minutiae set is an unordered set while the iris code is an ordered set. Therefore, the two feature vectors must be converted into a common representation. Moreover, the dimensions of the feature vectors can also be different and simply concatenating the two feature vectors may not be beneficial. The difference in the dimensionality of the two feature vectors can cause an adverse effect on the system performance. This problem is called the curse of dimensionality [30]. Therefore, in order to deal with this problem, the feature level fusion module is generally followed by a feature selection module in classical multi-biometric systems.

Moreover, one biometric trait may be performing better than the other in terms of verification performance (e.g., in general, iris performs better than face). This knowledge can be exploited in score level fusion systems by applying different weights to the individual biometric traits. In such systems, higher weight is given to the better performing biometric trait in the verification decision process. This kind of weighting can significantly improve the performance of multi-biometric system.

Since the match scores cannot be computed in key regeneration systems, classical score level fusion techniques cannot be used. Therefore, we propose a novel method in which the features are combined in feature domain and the error correction scheme is designed so that different weights can be applied to the individual biometric traits. This scheme also deals with the problem of curse of dimensionality. It can cope with the differences in the dimensions of individual feature vectors by carefully selecting the dimensions of the Level-1 ECC for the individual biometrics and minimize the effect of dimensions mismatch on the verification performance.

The enrollment and key regeneration modules of the proposed system are shown in Fig. 6.2(a) and 6.2(b). The error correction scheme in the proposed system consists of two levels. The Level-1 work on bit-errors occurring in blocks while the Level-2 ECC correct the block errors which are left after the Level-1 ECC action. Since the amount and nature of variations in biometric data are different for different modalities, and they also depend on the acquisition conditions, we need to select different Level-1 ECC for different modalities. The Level-1 ECC and their error correction capacity is selected by observing the Hamming distance distributions for genuine and impostor comparisons for the corresponding trait.

The application of different weights is carried out by assigning different number of blocks of the Level-2 ECC for different biometrics. As shown in Fig. 6.2(a), the output of the Level-2 codes (which is in form of n_s blocks) is split into two parts: Part-1 which consists of x blocks and Part-2 consisting of $y = (n_s - x)$ blocks. Higher weight can be applied to the Biometric-1 by having $x > y$ and vice versa.

The x blocks of Part-1 are further encoded and combined into x' bits by the Level-1 encoder for the first biometric (Biometric-1). The y blocks of Part-2 are encoded and combined into y' bits by the Level-1 encoder for the second biometric (Biometric-2). Here, x' and y' are equal to the number of effective bits in the feature vectors of Biometric-1 and Biometric-2, respectively. The number of bits in each

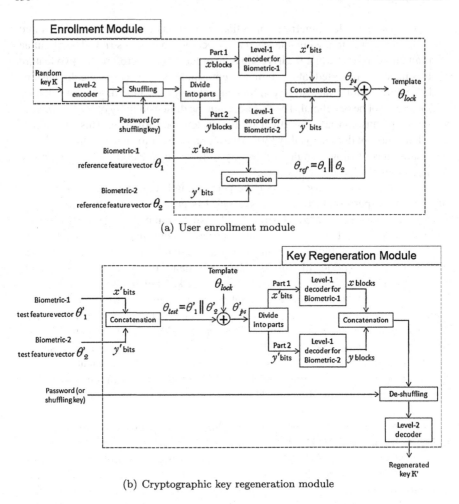

(a) User enrollment module

(b) Cryptographic key regeneration module

Fig. 6.2 Schematic diagram of the proposed multi-biometrics-based cryptographic key regeneration scheme using *FeaLingECc* (*Fea*ture *L*evel Fus*i*on through Weighted *E*rror *C*orrection)

input block of the Level-1 encoder should be equal to the number of bits in each output block of the Level-2 encoder. Alternatively, the input block size of the Level-1 encoder can be an integer multiple of the output block size of the Level-2 encoder. Concatenation of the outputs of the two Level-1 encoders yields the pseudo code θ_{ps}. This pseudo code is XORed with the multi-biometric reference feature vector θ_{ref} (which is obtained by concatenation of two individual feature vectors θ_1 and θ_2) to obtain the locked code θ_{lock}.

The weights are applied by changing the sizes of Part-1 and Part-2. In order to understand the concept, let us take a closer look into the error correction mechanism that takes place during the key regeneration step (see Fig. 6.3). When a multi-biometric test feature vector θ_{test} (which is obtained by concatenation of

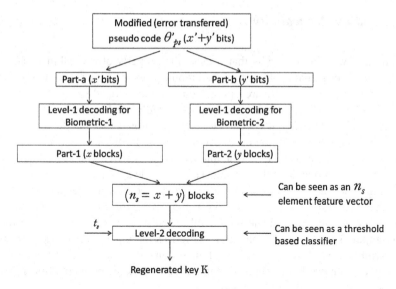

Fig. 6.3 Schematic diagram showing the proposed weighted error correction process. Note that *Part-b* is bigger than *Part-a*. When *Level-1* ECC are applied, this relationship changes. *Part-1* becomes bigger than *Part-2* which means that higher weight is applied to the *Biometric-1* than *Biometric-2*

two individual test feature vectors θ'_1 and θ'_2) is XORed with the locked code θ_{lock}, the errors between the reference and test feature codes are transferred onto the pseudo code θ_{ps}. Figure 6.3 shows the process of error correction that follows.

The modified (error transferred) pseudo code θ'_{ps} is divided into two parts: Part-a consists of the first x' bits while the Part-b consists of the remaining y' bits. The Level-1 decoder corresponding to Biometric-1 is applied on the x' bits to correct the bit errors caused by the Biometric-1. This process yields x blocks. Similarly, y blocks are obtained from the y' bits corresponding to the Biometric-2. These two parts are concatenated to form a single codeword which contains $n_s = (x + y)$ blocks. The Level-2 decoder corrects the erroneous blocks present in this codeword to obtain a trial value $\mathbf{K}'$ of the random key $\mathbf{K}$. The Level-2 decoder can correct up to t_s erroneous blocks where t_s is its error correction capacity. This Level-2 decoder can be seen as a threshold-based classifier which operates on an n_s element vector where t_s acts as a threshold. If the number of erroneous blocks are less than or equal to t_s, the key is successfully generated and the verification result is positive. Therefore, if we set $x > y$, a higher weight will be given to Biometric-1 than Biometric-2 in the decision process. The condition $x > y$ (or $x < y$ if required) is achieved by properly selecting the dimensions of the Level-1 ECC. However, this selection needs to take care of the error correction capacity which depends on the Hamming distance distribution of the biometric data.

6.3.2 Adding Revocability

The problem with biometrics is that it lacks the property of revocability and can compromise user's privacy. In order to overcome these drawbacks, some one-way transformations [20, 22, 29] are applied on the biometric data in case of uni-biometric systems. In a similar way, some cancelable mechanism should be used in the multi-biometrics-based system. One simple option is to apply the transformation on the two individual biometric feature vectors. In this way, revocability and privacy protection can be added to the multi-biometrics-based system.

But there is a loophole in this design. This loophole appears if the Level-2 error correcting codes used in the system (e.g., we use Reed–Solomon codes as Level-2 codes in our proposal) are of systematic nature. An error correcting code is said to be systematic in nature if the input to the code is present in its original form in the output. The output of such codes comprises the input data appended by the parity symbols, and thus, the locations of the original data and the parity symbols is known to an attacker. In this case, the attacker can attack the biometric information corresponding only to the data blocks.

For example, consider the case of Table 6.7, where $t_s = 8$. In this particular example, $n_s = 46$ which is the total number of blocks after Reed–Solomon (RS) encoding which are obtained by appending 16 parity blocks to the 30-block input data blocks ($n_s = k_s + 2t_s$). This encoded output is further encoded with the Level-1 encoders. The first 31 blocks of this output correspond to Biometric-1 and the remaining to Biometric-2. Therefore, an attacker can choose to attack only biometric-1 and obtain the 31 blocks, out of which the first 30 blocks constitute the actual key.

Clearly, this kind of attack can suppress the advantage gained by using multiple biometrics. The attacker may need only one set of biometric information to crack the multi-biometric system.

In order to overcome this drawback, we propose to apply the biometric data transformation mechanism (shuffling scheme in our case) after the Level-2 encoding instead of applying it on the biometric data. In this case, even if the Level-2 ECC are systematic, the shuffling process breaks the systematic nature of its output. The shuffled output of Level-2 ECC is further encoded with the Level-1 ECC. At the time of key regeneration, the original order of the Level-2 encoder output must be restored in order for the Level-2 decoder to function correctly. This is done by applying the de-shuffling process. For better understanding, the shuffling and de-shuffling processes are shown together in Fig. 6.4.

One might argue that revocability can be induced into the system by applying classical encryption on the fuzzy commitment (protected template), which is true in principle. However, this type of encryption of templates does not eliminate the security loophole cited above that occurs due to the systematic nature of the ECC. In this case, an attacker needs to decrypt the template and then crack only one biometric source in order to obtain the crypto-biometric key. By employing the shuffling scheme in the above mentioned manner, the attacker needs to crack the shuffling key and both the biometric sources.

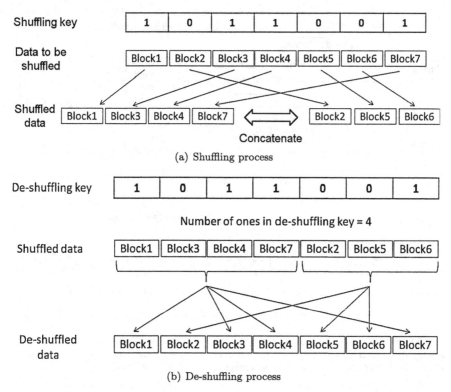

Fig. 6.4 A schematic diagram showing the shuffling and de-shuffling process. Note that the shuffling and de-shuffling key must be the same to recover the correct data

The generic multi-biometrics-based key regeneration scheme described in this section can be applied to a combination of two sets of biometric information. The pre-requisite for this system is that both the biometric data must be in form of binary vectors. We developed two systems based on this scheme:

- multi-unit type system that combines information from the left and the right irises of a person, and
- multi-modal type system that combines information from an iris with that from the face.

These systems are described in subsequent sections.

6.4 Multi-unit Type Multi-biometrics Based Key Regeneration

6.4.1 Algorithm for Multi-unit Biometrics Based Key Regeneration

We developed a multi-unit type multi-biometrics system to obtain cryptographic keys. Feature level fusion in multi-unit type systems is comparatively less com-

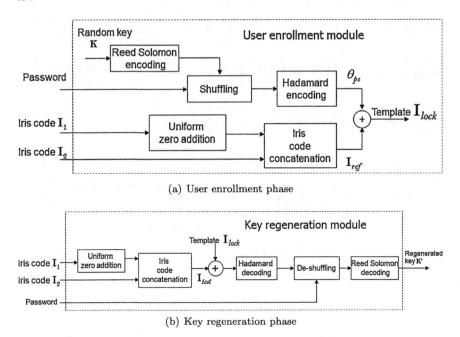

(a) User enrollment phase

(b) Key regeneration phase

Fig. 6.5 Schematic diagram of the proposed multi-unit type multi-biometrics-based crypto-graphic key regeneration scheme using feature level fusion, weighted error correction, and pass-word—(**a**) User enrollment phase; (**b**) cryptographic key regeneration phase

plicated than in the multi-modal type systems. The reason is that the feature sets obtained from different sources in a multi-unit system are generally similar in nature and dimensions. Our system incorporates information from left and right irises of a person in a fuzzy commitment-based key regeneration scheme. The information fusion is carried out in feature domain using the weighted error correction approach described in previous section.

The iris codes obtained from different iris images of the same user contain variabilities which are treated as errors. As pointed out by Hao et al. [9], there are two types of errors in iris codes: (1) background errors caused by the camera noise, image capture effects, etc., and (2) burst errors which are a result of specular reflections, occlusions, etc. Both these types of errors are corrected using the two level error correction scheme shown in Fig. 6.1.

The enrollment and key regeneration phases of the proposed multi-unit type system are shown in Fig. 6.5. We used Hadamard codes as Level-1 ECC and Reed–Solomon (RS) codes as Level-2 ECC for our two-iris-based system. A random bit string **K** is generated and assigned to a user and is then encoded using Reed–Solomon (RS) codes, the output of which is further encoded by the Hadamard codes. The Hadamard codes correct the background errors and RS codes correct burst errors. Details about these ECC can be found in [21]. The output of the encoder is called *pseudo code* θ_{ps}. In order to cope with the cascading structure of the two ECC, the number of bits in each symbol of RS and that in the input words of

Hadamard codes is set to be equal ($m = 7$). Iris codes I_1 and I_2 from the right and left iris images, respectively, are concatenated to form a reference (multi-) iris code I_{ref}. This I_{ref} is XORed with θ_{ps} to obtain the locked iris code template I_{lock}.

In the key regeneration phase, a test (multi-) iris code I_{test} is obtained similarly and XORed with I_{lock}. These XORing operations transfer the errors in the iris codes onto the pseudo code. The Hadamard codes can correct (up to) $2^{(k-2)} - 1$ errors in a 2^k-bit block. If a block has more than $2^{(k-2)} - 1$ errors, that block is not decoded correctly and results in an error. The second level of ECC consists of the RS codes. The output of the Hadamard decoding stage acts as the input to the RS decoder stage. The RS codes correct the errors caused due to the wrong decoding by the Hadamard codes and generate the key K'. If the total amount of errors is within the error correction capacity of the ECC, the errors are corrected and a key K' is regenerated which is the same as K. If the amount of errors is more than the error correction capacity of the ECC, $K' \neq K$.

In the proposed scheme, we apply higher weights to one iris than the other by employing the weighted error correction method described in Sect. 6.3.1. We use a bigger number of RS blocks for one iris than for the other to apply these weights. Kanade et al. [13] have shown that inserting certain amount of zeros in the biometric data can increase the error correction capacity of the Hadamard codes. Using this property, we applied the zero insertion scheme to one iris code in order to increase the error correction for it. Using the Hadamard codes without zero insertion scheme results in high false rejections but zero false acceptances. Thus, the increased error correction for the first iris code helps to increase acceptances while the low error correction for the second iris code increases rejections. The combined effect of the two is the improvement in the verification performance of the key regeneration system. The most important advantage of this scheme is that the feature vector is longer than in uni-biometrics-based system, and therefore, we can obtain longer keys. The biometric information is also larger compared to the uni-biometric systems resulting in higher entropy. Additionally, it experimentally validates our proposal of weighted error correction. The experimental results of this system are reported in the next subsection.

6.4.2 Results and Security Analysis of the Multi-unit (Two-Iris) Type System

In this section, we briefly describe the experimental setup, and then present the results and security analysis of the proposed multi-unit type system.

6.4.2.1 Experimental Setup

We used the OSIRISv1 (Open Source for Iris Recognition) system described in [28] and available online at [27] to extract a 1,188-bit binary string called iris code from

Table 6.1 Baseline
biometric system's
verification performance in
terms of EER in %. Single as
well as two-iris tests. Results
previously published in [15]

	CBS-BiosecureV1 (development)			NIST-ICE (evaluation)		
	Left	Right	Both irises	Left	Right	Both irises
	3.23	2.90	2.54	2.44	4.81	1.18

an iris image. In this system, the iris region in an image is detected, normalized, and then decomposed using Gabor filters having different scales and orientations. The phase information is then quantized to obtain the binary code. In order to cope with the iris rotations, the normalized test iris image is shifted 10 times in both directions and codes are extracted from them for comparison, leading to 21 comparisons.

The CBS database [28] is used for development to find out the ECC and error correction capacities. The system is then evaluated on the NIST-ICE database [26]. In the NIST-ICE database, there are 132 subjects out of which, only 112 subjects have recorded images of their both eyes. We select images of these 112 subjects for carrying out our tests. The right iris images are coupled with the left iris images for the multi-iris tests. The first such image pair of a person is considered for enrollment and a template is registered for that person. The genuine comparisons are carried out by comparing the remaining image pairs of that subject with the enrollment template leading to 1,099 genuine comparisons. For impostor comparisons, one image pair from each of the remaining subjects is randomly selected and these image pairs are compared with the enrollment template. Thus, for each person, we carry out 111 impostor comparisons. In summary, 1,099 genuine and 12,432 impostor comparisons are carried out on the NIST-ICE database for the two-iris experiment.

6.4.2.2 Experimental Results of the Multi-unit (Two-Iris) Type System

Since the proposed system is based on an iris recognition system, it is worthwhile to report the performance of the baseline biometric system for fair comparison. Such performance results are reported in Table 6.1. Note that the baseline iris system is based on OSIRISv1 with a re-implemented matching module. Classical multi-iris-based biometric system is also tested in which the iris codes are simply concatenated and compared. Note that, as expected, the combination of left and right irises results in reduction in the Equal Error Rate (EER).

For the cryptographic key regeneration system, we first report the results for the simple feature level fusion scheme in Table 6.2. The feature level fusion in this case is by simple concatenation of two feature vectors. For the sake of comparison, the key regeneration results (for CBS database) using single irises are also reported in the same table. The shuffling scheme is not used in any of these tests. It can be observed that the minimum FRR using single iris is 7.37 % with a key length of 6 bits. The combination of two irises reduces the FRR and also leads to longer keys such as 35-bit keys at 4.93 % FRR. In spite of the improvement, the FRR is still too high and hence we did not carry out these tests on the NIST-ICE database.

When the proposed *FeaLingECc* approach is used, a significant improvement is achieved that can be seen in Table 6.3. As is done in the uni-biometrics-based

Table 6.2 Key regeneration system results on the CBS-BiosecureV1 data set when two iris codes are combined using only feature level fusion; no weighting, no shuffling; FRR values are in %; length of key **K** is in bits; FAR is always zero for all these tests. t_s is the error correction capacity of RS codes. Results previously published in [15]

t_s	Left iris		Right iris		Both irises	
	FRR	Length (**K**)	FRR	Length (**K**)	FRR	Length (**K**)
16	9.80	30	14.13	30	4.93	35
17	8.60	18	13.10	18	4.57	21
18	**7.37**	**6**	**12.03**	**6**	**4.27**	**7**

Table 6.3 Key regeneration system results when two iris codes are combined using the proposed *FeaLingECc* method; FAR and FRR values are in %. Results previously published in [15]

t_s	Key length (in bits)	Without shuffling				With shuffling			
		CBS-Bio		NIST-ICE		CBS-Bio		NIST-ICE	
		FAR	FRR	FAR	FRR	FAR	FRR	FAR	FRR
6	259	0	8.37	0	13.28	0	8.50	0	13.74
9	217	0	5.37	0	5.19	0	5.63	0	5.46
10	203	0	4.50	0.016	3.37	0	4.60	0	3.28
11	189	0	4.10	0.06	2.09	0	4.10	0	2.09
12	175	0	3.63	0.38	1.64	0	3.67	0	1.36
13	161	0.10	3.40	1.49	0.55	0	3.50	0	1.00
14	147	0.70	3.30	2.98	0.27	0	3.30	0	0.18
15	133	1.87	3.13	10.46	0.18	0	3.03	0	0.18
16	119	6.40	2.80	15.86	0.09	0	2.37	0	0.09
21	49	84.47	0.23	91.37	0	0	0.30	0	0

system, we added certain amount of zeros to the right iris code to correct higher amount of errors in it whereas no zeros are added to left iris code. The Hadamard codes operate on 64-bit blocks and there are 49 such blocks resulting in a total amount of error correction equal to 735 bits. It also allows us to obtain much longer keys with low error rates, e.g., we can have 175-bit keys at 0.38 % False Acceptance Rate (FAR) and 1.64 % FRR for the NIST-ICE database.

Finally, the results for the key regeneration scheme with shuffling are presented in Table 6.3. These results are better than any previously published results in literature, e.g., we can generate 147-bit keys at 0.18 % FRR and 0 % FAR for ICE database. In our experiments, the number of blocks at the output of the RS encoder is 49. Hence we use a 49-bit shuffling key to shuffle those blocks. The shuffling key can be protected by a password of eight characters. Note that there is not much decrease in FRR due to the use of shuffling. The main improvement is in the FAR, which becomes zero, which means that the systems become more secure by using the shuffling.

The most appropriate work to compare with the proposed system is that by Nandakumar and Jain [24]. In their system, information from iris and fingerprints is combined and they succeed to obtain keys with 49-bit entropy while the verification error rates are FAR $= 0.02$ % and FRR $= 1.80$ %. For the proposed system, at FAR $= 0$ %, FRR $= 0.18$ % and the key entropy is 147 bits. This security analysis of the proposed system in terms of entropy is presented in the next subsection.

6.4.2.3 Security Analysis of the Multi-unit (Two-Iris) Type System

Since the main aim of the system is to provide security, it is required to analyze the security of the system. The entropy of the key can give us an estimate of the difficulty which an attacker has to face to obtain the key without having the proper credentials. It also indicates the strength of the template protection mechanism because once the attacker has the key, he can inverse the stored template and obtain the reference biometric data. Though the key is generated randomly at enrollment time, a lot of redundancy is added by the ECC and hence its entropy is bound to decrease. We use the same approach as used by Hao et al. [9] to estimate the entropy. They used the sphere packing bound [21] to roughly estimate the number of brute force attempts required for an attacker to guess the key $\mathbf{K}$ correctly. Let N be the number of degrees of freedom in the data being XORed with the pseudo code θ_{ps}, and P is the fraction of this information corresponding to the error correction capacity (i.e., $P = N \times$ error correction capacity). Then the number of brute force attacks an attacker needs to carry out is estimated by Equation (6.4) as

$$BF \approx \frac{2^N}{\binom{N}{P}}. \tag{6.4}$$

The number of degrees of freedom can be estimated by the procedure given by Daugman [6]. The iris codes used in our experiments are 1,188 bits long. We estimate the degrees of freedom in the iris codes to be 561. Collectively, in two iris codes, we have 1,122 degrees of freedom. In the weighted error correction configuration in the multi-iris system, the total amount of error correction is $\approx$30 %. If $N = 1,122$ and $P = 0.3 \times N \approx 336$, applying (6.4), an impostor needs approximately

$$BF \approx \frac{2^N}{\binom{N}{P}} \approx \frac{2^{1122}}{\binom{1122}{336}} \approx 2^{140}, \tag{6.5}$$

brute force calculations to successfully get the cryptographic key. Thus the entropy of the key is 140 bits, which is much higher than any other system reported in literature.

The shuffling scheme applied in the two-iris system needs a 49-bit shuffling key. This key is randomly generated and is protected by a password. We propose to use a randomly generated 8-character password which can have 52-bit entropy [4]. The shuffling process is embedded into the error correction process and hence the individual entropies add up together resulting in a total key entropy of $140 + 49 = 189$ bits. Thus the entropy of the key is

$$\text{Entropy} = \min(\text{Length}(\mathbf{K}), 189) \text{ bits.} \tag{6.6}$$

Recently, Stoianov [31] has proposed an attack on the iris-based key regeneration scheme of Kanade et al. [13] which targets the zero insertion scheme. This attack takes into consideration the known positions of the zeros inserted into the iris codes. Using this attack, a large amount of errors in the Hadamard codewords can be corrected and hence the crypto-biometric key can be recovered. The same zero insertion scheme is applied in the multi-unit type system described in this chapter. However, in this scheme, the de-shuffling process is done after the Hadamard codes error correction level. Therefore, even if an attacker successfully decodes the Hadamard codewords, he still needs to overcome the security offered by the shuffling/de-shuffling process. Moreover, this scheme involves multiple biometric information sources. The zeros are inserted into only one iris code, while the other iris code is left as it is. This provides another level of protection against the attack reported by Stoianov.

In order to carry out experimental security evaluation, we defined two extreme scenarios: (1) stolen biometric scenario, where an impostor always provides a stolen biometric sample of the genuine user, and (2) stolen key scenario, in which the impostor always provides a stolen shuffling key of the genuine user.

In the stolen biometric scenario, the FAR of the system remains unchanged (i.e., FAR $= 0\%$). The shuffling process prevents the impostor from being accepted when he provides the correct biometric data but a wrong shuffling key. Thus, use of shuffling completely eliminates the threat caused by compromised biometric data.

In the other security scenario, stolen key scenario, the system still has two iris codes which provide the security. The performance in this situation degrades but it is equivalent to that of the system without shuffling. Moreover, the performance degradation is only in terms of increase in FAR. The FRR remains unchanged even if the shuffling key is stolen. This is a distinct advantage of the proposed system.

6.5 Multi-modal Type Multi-biometrics Based Key Regeneration

6.5.1 Algorithm for Multi-modal Biometrics Based Key Regeneration

Multi-modal biometric systems combine biometric information from different traits. In this case, an attacker who wants to break into the system by creating fake biometric samples needs more efforts. Therefore, having multi-modal biometrics can significantly increase the security of the system. Combination of information from two biometric traits in the feature domain results in increase of the length of the feature vector. Additionally, the entropy of the crypto-bio keys also increases. We adapt the *FeaLingECc* scheme described in Sect. 6.3 in order to combine the information

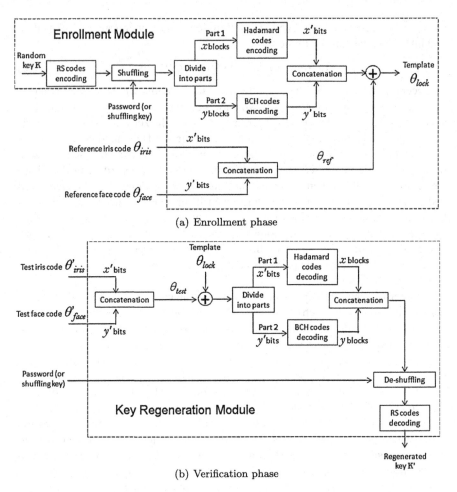

(a) Enrollment phase

(b) Verification phase

Fig. 6.6 Schematic diagram of the multi-modal biometrics-based template protection scheme using *FeaLingECc*: (**a**) Enrollment phase, (**b**) Key regeneration phase

from an iris and a face image of a person. The length of the iris feature vector is 1,188 bits, while that of the face feature vector is 3,200 bits. Following the notations of the general scheme described in Sect. 6.3, we consider iris as Biometric-1 and face as Biometric-2. Hadamard codes are used as Level-1 ECC for iris while Bose, Ray-Chaudhuri, Hocquengem (BCH) codes are used for face. These ECC are selected according to the Hamming distance distributions of the corresponding biometric data. Reed–Solomon (RS) codes are used as Level-2 ECC, which are common for iris and face. The schematic diagrams of the enrollment and key regeneration phase of the proposed multi-modal biometrics-based system are shown in Fig. 6.6(a) and 6.6(b), respectively.

The basic functioning of this scheme is the same as described in Sect. 6.3. But the involvement of two different types of biometric data raises many design complications. The two biometric data (iris and face) being combined are different in nature. The amount of variabilities, which is treated as errors, is different for iris and face images. In key regeneration systems, the goal is to correct only the intra-user variabilities. The amount of such errors to be corrected is highly dependent on the biometric data set. The error correction capacities for each of the biometric traits need to be set according to their respective Hamming distance distributions for genuine and impostor comparisons.

6.5.2 Experimental Setup—Multi-modal Biometrics Based Key Regeneration System

In this work, we created a virtual database created from two publicly available databases: the NIST-ICE database [26] for iris, and the NIST-FRGCv2 database [25] for face. In this selected data set, there are 175 subjects having five samples each of iris and face images. The face images are taken from the controlled data set of the FRGCv2 database. For each subject, data pairs are formed containing one iris image and one face image corresponding to that subject. Thus, we have five such pairs per subject for 175 subjects. For genuine comparisons, each data pair is compared with every other data pair corresponding to the same subject. Similarly, each data pair is compared with every other data pair of every other subject for impostor comparisons. This protocol results in 1,750 genuine comparisons and 380,625 impostor comparisons. For the sake of fair comparison with uni-biometric systems, similar protocol is followed to test the uni-biometrics-based systems' performance in this chapter.

We used a Gabor filter-based approach to extract features from the face image [19]. The face image is first geometrically normalized using the CSU Face Recognition System [1], and then processed using log-Gabor filters having four scales and eight orientations using the MATLAB source code available at [18]. Magnitude of the filtered output is calculated, downsampled, and concatenated to form a 3,200-element feature vector. The values in this vector are then binarized to obtain a 3,200-bit string called face code. The binarization process used is fairly simple. The median of the values in a feature vector is taken as a threshold for that feature vector. The elements having higher value than the threshold are made one while the remaining are made zeros.

By observing the Hamming distance distributions for genuine and impostor comparisons for iris on the development data set, we know that the iris data need nearly 35 % error correction. For face, we used only the controlled subset of the FRGCv2 data set. The error correction required on this subset is nearly 21 %. Note that these quantities of error correction requirements are specific to the data set concerned and will change according to the modality and acquisition conditions. Also the amount of error correction required for the iris is higher than for the face. However, this does not impact the verification performance. The verification performance depends on the separation between genuine and impostor Hamming distance distributions (see Table 6.4).

As shown in [13], Hadamard codes along with the zero insertion scheme can achieve the 35 % error correction requirement for iris. For face, BCH codes can be applied for correcting the 21 % errors. Therefore, we use Hadamard codes as Level-1 ECC for iris and BCH codes as Level-1 ECC for face. The Level-2 ECC are Reed–Solomon (RS) codes which is a common level for iris and face. But the error correction scheme in the proposed system is a cascaded structure where the dimensions of the Level-1 and Level-2 codes must be compatible. Each of the three ECC used in the system (RS, BCH, and Hadamard codes) has its own dimensional restrictions.

The Hadamard codes (which are used for iris) have a fixed relation between input and output size: a block of m bits is converted into a block of 2^{m-1} bits. The Reed–Solomon codes of block size m bits can have a maximum of 2^{m-1} blocks. The BCH codes having ≈ 21 % error correction capacity are: BCH(127, 15, 27), BCH(255, 21, 55), BCH(511, 28, 111), BCH(1023, 36, 223), BCH(2047, 56, 443), etc. The suitable ECC sizes also depend on the dimensions of the individual biometric feature vectors. For example, the face code is 3,200 bit. It has to be truncated such that its length is an integer multiple of the BCH code output size. Similarly, the effective iris code length must be an integer multiple of the Hadamard code output size (32 or 64 bits). Moreover, from our experiments, we know that the iris system performs better (from biometric recognition point of view) than the face system and hence, it is desirable to apply higher weights to iris than to face. This means that more blocks of RS codes output should be used for iris than for face.

Taking all these requirements into consideration, we fixed the size of the RS codes block to be equal to $m = 7$. The output of the RS codes encoder is also in form of blocks each of which is 7-bit. Hadamard codes of input size $m = 7$ should be used for compatibility. The output of these Hadamard codes is 64-bits. The length of the iris code after zero insertion is 1984 bits and thus there can be 31 blocks of Hadamard codes. This also means that 31 blocks of RS codes output are used for iris. The BCH codes should be selected such that the input size of BCH codes is an integer multiple of seven (7) but also keeping in mind that the total number of RS code blocks required for face remains less than 31. BCH(127, 15, 27) and BCH(255, 21, 55) will require 50 and 36 RS code blocks which is more than that required for iris. Therefore, these codes cannot be employed in the system. Hence we applied the next two possible BCH codes: BCH(511, 28, 111) and BCH(1023, 36, 223).

In case of BCH(511, 28, 111), four RS codes output blocks are concatenated to form a single input block. The 3,200-bit face code is truncated to 3,066 bits which is an integer multiple of 511. There are six such BCH code blocks which require 24 RS codes output blocks. Thus, the total number of output blocks required in the RS codes is $31 + 24 = 55$. The iris part has $31/55 = 56$ % weight in the final verification decision while the face part has 44 % weight.

For the other possible BCH codes, BCH(1023, 36, 223), five RS codes output blocks are concatenated and a zero is appended to it in order to obtain the required 36-bit input block. There can be three such BCH blocks requiring 15 RS

Table 6.4 Baseline biometric systems' user verification performances in terms of EER in % on subsets of NIST-ICE and NIST-FRGCv2 databases; values in bracket indicate the error margins for 90 % confidence interval; Baseline—corresponds to baseline biometric system; Shuffled—the shuffling scheme is applied. Results previously published in [16]

Exp.	Iris	Face	Iris+face
Baseline	1.29 [±0.23]	6.53 [±0.52]	1.06 [±0.22]
Shuffled	0.35 [±0.12]	0	0

code blocks. Thus the total number of RS code blocks is $31 + 15 = 46$. The iris is given 67 % weight in this scenario while the face is given 33 % weight.

It is also possible to combine BCH codes of different dimensions to apply different weights. For example, in a third setting, we applied 61 % weight to iris and 39 % to face. In order to achieve this, we employed one set of BCH(2047, 56, 443) codes in combination of four sets of BCH(255, 21, 55) codes. This requires $(8 + 12 =)20$ RS code blocks.

The experimental performance evaluation along with security analysis of this system is presented in the following subsection.

6.5.3 Results and Security Analysis for the Multi-modal (Iris and Face) Type System

The experimental results and theoretical as well as experimental security analysis are presented in this section.

6.5.3.1 Experimental Results of the Multi-modal (Iris and Face) Type System

For comparison purposes, the baseline biometric systems' verification performances are presented in Table 6.4. The BioSecure tool for performance evaluation [2] is used to calculate the EER and confidence intervals. This tool takes the number of comparisons and the match scores into account to calculate the error bounds on the verification error rates. The high improvement in the face verification system after shuffling is due to the high impact of shuffling on impostor face distribution. Shuffling makes the impostor distribution random. The randomness in un-shuffled iris data is higher than that of the face data, and hence, the impact of shuffling on face data is higher than that on iris data.

As said earlier, we evaluated the multi-modal system with three sets of experiments by applying different weights. In Set-1, RS codes having 55 blocks at the output are used. 31 out of these 55 (i.e., ≈56 %) are used for iris and remaining 24 (i.e., ≈44 %) are for face. The BCH codes used in this set are BCH(511, 28, 111). Since it requires 28-bit input, four RS code blocks are combined to form that block resulting in a total of 24 RS code blocks for face.

Table 6.5 Results for the proposed multi-modal biometrics-based key regeneration system—Set-1 (iris weight = 56 %, face weight = 44 %). FRR and FAR values are in %. $\|K\|$ indicates length of key K in bits; t_s denotes the error correction capacity of RS codes. Results previously published in [16]

t_s	$\|K\|$	Without shuffling		With shuffling	
		FRR	FAR	FRR	FAR
3	343	7.54	2.93	7.54	0
9	259	1.94	20.80	1.94	0
12	217	0.91	36.43	0.91	0
16	161	0.17	62.93	0.17	0

Table 6.6 Results for the proposed multi-modal biometrics-based key regeneration system—Set-2 (iris weight = 61 %, face weight = 39 %). Other signs have the same meaning as in Table 6.5

t_s	$\|K\|$	Without shuffling		With shuffling	
		FRR	FAR	FRR	FAR
3	315	6.46	3.89	6.46	0
6	273	2.74	13.41	2.74	0
8	245	1.66	22.70	1.66	0
10	217	0.86	32.70	0.86	0

In the second setting, Set-2, 61 % weight is applied to iris and 39 % is applied to face. The errors in face data are corrected by a combination of BCH(2047, 56, 443) and BCH(255, 21, 55) codes. BCH(2047, 56, 443) require concatenation of eight RS code blocks while each of the BCH(255, 21, 55) requires three RS code blocks. The total number of RS code blocks required in this setting is 51 out of which, 31 are used for iris and 20 for face.

In the third setting, Set-3, RS codes with 46-block output are selected, and 31 of them are used for iris (i.e., ≈67 %) and remaining 15 blocks for face (i.e., 33 %). BCH codes of higher output size are used so that the number of blocks coming from BCH codes will reduce. We selected BCH(1023, 36, 223) for which the error correction capacity is nearly the same. The 36-bit input required for these BCH codes is obtained by concatenating five RS code blocks appended with a zero. Thus, at the time of decoding, the last bit of the decoded value is discarded.

The results for these three experiments are reported in Tables 6.5, 6.6 and 6.7, respectively. For all the settings, we also carried out experiments without using shuffling, which are also reported.

The improvement in performance over uni-biometrics-based systems is threefold:

- better verification accuracy, e.g., at FRR of 0.91 %, FAR = 0 % for multi-biometric system while for iris-based uni-biometric system, FRR = 0.86 % at

Table 6.7 Results for the proposed multi-modal biometrics-based key regeneration system—Set-3 (iris weight = 67 %, face weight = 33 %). Other signs have the same meaning as in Table 6.5. Results previously published in [16]

t_s	$\|K\|$	Without shuffling		With shuffling	
		FRR	FAR	FRR	FAR
1	308	8.23	1.31	8.23	0
2	294	5.48	3.80	5.48	0
8	210	0.91	29.80	0.91	0
11	168	0.11	49.33	0.11	0

FAR = 0.21 %; similarly, for face-based uni-biometric system, FRR = 7.08 % at FAR = 0,

- longer keys, e.g., 186 and 217 bit keys for uni- and multi-biometric systems, respectively, at accuracies said above,
- higher key entropy, 183-bit for multi-biometric system while 83 for iris-based uni-biometric system.

The security of the multi-modal biometrics-based system is analyzed in the next subsection.

6.5.3.2 Security Analysis of the Multi-modal (Iris and Face) Type System

Theoretical as well as experimental security evaluation of the proposed system is presented in this section. Using the procedure of Daugman [6], the number of degrees of freedom in the iris and face codes are estimated to be equal to 556 and 243, respectively. Note that this estimation depends on the impostor Hamming distance distribution and can change with the data set being used for evaluation. The total number of degrees of freedom in the fused feature vector is $N = 556 + 243 = 799$. In total, the system can correct 27 % errors in this code (i.e., $P = N * 0.27 \approx 216$). Applying (6.4), an impostor needs,

$$\text{BF} \approx \frac{2^N}{\binom{N}{P}} \approx \frac{2^{799}}{\binom{799}{216}} \approx 2^{131}, \tag{6.7}$$

brute force calculations to obtain the key. Thus the entropy contributed by the biometric information is 131 bits. The shuffling scheme, which employs a shuffling key obtained with a password can add up to 52 bits of entropy to this estimate resulting in $131 + 52 = 183$ bits entropy. Therefore, the total entropy estimate for the multi-modal type key regeneration system can be given as

$$\text{Entropy} = \min\bigl(\text{Length}(\mathbf{K}), 183\bigr) \text{ bits.} \tag{6.8}$$

This entropy is significantly higher than that of the uni-biometrics-based system. The entropy of the keys reported for the iris-based uni-biometric system in [13] is 83 bits.

Experimental security evaluation of the multi-modal type key regeneration system is carried out in a way similar to that performed for the two-iris system. In the stolen biometric scenario, the performance of the system remains unchanged. None of the impostors who provide stolen biometric data along with a wrong shuffling key is accepted by the system. However, in the stolen key scenario, the FAR is equal to that of the system without shuffling.

An interesting observation from the results in the stolen key scenarios is that the system can better resist such attacks when higher weight is applied to the better performing modality. For example, in stolen key scenario, the FAR is equal to 36.43 % at FRR = 0.91 % for Set-1 where iris is given 56 % weight. At a similar FRR (0.86 %), the FAR is 32.70 % in the Set-3 when iris is given 61 % weight in Set-2. While at the FRR = 0.91 %, the FAR is equal to 29.80 % for Set-2 where iris is given 67 % weight.

6.6 Conclusions and Perspectives

Using multi-biometrics has several advantages over uni-biometrics such as: better verification accuracy, larger feature space to accommodate more subjects, and higher security against spoofing. We exploit these advantages and employ multi-biometrics for obtaining high entropy keys. Additionally, the systems described in this chapter also protect the biometric templates and enhance security and privacy.

In order to have keys with higher entropy and better security, we combine the biometric information in feature domain. We propose a novel method of *Feature Level Fusion* through Weighted *Error Correction* (*FeaLingECc*). With this method, different weights can be applied to different biometric data. The shuffling scheme, which we applied earlier to the biometric data, is used in this system to randomize the error correcting codes data which helps make the system more secure. Additionally, the shuffling scheme induces revocability, template diversity, and privacy protection in the system.

Two systems are discussed: (1) a multi-unit type system, and (2) a multi-modal type system. Information from the left and right iris of a person is combined in the multi-unit type system to obtain long and high entropy crypto-bio keys. The second scheme is a multi-modal biometrics-based system in which information from iris and face is combined.

The parameters (choice of ECC and correction capacity) of the systems are first tuned on development databases and the systems are evaluated on the evaluation databases. For the two-iris tests, we used the NIST-ICE database. On this database, we obtain 147-bit keys having 147-bit entropy with 0 % FAR and 0.18 % FRR.

The multi-modal system (iris + face) is evaluated on a virtual database created by combining images from the NIST-ICE and NIST-FRGCv2 databases. We succeed to obtain 210-bit keys having 183-bit entropy at 0.91 % FRR and 0 % FAR. There is a significant improvement over uni-modal biometrics-based systems, specifically in terms of the key entropy. The key entropies for iris- and face-based uni-modal systems are 83 and 110 bits, respectively, while the entropy for the multi-iris-based system is 147 bits and for iris-face-based system, it is 183 bits.

The proposed scheme can be adapted to other biometric modalities. The feature level fusion combined with weighted error correction method allows the fusion of biometric modalities having different performances (e.g., face + iris). This opens up new directions for combining biometric information from different sources and having different dimensions.

References

1. Beveridge JR, Bolme D, Raper BA, Teixeira M (2005) The CSU face identification evaluation system. Machine Vision and Applications 16(2):128–138
2. Biosecure Tool (2007) Performance evaluation of a biometric verification system. Online. http://svnext.it-sudparis.eu/svnview2-eph/ref_syst/Tools/PerformanceEvaluation/doc/
3. Boyen X (2004) Reusable cryptographic fuzzy extractors. In: 11th ACM Conference on Computer and Communications Security (CCS)
4. Burr WE, Dodson DF, Polk WT (2006) Electronic authentication guideline. Recommendations of the National Institute of Standards and Technology
5. Cimato S, Gamassi M, Piuri V, Sassi R, Scotti F (2008) Privacy-aware biometrics: design and implementation of a multimodal verification system. In: Annual Computer Security Applications Conference (ACSAC). doi:10.1109/ACSAC.2008.13
6. Daugman J (2003) The importance of being random: statistical principles of iris recognition. Pattern Recognition 36(2):279–291
7. Dodis Y, Reyzin L, Smith A (2004) Fuzzy extractors: how to generate strong keys from biometrics and other noisy data. In: Proceedings of the Eurocrypt 2004, pp 523–540
8. Fu B, Yang SX, Li J, Hu D (2009) Multibiometric cryptosystem: model structure and performance analysis. IEEE Transactions on Information Forensics and Security 4(4):867–882
9. Hao F, Anderson R, Daugman J (2006) Combining crypto with biometrics effectively. IEEE Transactions on Computers 55(9):1081–1088
10. Jain AK, Nandakumar K, Nagar A (2008) Biometric template security. EURASIP Journal on Advances in Signal Processing 2008:579416. 17 pp. doi:10.1155/2008/579416
11. Juels A, Sudan M (2002) A fuzzy vault scheme. In: Lapidoth A, Teletar E (eds) Proc IEEE Int Symp Information Theory. IEEE Press, New York, p 408
12. Juels A, Wattenberg M (1999) A fuzzy commitment scheme. In: Proceedings of the Sixth ACM Conference on Computer and Communication Security (CCCS), pp 28–36
13. Kanade S, Camara D, Krichen E, Petrovska-Delacrétaz D, Dorizzi B (2008) Three factor scheme for biometric-based cryptographic key regeneration using iris. In: The 6th Biometrics Symposium (BSYM)
14. Kanade S, Petrovska-Delacrétaz D, Dorizzi B (2009) Cancelable iris biometrics and using error correcting codes to reduce variability in biometric data. In: IEEE Computer Society Conference on Computer Vision and Pattern Recognition
15. Kanade S, Petrovska-Delacrétaz D, Dorizzi B (2009) Multi-biometrics based cryptographic key regeneration scheme. In: IEEE International Conference on Biometrics: Theory, Applications, and Systems (BTAS)
16. Kanade S, Petrovska-Delacrétaz D, Dorizzi B (2010) Obtaining cryptographic keys using feature level fusion of iris and face biometrics for secure user authentication. In: IEEE CVPR Workshop on Biometrics
17. Kelkboom E, Zhou X, Breebaart J, Veldhuis R, Busch C (2009) Multi-algorithm fusion with template protection. In: IEEE Second International Conference on Biometrics Theory, Applications and Systems

18. Kovesi P (2005) Matlab and octave functions for computer vision and image processing. Online. http://www.csse.uwa.edu.au/~pk/Research/MatlabFns/
19. Lades M, Vorbrüuggen JC, Buhmann J, Lange J, von der Malsburg C, Wüurtz RP, Konen W (1993) Distortion invariant object recognition in the dynamic link architecture. IEEE Transactions on Computers 42(3):300–311
20. Lumini A, Nanni L (2007) An improved biohashing for human authentication. Pattern Recognition 40(3):1057–1065. doi:10.1016/j.patcog.2006.05.030
21. MacWilliams FJ, Sloane NJA (1991) Theory of Error-Correcting Codes. North Holland, Amsterdam
22. Maiorana E, Campisi P, Ortega-Garcia J, Neri A (2008) Cancelable biometrics for HMM-based signature recognition. In: IEEE Conference on Biometrics: Theory, Applications and Systems (BTAS)
23. Nandakumar K (2008) Multibiometric systems: fusion strategies and template security. Phd thesis, Department of Computer Science and Engineering, Michigan State University
24. Nandakumar K, Jain AK (2008) Multibiometric template security using fuzzy vault. In: IEEE Second International Conference on Biometrics: Theory, Applications and Systems
25. National Institute of Science and Technology (NIST) (2005) Face recognition grand challenge. http://www.frvt.org/FRGC/
26. National Institute of Science and Technology (NIST) (2005) Iris challenge evaluation. http://iris.nist.gov/ice
27. Online. http://svnext.it-sudparis.eu/svnview2-eph/ref_syst/
28. Petrovska-Delacrétaz D, Chollet G, Dorizzi B (eds) (2009) Guide to Biometric Reference Systems and Performance Evaluation. Springer, Berlin
29. Ratha NK, Chikkerur S, Connell JH, Bolle RM (2007) Generating cancelable fingerprint templates. IEEE Transactions on Pattern Analysis and Machine Intelligence 29(4):561–572. doi:10.1109/TPAMI.2007.1004
30. Ross AA, Nandakumar K, Jain AK (2006) Handbook of Multibiometrics. International Series on Biometrics. Springer, Berlin
31. Stoianov A (2010) Security of error correcting code for biometric encryption (critical note). In: Eighth Annual International Conference on Privacy, Security and Trust
32. Sutcu Y, Li Q, Memon N (2007) Secure biometric templates from fingerprint-face features. In: IEEE Conference on Computer Vision and Pattern Recognition, pp 1–6. doi:10.1109/CVPR.2007.383385

Chapter 7
Privacy-Aware Processing of Biometric Templates by Means of Secure Two-Party Computation

Riccardo Lazzeretti, Pierluigi Failla, and Mauro Barni

Abstract The use of biometric data for person identification and access control is gaining more and more popularity. Handling biometric data, however, requires particular care, since biometric data is indissolubly tied to the identity of the owner hence raising important security and privacy issues. This chapter focuses on the latter, presenting an innovative approach that, by relying on tools borrowed from Secure Two Party Computation (STPC) theory, permits to process the biometric data in encrypted form, thus eliminating any risk that private biometric information is leaked during an identification process. The basic concepts behind STPC are reviewed together with the basic cryptographic primitives needed to achieve privacy-aware processing of biometric data in a STPC context. The two main approaches proposed so far, namely homomorphic encryption and garbled circuits, are discussed and the way such techniques can be used to develop a full biometric matching protocol described. Some general guidelines to be used in the design of a privacy-aware biometric system are given, so as to allow the reader to choose the most appropriate tools depending on the application at hand.

7.1 Introduction

Our world is becoming increasingly interconnected and by using the Internet we are able to share everything with everyone. Social networks (e.g. Facebook, LinkedIn, MySpace, Twitter) whereby people share thoughts, events, photos, and videos with friends are the most evident sign of this general trend. It is clear that behind the distribution and storage of such a massive amount of data there are several security and privacy issues. Potentially privacy sensitive data such as our age, health, preferences, locations, politics, and religious views are being stored in computers that we

R. Lazzeretti (✉) · P. Failla · M. Barni
Information Engineering and Mathematical Science Department, University of Siena, Siena, Italy
e-mail: riccardo.lazzeretti@gmail.com

P. Failla
e-mail: pierluigi.failla@gmail.com

M. Barni
e-mail: barni@dii.unisi.it

P. Campisi (ed.), *Security and Privacy in Biometrics*,
DOI 10.1007/978-1-4471-5230-9_7, © Springer-Verlag London 2013

do not own and we do not control. Even worse, the data is generally transferred to third parties in plain format (think about uploading photos or videos on Facebook): people believe in the good will of third parties to behave and handle their data in accordance to laws but also according to their own privacy policies that very often people do not know or do not care about. It is clear that these new platforms and networks are extremely vulnerable to private data disclosures. Current ad-hoc security methodologies, combined with a lack of security sometimes astonishing, will lead to more weaknesses as system complexity and the amount of to-be-handled data increases during the coming years. On the other side, laws aiming at protecting private data are continuously emanated, but legal assurance does not provide a complete answer. Once our private data, preferences or other sensitive information have been compromised, it is virtually impossible to "make them private" again. It is vital that privacy and security of sensitive data as well as its subsequent use be guaranteed a priori.

In some cases, privacy and security constraints are very stringent. Think about traveling. Many people in everyday life use airplanes to move around the world and as everyone knows following the September 11th attacks, controls in airports have been intensified. New electronic passports have been introduced for improved border controls containing personal data, including a *face picture* and *fingerprints*. Each time someone takes a flight the above information is made available to the airport staff and to the police for identity check. To exemplify how security and privacy can easily come at odds, let us consider the following scenario. There are two parties, say an Intelligence Agency and a remote controller (for example the security staff of an Airport). The Agency wants to trace the movements of a suspect person. To do so, it exploits some biometric information of the suspect person. In particular it tries to match the biometric sample it owns with the biometric of the people that are going to take a flight. The Agency wants to protect the identity of the suspect person (and hence the biometries stored in its database) while the Airport wants to protect the privacy of the passengers. From the point of view of the client, the question is: *if I am a good guy, why should I reveal my biometric data to other parties?* At the same time flight safety must be ensured, and from the point of view of the Agency, any possible measure to reduce the risk should be taken. More generally, we can affirm that the use of biometric data is becoming a common approach to handle people identities (at Disney World Resort in Florida customers use the fingerprint scanning for the clients that own a multiple-days ticket to ensure the non-re-usability [21]), thus raising the call for the adoption of stringent privacy protection measures.

Actually, when dealing with biometric data, the trade-off between the security of the system that needs to be protected and the privacy of the users who provides the biometries is not balanced and the privacy constraints are often overlooked for the sake of security. Often government and law enforcement agencies can access personal information to protect public safety and national security: however, abuses of personal information can cause untold harms, wasted resources, and generally lead to the detriment of society. Hence, there is a high demand for technologies that permit to protect the privacy of users while preserving the possibility of performing biometric analysis with the aim of achieving a greater security.

The most obvious and well-known way to secure personal data is to encrypt and store it in a (trusted) database. Such an approach works only when the owner of the data and the party in charge of processing or storing it trust each other, and the goal of the cryptographic module is only to protect the data from a third party. This is not the case in many practical situations where the owner of the to-be-protected data and the party that is in charge of storing or processing it do not trust each other. Possible examples include the storage of biometric information in a central database, the processing of personal (e.g. medical) data for statistical analysis, or the analysis of people behaviors (e.g. log files) for inspection purposes. How is it possible to combine the request for privacy and the need to analyze personal information for a legitimate purpose (possibly in the interest of the data owner itself)?

7.1.1 Processing Encrypted Signals

An effective and elegant way to answer the above question, it is to process the data while it is encrypted. In the last 30 years[1] the cryptographic community has worked hardly to build a set of tools that allow to compute with encrypted data. Though this may seem an almost impossible task, some solutions have been put forward recently by relying on the use of:

- *Homomorphic Encryption* whereby some algebraic operations are mapped into simple operations to be applied in the encrypted domain,
- *Secure Multi Party Computation—SMPC* where two or more non-trusted parties engage in an interactive protocol to carry out a computation without revealing their own inputs. The special case where only two parties are involved, such as a Client and a Server, is of particular interest for biometric applications and is usually referred to as Secure Two Party Computation (STPC).

Though the possibility of processing encrypted data (mainly by means of homomorphic encryption) has been advanced more than 30 years ago [63], processing encrypted biometric signals poses some new problems due to the peculiarities of this kind of data with respect to the type of data commonly encountered in the cryptographic literature, e.g. alphanumeric strings or bit sequences. The most straightforward difference is that biometric signals are often represented by means of real numbers (and processed by means of floating point arithmetic), while all the available cryptosystems work on integer rings. Other important differences include:

- the non-exact nature of biometric signals that can change significantly from a measurement to the other due to the presence of noise, time variability, pose, gesture etc. This property should be contrasted with the bit-precise nature of the data cryptosystems usually deal with;

---

[1]The first mention is in [63] 1978 by Rivest et al.

- the essential role played by the temporal or spatial structure of signals, in fact the spatio-temporal dependency between samples of the same process is a core peculiarity of signals.
- the large size of many signals such as audio files, still images, and video sequences, which poses very critical constraints on the complexity and storage requirements.

Despite the above difficulties, some recent studies have shown that the application of non-trivial signal processing tools to encrypted signals is practically feasible.

The great majority of cryptographic primitives used to process encrypted signals relies on two basic mechanisms: homomorphic encryption [62] and garbled circuits [68].

Homomorphic cryptosystems have the property that some elementary algebraic operations in the plain domain are mapped into elementary operations in the encrypted domain. For instance, in the Pailler cryptosystem [58], an addition in the plain domain corresponds to a multiplication in the encrypted domain. Other examples of homomorphic cryptosystems include RSA [64] that is multiplicatively homomorphic on product, Damgaard-Jurik's generalization of Pailler's cryptosystem [24] and the Bresson et al. cryptosystem [18] (that is additively homomorphic). If a homomorphic cryptosystem is used, it is possible for a party that does not posses the decryption key to perform some simple operations on the encrypted messages.

The current state of the art in homomorphic encryption does not allow the efficient simultaneous preservation of addition and multiplication. As a matter of fact a very recent result by Gentry in [32] shows that algebraically homomorphic cryptosystems are possible, however, actually such schemes are of theoretical interest only, given their extremely high complexity. Due to the unavailability of efficient algebraically homomorphic cryptosystems, homomorphic encryption does not allow the application of non-linear operators, which, on the other side, are essential ingredients of most non-trivial operation to be applied to the encrypted signals. To avoid the above limitation, the general approach is to use an interactive protocol whereby a Client and a Server collaborate and exchange data to securely compute a given functionality.

Garbled circuits have been introduced by Yao in 1982 [68] and later refined in [36], where it is shown that any function can be computed in a secure manner by implementing a boolean circuit of secure gates. With Yao's circuit approach one can evaluate circuits in a privacy preserving scenario by using either private-key or public-key primitives. Approaches based on symmetric primitives are several orders of magnitude faster than the asymmetric approaches. In its basic (two party computation) form, garbled circuits allow two users, namely the Client ($\mathcal{C}$) and the Server ($\mathcal{S}$), to securely evaluate a known function (usually in form of a boolean circuit) using their private inputs. In other words, executing the evaluation protocol does not reveal any knowledge about the inputs beyond what can be deduced merely from the computed output(s). The circuit approach can be relatively efficient in different security models even if it requires to transfer a large amount of data from one party to the other which yields an increase in the communication complexity of the protocol.

7.1.1.1 Application Scenarios

The techniques briefly outlined above have been used in a variety of application scenarios.

Biometry matching is one of the most important topics wherein secure computation can be used. In [27, 28] a privacy-enhanced face recognition system is proposed. The proposed construction is based on homomorphic encryption and allows to hide the biometric data using an encrypted version of Eigenfaces-based matching, and it is able to hide the result of the match to the server that actually performs the matching operation. A different STPC face matching algorithm based on garbled circuits has been proposed in [65]. Similarly, in [57] an ad hoc system for face recognition in a privacy preserving framework is proposed, specifically designed for usage in secure computation.

In [6, 7] the authors consider a scenario where a client equipped with a fingerprint reader is interested to learn if the acquired fingerprint belongs to a database of authorized entities managed by a server. Although privacy-preserving biometric identification usually focuses on selecting the best matching identity in the database, the solution proposed in [6, 7] also allows to select and report all the enrolled identities whose distance to the user's fingercode is under a given threshold.

In remote diagnosis [19] secure computation can be used to preserve the privacy of the patients. In [5] a privacy-preserving system is described whereby the Server classifies an ElectroCardioGram (ECG) signal without learning any information about the ECG signal and the Client is prevented from gaining knowledge about the classification algorithm used by the Server. The system relies on the concept of Linear Branching Programs (LBP) and a related cryptographic protocol for secure evaluation of private LBPs [5, 8] based on homomorphic encryption and garbled circuits. The paper faces the study of the trade-off between signal representation accuracy and system complexity both from practical and theoretical perspectives. As a result, the inputs to the system are represented with the minimum number of bits ensuring the same classification accuracy of a plain implementation. In [10] the same classification task is addressed by applying a neural network to the encrypted ECG signal. Quality evaluation of the ECG signals in the encrypted domain has been addressed in [9] to avoid that noisy signals are processed returning wrong classification results.

Many other application fields can benefit from privacy preserving techniques. In [30], a novel technique has been proposed to compute the well-known A^* algorithm, on the encrypted weights of a graph. A^* is a *best first* graph search algorithm that uses an heuristic function helping to choose the best candidates during the traversing of common graphs [39]. Graphs are data structures widely used to represent: social networks; computer networks; geographic maps; game moves; possible paths in a given environment and many more, and hence working on encrypted graphs may find several interesting applications. In the setting considered in [39] two parties are interested to compute the shortest path between two nodes in a context where: (i) part of the graph topology (only the number of nodes) is publicly known, (ii) the client knows the weights of each edge and (iii) the Server owns the heuristic used for searching. The Client wants to keep secret the weights and the Server the heuristic used.

In [31], a scenario in which two parties are interested in computing a given functionality in a privacy preserving way has been considered, but this functionality needs a sub-protocol that computes the *Gram–Schmidt Orthogonalization* on encrypted vectors. There are a lot of applications in which this kind of sub-protocol could be used as a basic privacy preserving primitive, including: QR decomposition [38]; linear least squares problems [15]; face recognition [70]; improving performances of neural networks [56]; wavelets computation [22]; principal component analysis [66] and image compression [50].

In [13] the authors analyze the implementation of the Fourier transform in a privacy preserving scenario. In [42] an efficient buyer-seller protocol embedding an encrypted watermark in a content is proposed, protecting the watermark secrets from the buyer and preventing false infringement accusations by the seller.

Other applications include data mining [1, 47]; secure compression [41]; access to encrypted databases [20]; encrypted strings comparison by using Levenshtein distance [61], etc.

7.1.2 Processing of Biometric Signals

Most tasks in biometric signal processing are based on pattern recognition, it is hence necessary to develop protocols that permit to apply at least the most basic pattern recognition operators to encrypted signals. The number of tools and tasks usually encompassed under the Pattern Recognition umbrella is virtually endless. An exhaustive discussion of how such tools could be applied in the encrypted domain is then impractical. For this reason we focus our discussion on the pattern recognition task most commonly used in biometric systems, namely *Pattern Matching*. There are two basic forms of Pattern Matching: (i) *Verification*, as a *one to one* matching problem, and (ii) *Identification*, as a typical *one to many* matching problem.

More specifically, the verification problem can be defined as follows: given two patterns V_1 and V_2 decide whether they represent the same object or not. On the other side, the identification problem answers the following question: given a pattern V and a set of patterns $\mathcal{V} = \{V_1, V_2, \ldots, V_n\}$, is there a pattern in $\mathcal{V}$ that corresponds to V? If yes, which is the index of such a pattern?

From a very general point of view, pattern matching can be seen as a two-step process. The first step is the so called feature extraction step, in which the pattern to be classified is transformed into an (m-long) vector whose components, called features, describe some particular characteristics of the to-be-classified pattern. As a first example, we may consider the classification of image regions. The region to be classified is the *pattern*, while the feature vector may contain the average gray level and the standard deviation of the pixels belonging to the region, the area of the region, its inertia moments, etc. A second example regards the classification of heart beats based on ECG signals. The *pattern* to be classified is the portion of ECG signal corresponding to a single heart beat, while the features may be the coefficients of the AR (autoregressive) model that better describes the signal, or a set of statistics extracted from the ECG.

Feature extraction is a crucial and necessary step since on one side it permits to simplify the pattern description by reducing it to a vector in $\mathbb{R}^m$, and on the other side the extracted features are supposed to describe some meaningful characteristics of the pattern to be classified. After feature extraction the *pattern* to be matched (or classified) is nothing but a vector V belonging to $\mathbb{R}^m$.

The second step is the actual matching step, in which a test pattern V is matched against one or several patterns $\{V_1, V_2, \ldots, V_n\}$.

The feature extraction step is highly application dependent and no general theory exists for it. For this reason, it is not possible to define the set of primitives that need to be developed to extract the features in the encrypted domain. Moreover, the involved operations are usually highly non-linear and their implementation in a STPC framework would be extremely cumbersome. Of course exceptions to this general rule exist, but in the majority of the cases we can assume that features are extracted in the plain domain and then processed securely by means of STPC techniques.

7.1.3 Goals and Outline of the Chapter

The goal of this chapter is to present some guidelines for developing a biometry matching protocol working in the encrypted domain, regardless of the kind of biometry being analyzed. Specifically, we will discuss several approaches to build the basic modules of any biometric matching protocol (distance computation and minimum selection), and show how such modules can be conveniently used in a great variety of different scenarios.

The rest of the chapter is organized as follows. The biometry matching problem is rigorously defined in Sect. 7.2. Then we show the cryptographic primitives necessary to the implementation of matching algorithms in the encrypted domain (Sect. 7.3). In Sect. 7.4 we describe how such primitives can be used to implement some of the most basic pattern recognition building blocks. In Sect. 7.5 we give some hints about how the building blocks can be assembled to carry out a given functionality. Finally in Sect. 7.6, some conclusions are provided.

7.2 Biometric Template Matching

As we said, regardless of the type of biometry and the feature extraction protocol, we can assume that any biometric template V is represented by a vector of m features, each assuming integer value (possibly resulting from a quantization problem) in the set $\{0, \ldots, b-1\}$, i.e. $V \in \mathbb{Z}_b^m$.

Table 7.1 Visibility of the values involved in the verification problem

	V_1	V_2	Intermediate values	Final result
C	Yes	No	No	Yes
S	No	Yes	No	Optional

7.2.1 The Verification Problem

As opposed to feature extraction, processing the feature vectors in a pattern matching application is a rather standard (though not easy) task always following a few number of fixed steps. It is then extremely important that these steps are defined and their privacy requirements identified, since doing so will allow to build a rather general theory. In this Section we start by considering the easiest problem, namely the verification problem: "Is he who he claims to be?".

The general verification problem can be summarized as follows:

- One party, say C knows a feature vector V_1.
- Another party, say S knows another feature vector V_2.
- We want to answer the question: is V_1 close enough to V_2?

As can be seen, the verification problem boils down to only two operations: (i) distance calculation and (ii) comparison against a threshold. As soon as an efficient protocol is available to perform these two tasks, a secure protocol for pattern verification can be built. In order to do so, it is necessary that the privacy requirements are defined. Though many different scenarios are possible, in most of the cases the requirements of the protocol can be defined as follows (see also the summary in Table 7.1):

- C gets yes/no.
- S gets nothing or yes/no.
- V_1 and V_2 are private inputs of C and S, respectively, and have to be kept secret.
- The distance function and the threshold may be assumed to be public parameters.
- Any intermediate value is not revealed to both parties.

7.2.2 The Identification Problem

While the verification problem involves a *one to one* matching, the identification problem corresponds to a *one to many* match and is used when two or more parties are interested to answer the question "Who is he?".

Specifically, pattern identification can be summarized as follows:

- One party, say C knows a feature vector V_{test}.
- Another party, say S knows a set of feature vectors $V = \{V_1, V_2, \ldots, V_n\}$.
- The possible questions to be answered are:

Table 7.2 Visibility of the values involved in the identification problem

	V_{test}	V_i	Intermediate values	Final result (yes/no or index)
C	Yes	No	No	Yes
S	No	Yes	No	No

Table 7.3 Visibility of the values involved in the access control problem

	V_{test}	V_i	Intermediate values	Final result (yes/no)
C	Yes	No	No	Yes
S	No	Yes	No	Yes

1. Is V_{test} close to at least one $V_i \in V$? Boiling down to: is the minimum distance between V_{test} and some elements in V smaller than a threshold?
2. Which is the index of the feature vector in V closest to V_{test}?
3. How many elements in V are close enough to V_{test}?

As can be seen, in most of the cases identification boils down to calculation of several distances, thresholding and/or computation of a minimum. Hence there are two main differences with respect to verification. The first one is quantitative, in that several distances and thresholds must be computed instead of one. The second is qualitative, since a new operator, namely minimum computation is needed.

With regard to the privacy requirements, the situation is slightly more complicated than in the verification case, however, it is still possible to define a standard set of requirements (see also Table 7.2):

- C gets (i) yes/no or (ii) the index of the minimum distance feature vector.
- S gets nothing.
- V_{test} (owned by C) and V (owned by S) are kept secret.
- The distance function and the threshold may be assumed to be public parameters.
- Intermediate values are not revealed to both parties.

A common alternative in which the identification is used by S to decide whether C belongs to a set of users allowed to access a given system is the following:

- C gets nothing or yes/no.
- S gets yes/no.
- V_{test} (owned by C) and V (owned by S) are kept secret.
- The distance function and the threshold may be assumed to be public parameters.
- Intermediate values are not revealed to both parties.

The privacy requirements of the access control problem are shown in Table 7.3.

7.3 Cryptographic Primitives

The problem of computing with encrypted data is a central one in the field of cryptography and goes back to the early days of modern cryptography, about 30 years ago [63]. The problem has a fundamental importance both from a theoretical and a practical perspective. Often and especially in the case of number theoretic cryptosystems, the possibility of computing with encrypted data is a direct consequence of a common property of the cryptosystems: the malleability. More in detail a cryptosystem is malleable if given an encryption of a plaintext m, it is possible to generate another ciphertext which decrypts to $f(m)$, for a known function f, without necessarily knowing or learning m.

Although from a security point of view malleability is a weakness of a cryptosystem because it allows to modify the plaintext using only the ciphertext, in our context it is the key that allows to compute on encrypted data. Starting from the pioneering works of Yao [68] and Goldreich, Micali and Widgerson [36] the problem has been extensively studied in a variety of settings and under different assumptions, up to homomorphic encryption and garbled circuits, the two main tools actually used in SMPC.

As we said in the introduction, a specific case of SMPC particularly interesting for biometric applications is Secure Two Party Computation where only two entities are involved: a server S (the service provider) and the client C (a user that needs to access to a functionality provided by the server).

Before introducing the main cryptographic tools available for STPC, we have to discuss two cornerstones of STPC: security and complexity.

Security   Mistrust among parties is usually modeled by assuming the existence of an adversary that is allowed to corrupt some partial set of the parties, so that the adversary can read (and possibly modify) the internal state of the corrupted players. A possible lack of reliability in the communication is modeled by allowing the adversary to control the communications involving corrupted players. The SMPC paradigm allows many settings and concerns to be modeled and is a strong tool in showing that solutions exist to very general cryptographic problems. The power of the framework is that under the assumption of partial corruption (and various settings and constraints) it is possible to compile any polynomial size function into a protocol that maintains the privacy of the inputs. Input privacy is ensured facing an adversary that is assumed to control the entire state (memory) of corrupted parties (passive adversary) and one that in addition may corrupt the memory arbitrarily (active adversary).

In STPC protocols we would like to have the same correctness and reciprocal privacy as in a trusted domain, but this is quite difficult to achieve. For this reason in many cases STPC developers adopt the *honest but curious* model (also called *semi-honest* model), according to which both parties are considered passive and follow the protocol but try to infer additional information from the transcript of messages seen in the protocol. So the parties may deviate from the protocol only in their internal computation, but the messages are constricted and sent in accordance to the protocol. Far from trivial, this model covers many typical practical settings such as protection against insider attacks. Further, designing and evaluating the performance of protocols in the honest but curious model is a first step toward protocols with stronger security guarantees. Indeed, most protocols for practical privacy-preserving applications focus on the honest but curious model [48]. In most cases sub-protocols are stacked together to obtain more complicated functionalities, in this context it is really important to know that if all sub-protocols are proven secure in the honest but curious model then their sequential composition inherits this security property [35].

Sometimes it is necessary to assume that one party can act maliciously, i.e. he behaves as an active adversary available to cheat to obtain information relative to the other party. For sake of brevity in this chapter we will not cover such scenarios.

Complexity General multiparty computation protocols allow to securely compute any function but this results in inefficient solutions when compared to plain protocols. For this reason, efficient ad hoc solutions have to be designed to solve specific cryptographic problems.

We can analyze complexity from three different points of view:

- *Number of Bit Operations*: this is also called computational complexity and indicates the number of basic operations that the protocol needs;
- *Number of Rounds*: the protocols we focus on are client-server protocols, i.e. they require some message exchanges to carry out the computation, a measure of the efficiency of this kind of protocols is the *number* of unidirectional transmission of information they require;
- *Bandwidth*: it is the amount of bits exchanged during protocol execution.

To measure the number of bit operations we use the Big-$\mathcal{O}$ notation [43]. Analyzing some basic operations needed in a STPC scenario and assuming that the largest number involved in the computation is represented by ℓ bits, i.e. the size of a ciphertext is ℓ bits, we see that the cost of an addition between two numbers is $\mathtt{add} = \mathcal{O}(\ell)$; that of a multiplication $\mathtt{mult} = \mathcal{O}(\ell^2)$; and that of an exponentiation $\mathtt{expo} = \mathcal{O}(\ell^3)$. Computing an hash function has a constant complexity that does not depend on ℓ. For the sake of simplicity in the rest of this chapter we will use as measure of computational complexity the operation having the largest complexity among all the operations involved in the protocol.

While the number of rounds is a very simple concept, we spend a few words about the bandwidth. The bandwidth depends on many factors, but probably the most important one is the cryptosystem and so the size of the ciphertext. Some cryptosystems require to transmit only the values used during the evaluation, while others need to transmit other information relative to the functionality, moreover each value is usually represented by long ciphertexts, resulting in big amount of data exchanged between the parties.

7.3.1 Symmetric vs. Asymmetric Encryption

Cryptographic systems can be divided in symmetric systems, where encryption and decryption are performed by using the same key, and asymmetric systems where the public encryption key and the secret decryption key are distinct.

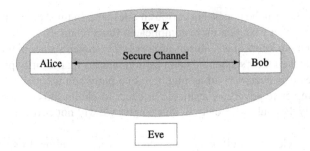

Fig. 7.1 The typical scenario for symmetric key cryptography. Alice and Bob are legitimate users of the system, whereas Eve is malicious and wants to eavesdrop the channel. The key K is the common secret key between Alice and Bob and creates a secure channel for communication between legitimate users

7.3.1.1 Symmetric Encryption

Symmetric key cryptography is one of the oldest methods in security systems and provides the confidentiality of a service. The most important properties of these algorithms are ease of operation and high speed [53]. In protocols based on symmetric encryption both the sender and receiver have a common secret key which is used for encryption and decryption of messages. It is assumed that decrypting a message is easy when the key is known and otherwise difficult. Indeed the encryption acts as a secure communication channel between sender and receiver (as shown in Fig. 7.1) an eavesdropped does not have access to.

There are several kinds of symmetric key systems proposed in the literature and used in practice like triple DES and AES (see [23] and [3]).

7.3.1.2 Asymmetric Encryption

Symmetric key systems are useful and efficient, but their application requires special infrastructures to be set up. Some examples are setting up the initial keys or managing keys among several users. A solution is using public key encryption in which encryption and decryption are performed using two different keys. The first one (public key) is published, whereas the second one (secret key) must be kept secret.

The first efficient public key encryption scheme was the RSA system [64], based on the difficulty of factoring large composite numbers.

An important class of public key cryptosystems are systems based on probabilistic encryption proposed for the first time in [37]. In these systems a given plaintext is encrypted into a different message at each new encryption. This is useful when, e.g., encrypting and transmitting single bits. If the encryption was deterministic, the adversary could encrypt the bits zero and one, and always see which of these encryptions has been transmitted.

Table 7.4 Homomorphic properties and homomorphic cryptosystem

Cryptosystem	Add	Mult	Both
RSA (*1978* [64])	No	Yes	No
Goldwasser–Micali (*1982* [37])	Yes	No	No
El-Gamal (*1985* [26])	No	Yes	No
Benaloh (*1994* [12])	Yes	No	No
Paillier (*1999* [58])	Yes	No	No
Boneh–Goh–Nissim (*2004* [17])	Yes	Only 1	Yes
Gentry (*2009* [32])	Yes	Yes	Yes

The most popular public key cryptosystem with semantic security (IND-CPA) is the Paillier cryptosystem (see Sect. 7.3.2.1), introduced for the first time in [58] and based on the difficulty of deciding if a number is an nth power in $\mathbb{Z}_{N^2}$, for a large enough N.

Many public key encryption schemes have homomorphic properties and can be used as cryptographic primitives in SMPC applications.

7.3.2 Homomorphic Encryption

A homomorphic encryption (HE) scheme over an algebraic ring, can allow additive, multiplicative or algebraically homomorphisms. In particular it permits to perform an algebraic operation $\bullet$ between encrypted numbers that returns, after decryption, the same result of the operation $+$ performed on the same values in the plain domain:

$$a + b = \mathcal{D}(\llbracket a \rrbracket \bullet \llbracket b \rrbracket); \qquad (7.1)$$

or permits an operation $\circ$ on ciphertexts such that

$$a * b = \mathcal{D}(\llbracket a \rrbracket \circ \llbracket b \rrbracket); \qquad (7.2)$$

where $\llbracket \cdot \rrbracket$ and $\mathcal{D}(\cdot)$ indicate, respectively, encryption and decryption. In the first case we say that the cryptosystem is additively homomorphic while in the second one it is multiplicatively homomorphic. Finally a cryptosystem is said to be algebraically homomorphic if both operations $\bullet$ and $\circ$ exist such that they have a mapping in the algebraic addition and multiplication.

Table 7.4 shows a list of cryptosystems with their homomorphic properties.

The most popular homomorphic cryptosystems permit to evaluate the sum among ciphertexts [58], while the El-Gamal cryptosystem [26] permits to evaluate the product. For several years the researcher community tried to propose a fully homomorphic cryptosystem with no significant results, but in 2009 in a breakthrough result by Gentry [32, 67], the first fully homomorphic encryption scheme was finally proposed. Gentry's paper shows how to use ideal lattices to construct an encryption scheme that allows to encrypt single bits and that is homomorphic with respect to addition and multiplication. Even though this result is a major theoretical achievement because secure fully homomorphic encryption was suspected to be impossible to achieve [16], the scheme itself and its recent improvements are still too inefficient to be used in practice. Very recently Melchor et al. in [52] and Gentry et al. in [33] have conceived less general forms of homomorphic encryption schemes based on lattices which are more efficient than existing fully homomorphic schemes but still unsuitable for most applications. Such schemes are less general in the sense that they allow only a limited number of multiplications.

7.3.2.1 Paillier Cryptosystem

The most popular homomorphic cryptosystem, used extensively in several SMPC protocols, is the Paillier cryptosystem. To illustrate the way the Paillier cryptosystem works, we start by defining its public and private keys generation, the encryption and the decryption.

- *Key generation*: given an RSA modulus $N = pq$ and $\lambda = \text{lcm}(p - 1, q - 1)$ and selected an integer generator $g \in \mathbb{Z}_{N^2}^*$ such that $N|\text{ord}(g)$ (N divides the order of g), meaning that

$$\text{GCD}\big(L\big(g^\lambda \bmod N^2\big), N\big) = 1,$$

the public (encryption) key is $\text{PuK} = (N, g)$ and the private (decryption) key is $\text{PrK} = (\lambda, \mu)$, where $\mu = (L(g^\lambda \bmod N^2))^{-1} \bmod N$, and $L(\cdot)$ is an integer function defined by

$$L(u) = \lfloor (u - 1)/N \rfloor.$$

- *Encryption*: the encryption of the message $m \in \mathbb{Z}_N$ is $[\![m]\!]$ when

$$[\![m]\!] = g^m r^N \bmod N^2, \tag{7.3}$$

where $r \in_R \mathbb{Z}_N^*$.
- *Decryption*: given the encryption $[\![m]\!] \in \mathbb{Z}_{N^2}$, the original message m can be obtained as:

$$m = L\big([\![m]\!]^\lambda \bmod N^2\big)\mu \bmod N.$$

The Paillier cryptosystem has several interesting properties. In the following we point out the most important ones.

Given $x, y, k, r \in \mathbb{Z}_N^*$ we have

Proposition 1 (Additive Homomorphism)

- $\mathcal{D}([\![x]\!][\![y]\!] \bmod N^2) = x + y \bmod N$.

Proposition 2 (Scalar Homomorphism)

- $\mathcal{D}([\![x]\!]^k \bmod N^2) = kx \bmod N$.

Proposition 3 (Self-blinding)

- $\mathcal{D}(\llbracket x \rrbracket r^N \bmod N^2) = x \bmod N$.

The security of the Paillier cryptosystem is provided under the Composite Residuosity Problem and Decisional Composite Residuosity Problem. These problems are considered intractable and so suitable as basis for a cryptosystem (a detailed discussion can be found in [58]). It can be also proven that under the assumption that the Decisional Composite Residuosity Problem is intractable, the Paillier cryptosystem is a randomized IND-CPA[2] cryptosystem.

In general we indicate with $T = \lceil \log_2 N \rceil$ the Paillier security parameter and we define $2T$ the bit size of a ciphertext. The most updated NIST[3] recommendation for security parameters is to use at least $T = 1024$ (more detail in [4]).

Note that for the Paillier cryptosystem the computational complexity is enc $\approx$ dec $\approx$ expo, hence the computation complexity of a homomorphic protocol can be related to the number of expo necessary to its execution.

7.3.2.2 Non-linear Computation by Using Blinding

Most protocols require that non-linear functions are computed. In a privacy preserving scenario such functions cannot be computed by relying on homomorphic properties only and interaction among the parties is required. In those cases S asks to C some help to carry out a portion of the computation. This introduces an interaction between the parties during which everything must be kept secret. Formally S has some data $\llbracket x \rrbracket$ encrypted with the public key of C and needs to compute the functionality $f(\cdot)$ with the help of C. Since C owns the private key, it is able to obtain x, but S does not want to reveal it to C, because it can be used to extrapolate some information owned by S. Hence S chooses a random r and by homomorphic properties computes $\llbracket x + r \rrbracket$ and sends it to C. C decrypts the message obtaining $x + r$ from which it cannot retrieve x. At this point C computes $\llbracket f(x + r) \rrbracket$ and sends it back to S that obtains the required computation. Obviously, it is necessary that $\tilde{f}(\cdot)$ exists such that

$$\tilde{f}\big(\llbracket f(x+r) \rrbracket, r\big) = \llbracket f(x) \rrbracket.$$

Figure 7.2 summarizes the flow of actions in blinding-based SMPC.

The security of this kind of schemes stems from the information theoretic security of additive blinding (the mutual information between x and $x + r$ decreases exponentially fast with the number of bits necessary to represent r), so it provides

---

[2]Indistinguishability under chosen-plaintext attack (IND-CPA) ensures that given two plain messages and the encryption of one of them, the adversary, cannot identify the message choice with probability significantly better than 1/2.

[3]National Institute of Standard and Technology. The mission of the Institute is to *"promote U.S. innovation and industrial competitiveness by advancing measurement science, standards, and technology in ways that enhance economic security and improve quality of life."*

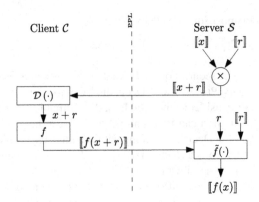

Fig. 7.2 Blind Computation with Encrypted Data (PPL indicates the Privacy Preserving Line and × denotes the product)

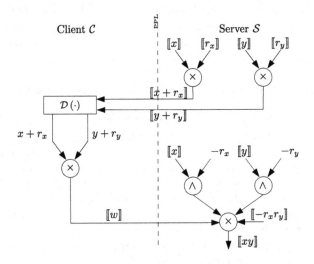

Fig. 7.3 The protocol EncMul (∧ denotes the exponentiation)

a perfectly secure and practical approach for computing on encrypted data. Additive blinding is used quite often, and several sub-protocols have been developed by using this approach. Here we present the EncMul, EncSquare and BitMin protocols that will be used later in Sect. 7.4.

- EncMul protocol: to exemplify the blinding procedure outlined above, we now describe the sub-protocol, EncMul, that allows to compute the product of two Paillier ciphertexts obtaining $[\![xy]\!] = \text{EncMul}([\![x]\!], [\![y]\!])$. Suppose (See Fig. 7.3) that S owns $[\![x]\!]$ and $[\![y]\!]$ encrypted with the public key of C. It can obfuscate both ciphertexts by adding two random numbers due to homomorphic additive properties and obtain $[\![x + r_x]\!]$ and $[\![y + r_y]\!]$. Upon reception of $[\![x + r_x]\!]$ and $[\![y + r_y]\!]$, C decrypts and multiplies them obtaining $w = xy + xr_y + yr_x + r_x r_y$. A this point C encrypts w and sends it back to S, which computes

$$[\![w]\!][\![x]\!]^{-r_y}[\![y]\!]^{-r_x}[\![-r_x r_y]\!] = [\![w]\!][\![-xr_y]\!][\![-yr_x]\!][\![-r_x r_y]\!]$$
$$= [\![w - xr_y - yr_x - r_x r_y]\!]$$

$$= [\![\underbrace{xy + xr_y + yr_x + r_xr_y}_{w} - xr_y - yr_x - r_xr_y]\!]$$

$$= [\![xy]\!]. \tag{7.4}$$

Computing EncMul requires two rounds (one from $\mathcal{S}$ to send the obfuscated ciphertexts and one from $\mathcal{C}$ to send back the result) and a bandwidth of $3 \times 2T$ bits (3 ciphertexts are exchanged having size $2T$ bits, where T is the Paillier security parameter introduced in Sect. 7.3.2.1) with a computational complexity equal to 3 enc to encrypt the obfuscation values r_x, r_y, $-r_xr_y$, 2 expo needed to compute $[\![x]\!]^{-r_y}$ and $[\![y]\!]^{-r_x}$; 5 mult needed to obfuscate $[\![x]\!]$, $[\![y]\!]$ and to compute the additions to $[\![w]\!]$; 2 dec to obtain in plain $x + r_x$ and $y + r_y$ and finally 1 enc to encrypt the result, for an asymptotic complexity of 8 expo operations.

- EncSquare protocol: the EncMul protocol can be optimized to compute the square of a value, resulting in the EncSquare protocol. $\mathcal{S}$ owns $[\![x]\!]$, obfuscates it by adding a random number r_x and obtains $[\![x + r_x]\!]$. At this point $\mathcal{S}$ sends the ciphertexts to $\mathcal{C}$ that decrypts it, computes the square value $w = (x + r_x)^2$ and sends it back to $\mathcal{S}$, after encryption. Finally $\mathcal{S}$ computes

$$[\![w]\!][\![x]\!]^{-2r_x}[\![-r_x^2]\!] = [\![w]\!][\![-2xr_x]\!][\![-r_x^2]\!]$$
$$= [\![w - 2xr_x - r_x^2]\!]$$
$$= [\![\underbrace{x^2 + 2xr_x + r_x^2}_{w} - 2xr_x - r_x^2]\!] = [\![x^2]\!] \tag{7.5}$$

obtaining the square value of x encrypted. The protocol EncSquare requires the same number of rounds of EncMul but only $2 \times 2T$ bits (2 ciphertexts) are transmitted. Even the computational complexity is reduced to a total asymptotic number of 5 expo operations.

- BitMin protocol: the protocol BitMin is a widely used building block that computes the minimum between two encrypted values. In Fig. 7.4 the flow of the protocol is depicted.

Given two encrypted values $[\![x]\!]$, $[\![y]\!]$, where x and y are ℓ-bit long, the main idea is to obtain the encryption of a bit b that assumes the value 0 if $x < y$, 1 otherwise. This can be done by computing the difference between the two values and extracting the sign bit. Even if this is a very simple operation when computed on plain values, it is not trivial when the values are encrypted. In the BitMin, $\mathcal{S}$ starts by computing $[\![z]\!] = [\![2^\ell + x - y]\!]$ by relying on homomorphic encryption, obtaining an $\ell + 1$-bit integer. The most significant bit of z (which we denote z_ℓ) is 0 if and only if $x < y$. Computing z_ℓ can be done as follows. $\mathcal{S}$ additively blinds z with a suitable random value r, obtaining $[\![d]\!]$, then it sends $[\![d]\!]$ to $\mathcal{C}$. At this point $\mathcal{S}$ and $\mathcal{C}$ run a comparison protocol [25] after which $\mathcal{S}$ will learn $[\![\rho]\!]$ such that $\rho = 0 \Leftrightarrow [\hat{d} < \hat{r}] = [d \bmod 2^\ell < r \bmod 2^\ell]$. We notice that given ρ it is possible to compute z_ℓ as:

$$b = z_\ell = 2^{-\ell}(z - \hat{z}) = 2^{-\ell}(z - ((d - r) \bmod 2^\ell)), \tag{7.6}$$

where $(d - r) \bmod 2^\ell = (d \bmod 2^\ell) - (r \bmod 2^\ell) + \rho \cdot 2^\ell$.

Fig. 7.4 The Protocol BitMin

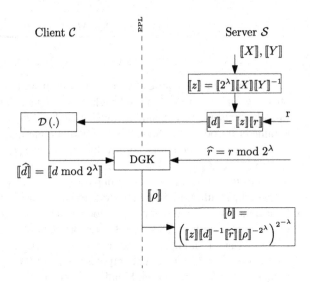

	#exp	Bandwidth	Rounds
Table 7.5 Computational Complexities—DGK sub-protocol	4ℓ	$\frac{2\ell T}{3} + 1$	3

The DGK comparison protocol allows both parties (i.e. $\mathcal{C}$ and $\mathcal{S}$) to learn the bit ρ of the predicate $d < r$, where d and r are two ℓ-bit integers owned by $\mathcal{C}$ and $\mathcal{S}$, respectively, by decomposing encrypted values into the encryptions of the single bits and returning the encryption of the most significant bit. For sake of brevity we do not describe the DGK protocol, interested readers may directly refer to [25].

Considering the DGK protocol complexities shown in Table 7.5, the BitMin requires a number of rounds equal to four: one to exchange the result and three due to DGK protocol. Only 1 ciphertext is sent from $\mathcal{S}$ to $\mathcal{C}$, so the bandwidth is a Paillier ciphertext plus the bandwidth of DGK, thus: $2T + \frac{2\ell T}{3} + 1 = 2T(1 + \frac{\ell}{3}) + 1$. Finally the asymptotic computation complexity is 1 expo to compute $[\![d]\!]$, 1 dec $+$ 1 enc to obtain $[\![\widehat{d}]\!]$ and 3 expo to compute $[\![b]\!]$; that is 6 expo. Considering that DGK requires 4ℓ exponentiations we have $(6 + 4\ell)$ expo.

7.3.2.3 Composite Signal Representation

A problem with the use of homomorphic encryption is that signals need to be encrypted sample-wise. Sample-wise encryption of signals poses some severe complexity problems since it introduces a huge expansion factor between the original signal sample and the encrypted one.

To fix the ideas, let us assume that the Paillier cryptosystem is used; in this case each encrypted sample is an element of $\mathbb{Z}_{N^2}$, i.e. the set of integer numbers modulo N^2 with N being at least 1024 bit long, that is, each encrypted sample needs at least 2048 bits to be represented. By considering that plain signal samples are usually represented by a few bits (e.g. 8 bits for images or 16 bits for ECG signals), we conclude that due to encryption, signals are expanded by a factor ranging from 125 to 250. For instance, the size of a gray level 1000×1000 image will pass from 1 Mbyte in the clear to 250 Mbytes in the encrypted domain. This huge expansion factor is clearly not affordable in many practical applications.

In order to solve these problems, in [14] an alternative representation of signals has been proposed. This representation permits to greatly reduce the expansion factor introduced by encryption, while still allowing the exploitation of the homomorphic properties of the underlying cryptosystem to process signals in the encrypted domain. In addition to limiting the storage requirement, this representation allows the parallel processing of different samples, thus providing a considerable reduction of computational complexity in terms of operations between encrypted messages.

The main idea behind the representation is to pad multiple data samples to form a composite encrypted message. To be specific, let $\mathcal{M}$ be the message space and $\mathcal{C}$ the cipher space and let signal samples be l-bit long. It is possible to bundle R l-bit messages $m_1, \ldots, m_R$ within a single composite message x as follows:

$$x = m_1 \cdot 2^0 + m_2 \cdot 2^L + \cdots + m_R \cdot 2^{L(R-1)}. \tag{7.7}$$

If L is larger than l, samples will remain distinct in the composite representation; moreover, if L is sufficiently large, adding two composite messages will result in the addition of the single messages composing them, and multiplying the composite message by a constant factor, will be equivalent to multiplying each single message by the same factor. In [14] other ways to pack more messages together that permit more complex operations, such as linear filtering, have been proposed.

7.3.3 Garbled Circuits

Yao demonstrated in [68] that any function can be securely evaluated in a constant number of rounds and polynomial communication and computation overhead, proposing the garbled circuit (GC) protocol. While Yao's protocol has been thought to be of theoretical interest only for a long time, recent works have shown its efficiency [44, 49, 60] and usability by compilers for automatic generation of GC-based STPC protocols [51, 59].

Yao's Garbled Circuit approach [69] is one of the most efficient methods for secure evaluation of a boolean circuit C. To describe garbled circuits in a few words, we can say that Yao's idea is to encrypt (or garble) the nodes and the transitions of a boolean circuit such that who evaluates it may follow only a single evaluation path, defined by the circuit and the input attribute vector. Given a public boolean function $y = f(\mathbf{x}_C, \mathbf{x}_S)$, where $\mathbf{x}_C$ is the set of (binary) inputs belonging to $\mathcal{C}$ and $\mathbf{x}_S$ those

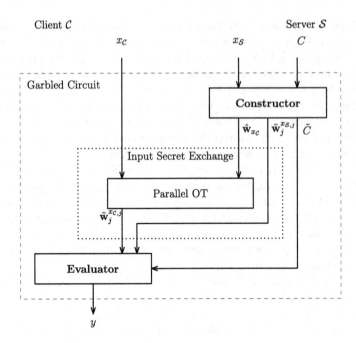

Fig. 7.5 General scheme for garbled circuits

to $\mathcal{S}$, it is possible to represent $f(\cdot)$ by a boolean circuit C. C and $\mathcal{S}$ are interested to evaluate the circuit, without disclosing their inputs. At the end of the protocol the output will be available to C and optionally to $\mathcal{S}$.

The circuit, together with $\mathbf{x}_C$ and $\mathbf{x}_\mathcal{S}$, is an input of a generic GC scheme, where one party ($\mathcal{S}$) constructs the circuit, then discloses the secrets necessary for the evaluation to the other party (C) and C uses them to evaluate the circuit.

A garbled circuit (Fig. 7.5) can be associated to any function described by a boolean circuit and is composed by the following blocks:

- *Constructor*: The circuit constructor, on $\mathcal{S}$ side, creates a *garbled circuit* $\widetilde{C}$:

  - for each input, intermediate and output wire W_i of the circuit, the constructor randomly chooses a complementary garbled value $\widehat{w}_i = \langle \widetilde{w}_i^0, \widetilde{w}_i^1 \rangle$ consisting of two secrets, $\widetilde{w}_i^0$ and $\widetilde{w}_i^1$, where $\widetilde{w}_i^j$ is the garbled value of W_i's value j, i.e. $\widetilde{w}_i^j$ is a randomly chosen secret associated to j that does not reveal j;
  - for each gate G_i, $\mathcal{S}$ creates a *garbled table* $\widetilde{T}_i$ with the following property: given a set of garbled values of G_i's inputs, $\widetilde{T}_i$ allows to recover the garbled value of the corresponding G_i's output, and nothing else.

  Each secret is randomly chosen and is uniformly distributed in the interval $(0, 2^t)$ (normally $t = 80$). Once the secrets are generated, for each gate, given the secrets $\widehat{w}_i$ and $\widehat{w}_j$ associated to the gate inputs wires and the secret $\widehat{w}_o$ associated to the gate output wire, the corresponding $\widetilde{T}$ is generated in the following way:

$$
\begin{bmatrix}
\mathcal{E}nc_{\widetilde{w}_i^0, \widetilde{w}_j^0}(\widetilde{w}_o^{g(0,0)}) \\
\mathcal{E}nc_{\widetilde{w}_i^0, \widetilde{w}_j^1}(\widetilde{w}_o^{g(0,1)}) \\
\mathcal{E}nc_{\widetilde{w}_i^1, \widetilde{w}_j^0}(\widetilde{w}_o^{g(1,0)}) \\
\mathcal{E}nc_{\widetilde{w}_i^1, \widetilde{w}_j^1}(\widetilde{w}_o^{g(1,1)})
\end{bmatrix}
\tag{7.8}
$$

where $g(b_i, b_j)$ is the output of the gate. As to symmetric encryption, any algorithm having the following properties can be used:

- *elusive range*: an encryption under one key is in the range of an encryption with a different key with negligible probability;
- *efficiently verifiable range*: given a key, a user can efficiently verify that a ciphertext is in the range of that key.

The rows of the tables are finally randomly scrambled to avoid that the evaluator understands the input values by the row successfully decrypted.

- *Input Secret Exchange*: Garbled values corresponding to $\mathcal{C}$'s inputs x_j are (obliviously) transferred to $\mathcal{C}$ with a parallel oblivious transfer (OT) protocol. An OT protocol [29] is a STPC tool where one party ($\mathcal{S}$) inputs two messages m_0 and m_1, while the other party ($\mathcal{C}$) inputs a bit b; at the end of the protocol $\mathcal{C}$ obtains the message m_b while nothing is revealed to $\mathcal{S}$. In the parallel OT inside the GC protocol, $\mathcal{S}$ inputs complementary garbled values $\widehat{w}_j$, while $\mathcal{C}$ inputs $x_{\mathcal{C},j}$ and obtains $\widetilde{w}_j^{x_{\mathcal{C},j}}$ as outputs. Oblivious Transfer can be instantiated efficiently as shown in [2, 54], and by relying on elliptic curve cryptography. In addition, as shown in [11], the OTs can be pre-computed in a set-up phase, such that they are not the performance bottleneck in Yao's protocol. Finally, the number of computationally expensive public-key operations in the set-up phase can be reduced to a constant number with the extensions proposed in [40]. By considering these instantiations, a parallel OT of n secrets each t-bit long requires two rounds where $2nt$ bits are transmitted. After the OT, $\mathcal{S}$ transmits the secrets $\widetilde{w}_j^{x_{\mathcal{S},j}}$ relative to its input $x_{\mathcal{S},j}$ and the tables $\widetilde{T}_i$ of the circuit.
- *Evaluator*: $\mathcal{C}$ simply evaluates the garbled circuit $\widetilde{C}$ gate by gate, using the garbled tables $\widetilde{T}_i$, to obtain the garbled output. In each table the evaluator decrypts each row by using the input secrets previously obtained until it successfully performs a decryption. In the first gates only input secrets are used, while successively input secrets and/or secrets obtained as output from other tables are used. Finally, $\mathcal{C}$ determines the plain values corresponding to the obtained garbled output values using output translation tables received by $\mathcal{S}$. If the output is needed by $\mathcal{S}$, $\mathcal{C}$ transmits the garbled output.

The basic GC protocol outlined above can be improved in many ways as shown in [51] and [44]. In particular, in [51] the authors suggest to replace encryption by Hash functions and the scheme proposed in [44] allows "free" evaluation of XOR gates so that a garbled XOR gate has no garbled table and its evaluation consists of XOR-ing its garbled input values, resulting in *no communication* and *negligible computation*.

From a computational point of view, GCs have lower complexity than homomorphic encryption protocols, replacing exponentiations computed on large numbers with simple hash functions. On the other side the amount of transmitted data can grow quickly, considering that, given the number of bits ℓ necessary to represent each input value, we have to transmit the secrets relative to the bits of the S inputs ($\mathcal{O}(\ell)$), the data necessary for the parallel OT that returns the secrets relative to C inputs ($\mathcal{O}(\ell)$) and the garbled table ($\mathcal{O}(f(\ell))$), where $f(\cdot)$ depends on the particular functionality implemented by the circuit. Finally the number of rounds is the same for any circuit (two) and it does not change if we assemble many building blocks together.

7.3.3.1 Basic Building Blocks

Many basic building blocks can be built by relying on GC theory. Figures 7.6 and 7.7 show the circuits implementing the blocks that we will use later in Sect. 7.4 to build the primitives necessary to construct pattern matching protocols working on encrypted data. Being the figures self-explicative, we refer to the original papers for their detailed descriptions. Only product and square circuits are here described.

- *Product* MULT_ℓ [45]: to multiply two unsigned integers x and y represented with ℓ bits, we can construct a circuit according to the scholar method for multiplication, i.e., adding up the bit-wise multiplications (logical AND) of y_i and x left shifted of i positions: $x \cdot y = \sum_{i=0}^{\ell-1}(y_i \wedge x)2^i$. The circuit is composed of ℓ^2 AND gates (Fig. 7.7(e)) yielding the matrix

$$
\begin{matrix}
y_0 x_{\ell-1} & \cdots & y_0 x_1 & y_0 x_0 \\
y_1 x_{\ell-1} & \cdots & y_1 x_1 & y_1 x_0 \\
& \cdots & & \\
y_{\ell-1} x_{\ell-1} & \cdots & y_{\ell-1} x_1 & y_{\ell-1} x_0
\end{matrix} \tag{7.9}
$$

and $\ell - 1$ adders (Fig. 7.7(f)). Instead of using adders of 2ℓ bits we can set $(x \cdot y)_0 = x_0 \wedge y_0$ and then add $(y_0 \cdot x)_{\ell-1,\dots,1}$ with $y_1 \cdot x$ setting $(x \cdot y)_1$ equal to the least significant bit of the result and then adding the other bits to $x_2 \cdot y$, etc. In this way adders of values represented with ℓ bits are used. The circuit requires $\ell^2 + (\ell - 1)\ell = 2\ell^2 - \ell$ non-XOR gates.

- *Square* SQUARE_ℓ: a circuit computing the square of an unsigned integer x can be obtained by optimizing the product circuit, that is, replacing the circuit of Fig. 7.7(e) with the circuit of Fig. 7.7(g). By considering that $x_i \wedge x_i = x_i$ and $x_i \wedge x_j = x_j \wedge x_i$ we can rebuild the matrix of (7.9) as:

$$
\begin{matrix}
x_0 x_{\ell-1} & \cdots & x_0 x_1 & x_0 \\
x_1 x_{\ell-1} & \cdots & x_1 & x_0 x_1 \\
& \cdots & & \\
x_{\ell-1} & \cdots & x_1 x_{\ell-1} & x_0 x_{\ell-1}
\end{matrix} \tag{7.10}
$$

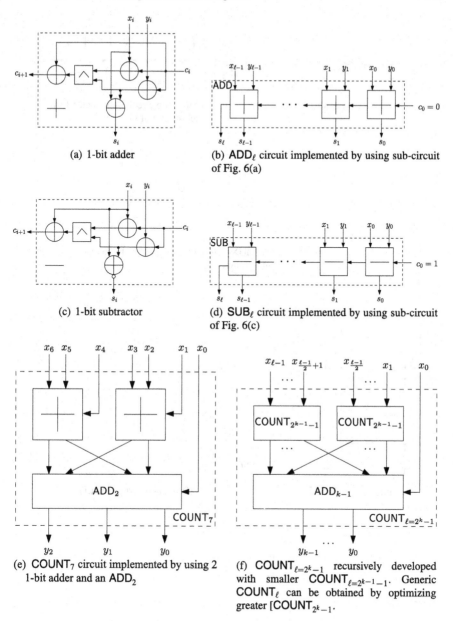

(a) 1-bit adder

(b) $\mathbf{ADD}_\ell$ circuit implemented by using sub-circuit of Fig. 6(a)

(c) 1-bit subtractor

(d) $\mathbf{SUB}_\ell$ circuit implemented by using sub-circuit of Fig. 6(c)

(e) $\mathbf{COUNT}_7$ circuit implemented by using 2 1-bit adder and an $\mathbf{ADD}_2$

(f) $\mathbf{COUNT}_{\ell=2^k-1}$ recursively developed with smaller $\mathbf{COUNT}_{\ell=2^{k-1}-1}$. Generic $\mathbf{COUNT}_\ell$ can be obtained by optimizing greater [$\mathbf{COUNT}_{2^k-1}$].

Fig. 7.6 Logical circuits implementing the basic building blocks used in Sect. 7.4 (*first part*)

In this way only $\ell - 1 + \ell - 2 + \cdots + 1 = \ell(\ell - 1)/2$ AND gates are evaluated, obtaining $\frac{3}{2}\ell(\ell - 1)$ gates for the whole circuit.

Reminding the reader that the circuit complexity is related to the number of non-XOR gates (each having a table of size $4t$ bits associated), we note that Table 7.6 shows the complexity of the circuits as a function of the number of non-XOR gates.

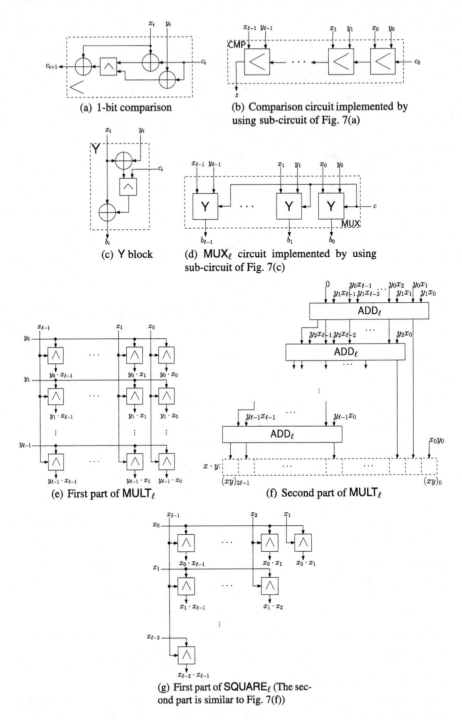

(a) 1-bit comparison

(b) Comparison circuit implemented by using sub-circuit of Fig. 7(a)

(c) Y block

(d) MUX$_\ell$ circuit implemented by using sub-circuit of Fig. 7(c)

(e) First part of MULT$_\ell$

(f) Second part of MULT$_\ell$

(g) First part of SQUARE$_\ell$ (The second part is similar to Fig. 7(f))

Fig. 7.7 Logical circuits implementing the basic building blocks used in Sect. 7.4 (*second part*)

Table 7.6 Complexity of GCs implementing the basic building blocks used in Sect. 7.4

Circuit	Inputs (bit length)	Output (bitlength)	# Non-XOR gates
ADD_ℓ [45], Fig. 7.6(b)	x (ℓ), y (ℓ)	s ($\ell + 1$)	ℓ
SUB_ℓ [45], Fig. 7.6(d)	x (ℓ), y (ℓ)	s ($\ell + 1$)	ℓ
$COUNT_\ell$ [9], Fig. 7.6(f)	x (ℓ)	y ($k \approx \log_2(\ell + 1)$)	$\approx \ell - k$
$<_\ell$ [45], Fig. 7.6(d)	x (ℓ), y (ℓ)	z (1)	ℓ
MUX_ℓ [44], Fig. 7.7(d)	x (ℓ), y (ℓ), c (1)	b (ℓ)	ℓ
$MULT_\ell$ [45], Fig. 7.7(e), 7.7(f)	x (ℓ), y (ℓ)	z (2ℓ)	$2\ell^2 - \ell$
$SQUARE_\ell$, Fig. 7.7(g)	x (ℓ)	z (2ℓ)	$\frac{3}{2}\ell^2 - \frac{3}{2}\ell$

7.3.4 Hybrid Protocols

Given STPC protocols implementing several basic functions, it is possible to obtain more complicated protocols by composing them. Homomorphic Encryption is particularly useful when it is possible to move the computation on S's side (almost) without interaction, while Garbled Circuits are more performing when the data is represented by few bits or whenever it is not possible to perform some operations by HE. As a result, it is possible that complex protocols contain blocks having an efficient HE implementation, while others can be more efficiently implemented by using GCs. To pass from HE to GC and vice versa it is necessary to disclose intermediate values to C (which owns the decryption key of the homomorphic cryptosystem), but this involves a privacy leakage. To solve this problem we can use blinding [46]: the intermediate data is first of all blinded by adding a random value (known only by S) and then disclosed to C. The following HE or GC sub-protocol will remove the obfuscation before continuing the computation.

For example, to convert an Homomorphic value $[\![x]\!]$ into a Garbled value $\tilde{x}$, S adds a random value r under homomorphic encryption, sends the blinded value $[\![\bar{x}]\!] = [\![x + r]\!] = [\![x]\!] \cdot [\![r]\!]$ to C who decrypts it and uses the $\bar{x}$ value as input to the subsequenting GC. S inputs the value r to the GC and the constructor will prepare a garbled circuit that first computes the subtraction between $\bar{x}$ and r and then evaluates the desired block. A similar method can be used for converting a garbled value $\tilde{x}$ into a homomorphic value $[\![x]\!]$.

7.4 Building Blocks for Privacy-Aware Pattern Matching

We now describe the building blocks necessary to carry out the general secure pattern matching algorithms described in Sect. 7.2.

The first problem to be considered is the verification problem. Pattern verification boils down to the computation of a certain distance function and its comparison against a threshold, as shown in Fig. 7.8(a). It is easy to realize that the verification problem can be considered as special case of the identification problem, shown in

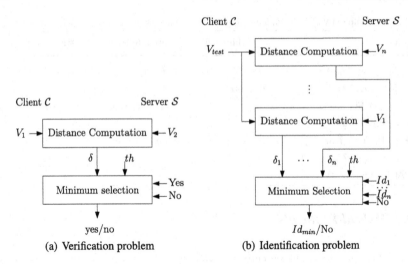

Fig. 7.8 STPC blocks necessary for the Matching problems

Fig. 7.8(b). Verification only needs that the distance between V_1 (now playing the role of V_{test}) and V_2 is computed and the minimum between such a distance and the verification threshold evaluated. So, in the following we will treat the two problems together.

Specifically we will describe the single blocks necessary for secure evaluation of the Matching Problems: *distance computation* and *minimum selection*. For each block the implementation by using HE and GC will be provided. The comparison among the different implementations and their composition will then be analyzed in Sect. 7.5.

7.4.1 Distance Computation

This section is devoted to sketch the sub-protocols for securely computing the distance δ between two feature vectors. We will describe two possible solutions: the former relying on homomorphic encryption, the latter on garbled circuits. Due to the great difference in complexities and performances of these approaches, we will provide an analysis of our constructions in the following Sect. 7.5, trying to delineate the different contexts in which one approach should be preferred to the other. Considering the verification problem the distance δ is computed between V_1 and V_2, while in the identification problem n distances δ_i are evaluated between the feature vector V_{test} provided by C and the feature vectors V_i stored in the database owned by S. Reminding the reader that each biometry feature vector can be represented by a point in $\mathbb{Z}_b^m$, as presented in Sect. 7.2, for the sake of notational simplicity the distance computation is here evaluated between two points $P, Q \in \mathbb{Z}_b^m$ and the final result belongs to $\mathbb{Z}_{m'}$, where m' is chosen to correctly represent the distance.

Fig. 7.9 Euclidean distance via homomorphic encryption

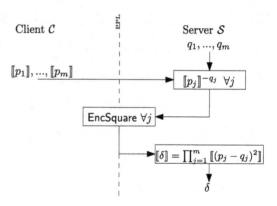

Fig. 7.9 Euclidean distance via homomorphic encryption

7.4.1.1 Euclidean Distance

The Euclidean distance is defined as

$$\delta = d_E(P, Q) := \sqrt{\sum_{j=1}^{m} (p_j - q_j)^2}$$

for $j = 1, \ldots, m : p_j, q_j \in [0, \ldots, b) \subseteq \{0, 1\}^\ell$. As the Euclidean distance is non-negative, in many cases it is replaced by $\delta^2 = \sum_{j=1}^{m} (p_j - q_j)^2$, namely the square of the Euclidean distance, whose minimum coincides with the minimum among Euclidean distances. Considering that $P, Q \in \mathbb{Z}_b^m$, we can observe easily that $\delta^2 \in \mathbb{Z}_{m'}$, where $m' = m * (2b)^2$.

Homomorphic Protocol The encryption of the square of the Euclidean distance $[\![\delta_i^2]\!] = [\![d_E(P_i, Q)^2]\!]$ can be computed by using additively homomorphic encryption together with an additional round for squaring as proposed in [28]. As depicted in Fig. 7.9, S is able to compute all the differences $[\![p_j - q_j]\!]$ by using the additive homomorphic property, then the interactive EncSquare protocol is needed to compute the squared values of the summands, to let S obtain $[\![(p_j - q_j)^2]\!]$.

Considering that many calls to EncSquare are required, they can be evaluated in parallel. In this way, with just two rounds $2mn$ ciphertexts of size $2T$ bits are exchanged between C and S ($n > 1$ when more distances are parallel evaluated).

Finally by the homomorphic properties S can compute δ^2 by multiplying in the encrypted domain (equivalent to adding in the plain domain) all the squared values.

GC Protocol To build a GC-based STPC for computing the Euclidean distance, we need to pay particular attention to the correct number of bits used to represent each value involved in the computation. In this case a Boolean circuit computing $\sum_{j=1}^{m} (p_j - q_j)^2$ is evaluated. Supposing that each feature of the biometry is represented with ℓ bits (the base used for the feature representation is $2^{\ell-1} \leq b < 2^\ell$), the point P and Q are represented with $m\ell$ bits each. The differences between each

Fig. 7.10 Euclidean distance via garbled circuits

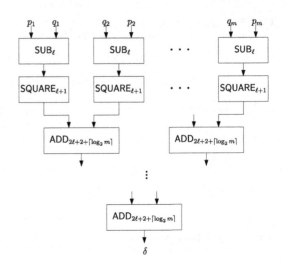

couple of features are represented with $\ell + 1$ bits and the square values of the difference needs $2\ell + 2$ bits for their representation. Finally δ is obtained by adding all the square differences and is represented with $2\ell + 2 + \lceil \log_2 m \rceil$ bits.

The circuit, shown in Fig. 7.10, requires m SUB_ℓ, m $\mathsf{SQUARE}_{\ell+1}$ and $(m-1)\,\mathsf{ADD}_{2\ell+2+\lceil \log_2 m \rceil}$.

To transmit the circuit $(m\ell + \frac{3m}{2}(\ell+1)\ell + (m-1)(2\ell + 2 + \lceil \log_2 m \rceil))4t$ bits are transferred from $\mathcal{S}$ to $\mathcal{C}$.

7.4.1.2 Hamming Distance

The Hamming distance is often used when biometries are represented by vectors of boolean features (i.e. points $P, Q \in \mathbb{Z}_2^m$), and is defined as $d_H(P, Q) := \sum_{j=1}^{m} p_j \oplus q_j \in \mathbb{Z}_{m'}$, where $m' = \lceil \log_2 m \rceil$.

Homomorphic Protocol To evaluate the Hamming distance in a privacy preserving fashion, the m XOR operators needed for the distance evaluation are computed by using homomorphic encryption. Let us assume that we want to evaluate a generic $[\![p_j \oplus q_j]\!]$ where p_j and q_j are bit values available in encrypted format, i.e. $\mathcal{S}$ knows $[\![p_j]\!]$ and $[\![q_j]\!]$, where encryption is carried out by using $\mathcal{C}$'s PuK. In this setting $\mathcal{S}$ does not want to reveal neither p_j nor q_j to $\mathcal{C}$, so it chooses two additional random bits r_{p_j} and r_{q_j} and computes $[\![p_j \oplus r_{p_j}]\!] = [\![p_j + r_{p_j} - 2p_j r_{p_j}]\!] = [\![p_j]\!]^{1-2r_{p_j}}[\![r_{p_j}]\!]$ and similarly $[\![q_j \oplus r_{q_j}]\!]$ then it sends these values to $\mathcal{C}$. The obfuscated bits can be packed in a single ciphertext by computing $[\![p_j \oplus r_{p_j}]\!]^2[\![q_j \oplus r_{q_j}]\!] = [\![2(p_j \oplus r_{p_j}) + (p_j \oplus r_{p_j})]\!]$. Note that p_j and q_j are perfectly obfuscated by the xor-ing with r_{p_j} and r_{q_j}, so $\mathcal{C}$ can safely decrypt the ciphertexts, obtain the single bits, compute the encryption of $[\![(p_j \oplus r_{p_j}) \oplus (q_j \oplus r_{q_j})]\!]$

Fig. 7.11 Sub protocol XOR
with $[\![x]\!]$ and $[\![y]\!]$

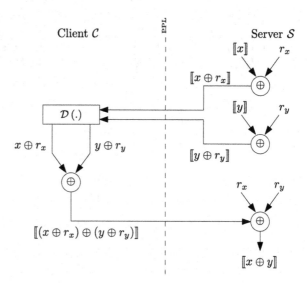

and send the result back to S. At this point S can remove $r_{p_j} \oplus r_{q_j}$ from the result and obtain $[\![p_j \oplus q_j]\!]$. The whole protocol is shown in Fig. 7.11.

Since S needs to compute the XOR function, C computes two decryptions and one encryption and the complexity is $4\ \mathsf{expo} + 2\ \mathsf{dec} + 1\ \mathsf{enc} \simeq 7\ \mathsf{expo}$.

Since computing the Hamming distance requires m XOR operations, the communication complexity can be reduced by packing all the $nm\ p_j \oplus r_{p_j}$ ($n > 1$ when several distances are parallel computed) and all the $nm\ q_j \oplus r_{q_j}$ in a single ciphertext during the transmission from S to C answers with nm ciphertexts. The round complexity is 2.

GC Protocol   In Hamming distance calculation each feature is represented by 1 bit, hence the points P and Q are represented with m bits. The XOR among the two points is again represented with m bits, while the distance can be represented with $\lceil \log_2(m) \rceil$ bits. The circuit computing the Hamming distance is composed by m XOR (having no tables associated thanks to the Free-XOR) and their binary results are summed together by using a COUNT_m having $\lesssim m - \log_2(m+1)$ non-XOR gates. The garbled gates transmitted are hence relative only to the COUNT circuit, implying the transmission of less than $(m - \log_2(m+1))4t$ bits.

7.4.2 Minimum Selection

The computation of the minimum among a set of values is the second essential operation needed in a matching protocol. When the minimum has to be computed among $n + 1$ values, and the index of the minimum value is required, we can use the cascade of several minimum blocks as depicted in Fig. 7.12.

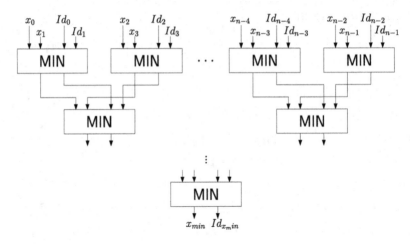

Fig. 7.12 Circuit for minimum search among n values

Due to this we can solve the problem of Minimum Selection by repeatedly application of a basic building block able to compute the minimum and the related index on a couple of values.

Suppose we have two integer values x, y represented with ℓ bits obtained from a previous computation and two identification labels Id_x, Id_y associated to x and y, respectively, and represented with κ bits. The goal of Minimum Selection is to select $\min\{x, y\}$ and the $\mathrm{Id}_{\{x,y\}}$ associated to the minimum.

Homomorphic Protocol   Given the sub-protocol BitMin described in Sect. 7.3.2.2, allowing $\mathcal{S}$ to compute the encrypted bit $[\![b]\!]$ such that

$$b = \begin{cases} 0 & \text{if } x < y, \\ 1 & \text{if } x \geq y, \end{cases} \tag{7.11}$$

$\mathcal{S}$ can compute $[\![\min\{x, y\}]\!] = \mathsf{EncMul}([\![1-b]\!], [\![x]\!][\![y]\!]^{-1})[\![y]\!] = [\![(1-b)(x-y)+y]\!]$ and $[\![\mathrm{Id}_{\min\{x,y\}}]\!] = \mathsf{EncMul}([\![1-b]\!], [\![\mathrm{Id}_x]\!][\![\mathrm{Id}_y]\!]^{-1})[\![\mathrm{Id}_y]\!] = [\![(1-b)(\mathrm{Id}_x - \mathrm{Id}_y)+\mathrm{Id}_y]\!]$. Note that the two EncMul can be performed in parallel and b is transmitted only once, resulting in the transmission of 5 ciphertexts.

When the minimum among $n + 1$ values is evaluated returning its index, as in the identification problem where there is the necessity to choose among n distances and a threshold, we need to evaluate n minimum functions as shown in Fig. 7.12. For each minimum block $2T(6 + \frac{\ell}{3}) + 1$ bits are transmitted and $14 + 4\ell$ expo are evaluated during the computation. The reverse tree has $\lceil \log_2(n + 1)\rceil$ levels and six rounds are required for each level.

GC Protocol   The minimum circuit (MIN) which selects the minimum value $\min\{x, y\}$ among two values x and y together with the associated Id is shown in Fig. 7.13. The circuit is composed by a comparison circuit having ℓ non-XOR gates and two MUX circuits. The one that selects among x, y has ℓ non-XOR gates, while

Fig. 7.13 The circuit which
selects the minimum value
$\min\{x, y\}$ among x and y
together with the Id
associated

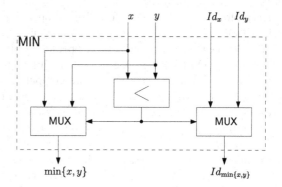

$$\min\{x, y\} \qquad\qquad Id_{\min\{x,y\}}$$

that selecting among the Ids has κ non-XOR gates, totally resulting in $2\ell + \kappa$ tables of size $4t$ bits each. If only the Id of the minimum value is required the MUX
selecting among x and y has to be removed, resulting in a total size of $\ell + \kappa$ gates.

When the minimum has to be computed among more than two values we can
use a reverse tree structure, as in Fig. 7.12. The minimum value and minimum identifier are selected pair-wise in a tournament-like way using a reverse tree of minimum blocks, were the intermediate blocks choose among the outputs of the previous
blocks. Given $n + 1$ pairs (x_i, Id_i) the circuit needs n MIN block, hence the total size
of the garbled circuit is $n(2\ell + \kappa)$ tables of $4t$ bits. If only the Id of the minimum
value is required, in the last MIN block the MUX selecting among the values can be
removed, resulting in a total size of $n(2\ell + \kappa) - \ell$ gates.

7.5 Design Principles for Privacy-Aware Biometric Matching

By composing the building blocks described in Sect. 7.4, a privacy-aware matching
protocol can be easily built. In this Section we give some general guidelines that
can be used to choose the proper implementation of the basic building blocks so to
achieve an efficient protocol suited to the application at hand.

From a computational point of view, HE is preferable when the parties have
enough computing power since they need to compute many exponentiations, while
GC requires the computation of (many) simple Hash functions. From a communication point of view HE protocols transmit few long ciphertexts ($2T$ bits each, where
T is at least 1024) in a number of rounds that depends on the application, while GC
has to transfer a secret for any S input bit ($t = 80$ bits long each), a table for each
non-XOR gate ($4t$ bits) and exchange the secrets relative to the C input bits by OT
($2t$ bits transferred for each input bit), resulting in a high bandwidth, even if all the
transmissions are performed in only two rounds.

Comparing the HE and the GC implementations of the sub-protocol (detailed in
Sect. 7.4) from a computational point of view is not easy, since the answer finally
depends on the number of bits used to represented biometric vectors and hence on
the representation accuracy needed to achieve a given recognition rate. Usually a

HE protocol is composed by few difficult operations performed on large numbers; in a Paillier homomorphic protocol, where ciphertexts are represented by $2T$ bits ($T = 1024$), the most complex basic operation is the exponentiation, having $\mathcal{O}(T^3)$ complexity. On the other side to evaluate a GC a big number of hash functions, having small constant complexity, are computed. Moreover we have to consider that the complexity of these operations can change from one system to another, for example in the presence of dedicated hardware. Finally we have to consider that in the future longer ciphertexts will be required to guarantee security, due to the increase of available computational resources. While the security parameter T of an asymmetric scheme (necessary to HE) grows exponentially, the security parameter t of the symmetric cryptosystem (used in GC) grows linearly [34], making GC more performing than HE.

We now analyze the different implementations of the building blocks described in Sect. 7.4, from a communication point of view.

We remind the reader that any matching protocol starts with the computation of distances (1 distance in the verification scenario and n distances in the identification scenario), and then terminates with a minimum selection, computed between two values (the distance and a threshold) in the verification protocol or $n + 1$ values (the n distances and a threshold) in the identification protocol. A label represented with κ bits is associated to each distance (for example "Yes" in the verification protocol or an identifier in the identification protocol) and to the threshold (the "No" string).

Given a feature vector composed by m features represented with $\ell < T$ (usually $\ell \ll T$) bits each, if the Euclidean distance is computed by HE, $\mathcal{C}$ transmits m ciphertexts to $\mathcal{S}$ and during the computation other $2m$ ciphertexts are transmitted for each distance (note that it is possible to reduce the transmission from $\mathcal{S}$ to $\mathcal{C}$ by packing several values in a single ciphertext), resulting in the transmission of $\mathcal{O}(nmT)$ bits in three rounds and the distances are finally available to $\mathcal{S}$ in encrypted form. In a GC protocol $\mathcal{C}$ has to obtain $m\ell$ secrets by the parallel OT ($2m\ell t$ bits); receives $nm\ell$ secrets relative to the feature vectors representing the biometries owned by $\mathcal{S}$ ($nm\ell t$ bits); receives $m\ell + \frac{3m}{2}(\ell + 1)\ell + (m - 1)(2\ell + 2 + \lceil \log_2 m \rceil)$ garbled tables for each distance computation ($n(m\ell + \frac{3m}{2}(\ell + 1)\ell + (m - 1)(2\ell + 2 + \lceil \log_2 m \rceil))4t$ bits), obtaining a total communication complexity of $\mathcal{O}(nm\ell^2 t)$ bits. Finally the output secrets are available to $\mathcal{C}$. We can observe easily that GC is preferable to HE only when ℓ is small.

When $\ell = 1$, Euclidean distance is replaced by Hamming distance. HE still requires the transmission of m ciphertexts from $\mathcal{C}$ to $\mathcal{S}$ at the beginning of the protocol, but then the communication complexity is reduced to $nm + 1$ ciphertexts. The asymptotic communication complexity results $\mathcal{O}(nmT)$ bits. The GC computing the Hamming distance requires a parallel OT for m secrets ($2mt$ bits), the transmission of nm secrets (nmt bits) and $\lesssim n(m - \log_2(m + 1))$ non-XOR gates of size $4t$ bits, with an asymptotic communication complexity of $\mathcal{O}(nmt)$ bits. Concluding, when the Hamming distance can be computed, GC is preferable to HE also from a communication complexity point of view.

Regarding the minimum selection GC is indeed more efficient than HE. In fact in a GC solution only two rounds are necessary (there are no additional rounds if the

Table 7.7 Asymptotic communication complexities of the different implementation for the addressed sub-protocols

	Euclidean distance		Hamming distance		Minimum selection	
	Bandwidth	Rounds	Bandwidth	Rounds	Bandwidth	Rounds
HE	$\mathcal{O}(nmT)$	3	$\mathcal{O}(nmT)$	3	$\mathcal{O}(n\ell_d T)$	$6\log_2(n+1)$
GC	$\mathcal{O}(nm\ell^2 t)$	2	$\mathcal{O}(nmt)$	2	$\mathcal{O}(n\ell_d t)$	2

distance computation is also carried out by GC) and $\mathcal{O}(n\ell_d t)$ bits are transferred, where ℓ_d is the number of bits necessary to represent a distance, while the HE solution requires $6\log_2(n+1)$ rounds where $\mathcal{O}(n\ell_d T)$ bits are transmitted.

The asymptotic complexities are summarized in Table 7.7.

To conclude, for both verification and identification, we suggest to use a hybrid protocol where the distance is computed by HE and the minimum is selected by GC. When the biometries can be represented by binary vectors, we suggest to evaluate the Hamming distance by using GC, obtaining a unique GC that computes distances and the minimum index.

7.6 Conclusions

Multiparty computation has been studied for three decades by cryptographers, however, only recently the state of the art in the field, and the computational power and bandwidth made available by information and communication technology have permitted to deploy such techniques for real life applications. Among the most promising applications of SMPC (and specifically STPC), privacy-aware processing of biometric data occupies a central role. As a matter of fact, biometric applications raise important privacy issues that can be conveniently solved by resorting to STPC. In this chapter we have reviewed the basic concepts behind STPC and described the basic cryptographic primitives needed to achieve privacy-aware processing of biometric data in a STPC context. The two main approaches proposed so far, namely homomorphic encryption and garbled circuits have been discussed and the way such techniques can be used to develop a full biometric matching protocol described. Some general rules designers should follow to select the most appropriate tools have also been given.

Even if the state of the art already permits the development of real-life applications based on the tools described in this chapter, several advances are still needed before we assist to a widespread use of STPC techniques in biometric applications.

The most pressing demand is surely a request for a better efficiency. The importance of this request lies in a very simple fact: privacy has a price and if we want that someone pays for improving the privacy of a system this price must be reasonably low. Actually it is surprising how few people are willing to pay for privacy measures despite the continuous call for privacy raising from various sources. While everybody agrees that sensitive data needs to be protected and that personal privacy is worth protection, very few users would be willing to pay for a secure service if an insecure, but faster, service is offered to them for free or at a lower price.

A second line of research that needs to be considered regards the security model. According to the current state of the art, efficient privacy preserving protocols are available only under the assumption of semi-honest parties. This is a rather common assumption, however, its applicability in practical scenarios is doubtful. In most cases, in fact, we should assume that our adversary is willing to deviate from the correct protocol if in this way he can steal some supposed-to-be-secret information. Some interesting results in this sense have been shown in [55]. We expect that further improvements will follow hence making privacy protection in the presence of a malicious adversary practical.

Finally, we mention the importance that specific biometric processing algorithms are devised tailored to the need of a privacy-preserving implementation. Indeed, the approach used so far has been that of taking a classical algorithm and transforming it into a protocol to be run on encrypted signals. It is arguable that much better results could be obtained by developing a class of processing tools that are explicitly thought to ease a STPC implementations, e.g. by considering in advance which are the most complex operations to be carried out in a secure way and try to avoid them, or by trying to minimize the number of bits used to represent the biometric templates to reduce the communication or computational complexity of the protocols.

References

1. Agrawal R, Srikant R (2000) Privacy-preserving data mining. SIGMOD Record 29(2):439–450
2. Aiello B, Ishai Y, Reingold O (2001) Priced oblivious transfer: how to sell digital goods. Advances in Cryptology—EUROCRYPT 2001:119–135
3. Barker WC (2004) Recommendation for the triple data encryption algorithm (TDEA) block cipher. NIST special publication, May 2004
4. Barker E, Burr W, Jones A, Polk T, Rose S, Smid M, Dang Q (2009) Recommendation for key management. NASA Special Publication 800:57
5. Barni M, Failla P, Kolensikov V, Lazzeretti R, Paus A, Sadeghi A, Schneider T (2009) Efficient privacy-preserving classification of ECG signals. In: Workshop on Information Forensics and Security—WIFS 2009
6. Barni M, Bianchi T, Catalano D, Di Raimondo M, Donida Labati R, Failla P, Fiore D, Lazzeretti R, Piuri V, Scotti F, Piva A (2010) Privacy-preserving fingercode authentication. In: Proceedings of the 12th ACM Workshop on Multimedia and Security. ACM, New York, pp 231–240
7. Barni M, Bianchi T, Catalano D, Di Raimondo M, Labati RD, Failla P, Fiore D, Lazzeretti R, Piuri V, Piva A, Scotti F (2010) A privacy-compliant fingerprint recognition system based on homomorphic encryption and fingercode templates. In: Fourth IEEE International Conference on Biometrics: Theory Applications and Systems—BTAS 2010. IEEE Press, New York, pp 1–7
8. Barni M, Failla P, Kolesnikov V, Lazzeretti R, Sadeghi AR, Schneider T (2010) Secure evaluation of private linear branching programs with medical applications. In: European Symposium on Research in Computer Security—ESORICS 2009, pp 424–439

9. Barni M, Guajardo J, Lazzeretti R (2010) Privacy preserving evaluation of signal quality with application to ECG analysis. In: IEEE International Workshop on Information Forensics and Security—WIFS 2010. IEEE Press, New York, pp 1–6
10. Barni M, Failla P, Lazzeretti R, Sadeghi AR, Schneider T (2011) Privacy-preserving ECG classification with branching programs and neural networks. In: IEEE Transactions on Information Forensics and Security—TIFS, June 2011
11. Beaver D (1995) Precomputing oblivious transfer. In: Advances in Cryptology—CRYPTO'95. LNCS, vol 963. Springer, Berlin, pp 97–109
12. Benaloh J (1994) Dense probabilistic encryption. In: Proceedings of the Workshop on Selected Areas of Cryptography. Citeseer, pp 120–128
13. Bianchi T, Piva A, Barni M (2009) On the implementation of the discrete Fourier transform in the encrypted domain. IEEE Transactions on Information Forensics and Security 4(1):86–97
14. Bianchi T, Piva A, Barni M (2010) Composite signal representation for fast and storage-efficient processing of encrypted signals. IEEE Transactions on Information Forensics and Security 5(1):180–187
15. Bjorck A (1967) Solving linear least squares problems by Gram–Schmidt orthogonalization. BIT Numerical Mathematics 7(1):1–21
16. Boneh D, Lipton R (1996) Algorithms for black-box fields and their application to cryptography. In: Advances in Cryptology—CRYPTO'96. Springer, Berlin, pp 283–297
17. Boneh D, Goh EJ, Nissim K (2005) Evaluating 2-DNF formulas on ciphertexts. Theory of Cryptography 325–341
18. Bresson E, Catalano D, Pointcheval D (2003) A simple public-key cryptosystem with a double trapdoor decryption mechanism and its applications. Advances in Cryptology—ASIACRYPT 2003(1):37–54
19. Brickell J, Porter DE, Shmatikov V, Witchel E (2007) Privacy-preserving remote diagnostics. In: Proceedings of the 14th ACM Conference on Computer and Communications Security. ACM, New York, p 507
20. Brinkman R, Doumen J, Jonker W (2004) Using secret sharing for searching in encrypted data. Secure Data Management 1:18–27
21. Camp JL (2004) Digital identity. IEEE Technology & Society Magazine 23(3):34–41
22. Chui CK, Quak E (1992) Wavelets on a bounded interval. Numerical Methods of Approximation Theory 9(1):53–57
23. Daemen J, Rijmen V (1999) The Rijndael block cipher. AES Proposal, Mar 1999
24. Damgård I, Jurik M (2001) A generalization, a simplification and some applications of Paillier's probabilistic public-key system. In: Public Key Cryptography. Springer, Berlin, pp 119–136
25. Damgård I, Geisler M, Krøigaard M (2007) Efficient and secure comparison for on-line auctions. In: Information Security and Privacy. Springer, Berlin, pp 416–430
26. ElGamal T (1985) A public key cryptosystem and a signature scheme based on discrete logarithms. IEEE Transactions on Information Theory IT-31(4):469–472
27. Erkin Z (2010) Secure signal processing: privacy preserving cryptographic protocols for multimedia. PhD thesis, Delft University of Technology, The Netherlands
28. Erkin Z, Franz M, Guajardo J, Katzenbeisser S, Lagendijk I, Toft T (2009) Privacy-preserving face recognition. In: Privacy Enhancing Technologies. Springer, Berlin, pp 235–253
29. Even S, Goldreich O, Lempel A (1985) A randomized protocol for signing contracts. Communications of the ACM 28(6):647
30. Failla P (2010) Heuristic search in encrypted graphs. In: Fourth International Conference on Emerging Security Information, Systems and Technologies—SECURWARE'10, pp 82–87
31. Failla P, Barni M (2010) Gram–Schmidt orthogonalization on encrypted vectors. In: 21st International Tyrrhenian Workshop on Digital Communications—ITWDC 2010
32. Gentry C (2009) Fully homomorphic encryption using ideal lattices. In: Proceedings of the 41st Annual ACM Symposium on Theory of Computing. ACM, New York, pp 169–178
33. Gentry C, Halevi S, Vaikuntanathan V (2010) A simple BGN-type cryptosystem from LWE. Advances in Cryptology—EUROCRYPT 2010:506–522

34. Giry D, Quisquater JJ (2010) Cryptographic key length recommendation
35. Goldreich O (2004) Foundations of Cryptography. Cambridge University Press, Cambridge
36. Goldreich O, Micali S, Wigderson A (1987) How to play any mental game. In: Proceedings of the Nineteenth Annual ACM Symposium on Theory of Computing. ACM, New York, pp 218–229
37. Goldwasser S, Micali S (1984) Probabilistic encryption. Journal of Computer and System Sciences 28(2):270–299
38. Golub GH, Van Loan CF (1996) Matrix Computations. Johns Hopkins University Press, Baltimore
39. Hart PE, Nilsson NJ, Raphael B (1968) A formal basis for the heuristic determination of minimum cost paths. IEEE Transactions on Systems Science and Cybernetics 4(2):100–107
40. Ishai Y, Kilian J, Nissim K, Petrank E (2003) Extending oblivious transfers efficiently. In: Advances in Cryptology—CRYPTO'03. LNCS, vol 2729. Springer, Berlin
41. Johnson M, Ishwar P, Prabhakaran V, Schonberg D, Ramchandran K (2004) On compressing encrypted data. IEEE Transactions on Signal Processing 52(10):2992–3006
42. Katzenbeisser S, Lemma A, Celik MU, van der Veen M, Maas M (2008) A buyer–seller watermarking protocol based on secure embedding. IEEE Transactions on Information Forensics and Security 3(4):783–786
43. Koblitz N (1994) A Course in Number Theory and Cryptography. Springer, Berlin
44. Kolesnikov V, Schneider T (2008) Improved garbled circuit: free XOR gates and applications. In: International Colloquium on Automata, Languages and Programming (ICALP'08). LNCS, vol 5126. Springer, Berlin, pp 486–498
45. Kolesnikov V, Sadeghi AR, Schneider T (2009) Improved garbled circuit building blocks and applications to auctions and computing minima. Cryptology and Network Security 1–20
46. Kolesnikov V, Sadeghi AR, Schneider T (2010) Modular design of efficient secure function evaluation protocols. Technical report, cryptology ePrint archive, report 2010/079, http:// eprint.iacr.org/2010/079/. [Online]. Available: http://thomaschneider.de/papers/KSS10.pdf
47. Lindell Y, Pinkas B (2008) Privacy preserving data mining. Journal of Cryptology 15(3):177–206
48. Lindell Y, Pinkas B (2009) A proof of security of Yao's protocol for two-party computation. Journal of Cryptology 22(2):161–188
49. Lindell Y, Pinkas B, Smart N (2008) Implementing two-party computation efficiently with security against malicious adversaries. In: Security and Cryptography for Networks—SCN'08. LNCS, vol 5229. Springer, Berlin, pp 2–20
50. Ma YD, Qi CL, Qian ZB, Shi F, Zhang ZF (2006) A novel image compression coding algorithm based on pulse-coupled neural network and Gram–Schmidt orthogonal base. Dianzi Xuebao (Acta Electronica Sinica) 34(7):1255–1259
51. Malkhi D, Nisan N, Pinkas B, Sella Y (2004) Fairplay—a secure two-party computation system. In: USENIX. http://fairplayproject.net
52. Melchor CA, Gaborit P, Herranz J (1996) Additively homomorphic encryption with t-operand multiplications. Crypto 2010
53. Menezes AJ, Van Oorschot PC, Vanstone SA (1997) Handbook of Applied Cryptography. CRC Press, Boca Raton
54. Naor M, Pinkas B (2001) Efficient oblivious transfer protocols. In: ACM-SIAM Symposium on Discrete Algorithms—SODA'01. Society for Industrial and Applied Mathematics, Philadelphia, pp 448–457
55. Nielsen JB, Nordholt PS, Orlandi C, Burra SS (2011) A new approach to practical active-secure two-party computation. Cryptology ePrint archive, report 2011/091. http://eprint. iacr.org/
56. Orfanidis SJ (1990) Gram–Schmidt neural nets. Neural Computation 2(1):116–126
57. Osadchy M, Pinkas B, Jarrous A, Moskovich B (2010) SCiFI-a system for secure face identification. In: 2010 IEEE Symposium on Security and Privacy. IEEE Press, New York, pp 239–254

58. Paillier P (1999) Public-key cryptosystems based on composite degree residuosity classes. In: Advances in Cryptology—EUROCRYPT'99. Springer, Berlin, pp 223–238
59. Paus A, Sadeghi A-R, Schneider T (2009) Practical secure evaluation of semi-private functions. In: Applied Cryptography and Network Security—ACNS'09. LNCS, vol 5536. Springer, Berlin, pp 89–106. http://www.trust.rub.de/FairplaySPF
60. Pinkas B, Schneider T, Smart NP, Williams SC (2009) Secure two-party computation is practical. In: Advances in Cryptology—ASIACRYPT 2009, Dec 2009. LNCS, vol 5912. Springer, Berlin. Full version available at http://eprint.iacr.org/2009/314
61. Rane S, Sun W (2010) Privacy preserving string comparisons based on Levenshtein distance. In: IEEE International Workshop on Information Forensics and Security—WIFS 2010. IEEE Press, New York, pp 1–6
62. Rappe DK (2004) Homomorphic cryptosystems and their applications. Volume PhD
63. Rivest RL, Adleman L, Dertouzos ML (1978) On data banks and privacy homomorphisms. Foundations of Secure Computation 169–178
64. Rivest RL, Shamir A, Adleman L (1978) A method for obtaining digital signatures and public-key cryptosystems. Communications of the ACM 21(2):126
65. Sadeghi AR, Schneider T, Wehrenberg I (2009) Efficient privacy-preserving face recognition. In: International Conference on Information Security and Cryptology—ICISC 2009. Springer, Berlin
66. Sharma A, Paliwal KK (2007) Fast principal component analysis using fixed-point algorithm. Pattern Recognition Letters 28(10):1151–1155
67. van Dijk M, Gentry C, Halevi S, Vaikuntanathan V (2010) Fully homomorphic encryption over the integers. In: Advances in Cryptology–EUROCRYPT, pp 24–43
68. Yao AC (1982) Protocols for secure computations. In: Proceedings of the 23rd Annual IEEE Symposium on Foundations of Computer Science, vol 23. Citeseer, pp 160–164
69. Yao AC (1986) How to generate and exchange secrets. In: IEEE Symposium on Foundations of Computer Science (FOCS'86). IEEE Press, New York, pp 162–167
70. Zheng W, Zou C, Zhao L (2004) Real-time face recognition using Gram–Schmidt orthogonalization for LDA. Pattern Recognition 2:403–406

Chapter 8
Fingerprint Template Protection: From Theory to Practice

Anil K. Jain, Karthik Nandakumar, and Abhishek Nagar

Abstract One of the potential vulnerabilities in a biometric system is the leakage of biometric template information, which may lead to serious security and privacy threats. Most of the available template protection techniques fail to meet all the desired requirements of a practical biometric system like revocability, security, privacy, and high matching accuracy. In particular, protecting the fingerprint templates has been a difficult problem due to large intra-user variations (e.g., rotation, translation, nonlinear deformation, and partial prints). There are two fundamental challenges in any fingerprint template protection scheme. First, we need to select an appropriate representation scheme that captures most of the discriminatory information, but is sufficiently invariant to changes in finger placement and can be secured using available template protection algorithms. Secondly, we need to automatically align or register the fingerprints obtained during enrollment and matching without using any information that could reveal the features, which uniquely characterize a fingerprint. This chapter analyzes how these two challenges are being addressed in practice and how the design choices affect the trade-off between the security and matching accuracy. Though much progress has been made over the last decade, we believe that fingerprint template protection algorithms are still not sufficiently robust to be incorporated into practical fingerprint recognition systems.

A.K. Jain (✉) · A. Nagar
Department of Computer Science & Engineering, Michigan State University, East Lansing, MI 48824, USA
e-mail: jain@cse.msu.edu

A. Nagar
e-mail: nagarabh@cse.msu.edu

A.K. Jain
Department of Brain & Cognitive Engineering, Korea University, Seoul, South Korea

K. Nandakumar
Institute for Infocomm Research, A*STAR, Fusionopolis, Singapore, Singapore
e-mail: knandakumar@i2r.a-star.edu.sg

P. Campisi (ed.), *Security and Privacy in Biometrics*,
DOI 10.1007/978-1-4471-5230-9_8, © Springer-Verlag London 2013

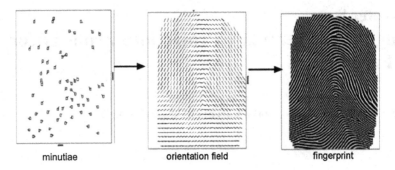

minutiae   orientation field   fingerprint

Fig. 8.1 Reconstruction of a fingerprint image from the minutiae template [18]

8.1 Introduction

The primary purpose of using a biometric system is to provide non-repudiable authentication. Authentication implies that (i) only legitimate or authorized users are able to access the physical or logical resources protected by the biometric system and (ii) impostors are prevented from accessing the protected resources. Non-repudiation ensures that an individual who accesses a certain resource cannot later deny using it. From the perspective of the users, there are two main requirements that a biometric system must meet. Firstly, the legitimate users must have timely and reliable access to the protected resource/service. Secondly, the biometric system and the personal data stored in it must be used only for the intended functionality, which is to control access to a specific resource and not for other unintended purposes. However, attacks by adversaries may prevent the biometric system from satisfying the above functionalities and requirements.

While a biometric system can be compromised in a number of ways, one of the potentially damaging attacks is the leakage of biometric template information. The leakage of this template information to unauthorized individuals constitutes a serious security and privacy threat due to the following two reasons:

1. *Intrusion attack*: If an attacker can hack into a biometric database, he can easily obtain the stored biometric information of a user. This information can be used to gain unauthorized access to the system by either reverse engineering the template to create a physical spoof or replaying the stolen template. For example, it has been shown that fingerprint images can be reconstructed from minutiae templates (see Fig. 8.1), which may in turn be used to construct a spoof [6, 18, 44].
2. *Function creep*: An adversary can exploit the biometric template information for unintended purposes (e.g., covertly track a user across different applications by cross-matching the templates from the associated databases), compromising user privacy.

Due to these reasons, biometric templates (or the raw biometric images) should not be stored in plaintext form and fool-proof techniques are required to securely store the templates such that both the security of the application and the users' pri-

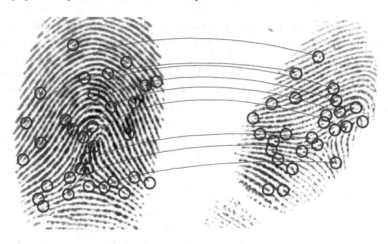

Fig. 8.2 Illustration of fingerprint intra-class variability. Two different impressions of the same finger with differences in the number and location of minutiae are shown. Among the 33 and 26 minutiae in the *left* and *right images*, respectively, only 16 minutiae match and some of these matches are marked

vacy are not compromised by adversary attacks. The fundamental challenge in designing a biometric template protection scheme is to overcome the large intra-user variability among multiple acquisitions of the same biometric trait (see Fig. 8.2).

8.1.1 Biometric Template Security Requirements

A biometric template protection scheme should have the following three properties.

1. *Cryptographic security*: Given a secure template, it must be computationally difficult to find a biometric feature set (commonly known as a *pre-image*) that will match with the secure template. This pre-image resistant property defends against the possibility of an attacker intruding into the biometric system under consideration by replaying the pre-image.

   The concept of pre-image resistance is also related to *one-way* or *non-invertible* mathematical functions. A function **f** is referred to as a one-way function if it is "easy to compute" (in polynomial time) but "hard to invert" (given **f(x)**, the probability of finding **x** in polynomial-time is small). A non-invertible template protection scheme implies that it will be computationally hard to obtain the original biometric features from the secure template. This prevents an adversary from creating a physical spoof of the biometric trait and intruding another biometric system that makes use of the same biometric trait. Thus, a secure template must be pre-image resistant and non-invertible.

2. *Performance*: The biometric template protection scheme should not degrade the recognition performance (False Match Rate (FMR) and False Non-Match Rate (FNMR)) of the biometric system.

3. *Revocability*: It is desirable to have a template protection scheme that can generate multiple secure templates from the same biometric data. These multiple secure templates must be such that even if an adversary obtains two or more of them, it must be computationally hard to: (i) identify that they are derived from the same biometric data, and (ii) obtain the original biometric features of the user. This revocability or cancelability property ensures that cross-matching across biometric databases is not possible, thereby preserving the user's privacy. Revocability also makes it straightforward to discard a compromised template and reissue a new one based on the same biometric data.

Ideally, the template protection scheme should satisfy all the three requirements simultaneously. However, it is quite a challenge to design such a technique. The simplest way to secure biometric templates is to encrypt them using standard cryptographic techniques like RSA and AES. This is the methodology deployed in most of the existing commercial biometric systems. However, it must be emphasized that multiple acquisitions of the same biometric trait do not result in the same feature set. Typically, standard encryption functions are not smooth functions and a small difference in the values of the feature sets extracted from the raw biometric data would lead to very large difference in the resulting encrypted features. Consequently, one cannot perform biometric matching directly in the encrypted domain. Rather, the template must be decrypted in order to be matched with the query features. As a result, the original biometric features are exposed during every authentication attempt, irrespective of whether the authentication is eventually successful. Therefore, the encryption solution is secure and revocable only under ideal conditions (key is kept secret and matching is done at a trusted location). If practical issues such as key management or susceptibility to template theft during a matching attempt are taken into account, the standard encryption technique is not good enough for securing biometric templates.

8.1.2 Biometric Template Protection Approaches

To overcome the limitations of the standard encryption approach, a number of techniques have been proposed to secure biometric templates (see [23] for a detailed review). These techniques can be categorized into two main classes (see Fig. 8.3):

- *Biometric cryptosystems*: In a biometric cryptosystem, secure sketch ($\mathbf{y}_c$) is derived from the enrolled biometric template ($\mathbf{x}^E$) and stored in the system database instead of the original template. In the absence of the genuine user's biometric data, it must be computationally hard to reconstruct the template from the sketch. On the other hand, given an authentication query ($\mathbf{x}^A$) that is *sufficiently close* to the enrolled template ($\mathbf{x}^E$), it should be easy to decode the sketch and recover the template. Typically, the sketch is obtained by binding the template with a codeword from an error correcting code, where the codeword itself is de-

Fig. 8.3 Biometric template protection based on (**a**) biometric cryptosystem and (**b**) template transformation

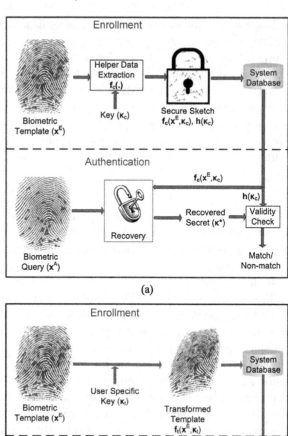

fined by a key (κ_c). Therefore, the sketch ($\mathbf{y}_c$) can be written as $\mathbf{f}_c(\mathbf{x}^E, \kappa_c)$, where $\mathbf{f}_c$ is the sketch generation function. The error correction mechanism facilitates the recovery of the original template and hence, the associated key. Thus, a biometric cryptosystem not only secures the biometric template, but also facilitates secure key management, which is one of the challenging issues in cryptographic systems. Examples of biometric cryptosystems include fuzzy vault [26], fuzzy commitment [27], PinSketch [14], and secret-sharing approaches [20].

- *Template transformation*: Template transformation techniques modify the template ($\mathbf{x}^E$) with a user specific key (κ_t) such that it is difficult to recover the original template from the transformed template ($\mathbf{y}_t$). During authentication, the same transformation is applied to the biometric query ($\mathbf{x}^A$) and the matching is performed in the transformed domain to avoid exposure of the original biometric template. Since the key κ_t needs to be stored in the system along with $\mathbf{y}_t$, the template security is guaranteed only if the transformation function is non-invertible even when κ_t is known to the attacker. Some well-known examples of template transformation include Bio-Hashing [49] and cancelable biometrics [42].

Different combinations of the above two basic approaches, called hybrid biometric cryptosystems, have also been proposed [37, 46]. The template protection schemes described above have their own advantages and limitations in terms of template security, computational cost, storage requirements, applicability to different kinds of biometric representations and ability to handle intra-class variations in biometric data [52].

In this chapter, we will focus on the practical issues involved in applying the available template protection algorithms to secure fingerprint templates. Features representing fingerprint images may exhibit intra-user variations due to various factors like rotation, translation, nonlinear deformation, and partial overlap between multiple impressions of the same finger. As a result, protecting fingerprint templates is a challenging task. Fingerprint recognition is typically based on the location and orientation of minutia points, which represent ridge endings or ridge bifurcations [31]. Minutiae sets are unordered and there may be variations (see Fig. 8.2) in the number and location of minutia points due to intra-user variations. The similarity between two fingerprints is measured based on the number of minutia correspondences. Furthermore, the template and query minutiae sets need to be aligned before the minutia correspondences can be found. Hence, there are two key challenges in securely matching fingerprints: (i) How to align query minutiae set with template without leaking information about the original minutiae template? and (ii) Even after aligning the query and the template, the minutiae in the two sets will not match exactly in location and orientation due to nonlinear deformation (hence, a simple set difference metric may not be good enough). Finding a good representation scheme for fingerprints that can overcome the above problem is a challenge.

The rest of the chapter is organized as follows. Section 8.2 gives a brief overview of the major template protection algorithms that have been applied for securing fingerprint templates. Next, Sect. 8.3 gives some examples of how the fingerprint features need to be adapted so that biometric cryptosystems can be applied to secure them. Section 8.4 describes the various approaches that have been proposed for aligning the query fingerprint with the secure template. The matching performance and security of the state-of-the-art fingerprint template protection schemes are discussed in Sect. 8.5. Finally, our conclusions and pointers for future research are highlighted in Sect. 8.6.

8.2 Fingerprint Template Protection Schemes

Depending on the features used for recognition, existing solutions for fingerprint template security can be categorized as minutiae-based or pattern-based approaches. Minutiae-based template protection schemes can be further classified into three types: (i) directly secure the unordered set representation of minutiae, (ii) secure a new set of unordered features derived from the minutiae (e.g., distances between pairs of minutiae), and (iii) secure a fixed-length feature vector derived from the minutiae. On the other hand, pattern-based schemes directly derive a fixed-length feature vector based on the global texture of the fingerprint pattern. When the representation to be secured is an unordered set, a *non-invertible template transformation* approach or a biometric cryptosystem called *fuzzy vault* can be used. When the representation is a fixed-length binary vector, a biometric cryptosystem called *fuzzy commitment* can be used to secure it. We will now discuss these three schemes in detail.

8.2.1 Non-invertible Fingerprint Template Transformation

Ratha et al. [42] proposed and analyzed three non-invertible transforms for generating cancelable fingerprint templates. The three transformation functions are Cartesian, polar and functional. These functions were used to transform fingerprint minutiae data such that a minutiae matcher can still be applied to the transformed minutiae. In Cartesian transformation, the minutiae space (fingerprint image) is tessellated into a rectangular grid and each cell (possibly containing some minutiae) is shifted to a new position in the grid corresponding to the translations set by the user-specific key. The polar transformation is similar to Cartesian transformation with the difference that the image is now tessellated into a number of concentric shells and each shell is divided into sectors. Since the size of sectors can be different (sectors near the center are smaller than the ones far from the center), restrictions are placed on the translation vector generated from the key so that the radial distance of the transformed sector is not very different from the radial distance of the original position. Examples of minutiae before and after polar and Cartesian transformations are shown in Fig. 8.4.

For the functional transformation, Ratha et al. [42] used a mixture of 2D Gaussians and electric potential field in a 2D random charge distribution as a means to translate the minutia points. The magnitude of these functions at the point corresponding to a minutia is used as a measure of the magnitude of the translation and the gradient of these functions is used to estimate the direction of translation of the minutiae. In all the three transforms, two or more minutiae can possibly map to the same point in the transformed domain. For example, in the Cartesian transformation, two or more cells can be mapped onto a single cell so that even if an adversary knows the key and hence the transformation between cells, he cannot determine the original cell to which a minutia belongs because each

Fig. 8.4 Illustration of
Cartesian and polar
transformation functions used
in [42] for generating
cancelable biometrics.
(**a**) Original minutiae on
radial grid, (**b**) transformed
minutiae after polar
transformation, (**c**) original
minutiae on rectangular grid,
and (**d**) transformed minutiae
after Cartesian transformation

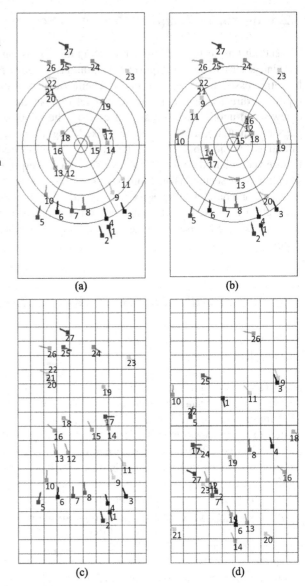

minutia can independently belong to one of the possible cells. This provides a
limited amount of non-invertibility to the transform. Also since the transformations used are locally smooth, the error rates are not affected significantly and
the discriminability of minutiae is preserved to a large extent. Note that the key
to achieving good recognition performance is the availability of an alignment algorithm that can accurately pre-align (register) the fingerprint images or minutiae
features prior to the transformation (e.g., based on core and delta points in the fingerprint).

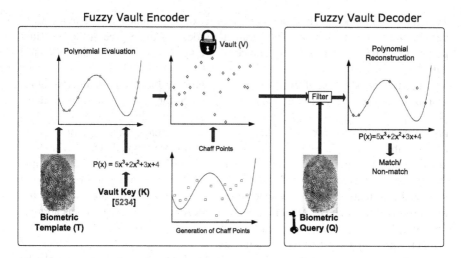

Fig. 8.5 Securing a fingerprint minutiae template using fuzzy vault

8.2.2 Fingerprint Fuzzy Vault

Fuzzy vault is a cryptographic construct that is designed to work with biometric features represented as an unordered set (e.g., minutiae in fingerprints). The security of the fuzzy vault scheme is based on the computational difficulty in solving the polynomial reconstruction problem, which is a special case of the Reed–Solomon list decoding problem [2]. The fuzzy vault scheme works as follows (see Fig. 8.5). Let $s^E = \{x_1, x_2, \ldots, x_r\}$ denote a biometric template consisting of a set of r points from a finite field $\mathcal{F}$. In order to secure s^E, a uniformly random cryptographic key κ_c of length L bits is generated and this key is transformed into a polynomial P of degree k ($k < r$) over $\mathcal{F}$. All the elements in s^E are then evaluated on this polynomial to obtain the set $\{P(x_i)\}_{i=1}^r$. The set of points $\{(x_i, P(x_i))\}_{i=1}^r$ is then secured by hiding them among a large set of q randomly generated chaff points $\{(a_j, b_j)\}_{j=1}^q$ that do not lie on the polynomial P (i.e., $b_j \neq P(a_j)$ and $a_j \notin s^E, \forall j = 1, 2, \ldots, q$). The set of genuine and chaff points along with their polynomial evaluations constitute the sketch or vault $\mathbf{y}_c$. During authentication, if the query biometric set s^A is sufficiently close to s^E, the polynomial P can be successfully reconstructed by identifying the genuine points in $\mathbf{y}_c$ that are associated with s^E. Note that for successful reconstruction of P of degree k, a minimum of $(k + 1)$ genuine points need to be identified from $\mathbf{y}_c$.

The three main parameters in the fuzzy vault scheme are r, q and k. The parameter r denotes the number of points in the vault that lie on the polynomial P and it depends on the number of features that can be extracted from the template (e.g., number of minutia points in the user's fingerprint). The parameter q represents the number of chaff points that are added and this parameter influences the security of the vault. If no chaff points are added, the vault reveals the information about the template and the secret. As more chaff points are added, the security increases.

Typically, the number of chaff points is an order of magnitude larger than the number of genuine points ($q \gg r$). The parameter k denotes the degree of the encoding polynomial and it controls the tolerance of the system to errors in the biometric data.

Since the introduction of the fuzzy vault scheme by Juels and Sudan, several researchers have attempted to implement it in practice for securing fingerprint minutiae templates. Clancy et al. [12] proposed a fuzzy vault scheme based on the location of minutia points (row and column indices in the image) in a fingerprint. They assumed that the template and query minutiae sets are pre-aligned, which is not a realistic assumption in practical fingerprint authentication systems. Further, multiple (four) fingerprint impressions of a user were used during enrollment for identifying the reliable minutia points. The error correction step was simulated without being actually implemented. The False Non-Match Rate of their system was approximately 20–30 % and they claimed that retrieving the secret was 2^{69} times more difficult for an attacker than for a genuine user.

The fingerprint-based fuzzy vault proposed by Yang et al. [56] also used only the location information about the minutia points. Four impressions were used during enrollment to identify a reference minutia, and the relative position of the remaining minutia points with respect to the reference minutiae was represented in the polar coordinate system. This scheme was evaluated on a small database of 10 fingers and a FNMR of 17 % was reported. Chung et al. [11] proposed a geometric hashing technique to perform alignment in a minutiae-based fingerprint fuzzy vault. Uludag et al. [53] introduced a modification to the fuzzy vault scheme, which eliminated the need for error correction coding. Uludag and Jain [51] also proposed the use of high curvature points derived from the fingerprint orientation field to automatically align the template and query minutiae sets (see Sect. 8.4 for details).

Nandakumar et al. [36] proposed a fuzzy vault framework that secures both minutiae locations and directions. During vault encoding a ($16 \times k$) bit key (κ_c) is appended with a 16-bit Cyclic Redundancy Check (CRC) code and divided into ($k + 1$) blocks of 16 bits each. These ($k + 1$) values serve as the coefficients of a polynomial P of degree k in the Galois field $GF(2^{16})$. The template minutiae are sorted according to their quality and only well-separated minutiae [36] are selected for constructing the vault. If the desired number of minutiae (say r) cannot be obtained, it is counted as a Failure to Capture error (FTCR). The location and orientation of each minutia is encoded as an element in $GF(2^{16})$. Points with high ridge curvature are extracted from the fingerprint and stored along with the vault to be used for alignment during authentication.

During authentication, the high curvature points are used to align the template and query fingerprints. Then, r well separated and good quality minutiae are selected from the query and are coarsely matched with the points in the vault in order to filter out most of the chaff points. At this stage, a minutiae matcher [22] is applied to determine the corresponding pairs of minutiae in the filtered set of chaff points and the query minutiae set. To find the coefficients of a polynomial of degree k, ($k + 1$) unique projections are necessary. If the number of correspondences found is less than ($k + 1$), it results in authentication failure. Otherwise, all possible subsets

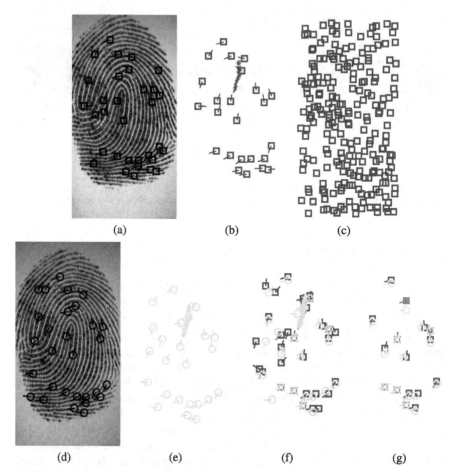

Fig. 8.6 An example of successful operation of the fingerprint fuzzy vault proposed in [36].
(a) Enrolled fingerprint image with minutiae template, (b) selected template minutiae and high curvature points extracted from the enrolled image, (c) vault in which the selected template minutiae are hidden among chaff points (for clarity, minutiae directions are not shown), (d) query fingerprint image with minutiae, (e) selected query minutiae and high curvature points extracted from the query image, (f) alignment of template and query high curvature points and coarse filtering of chaff points, and (g) unlocking set obtained by applying a minutiae matcher which eliminates almost all the chaff points. The two points shown in filled squares in (g) are the only chaff points that remain in the unlocking set

of size $(k + 1)$ of the obtained correspondences are selected and for each subset, a polynomial P^* is constructed using Lagrange interpolation. The coefficients of the polynomial P^* are 16-bit values, which are concatenated to obtain a $16(k + 1)$-bit string κ^* and CRC error detection is applied to κ^*. If an error is detected, it indicates that an incorrect key has been decoded and the same procedure is repeated for the next candidate subset. If no error is detected, it indicates that $\kappa^* = \kappa_c$ with very high probability. A successful operation of the fuzzy vault scheme proposed in [36] is shown in Fig. 8.6.

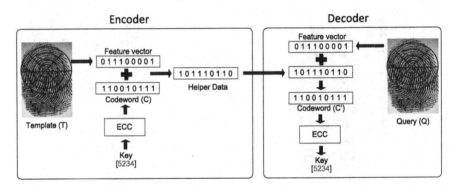

Fig. 8.7 Securing a fingerprint template using fuzzy commitment. Here, ECC denotes error correction coding

8.2.3 Fingerprint Fuzzy Commitment

Fuzzy commitment [27] is a biometric cryptosystem that can be used to secure biometric traits represented in the form of binary vectors (see Fig. 8.7). Suppose that the enrolled biometric template $\mathbf{b}^E$ is an N-bit binary string. In fuzzy commitment, a uniformly random key κ_c of length L ($L \leq N$) bits is generated and used to uniquely index a N-bit codeword $\mathbf{c}$ of an appropriate error correcting code. The sketch is then extracted from the template as $\mathbf{y}_c = \mathbf{c} \oplus \mathbf{b}^E$, where $\oplus$ indicates the modulo-2 addition. The sketch $\mathbf{y}_c$ is stored in the database along with $\mathbf{h}(\kappa_c)$, where $\mathbf{h}(.)$ is a cryptographic hash function. During authentication, the codeword is obtained from the query biometric $\mathbf{b}^A$ and the sketch $\mathbf{y}_c$ as follows: $\mathbf{c}^* = \mathbf{y}_c \oplus \mathbf{b}^A = \mathbf{c} \oplus (\mathbf{b}^E \oplus \mathbf{b}^A)$. This codeword $\mathbf{c}^*$, which is generally a corrupted version of the original codeword $\mathbf{c}$, can be decoded to get the key κ^*. The authentication is deemed successful if $\mathbf{h}(\kappa^*)$ is the same as $\mathbf{h}(\kappa_c)$. If the Hamming distance between $\mathbf{b}^E$ and $\mathbf{b}^A$ is not greater than the error correcting capacity of the code, κ^* would be the same as κ and the matching will be successful.

8.3 Adapting Fingerprint Representations for Cryptosystems

While minutiae-based schemes are widely used for fingerprint matching, the following characteristics of minutiae-based representation make it difficult to secure the minutiae templates directly.

1. *Unordered Set Representation*: Minutiae sets are *unordered* and the correspondence between individual minutiae in the enrollment and query minutiae sets are not known in advance. Furthermore, the number of minutiae in the two sets may be different (see Fig. 8.2).
2. *Alignment Issues*: A template protection scheme for minutiae templates generally precludes the use of sophisticated minutiae matchers to align the minutiae sets. The alignment issue is handled either by using external information such

Table 8.1 Different techniques to transform fingerprint features for template protection

Technique	Features	Transformation	Final representation
Spectral minutiae [55]	Minutiae	Fourier transform of 2D-delta functions at minutiae locations	Vector
BioPhasor [49]	FingerCode	Nonlinear	Vector
Biometric encryption [47]	Fingerprint image	Apply a secure filter	Vector
Minutiae indicator [15]	Minutiae	Minutiae locations are marked as '1'	Vector
Histogram of minutiae triplets [16]	Minutiae	Hashing the histogram of minutiae triplet features	Vector
Cuboid based minutiae Aggregates [48]	Minutiae	Minutiae aggregate selection from random local regions	Vector
Symmetric hash [50]	Minutiae as complex numbers	Set of order invariant functions of minutiae	Minutiae
Cancelable fingerprints [42]	Minutiae	Image folding	Minutiae
Alignment free cancelable fingerprint[29]	Minutiae, orientation field	Transform minutiae according to surrounding orientation field	Minutiae
Minutiae structures [25]	Minutiae	Local minutiae structures	Minutiae

as reference points or by using rotation- and translation-invariant local minutiae structures.

3. *Nonlinear distortion*: Even when two minutiae sets are aligned with respect to linear transformations like rotation and translation, the locations and directions of the corresponding minutiae do not match exactly due to nonlinear distortion. Though quantization of minutiae attributes can reduce the effect of distortion to some extent, it cannot be eliminated completely.

While some template protection schemes have been designed specifically to work with unordered sets like minutiae (e.g., fuzzy vault [26] and non-invertible transformation [42]), these schemes tend to significantly degrade the matching accuracy due to alignment issues and nonlinear distortion. Furthermore, other template protection schemes like fuzzy commitment, which have been successfully used with other biometric modalities like iris [19], cannot be directly used for securing fingerprint minutiae. On the other hand, feature representations that characterize the global texture pattern of the fingerprint image are typically fixed-length real-valued vectors, which are again difficult to secure. To overcome these limitations, several techniques have been proposed to adapt the given fingerprint representation into a form that can be more easily secured using biometric cryptosystems like fuzzy vault and fuzzy commitment (see Table 8.1).

We now discuss four different fingerprint feature adaptation approaches that have been proposed in the literature, namely, (i) local aggregates, (ii) spectral minutiae, (iii) local minutia structure, and (iv) quantization and reliable component selection. The goal of local aggregates and spectral minutiae approaches is to convert the minutiae set into a fixed-length binary feature vector that can be secured using fuzzy commitment. The local minutia structure approach is primarily designed to overcome the alignment problem by deriving new features from the minutiae that are invariant under rotation and translation. The new features derived from the minutiae can be secured using fuzzy vault, fuzzy commitment, or other hybrid biometric cryptosystems. Quantization and reliable component selection converts a fixed-length real-valued feature vector into a compact binary vector, thereby enabling the use of a fuzzy commitment.

8.3.1 Local Aggregates Approach

In this approach, the fingerprint region is divided into a number of randomized local regions (could be over-lapping) and features are computed based on the minutiae falling within each local region. For example, Chang and Roy [8] consider a finite number of lines in the fingerprint area and use the difference in the number of minutiae on the two sides of the line as the feature vector. This feature vector is further converted into a binary representation using the techniques described in Sect. 8.3.4. Note that the fingerprints need to be aligned before feature extraction in order for the local aggregates approach to work.

Sutcu et al. [48] used a set of axis-aligned variable-sized cuboids as the local region. Each cuboid is parameterized by its location and range along each of the x and y coordinates and the minutia orientation angle θ (see Fig. 8.8 for a typical cuboid configuration). A vector consisting of the number of minutiae falling into each of the cuboids is obtained and binarized to derive the final representation. This approach was further improved in [33] by including additional statistics related to minutiae falling in each cuboid. The statistics computed are

1. *Aggregate wall distance (δ)*: For a cuboid bounded by ($x_{min}, x_{max}, y_{min}, y_{max}, \theta_{min}, \theta_{max}$), δ is computed as:

$$\delta = \sum_{i=1}^{t} \min\left(\delta_x^i, \delta_y^i, \delta_\theta^i, \tau_\delta\right), \tag{8.1}$$

where t is the number of minutiae in the given cuboid, τ_δ is a threshold used for wall distance, and δ_x^i, δ_y^i, and δ_θ^i are given by $\min(|x_i - x_{min}|, |x_i - x_{max}|)$, $\min(|y_i - y_{min}|, |y_i - y_{max}|)$, and $\min(|\theta_i - \theta_{min}|, |\theta_i - \theta_{max}|)$, respectively.
2. *Minutiae Average*: Average coordinate of all the minutiae present in each cuboid in a given measurement.
3. *Minutiae Deviation*: Standard deviation of minutiae coordinates present in each cuboid in a given measurement.

Fig. 8.8 A cuboid bounded by $(x_{min}, x_{max}, y_{min}, y_{max}, \theta_{min}, \theta_{max})$ overlaid over the minutia points. The local aggregate features are computed based on the statistics of minutiae that fall within the cuboid [33, 48]

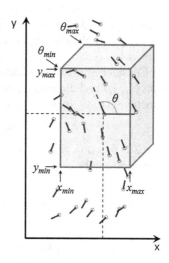

Additional information related to ridge orientation as well as ridge frequency present inside a local rectangular region can also be added to the local aggregate representation [34]. To obtain the orientation-based features, the fingerprint is filtered using four different Gabor filters oriented along 0, 45, 90, and 135 degrees. Given a local aggregate region, four different values are obtained corresponding to the standard deviations of the values associated with the four Gabor responses. The ridge frequency based features are computed as the average ridge frequency inside the aggregate region.

8.3.2 Spectral Minutiae Representation

The spectral minutiae representation is obtained by considering the minutiae set as a collection of 2-dimensional Dirac-delta functions and obtaining its Fourier spectrum after low pass filtering [55]. Only the magnitude spectrum is considered and it is sampled on a log polar grid to obtain a fixed-length vector. Theoretically, the magnitude spectrum is invariant to rotation and translation due to the shift, scale, and rotation properties of the Fourier transform. Hence, it is possible to perform matching between two spectral minutiae vectors without aligning them first. However, in practice, alignment based on singular points is required to achieve good matching performance [55] because large rotation or translation may lead to partial overlap between different impressions of the same finger.

Another variation of the spectral minutiae approach is the Binarized Phase Spectrum (BiPS) representation proposed in [35]. To incorporate translation- and rotation-invariance, only the magnitude spectrum is considered in [55] and the phase spectrum is ignored. In [35], alignment is achieved through the use of external information such as reference points. Therefore, only the phase spectrum of the minutiae is considered. The phase spectrum can be sampled along a log-polar grid to obtain the fixed-length minutiae representation. Furthermore, these phase samples can be easily quantized into two bits depending on which quadrant they fall into. The resulting binarized phase spectrum can be directly secured using the fuzzy commitment approach.

Consider a minutiae set $M = \{\mathbf{m}_i\}_{i=1}^n$, where $\mathbf{m}_i$ is the ith minutia with location (x_i, y_i) and direction θ_i, and n is the number of minutiae. We can associate a function $g(x, y)$ to each minutia $\mathbf{m}_i$ as follows.

$$g(x, y; \mathbf{m}_i) = \delta(x - x_i, y - y_i) \exp(j\theta_i). \tag{8.2}$$

The 2-D function $f(x, y)$ that defines the minutiae set M and its continuous Fourier transform can be expressed as

$$f(x, y) = \sum_{i=1}^n \delta(x - x_i, y - y_i) \exp(j\theta_i), \tag{8.3}$$

$$F(u, v) = \sum_{i=1}^n \exp\left(j\left(2\pi(ux_i + vy_i) + \theta_i\right)\right). \tag{8.4}$$

The phase of the Fourier spectrum of $f(x, y)$ is denoted as $\Psi(F(u, v))$ and is given by the following equation:

$$\Psi\left(F(u, v)\right) = \arctan \frac{\sum_{i=1}^n \sin(2\pi(ux_i + vy_i) + \theta_i)}{\sum_{i=1}^n \cos(2\pi(ux_i + vy_i) + \theta_i)}. \tag{8.5}$$

$\Psi(F(u, v))$ can take values in $[0, 2\pi]$. To binarize the phase spectrum, $\Psi(F(u, v))$ is quantized into four distinct values based on the quadrant in which it falls and is represented using two bits. Thus, the phase spectrum can be represented as a fixed length binary string $\mathbf{x} = [b_1, b_2, b_3, \dots, b_{2N}]$ as follows:

$$\begin{aligned} b_{2j-1} &= \mathrm{sgn}\left(\mathrm{Re}\left(F(u_j, v_j)\right)\right), \\ b_{2j} &= \mathrm{sgn}\left(\mathrm{Im}\left(F(u_j, v_j)\right)\right), \end{aligned} \tag{8.6}$$

where $\mathrm{sgn}(y) = 1$, if $y \geq 0$, zero, otherwise, $\mathrm{Re}(.)$ and $\mathrm{Im}(.)$ are the real and imaginary parts of a complex number, and (u_j, v_j) denotes the jth frequency sample, $j = 1, \dots, N$. On a log-polar grid, $u = v\cos(\phi)$ and $v = v\sin(\phi)$, where v is the radial distance and ϕ is the radial angle. If we choose N_v logarithmically spaced samples between $v_{\min}$ and $v_{\max}$ and N_ϕ linearly spaced samples between 0 and π, the total number of samples is $N = N_v N_\phi$ and the length of the binary string obtained from a minutiae set is $2N$ bits. An illustration of the BiPS representation of minutiae is shown in Fig. 8.9.

8.3.3 Local Minutiae Structures

Local minutiae structures consist of features that characterize the relative information between two or more minutiae (e.g., distance between two minutiae) [7]. The main advantage of this approach is that since the features are relative, they are invariant to global rotation and translation of the fingerprint. Hence, no a priori alignment

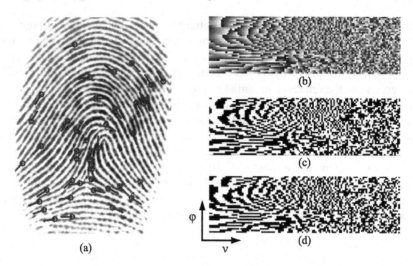

Fig. 8.9 Illustration of binarized phase spectrum of fingerprint minutiae [35]. (a) A fingerprint image with minutiae marked on it, (b) phase spectrum: $\Psi(F(u,v))$, (c) odd bits of the binarized phase spectrum: sgn(Re($F(u_j, v_j)$)), and (d) even bits of the binarized phase spectrum: sgn(Im($F(u_j, v_j)$))

is needed before matching. An additional benefit is that such features are robust to nonlinear distortion. However, if the matching is based only on the local minutiae information and the global spatial relationships between minutiae (which are highly distinctive) is ignored, it may lead to degradation in the matching accuracy.

The simplest local minutiae structure is based on minutia pairs, where the distance between the pair and the orientation of each minutia with respect to the line connecting them can be used as the invariant attributes. Boult et al. [4] proposed a hybrid biometric cryptosystem to secure such a representation. The fundamental idea is to split the value of each feature (relative distances and angles) into stable and unstable parts. The stable parts are encrypted, while the unstable parts are left unprotected. A robust distance measure was proposed to match minutia pairs by combining the results of the stable part matching that takes place in the encrypted domain and the unstable part matching in the plaintext domain.

Another commonly used local minutiae structure is the minutia triplet, where relative features (distances and angles) are computed from combinations of three minutiae. Farooq et al. [16] proposed a non-invertible feature transformation approach for secure fingerprint matching based on minutia triplets. The relative features in a triplet are quantized such that only a finite number of triplets (say N) are possible. A N-dimensional histogram characterizing the distribution of different triplets in the given fingerprint image is obtained. This histogram is binarized and transformed in a non-invertible manner by randomly modifying some of the bits in the binary string.

A number of other local minutiae structures have also been proposed. For example, Jeffers and Arakala [24] showed that it is possible to use a fuzzy vault to secure triplet-based, five nearest neighbor-based, and Voronoi neighbor-based minutia structures. Another interesting structure is the Minutia Cylinder Code proposed by Cappelli et al. [7]. This local minutia structure divides a cylindrical region (with its axis along the minutia orientation) around each minutia into a finite number of cells and encodes the likelihood of another minutia in the fingerprint with a specific angle difference from the reference minutia being present in the specific cell.

Finally, it is also possible to exploit additional descriptors such as ridge orientation and ridge frequency in the neighborhood of a minutia [17] for more accurate fingerprint matching. For instance, Nagar et al. [32] use the ridge orientation and ridge frequency values, which are sampled at a set of points around each minutia, to encrypt the polynomial evaluations of the corresponding minutia in a fuzzy vault. As a result, an attacker who only guesses the set of genuine minutiae from the vault can no longer recover the key; he also needs to know the values corresponding to the associated descriptors in order to fully decode the vault.

8.3.4 Quantization and Reliable Component Selection

Most of the fingerprint feature adaptation techniques initially output a fixed-length real-valued feature vector. This feature vector could be either derived from the minutiae [34, 55] or based on the global texture pattern [5]. Typically, this real-valued feature vector is quantized by assigning bits to each element in order to obtain a binary representation. In some cases, only a fixed-number of reliable bits are selected to obtain the final binary representation, which is secured using a fuzzy commitment scheme.

Rohde [43] proposed two basic Binary Multidimensional Scaling techniques with the objective of obtaining a lower dimensional set of binary vectors whose pairwise distances closely follow the pairwise distances between the associated original data points. In the first approach, a singular value decomposition was performed on the original real-valued vectors and the resultant projections were binarized using unary encoding.[1] In the second technique, a projection matrix was obtained using the gradient descent method with the objective of minimizing the stress between the pairwise distances in the original space and the scaled pairwise distances in the transformed space. The original vectors were projected using the obtained projection matrix and the resultant vectors were binarized based on the sign of each vector-element.

Andoni et al. [1] proposed a technique referred to as Locality Sensitive Hashing (LSH), where the original real-valued vectors are projected using random matrices and the resultant projections are binarized using unary coding in order to obtain the final binary vector. LSH is mostly used in image retrieval applications, where the objective is to efficiently compute an approximate nearest neighbor of a query. Chen

---

[1] A unary encoding works as follows. Suppose that a real-value a needs to be encoded using t bits. The range of a, say $[a_{min}, a_{max}]$, is quantized into $(t + 1)$ bins. If a falls into the ith bin, it is represented as $(t - i + 1)$ ones followed by $(i - 1)$ zeros, where $i = 1, 2, \ldots, (t + 1)$.

et al. [10] associated multiple bits with each real valued feature element based on its discriminability. The bit values were determined based on binary representation. Chen et al. [9] also proposed a binarization technique, where pairs of elements of real vectors were converted to polar coordinates and then quantized.

Given binarized features, it is a common practice to select a subset of reliable bits either because the specific biometric cryptosystem requires the binary vector to be of a desired length or there are a large number of unreliable bits and removing them will improve the system accuracy. Selecting a subset of bits that provides the best performance would, in general, require evaluating all the 2^n possible subsets where there are n bits in the original binary vector. However, a number of efficient approximations have been proposed in literature. Examples include the sequential forward floating search [40], where features are successively added and removed to the selection based on the performance of the selected set of features till a stable performance is reached, mutual information based feature selection [39], and other simple selection procedures based on correlation and feature discriminability [33].

8.4 Alignment with Secure Fingerprint Templates

The first step in matching two fingerprint images is to align them and determine the area of overlap. Although aligning two fingerprints is a difficult problem in any fingerprint authentication system, it is much more difficult when the information about the template must not be leaked. One way to solve this problem is to use local minutiae structures, which are invariant to rotation and translation because such features are typically obtained relative to the location and orientation attributes of each minutia point. We have already discussed this approach in Sect. 8.3.3. The alternate approach is to extract and store some reference points from the enrolled fingerprint image that do not leak excessive information about the minutiae template. During authentication, the reference points can also be obtained from the query fingerprint image. The template and query minutiae sets can be aligned based on the parameters obtained by aligning the corresponding sets of reference points.

The most commonly used reference points for fingerprint alignment are the *singular points* (e.g., core and delta) [31]. There are many approaches like Poincare index method [31], geometric method [41], complex filter method [38], etc. to determine the singular points in a fingerprint image. However, the accuracy of these techniques is limited by the following three issues: (i) low quality of the captured fingerprint image, (ii) the absence of clearly defined core points in arch and tented-arch fingerprint patterns, and (iii) partial nature of many fingerprint images captured using live-scan sensors.

One promising approach for reference point detection is the focal point localization algorithm proposed by Boonchaiseree and Areekul [3], which overcomes the problems associated with singular points. The focal point is defined as the average center of curvature of a fingerprint. In other words, the focal point is the centroid of all the crossing points, where a crossing point is a point of intersection of two normal lines of curved ridges. The algorithm proposed in [3] is iterative and in each iteration, only the orientation field in the semi-circular region of a specified radius centered at the current focal point is used to generate the crossing points. The limitations of this algorithm are its iterative nature (hence high computational requirement) and the need for carefully selecting the focal point for the first iteration.

Another alternative candidate for a reference point is a stable minutia point in the given fingerprint [56]. While the alignment based on such a reference point is simple and computationally efficient, it is difficult to determine the stable minutia point reliably. Even a small error in locating the reference point could lead to a false reject.

Uludag and Jain [51] extracted a set of points with high curvature from the fingerprint orientation field. A trimmed Iterative Closest Point (ICP) algorithm was used to determine the alignment between the template and the query based on these high curvature points. Since high curvature points are global features in the fingerprint pattern, they do not reveal any information about the minutia attributes, which are local characteristics in the fingerprint. Nandakumar et al. [36] have made significant enhancements to the alignment algorithm in [51], resulting in more accurate alignment between the template and query.

The high curvature points can be extracted as follows (see Fig. 8.10). First a set of orientation field flow curves are extracted from the fingerprint. An orientation field flow curve [13] is a set of piecewise linear segments whose tangent direction at each point is parallel to the orientation field direction at that point. Although flow curves are similar to fingerprint ridges, extraction of flow curves is not affected by breaks and discontinuities, which are commonly encountered in ridge extraction. Points of maximum curvature in the flow curves along with their curvature values can be used for alignment. These high curvature points tend to occur near the singular points in the fingerprint image. If the image has more than one singularity, high curvature points may have many clusters, which can be identified by applying a single-link clustering algorithm. While this alignment technique is more accurate than alignment based on singular points [36], it is not computationally efficient and storing many high curvature points may leak more information about the fingerprint pattern. To overcome this problem, a single focal point was estimated from each cluster of high curvature points in [35].

8.5 Matching Performance and Security

The effectiveness of a fingerprint template protection technique can be measured in terms of the resulting (i) matching performance and (ii) template security. Matching performance is usually quantified by the False Accept Rate (FAR) and the Genuine Accept Rate (GAR) of the biometric system. Security is measured in terms of the in-

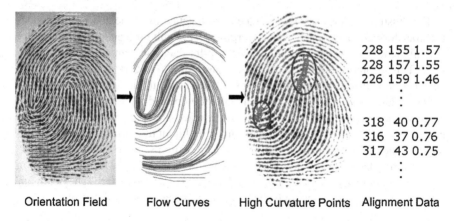

| Orientation Field | Flow Curves | High Curvature Points | Alignment Data |

Fig. 8.10 Algorithm for extraction of high curvature points

formation leakage rate[2] or the computational complexity involved in recovering the original template from the secure sketch or the transformed template [20, 28]. Due to intra-user variability in fingerprint images, there is usually a trade-off between the GAR and the security in most template protection schemes. Schemes with higher security tend to have lower GAR and vice versa.

While a number of fingerprint template protection schemes have been proposed, many of them have not been carefully evaluated in terms of their matching performance and template security. For example, the matching performance of traditional fingerprint recognition systems have been evaluated on large databases containing several thousand unique fingerprints by independent third-parties (e.g., Fingerprint Vendor Technology Evaluation [54]). Such large scale independent evaluations allow us to determine whether the performance differences between competing algorithms are statistical significant. However, most fingerprint template protection schemes have been tested using small (sometimes proprietary) databases containing at most a few hundred users. Hence, it is difficult to judge the relative differences in matching performance among various fingerprint template security schemes. Similarly, accurate estimation of the security provided by a template protection scheme requires good statistical models for the distribution of fingerprint features (e.g., minutiae). Given the absence of such models, most of the schemes make unrealistic assumptions such as uniform distribution of features, resulting in over-optimistic estimates of security. Furthermore, in addition to the information leakage rate from the secure sketch or transformed template, one must also carefully analyze the security in scenarios where the adversary may get access to ancillary information (e.g., alignment information stored with a secure sketch or the user-specific key used to derive a transformed template) along with the protected template.

---

[2]Given the secure sketch, leakage rate quantifies the information available to adversary about the original biometric template (known as privacy leakage) or the cryptographic key associated to it (secret key leakage).

For illustration purposes, we evaluate implementations of the non-invertible feature transformation approach [42], fingerprint fuzzy vault [36], and fingerprint fuzzy commitment [35] on a public-domain fingerprint database, namely the FVC2002-DB2. This database [30] consists of 800 images of 100 fingers with 8 impressions per finger obtained using an optical sensor. The size of the images in this database is 560 × 296, the resolution of the sensor is 569 dpi and the images are generally of good quality. Our goal here is not to determine the superiority of one template protection method over the other but to simply highlight the various issues that need to be considered in implementing a template protection scheme. Of course, performance varies depending on the choice of the features, the selected feature adaptation scheme, database used, and the values of the parameters used in each scheme. In our implementation, we consider only the location and orientation attributes of minutiae.

8.5.1 Non-invertible Transform

We implemented two non-invertible transforms, namely, polar and functional (with a mixture of Gaussian as the transformation function) defined in [42]. For the polar transform, the central region of the image was tessellated into $n = 6$ sectors of equal angular width and 30-pixel wide concentric shells. The transformation here is constrained such that it only shifts the sector number of the minutiae without changing the shell. There are $n!$ ways in which the n sectors in each shell can be reassigned. Given k shells in the image (constrained by the width of the image and ignoring the central region of radius 15 pixels), the number of different ways a transformation can be constructed is $(n!)^k$ which is equivalent to $\log_2 (n!)^k$ bits of security.

For the functional transformation, we used a mixture of 24 Gaussians with the same isotropic standard deviation of 30 pixels (where the peaks can correspond to $+1$ or -1 as used in [42]) for calculating the displacement and used the direction of gradient of the mixture of Gaussian functions as the direction of minutiae displacement. Since the mean vector of the Gaussians can fall anywhere in the image, there are 296 × 560 possible different values of means of each Gaussian component. As there are 24 Gaussian components and each one can peak at $+1$ or -1, there are $(296 * 560 * 2)^{24}$ possible transformations. However, two transformations with slightly shifted component means will produce two similar templates such that one template can be used to verify the other.

To analyze the security of the functional transformation, Ratha et al. [42] assumed that for each minutia in the fingerprint, its transformed counterpart could be present in a shell of width d pixels at a distance of K pixels from the minutiae. Further, assuming that the matcher cannot distinguish minutiae that are within δr pixels and their orientations are within $\delta\theta$ degrees, each transformed minutia encodes $I_m = \log_2 (\pi \frac{((K+d)^2 - K^2)}{(\delta r)^2} * \frac{\pi}{\delta\theta})$ bits of information. Assuming that there are N minutiae in template fingerprint and one needs to match at least m minutiae to get accepted, the adversary needs to make $2^{I_m * m - \log_2 \binom{N}{m}}$ attempts. Note that this

Fig. 8.11 ROC curves corresponding to two non-invertible transforms (Gaussian and polar) on FVC2002-DB2. The *"Original" curve* represents the case where no transformation is applied to the template, *"Gaussian" curve* corresponds to the functional transformation of the template and *"Polar"* corresponds to the polar transformation of the template

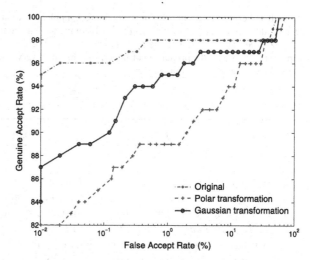

analysis is based on the simplifying assumption that each minutia is transformed independently. This overestimates the number of attempts needed by an adversary to guess the minutiae template.

Among the eight impressions available for each of the 100 fingers in FVC2002-DB2, we use only the first two impressions in this experiment because they have the best image quality. The results, based on the minutiae matcher in [22], are shown in Fig. 8.11, which indicates a decrease of about 6 % in the GAR at a FAR of 0.1 %. In terms of security, non-invertible transformation is one of the better approaches since it is computationally hard (in terms of brute force complexity) to invert the stored template and obtain the true template. The true template is never revealed especially in case when the transformation of the biometric template is done on a separate module (possibly a hand held device [21]), which does not save the original template in memory and is not accessible to an adversary.

8.5.2 Fingerprint Fuzzy Vault

We implemented the fuzzy vault as proposed in [36] using the first two impressions of each of the 100 fingers in the FVC2002-DB2. Table 8.2 shows the error rates corresponding to different key sizes used in binding. Compared to the "original" ROC curve in Fig. 8.11, we observe that the fuzzy vault scheme has a lower genuine accept rate by about 4 %. Further, this scheme also has failure to capture errors if the number of minutiae in the fingerprint image is not sufficient for vault construction (18 in our implementation).

Suppose an attacker launches a brute-force attack on the fuzzy vault by trying to decode the key using all possible combinations of $(k + 1)$ points in the vault. If $k = 10$ and the number of genuine and chaff points in the vault are 24 and 200, respectively, the security of the minutiae template is approximately 39 bits. Note that

Table 8.2 Performance summary of the fuzzy vault implementation for FVC2002-DB2 database. Here, k denotes the degree of the encoding polynomial used in vault construction. The maximum key size that can be bound to the minutiae template is $16k$ bits. FTCR refers to the failure to capture rate, which is the proportion of fingerprints having a very small number of minutiae that is not sufficient for vault construction

FTCR	$k = 7$		$k = 8$		$k = 10$	
	GAR	FAR	GAR	FAR	GAR	FAR
2 %	91 %	0.13 %	91 %	0.01 %	86	0 %

this estimate is based on the assumption that minutia points are distributed uniformly over the fingerprint image area, which is not true in practice. Moreover, there are some specific attacks that can be staged against a fuzzy vault, e.g., *attacks via record multiplicity, stolen key inversion attack*, and *blended substitution attack* [45]. If an adversary has access to two different vaults (say from two different applications) obtained from the same biometric data, he can easily identify the genuine points in the two vaults and decode the vault. Thus, the fuzzy vault scheme does not provide revocability. In a stolen key inversion attack, if an adversary somehow recovers the key embedded in the vault, he can decode the vault to obtain the biometric template. Since the vault contains a large number of chaff points, it is possible for an adversary to substitute a few points in the vault using his own biometric features. This allows both the genuine user and the adversary to be successfully authenticated using the same identity and such an attack is known as blended substitution.

8.5.3 Fingerprint Fuzzy Commitment

The fingerprint fuzzy commitment scheme based on the Binarized Phase Spectrum representation of minutiae proposed in [35] was implemented with the following parameter settings: $\nu_{min} = 0.01$, $\nu_{max} = 0.25$, $N_\nu = 128$, $N_\phi = 37$. At the time of enrollment, $N = 2,048$ most reliable bits are selected from the available bits using the bit selection algorithm described in [35]. During enrollment, we select a codeword c of the same length N by adding error correction bits to a uniformly random key (κ_c) of length L bits generated independently. The length of the key (L) is varied from 224 to 256 bits to obtain different false accept rates (FAR). A turbo encoder with a recursive convolutional code of rate $1/4$ as the component encoder is used for error correction. For these settings, the turbo code can recover the key κ from the secure sketch even if approximately 30 % of bits in b^E and b^A are different.

The genuine accept rate (GAR) at zero, 0.02 %, and 0.1 % FAR are shown in Table 8.3. Note that these GAR values are based on all the impressions for each user. In the case of fingerprint fuzzy vault (see Table 8.2), the GAR is 86 % at zero-FAR compared to a GAR of 87.4 % for the fingerprint fuzzy commitment. However, only the 100 genuine matches based on the first two impressions for each user were considered in the fuzzy vault. For this subset of FVC2002-DB2, the GAR of the fuzzy

Table 8.3 Genuine Accept Rate (GAR) of fingerprint fuzzy commitment based on Binarized Phase Spectrum representation of minutiae proposed in [35]. Here, FAR denotes the false accept rate

0 % FAR	0.02 % FAR	0.1 % FAR
87.4 %	90.4 %	91.1 %

commitment is 94 % at zero-FAR. Even after considering the correlation between the bits, a security of 43 bits was reported in [35].

8.6 Conclusions and Future Research Directions

Among the various vulnerabilities of a biometric system, leakage of biometric template information is a major security and privacy concern due to the strong linkage between a user's template and his identity and the irrevocable nature of biometric templates. In this chapter, we briefly reviewed the three basic theoretical frameworks for biometric template protection, namely, encryption, template transformation, and biometric cryptosystems and discussed the practical issues involved in applying these techniques to secure a fingerprint template. Due to variations in finger placement and pressure applied on the sensor, there are two fundamental challenges in any fingerprint template protection scheme. First, we need to automatically align or register the fingerprints obtained during enrollment and matching, without revealing excessive information about the features that uniquely characterize a fingerprint. Secondly, we need to select an appropriate representation scheme that captures most of the discriminatory information, but is relatively invariant to changes in finger placement. Finally, specific implementations of three different template protection schemes on a common fingerprint database was presented to illustrate the issues concerning matching accuracy and template security.

We believe that as yet, there is no "best" approach for template protection that completely satisfies the three main requirements of template security, matching accuracy, and revocability. The application scenario and requirements play a major role in the selection of a template protection scheme. In an airport watch list application, non-invertible transform may be a more suitable approach because it provides both template security and revocability without relying on any other input from the user. Biometric cryptosystems may be more appropriate in match-on-card applications because such systems typically release a key to the associated application in order to indicate a successful match. In general, more than one template protection scheme may be admissible and the choice of the suitable approach may be based on a number of factors such as matching performance, computational complexity, memory requirements, and user acceptance and co-operation. Further research in the area of fingerprint template security is expected to progress along the following three main directions.

1. What is the "optimal" feature transformation function or biometric cryptosystem for matching fingerprints securely? Optimality generally refers to the best trade-off between template security and matching performance.
2. Suppose that there is a good template protection algorithm for a specific feature type (e.g., a binary string); what is the best way to embed other types of features (e.g., minutiae set) in the desired feature domain? This question is also relevant in case there is a need to secure templates from multiple biometric traits as a single entity. Note that the best representation should be compact, preserve accuracy, and preferably have a uniform distribution.
3. Finally, one of the important but difficult tasks in the design of a template protection algorithm is: how to quantify the security provided by the algorithm? Most of the existing methodologies for security analysis are based on unrealistic assumptions (e.g., uniform distribution of minutiae). A related issue is the need to quantify the inherent entropy in (or the individuality of) a fingerprint or the features extracted from it.

References

1. Andoni A, Indyk P (2008) Near-optimal hashing algorithms for approximate nearest neighbor in high dimensions. Communications of the ACM 51(1):117–122
2. Bleichenbacher D, Nguyen PQ (2000) Noisy polynomial interpolation and noisy Chinese remaindering. In: Proc Nineteenth IACR Eurocrypt, Bruges, Belgium, pp 53–69
3. Boonchaiseree N, Areekul V (2009) Focal point detection based on half concentric lens model for singular point extraction in fingerprint. In: Proceedings of International Conference on Biometrics, pp 637–646
4. Boult TE, Scheirer WJ, Woodworth R (2007) Fingerprint revocable biotokens: accuracy and security analysis. In: Proceedings of IEEE Computer Society Conference on Computer Vision and Pattern Recognition, pp 1–8
5. Bringer J, Chabanne H, Cohen G, Kindarji B, Zémor G (2008) Theoretical and practical boundaries of binary secure sketches. IEEE Transactions on Information Forensics and Security 3(4):673–683
6. Cappelli R, Lumini A, Maio D, Maltoni D (2007) Fingerprint image reconstruction from standard templates. IEEE Transactions on Pattern Analysis and Machine Intelligence 29(9):1489–1503
7. Cappelli R, Ferrara M, Maltoni D (2010) Minutia cylinder-code: a new representation and matching technique for fingerprint recognition. IEEE Transactions on Pattern Analysis and Machine Intelligence 32(12):2128–2141
8. Chang EC, Roy S (2007) Robust extraction of secret bits from minutiae. In: Proc Second International Conference on Biometrics, Seoul, South Korea, pp 750–759
9. Chen C, Veldhuis R (2009) Binary biometric representation through pairwise polar quantization. In: Proc International Conference on Biometrics, pp 72–81
10. Chen C, Veldhuis RNJ, Kevenaar TAM, Akkermans AHM (2009) Biometric quantization through detection rate optimized bit allocation. EURASIP Journal on Advances in Signal Processing
11. Chung Y, Moon D, Lee S, Jung S, Kim T, Ahn D (2005) Automatic alignment of fingerprint features for fuzzy fingerprint vault. In: Proc Conference on Information Security and Cryptology, Beijing, China, pp 358–369
12. Clancy T, Lin D, Kiyavash N (2003) Secure smartcard-based fingerprint authentication. In: Proc ACM SIGMM Workshop on Biometric Methods and Applications, Berkley, USA, pp 45–52

13. Dass SC, Jain AK (2004) Fingerprint classification using orientation field flow curves. In: Proc Indian Conference on Computer Vision, Graphics and Image Processing, Kolkata, India, pp 650–655
14. Dodis Y, Ostrovsky R, Reyzin L, Smith A (2006) Fuzzy extractors: how to generate strong keys from biometrics and other noisy data. Tech rep 235, Cryptology ePrint archive. A preliminary version of this work appeared in EUROCRYPT 2004
15. Draper SC, Khisti A, Martinian E, Vetro A, Yedidia JS (2007) Using distributed source coding to secure fingerprint biometrics. In: Proc IEEE International Conference on Acoustics, Speech, and Signal Processing (ICASSP), Hawaii, USA, vol 2, pp 129–132
16. Farooq F, Bolle R, Jea T, Ratha N (2007) Anonymous and revocable fingerprint recognition. In: Proc IEEE Computer Vision and Pattern Recognition
17. Feng J (2008) Combining minutiae descriptors for fingerprint matching. Pattern Recognition 41(1):342–352
18. Feng J, Jain A (2009) FM model based fingerprint reconstruction from minutiae template. In: International Conference on Biometrics (ICB)
19. Hao F, Anderson R, Daugman J (2006) Combining crypto with biometrics effectively. IEEE Transactions on Computers 55(9):1081–1088
20. Ignatenko T, Willems FMJ (2009) Biometric systems: privacy and secrecy aspects. IEEE Transactions on Information Forensics and Security 4(4):956–973
21. Jain AK, Pankanti S (2006) A touch of money. IEEE Spectrum 3(7):22–27
22. Jain AK, Hong L, Bolle R (1997) On-line fingerprint verification. IEEE Transactions on Pattern Analysis and Machine Intelligence 19(4):302–314
23. Jain A, Nandakumar K, Nagar A (2008) Biometric template security. EURASIP Journal on Advances in Signal Processing
24. Jeffers J, Arakala A (2006) Minutiae-based structures for a fuzzy vault. In: Proc Biometric Symposium, BCC, Baltimore, MD, pp 1–6
25. Jeffers J, Arakala A (2007) Fingerprint alignment for a minutiae-based fuzzy vault. In: Proc Biometric Symposium, BCC, Baltimore, MD
26. Juels A, Sudan M (2002) A fuzzy vault scheme. In: Proc IEEE International Symposium on Information Theory, Lausanne, Switzerland, p 408
27. Juels A, Wattenberg M (1999) A fuzzy commitment scheme. In: Proc Sixth ACM Conference on Computer and Communications Security, Singapore, pp 28–36
28. Lai L, Ho SW, Poor HV (2008) Privacy-security tradeoffs in biometric security systems. In: Annual Allerton Conference on Communication, Control, and Computing, Monticello, IL, pp 23–26
29. Lee C, Choi JY, Toh KA, Lee S (2007) Alignment-free cancelable fingerprint templates based on local minutiae information. IEEE Transactions on Systems, Man and Cybernetics. Part B. Cybernetics 37(4):980–992
30. Maio D, Maltoni D, Wayman JL, Jain AK (2002) FVC2002: second fingerprint verification competition. In: Proc International Conference on Pattern Recognition (ICPR), Quebec City, Canada, pp 811–814
31. Maltoni D, Maio D, Jain AK, Prabhakar S (2009) Handbook of Fingerprint Recognition, 2nd edn. Springer, Berlin
32. Nagar A, Nandakumar K, Jain AK (2008) Securing fingerprint template: fuzzy vault with minutiae descriptors. In: Proc IEEE International Conference on Pattern Recognition, Tampa, FL
33. Nagar A, Rane S, Vetro A (2010) Privacy and security of features extracted from minutiae aggregates. In: Proceedings IEEE International Conf on Acoustics, Speech and Signal Processing, Dallas, TX, pp 524–531
34. Nagar A, Rane SD, Vetro A (2010) Alignment and bit extraction for secure fingerprint biometrics. In: SPIE Conference on Electronic Imaging (Special Collection), vol 7541
35. Nandakumar K (2010) A fingerprint cryptosystem based on minutiae phase spectrum. In: Proc of Second IEEE Workshop on Info Forensics & Security, Seattle, USA

36. Nandakumar K, Jain AK, Pankanti S (2007) Fingerprint-based fuzzy vault: implementation and performance. IEEE Transactions on Information Forensics and Security 2(4):744–757
37. Nandakumar K, Nagar A, Jain AK (2007) Hardening fingerprint fuzzy vault using password. In: Proc Second Intl Conf on Biometrics, Seoul, South Korea, pp 927–937
38. Nilsson K, Bigun J (2002) Complex filters applied to fingerprint images detecting prominent symmetry points used for alignment. In: Proceedings of International Conference on Biometric Authentication, pp 39–47
39. Peng HC, Long F, Ding C (2005) Feature selection based on mutual information: criteria of max-dependency, max-relevance, and min-redundancy. IEEE Transactions on Pattern Analysis and Machine Intelligence 27(8):1226–1238
40. Pudil P, Novovicova J, Kittler J (1994) Floating search methods in feature selection. Pattern Recognition Letters 15:1119–1125
41. Ramo P, Tico M, Onnia V, Saarinen J (2001) Optimized singular point detection algorithm for fingerprint images. In: Proceedings of ICIP, pp 242–245
42. Ratha NK, Chikkerur S, Connell JH, Bolle RM (2007) Generating cancelable fingerprint templates. IEEE Transactions on Pattern Analysis and Machine Intelligence 29(4):561–572
43. Rhodes D (2002) Methods for binary multidimensional scaling. Neural Computation 14:1195–1232
44. Ross AK, Shah J, Jain AK (2007) From templates to images: reconstructing fingerprints from minutiae points. IEEE Transactions on Pattern Analysis and Machine Intelligence 29(4):544–560
45. Scheirer WJ, Boult TE (2007) Cracking fuzzy vaults and biometric encryption. In: Proceedings of Biometrics Symposium
46. Scheirer W, Boult T (2008) Bio-cryptographic protocols with bipartite biotokens. In: Proc Biometric Symposium
47. Soutar C, Roberge D, Stoianov A, Gilroy R, Kumar BVKV (1998) Biometric encryption using image processing. In: Proc of SPIE, vol 3314, pp 178–188
48. Sutcu Y, Rane S, Yedidia J, Draper S, Vetro A (2008) Feature extraction for a Slepian-Wolf biometric system using ldpc codes. In: Proc the IEEE International Symposium on Information Theory, Toronto, Canada
49. Teoh ABJ, Toh KA, Yip WK (2007) 2^N discretisation of BioPhasor in cancelable biometrics. In: Proc Second Intl Conf on Biometrics, Seoul, South Korea, pp 435–444
50. Tulyakov S, Farooq F, Mansukhani P, Govindaraju V (2007) Symmetric hash functions for secure fingerprint biometric systems. Pattern Recognition Letters 28(16):2427–2436
51. Uludag U, Jain AK (2006) Securing fingerprint template: fuzzy vault with helper data. In: Proc CVPR Workshop on Privacy Research in Vision, New York, USA, p 163
52. Uludag U, Pankanti S, Prabhakar S, Jain AK (2004) Biometric cryptosystems: issues and challenges. Proceedings of the IEEE 92(6):948–960. Special issue on multimedia security for digital rights management
53. Uludag U, Pankanti S, Jain AK (2005) Fuzzy vault for fingerprints. In: Proc Fifth International Conference on Audio- and Video-Based Biometric Person Authentication, Rye Town, USA, pp 310–319
54. Wilson C, Hicklin AR, Bone M, Korves H, Grother P, Ulery B, Micheals R, Zoepfl M, Otto S, Watson C (2004) Fingerprint vendor technology evaluation 2003: summary of results and analysis report. Technical report NISTIR 7123, NIST
55. Xu H, Veldhuis RNJ, Bazen AM, Kevenaar TAM, Akkermans TAHM, Gokberk B (2009) Fingerprint verification using spectral minutiae representations. IEEE Transactions on Information Forensics and Security 4(3):397–409
56. Yang S, Verbauwhede I (2005) Automatic secure fingerprint verification system based on fuzzy vault scheme. In: Proc IEEE International Conference on Acoustics, Speech, and Signal Processing, Philadelphia, USA, vol 5, pp 609–612

Chapter 9
Biometric Encryption: Creating a Privacy-Preserving 'Watch-List' Facial Recognition System

Ann Cavoukian, Tom Marinelli, Alex Stoianov, Karl Martin,
Konstantinos N. Plataniotis, Michelle Chibba, Les DeSouza,
and Soren Frederiksen

Abstract This paper presents the proof of concept of a facial recognition (FR) system combined with Biometric Encryption (BE) in a watch-list scenario. The system was successfully deployed for Ontario Lottery and Gaming Corporation (OLG) self-exclusion (SE) program. The system is hybrid in nature and comprises a commercial facial recognition module with anonymous templates sequentially combined with a BE module. BE is used to conceal the relationship between a self-excluded person's FR template and their other personal information (PI). To reveal the corresponding PI record for a matched FR record, BE will attempt to release the pointer key. The FR templates and BE helper data use different biometric feature vectors to prevent interoperability between two modules. In case of a positive match, the final decision is made by a human operator. The BE scheme is based on improved Quantization Index Modulation (QIM) method. It is shown that, unlike other BE schemes, QIM offers a curve of operating points, thus allowing optimal tuning of the entire system. The simulations were performed on a subset of the CMU PIE face image database and then on the actual live test database involving OLG control group participants (simulating the self-excluded persons) and the general public. The maximum Correct Identification Rate was 91 % without BE and 90 % with BE, while FAR (before manual inspection) was of the order of 1 % (depending on the SE database size) without BE and by 30 % to 50 % lower with BE. This system, which we consider an example of Privacy by Design approach, was shown to enhance patron privacy

A. Cavoukian · A. Stoianov · M. Chibba
Office of Information and Privacy Commissioner of Ontario, Toronto, Canada

T. Marinelli · L. DeSouza
Ontario Lottery and Gaming Corporation, Toronto, Canada

K. Martin
Bionymity Inc., Toronto, Canada

K.N. Plataniotis
University of Toronto, Toronto, Canada

S. Frederiksen
iView Systems, Oakville, ON, Canada

P. Campisi (ed.), *Security and Privacy in Biometrics*,
DOI 10.1007/978-1-4471-5230-9_9, © Springer-Verlag London 2013

(both for those on the watch list, and regular patrons), system security, and over-all accuracy of the watch list system within the context of the OLG self-exclusion program.

9.1 Introduction

The rapid, accurate authentication of individuals has become a challenge across many sectors and jurisdictions, as organizations express a need to know who they are dealing with. Current security models allow for three primary forms of authentication: something you know (e.g. a password or other shared secret), something you have (e.g. an identification card), or something you are (biometrics). Increasingly, the third type of authentication—biometrics—is being viewed as the ultimate means of verification or identification, and many agencies begin to deploy biometric systems (such as fingerprinting or facial recognition) across a broad range of applications.

In 2007, the Ontario Lottery and Gaming Corporation (OLG)[1] approached the Information and Privacy Commissioner of Ontario, Canada (IPC) to discuss the use of facial biometrics to enhance their ability to identify individuals entering gaming sites who had enrolled in OLG's voluntary 'self-exclusion' program [1]. Although the program is entirely voluntary (opt-in), seeking to recognize only those individuals who have provided positive consent, the increased use of facial recognition technology raises a number of privacy and security concerns. The IPC and OLG agreed that the application of an emerging privacy-enhancing technology—Biometric Encryption (BE) [2]—to a facial recognition system at an OLG casino could ensure that the use and storage of problem gambler records receives a high degree of privacy assurance. This use of *Privacy by Design* approach—in which privacy protections are designed directly into technologies, from the outset—would make it possible to achieve a "positive-sum" outcome, in which both the functionality of the biometric system and the privacy of individuals are respected.

In this paper, we describe the proof of concept research and development work of a collaborative team consisting of OLG, IPC, members of the University of Toronto (U of T)'s Electrical and Computer Engineering Department, and incident reporting and biometrics firm iView Systems. This project looked to integrate a BE algorithm developed by the University of Toronto researchers [3, 4] into a commercially available facial recognition system. The end goal of this collaboration was to develop a technology that could function in a real-world environment, and would offer dramatically improved privacy protection over simple facial recognition, without compromising functionality, security or performance—the hallmarks of a positive-sum, *Privacy by Design* application.

---

[1]The Ontario Lottery and Gaming Corporation is designated as an institution for the purposes of the *Freedom of Information and Protection of Privacy Act*, R.S.O. 1990, c. F.31.

9.2 Facial Recognition and Voluntary Self-exclusion Programs

9.2.1 Voluntary Self-exclusion

In a commitment to fostering an environment of responsible gambling within their gaming sites, many partnerships and programs have been developed by Canadian (and global) gaming authorities to provide both patrons and employees with support and information about addiction issues. In many jurisdictions, these initiatives include a program called "voluntary self-exclusion," which allows individuals the opportunity to opt for a self-imposed ban from one or more gaming sites. All Canadian casinos offer some form of self-exclusion program, though these programs vary in scope (individual casino vs. all gaming sites overseen by a particular gaming authority), length (six months to indefinite), and penalty for breaches (removal from premises, trespassing notice, fine, escalation to a non-voluntary ban, etc.) [5].

In Ontario, the self-exclusion program offered by the OLG allows individuals to voluntarily have their names removed from OLG marketing and promotional databases [1]. Enrollees in this program, if found by OLG staff at a gaming site, will also be escorted from the premises by Security staff and issued a trespass notice. An OLG self-exclusion extends for an indefinite period, with a minimum length of six months, after which an individual can submit a written application for reinstatement. Though it is first and foremost the responsibility of self-excluded individuals to remain away, OLG looks to provide assistance, as necessary, by detecting enrollees who attempt to enter a gaming site. Improving detection helps OLG create a key disincentive for self-excluded individuals returning to a site. Of course, this presents a challenge—how best to identify self-excluded individuals amongst a large number of regular patrons?

9.2.2 Detecting Self-excluded Individuals

Until recently, OLG's process of detecting self-excluded individuals was largely manual. Enrollees were voluntarily photographed and personal information about them was collected, at their request, to be used in subsequent identification. These photos and associated information were then distributed to OLG gaming sites where they were printed and stored in secure binders accessible by security personnel who, among other responsibilities, would undertake the arduous task of trying to match faces in the casino with photos in the binders. Such a process of manual facial recognition suffers many obvious challenges, due to the limits of staff (and human) capability. Of particular note, humans are not generally good at recognizing the faces of people they do not know [6], and may quickly be overloaded by the task of reviewing the many faces that appear in a busy casino environment (particularly as staff are not searching for a single individual, but instead must watch for *any* self-enrolled person).

As there are thousands of self-identified problem gamblers enrolled in the program, OLG wanted to examine whether technological tools could aid them in more efficiently and effectively meeting their objectives for the self-exclusion program. Such a tool would be required to:

- Reliably detect most self-excluded problem gamblers;
- Not interfere with the smooth flow of other patrons into the casino;
- Be cost-effective; and
- Respect all casino patrons' privacy.

An automated facial recognition system was thought to be an attractive tool to enhance and support the manual inspection process. Such a solution seemed feasible within a casino environment, in which patrons are already aware of and accustomed to the presence of video surveillance. From a business perspective, the general patron experience would also be unaffected by such an approach since facial images may be captured at a distance, with no requirement for any direct physical interaction.

9.2.3 Facial Recognition: One-to-One vs. One-to-Many

Biometric systems such as facial recognition can be deployed in 1:1 ("one-to-one") or 1:many ("one-to-many") modes, depending on the application. 1:1 comparisons are generally used to provide access control, while 1:many systems are generally applied as a 'watch list' system (e.g. a system designed to find one or more particular individuals in a crowd) or a system preventing multiple enrollments. Access control systems are typically concerned with letting the correct person in; watch list systems are typically concerned with keeping specific people out.

Facial recognition, like most biometric systems, is easier to deploy for a 1:1 application. The authentication process for a 1:1 matching system involves two stages. First, the person requiring access makes an identity claim (for example, by presenting an employee ID), which is used as an index to retrieve a single template from a database of biometrics collected by the organization during the enrollment phase. The system then captures the individual's live biometric (e.g. an image of his or her face), and compares it against the retrieved template to verify whether the person is who he or she claims to be.

In 1:many watch list mode the system must compare each 'live' biometric captured against a full list of stored templates (a "watch list")—in effect, rapidly performing a matching task against all individuals in the database. The identification process for a 1:many facial recognition system is as follows: once a watch list has been created, and the system is installed, an image of each individual within range of a camera is temporarily captured. Biometric features are extracted from these new images, which are then compared against each of the templates collected during the enrollment phase. Each comparison yields a matching score, which represents the degree of similarity between the image of the patron and a stored biometric template.

The process concludes by determining whether any of the scores are high enough to be included on the list of top matches (the number of top matches is called the rank), which may then be followed by manual inspection for purpose of confirmation.

In biometric systems, scoring rules (e.g. the minimum score required to declare a match) are generally administrator configurable. This allows for the management of the rates of false acceptance (i.e. wrongly matching captured images with those of others) and false rejection (i.e. failing to positively identify images of individuals who are on the watch list), to which biometric systems are subject. Typically, there is an inverse relationship between the false acceptance rate (FAR) and the false rejection rate (FRR), in which the reduction of one causes an increase in the other. Most biometric systems (including most generic face recognition systems reported in the literature) are required to maintain a very low (e.g., 1 in 10,000) false acceptance rate and an acceptable false rejection rate. In an access control system, for example, it will generally be less problematic to correct a false rejection (via a secondary access mechanism, or a re-scan of the biometric) than a false acceptance (which permits access to an unauthorized individual). In the OLG scenario, the requirements are to maintain an acceptable FAR with a low FRR to assist as many self-excluded individuals as possible.

9.3 Biometric Encryption—The Privacy by Design Approach to Biometric Systems

It should be noted that a decision regarding the adoption of facial recognition technology to aid the OLG's self-exclusion program could not be made based on technical considerations alone—sound technology does not necessarily mean good public policy. For instance, privacy advocates have long held that surveillance and biometric systems represent significant privacy concerns. Potential issues that have been identified include [2, 7]:

1. *Function creep*—When personal data is collected, organizations often face suggestions as to why they ought to do something more with it, or temptations to expand the scope of a system—in this case, to use the biometric data for purposes other than those initially intended and described upon collection of the information.
2. *Data linkage*—The uniqueness of biometric templates across individuals allows for the possibility that biometric databases, even if they store only templates (i.e. no images) and are anonymous, can be algorithmically linked for data mining, profiling, investigation, and other purposes.
3. *Data misuse*—Unlike tokens and passwords, biometrics are not the sort of things that can be replaced or reset. Care must be taken to ensure that they are not vulnerable to threat or abuse.
4. *Security vulnerabilities*—Biometric systems are potentially vulnerable to a range of attacks, including: spoofing, interception, replay, substitution, masquerade and Trojan horse attacks; tampering; overriding Yes/No response, etc.

The need to develop a privacy-protective facial recognition system presented an excellent opportunity to practice "*Privacy by Design*." *Privacy by Design (PbD)* is predicated on the notion that technology can be enlisted to *protect* privacy, rather than encroaching upon it. Practicing *PbD* requires embedding internationally accepted fair information practices and the seven Foundational Principles of *PbD* directly into the design of technologies, at the architecture level [8, 9]. *PbD* emphasizes the "positive-sum paradigm," in which it is recognized that embedding privacy measures need not weaken security, functionality or performance—quite the opposite. As opposed to a zero-sum paradigm, which brings unnecessary trade-offs and false dichotomies, *Privacy by Design* serves to enhance the overall design by creating technologies that achieve strong privacy without compromising performance— a doubly enabling "win-win" outcome.

Biometric Encryption (BE)—explained in detail in [2]—uses *Privacy by Design* to directly address the privacy and security concerns associated with biometric systems. BE is a process that securely binds a key to, or extracts a key from, a biometric. It is computationally difficult to retrieve either the key or the biometric from the "helper data" (also called a "private template") created by this process and stored by the application, except upon presentation of the correct live biometric sample for authentication. In essence, the key is "encrypted" with the biometric—a 'fuzzy' process due to the natural variability of biometric samples. The key can represent any value required by the particular application—for instance, it may be a cryptographic key or a pointer into a related private information database.

The concept of Biometric Encryption (BE) was first introduced in the mid-90s by Tomko et al. [10]. In subsequent works, many BE solutions were proposed (more information on BE and related technologies can be found in [2, 11–13]. It should be noted that while some of the BE solutions (see, for example, [14] hinted at the possibility of a secure application, no explicit treatment of this type of construction has been considered by the existing solutions. In most cases, the cryptographic key was simply assumed to be the output of a BE verification algorithm. Although some BE-style 1:many biometric systems have been proposed [15, 16], a BE application in a watch list scenario has never been discussed let alone implemented, to the best of our knowledge.

In general, Biometric Encryption schemes offer a number of advantages over traditional biometric systems. With BE, the user has greater control over his or her biometric, since images, biometric templates and keys are not stored. There is considerably less risk associated with storing private templates, even in centralized databases. BE is less susceptible to high level attacks, such as substitution, Trojan horse, and masquerade attacks, tampering, overriding Yes/No response, etc. BE can work in a non-trusted or, at least, in less trusted environment, and is less dependent on hardware, procedures, and policies. Even though the random keys are longer than conventional passwords, they do not require user memorization. The BE keys and helper data are revocable and renewable. Overall, BE can enhance both privacy and security of a biometric system, thereby resulting in greater public confidence, acceptance, and use, and better compliance with privacy laws.

Another group of privacy-enhancing biometric technologies was called "Cancelable Biometrics" (CB) [17–20]. It does the feature transformation and stores the transformed template. The same transform is applied on verification and the transformed samples are compared. There is a large number of transforms available, so that the templates are revocable. The difficulty with this approach is that in most cases the transform is fully or partially reversible [2], which necessitates keeping it secret (i.e. the transform cannot be stored alongside with the template). Therefore, the CB approach is not applicable to watch list systems, since it would require the same transform for all the users (on authentication, the patrons are unknown to the system). Eventually, this transform would become public and the system would be cracked.

It was shown in [3] that BE could, in theory, be effectively integrated into a watch list facial recognition system. What remained was the practical development and deployment of such a system—an opportunity presented through a partnership with OLG and its self-exclusion program.

9.4 OLG FR + BE Application

As previously mentioned, for the OLG's self-exclusion program, an automated facial recognition system was determined to be the best technology to enhance the effectiveness of a manual inspection/detection process. First, such a system captures facial images at a distance, with no need for user interaction. This is an important consideration as, in Ontario, casino visitors do not generally need to provide identification upon entry (except for age verification)—thus, a remote system is needed in order to preserve the current entrance experience for non-enrolled individuals. Secondly, a facial recognition system will be able to operate in conjunction with the legacy, photograph-based system, without the need for re-enrollment of individuals (which would require a visit by each enrollee to a gaming site). Other remote biometric modalities, such as iris-on-the-move or gait recognition, are not yet sufficiently advanced for OLG's application, and would not satisfy the legacy requirement.

It should be mentioned, however, that facial recognition at a distance is quite challenging: there are illumination, camera position, pose, facial expression, etc. problems that seriously impact system accuracy. As a result, the accuracy numbers for live facial recognition significantly vary in the literature: from FRR ~ 0.3 %–3 % at FAR $= 0.1$ % in the controlled MBE 2010 NIST test [21] to FRR ~ 40 %–70 % in the German Federal Criminal Police Office study at a railway station [22]. The conditions of the latter test are much closer to the OLG environment. The accuracy of facial recognition has, however, significantly improved over the past decade [21, 23], increasing the chance for a successful deployment (compared, for example, to the failed facial recognition watch-list test in Tampa in 2001 [24, 25]).

In relation to the above challenges, some representatives of the U.S. Federal Bureau of Investigation (FBI) blasted facial recognition technology in general for its alleged failure "to deliver the highly reliable verification required" [26]. While this opinion is not shared by many biometrics experts, it is true that live facial recognition at a distance does not have accuracy levels comparable to fingerprints, DNA, or iris scan for massive 1:many applications, which require searches through a database of tens of millions of records. However, in the context of the OLG application, where the database size is much smaller (about 20,000 records), facial recognition is expected (based on the German test [22]) to identify at least two out of three self-excluded persons with a manageable rate of false alarms. While this level is less than ideal, it must be recalled that the current system of manual identification is significantly less accurate. As well, it will be shown that a novel system design alongside a gradual approach of several field tests can help to bring the overall performance of facial recognition to a level acceptable for the OLG application. In addition, the final decision of whether a match is declared is made by a human operator, and a number of manual or alternative recognition methods (checking for license plates of enrollees, monitoring for use of enrollees' 'frequent player' cards, etc.) is kept in place. This recognizes, and mitigates, the potential fallibility [27] of any biometrics-based system. In fact, facial recognition has become a part of the FBI's Next Generation Identification (NGI) program [28].

Along with the challenges associated with properly deploying a biometric system, the integration of Biometric Encryption into a facial recognition system, as required by the application proposed by OLG, is far from a trivial task, as it requires a re-engineering of the underlying architecture of a commercial facial recognition product. In this section, we also describe the issues faced by the collaborative team of researchers from OLG, the University of Toronto, iView Systems, and the IPC, the means by which they were addressed, the privacy protections made available through use of *Privacy by Design*, and discuss the results of proof of concept testing of the system.

9.4.1 System Overview

The self-exclusion context at OLG is a 1:many (watch list) scenario in which the system must identify self-excluded individuals amongst a crowd of other patrons. Biometric Encryption alone is not recommended in a pure watch list scenario such as this, as the computing power required to perform the 1:many comparisons would be daunting. However, a standard facial recognition system can be used to reduce the normal 1:many comparison to a near-1:1 comparison, by filtering out all but the top few matches. Thus, a system was developed which was composed of two distinct components (Fig. 9.1):

- A *watch list module*, which uses traditional facial recognition technology in a 1:many mode to produce a top-matches list for every patron walking into a casino. The list can contain zero or more potential matches, but typically has fewer than five; and,
- A *BE module*, which attempts to release keys for each of the subjects on the top matches list. If a key is successfully released, a match alert is generated for review by a security officer.

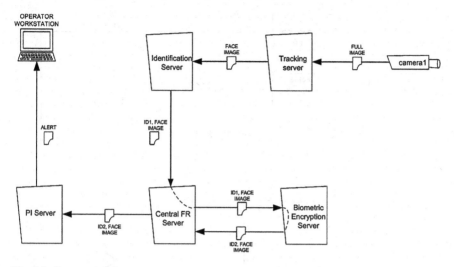

Fig. 9.1 System overview

Such a configuration has accuracy benefits on top of the privacy enhancements generally gained through the use of BE. For instance, in contrast to many biometric systems, the OLG operating scenario requires a minimized FRR (since this represents the rate at which enrolled self-exclusion subjects would go undetected and allowed into the gaming premises), while maintaining an acceptable FAR (as large numbers of false matches may increase staff frustration and inspire distrust in the system). In proof of concept testing (as described later in this document) of a watch list facial recognition system with the described configuration, the FAR results improved when compared to the watch list system without BE—with a minimal (or near zero) increase in FRR. The same wording was used in Sect. 9.5 so I had to change it. In other words, BE module, which acts as a second classifier after the watch list identification module, cannot introduce any additional false acceptances (i.e., add to the list of potential matches), but may reject some. By carefully tuning the system parameters, it is possible to minimize or even nullify the negative impact on FRR. More details can be found in Sect. 9.5 and [3, 4].

9.4.2 Enrollment and Identification

In the proposed system design, the "self-excluded" subject identification is performed using a vendor-supplied facial recognition system—iGWatch IP from iView Systems, which uses an FR algorithm SDK from Cognitec Systems, Germany. A biometrics-based cryptosystem (another term for BE) is implemented in tandem to offer privacy protection of the subject's personal information by way of a bound pointer key.

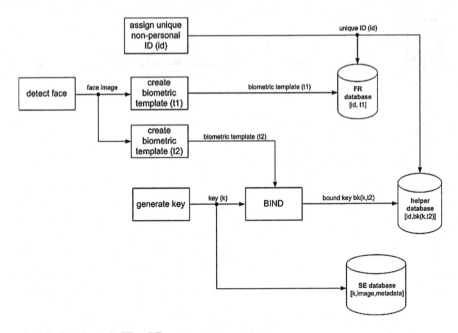

Fig. 9.2 Enrollment in FR + BE system

As shown in Fig. 9.2, in the enrollment phase, the subject's facial image is captured, and he or she is assigned a non-identifying, unique enrollee ID (*id*). A commercial facial recognition system then extracts biometric features and generates a template (*t1*) that is stored in the face recognition database (*FR database*), indexed by the enrollee ID. Another set of biometric features (*t2*) is sent to the BE key binding algorithm, which creates BE helper data (or a 'private template') from the biometric data and a pointer key. This pointer key represents the location of the subject's facial image and other personal information (PI) within a database of self-excluded individuals (*SE database*), and is generated at random. Finally, the BE helper data, *bk(k, t2)*, is stored in another database (*helper database*), again indexed by the same enrollee ID. For the OLG implementation *t1* and *t2* use different facial algorithms to extract features and are not interoperable, which increases the security and privacy of the system.

During identification (Fig. 9.3), the vendor-supplied system will attempt to do a one-to-many match of subjects entering the monitored facility to those in the FR database. This "Preliminary Identification" stage is typical of a "watch list" scenario. The enrollee IDs of the top matches are then output to the BE key retrieval algorithm. If a key can be retrieved from the BE helper data associated with one of the potential matches, the final verification stage is entered. Here, the pointer to the stored personal information associated with the potential match is regenerated (from the BE helper data), and the record at that location is retrieved. An operator then manually compares the retrieved facial image with the image of the casino patron in question. As such, the final decision of whether to approach a person and ask

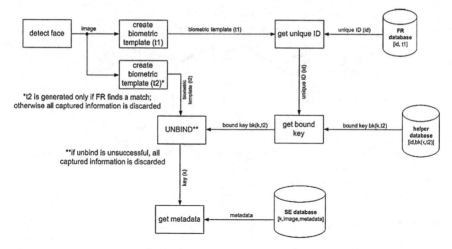

Fig. 9.3 Identification in FR + BE system

to confirm his or her identity is left to a human operator. It is important to note, with regard to the privacy of those patrons not registered in the self-exclusion program, that though an image of each individual entering the facility will be captured and analysed by the facial recognition system, no captured or derived information (e.g. images or biometric templates) is stored by this system should there be no match identified. In the event that a match is declared by a human operator, the captured image is planned to be securely stored in the system for one year to be provided in cases of legal challenges.

9.4.3 Privacy Protections

As stated, this is the first BE application proposed for a biometric watch list scenario. This scenario, though, differs from most other watch lists. A common application of a watch list involves the detection of subjects who have been identified as posing a risk to public safety or security. In such a system, the primary privacy issues are associated with the general public. It is important that any information—such as captured images or biometric templates—related to non-watch listed individuals is not stored. Such a system must also have a sufficiently low false acceptance rate (FAR) to prevent excessive numbers of incorrect alarms which will burden the security staff unnecessarily. Note that individuals are approached by security personnel to confirm their identity only after a manual inspection of biometrics, and it is crucial that this would rarely occur for non-watch listed individuals.

However, there are some additional privacy considerations for the OLG Self-Exclusion Program, which consists of individuals who have voluntarily put themselves on the watch list. In addition to maintaining the privacy of non-enrolled indi-

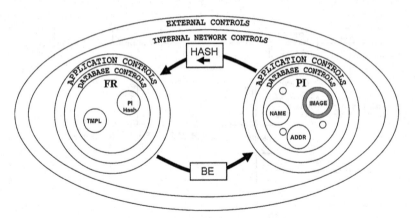

Fig. 9.4 *Privacy by Design*: a multi-layered approach to privacy

viduals (which OLG accomplishes by not storing any captured or derived information when the system does not find a match), the personal information of enrollees
should enjoy the highest possible level of privacy protection (similar to that of health
records) while it is in OLG's custody. BE can be a significant aid in achieving this
important standard.

The above-described system architecture uses several techniques to increase the
privacy and security of the enrollee records throughout the system (as shown in
Fig. 9.4). Conventional cryptography is used to encrypt all images in the PI database;
these images must be stored in order for a small set of authorized users to use non-
biometric means (e.g. visual comparisons) to spot or verify a self-excluded patron.
The databases themselves are encrypted to protect data while it is 'at rest,' while
communication between clients and the databases also occur through encrypted
pathways, to protect data 'in motion.' Both the databases and the application clients
are access controlled, and the entire system is deployed on a secure internal network,
which is protected from the external world.

One of the principal privacy protections of this system, though, is that the link
to the photo and other personal information of a self-excluded person can only be
determined by accessing a key that is bound to the person's biometric. In order to
reveal the stored information, the BE key retrieval algorithm must be able to regenerate a biometrically encrypted pointer key. To achieve this, the person's live facial
image is required—control, thus, rests with the individual. This control also makes it
much more difficult for the information to be linked with other, third party databases
without the user's consent. The OLG system further uses different template generation algorithms which are independent of each other, to ensure that the two biometric
templates (used by the facial recognition and BE modules, respectively) are not the
same or interoperable. This greatly reduces the possibility that the vendor's template
could be transformed and used to retrieve a key from the corresponding BE helper
data.

In the OLG application, the connection between a PI record and the FR database
must also be accessible, to allow for updates to records in the FR database (for

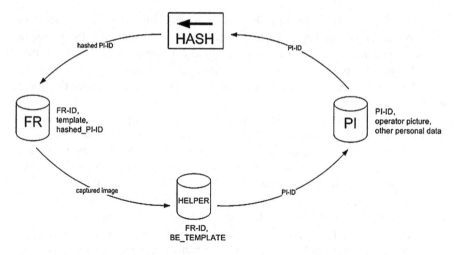

Fig. 9.5 BE in the proposed OLG application

example, to de-enroll someone from face recognition). To ensure that BE cannot be circumvented to reveal the link from an FR record to the PI record, a one-way hashing algorithm is used to reveal the link between a PI record and a corresponding FR record (see Fig. 9.5).

BE may also enhance privacy protection for the casino patrons who are not self-excluded—the general public. BE works as a second classifier that follows the vendor's biometric engine. As shown in Sects. 9.5 and 9.6 (see also [3]), this can substantially reduce the system FAR without a significant impact on FRR and, thus, should help the security personnel minimize the level of false alarms (i.e. when a legitimate user is approached for identity check).

It is interesting to note that BE has the future potential of allowing the consensual sharing of personal data with some user-authorized third parties, such as a self-help workgroup of gambling addicts. In this situation, the personal data would be encrypted with the BE key, so that the self-excluded person retains full control over the data, since accessing it would require his physical presence at the workgroup. Further, by providing an extra security layer, the system with BE would offer better safeguards over information either stored or transmitted to such third party. To access and decrypt personal data, a would-be attacker would face the added task of cracking the BE helper data. Even if successful, such an attack would be limited in scope, as though a 'crack' would cause a breach of one person's information, the rest of the system would remain uncompromised (as there is no single key or template to decrypt all records).

It is acknowledged that a facial recognition BE solution for a watch list system, such as that proposed for OLG's application, does not necessarily capture all the privacy benefits that could be provided by BE in a 1:1 application [2]. As a biometric modality, facial recognition is weaker in terms of entropy than, for example, iris and fingerprints [2, 29]. This means that only a relatively short key can be bound to the biometric. Overall, face-based BE is also more susceptible to offline attacks. As a caution, developers and system administrators should be aware that facial images are more generally available than other biometrics (through social networking sites, etc.). As such, the potential should be addressed that such an image could be reformatted and submitted to the facial recognition system in order to retrieve the stored information.

With regard to the OLG application in particular, privacy concerns may arise from the fact that personal data, including facial images, from the OLG self-exclusion program are already, and will likely continue to be, held by OLG in a central database(s). Access to these databases is limited and strictly regulated, however. Further, access to personal data which bypasses the BE system must be available, for a number of purposes. Should a self-excluded individual need to update his or her personal information (such as address, to remain free from marketing materials), it would be a poor practice to require the individual to visit a gaming site to present his or her biometrics. As such, a mechanism is required to allow non-BE access to a self-excluded person's own data. OLG may also use some non-biometric means to spot a self-excluded person, such as automobile license plate numbers or monitoring use of the person's loyalty card number (some self-excluded people still try to use the card after sneaking into the facilities). In this case, as well, the system operator will need to access some of the self-excluded person's data. To minimize those privacy concerns, the PI and FR systems are kept autonomous, as shown in Fig. 9.4.

Overall, though, it is felt that BE in the OLG watch list scenario, even given any real or potential challenges, provides significant *privacy protection* both to self-excluded persons and to the general public. This privacy protection is achieved mainly on the operational level. BE also offers a more *secure system architecture*— an attacker must still penetrate all of the standard security safeguards in order to access BE helper data. BE may even improve the *overall accuracy* of the watch list system. In other words, BE could bring a "triple-win" advantage to a conventional watch list system by transforming its surveillance nature.

9.5 QIM-Based Biometric Encryption

Among all BE schemes, the most popular are Fuzzy Vault [30], which is suitable for unordered data with arbitrary dimensionality (e.g., fingerprint minutiae), and the XOR-based Fuzzy Commitment, which is applicable to an ordered biometric feature set of a fixed length.

The BE solutions based on the Fuzzy Commitment scheme [31] are implemented in the commercial priv-ID^{TM} system for fingerprints. From the available literature, there are essentially two notable classes of priv-ID^{TM} BE variants: the so-called Helper Data System (HDS) [32], and the Multi-Bit Quantization Using Likelihood Ratio [33].

We adopted an alternative approach [3, 4], called Quantization Index Modulation (QIM), for generating helper data from a key and the feature vector. Originally proposed for watermarking applications [34], QIM was first applied to BE by Linnartz and Tuyls [35] and generalized by Buhan et al. [36]. However, neither a complete system description nor practical simulation results were presented. Compared to the HDS and the Multi-Bit Likelihood Ratio approaches, the most significant distinguishing feature of the QIM scheme is its elimination of the necessity to explicitly binarize the extracted features. This is made possible by employing an ensemble of quantizers to process the continuous-input features. The information to be embedded (i.e., the cryptographic key) determines which quantizer needs to be used, as specified by an associated codebook. In other words, the objective is to utilize a feature vector to securely bind the encoded cryptographic key, i.e., to generate a secure helper data (or "sketch") suitable for storage. Also, due to its structure and design parameters, the QIM framework provides more flexibility in balancing the trade-off between FAR and FRR requirements. In particular, the quantizer step size can be used to tune the system towards a particular operating point, with an associated pair of (FAR, FRR) values. This property is useful in designing practical BE systems, which are potentially subject to a wide range of operating conditions.

Of particular interest is the QIM class implemented using dither modulation [34]. In this case, the quantization partitions and reconstruction points of the quantizer ensemble can be defined as shifted versions of a basis quantizer. The advantage is that the encoding and decoding procedures are simplified, due to the well-defined structure offered by the dither quantizers. Using dither quantizers, we were able to extend the one-bit per component strategy described in the previous works [35, 36] to the multi-bit per component QIM.

9.5.1 QIM Parameters and General Construction

In this subsection, the general mechanisms of QIM for key binding are described.

QIM Function: Given an ensemble of N quantizers $\{Q_1, Q_2, \ldots, Q_N\}$, the QIM function takes a continuous input feature X and a discrete message M to produce a reconstruction point $Q = \text{QIM}(X, M) = Q_M(X)$.

Key Binding using QIM: Given a message M (e.g., an encoded cryptographic key) to be bound using a signal vector X (e.g., a feature vector during enrollment), a pair of encoder and decoder can be defined based on QIM as follows:

Encoder: an encoded sketch W (a continuous output signal) is obtained using an underlying QIM function as:

$$W = \text{Enc}(X, M) = \text{QIM}(X, M) - X = Q_M(X) - X.$$

The encoded sketch W is the offset (also called correction vector) between the input and the closest reconstruction point of the quantizer Q_M.

A Gray coding scheme is appropriate for mapping the quantizers using the message M. This is so that, for M being a binary cryptographic key, incremental changes in the feature vectors result in incremental changes in the recovered key.

Decoder: from a noisy signal vector Y (e.g., a feature vector obtained during verification) and a given sketch W, the decoder extracts the embedded message using a minimum distance scheme as follows:

$$M_{ext} = Dec(Y, W) = \underset{m \in M}{\arg\min}\, d(Y + W, Q_m),$$

where $d(.)$ is an appropriate distance metric.
In other words, the decoder performs the following steps:

- Compensates for the offset
- Searches for the closest reconstruction point from all the N quantizers
- The label m of the quantizer with the closest reconstruction point corresponds to the embedded message.

9.5.2 QIM Implementations and Bit Allocation

In case of dither quantizers, the number of quantizers in the ensemble is equal to $L = 2^{n_b}$, where n_b represents the number of information bits to be embedded.

When using dither lattice quantizers, the reconstruction points of the quantizers are all constructed as shifts of a base quantizer $Q_1 = [P_1, C_1]$, where P_1 and C_1 represent, respectively, the quantization partition and reconstruction points. Then, the subsequent quantizers are computed with shifted codebooks. The min and max reconstruction points are, respectively, q_m and q_p. The following construction is made:

$$P_1 = (q_m + q_p)/2, \tag{9.1}$$

$$C_1 = [q_m, q_p], \tag{9.2}$$

where

$$q_m = \mu - (f_q \times \sigma), \qquad q_p = \mu + (f_q \times \sigma)$$

with μ being the mean, σ the standard deviation of the feature component, and f_q a scaling factor. The value of f_q provides the tolerance for the quantizer ensemble.

The remaining quantizers $Q_2, Q_3, \ldots, Q_L$ are constructed as dither quantizers, with shift step-size

$$s_q = \frac{q_p - q_m}{L}.$$

In other words, these partitions and reconstruction points are all shifted by s_q from the basis quantizer Q_1 for the remaining quantizers.

With the given design, the two key results are:
Range of output helper data:

$$|w| \le \frac{q_p - q_m}{L}.$$

Tolerance of QIM decoder:

Admissible $|E| = |Y - X| < \frac{s_q}{2}$.

From the above, it is easy to see that the quantizer range $[q_m, q_p]$ should be proportional to the dynamic range of the input features. The values of fq may need to be larger to deliver acceptable tolerance.

In addition, depending on how the feature components are used to bind a secret message, several specific implementations of the QIM framework can be distinguished. This is related to the bit allocation problem, in which two general strategies can be summarized as follows.

1. One-Bit per component strategy: each component is used to embed one bit of the encoded key sequence. For example, when using a BCH code (255, 131, 18), in order to embed a 131-bit key, a codeword of 255 bits is generated by the error correcting code (ECC) module. Then, at least 255 components are required for the one-bit per component procedure.
2. M-Bit per component strategy: each component is used to embed a variable number of bits from the encoded key sequence. For example, each component can be used to embed 3 bits of the encoded key. Then, to embed a 131-bit cryptographic key (which is ECC-encoded to 255 bits), 85 components would be required.

In all cases, the number of components that should be kept depends on the reliability of the components.

9.5.3 Simulation Setup and Protocol

The simulations were performed on a subset of the CMU PIE face image database [37].

The database was partitioned into a gallery set containing all but one of the images for each of the subjects, and a probe set containing the single remaining image for each subject. The gallery set was used for training the feature extractor and the BE modules as well as enrollment of the subjects. The probe set was used for verification/identification of each of the subjects.

PCA feature extraction [38] was trained on the gallery set and applied to all images. For most cases, the first 154 PCA components were retained for each image, constituting up to 95 % of the signal energy.

BE verification performance was first tested in isolation, and then as part of the whole system employing Watch List subject identification before applying BE. In the case where the entire system is simulated, the Watch List subject identification process produces a ranked list of candidate gallery (enrolled) subjects for each probe subject tested. This list of claimed identities for each probe subject is passed to the BE module where verification is performed on each one individually. The length of the list of claimed identities may vary between 0 (i.e., unidentified—no matching subject found in the gallery) and r (the maximum rank allowed for identification). The system parameter r is to be chosen based on the application requirements.

Table 9.1 Selected QIM configurations for different key lengths

Achieved key length (bits)	Closest standard key length (bits)	Code length (bits)
16	16	63
36	32	63
64	64	127
131	128	255

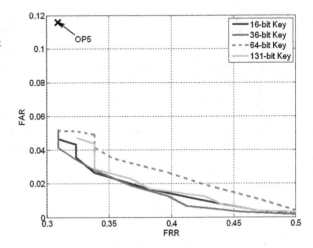

Fig. 9.6 ROC curve for full Watch List system with QIM BE and $r = 5$ operating point (OP5). Simulation results for CMU PIE face image database; PCA feature extraction

9.5.4 QIM Recognition Performance

The recognition performance of the QIM BE was first simulated in isolation as a verification operation. Out of several variants (they differ by the bit allocation method) of the QIM BE, the best results were achieved for the basic QIM with uniform bit allocation using the first 154 PCA components, based on 95 % of the total energy.

The results were grouped according to the achieved key length. The configurations that were selected for simulation of the full Watch List system are listed in Table 9.1.

The full Watch List system with the QIM BE module was simulated using the selected operating points OP5, OP10, and OP20 (for $r = 5$, 10, and 20, respectively) and the four key length configurations described in Table 9.1. The results are shown in Fig. 9.6 for OP5. As can be seen, for all tested key lengths, the addition of the QIM BE is in fact able to provide *improved* recognition results, compared to the operating point without BE. Specifically, the use of the QIM BE is able to significantly reduce FAR while achieving approximately the same FRR. Additionally, to reduce the FAR even further, the FRR can be increased. Alternatively, by maintaining the same FAR as was without BE, it is possible to reduce FRR by increasing the rank list length, r, from 5 to 20 and applying BE (not shown in Fig. 9.6).

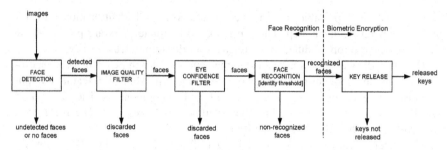

Fig. 9.7 Integration of vendor's FR algorithm and Biometric Encryption into iGWatch IP

Upon simulation of the full Watch List system, BE exhibited behavior whereby the FAR results *improved* when compared to the Watch List system without BE. This could be understood by the fact that the BE module receives a candidate list of identities from the Watch List module—falsely accepted imposter subjects are placed on the list by the Watch List module—the BE module cannot add to this list (i.e., the BE module cannot increase the number of subjects falsely accepted). This is inherent in the system design that has the Watch List identification module in series with the BE module, which acts as a second classifier. In all simulation cases, the BE module in fact rejected many imposter candidates, thus reducing the FAR. Even though the BE module may falsely reject legitimate subjects placed on the candidate list, thus increasing FRR, it is possible to compensate for that by increasing the size of the candidate list, i.e. the rank r. If the rank remains the same, all simulation cases showed the possibility of BE significantly reducing the FAR (from the Watch List alone) with a minimal (or zero) increase in FRR.

It can be seen that the QIM method is able to generate a curve of operating points, offering system implementers an important degree of freedom to control the choice of operating point. It was shown that out of the QIM variants, the basic QIM approach yielded the best performance. More details can be found in [3, 4].

9.6 Integration of Commercial FR System and QIM BE

iView Systems integrated Cognitec FR algorithms and Biometric Encryption [3, 4] into their iGWatch IP module, as shown in Fig. 9.7:

As the person walks into the OLG facility, his/her face is detected and tracked. All detected face images constitute a session. The session images go through a series of filters (such as image quality and eye confidence filters) that discard some images based on pre-selected thresholds. The remaining images are converted into templates and run against the database of FR templates. Each record in the database may contain multiple (up to 5) FR templates that were created from different face images of the same person. The FR matching score is computed between each remaining image in the session and each template in the record. The top session vs. record matches (where the rank r typically varies from 1 to 5) are selected by thresholding and by a voting technique. Since the FR algorithm is implemented in a very efficient way, it is possible to combine both filtering and identification into one multi-parameter decision step. The top image-to-template pairs are passed to the Biometric Encryption module, which releases (or does not release) a key.

The QIM BE was implemented using the vendor's FR templates that are incompatible with the templates used for the one-to-many step. About 600 feature components were selected out of several thousand template components. They were used in QIM encoder to obtain 511 bits that in turn encode key bits. The BCH error correcting code (511, 67, 87) was chosen.

The system parameters were tuned using a FR database of 114 OLG employees. The database contains 61824 images captured in 23788 live sessions. By varying the size of the QIM quantization interval and the number of bits per component (either one or two), it was possible to optimize the overall system performance. At the end, BE had very little impact on the false rejection rate but significantly reduced the false acceptance rate. Thus, the results of the previous section were confirmed using the vendor supplied FR algorithm.

9.7 Proof of Concept and Deployment

The system described above has moved beyond the conceptual phase. In fact, proof of concept testing has allowed OLG, in collaboration with iView Systems, U of T and the IPC, to demonstrate that a face recognition application with BE is viable for development and deployment in a casino environment. As this was a first-of-its-kind effort, expectations were unknown. The proof of concept testing had the following main steps and results:

- Facial recognition technology was proven effective in a casino environment through several tests in real field conditions (up to 20,000 visitors on Saturday) involving OLG control group participants (simulating the self-excluded persons) and the general public. During the course of field tests, there were several control groups containing from 10 to 64 participants. The groups were comprised of different individuals to minimize the learning curve effect. Each participant made on average 12 attempts to enter the facilities on different dates. The control group data samples were used to estimate the Correct Identification Rate (CIR).
- The general public data sample was used to measure the False Acceptance Rate (FAR). When there was a match from the face recognition (FR) system, the test operator manually compared the image of the person in question with the corresponding enrolled image of a self-excluded person and decided whether the person should be approached. At the end, it was known if the system detected a real self-excluded person (correct match) or if a false match was produced by the FR system.
- The Correct Identification Rate was increased to a maximum of approximately 91 % from a starting point of approximately 30 %. The CIR of 91 % is a best case result achieved by controlling participant pose; a more realistic CIR range for the field is between 60 % and 80 %. The advances in CIR were achieved using

a measured approach of several field tests and were mainly due to corrections in lighting, camera position and subject pose through the use of "attention-getting" devices like marketing screens. This compares positively to, for instance, a 2007 German Federal Criminal Police Office study which achieved a 30-60 % recognition rate for a facial recognition watch list field tested at a railway station [22].

- The False Acceptance Rate was of the order of 1 %. The FAR depends on the self-excluded database size, i.e. increases with the number of enrollees. However, it was observed that this dependence is slower than linear. For the latest tests, the self-excluded FR database contained about 13000 records. In all the tests, the FAR remained at manageable levels.

- Biometric Encryption did not decrease the accuracy or efficiency of face recognition in a pipeline test. Positive matches from face recognition were fed into the BE system; the BE system marginally affected the original CIR (by less than 1 %) while reducing the FAR by 30 % to 50 %. This result was an unexpected benefit, which, as described prior, occurs due to the status of the BE module as a secondary classifier.

- Face recognition was field tested using the actual OLG self-excluded images to determine the degree to which detection rates would improve. Preliminary results show that FR is a valuable tool in the overall goal of assisting self-excluded patrons from staying out of gaming facilities.

- The system architecture was successfully created to integrate BE into a commercial face recognition product (iGWatch IP from iView Systems) while maintaining OLG's core requirements. This architecture treated BE as an important component in a multi-layered approach to privacy and security of the overall system in line with the *Privacy by Design* approach.

- By the summer of 2011, the system was successfully deployed and is fully operational in most of Ontario's 27 gaming sites. To the best of our knowledge, this is by far the largest installation of a BE system and the first ever application of BE in a watch list scenario. The overall identification accuracy of self-excluded people has already improved by more than one order of magnitude compared to the previous manual system.

9.8 Conclusions

The Ontario Lottery and Gaming Corporation's self-exclusion program was identified as an ideal opportunity to deploy, for the first time, Biometric Encryption (BE) as a Privacy-Enhancing Technology in a biometric watch list scenario. The system, as designed, sequentially combined a commercial, one-to-many face recognition system with a BE module. This use of BE as a secondary classifier was shown to enhance patron privacy (both for those on the watch list, and regular patrons), system security, and even overall accuracy of the watch list system within the context of the OLG self-exclusion program. Based on the results of a field test of the system, it was also shown that facial recognition technology can contribute to OLG's program objectives. This technology serves as one part of OLG's Responsible Gaming program, to assist self-excluded patrons to keep their self-expressed commitment not to enter gaming sites.

The development of a facially oriented, Biometric Encryption application that may be integrated with commercially available facial recognition systems holds great promise. We firmly believe that this exciting and innovative project will generate considerable interest for other applications at OLG, and from other casinos across the country, and around the world. This leading-edge research should foster the development of a commercially available product that will facilitate the conduct of responsible management with respect to gaming and privacy—a positive-sum approach.

References

1. Self Exclusion (2009) Ontario Lottery and Gaming Corporation. http://www.knowyourlimit.ca/self-exclusion.html
2. Cavoukian A, Stoianov A (2009) Biometric encryption: the new breed of untraceable biometrics. In: Boulgouris NV, Plataniotis KN, Micheli-Tzanakou E (eds) Biometrics: Fundamentals, Theory, and Systems. Wiley/IEEE Press, New York, pp 655–718. Chapter 26
3. Martin K, Lu H, Bui F, Plataniotis KN, Hatzinakos D (2009) A biometric encryption system for the self-exclusion scenario of face recognition. IEEE Systems Journal 3(4):440–450. Special issue on biometrics systems
4. Bui FM, Martin K, Lu H, Plataniotis KN, Hatzinakos D (2010) Fuzzy key binding strategies based on quantization index modulation (QIM) for biometric encryption (BE) applications. IEEE Transactions on Information Forensics and Security 5(1):118–132
5. For information on casino self-exclusion programs in Canada, see: *British Columbia*: http://www.bclc.com/cm/gamesense/voluntary-self-exclusion.htm; *Alberta*: http://www.aglc.gov.ab.ca/responsiblegambling/selfexclusionprogram.asp; *Saskatchewan* (Indian Gaming Authority): http://www.siga.sk.ca/Self~%20Exlusion~%20Broch.pdf; *Manitoba*: http://www.mlc.mb.ca/MLC/content.php?pageid=420&langdir=E; *Ontario*: http://www.olg.ca/about/responsible_gaming/practices.jsp; *Quebec*: http://lotoquebec.com/corporatif/nav/en/responsible-gaming/self-exclusion-program; *Nova Scotia*: http://www.nsgc.ca/rgVoluntary.php; *PEI*: http://www.alc.ca/PlayResponsibly.aspx?id=2041
6. Hancock P, Bruce V, Burton AM (2000) Recognition of unfamiliar faces. Trends in Cognitive Sciences 4(9):330–337
7. Ratha NK, Connell JH, Bolle RM (2001) Enhancing security and privacy in biometrics-based authentication systems. IBM Systems Journal 40(3):614–634
8. Cavoukian A (2010) The 7 foundational principles: implementation and mapping of fair information practices. IPC, May 2010. http://www.ipc.on.ca/images/Resources/pbd-implement-7found-principles.pdf
9. Privacy by Design Resolution (2010) 32nd international conference of data protection and privacy commissioners, Jerusalem, Israel, 27–29 October 2010
10. Tomko GJ, Soutar C, Schmidt GJ (1996) Fingerprint controlled public key cryptographic system. US Patent 5541994, 30 July 1996 (Filing date: 7 Sept 1994)
11. Jain AK, Nandakumar K, Nagar A (2008) Biometric template security. EURASIP Journal on Advances in Signal Processing 2008:1–17. Article ID 579416
12. Tuyls P, Škorić B, Kevenaar T (eds) (2007) Security with Noisy Data: Private Biometrics, Secure Key Storage and Anti-counterfeiting. Springer, London

13. Rathgeb C, Uhl A (2011) A survey on biometric cryptosystems and cancelable biometrics. EURASIP Journal on Information Security 2011:3–25. http://jis.eurasipjournals.com/content/2011/1/3

14. Delvaux N, Bringer J, Grave J, Kratsev K, Lindeberg P, Midgren J, Breebaart J, Akkermans T, Van der Veen M, Veldhuis R, Kindt E, Simoens K, Busch C, Bours P, Gafurov D, Yang B, Stern J, Rust C, Cucinelli B, Skepastianos D (2008) Pseudo identities based on fingerprint characteristics. In: IEEE 4th International Conference on Intelligent Information Hiding and Multimedia Signal Processing (IIH-MSP 2008), Harbin, China, 15–17 August

15. Adjedj M, Bringer J, Chabanne H, Kindarji B (2009) Biometric identification over encrypted data made feasible. In: Lecture Notes in Computer Science, vol 5905. Springer, Berlin, pp 86–100

16. Ultra fast fingerprint matching for large scale databases (2010) Product Brochure FastAFIS® SDK, priv-ID BV. http://www.priv-id.com/wp-content/uploads/priv-ID-Product-Brochure-FastAFIS-SDK.pdf

17. Ratha NK, Chikkerur S, Connell JH, Bolle RM (2007) Generating cancelable fingerprint templates. IEEE Transactions on Pattern Analysis and Machine Intelligence 29(4):561–572

18. Savvides M, Vijaya Kumar BVK, Khosla PK (2004) Cancelable biometric filters for face recognition. In: Proc 17th International Conference on Pattern Recognition (ICPR'04), vol 3 Cambridge, England, pp 922–925

19. Teoh ABJ, Yuang CT (2007) Cancelable biometrics realization with multispace random projections. IEEE Transactions on Systems, Man and Cybernetics. Part B. Cybernetics 37(5):1096–1106

20. Boult T (2006) Robust distance measures for face recognition supporting revocable biometric tokens. In: Proceedings of the 7th International Conference on Automatic Face and Gesture Recognition, 10–12 April 2006. IEEE Computer Society, Washington, pp 560–566

21. Grother PJ, Quinn GW, Phillips JP (2010) Report on the evaluation of 2D still-image face recognition algorithms. NIST interagency report 7709, multiple-biometric evaluation (MBE), 22 June 2010

22. Face recognition as a search tool: Bundeskriminalamt, final report. http://www.eucpn.org/download/?file=GER%20FAce%20Recognition.pdf&type=14

23. Phillips PJ, Scruggs WT, O'Toole AJ, Flynn PJ, Bowyer KW, Schott CL, Sharpe M (2007) FRVT 2006 and ICE 2006 large-scale results. NIST report NISTIR 7408, 29 March 2007

24. Bonson K, Johnson R How facial recognition systems work. http://electronics.howstuffworks.com/facial-recognition.htm

25. Olsen S ACLU decries face-recognition tools. http://news.cnet.com/ACLU-decries-face-recognition-tools/2100-1023_3-800864.html

26. Moss D (2009) FBI techs shy away from facial recognition: spends 40 years losing face, 3 Nov 2009. http://www.theregister.co.uk/2009/11/03/fbio_face_recognition/

27. Pato JN, Millett LI (eds) (2010) Biometric recognition: challenges and opportunities. Whither biometrics committee, computer science and telecommunications board, Division on Engineering and Physical Sciences, National Research Council, 24 Sept 2010. http://www.nap.edu/catalog/12720.html

28. Pender JM What facial recognition technology means for privacy and civil liberties. Statement before the subcommittee on privacy, technology and the law committee on the judiciary. United States Senate, 18 July 2012. http://www.judiciary.senate.gov/pdf/12-7-18PenderTestimony.pdf

29. Youmaran R, Adler A, Loyka S (2006) Towards a measure of biometric information. In: Can Conf Computer Elec Eng (CCECE), Ottawa, Canada, 7–10 May 2006

30. Nandakumar K, Jain AK (2008) Multibiometric template security using fuzzy vault. In: 2nd IEEE International Conference on Biometrics: Theory, Applications and Systems (BTAS 2008), Arlington, VA, 29 Sept–1 Oct 2008, pp 1–6

31. Tuyls P, Akkermans AHM, Kevenaar TAM, Schrijen G-J, Bazen AM, Veldhuis RNJ (2005) Practical biometric authentication with template protection. In: 5th International Conference,

AVBPA 2005, Hilton Rye Town, NY, USA, 20–22 July 2005. Lecture Notes in Computer Science, vol 3546. Springer, Berlin, pp 436–446

32. Van der Veen M, Kevenaar T, Schrijen G-J, Akkermans TH, Zuo F (2006) Face biometrics with renewable templates. In: Proceedings of SPIE: Security, Steganography, and Watermarking of Multimedia Contents VIII, vol 6072

33. Chen C, Veldhuis R, Kevenaar T, Akkermans T (2007) Multi-bits biometric string generation based on the likelihood ratio. In: IEEE Conference on Biometrics: Theory, Applications and Systems, Washington, DC, 27–29 September 2007

34. Chen B, Wornell GW (2001) Quantization index modulation methods for digital watermarking and information embedding of multimedia. Journal of VLSI Signal Processing 27(1):7–33

35. Linnartz J-P, Tuyls P (2003) New shielding functions to enhance privacy and prevent misuse of biometric templates. In: Proc of the 4th Int Conf on Audio and Video Based Biometric Person Authentication, Guildford, UK, pp 393–402

36. Buhan IR, Doumen JM, Hartel PH, Veldhuis RNJ (2007) Constructing practical fuzzy extractors using QIM. Technical report TR-CTIT-07-52, Centre for Telematics and Information Technology, University of Twente, Enschede

37. Sim T, Baker S, Bsat M (2003) The CMU pose, illumination, and expression database. IEEE Transactions on Pattern Analysis and Machine Intelligence 25(12):1615–1618

38. Turk MA, Pentland AP (1991) Face recognition using eigenfaces. In: IEEE Conference on Computer Vision and Pattern Recognition, pp 589–591

Chapter 10
Smart Cards to Enhance Security and Privacy in Biometrics

Raul Sanchez-Reillo, Raul Alonso-Moreno, and Judith Liu-Jimenez

Abstract Smart cards are portable secure devices designed to hold personal and service information for many kind of applications. Examples of the use of smart cards are cell phone user identification (e.g. GSM SIM card), banking cards (e.g. EMV credit/debit cards) or citizen cards. Smart cards and Biometrics can be used jointly in different kinds of scenarios. Being a secure portable device, smart cards can be used for storing securely biometric references (e.g. templates) of the cardholder, perform biometric operations such as the comparison of an external biometric sample with the on-card stored biometric reference, or even relate operations within the card to the correct execution and result of those biometric operations.

In order to provide the reader of the book with an overview of this technology, this chapter provides a description of smart cards, from their origin till the current technology involved, focusing especially in the security services they provide. Once the technology and the security services are introduced, the chapter will detail how smart cards can be integrated in biometric systems, which will be summarized in four different strategies: Store-on-Card, On-Card Biometric Comparison, Worksharing Mechanism, and System-on-Card.

Also the way to evaluate the joint use of smart cards and Biometrics will be described; both at the performance level, as well as its security. Last, but not least, this chapter will illustrate the collaboration of both technologies by providing two examples of current major deployments.

10.1 Introduction

Identification cards are a kind of token that can be used for identifying their holder, and that are typically of the size of a credit card. Different technologies are related

R. Sanchez-Reillo (✉) · R. Alonso-Moreno · J. Liu-Jimenez
Carlos III University of Madrid, Avda. Universidad, 30, 28911 Leganes, Madrid, Spain
e-mail: rsreillo@ing.uc3m.es

R. Alonso-Moreno
e-mail: ramoreno@ing.uc3m.es

J. Liu-Jimenez
e-mail: jliu@ing.uc3m.es

P. Campisi (ed.), *Security and Privacy in Biometrics*,
DOI 10.1007/978-1-4471-5230-9_10, © Springer-Verlag London 2013

to identification cards: business cards, plastic cards, magnetic stripe cards (such as banking cards), laser cards (also called optical cards) or integrated circuit cards (such as memory cards or smart cards). Smart cards are identification cards that contain a microprocessor embedded within its body. Their existence is dated back to the early 1970s, when Dr. Kunitake Arimura [1] invented the idea of a plastic card with an integrated circuit, as to overcome the limitations that magnetic stripe cards had. Those limitations were mainly the lack of storage capacity (about 225 characters/digits), endurance (the magnetic stripe can be easily erased) and security (there are no mechanisms that avoid their copy). Dr. Arimura patented the technology in Japan and started to develop several products based on this initial idea.

But the international expansion of this technology began with Mr. Roland Moreno [2], a French journalist, who also had the same idea, patenting it worldwide in 1976 (patent number US3971916). With the creation of Innovatron, he licensed that patent (and the following ones coming out as a derivative of the first one, such as US4007355, US4092524, US4102493 or US4404464) to several companies. Among these companies, there were three of them that played a major role in the manufacturing of Integrated Circuit Cards (ICC). On one hand, Schlumberger [1] implemented the idea of an ICC by embedding within the card a semiconductor memory with some access logic that will protect its writing. The focus of this implementation was to manufacture a card that could even compete in price with the magnetic stripe card. On the other hand, Bull (in association with Motorola) and Philips developed cards where the integrated circuit was based on a microcontroller [1] (i.e. a microprocessor with a memory attached, plus some other peripherals). The main idea behind this implementation was to create a product with a high level of security.

These two lines of products were tested in France at the end of the 1970s and the early 1980s in different scenarios [1, 2]. The outcome of those tests showed that the Schlumberger product was ideal for applications like prepaid phone cards, due to its low cost, while the Bull and Philips products were the best option for applications requiring security, such as banking cards. This led to two different technologies within ICC products: Memory Cards (the ones based on Schlumberger implementation) and Smart Cards (the ones based on Bull and Philips implementations). These two technologies are completely different in nature and performance, especially in processing capabilities and the security level achieved, it being obvious that these features were much better in smart cards than in memory cards.

Throughout chapter only smart cards will be considered due to the security they provide that allows their integration within a biometric system. Next section will describe smart card technology, from its architecture to its different interfaces. After that, an overview to the security services that smart cards can provide will be detailed. This will settle the basis to explain the different ways that smart cards can be used to protect Biometrics. This will be followed by a section that will cover the evaluation of smartcard-based biometrics systems, both their performance and their security. In the last section two current use cases of the integration of smart cards and Biometrics will be described.

Fig. 10.1 Smart card block diagram

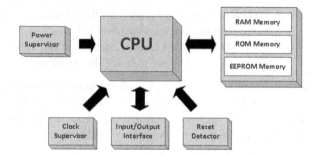

10.2 Smart Card Technology

Once the first smart card products were integrated in several sectors and applications, the technology of smart cards started to improve providing better solutions. The subsequent evolutions were also based on a series of international standards that were developed in parallel [3], targeting interoperability among products and systems. From the very beginning smart cards were considered as identification cards, and therefore their physical characteristics follow ISO/IEC 7810 specifications, which also rules magnetic stripe cards. Later on, other physical layouts were allowed, such as the plug-in format developed for applications such as the subscriber identification card in mobile phones in the GSM architecture.

But smart card technology requested further specifications, and that lead to the definition of the series of standards under the number ISO/IEC 7816, which define all different layers of the technology of smart cards with contacts, plus many other medium and high level specifications that can also be applied to contactless smart cards. Some of all these specifications will be described in the following subsections.

10.2.1 Architecture

As previously mentioned, a smart card is a microprocessor-based system, whose architecture can be described as the block diagram in Fig. 10.1. In few words, these blocks are:

- A central low-power *microprocessor* that is in charge of the whole control of the card. In the early days, this microprocessor was based on an 8-bit architecture. Nowadays, although this kind of microprocessors is still able to hold the control of a smart card, architectures of 16 or 32 bits are used. This evolution is mainly based on the evolution of the product of semiconductor manufacturers, benefiting for the new technologies of low-power consumption.
- A set of *memories* connected to the microprocessor:

  – A *ROM memory* (non-volatile and non-modifiable), which will hold the Operating System that will control the information flow and processing.

- A *RAM memory* (volatile) used for the temporal data needed by the Operating System, such as the communication buffer.
- An *EEPROM memory bank* (non-volatile but modifiable) that will hold the information stored by the user and the application.

• A *serial input/output interface* that allows the communication with the outside world. This will be detailed later in the interfaces subsection.
• A set of *control circuits* that will supervise the sources needed by the microprocessor, such as power, clock source, and reset mechanisms.

10.2.2 Operating System

The strength of smart cards compared to any other identification technology is the fact that the card is ruled by an Operating System (*Smart Card Operating System—SCOS*). The SCOS [4] is the element that is going to protect the card from any misleading use, and manage all the information and security mechanisms. In few words, the SCOS:

• Manages information storage in data structures such as files, directories or complex objects.
• Provides a set of commands to be executed in the card.
• Provides a security architecture (e.g. ciphering, authentication, etc.).
• Control the command-response exchange with the external world. For example, whenever the card receives a command, it will:

  - check that the command is a valid one,
  - check that its parameters and fields are well defined,
  - verify the security conditions,
  - verify the status of the data stored in the card, and
  - if all verifications are valid, then the command is executed, providing afterwards a feedback to the outer world, or
  - if any of the verifications fail, then an error occurs and provides a short feedback about the error to the outer world.

• Control the life cycle of the card.
• Hide all internal resources of the card architecture to the external world, only allowing the knowledge about:

  - the information structures in the card,
  - the security architecture,
  - the command set, and
  - the amount of EEPROM memory available (other memory banks are completely inaccessible to the outer world).

Traditionally SCOS are proprietary and therefore the interoperability among different smart cards is not fully achieved. Several parts within the ISO/IEC 7816 family of standards define interindustry commands as to allow reaching such interoperability, but there are still some open issues, options and alternatives that make each smart card model unique from others in the market.

But within the smart card industry, during the late 1990s the idea of developing smart cards with an Open Operating System was launched, being the most popular approach the one launched in conjunction with Sun Microsystems using Java programming language: JavaCards [5]. Most of the smart card manufacturers develop at least one JavaCard product. This kind of SCOS allows the developer to design and develop its own data structures, command set and processes, being able to adjust the card to any specific application. It is even possible to emulate the behaviour of the SCOS from any other manufacturer as to provide an interoperable alternative to the cards that are being used currently in any application.

10.2.3 Communication Interfaces

The command and information exchange between a smart card and the external world is done through a serial interface. Depending on the product, there could be different serial interfaces used. Initially interfaces used contacts, but afterwards also contactless interfaces were defined. This section describes briefly these possibilities. In addition to this, it has to be mentioned that there are products that implement more than one interface. These are hybrid cards that have contact and contactless interfaces. Within these products it can happen that both interfaces provide communication with the same integrated circuit. But there are also hybrid cards where each interface connects to a different integrated circuit (i.e. having more than one smart card in the same embodiment).

10.2.3.1 Interfaces Through Contacts

The traditional interface for smart cards is a half-duplex bidirectional base-band asynchronous interface using a set of 5 superficial contacts on the card (although the card module can show 6 or 8 contacts). This is defined in ISO/IEC 7816-3 and can be implemented, either based on a char-control protocol called $T = 0$, or on a frame-control protocol called $T = 1$, or on both.

The 5 contacts are providing power to the card (Vcc and GND), the clock for the microprocessor (CLK), a Reset signal (RST) for re-starting the communication and execution of the SCOS and the serial bidirectional line (I/O). The starting conditions for establishing a connection with a smart card are fixed in power (5 or 3.3 volts, other voltages being possible in the near future), and in clock frequency (from 1 to 5 MHz). After applying a reset, the card reports to the external world with a sequence of bytes called *Answer To Reset* (*ATR*) that provides the actual communication parameters for the protocol to be used. After such ATR is sent, the external world can send commands to the smart card, receiving its responses. Figure 10.2

Case 1: No data transfer between the IFD and the ICC

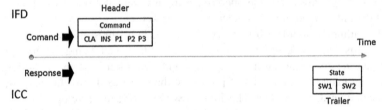

Case 2: Data transfer between the IFD and the ICC

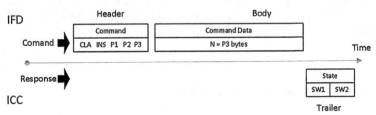

Case 3: Data transfer between the ICC and the IFD

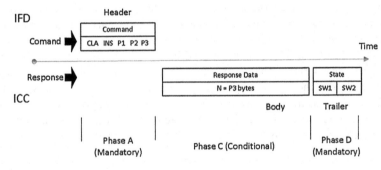

Fig. 10.2 Summary of the $T = 0$ protocol for smart cards with contacts

provides a simplified and brief overview to the $T = 0$ protocol defined for smart cards.

In such a figure it can be seen that the communication exchange is done using a command-response pair, where the command is always sent by the interface device (IFD), and the response is always sent by the card (ICC). The command is composed of a compulsory 5-byte block called *header*, and an optional data block, whose length is of P3-bytes (P3 being the 5th byte of the Header). This data block is only part of the command if the command sent is also providing data to the smart card. The response has an optional P3-byte data block, which is sent by the card when the command is requesting data from the card. The response always finishes with a 2-byte mandatory *trailer* called Status Word, which provides the feedback about how the command-response pair has been executed. It is important to note that in $T = 0$ protocol is not allowed to have commands that have, at the same time, data sent to the card and received from the card.

In recent years it has been considered that the initial contact interface for smart cards could be highly improved and an USB contact interface has also been defined for smart cards (ISO/IEC 7816-12:2005). This interface provides faster communication and a more universal way to exchange commands and information. Unfortunately, although this alternative is already published and some products are currently available, it has not reached a massive deployment yet.

10.2.3.2 Contactless Interface

An alternative interface from the contact-based ones was proposed in 1978. Dr. Arimura defined the idea of having an ICC with a contactless interface. This idea was initially implemented contactless tags to be used for registering animals (i.e. attaching the tag in one of the ears of farm animals, or implanting the chip in the neck of pets). In these cases some variations were introduced from the concept of an identification card. None of these products were designed as a plastic card, and some of them, especially those for farm animals, had a battery included, as to allow larger distances for reading and writing in the tag. All these products are still in use, with a high level of satisfaction. But it has to be mentioned that all those products are based on the technology of memory cards, not being smart cards.

By the end of the 1980s there were products launched with contactless interfaces and with the same specifications of identification cards, some of them being smart cards. Also, the standardization of these interfaces began. As there were different requirements that contactless cards could cover and also different technologies could be used, three families of standards were developed:

- ISO/IEC 10536 "Identification cards—Contactless integrated circuit(s) cards—Close-coupled cards". This technology is based on capacitive and/or inductive coupling between the card and the terminal, and requires that the card fully touches the sensor part of the terminal. They have been used in some physical access control systems. Nowadays Proximity Cards are taking most of the business case of this technology.
- ISO/IEC 14443 "Identification cards—Contactless integrated circuit(s) cards—Proximity cards". This technology, based on radiofrequency transmissions, allows the reading and writing of the card at a distance between 0 and 10 cm from the card to the terminal. The interface is fully defined as to allow multiple cards to be present within the same field of the reader, allowing interactions with several cards at the same time. This is, by no doubt, the technology that is mostly used nowadays, and the one tested more thoroughly. This standard allows more than one specification for the electrical interface and the low level protocol, defining cards of different types, being the most widely used those known as Type A and Type B.
- ISO/IEC 15693 "Identification cards—Contactless integrated circuit(s) cards—Vicinity cards". In certain applications and scenarios the identification below the 10 cm limit is not possible, requiring longer distances between cards and terminals. This standard provides specifications for those products that are meant to provide communication with a more powerful radiofrequency field.

It is important to note that contactless smart cards can be considered as one kind of RFID solution, but one where the token/tag is not only a memory, but a microprocessor with a SCOS installed, which provides a high level of security as well as many other functionalities.

Last, but not least, is shall be mentioned that some parts of the ISO/IEC 7816 family of standards contain specifications that are applicable to both contact and contactless interfaces. From these parts, the most important one can be considered the fourth one [6], which standardizes data structures, data objects and interindustry commands.

10.3 Smart Card Readers and Terminals

In order to use smart cards, the application can be installed into a computer-based system, or using a programmable standalone terminal (i.e. a device that integrates the application with the smart card reader plus some other peripherals such as displays, keyboards, speakers, etc.).

Considering the former case, the usual situation up to the late 90s was that the application programmer had to implement the solution oriented not only to a specific smart card, but also to a specific reader. But with the appearance of PC/SC [7] and other initiatives, an intermediate layer was defined so that applications could be programmed independently of the reader used. The only requirement is that the reader manufacturer has to provide a PC/SC compliant driver, which will interface between that intermediate layer and the physical reader. Nowadays PC/SC is considered the de-facto standard for interfacing smart card readers, no matter whether the reader is connected via RS-232, USB, PCMCIA, ExpressCard or any other interface, or if it is prepared for contact cards or contactless ones, or even both interfaces. This standard, designed initially for Microsoft Windows, has also been adapted to other platforms, such as Linux.

Unfortunately using terminals instead of readers does not benefit from any common application programming interface (API). This is because each terminal is considered as an embedded system, based on a specific microprocessor and using a programming language (typically C) with a proprietary set of libraries. The decision on which terminal to use will come on those requirements that the solution will have to fulfil, instead of the smart card interface, as, in most cases, this is considered as something that is solved via one of the above mentioned libraries.

10.4 Smart Card Technology Applied to Other Tokens

The smart card technology is applicable to other embodiments different from the ones of identification banking card. As previously mentioned, it is quite known from long time ago that smart cards can be used in a tiny plastic format called *plug-in*, which is currently used when the cards are used as mobile subscriber cards (such as in the GSM-based mobile telephony), or as a module to be integrated into a Point of Service terminal for performing the security operations (i.e. a SAM card that will be described later in this chapter).

But it can also be implemented into different formats that could adjust better to the application that is targeted. For example, they can be embedded into a key-shape, as to be used for physical access applications, or as a USB Token for using it in logical access control applications. Figure 10.3 shows several smart card formats in addition to the standardized formats: an USB Token, a USB Token with fingerprint user verification, a super-smart card with fingerprint verification and display. As a reference also the standardized formats and the detail of the plug-in format is given. They can also have other device embedded, such as a display, a fingerprint sensor or a keyboard. In all these cases, they can be conformant to all smart card standards except for those dealing with the physical characteristics (e.g. shape or flexibility).

The most widely known implementation of a smart card in an embodiment different from the plastic identification card is its use in current electronic passports (as it will be described later in this chapter). Current electronic passports carry, embedded into one of their covers, a contactless smart card where the identification information, plus some biometric information is stored. This way, the electronic use of the passport is available, while allowing, at the same time, the stamping of migration controls and visas.

10.5 Security in Smart Cards

The major difference between smart cards and the rest of the identification technologies is the level of security they provide. This high level of security is reached by both the security mechanisms embedded within the product to avoid misuse or reverse engineering (i.e. physical security), and the security mechanisms they provide to the external world, as to secure information exchange and allow trusted authentication of both the terminal and the card (i.e. logical security).

If all mechanisms are integrated successfully, then attacking a smart card-based system will have to be based on attacking each single card, and for each of these attacks, the smart card will react denying them, either by not responding or by stopping its functionality temporally or permanently. For example, in the case of a certain number of consecutive incorrect presentations of the PIN code, the card will block the information protected by such code. And if there has not been defined an unblocking mechanisms for such code, then access to such information will be permanently blocked.

Therefore this section of this chapter will cover the different security mechanisms integrated into smart cards, which could be of benefit for many different applications and services, including the use of biometrics. First, the physical security mechanisms will be explained, followed by those dedicated to logical security (mainly based on cryptographic approaches). Then the concept of a SAM card will be introduced, so as to show that smart cards can work not only as a secure storage device for the citizen, but also as a security engine for devices and systems. This section will end by noting the different kind of attacks that a smart card can suffer.

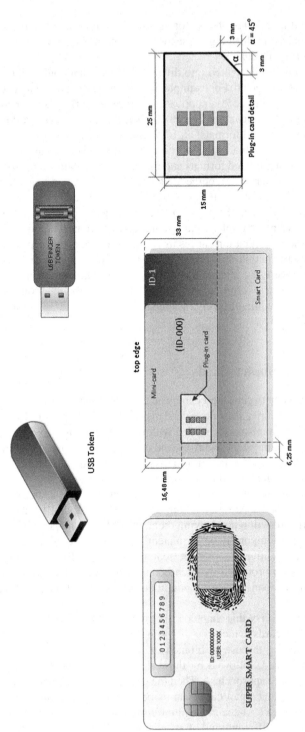

Fig. 10.3 Different layouts for smart card-based products

10.5.1 Physical Security Mechanisms in Smart Cards

It is important to highlight that the benefits on using smart cards compared to, for example, centralized systems, are not in the use of cryptographic protocols (which can be used in both cases), but in the fact that smart cards are portable devices that are built following tamper-proof approaches. Tamper-proof devices refer to those ones that provide resistance to their deliberate alteration or adulteration. In other words, they are designed to avoid success of any kind of attacks intended to either misuse the card, perform reverse engineering and/or accessing the information stored in it by fraudulent means. That information can be cardholder data, application data, or even the security keys and secret codes stored in the card.

The most reliable smart cards are built using tamper-resistant microcontrollers. To prevent an attacker from retrieving or changing the information stored, the chips are designed so that the information is not accessible through any external mean, being only accessible through their embedded SCOS, which contain the logical security mechanisms that will be mentioned in subsections below. But it is clear that designing and manufacturing such a tamper-resistant microcontroller is extremely difficult, as attacks could come in many different ways (e.g. applying voltages and frequencies out of specified ranges, freezing and/or overheating the chip, de-encapsulating the chip, irradiating certain zones of the microcontroller, analysing the variation of timing or power consumption related to input data, etc.).

The physical security mechanisms of a smart card microcontroller are extremely variable and most of the time they are secret and proprietary, but some basic ones are the following [8]:

- Faraday cage embodiment. By adding a set of power planes to the whole surface of the chip, the effect of a Faraday cage is obtained, eliminating the flow of electromagnetic fields out of the chip, and also avoiding the inspection of the inner parts of the chip by electromagnetic based sensors.
- Light detection. In order to detect that the module (i.e. the chip plus the contacts) is separated from the plastic, or the passivation of the chip is being removed, light sensible cells provoke the immediate alteration of parts of the smart card memory, stopping it from working permanently. This can also be applied to certain memory areas containing sensible data, such as keys and codes.
- Pseudo-random placement of chip cells. Instead of manufacturing the chip following a traditional structure, all its components are divided in cells and then placed randomly in the substrate. This makes the interconnection less optimal, but acts as a defence against reverse engineering.
- Scrambled addressing of memory blocks. In addition to dividing the memory blocks in parts and placing those parts randomly in the chip, the addressing of each of the memory position is scrambled, so even within the same part of memory the information does not follow a logical structure.
- Ciphering of the information stored in the non-volatile memory. By the use of the logical security mechanisms that will be explained below, the smart card can be manufactured to store all data in the card in a ciphered way, making it even more difficult to look for any kind of relation between data cells.

- Attack detection through variation in power supply (static and dynamic). Smart cards have a set of circuits in the power supply entry point, to detect the variations in the voltage value, both in absolute value and in the frequency of such variation. If the supply voltage does not fit the specifications, or the voltage variations have non-acceptable frequency, the smart card stops its functionality and, depending on the designed rule, even blocks itself temporally or permanently.
- Attack detection through illegal variation in clock source. The same kind of philosophy as the one with the power supply is also used with the clock source, where both, the voltage and the frequency are fully analyzed.

All these mechanisms are included to avoid direct attacks either for destroying the card, for reverse engineering and for accessing sensible information inside the card. But there are indirect means for gaining information, such as Differential Power Analysis (DPA), which, in few words, study statistically the variations of power consumption depending on the variation of the input data. After subsequent studies, information about the secret keys and codes inside the card can be extracted. In order to avoid this, some additional mechanisms are included, such as:

- From the stable clock source received by the card, the microcontroller manipulates it to provide a random clock fluctuation that will change both the timing and the power consumption of the card.
- Also, the microcontroller, by using interruptions, can provide an unpredictable behaviour, which does not change the processing of the SCOS, but modifies completely the behaviour of the chip both in timing and power consumption. By provoking randomly that interruption, the statistical value of the information acquired gets highly reduced.
- By using the most recent advances in technology, the chip can benefit from reduction in size and in power consumption, reducing at the same time the information offered to those indirect attack methods.

As already mentioned, when any kind of attack is detected, the smart card can react by not responding with any information, by erasing the information stored and/or by erasing the SCOS disrupting its functionality. For the erasing of sensible information (e.g. keys and secret codes), the microcontroller can be designed to write those memory areas with either '0's or '1's, even if power supply is not provided.

In order to finish this section, it is important to highlight one fact. The major inconvenience of smart cards for achieving practical resistance against physical attacks is the fact that the attacker will be in possession of the smart card, for whatever time he/she may need and in the place he/she prefers. Even more, the attacker may have more than one unit to work with. Therefore the attacker is free of any kind of constraints dealing with time and location, and a seriously motivated attacker (or group of attackers) may be able to get to a successful end, as long as he/she has the resources to execute the attacks.

10.5.2 Logical Security Mechanisms Within Smart Card Technology

In addition to the physical security mechanisms described above, the smart card, within its SCOS, includes a whole set of logical mechanisms to protect data access and information exchange from the external world. These mechanisms are based on cryptographic algorithms and security policies.

This is an extremely wide field of knowledge and this subsection pretends only to provide an overview of the basic concepts involved. In order to do so, it will first introduce the concepts dealing with cryptography, mainly based on the services provided. Afterwards, and due to its importance in smart cards, one of these services, Authentication, will be deeply studied, as to see how the different actors involved in the information exchange can be considered reliable.

Later on, once the major basic concepts are introduced, the combination of them with security policies will be explained, as to detail one of the most important concepts in smart card-based information exchange: the secure channel. The building of a robust secure channel will provide the three security services introduced in the above introduced subsection on cryptography.

Finally, as all logical security mechanisms rely on keys and secret codes, a final subsection will focus on key management, illustrating many of the security policies that the SCOS implements.

10.5.2.1 Cryptographic Mechanisms

Most of smart cards in the market include cryptographic algorithms [9] within the SCOS. These algorithms are mainly symmetric ones such as DES, Triple-DES or AES. But there are also some products that are able to perform asymmetric cryptography, such as RSA or ECC.

Based on these algorithms, the SCOS can provide mechanisms to cipher all information exchange between the card and the external world in any of both directions. Furthermore, these algorithms can be used in a variety of ways, providing some, or all, of the following services:

- *Confidentiality*: the information exchanged is sent in a way that only the meant receiver is able to understand it. The mechanisms shall be strong enough to avoid any information leakage by using man-in-the-middle attacks.
- *Authentication* of the sender of the information. This same concept can be extrapolated to the authentication of both ends in the information exchange, as will be seen in the following subsection.
- *Integrity* of the information and/or command, as to deny any message alteration during the information exchange.

When using smart cards with asymmetric algorithms (e.g. RSA), the card can be part of a *Public Key Infrastructure* (PKI), performing the electronic signature of documents and forms in a trustable and tamper-proof way. This is currently being implemented within some National ID Cards in several countries around the world. This kind of solutions allows the elimination of those attacks based on stealing the electronic identity of a citizen, by exploiting security holes in the operating system of desktop computers and accessing the private keys stored in their storage media.

In the rest of this chapter, an algorithm-independent approach will be used, so as to describe the main concepts involved. In some cases there will be some references to examples using symmetric keys, as they are simpler to understand. Readers interested in the application of all these security mechanisms using PKI, are requested to relevant references such as [9, 10] or [11].

10.5.2.2 Authentication Methods

From all the security services mentioned above, the most interesting one is the authentication of all actors involved in the information exchange. The use of different ways of combining cryptographic algorithms, plus the storage of different keys within a single card, allows solving certain problems when trying to authenticate both ends in an information and/or command exchange [12].

Authentication Mechanisms are based on the common calculation of a certain data by using stored internal keys and some random data used as a challenge. If the random data (the challenge) is generated by the terminal and sent to the card, it is called *Internal Authentication* because the terminal is authenticating the card (as the terminal is the one forcing to have a calculation with new input data, i.e. the challenge, and the one verifying the success in the result of the procedure). In this case, once the card has received the challenge, it uses some internal keys and algorithm to calculate a resulting data from the challenge, sending it to the terminal. The terminal, which should also know the internal keys and algorithm performs the same calculation and compares its result with the one sent by the card. If the result is the same, then the terminal is sure that the card is a trustable one, as long as the secrets have not been disclosed. Figure 10.4 shows this process graphically.

The same mechanism can be used but there is a challenge generated by the smart card. In such case also the verification is done by the card. When the result matches the one sent by the terminal, the card can consider trustable the terminal where it is connected. This process is called *External Authentication*.

Some cards also implement a *Mutual Authentication* mechanism that, in few words, provides the same service as a consecutive execution of an *Internal* and an *External Authentication*, but as a single operation. It is important to note that none of these three mechanisms exchange any kind of keys, keeping them secretly stored in both the terminal and the card.

In addition to these authentication mechanisms, smart cards also provide another authentication mechanism that implies the authentication of the cardholder. This is known as *CardHolder Verification* (CHV), although most of the times people refers to it as *Presentation of the PIN code*. Through this mechanism, the terminal requests the cardholder for a *Personal Identification Number* (PIN). After typing such PIN, the terminal generates a CHV-Key, which is sent to the card. The card then compares

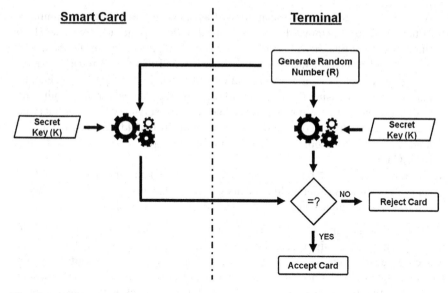

Fig. 10.4 Block diagram for the internal authentication

such CHV-Key with the one stored in the card. If a mismatch is found, then the number of the incorrect presentations counter is increased, and if it reaches a certain number, the whole mechanism becomes blocked. On the other hand, if a match occurs, then the cardholder is authenticated and the incorrect presentation counter is reset.

The same idea of the CHV-Key presentation can be used with application-specific keys for performing application authentications. But as this mechanism involves the submission of a key to the card (i.e. the transmission of a key between the terminal and the card), this mechanism is considered deprecated. It is preferable to use the previously mentioned authentication mechanisms using application-specific keys and/or algorithms.

10.5.2.3 Secure Channels

Once the main logical security mechanisms have been introduced in the previous two subsections, the application of certain security policies can provide the means to exchange information and commands between the card and the external world. This can ensure all three requirements: confidentiality, authenticity and integrity. When this is achieved we can consider that a *Secure Channel* has been created for using the smart card [10]. The principles to build a secure channel are as follows:

- By using mutual authentication, both ends of the communication are authenticated, and therefore the authentication requirement is fulfilled. Even more, during the mutual authentication process, both ends of the communication knows the same key, which could be used for other cryptographic mechanisms.

- Any cryptographic algorithm can be used as an algorithm to create a summary of the data and/or command to be exchanged, following the rules of those algorithms used for integrity checking (i.e. that any single change in the data, will create a full change of the summary generated, and that the summary is small enough as to not allow the reconstruction of the whole message from the summary). Therefore, using the same known key and the same algorithm, both ends of the communication can generate and check such a summary. That summary is, therefore, added to the command or data, as an integrity field. An example of this kind of algorithms is obtaining the result of the final round of an AES ciphering in CBC mode.
- Last but not least, with both ends authenticated, which know the same key and the same algorithm, and after adding the integrity field, the whole data involved in the information exchange can be ciphered, providing confidentiality to the channel.

If the key is the same for all cards, then a brute force attack can be applied if the attacker can acquire a significant number of cards. As smart cards can have a limit in the consecutive number of incorrect uses of the key, this kind of attack, being theoretically possible, is not viable in practice as the number of cards needed would be so large that the manufacturer will discover that an attack is being performed. Then the manufacturer can act in accordance to reject this attack before the attack is successful.

But another problem is that, if by any chance an attacker discovers the key for one card, then he/she will know the key for all cards, compromising the security of the whole system. In order to avoid this, each card has its own key, which is derived from a common seed, by using some unique data from the card (e.g. serial number plus some invariant personal data from the cardholder). The terminal requests that unique information from the card, and performs the derivation algorithm to obtain the key for such specific card. This process is called *Key Diversification*.

Another principle to consider is avoiding any cryptanalysis based on obtaining several ciphered data from a single card. If an attacker grabs a significant number of messages that are ciphered with the same card, then cryptanalysis can be a successful tool. In order to avoid this possibility, it is recommended that during each session, the key is different from the previous session. As keys are different, then the cryptanalysis is not possible unless the cryptographic algorithm is too weak. The way to create *Session Keys* (SK) is to use some random data generated by both parties (e.g. the ones used during *External* and *Internal Authentication*) after the process of *Key Diversification*. As in each session the random data is different, the key used in each session will be different. As the SK is generated in both ends of the communication, it is never exchanged, and therefore any security breach is avoided. Whenever the session is voluntarily ended, the card disconnected, or a security error detected, the session is considered finished, and the application shall generate new SKs to continue with the communication. A graphical representation of how the SK is generated from the original seed including the Diversification is shown in Fig. 10.5.

By using all the above mentioned mechanisms, a robust *Secure Channel* can be created to guarantee data and command exchanges between the terminal and the

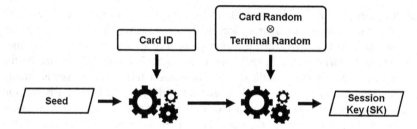

Fig. 10.5 Generation of the SK from the original seed

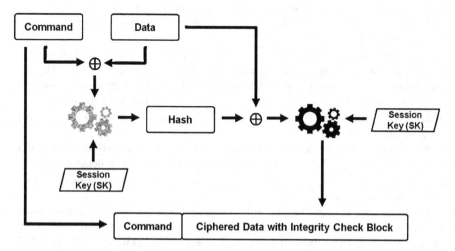

Fig. 10.6 An implementation of the Secure Messaging mechanism

card. The fourth part of ISO/IEC 7816 standard defines a mechanism called *Secure Messaging* (*SM*) that can be used for part or all of the principles here explained. Figure 10.6 illustrates one of the different ways to implement secure messaging can be implemented, provided that previously the Session Key has been calculated as explained above.

10.5.2.4 Key Management

Once the general ideas about security mechanisms have been provided, it is important to emphasize one of the major potential vulnerabilities that this kind of mechanisms may suffer: the management of the keys involved in the process.

It is important to mention that the added value that smart cards provide to any kind of cryptographic mechanism, is that a smart card keeps the keys stored securely, not allowing the external world to read their values. Also, the smart card can block temporally or permanently the use of any of such keys, if a certain number of consecutive erroneous uses is detected. The smart card can even force the external world to use those keys only after a successful secure channel has been established.

Within the smart card industry, the management of keys start from the very moment of manufacturing them. In such a process, all cards are fully protected by the use of a diversified key stored at the moment of manufacturing. Such a key is usually known as Manufacturing Key or as Personalization Key. When these cards are sent to the issuer, they are sent without disclosing the seed and the algorithm to diversify all related keys. Only when the issuer has reported that all cards (after counting all of them) have been received, the manufacturer sends the issuer the seed and the algorithm to calculate all the diversified keys. In case the number of units received is not the same as the ones sent, an alarm is provided to the system, and the seed and algorithm will never be released, denying the possibility of using those cards for their whole life.

After receiving the cards, the seed and the algorithm, the issuer proceeds to personalize the cards, changing the personalization keys with those ones needed by the specific application, usually called Administrative Keys. An obvious requirement is that those new keys are also diversified. Usually the calculation of the new keys is provided by a SAM card (explained later in this chapter) or another kind of Hardware Security Module (HSM).

Therefore, when cards are sent to the citizens, the keys are already securely stored in the cards. In case of public key cryptography, due to its own benefits, there is no further need for key management, apart from those mechanisms dealing with renewal or revocation of the keys.

But in the case of secret key algorithms, key management becomes a major issue as both the seeds and the diversification algorithm has to be distributed securely among all terminals of the system (e.g. all Point of Sell units and ATMs). SAM cards, as explained below, provide a solution for that.

These same rules are applicable to all kind of keys involved in the system: Session Keys, Administrative Keys, CHV-Keys, etc. Those keys are calculated using diversification algorithms that are embedded into SAM cards, and those SAMs have to have the seeds needed for those algorithms securely stored. Those seeds are issued and distributed by the issuing authority, by means of issuing those SAM modules required. Table 10.1 shows a summary of the different keys a smart card can handle and the origins for their creation, their distribution and which management is handled inside the card and which one outside the card.

10.5.3 Security Aid Modules (SAM)

With all the information provided above, it is clear that if all the mentioned security mechanisms are used, then the weakest point in a smart card system is located at the terminal. The terminal can be tampered and extracting information about seeds and algorithms. Therefore the terminal should have the same security mechanisms that a smart card has. This will make the terminal extremely expensive, which will make them not economically viable for most applications.

Table 10.1 Management for the different keys that smart cards handle

Key	Created by	Distributed by	Management inside the card	Management outside the card
Manufacturing Key	Manufacturer	Manufacturer	Verification Blocking Access control	Presentation Request for update
Administrative Keys	Issuer (SAM/HSM)	SAM	Use for internal calculations Blocking Access control	Request for update
Session Keys	Card	Not applicable	Creation Access control Blocking Use for internal calculations	None
Secret Codes	Issuer (SAM/HSM)	SAM	Verification Blocking Access control	Presentation
CHV-Keys	Issuer	Issuer (through a confidential letter to the citizen)	Verification Blocking Access control	Presentation
PKI-Public Keys	Issuer (HSM) or Card	Publicly through PKI	Use for internal calculation Expiration and revocation	None
PKI-Secret Keys	Issuer (HSM) or Card	Not applicable	Use for internal calculation Expiration and revocation	None

The best solution for this problem is securing only the part of the terminal that is in charge of all cryptographic mechanisms. That being the case, and knowing that a smart card is already a tamper-proof device that is able to perform cryptographic operations, the use of a smart card for performing all cryptographic mechanisms is meant to be the most reasonable solution.

When a smart card is used for being in charge of all cryptographic operations, then it is called a *Security Aid Module* (SAM card), also named as *Secure Authentication Module*. SAM cards are usually used with the plug-in format, as to reduce the size of the terminal, and especially due to the fact that the SAM card is not meant to be extracted from the terminal.

By using SAM cards, the terminal can reduce their computational load as they are no longer required to perform the complex mathematical operations required by cryptographic algorithms. Lower computational requirements will mean lower processor requirements and, therefore, lower costs.

To better explain how a SAM card works within a terminal, let's consider the example of the need of diversifying keys. Imagine that the diversification algorithm is based on AES algorithm (already included into the SAM), using a seed as the key of such algorithm (the seed is also included securely in the SAM as an Administrative Key), and diversifying with some 16-byte input data obtained from the smart card to be used. Therefore, the terminal will have to read from the user's smart card the freely available information to compose those 16 bytes. Then the terminal sends those 16 bytes to the SAM card, indicating that the operation to be done is to cipher those 16 bytes with the AES algorithm and using the administrative key that has the seed. The SAM card computes internally the requested ciphering and provides the result, which will be the key to be used with the user's smart card. This schema can be sophisticated in many ways, as to provide secure channel communications between the terminal and the SAM module, or even providing a three-way communication between the terminal, the user's smart card, and the SAM card.

10.5.4 Attack Efforts in Smart Cards Compared to Other Architectures

With all the above information given, it is possible for the reader to have a clear idea of the difficulty for an attacker to try to break the security of a whole authentication system. First of all, as the use of smart cards implies the design of the authentication system in a distributed way, and due to diversification and other cryptographic mechanisms, the attack will have to be focused on a single smart card. In case that such attack is satisfactory, there will only be one user of the system with his/her identity disclosed, but the rest of the system will not be affected. So, in order to attack the whole system, the attacker should tamper with as many as smart cards are distributed, which is unviable in terms of time (both, for acquiring the cards and for attacking them) and money, plus the high level of probability that such major attack is detected by system administrators, who will act against it.

But coming back to the attack to a single card, due to the denial of service directives of the SCOS and the physical protection of the device, the attacker has only a very limited number of tries to tamper the card. It is also important to note that in order to overcome some of the physical mechanisms, the equipment needed is extremely expensive, which reduces to a very minimum the population of potential attackers.

Last, but not least, the attacker might want to gain access to the system by tampering with terminals, as to obtain information for the diversification of keys, the seeds used, algorithms, logs, etc. Some terminal manufacturers also provide tamper-proof mechanisms to their products. But even not including that, as all the cryptography is done via the SAM card embedded in the terminal, this takes the attacker to the same problem as with tampering with high-quality smart cards. But this is with the addition of, firstly, not having so many cards to attack, as there are less terminals than users, and secondly, system and terminal policies will launch an immediate alert if a SAM card is considered out of control.

Other kind of architectures, such as distributed ones using information stored in computers or non-tamper-proof devices, or those centralized, are exposed to the potential attacks coming from Virus, Trojans, Replay Attacks, Man-in-the-Middle, etc. But many of those attacks can be avoided in those applications by having a detailed security protection design for the whole system.

10.6 Protecting Biometrics Using Smart Cards

With all the knowledge acquired in the previous sections of this chapter, it is time to study the different ways in which smart cards can benefit Biometrics. Obviously, as with other identification tokens, smart cards can be used by the citizen as a mean to claim his/her identity to a biometric system. But the major benefits that smart cards can provide to Biometrics come from the protection of biometric data and/or operations [13, 14].

Therefore this section of the chapter will start introducing the relationships between privacy and biometrics, as to understand the need of protecting biometric data. This will include also a study of the different Potential Vulnerable Points (PVPs) of a biometric system, as to establish the basis for the different ways that smart cards can be included into a biometric system. From this point, four different architectures will be introduced, which will subsequently remove PVPs from the biometric system.

10.6.1 Privacy and Biometrics

The major problem when talking about privacy is that it is not a universal concept, but depends a lot on the culture and society where the citizen is involved. From the western world point of view, privacy is the ability of a human being (or group of people) to keep him, his acts and/or his information out of the scope of any selected section of the society. From the information point of view, privacy can be understood as the right that a citizen has to decide with whom he/she is sharing or not sharing a specific portion of data which is related to him/her. Considering this definition, Biometrics plays a double role in privacy:

- Biometric data is a piece of personal data and in such scenario biometric data shall be protected as any other kind of personal data, which will be under the personal consideration of the citizen about its privacy.
- Biometric data is a mean of identification, and therefore, it may be used as a credential to access further private data. In this case, the disclosure of the biometric

data may lead to disclose all personal data protected by such biometric information, and therefore attack the privacy of the citizen in an indirect way. Therefore, depending on the way the biometric system is implemented, implications to citizens' privacy may differ.

If the biometric identification system is implemented using a centralized database, citizens may reject the system as they feel that part of their personal data is stored out of their control. Therefore they may thought of as being, for example, tracked by police, governmental agencies or even private companies. This is what is called "the Big Brother effect", which may raise a lot of citizen concerns, even without having any evidence any illegal or illicit act that support those concerns. Also, from the security point of view, if the centralized database is compromised, then the privacy of the whole population enrolled in such database is compromised, creating a social problem of a great scale.

Using a distributed architecture like the one based on smart cards, will allow citizens to become aware that their personal data is stored in a token that belongs to them, and not stored in a central database out of their control. Therefore they will be in the position of knowing or authorizing when, where and who is demanding his authentication, being able to deny that demand. Furthermore, considering the news appearing on mass media about how hackers have been able to access central databases obtaining personal information, such as bank accounts, citizens will prefer to have a full control of their personal data (especially that one that is not expected to be changed for their whole life), in a personal and secured device. From the security point of view, if an attack is successful, it will only compromise the privacy of a single citizen, avoiding the appearance of an important social problem.

Therefore a distributed architecture is preferred for those systems involving personal information, and especially those that involve credentials to access further information for the citizen. But even having many advantages, the use of biometrics in a distributed way may face several vulnerabilities, as stated in the following subsection. As it will be shown, if the distributed system is implemented using smart cards, dealing to the security they provide, many of the vulnerabilities will be removed.

10.6.1.1 Potential Vulnerable Points

Within a biometric system there are several vulnerabilities to be considered. Figure 10.7 is a representation of those Potential Vulnerable Points (PVPs) that a biometric system might have, removing those that might appear during enrolment as enrolment is considered to be performed under security conditions.

The first PVP (PVP1) is related to the user attitude at the system front-end (capture device). Unfortunately smart cards will never remove this PVP. Only by the integration of anti-spoofing mechanisms within the capture device, this PVP can be partially removed.

PVP2 is located at the capture device back-end, as well as the front-end of the biometric algorithm. The captured sample could be intercepted and/or injected, to provide a replay-attack. If this PVP is exploitable, a major concern is raised as the

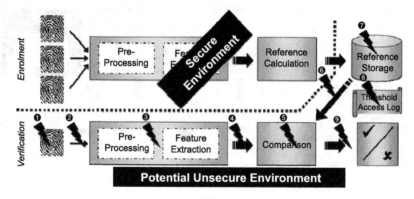

Fig. 10.7   Potential vulnerable points in a biometric system

citizen might lose the validity of his/her identity credentials. Another kind of attack at this PVP are hill-climbing attacks by injecting successive biometric samples based on the feedback that the biometric system supplies.

A large number of the remaining PVPs (i.e. 3–8) are potential vulnerabilities that also exist in any IT system. Hacking tools such as Trojans, Viruses, Man-In-The-Middle attacks for further data injection, hill climbing attacks or replay attacks can be used to override the identification process. PVPs 3 and 5 are related to the manipulation of algorithms, parameters and/or temporal data used for calculations. PVPs 4 and 6 deal with the interception of data exchanged from one module to another. From these two, PVP6 is more sensitive as the template (or other kind of biometric reference) is the data involved, which is the one that officially relates to the citizen. Last but not least, PVPs 7 and 8 refer to vulnerabilities in the storage of sensitive data such as biometric references, thresholds and logs.

Finally, even considering that PVP9 (i.e. exploiting the outcome from the biometric identification process) is also a typical point of study in any IT system, has here more importance depending on the information that could be provided by the system to the external world. If the comparison result is not given as just an OK/ERROR message, but also carries information about the level of matching acquired, an attacker can use this information to build an artificial sample using hill-climbing techniques.

These PVPs (some or most of them) can be removed by using smart cards. In order to achieve this target, several architectures can be proposed, which will be explained in the following sections. The following alternatives are defined in ISO/IEC 24787 standard [15]:

- Store on Card
- On-Card Biometric Comparison
- Work-sharing between the card and the biometric system
- System on Card

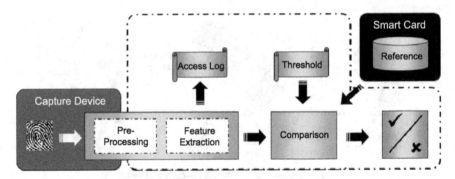

Fig. 10.8 Store on card architecture

10.6.2 Store on Card

The first idea in using smart cards for protecting Biometrics is based on using a smart card to store the biometric reference (e.g. the template) of each citizen (see Fig. 10.8). This solution presents a series of benefits. As smart cards are tamper-proof devices, they can store securely the sensible information that represents the user biometric reference. Also, its SCOS can force the biometric system to establish a secure channel, after a successful mutual authentication, in order to read the user's biometric reference. Furthermore, the smart card can send the biometric reference to the biometric system ciphered with the session key (SK), as to avoid any success in Man-in-the-Middle attacks [13]. Therefore, it can be considered that PVP6 and PVP7 are already covered by this approach.

This solution is currently available and can be implemented in any biometric system, with the only need of providing cards to the users, and incorporating a smart card reader to all terminals. This can be applied to any system used nowadays that uses Biometrics, or another kind of identification mechanism, such as passwords. This approach can be used with all modalities existing nowadays, with the following constraints:

- Data storage capacity of the card. Depending on the card capacity, and the amount of information that is needed to be stored in the card, some modalities might experience difficulties in being implemented (at least when storing the raw sample, instead of a feature vector). Being aware of this, several compact formats for storing data have been defined (for example in ISO/IEC 19794 series of standards). Currently, the memory needed for storing raw data such as face, fingerprints or iris, is sufficiently low so as to be able to store more than one sample, or even more than one modality. In other cases, such as voice or handwritten signature, the use of statistical models may compromise the storage capacity of the card depending on the complexity of the model. The storage of raw voice data is, at this moment, discouraged for the large amount of storage capacity needed. The reader should be aware that the current storage capacity of a smart card is below 100 KB (e.g. some ePassport chips allow storage of information up to a little more than 70 KB).

- The amount of data to be transmitted in and/or out of the card in any verification attempt. Considering that the communication channel in a smart card is not as fast as in other technologies, the exchange of large amounts of data can delay the whole authentication process. Current limit for contactless smart cards is 424 Kbps. Also, it is important to note that in some cases the internal communication buffer might experience overflows. Nowadays this is not a problem in modalities such as face, fingerprint or iris, and nearly in any of them where what is transferred is a feature vector, instead of a raw sample.

10.6.3   On-card Biometric Comparison

The previous approach has the inconvenience that the biometric reference is transferred to the terminal, which may be tampered as to acquire the citizen's template. In addition, the comparison and decision is taken at the biometric system and this can also be manipulated by an attacker. Last but not least, if the cardholder verification was requested to activate a certain service or access certain information in the card, this will have to be checked by the biometric system and then the biometric system will have to submit an administrative key (which could also be called CHV-Key as it will be related to the user identity, although not directly known by the cardholder) to the card as to gain access to such services or information.

In order to solve these problems, a smart card can be developed so as to be able to substitute or complement its current cardholder verification mechanisms, with a biometric verification of the cardholder. In such a case, the smart card will be able, not only to store the biometric reference, but also to keep the comparison threshold and the comparison algorithm, providing the final decision on such process [16].

The benefits of this kind of solution is that, as happens with smart card keys, the biometric reference is never released by the card, and a successful verification can be used to open access to internal data and/or operations in the card. The SCOS will also have control of the number of consecutive unsuccessful verifications of the biometric reference, it being able to block this verification mechanism if it gets over a predefined threshold. Also, as in the previous case, the card can force the biometric system to establish a Secure Channel prior to the submission of the feature vector, or other biometric data, that will be sent to the card.

Tampering with the biometric reference, the threshold, the algorithm, or even with the result provided is denied. Also, following smart card sector best practices, the information that the card provides to the external world will be minimal, as to acknowledge a successful comparison, a non-successful result, or a rejection of the biometric data submitted (e.g. because the security mechanisms have not been fulfilled or some quality thresholds have not been reached).

The level of security achieved with this approach is such that PVPs 4–9 could be considered solved, as can be seen in Fig. 10.9.

Within ISO/IEC JTC1/SC17 the ISO/IEC 24787:2011 standard has been written to specify the different implementations that can be followed for an on-card

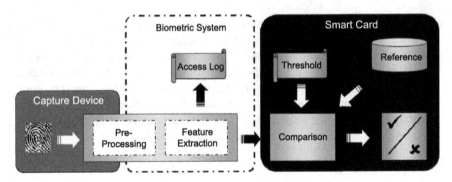

Fig. 10.9 On-card biometric comparison architecture

biometric comparison architecture (also known as *Match-on-Card*). The biometric reference can be used for the whole set of applications using the card, or a different reference can be used for each of those applications. This standard also defines the possibility of using the same biometric reference with different thresholds for different applications, depending on the security level that is meant to be reached, both locally and globally.

This concept can be applied to several biometric modalities, although there are others that, in addition to the limitations shown in the Store-on-Card section, may have a comparison algorithm with a high level of complexity. For example, the comparison algorithms used nowadays in most implementations of face, voice, and signature, do not allow to be integrated into the SCOS, although the near future can change the processing capabilities of the smart cards, and therefore allow the inclusion of any of these modalities. Currently there are a number of commercial products available based on fingerprints (e.g. [17–19] and the products listed in [20]), and some prototypes based on face [21], iris and hand geometry [22].

Due to the time consumption of the virtual machine of JavaCards (JCVM), all commercial products are based on native code, while some prototypes are implemented on JavaCards as to provide a proof of concept for further development of a product in native code. If in the future, the optimization of the JCVM reduces the loss in processing time, and microprocessors embedded in smart cards evolve enough, it will be possible to see implementations of on-card biometric comparison as JavaCard applets.

It is also important to note that due to the lower processing power of smart cards, compared to desktop computers, the performance achieved by smart card implementation of the biometric comparison algorithms can be lower than the one obtained by the equivalent desktop solution. This was part of the analysis of the MINEX II initiative by NIST [23], which also led to the creation of a standard within ISO/IEC JTC1/SC37, which provides the methodology to analyze these differences (ISO/IEC 19795-7).

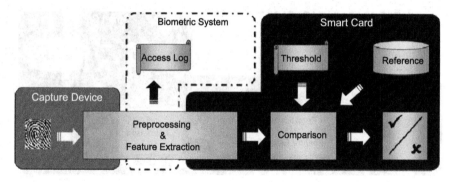

Fig. 10.10 Work-sharing mechanism for improving biometrics

10.6.4 Work-Sharing Mechanism

ISO/IEC 24787:2011 also defines a mechanism called *Work-sharing* for those cards meant to be used as on-card biometric comparison products, but where the computational needs of the comparison algorithm request that part of the algorithm is done in the biometric system. This process is done without sending any part of the biometric reference to the biometric system.

In this case, certain activities that are computationally intensive, for example, a mathematical transformation, are sent to the biometric system to perform the calculation. The result of the computation is sent back to the smart card so that the final determination of the matching score is calculated on the card, as well as taking the proper decision considered the defined threshold. During the pre-comparison calculation, communication takes place between the card and the biometric verification system. A secure and trusted channel is used to protect the communication between the terminal and the card unless the need for such protection is explicitly not required for a particular operational environment. The final comparison should be performed in the card. Figure 10.10 shows a block diagram of this architecture.

This same idea can be used for expanding the role that the smart card has in the citizen authentication process, and reducing the PVPs of the whole system. With this idea in mind, part of the Pre-processing and/or Feature Extraction processes can be executed inside the smart card, while the rest is executed in the biometric system.

The extension of this architecture will be executing the whole processing inside the card. In that case, the only part of the biometric system that is out of the card is the capture device. The benefit of this solution is that, being based on standardized data formats (i.e. the ones defined in ISO/IEC 19794 series of standard), the solution will be fully interoperable among manufacturers, with the only concern of the performance achieved by each of the products on the market. With this approach, PVPs 4–9 are considered secured, while some part of PVP3 can still be considered vulnerable.

Nowadays this architecture is only at the design and prototype phase, without attracting much interest from the industry. The main advantage of this approach

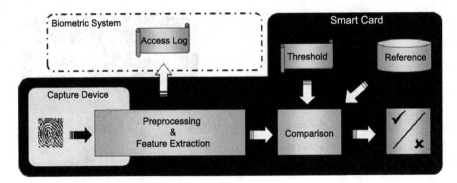

Fig. 10.11 System-on-card architecture

compared with the System-on-Card one (to be explained in the following subsection), is that it can be applied to most of the biometric modalities, as there will be no physical restrictions due to the capture device size and the mechanics involved.

10.6.5 System on Card

The last approach comes as an extension of the previous one. In this case even the capture device (i.e. the biometric sensor) is embedded in the card. There are currently prototypes and even products that implement this idea using fingerprints, but unfortunately they are not conformant to the physical and mechanical specifications of a smart card (e.g. thickness and flexibility). Manufacturers are working in new sensor technologies that could overcome these difficulties, with the expectations to have some prototypes by the end of 2012. These new inputs are promoting the initiation of some standardization works in the scope of ISO/IEC JTC1/SC17 WG11.

With this architecture the whole biometric system is included in a product that is carried out by the citizen, and it could interact electronically with any kind of application requesting biometric authentication for physical and/or logical access. As can be seen in Fig. 10.11, all PVPs can be considered as secured, although PVP1 can never be considered completely solved.

The major drawback of this approach is that currently this idea is only applicable to fingerprints. Also voice biometrics could benefit of this scheme due to the existence of small size microphones, although the processing capabilities could be too demanding. But it would be very difficult to think that in a near future an iris or vascular sensor could be embedded in a plastic identification card following the ISO/IEC 7816 standard.

On the contrary, this same idea, without considering the physical restrictions of a plastic card, can be implemented in other kind of embodiments, such as a USB-Token. This can allow the extension of this same architecture to other biometric modalities in a short term. The only requirement to focus on would be that such a token shall be fully compliant with all security mechanisms that the smart card industry has defined.

Another approach to consider could be to allow the sensor to be out of the card, and through the card interface and with the security requirements of the SCOS, to exchange information between the sensor and the smart card. In such a case, advances such as the incorporation of the USB interface into the contacts of the smart card (i.e. ISO/IEC 7816-12), or the increase of data transfer rate in the contactless interfaces could help to provide this kind of solution. This may be considered in the new efforts that are being started within the standardization bodies. This kind of approach will secure all kind of PVPs except PVP1, which will have to be handled directly with the sensor used.

10.7 Evaluation of Smart Card-Based Biometrics

Once the technology and its potential use have been described, it is time to study how this kind of solutions can be evaluated, as to check whether the claimed benefits have been reached or not. This section will cover two major points for evaluation when the biometric system is using smart cards: performance and security. Out of the scope of this chapter is the evaluation of Biometrics, which is covered in other chapters of this book.

10.7.1 Performance Evaluation

Smart Cards technology is mature enough to have developed over the years a large number of Test Methods for all different aspects of the technology involved. In fact, the family of international standards ISO/IEC 10373 cover most of those tests at the physical, electrical and even protocol levels. In addition to this, other organizations, such as VISA or MasterCard, have also developed their own testing procedures for checking the conformance of a smart card for their own applications. This has also created the business case for evaluation laboratories and nowadays there are a significant number of accredited laboratories to carry on some or all of these tests.

But if we focus on the use of Biometrics with smart cards, there is still the need of developing some testing methods and publishing them as standard. In this line, it is expected that in the near future a new standard will be developed to test the conformance with ISO/IEC 24787 within ISO/IEC JTC1/SC17.

On the meantime, as it was mentioned before, one step ahead was taken by ISO/IEC JTC1/SC37, developing a standard that test the performance achieved by the comparison algorithms embedded into a smart card under the on-card biometric comparison architecture. Such standard is the ISO/IEC 19795-7:2011 and was inspired by the MINEX II evaluation that the NIST carried out between 2007 and 2009 [23], and continued till 2010 with new products [20]. This standard studies how performance in the comparison algorithm could be changed when implemented within the processing limitations of a smart card, compared to its performance in a desktop computer system. Performance is analyzed in terms of error rates and execution time.

On-card biometric comparison products based on fingerprints were the ones used for the MINEX-II evaluation. From the 2011 report [20] the major conclusions from MINEX II have been:

- From the 36 participants, five providers are able to meet the minimum error rate interoperability specification of the PIV card defined by the United States (i.e. FNMR ≤ 0.01 at FMR ≤ 0.01).
- As important as the On-card biometric comparison algorithm, are other stages in the process, such as the minutiae detection algorithm used.
- As there were some providers whose solution for the store-on-card version of the PIV outperforms their own on-card biometric comparison solution, it can be said that translating comparison algorithms into a smart card is not trivial and introduces significant error rates.
- The checking of the quality values of the biometric sample is encouraged, as they have been shown to be vital for creating the compact-format templates to be sent to the card.
- Although biometric providers usually do not publish operating thresholds needed to achieve target false match rates (FMRs), MINEX II has included FMR threshold calibration information, based on minutiae coming from more than 20 minutiae detection algorithms, as to fit with the scenario of multiple algorithm providers.
- There are current implementations that performs the verification process is less than 0.25 seconds, which it can be considered imperceptible for an identification system with human interaction, as it happens in all biometric systems.
- The improvement of products during the three years of this evaluation has been enormous, having products that are able to work even 15 times faster from those initially submitted in 2007. It is out of the scope of MINEX II to evaluate if such improvements are dependent on the cost of the product.
- That same level of improvement has not been extrapolated to the computer based feature extraction algorithms, some of them behaving quite poorly. A conclusion is that manufacturers should also spend resources in improving the earlier stages of the biometric verification, mainly based on ISO/IEC 19794-2 and ISO/IEC 29109-2.
- And, as it has already been said, the testing protocol has become an international standard (ISO/IEC 19795-7:2011).

10.7.2 Security Evaluation

In terms of security, the best reference for its evaluation is Common Criteria [24], which is subsequently being standardized under ISO/IEC JTC1/SC27. We will refer here directly to Common Criteria (CC) as its evolution cycles are faster than the ones allowed by the standardization mechanisms. CC is a worldwide and well recognized scheme for the evaluation of security in IT products and systems. At the time of writing of this book, CC current version is 3.1 in its third release. All documents are freely available at http://www.commoncriteriaportal.org, as well as references to the products that have already obtained a CC certificate.

CC is a set of specifications for the design and development of security products that, together with a Common Evaluation Methodology (CEM), allows testing the level of assurance that a product can provide. As IT products can be of different nature, and security can also be dependent on the scenario to be applied, the evaluation is carried out based on a specific Protection Profile (PP) and/or a Security Target (ST) previously defined for such a kind of product, scenario and/or application.

As has already been mentioned, smart cards are considered a secured device and therefore an element to be used in security systems and applications. This has made the smart card industry to be seriously involved in claiming for CC evaluations. This can be checked easily in the CC website, as a large number of Protection Profiles are defined for smart cards and smart card related devices and systems. Currently more than 50 PPs are published, including those dealing with ePassports, Residence Permits and Health Service Cards. The number of products that are currently available with a CC certificate is much larger, as it can be checked in the same website, getting many of them the Common Criteria EAL4+ certification and even some of them reaching the EAL5+ certification.

Considering the embedding of Biometrics in smart cards, currently there are PPs and certified products that cover the store-on-card architecture (e.g. the ePassport related ones). There are also some On-Card Biometric Comparison products that have obtained the CC certification (e.g. the Spanish National ID Card—DNIe), but in these cases the security evaluation is more focused on the smart card level than on the Biometrics level, which is an issue to be targeted in the near future.

10.8 Current Use Cases on the Integration of Biometrics and Smart Cards

This last section of this chapter will illustrate how Biometrics and smart cards can be integrated into large scale products. This is going to be illustrated using two major applications: ePassports and the Spanish National ID Card (DNIe). While the first case is a contactless store-on-card solution, the second one is a contact card embedding also on-card biometric comparison. The explanation will be simply descriptive, forwarding the reader to those relevant documents for further study.

10.8.1 ePassport

After the terrorist attacks in September 2001, it was decided that a new generation of passports should be defined. The previous passport was a booklet that contained

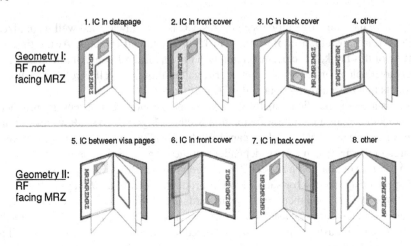

Fig. 10.12 Different locations for the contactless smart card in an ePassport (image taken from [25])

a standardized page holding all relevant information, security features, and an area where certain printed information was placed as to be read automatically by a machine (called MRZ—*Machine Readable Zone*). Due to the existence of the MRZ is why the previous generation of passports were considered as a *Machine Readable Travel Document (MRTD)*.

For going one step beyond in all areas of interest for using a MRTD, the decision taken was not only to improve the printed information and emphasize all the security mechanisms, but also to use smart card technology and allow the use of biometric recognition technologies. In order to accomplish these requirements, it was decided to use a contactless approach based on ISO/IEC 14443, being the smart card chip and the antenna embedded in the passport booklet. Therefore a new era on MRTDs started, with the so called Electronic Passport, or just ePassport, where contactless and store-on-card technologies are being used. Figure 10.12 shows how the contactless smart card (and its antenna) can be embedded into an ePassport. One of the most popular implementations is embedding the chip and the antenna in one of the booklet covers not facing the MRZ. This has required manufacturing the booklet cover with a more rigid material than the one used in previous generations of passports.

Within the smart card, all the printed information on the standardized page was stored, plus many other data fields. From those new data fields, some biometric information was included, the minimum requirement being the storage of a standardized image of the face of the passport holder. In addition to this information, other additional biometric features could be stored depending on the decision of the country issuing the passport. Initially those additional features are considered to be the image of one or several fingerprints, or the image of one or two of the passport holder irises. All this is defined by the International Civil Aviation Organization (ICAO) in its document 9303 [25]. Figure 10.13 shows an excerpt of the Logical Data Structure (LDS) to be stored into the ePassport smart card. It shows all the

Fig. 10.13 Excerpt of the LDS of the ePassport (image taken from [25])

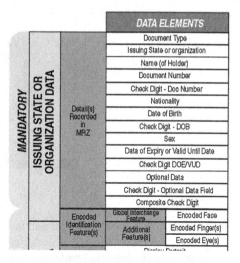

			DATA ELEMENTS		
MANDATORY	ISSUING STATE OR ORGANIZATION DATA	Detail(s) Recorded in MRZ	Document Type		
			Issuing State or organization		
			Name (of Holder)		
			Document Number		
			Check Digit - Doc Number		
			Nationality		
			Date of Birth		
			Check Digit - DOB		
			Sex		
			Data of Expiry or Valid Until Date		
			Check Digit DOE/VUD		
			Optional Data		
			Check Digit - Optional Data Field		
			Composite Check Digit		
		Encoded Identification Feature(s)	Global Interchange Feature	Encoded Face	
			Additional Feature(s)	Encoded Finger(s)	
				Encoded Eye(s)	

information also printed in the MRZ and the encoded biometrics (mandatory and optional).

The idea behind storing images instead of templates or models, is reaching a worldwide interoperability, not having to be dependent on the algorithm that each country has decided to integrate into their immigration system. Then, at the immigration control, the system can extract the biometric information from the smart card, can also scan the photograph on the passport page, and can take live samples from the passport holder, and use their own tools to determine the authenticity of the passport holder.

In order to protect the information stored at the contactless chip much of a controversy took place in the very beginning. The solution adopted was a compromise about security, worldwide interoperability and citizens' privacy. The worldwide interoperability presented a lot of restrictions in implementing high-level security mechanisms. But there was also the requirement that no-one could obtain the information stored in the passport without the consent of the passport holder. Therefore the solution adopted was based in protecting the access to the information in the passport by a secret code, which will be different for each ePassport. In order to allow every country in the world to know such secret code, an algorithm was defined to calculate it from the information printed in the MRZ of the passport page. Citizen's privacy is ensured by the fact that the MRZ cannot be read if the passport is not opened by the page containing the MRZ and properly scanned.

10.8.2 Spanish National ID Card (DNIe)

The other use case to be shown is the Electronic Spanish National ID Card (*Documento Nacional de Identidad electrónico—DNIe*). In Spain there is a well-established tradition of a mandatory identification document for all Spanish citizens

Fig. 10.14 Block diagram of
the authentication services
provided by the DNIe

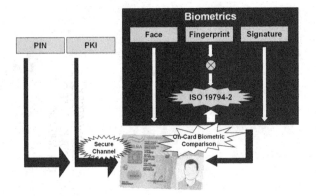

and residents. This document is present in most of the acts that the inhabitant is doing in his/her normal life, such as declaring his/her identity for banking operations, to access security controlled buildings, or even claiming the identity before paying with a debit or credit card at any shop.

Spanish Police decided to improve the capacities of the traditional Spanish National ID Card by including, not only the physical identity of the inhabitant, but also to add a National accredited digital identity [17]. It was decided to implement this using a public key powered smart card with contacts, based on ISO/IEC 7816 and PKCS #11 [10] and #15 [11]. Two certificates are issued by the Spanish Administration for the electronic identity of the Spanish inhabitant, one for authentication, and the other for signing documents. The use of each of those certificates is protected by a PIN code. In order to guarantee citizens' privacy, it was decided that the PIN code should be an alphanumeric password of 8 bytes.

Regarding Biometrics, three modalities are included in the chip (face, fingerprint and handwritten signature), two of them being also printed in the smart card body. These two are the face image and the handwritten signature. This two modalities are stored in the card as an image, and could be extracted through a secure channel to allow double checking of the identity of the cardholder (store-on-card technology). But the fingerprint information is not stored as an image, but only the features, which are coded following the compact format in ISO/IEC 19794-2. In addition to this, the fingerprint template cannot be extracted from the card, but only compared inside the card (on-card biometric comparison technology). All the above mentioned capabilities of the Spanish National ID Card are illustrated in Fig. 10.14.

Currently, the use of Biometrics within the DNIe is restricted, and only the Spanish Administration (specifically the national security bodies, such as the police) can use it. But a very useful service is provided to citizens using the fingerprint. This service is to unblock and/or change the PIN code. As it has been mentioned above, the PIN code was decided to be long and complex (8 alphanumerical characters). This can lead to the users to either forget it, or to erroneously entering the code. As only three consecutive wrong presentations are allowed, the probability of blocking the use of the certificates is not discardable. Therefore in all Police Stations, there is an ATM where each inhabitant can go and unblock his/her PIN code by verifying his/her fingerprint. There is no need to wait queues or requesting attention from an officer at the Police Station. If the fingerprint is matched, then the cardholder can define a new PIN code.

10.9 Conclusions

This chapter has provided an overview to the smart card technology, as to show the benefits that this technology can provide to biometric systems. Special emphasis has been applied to explain the security mechanisms included in most smart cards, and how these security mechanisms can protect biometric data and processes.

Different architectures for the integration of Biometrics and smart cards have been presented (Store-on-Card, On-Card Biometric Comparison, Work-sharing mechanisms, and System-on-Card), some of them still being in prototyping stages. Each of the architectures has its own advantages and disadvantages, so it will depend on the final application where it is going to be used, to decide which architecture fits better. Currently there are major deployments, such as ePassports that already include the store-on-card approach, while others, such as the Electronic Spanish National ID Card includes the on-card biometric comparison architecture.

This chapter has also described the different levels for the evaluation of the technology, both at performance and security levels.

In a few words, it can be said that the technology is ready to be used for implementing any kind of biometric system under an authentication scheme using smart cards, although technology is continuously evolving as to provide further improvements.

References

1. Zoreda JL, Oton JM (1994) Smart Cards. Artech House, Norwood
2. Bright R (1988) Smart Cards: Principles, Practice, Applications. Ellis Horwood Books in Information Technology
3. International Organization for Standardization (ISO). ISO/IEC 7816 identification cards—integrated circuit cards. http://www.iso.org
4. Rankl W, Effing W (1997) Smart Card Handbook. Wiley, New York
5. Oracle. Java card. http://www.oracle.com/technetwork/java/javacard/overview/index.html
6. International Organization for Standardization (ISO). ISO/IEC 7816 identification cards—integrated circuit cards—part 4: organization, security and commands for interchange. http://www.iso.org
7. PC/SC Workgroup. http://www.pcscworkgroup.com/
8. Kömmerling O, Kuhn MG (1999) Design principles for tamper-resistant smartcard processors. In: Proceedings of the USENIX Workshop on Smartcard Technology on USENIX Workshop on Smartcard Technology (WOST'99). USENIX Association, Berkeley
9. Schneier B (1995) Applied Cryptography. Wiley, New York
10. RSA Laboratories. PKCS #11 cryptographic token interface (cryptoki). http://www.rsa.com/rsalabs/node.asp?id=2133

11. RSA Laboratories. PKCS #15 cryptographic token information format standard. http://www.rsa.com/rsalabs/node.asp?id=2124
12. Sanchez-Reillo R (2002) Achieving security in integrated circuit card applications: reality or desire? IEEE Aerospace and Electronic Systems Magazine 17(6):4–8
13. Ratha NK, Connell JHBRM (2001) Enhancing security and privacy in biometrics-based authentication systems. IBM Systems Journal 40(3):614–634
14. Sanchez-Reillo R (2009) Tamper-Proof Operating System. Encyclopaedia of Biometrics, vol 2. Springer, Berlin, pp 1315–1321
15. International Organization for Standardization (ISO). ISO/IEC 24787 information technology—identification cards—on-card biometric comparison. http://www.iso.org
16. Sanchez-Reillo R, Gonzalez-Marcos A (1999) Access control system with hand geometry verification and smart cards. In: IEEE 33rd Annual 1999 International Carnahan Conference on Security Technology, pp 485–487
17. Cuerpo Nacional de Policia. DNI electrónico. http://www.dnielectronico.es/
18. Precise Biometrics. Precise match-on-card. http://www.precisebiometrics.com/?id=136
19. Gemalto. NET bio. http://www.gemalto.com/products/dotnet_bio/
20. NIST. MINEX II—performance of fingerprint match-on-card algorithms—phase IV report, NIST interagency report 7477 (revision II), http://biometrics.nist.gov/cs_links/minex/minexII/minex_report.pdf
21. NEUROtechnology. Megamatcher on card SDK. http://www.neurotechnology.com/megamatcher-on-card.html
22. Sanchez-Reillo R (2001) Including Biometric Authentication in a Smart Card Operating System. International conference on audio and video-based biometric person authentication (AVBPA). Lecture Notes on Computer Science, vol 2091. Springer, Berlin. pp 342–347
23. NIST. MINEX minutia exchange homepage. http://www.nist.gov/itl/iad/ig/minex.cfm
24. Common Criteria Portal. http://www.commoncriteriaportal.org/pps/
25. International Civil Aviation Organization (ICAO) (2006) Doc 9303: machine readable travel documents—part 1: machine readable passports—vol 2: specifications for electronically enabled passports with biometric identification capability, 6th edn. http://www.icao.org/

Chapter 11
Two Efficient Architectures for Handling Biometric Data While Taking Care of Their Privacy

Julien Bringer and Hervé Chabanne

Abstract We present two architecture examples that illustrate what can be done today in terms of Privacy and Security in Biometrics. Our choice corresponds to the base of two demonstrators developed for the European FP7 cooperative project TURBINE. These solutions have been conceived for two distinct kinds of applications as the first one deals with private remote biometric authentication while the second one is devoted to local biometric identification which corresponds to a physical access control scenario. Moreover, the techniques on which they rely are quite different. Our scope is here mainly dedicated to describe the cryptographic protocols, their implementations and their security analysis.

11.1 Introduction

The biometric industry has grown over the years. The applications now vary from criminal investigations to identity documents, involving millions of people. The simplicity of the principle of biometric authentication is one of the reasons of its success; a biometric trait is captured to be compared to a reference, also known as biometric template. With this development, the issues related to the protection of the privacy of the used biometric traits have received particular attention. As biometric traits can serve to track people, their confidentiality is often needed. A first answer to this need of confidentiality can be brought by making the computations involving biometric data only in places physically protected against intruders. For personal need, such as biometric authentication, a smartcard, for instance, can be used. In this case, the tamper resistance of the hardware component of the smartcard ensures the confidentiality of the computations made within it. A technology known as Match-on-Card (MOC, see Sect. 11.2.1) has been developed to realize the

J. Bringer (✉)
Morpho, 11, Boulevard Gallieni, 92130 Issy les Moulineaux, France
e-mail: julien.bringer@morpho.com

H. Chabanne
Morpho & Télécom ParisTech, 11, Boulevard Gallieni, 92130 Issy les Moulineaux, France
e-mail: herve.chabanne@morpho.com

P. Campisi (ed.), *Security and Privacy in Biometrics*,
DOI 10.1007/978-1-4471-5230-9_11, © Springer-Verlag London 2013

comparison—also called the matching—of the fresh biometric trait to a biometric template stored inside the smartcard.

Some researchers suggest to replace the traditional algorithms to compare biometric traits by an error correction procedure by means of Secure Sketch (see Sect. 11.2.2). In fact, in a secure sketch, biometric data are quantized and then combined with a codeword to exploit its correction capacity. In this case, the biometric template—the secure sketch—partially hides the biometric reference which was used in its creation. However, secure sketch suffers from two drawbacks. The first one is that the error correction is, usually, less effective than the traditional matching algorithm to compare two biometric traits regarding the accuracy of the performances. The second one is that secure sketch is not sufficient to ensure the confidentiality of the underlying biometric trait used alone [9, 29].

A potential benefit of the secure sketch is the simplification of the biometric matching. This opens the possibility to encrypt the secure sketch with a homomorphic cryptosystem to perform the comparison with encrypted biometric data, i.e. without decrypting them. Homomorphic encryption indeed enables to realize one simple operation on cleartexts by manipulating their ciphertexts. This may suffice for some biometric protocols. Moreover, homomorphic encryption has received great attention since the recent introduction of a cryptosystem which can handle more complex operations at the same time. This is certainly a promising direction for future works but it today requires a lot of computations.

We here want to focus to solutions which can be deployed today without losing too much performances either in speed of computations or in accuracy and without sacrificing the security of our schemes. To make that happen, we have to mix different existing components: MOC, secure sketch, advanced cryptographic protocols. At the end, we obtain two different systems, one dedicated to remote biometric authentication described in Sect. 11.3 (first results on this system have been published in [11]) and the other one to access control (see Sect. 11.4 or [12] for the earliest version of this work). The first protocol corresponds to a remote authentication scenario. It combines local authentication on a local client, based either on a traditional biometric comparison or on a secure sketch biometric comparison. After this local authentication, a specific anonymous remote authentication is executed where the server can only verify the validity of the individual without learning its identity. The second protocol corresponds to a local access control scenario. It uses a security module embedded in a local terminal to ensure the protection of the reference data. The protocol enables to achieve authorization checking. In both cases, we describe their design, the details of their implementation and the security results we can obtain with them.

These systems have been analyzed and demonstrated within the TURBINE project, see http://www.turbine-project.eu/index.php. Based on innovative developments in cryptography and fingerprint biometrics, it aimed at establishing protocols to handle fingerprint biometrics for ID management with good privacy properties. The objectives of this TURBINE project concerning the security are, according to [18]:

Fig. 11.1 A schematic view of Match-on-Card authentication

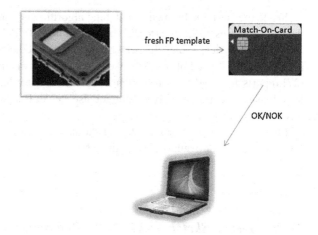

fresh FP template

Match-On-Card

OK/NOK

- Ensure that the "protected" biometric information cannot be used to derive the original biometric data (image or minutiae)
- Ensure that the "protected" biometric information can be canceled and a new replacement can be readily and securely generated
- Ensure that a protected biometric sample can be processed to generate different application specific results and that such capabilities are supported in the replacement biometric reference in the event of cancelation for whatever reasons.

This has to be understood as general requirements valid not only for external adversaries but also for malicious internal ones.

After this Introduction, Sect. 11.2 recalls some already known techniques which are useful to define our architectures. Section 11.3 deals with our first solution dedicated to remote biometric authentication. Section 11.4 describes our second system for local biometric identification on an access control terminal. Section 11.5 concludes.

11.2 Preliminaries

11.2.1 Match-on-Card Technology

Match-on-Card (MOC) Technology is a solution for keeping biometric data private. It can be seen as the opposite to central database as the holder of the card has his reference biometric data stored in the card. Moreover, the comparison between this reference and a fresh capture is performed by and inside the smartcard. More precisely, a sensor outside the card captures the biometric data and processes them to put them in an adequate format (for instance, a fingerprint is stored on about 512 bytes according to compact-size ISO minutiae template, [22]). They are then sent to the smartcard to authenticate its holder, cf. Fig. 11.1.

Inside the card, the biometric matching algorithm is thought to take into account the low resources of the smartcard which is limited in CPU processing power and in available memories. Today, the performances are nonetheless good, both in terms of accuracy and of speed of the response of the card. Typically, the NIST MINEX test [27] reports for a MOC of less than 2 seconds, a False Reject Rate of 4.7×10^{-3} for a False Accept Rate of 10^{-2}, and a False Reject Rate of 8.6×10^{-3} for a False Accept Rate of 10^{-3}.

MOC is sometimes considered as an alternative to cardholder PIN authentication. It can also be used to authorize repetitive but sensitive operations to be made by the card.

11.2.2 Secure Sketch as Biometric Templates

Let V stand for a biometric trait. Let $v \leftarrow V$ indicate that v is a capture of V. For instance, $v, v' \leftarrow V$ are two captures of the same biometric trait V. As we will see later (see next Sect. 11.2.4) the values of v and v' can be very different.

Iriscodes are a common way of representing iris trait as binary vectors. To represent iris, biometric data are quantized (binarized) in such a way that for comparing two iriscodes one has to look at the number of coordinates in which they differ.

Remark 11.1 Measuring the number of coordinates in which two vectors are different is known as computing their Hamming distance. In the following, we will frequently refer to this distance.

This clearly leads to a very convenient matching algorithm. The paradigm that makes things work can be simply stated as:

1. Two different captures v, v' from the same user are close for the Hamming distance
2. Captures v_1, v_2 of different users are far away for the Hamming distance

Roughly speaking, a secure sketch scheme allows recovery of a hidden value from any element close to this hidden value. The goal is to manage noisy data such as biometric acquisitions. The general idea is to absorb the differences occurring between two captures by viewing them as errors over a codeword. More precisely, binarized biometric data v are added to a codeword c of an error-correcting code to form the secure sketch $s = v \oplus c$, the addition being made thanks to an exclusive or. Let v' be a fresh capture of the biometric data. To compare v and v', one has to compute $s \oplus v' = c \oplus (v \oplus v') = c \oplus e$ where e stands for some errors to be corrected by the property of the underlying error-correcting code. Thanks to the hypothesis we made, whenever v, v' come from the same user, they will be close and e can be corrected.

Unfortunately, for biometric data, the security constraints of secure sketch are difficult to fulfill. It has been proved that secure sketches are not as secure as one can think initially [9, 29], and in practice, it is easy to recover v from s. Consequently, there have been a lot of papers integrating secure sketches into cryptographic protocols to reinforce their security [2, 4, 7, 8, 20, 28, 30].

The are a lot of propositions to apply this construction to real biometrics data. And in fact, to get good accuracy performances, the binarization of biometric data could be difficult. We will now give an example for fingerprints that is the subject of a lot of scientific works [10, 17, 19, 21, 23, 26, 31–33].

11.2.3 Encoding Fingerprint Templates into Fixed-Length Binary Vectors

One natural solution to binarize a fingerprint is to start from the image, to extract the global pattern (ridge direction field) of the fingerprint and then to adapt state-of-the-art quantization techniques. For instance, this approach is studied and experimented in [31] and improved later in [10]. From the fingerprint approach, a real vector is extracted via the computation of the ridge direction field and some responses to Gabor filters. Then, using several captures of the same fingerprint which are aligned one by one, the corresponding vectors are fed into a reliable component selection algorithm that selects for each user a small subset of the vectors coordinates based on the stability of the values and a quantization step that binarizes the value by comparison to a mean value. However, this method has several disadvantages. The encoding is not based on classical fingerprint templates [22] that use minutiae and for which performances are known to be far better than with the fingerprint pattern. Moreover, the representation—as most of the state-of-the-art techniques—is not resilient to translation and rotation of the fingerprint. This is a great issue for fingerprint applications.

In TURBINE project, research has been conducted to design encoding algorithms [6, 32, 33] that apply upon minutiae templates that address the misalignment resilience problem and that achieve good biometric performances. In particular, [6] introduces a minutiae template transformation that is based on comparisons of local neighborhood of a minutia (a vicinity centered around the minutia) with a representative dataset. This doing, it enables to convert the template into a fixed-length binary vector which is resilient to translation and orientation of the fingerprint. The algorithm can be summed up as follows:

- Extract all minutiae from a fingerprint to obtain a set of minutiae $M = \{m_i\}_i$;
- For each minutia, construct the vicinity centered in this minutia—i.e. a subset of the minutiae contained in a disk of fixed radius (cf. Fig. 11.2)—to obtain a list of vicinities $\{V(M)_i\}_i$;
- Let $R_1, \ldots, R_N$ be the representative data (which have been collected in a training phase of the algorithm, i.e. they are user-independent);

Fig. 11.2 Example of four different kinds of vicinities

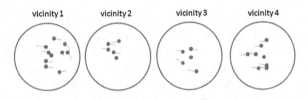

Fig. 11.3 Summary of the feature vector construction process

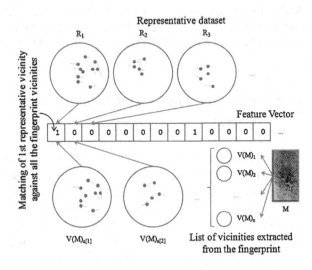

- For i from 1 to N

  - compare all constructed vicinities to R_i
  - if one gives a matching score above a given threshold, then define $V_i = 1$, else $V_i = 0$

- Output V.

The overall process is illustrated by Fig. 11.3 and the details of the comparison between representative vicinities and fingerprint vicinities are given in Fig. 11.4.

What makes the encoding translation and rotation invariant is that each vicinity and representative data are self-aligned based on the central minutia. Moreover, as the encoding is based only on local comparisons, it helps to deal with local distortions that may occur during acquisition. This gives relatively good performances compared to state-of-the-art binary encodings of minutiae templates and the algorithm is easy to adapt to several captures at enrollment to increase further the performances.

Bringer and Despiegel [6] present results of experiments on FVC2000 DB2 [24] and FVC2002 DB2 [25] with $N = 50,000$ representative vicinities that lead to vectors of 50,000 bits. On FVC2002 DB2, the given EER (Equal Error Rate) is of 5.3 %, and 1.7 % with four samples at enrollment. Figure 11.5 establishes the comparison between FAR and FRR for this type of representation.

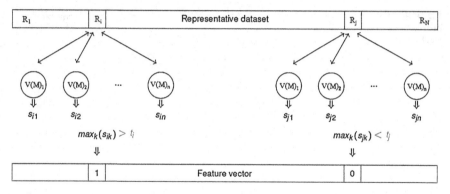

Fig. 11.4 Binarization based on comparison of a representative vicinity with the list of the fingerprint vicinities

Fig. 11.5 FAR vs. FRR on FVC2002 DB2 and FVC2000 DB2 with mono-sample enrollment and multi-samples (4) enrollment

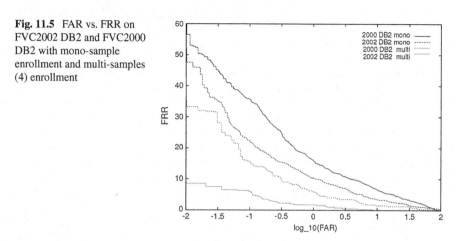

Remark 11.2 This 50,000-bits long vector contains lot of redundancy compared to the traditional minutiae-based representation (at least 20 times more bits). The reduction of the size of representative vicinities vectors would be useful for constrained environments, see for instance Sect. 11.4.3.2.

11.2.4 Some Elements on Volatility of Biometric Acquisitions

For the binary encoding technique described above, the comparison between two vectors is based on a bit-by-bit AND, normalized by the number of ones for each vector. Besides the error rates of such a biometric system that depends on a decision threshold, the range of possible variations occurring between two acquisitions of the same biometric trait matters also a lot.

We give here some details about the level of noise that can occur. Based on all possible comparisons (matching and non-matching pairs) from fingerprint of the

Fig. 11.6 Hamming distance distributions over FVC 2000 DB2

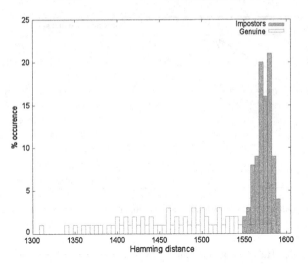

Fig. 11.7 Hamming distance distributions over FVC 2002 DB2

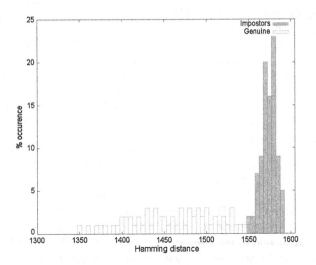

FVC2000 database 2 [24] (resp. FVC2002 database 2 [25]), we compute the corresponding Hamming distance and we obtain the genuine and impostor distributions from Fig. 11.6 (resp. Fig. 11.7). We remark that there is a large amount of errors to tolerate between two genuine fingerprint images. There are at least 1,000 bits that differ.

Consequently, due to the high number of differences between two different captures of the same trait, it is very hard to determine the value of one specific capture even when knowing another one. This specific property—i.e. the secrecy of a given capture—is exploited in next section for a new way to generate cryptographic keys.

11.3 Private Remote Biometric Authentication

11.3.1 A Simple Solution for Biometric Cryptographic Keys

In this section, we give a simple idea to obtain biometric cryptographic keys. Biometric data are often quite easy to capture; think at a face in the crowd or latents of the fingerprints you leave on the glass that you take. For this reason, it is wise to build systems on the assumption that they are public data. Moreover, such captures are quite volatile and as we have seen before in Sects. 11.2.2 and 11.2.4 the problem of getting the same key through a reproducible process is, today, quite challenging. That said, we will explain why these two objections put together lead to a simple solution for biometric key.

One has to remark that while a biometric trait cannot be considered as secret, its different captures—thanks to their volatility—have a large unknown part. Treating the capture made at the enrollment as confidential will give us our biometric key. This means that this particular enrollment capture has to be kept hidden on a specific support (for instance, on a personal card) by its holder. An adversary will have access to different captures of the same biometric trait but cannot be able to determine which one is hold.

11.3.2 An Application

Let v be a biometric template extracted and encoded from a specific capture of a user's biometric trait. The user keeps a token on his own with v stored in it. Due to the secrecy of this specific template, it can be used as a password or a secret for cryptographic key generation. Moreover, a new capture of the biometric trait will enable to check that the user is the legitimate bearer of the token.

Assume that a remote database stores $H(v)$, a basic protocol for remote authentication of the user would be:

- capture and extract a fresh v' from the user;
- check at the client side the proximity between v' and the template v stored in the user's token;
- if v and v' match, then proceed to the remote authentication via $H(v)$.

[11] extends this basic approach to enable a privacy-enhanced remote authentication while still linking the authentication process to a biometric key. The protocol uses a cryptographic scheme named group signature scheme to this aim.

A group signature scheme is a cryptographic scheme with the following algorithms:

- *Join* allows a user to be registered as a group member. This registration finishes with the generation of a user secret key *sk*.
- *Sign* is the signature procedure that a user can use with his secret key *sk* to sign a message on behalf of the group.

Fig. 11.8 Enrolment process for the remote authentication protocol

User   Token   Enrollment office
        v $Join, v$
    ──────→ Store v ──────→ Generate $sk = f(t, v)$
              Store t ←──────t────

Fig. 11.9 Overview of the authentication phase for the private remote biometric authentication scheme

- *Verify* is the algorithm for a server to check if a given signature is valid. The main difference with classical signature scheme is here that the server will not be able to determine the identity of the original signer. Indeed, the group signature scheme allows the verifier to only check if the signature is valid with respect to the group but disallows the retrieval of the identity. This process includes in particular a revocation check for the verifier to know whether the signer user has been revoked or not. Would it be the case, the verifier would retrieve the identity of the user.

Based on a group signature scheme, a private remote authentication protocol relying on biometric keys is explained below.

Registration   The registration of a new user, as illustrated by Fig. 11.8, works as follows.

- A user asks an enrollment officer to register to the service.
- A biometric template v is extracted from a given capture of the user's biometric trait
- The enrollment officer uses v and *Join* algorithm to register the user in the group and to generate a key sk that is derived partially from v.
- v and the other data (denoted t) needed to generate again sk are stored inside the user's token.

Authentication   The general overview of the authentication procedure is illustrated by Fig. 11.9.

- A fresh template v' is computed;
- v' is compared with v (if possible inside the token via a Match-on-Card technique);
- if this is determined as a matching pair, generate back sk;
- the server sends a challenge C to be signed;
- the user signs the challenge C, with the secret key sk, on behalf of the group (on the token or a local client) and sends the corresponding value R to the server;

User   Token   Remote Server

$\xrightarrow{v'}$ Compare v with v'

If no match, abort

If match, compute $sk = f(t,v)$ $\xrightarrow{\text{Auth. query}}$

$\xleftarrow{\quad C \quad}$ Generate a random challenge C

$R = Sign(C, sk)$ $\xrightarrow{\quad R \quad}$ Check R

Fig. 11.10 Authentication process for the remote authentication protocol

- the server verifies if the signature is valid and the user not revoked;
- if so, access to the service is granted (anonymously with respect to the other group members).

The process in the case of on-token comparison is given in Fig. 11.10.

A very important feature in this protocol is that the biometric error rates are not altered by the combination with the cryptographic protocol. Classical matching can be used locally to generate the secret key and gives the right to sign the challenge.

Bringeret al. [11] suggested the use of the Boneh–Shacham group signature scheme [3]. An interesting property of this scheme is the Verifier-Local Revocation (VLR) property that enables the verifier to run revocation check without any interaction with the signer or with the group manager.

11.3.3 Security

As explained in Sect. 11.2.4, secrecy of the key used for authentication is based on the confidentiality of the enrolled biometric template (even if an adversary knows another capture of the same trait). When based on a group signature scheme, the protocol enables to enhance the privacy of the users. This is related to the anonymity properties that are explained below.

Selfless-Anonymity A group member can say if he produced a particular signature. If it was not him, he has no information about the user who produced it.

Full-Anonymity The signatures do not reveal the identity of the signer. A coalition of all users, not given the master secret key, cannot find who signed a particular message.

Following those notions, if the group signature scheme fulfills either selfless or full anonymity (which is the case for [3]), then the privacy of the user is ensured with respect to the remote server.

11.3.4 Implementation

This scheme has been implemented and tested in the TURBINE project for one of the demonstrators to prove the feasibility of this solution. On a PC (Intel® Xeon®

CPU X3320 @ 2.50 GHz, 3 GB RAM) with the choice of elliptic curve with 512-bit-long order, the total time for a remote authentication, included a fingerprint capture and local comparison, is around 3 seconds with a revocation list with 50 revoked users. The size of the revocation list is an important factor. Concretely, when one checks a signature, one first verifies if the signature is valid using the public parameters of the group, to verify whether the signer has a secret key delivered by the group manager, and then the verifier tests whether the user has been revoked or not by comparing values derived from the signature with revocation tokens stored in a revocation list (and the comparison is linear in the number of revoked users).

To decrease the time needed for signature and revocation checks, it is possible to use recent VLR group signature schemes that are more efficient, e.g. [16]. For instance, the time needed (on a PC with a 2.93 GHz Intel® Core™ 2 Duo processor) with [16] for a signature check (resp. verification check, revocation check per revoked user) is 400 ms (resp. 350 ms, 45 ms) whereas it takes 1,000 ms (resp. 1170 ms, 180 ms) with [3].

11.4 Local Identification for Access Control

11.4.1 A New Way of Using Secure Sketch

Application of secure sketch to biometrics most often comes with two interesting flavors: traditional biometric templates are converted following specific transformations to obtain quantized fixed-length vectors and that can be compared simply by means of a Hamming distance-like comparison algorithm. This enables the use of error correcting codes for sketching and reconstruction functions. Moreover, for efficiency of error correction, the size of the converted templates is made quite small (a few hundreds to thousands of bits).

Taken into account the facts that secure sketches cannot ensure alone the security of biometric data and that their performances accuracy is not as good today for some biometric modalities as the one we get with classical algorithms, we here suggest a novel architecture:

- sensitive operations are made inside a Secure Access Module (SAM),
- the comparison of biometric data is performed with a classical matching algorithm inside this SAM using MOC technology,
- secure sketches are stored inside the SAM,
- biometric data are stored outside the SAM but they are encrypted/decrypted by a key which stays in the SAM,
- secure sketches enable us to minimize the number of biometric data that will be sent to the SAM to be decrypted and matched using MOC.

Fig. 11.11 Biometric
terminal architecture for
private access control

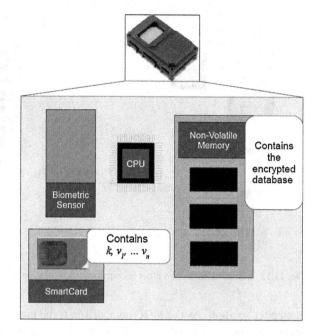

11.4.2 Our System

We conceive a biometric terminal for which the confidentiality is brought thanks to
a dedicated hardware element (think of a smartcard as a SIM card in a cell phone).
The device is made of different elements (cf. Fig. 11.11):

- a main processing unit (CPU),
- a sensor,
- some non-volatile memory,
- a Secure Access Module (SAM) dedicated to the terminal.

11.4.2.1 Enrollment

As illustrated by Fig. 11.12, the secure sketches of the registered users $v_1, \ldots, v_n$
are stored inside the SAM. The references for the biometric data are stored inside a
non-volatile memory, encrypted under a key k stored in the SAM. For this reason,
we will refer to this memory in the following as the encrypted database. Finally, the
SAM has the capacity to compare biometric data thanks to MOC technology.

11.4.2.2 Authorization Checking

A simple solution to determine whether a user is registered or not would be to compare its biometric trait to all those which are stored inside the terminal. We can think

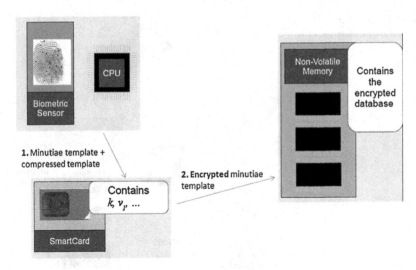

Fig. 11.12 The enrollment flow chart for our local identification procedure

at a better solution. As the MOC comparison is the most time costly operation, we will instead proceed as summarized by Fig. 11.13. We introduce a pretreatment step where the distances between secure sketches are computed; this only involves simple operations and goes fast. This way, we obtain a list of best candidates on which we can focus on.

When a user wants to be identified by the biometric terminal:

1. its biometric trait is captured by the sensor,
2. the main processor computes the secure sketch corresponding to this fresh biometric data. It sends it to the SAM along with the captured biometric data,
3. the SAM compares this secure sketch with $v_1, \ldots, v_n$, the ones it stored. It sorts them from the closest to the farthest,
4. the SAM sequentially retrieves the encrypted biometric data from encrypted database. It proceeds following the order it has established before (from the closest to the farthest),
5. the SAM decrypts with k this biometric data and compares it with the fresh one thanks to its MOC capacity to grant or not access.

11.4.3 Implementation

In this section, we give more details about the implementation and performances issues for the local access control system and then describe practical experimentations of the protocol.

The sorting step based on the comparisons between the sketches could be seen as the selection of a small number of candidates that will be retrieved from the

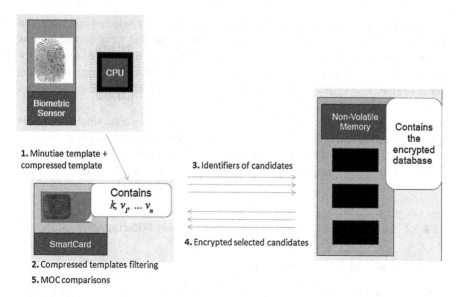

1. Minutiae template + compressed template

2. Compressed templates filtering

3. Identifiers of candidates

4. Encrypted selected candidates

5. MOC comparisons

Fig. 11.13 The verification flow chart for our local identification procedure

encrypted database to be matched using the MOC functionality. The time needed for a MOC execution (hundreds of ms) is very long compared to a classical matching executed on a powerful CPU. Thus, for performances issues, several constraints should be analyzed:

- A threshold δ on the maximal number of MOC comparisons to be executed is set such as the time needed for δ MOC executions remains acceptable for usability (a few seconds).
- This threshold implies that if the genuine candidate is not a member of the δ closest secure sketches, then the system will wrongly reject the user. Consequently, there is a trade-off with the accuracy at rank δ when considering classification based on secure sketches comparison.
- Finally, as we are dealing with a smartcard environment, timings of all operations (including the communication with the SAM) and sizes of involved data are important. For the secure sketches, the time complexity of the comparisons and transmission is directly related to the length of the sketches. So the shortest they are, the better, but we have again a trade-off with the accuracy.

11.4.3.1 Straightforward Applications of Secure Sketches

An experimentation of this protocol has first been described in [12] for fingerprint biometric data. The proposal relies on the use of the secure sketches from [10, 31] that are based on reliable component quantization. From the image, the ridges directional field is used to obtain a real vector of fixed length 1,984. Then with M

several enrolled vectors per user, k reliable components are selected and binarized for each user following some statistics (in particular mean and variance within-class and between-class). For each user i, this leads to binary vectors v_i of length k together with a list p_i of the selected indices. For vectors of 128 bits, the SAM thus needs to store $s_i = c_i \oplus v_i$ and p_i for each user (i.e. about $128 + 128 \times 12 = 1,664$ bits).

According to [31], a practical choice of an error correcting code would be a BCH code of length 128. But for efficient comparison within the SAM, the best choice is to avoid the execution of any decoding algorithm. We set c_i as the all-zero vector for all users. Hence, the comparison is equivalent to an Hamming distance comparison.

11.4.3.2 Adaptations of Secure Sketches for Efficient Filtering

This approach underlines some problems:

- the size needed to store the secure sketch is important, due to the list p_i of indices. For instance, for $n = 100$ enrolled users, this would require more than 20 kbytes to store the data;
- the comparison, even if reduced to an Hamming distance, is very dependent on the user indices.

Bringer et al. [12] overcome these problems by adapting techniques from [10, 31] to take into account the application to a one-to-many scenario by selecting the same choice of indices for all users. This way the memory needed in the SAM and the comparison efficiency are improved. For 100 users, less than 2 kbytes are now needed and all comparisons are made on the same coordinates. On FVC2000 DB2, with $M = 6$ images per user at enrollment and the two others for authorization experiments, [12] obtains an accuracy of 90 % at rank 8 with 128 bits vectors. With 256 bits vectors, results are 90 % at rank 5. In that case, the number of needed MOC executions might be acceptable but the accuracy needs to be improved for operational use.

As explained in Sect. 11.2.3, the performances of the secure sketches and quantization techniques from [10, 31] are now known to be far from the best ones, and their adaptation—that was originally made for one-to-one comparison—to the case of one-to-many comparisons makes this situation worse. One additional drawback for real applications of the above method is that all users need to be enrolled at the same time in order to select the same "reliable" coordinates for everyone.

We show below how to exploit the more accurate minutiae-based binarization technique from [6] to obtain an efficient solution for an implementation of our local identification system. In Sect. 11.2.3, the length of the binary vectors is 50,000. To reduce the overhead on communication complexity from the terminal to the SAM and the time to convert a minutiae template for computation complexity in the terminal CPU (as the complexity of the algorithm from [6] is linear in the length), an almost[1] randomly chosen subset of 5,000 representative vicinities is selected from the original set of 50,000 vicinities.

- For the access control phase, binary vectors of $N = 5,000$ will be used accordingly.
- For the enrollment phase, we decrease the storage size for one v_i to 520 bits given the following principle: as described in Sect. 11.2.3, the conversion of a minutiae template into a binary vector relies on the computation of N similarity scores between the fingerprint (more precisely its vicinities) and the N representative vicinities. One coordinate is lightened at 1 if the fingerprint is sufficiently close to the corresponding representative vicinities. For compressing the representation, we decide to keep in memory only the information of the 40 indices of the closest representative vicinities. As an index is encoded on 13 bits, this gives 520 bits in total. Consequently the memory needed in the SAM for the secure sketches of $n = 100$ users is less than 7 kbytes.
- The comparison between a fresh binary vector of 5,000 bits and a enrolled set of 40 indices is simply a counting of the number of lightened 1 in the 5,000-bits vector at the coordinates determined by those indices. Scores are thus always smaller than 40 and the sorting of all results to obtain the δ closest candidates is very fast.

On FVC2000 DB2, with only one image enrolled per user, this leads to about 80 % at rank 5 and around 95 % with four images enrolled. Such an approach has been implemented and demonstrated during TURBINE project. This enabled to prove that the solution is feasible in practice. On a smartcard, the total time measured for secure sketches comparisons followed by the remaining MOC comparisons with 100 enrolled users is around 5 seconds.

11.4.4 Security

The security of the protocol as explained in [12] relies on the SAM-based physical protection: either data are stored directly in the card or stored encrypted outside the card. In all cases, all enrolled data are available in cleartext within the smartcard only.

Consequently, the higher the level of security of the SAM is, the higher the confidentiality of enrolled templates is. Indeed, thanks to the SAM protection, there is no way to learn information neither about the encryption/decryption key nor on the biometric templates stored encrypted in the main memory. In [14], the security analysis is pushed further to determine to what extent an adversary would be able to gain information on the secure sketches stored in the SAM's memory.

---

[1]The validity of the selection is checked with some experiments and if needed a new subset is drawn.

If an adversary were able to open the terminal (physical breach), then he would have a direct access to the SAM interface or the inputs/outputs from the communication channel between the main terminal components (CPU, main memory unit, SAM). A possible information leakage that might be exploited is then the list of candidates (the identifiers or the encrypted templates) that the SAM will request to the main memory unit before the Match-on-Card comparisons.

The strategy in [14] is a kind of blackbox attack that uses the SAM as an oracle as follows:

- send several binary vectors v'_j,
- eavesdrop which identifiers and encrypted templates are requested by the SAM to learn the list of the δ candidates related to an input vector v'_j,
- iterate while executing a hill climbing reconstruction of an enrolled compressed vector.

The idea is in fact to send first some random vectors, then to construct new vectors adaptively by taking into account the indices of the SAM outputs. By observing the difference in the list of candidates from one chosen vector to another one (for instance where only one bit has been switched), the adversary can gain information on some bits of the stored vectors (and guess the good bits via a kind of majority voting).

From the implementation experimented in [12], the fact that the binary vectors derived from a fingerprint are stored together with a mask (list of erased positions) is further exploited. For instance, the adversary can send a v'_j with its first bit non-erased and erasures in all the $k-1$ last bits, and if we have three quantized templates v_1, v_2 and v_3 that have as first bit 0, 1 and erasure, respectively, by switching the first bit of v'_j from 0 to 1, the closest vector will change (from v_1 to v_2). Bringer et al. [14] show with an adaptive attack that about 75 % of the 128 bits of an enrolled compressed templates can be recovered after 200 queries to the SAM. Note that, however, no additional information on the full enrolled templates can be retrieved.

Several countermeasures are suggested in [14], such as random delays between requests, periodical re-shuffling the data, muting the SAM if queries are too far, randomizing the order of the candidates, adding noise in the list of candidates, ... The effect of some of these countermeasures has been analyzed in the TURBINE project on the implementation (based on [6]'s binary representation) described in the previous section and this helps to limit the leakage to a very few percent of the representation of the enrolled compressed templates.

11.5 Conclusion

In this chapter, we try to be pragmatic and to conciliate different objectives: security, performances, accuracy. Moreover, we have in mind two kinds of biometric applications: one devoted to local access control and the other one to remote identification. Thanks to the progress made during the last years, we are able to achieve our goal and to deliver two corresponding prototypes. To do so, we have to combine techniques coming from several horizons: biometric secure sketch, Match-on-Card, cryptographic protocols. From our experience, one technique alone is not sufficient today for reaching these three objectives at the same time:

- confidentiality of private data is ensured by the tamper resistance of the smartcard executing MOC,
- secure sketch facilitates the treatment of raw biometric data as it is more easy to handle,
- group signature scheme brings the anonymity searched during the identification.

This fact can—of course—change with a significant improvement of one of these techniques. For instance, enhancing the accuracy of secure sketch and in particular lowering their FAR score dramatically, would also increase the security of the biometric data they represent. Increasing biometric processing capabilities of secure hardware should also permit to envisage more elaborate scenarios. A development that would be desirable would be to move from private one-to-one (authentication) or one-to-few biometric verifications such as in the prototypes we just described to huge biometric identification system as encountered, for instance, in today's AFIS (Automatic Fingerprint Identification System). Some theoretical articles have been published recently [1, 5, 13, 15]; it would be interesting if they were followed by proposals for implementations.

Acknowledgements   This work was sponsored in part by the EU project TURBINE, which is funded by the European Community's Seventh Framework Programme (FP7/2007-2011) under grant agreement nb. ICT-2007-216339. The authors acknowledge their partners, and especially Nicolas Delvaux (coordinator of the TURBINE project), Vincent Despiegel, Mélanie Favre, Tom Kevenaar, Bruno Kindarji, Alain Patey, David Pointcheval, Koen Simoens, Stefaan Seys, Sébastien Zimmer, their co-authors on works related to this chapter.

References

1. Adjedj M, Bringer J, Chabanne H, Kindarji B (2009) Biometric identification over encrypted data made feasible. In: Prakash A, Gupta I (eds) ICISS. Lecture Notes in Computer Science, vol 5905. Springer, Berlin, pp 86–100
2. Barbosa M, Brouard T, Cauchie S, de Sousa SM (2008) Secure biometric authentication with improved accuracy. In: Mu Y, Susilo W, Seberry J (eds) ACISP. Lecture Notes in Computer Science, vol 5107. Springer, Berlin, pp 21–36
3. Boneh D, Shacham H (2004) Group signatures with verifier-local revocation. In: Atluri V, Pfitzmann B, McDaniel PD (eds) ACM Conference on Computer and Communications Security. ACM, New York, pp 168–177
4. Bringer J, Chabanne H (2008) An authentication protocol with encrypted biometric data. In: Vaudenay S (ed) AFRICACRYPT. Lecture Notes in Computer Science, vol 5023. Springer, Berlin, pp 109–124
5. Bringer J, Chabanne H (2011) Biometric identification paradigm: towards privacy and confidentiality protection. In: Nichols ER (ed) Biometrics: Theory, Applications, and Issues. Nova Science Publishers, New York

6. Bringer J, Despiegel V (2010) Binary feature vector fingerprint representation from minutiae vicinities. In: IEEE 4th International Conference on Biometrics: Theory, Applications, and Systems, BTAS'10

7. Bringer J, Chabanne H, Izabachène M, Pointcheval D, Tang Q, Zimmer S (2007) An application of the Goldwasser–Micali cryptosystem to biometric authentication. In: Pieprzyk J, Ghodosi H, Dawson E (eds) ACISP. Lecture Notes in Computer Science, vol 4586. Springer, Berlin, pp 96–106

8. Bringer J, Chabanne H, Pointcheval D, Tang Q (2007) Extended private information retrieval and its application in biometrics authentications. In: Bao F, Ling S, Okamoto T, Wang H, Xing C (eds) CANS. Lecture Notes in Computer Science, vol 4856. Springer, Berlin, pp 175–193

9. Bringer J, Chabanne H, Cohen G, Kindarji B, Zémor G (2008) Theoretical and practical boundaries of binary secure sketches. IEEE Transactions on Information Forensics and Security 3(4):673–683. doi:10.1109/TIFS.2008.2002937

10. Bringer J, Chabanne H, Kindarji B (2008) The best of both worlds: applying secure sketches to cancelable biometrics. Science of Computer Programming 74(1–2):43–51. doi:10.1016/j.scico.2008.09.016. Special issue on security and trust

11. Bringer J, Chabanne H, Pointcheval D, Zimmer S (2008) An application of the Boneh and Shacham group signature scheme to biometric authentication. In: IWSEC. Lecture Notes in Computer Science. Springer, Berlin

12. Bringer J, Chabanne H, Kevenaar TAM, Kindarji B (2009) Extending match-on-card to local biometric identification. In: Biometric ID Management and Multimodal Communication, BioID-Multicomm 2009. Lecture Notes in Computer Science, vol 5707

13. Bringer J, Chabanne H, Kindarji B (2009) Error-tolerant searchable encryption. In: International Conference on Communications

14. Bringer J, Chabanne H, Simoens K (2010) Blackbox security of biometrics. In: IIH-MSP

15. Bringer J, Chabanne H, Kindarji B (2011) Identification with encrypted biometric data. Journal Security and Communication Networks 4(5):548–562

16. Chen L, Li J (2010) Vlr group signatures with indisputable exculpability and efficient revocation. In: Elmagarmid AK, Agrawal D (eds) SocialCom/PASSAT. IEEE Computer Society, Los Alamitos, pp 727–734

17. Chen C, Veldhuis RNJ (2009) Binary biometric representation through pairwise polar quantization. In: Tistarelli M, Nixon MS (eds) ICB. Lecture Notes in Computer Science, vol 5558. Springer, Berlin, pp 72–81

18. Delvaux N, Chabanne H, Bringer J, Kindarji B, Lindeberg P, Midgren J, Breebaart J, Akkermans T, van der Veen M, Veldhuis R, Kindt E, Simoens K, Busch C, Bours P, Gafurov D, Yang B, Stern J, Rust C, Cucinelli B, Skepastianos D (2008) Pseudo identities based on fingerprint characteristics. In: International Conference on Intelligent Information Hiding and Multimedia Signal Processing, IIHMSP'08, pp 1063–1068. http://doi.ieeecomputersociety.org/10.1109/IIH-MSP.2008.327

19. Draper S, Yedidia J, Draper SC, Khisti A, Khisti A, Martinian E, Martinian E, Vetro A, Vetro A, Yedidia JS (2007) Using distributed source coding to secure fingerprint biometrics. In: Int Conf Acoustics Speech Signal Proc, pp 129–132

20. Failla P, Sutcu Y, Barni M (2010) Esketch: a privacy-preserving fuzzy commitment scheme for authentication using encrypted biometrics. In: ACM MMSec'10,

21. Farooq F, Bolle RM, Jea TY, Ratha NK (2007) Anonymous and revocable fingerprint recognition. In: CVPR. IEEE Computer Society, Los Alamitos

22. ISO/IEC 19794-2:2005 (2005) Information technology, biometric data interchange formats, part 2: finger minutiae data. Tech rep, ISO/IEC

23. Jain AK, Prabhakar S, Hong L, Pankanti S (1999) Fingercode: a filterbank for fingerprint representation and matching. In: CVPR. IEEE Computer Society, Los Alamitos, p 2187

24. Maio D, Maltoni D, Cappelli R, Wayman JL, Jain AK (2002) FVC2000: fingerprint verification competition. IEEE Transactions on Pattern Analysis and Machine Intelligence 24(3):402–412

25. Maio D, Maltoni D, Cappelli R, Wayman JL, Jain AK (2002) FVC2002: second fingerprint verification competition. International Conference on Pattern Recognition 3:30811. doi: 10.1109/ICPR.2002.1048144
26. Nagar A, Rane S, Vetro A (2010) Alignment and bit extraction for secure fingerprint biometrics. In: SPIE Conference on Electronic Imaging 2010
27. National Institute of Standards and Technology (NIST): MINEX II—an assessment of match-on-card technology. http://fingerprint.nist.gov/minex/
28. Raimondo MD, Barni M, Catalano D, Labati RD, Failla P, Bianchi T, Fiore D, Lazzeretti R, Piuri V, Scotti F, Piva A (2010) Privacy-preserving fingercode authentication. In: ACM MMSec'10
29. Simoens K, Tuyls P, Preneel B (2009) Privacy weaknesses in biometric sketches. In: 2009 30th IEEE Symposium on Security and Privacy, pp 188–203. doi:10.1109/SP.2009.24
30. Stoianov A (2010) Cryptographically Secure Biometric. SPIE Biometric Technology for Human Identification VII, vol 7667
31. Tuyls P, Akkermans AHM, Kevenaar TAM, Schrijen GJ, Bazen AM, Veldhuis RNJ (2005) Practical biometric authentication with template protection. In: Kanade T, Jain AK, Ratha NK (eds) AVBPA. Lecture Notes in Computer Science, vol 3546. Springer, Berlin, pp 436–446
32. Xu H, Veldhuis RN, Kevenaar TA, Akkermans AH, Bazen AM (2008) Spectral minutiae: a fixed-length representation of a minutiae set. In: Computer Vision and Pattern Recognition Workshop, pp 1–6. http://doi.ieeecomputersociety.org/10.1109/CVPRW.2008.4563120
33. Yang B, Busch C, Bours P, Gafurov D (2010) Robust Minutiae Hash for Fingerprint Template Protection. SPIE, Bellingham. doi:10.1117/12.838998. http://link.aip.org/link/?PSI/7541/75410R/1

Chapter 12
Standards for Biometric Data Protection

Catherine J. Tilton and Matthew Young

Abstract This chapter discusses biometric data protection from the perspective of standardization. It covers technical standards developed at ISO (e.g., SC27, SC37, and TC68) and other standards development organizations as well as technical reports developed by these groups. In addition to those that address the confidentiality and integrity of biometric/identity data directly, other standards covering security of biometric systems in general are discussed.

12.1 Introduction

Outside of the law enforcement community, the use of biometrics is considered relatively new. However, the development of related technical standards began fairly soon after the technology began use within civil and commercial applications. Interestingly, work on standards related to the security of biometric data and systems began about the same time as those related to interoperability, underscoring the importance of security and privacy considerations to the biometric community and its users.

Standards are developed within formal (national and international) and informal (e.g., consortia) organizations. Many of the biometric security standards that began at the informal level soon migrated into the formal standards development organizations (SDOs). In particular, the International Organization for Standardization (ISO) has played a major role, especially since the establishment of ISO/IEC JTC1 SC37 (Subcommittee on Biometrics) was formed in 2002. But even before that, work was in progress and some standards had been published.

At the international level, a number of groups are involved in biometric standardization. These are depicted in Fig. 12.1.

C.J. Tilton
Daon, 11955 Freedom Drive, Suite 16000, Reston, VA 20190, USA

M. Young
Booz Allen Hamilton, Sotera Defense Solutions, 2121 Cooperative Way, Suite 400, Herndon, VA 20171, USA

P. Campisi (ed.), *Security and Privacy in Biometrics*,
DOI 10.1007/978-1-4471-5230-9_12, © Springer-Verlag London 2013

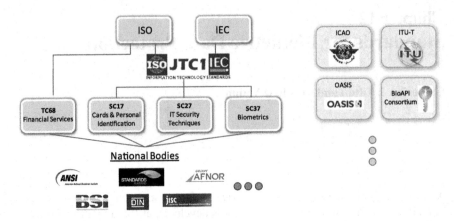

Fig. 12.1 Organizations involved in biometric standards

Within these organizations, three have made major contributions towards biometric security standards:

- ISO TC 68, *Financial Services*
- ISO/IEC JTC1 SC37, *Biometrics*
- ISO/IEC JTC1 SC27, *IT Security Techniques*

Joint Technical Committee (JTC) 1 is a joint committee of ISO and the International Electrotechnical Commission (IEC) that is responsible for the development of international standards in the realm of information and communication technologies (ICT). It manages 18 subcommittees which together have published over 2000 ISO standards since its establishment in 1987.

Standards on this topic generally fall into one of the following categories:

- Protection of biometric data itself
- Security of biometric systems and transactions
- Security evaluation

These are addressed in further detail in the following sections. As standards are continuously evolving, both published standards and those in progress are described.

12.2 Standards Developed by the Financial Services Community

Biometrics have been used in the financial sector for a variety of purposes—both in the "back office" by staff (for network and application login, single sign-on, supervisor overrides, etc.) and in customer facing applications such as check cashing, safe deposit box access, transactions at "virtual branches," and even online banking. Account holder authentication and transaction security are important in the financial world, so it is not surprising that the security aspects of biometrics would be of interest to this group.

12.2.1 ANSI X9.84

One of the first standards to address biometric data protection was developed in the US by the American National Standards Institute (ANSI) Accredited Standards Committee (ASC) X9, Financial Industry Standards [1]. In 2001, they published (and in 2010 revised) ANSI X9.84, *"Biometric Information Management and Security for the Financial Services Industry."* [2]

The scope of X9.84 includes:

- Security for the collection, distribution, and processing of biometric data, encompassing data integrity, authenticity, and non-repudiation.
- Management of biometric data across its life cycle comprised of the enrollment, transmission and storage, verification, identification, and termination processes.
- Usage of biometric technology, including one-to-one and one-to-many matching, for the identification and authentication of banking customers and employees.
- Application of biometric technology for internal and external, as well as logical and physical, access control.
- Encapsulation of biometric data.
- Techniques for the secure transmission and storage of biometric data.
- Security of the physical hardware used throughout the biometric data life cycle.
- Techniques for integrity and privacy protection of biometric data.

The philosophy of X9.84 is that since biometrics are not generally considered "secrets", any system utilizing them cannot depend upon their secrecy for their security; however, confidentiality is still important for privacy protection. Instead, there is a greater emphasis placed on integrity of the biometric data.

In addition to providing an overview and architectural framework for biometric systems, X9.84 provides a set of management and security requirements. Core requirements for applications/environments using biometric information are the use of cryptographic mechanisms and physical protection to:

1. Maintain the integrity of biometric data and matching results between any two components
2. Mutually authenticate the source and destination of biometric data and matching results, and
3. If desired, ensure the confidentiality of the biometric data between any two components and within any single component.

Additional requirements are specified for enrollment, verification, identification, transmission and storage, termination, archiving, and audit. Specific security techniques are also specified and an annex describes potential attacks and countermeasures. Annex F delineates control objectives against which a given implementation can be audited for compliance.

X9.84 defines a biometric object which is conformant to the Common Biometric Exchange Formats Framework (CBEFF) (see SC37 standards, below). This object is encoded in Abstract Syntax Notation (ASN.1) [3] and has different levels of integrity and privacy protections available—none, privacy only, integrity only, and privacy and integrity. Figure 12.2 shows the last of these four options.

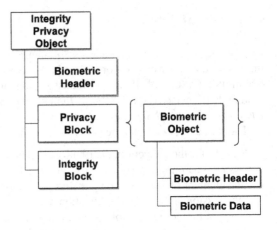

Fig. 12.2 X9.84 biometric object with privacy and integrity protections

The privacy block contains an encrypted biometric object along with the associated encryption information (e.g., algorithm, key length). The integrity block contains integrity/authenticity data such as a digital signature or message authentication code (MAC). Four different cryptologic message syntax (CMS) options are specified for each block.

12.2.2 ISO 19092

Subsequent to the publication in the US of X9.84, ISO Technical Committee 68 (TC68) undertook an international standard based upon it, but broken into initially two parts—a security framework and a message syntax. In 2008, the first part was published (ISO 19092:2008, Financial Services—Biometrics—Security framework) [4]. This part is very similar to X9.84; however, it deviates in some specifics. For example, X9.84 set a maximum verification false match rate of 10^{-4} and a maximum false non-match rate of 10^{-2}; however, ISO 19092 did not set a specific false match rate requirement.

The second part, planned to be entitled "Part 2: Message syntax and cryptographic requirements," was not completed.

12.3 Standards Developed in SC37 and Their Application

In the wake of the tragic events of 9/11, biometric technology was looked to as a potential tool to improve national security. However, to do so effectively would require that standards exist to provide needed interoperability. But outside law enforcement, few biometric standards existed. Therefore, in June of 2002, ISO approved the establishment of a new subcommittee on biometrics under JTC1. This new subcommittee first met in December of 2002 with 17 countries participating.

By early 2013, ISO/IEC JTC1 SC37 had published 52 biometric standards and technical reports in the areas of vocabulary, technical interfaces, data interchange formats, performance testing, and societal considerations. Its scope excluded work under the purview of other JTC1 subcommittees, such as SC17 (smart cards) and SC27 (IT security techniques); however, security and privacy are by necessity a consideration within more generic areas. As a result, several of the SC37 standards include such provisions. It is worth noting that SC37 and SC27 (addressed in next section) have a close liaison relationship and cooperate on standards that contain both biometric and security components.

12.3.1 ISO/IEC 19785—CBEFF

The Common Biometric Exchange Formats Framework (CBEFF) is a multi-part standard that defines a common structure and metadata elements for exchanging biometric data [5]. This standard was conceived in 1999 as the result of a workshop sponsored by the National Institute for Standards and Technology (NIST) in the US. It then progressed as a national standard (ANSI INCITS 398) and in 2006 became an international standard eventually consisting of four parts:

Information Technology—Biometrics—Common Biometric Formats Framework:

- Part 1: Data element specification (ISO/IEC 19785-1:2006)
- Part 2: Procedures for the operation of the Biometric Registration Authority (ISO/IEC 19785-2:2006)
- Part 3: Patron format specifications (ISO/IEC 19785-3:2007)
- Part 4: Security block format specifications (ISO/IEC 19785-4:2010)

The CBEFF structure is called a biometric information record (BIR) and consists of three parts as shown in Fig. 12.3.

The CBEFF header contains metadata describing the biometric data contained within the BDB; for example, the type (modality) of the data (e.g., fingerprint, iris), the date at which it was created, and an identifier of its format. Part 1 defines the mandatory and optional header elements, but does not prescribe its encoding—this is done by a "patron" specification, which specifies an implementation of CBEFF for a particular application domain. Some patron formats are provided in Part 3, however, others are defined independently from ISO.

Standard Biometric Header (SBH)	Biometric Data Block (BDB)	Security Block (SB)*

*Optional

Fig. 12.3 CBEFF BIR structure

The security block (SB) is an optional component that contains security information similar to that described for the X9.84 biometric object. If the BDB is encrypted, it may contain information related to how it was encrypted (e.g., encryption algorithm used, key length, key name). It may also contain information related to integrity and authenticity, such as a digital signature or MAC covering the SBH plus BDB. Part 4 specifies some security block formats, but others may be defined independently from ISO (i.e., by a given patron or implementation).

From a security and privacy perspective, the following CBEFF header elements are of interest:

- *Security options.* This mandatory element indicates if the BDB is signed, encrypted, or both.
- *Purpose.* This optional element identifies if the data contained in the BDB is intended for enrollment, verification, or identification.
- *Validity period.* This optional field allows a start and end date/time for which the BIR is valid.
- *Security block format.* This element is required whenever a security block is present and identifies the format of the content of the SB.

The use of the security options element and the security block are easily understood; however, that of the purpose element is perhaps less obvious. During enrollment, the biometric record that is produced may be identified in the purpose field as an enrollment record. If the BIR is signed, then that purpose cannot be subsequently changed without detection. Therefore, if the storage location is compromised and an attacker attempts to replay the disclosed enrollment BIR as a live sample during a verification (or identification) transaction, the verifier can check the header and discover that it is an enrollment rather than a verification record and deny access.

12.3.2 ISO/IEC 19795—Biometric Performance Testing

Unlike cryptographic algorithms, whose strength is openly validated through peer review; the strength of a biometric algorithm is generally evaluated through 3rd party black box performance testing. This testing assesses the accuracy of the algorithm in terms of error rates—false match and false non-match rates. However, a standard methodology is needed to ensure that such performance testing is conducted properly and that results are understandable, comparable, and statistically valid.

SC37 Working Group 5 (WG5) has developed a set of standards which provide such a methodology. As of early 2013 the ISO/IEC 19795 series [6] consisted of the following parts, with others in progress:

Information technology—Biometric performance testing and reporting:

- Part 1: Principles and framework (ISO/IEC 19795-1:2006)
- Part 2: Testing methodologies for technology and scenario evaluation (ISO/IEC 19795-2:2007)

- Part 3: Technical Report—Modality-specific testing (ISO/IEC TR 19795-3:2007)
- Part 4: Performance and interoperability testing of interchange formats (ISO/IEC 19795-4:2008)
- Part 5: Access control scenario and grading scheme (ISO/IEC 19795-5:2011)
- Part 6: Testing methodologies for operational evaluation
- Part 7: Testing of on-card biometric comparison algorithms (ISO/IEC 19795-7:2011)

These standard testing methodologies are applicable to biometric security evaluations defined in ISO/IEC 19792 (Security evaluation of biometrics—see SC27 section) and common criteria evaluation of biometric systems.

In addition to defining biometric performance metrics, some of the other areas addressed by ISO/IEC 19795 relate to data collection requirements, sample sizes, test conditions, analysis methods, and factors affecting performance.

12.3.3   ISO/IEC TR 24714—Societal Considerations

SC37 WG6 addresses considerations related to societal and cross-jurisdictional aspects of biometric systems. One of the primary areas of consideration is that of security and privacy. These are addressed in their first publication:

- ISO/IEC TR 24714-1:2008, Jurisdictional and societal considerations for commercial applications—Part 1: General guidance [7]

This technical report (which does not carry the weight of a standard) gives guidelines for the stages in the life cycle of a system's biometric and associated elements, covering data storage and security, system evaluation and audit, and legal and societal constraints on the use of biometric data, among others.

12.4   Standards Developed in SC27 and Their Application

ISO/IEC JTC1 SC27 handles standardization of IT Security Techniques. Formed in 1990, SC27 recently celebrated its 20th anniversary. As biometric technologies have matured, the need for biometric standards to incorporate security mechanisms has remained prominent. The relationship between biometrics and security has many aspects, including protection of biometric data during transmission and storage, evaluating security threats of a biometric system, and the role of biometrics as an authentication mechanism in support of larger identity management systems. Since SC37 was formed in 2002, a spirit of collaboration has existed between the two subcommittees through liaison relationships, cross membership, and similar awareness of industry needs. The following lists SC27 standards projects which have either been published as international standards (IS), or are currently in development, and which have relevance to biometric technologies.

Published:

- ISO/IEC 19792:2009—Security evaluation of biometrics
- ISO/IEC 24761:2009—Authentication context for biometrics (ACBio)
- ISO/IEC 24745:2011—Biometric information protection
- ISO/IEC 24760:2011—Framework for Identity Management
- ISO/IEC 29115:2013—Entity Authentication Assurance Framework

In Development:

- ISO/IEC 29101—Privacy Architecture Framework
- ISO/IEC 29146—A Framework for Access Management

12.4.1 ISO/IEC 19792:2009—Security Evaluation of Biometrics

ISO/IEC 19792 [8] provides a comprehensive approach to evaluating the security aspects of biometric systems; however, it is generic enough to apply to a range of environments. This standard does not define strict requirements for how security must be implemented for biometric systems, but rather provides a general methodology and considerations for both developers and evaluators when assessing the vulnerabilities of a biometric system. This standard maintains a strong tie to the work being performed by SC37 WG5 (Biometric Testing and Reporting) and ISO/IEC 19795, Part 1 in particular (see SC37 standards, above), which it normatively references. Though not tied to a particular certification scheme, it is compatible with the common criteria of ISO/IEC 15408 [9].

The purpose of this standard is to both educate the reader on biometric terms as they relate to security and also to provide known areas to be evaluated. In particular, the document describes an evaluation based on the following three concepts:

- Measurement of Statistical Error Rates
- Biometric Specific Vulnerabilities
- Privacy

Matching (comparison) of biometric data is an inherently probabilistic process which involves error rates. Knowledge of these error rates and their relation to overall system security (strength of function) is an important element of an evaluation. The statistical error rates section of the standard poses questions, considerations, and approaches to be used in the evaluation process.

Biometric systems exhibit unique vulnerabilities not found in other authentication mechanisms because of the nature of the processes and subsystems involved with performing biometric comparisons. The vulnerabilities section of the standard provides a description of common biometric vulnerabilities, ways to assess each particular vulnerability, and countermeasures to mitigate the vulnerability. The list is not meant to be holistic, but does provide a baseline of those vulnerabilities known to the community.

Privacy is a topic which draws considerable attention when discussed in the context of biometrics. The close association of one's biometric data to their own individual identity naturally raises privacy concerns with biometric systems. Environments which call for biometric data to be transmitted, stored and processed by external parties further exacerbate these concerns. The privacy section of the standard focuses on reducing the risk of inappropriate data handling, as well as procedures which could be implemented and evaluated should data compromise occur.

This international standard was one of the first to focus on broader aspects in security of biometric systems and is a good primer for additional work in the field. Many of the other projects discussed in this section relate in some way to ISO/IEC 19792.

12.4.2 ISO/IEC 24761:2009—ACBio

ISO/IEC 24761 [10] provides a solution for validating the integrity and authenticity of biometric data during transmission, processing, and storage as part of the biometric system process/lifecycle. The scope of ACBio incorporates the enrollment and verification biometric system processes when either (or both) is performed in a remote environment. The remote transmission scenario involves the biometric data being sent over an untrusted network such as the Internet, thus introducing the potential for malicious activity which may compromise the integrity of the biometric data. The intent of ACBio is to protect the biometric system against the alteration of the data from its originally intended purpose as presented by a valid system user. Such threats include manipulation of the data, insertion of imposter data, or replay of data by a source not associated with the current transaction. This standard is not meant to protect against threats related to the confidentially or availability of the biometric data in the system, so privacy concerns related to data leakage or exposure of data to unintended parties are not within scope. (However, other standards such as ISO/IEC 24745 do apply—see next section).

The title, "Authentication context for biometrics," is derived from the fact that ACBio appends contextual security information about the biometric data as it is being transmitted and processed through each step of both the enrollment and verification processes. In relation to an ACBio environment, the following sub processes are identified and covered in the standard.

- *Data Capture*—The entry point into the system where the initial raw biometric data is collected and packaged for processing.
- *Intermediate Signal Processing*—The initial signal processing includes normalization of the biometric data so that all data captured can be adequately transformed in a common way.
- *Final Signal Processing*—The final signal processing involves transforming the data into the biometric reference format for storage and comparison.
- *Storage*—After the biometric reference is created during enrollment, it is stored in the database for use later in biometric data comparisons.

- *Comparison* (verification only)—Using the stored enrolled biometric reference and the acquired verification biometric sample as inputs, the comparison sub process performs a determination of similarity.
- *Decision* (verification only)—Based on the similarly score of the comparison sub process, an overall matching decision is made.

As the biometric data progresses through the enrollment or verification processes, the system generates and stores several pieces of data at each of the sub processes. This data is packed into one ACBio instance from the capture to the decision transaction. Of particular importance is the cryptographic signature which is generated by the biometric processing unit (BPU), the entity that performs the sub process, and which is subsequently stored with the ACBio instance. These signature values are eventually used by the validator to determine whether or not the biometric data was altered from the time it was first captured until the time it was used for decision purposes. If the cryptographic signatures from the sub processes prove to be authentic, then the integrity of the biometric data is trustworthy. If the cryptographic signatures from the sub processes prove to not be authentic, then the integrity of the biometric data cannot be trusted. Ultimately, ACBio provides another piece of information to the overall decision making ability of the biometric system. A degree of trust in the integrity of the biometric data can aid in the final identity determination produced by the system.

12.4.3 ISO/IEC 24745:2011—Biometric Information Protection

When initiated, ISO/IEC 24745 [11] was originally titled "Biometric Template Protection," with the scope focused primarily on biometric templates (only a small subset of biometric information). Since that time, the project has evolved to cover broader biometric information concepts including biometric system application models, secure storage of biometric references and comparisons, and guidance on the protection of an individual's privacy.

The project blends together some concepts of both ISO/IEC 19792 and ISO/IEC 24761 (described above); however, its scope is slightly different from that of these other two standards. While ISO/IEC 19792 is focused on overall threats and countermeasures for biometric systems and ACBio is focused on integrity of biometric data, ISO/IEC 24745 adds protections for the confidentially as well as the "renewability" of the biometric data. Thus, although the project discusses the vulnerability and threats related to biometric systems, it provides more detailed guidance on countermeasures in order to meet specific security requirements related to all three areas of integrity, confidentially, and renewability.

ISO/IEC 24745 makes a distinction between an identity reference (IR) and a biometric reference (BR). An example of an identity reference would be a name, social security number and/or driver license's number; whereas a biometric reference example would be a fingerprint image, face image and/or finger minutia data. This allows the standard to be applied to scenarios where the IR and BR are either

Fig. 12.4 Segregated storage
system

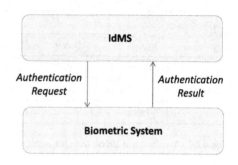

Fig. 12.4 Segregated storage
system

co-located in the same data storage subsystem, or stored in separate data storage subsystems. A co-located system may be self-contained to reduce processing time through limited data transfer. On the other hand, some systems appreciate segregation of duties between the identity management system (IdMS), which makes an authentication request, and the biometric system, which delivers the authentication result, as shown in Fig. 12.4. It is worth noting that ISO/IEC 24760—"Framework for Identity Management" [12], discussed later in this chapter, goes into further detail on identity management. In both co-located and separate storage scenarios, this standard describes protection requirements for the IR and BR in terms of encryption as it relates to the three security aspects mentioned previously (integrity, confidentially, and renewability/revocability).

This standard discusses privacy of biometric data from a proactive perspective to prevent personally identifiable information (PII) from being compromised. Cryptographically binding the IR and the BR can produce a range of privacy benefits including the characteristics of irreversibility, unlinkability, and confidentially. Other privacy related topics covered include regulatory and policy requirements, biometric information lifecycle, privacy management, and responsibilities of a biometric system owner.

A "renewable" biometric reference (RBR) in this standard is a "revocable/renewable identifier that represents an individual or data subject within a certain domain by means of a protected binary identity (re)constructed from the captured biometric sample." [11] It consists of two data elements—a pseudonymous identifier (PI) and corresponding auxiliary data (AD). The original biometric reference data is discarded and comparison is done between the stored PI and PI', the latter calculated from the probe biometric data and the AD.

When a comparison of a collected biometric sample and a biometric reference (stored during biometric enrollment) is performed, two key factors are the storage location of the biometric reference and the matching location where the comparison is performed. These alternatives in the application model of the biometric system are a driving force for how the biometric information needs to be protected. ISO/IEC 24745 outlines requirements for the following eight scenarios in Fig. 12.5 below.

Other work, such as the Ad Hoc Group on Biometrics and E-Authentication (AHGBEA), cited by this standard, has taken similar approaches to assessing security for the most common storage and comparison locations [13].

		Storage			
		Server	Client	Token	Distributed
Comparison	Server	A		B	G
	Client	C	D	E	H
	Token			F	

Fig. 12.5 Architectural alternatives for storage and matching locations

12.4.4 ISO/IEC 24760—Framework for Identity Management

ISO/IEC 24760-1:2011. Part 1: Terminology and concepts [15] includes a handful of references to biometrics as they relate to Identity Management (IdM). First and foremost, biometrics can be a valuable technique during the identity proofing stage of enrollment. Performing biometric uniqueness checks on the identity being enrolled in the system can greatly reduce the chance of a false or duplicate identity being created in the system. Subsequently, biometric data can be enrolled into the system as an identity attribute and used as an authentication mechanism to verify the identity in the future. Part 2: Reference architecture and requirements as well as Part 3: Practice are both currently under development.

12.4.5 ISO/IEC 29115—Entity Authentication Assurance Framework

ISO/IEC 29115:2013 [16] was jointly developed between ISO/IEC JTC1 SC27 and the International Telecommunication Union (ITU-T). The purpose of the project is to define requirements for entity authentication assurance in a given context. An entity in the scope of this work can be generalized as either an individual system user or a computing device. To do this, the project outlines four levels of authentication assurance from low to very high. These levels of assurance are then mapped to use case scenarios based on risk. Higher risk scenarios require a higher level of assurance to be satisfied. Naturally, biometric authentication is not possible when computing devices are authenticating to each other.

In the context of this project, biometric authentication is acceptable at level 3 (high) and level 4 (very high) for authentication of system users. At both assurance levels, biometric authentication can be used as a means of activating a credential. For instance, a user could use a biometric trait to authenticate him/herself as the valid user of a cryptographic certificate, which would then be recognized as the authentication credential. Therefore, biometric authentication as a standalone form of authentication is not acceptable at any level. However, during the enrollment stage, biometric data can be used for identity proofing (as also addressed in ISO/IEC

29146, above). These authentication levels and restriction on the use of biometrics is quite similar to that of NIST SP 800-63, *Electric Authentication Guidelines* [17].

12.4.6 ISO/IEC 29101—Privacy Architecture Framework

ISO/IEC 29101 [14] is currently (early 2013) a Final Draft International Standard (FDIS) stage project within SC27 which makes mention of biometric encryption as one method to secure data, access control, storage and processing. Biometric encryption differs from other biometric operations in that the collected biometric sample itself is not stored in the database. Alternatively, a code or other secretive value encrypted by the biometric sample is stored in the database. The biometric sample itself acts as the encryption key in this scenario, ideally with only the person who processes the biometric sample being able to decrypt the code or other secret value stored in the database. Therefore, the identifying features of the biometric data are still useful, while the privacy concerns of storing biometric information in a central database are diminished. This can be considered as one type of renewable biometric reference cited in ISO/IEC 24745 (above).

12.4.7 ISO/IEC 29146—A Framework for Access Management

ISO/IEC 29146 [15] is currently (early 2013) a project under development that includes biometric authentication as an acceptable form of authentication. Biometric data does not play a large role in traditional access management, which includes access privileges and the levels of access to information (authorization). However, biometric characteristics are a valuable mechanism for authentication, which in most cases is a process performed prior to granting privileges to the requesting entity. Due to the unique properties of biometric data, the resulting level of confidence for a biometric authentication may influence the business rules associated with the access privileges granted following authentication.

12.5 Conclusion

Unlike even a few years ago, a number of standards exist related to biometric data protection and biometric system security, and others are in progress. Those described above provide valuable guidance on security and privacy approaches that can be implemented within biometrically enabled systems. Practitioners should review such standards to determine which best fit within their architecture and concept of operations and which meet their overall security/privacy goals and requirements.

References

1. ANSI ASC X9. www.x9.org
2. ANSI X9.84:2010. Biometric information management and security for the financial services industry
3. ASN.1 ISO/IEC 8824:2001 (All parts) | ITU-T recommendation X.680:3 (2000) Information technology—abstract syntax notation one (ASN.1)
4. ISO 19092:2008. Financial services—biometrics—security framework
5. ISO/IEC 19785. Information technology—biometrics—common biometric formats framework (CBEFF)
6. ISO/IEC 19795. Information technology—biometric performance testing and reporting
7. ISO/IEC TR 24714-1:2008. Information technology—biometrics—jurisdictional and societal considerations for commercial applications—part 1: general guidance
8. ISO/IEC 19792:2009. Information technology—security techniques security evaluation of biometrics
9. ISO/IEC 15408. Information technology—security techniques—evaluation criteria for IT security
10. ISO/IEC 24761:2009. Information technology—security techniques—authentication context for biometrics (ACBio)
11. ISO/IEC 24745:2011. Information technology—security techniques—biometric information protection
12. ISO/IEC FDIS 24760. Information technology—security techniques—framework for identity management
13. InterNational Committee for Information Technology Standards (INCITS) Technical committee M1 (biometrics). Study report on biometrics in e-authentication, INCITS M1/07-0185rev, 30 March 2007. http://www.incits.org/tc_home/m1htm/m1070185rev.pdf
14. ISO/IEC CD3 29101. Information technology—security techniques—privacy reference architecture
15. ISO/IEC WD5 29146. Information technology—security techniques—a framework for access management
16. ISO/IEC CD3 29115. Information technology—security techniques—entity authentication assurance framework
17. NIST SP800-63-2. Electric authentication guidelines, 1 February 2013. http://csrc.nist.gov/publications/drafts/800-63-2/sp800_63_2_draft.pdf

Chapter 13
Nameless and Faceless: The Role of Biometrics in Realising Quantum (In)security and (Un)accountability

Juliet Lodge

Abstract This chapter explores the contradictions between the claims that bio-metrics will boost security and prevent identity theft, and the growing evidence of how, as more biometric documents are introduced, there is increasing e-crime that threatens personal identity and security, and collective security in the e-spaces of egovernment and personal life. It considers the impact on and ethical implications for society of widening biometric applications to daily life; and for those responsible for ensuring security and accountability as traditional controls are eroded. It concludes with a series of suggestions for avoiding dystopia.

'Though all the new technologies will make their mark on the new society, the information technologies will cause upheaval and completely transform it.'

European Parliament Working Document A2-109/85/B (30 Sept 1985)

'The European Council and the Council have … repeatedly underlined the importance of using biometrics in databases and travel documents to enhance the level of security of the European Union.'

Commission of the European Communities, COM(2008) 69 final (13 Feb 2008)

Biometrics are a feature of communication technologies (ICTs). Their disproportionate use and the lax and arbitrary way in which they are defined and implemented endangers values, norms and practices central to accepted conceptions in the EU27 of transparency, accountability, legitimacy, data protection and data privacy. Concern over the indiscriminate and growing use of biometrics for increasingly mundane and imprecise purposes results in a breach of the earlier intention to ensure their proportionate deployment based on the principle of necessity. Deviation from this is now justified by reference to loose arguments about the alleged 'certainty' that biometric identifiers bring to cutting risk and so enhancing 'security', however that is defined.

J. Lodge (✉)
AIMTECH, University of Leeds, Leeds, UK
e-mail: J.E.Lodge@leeds.ac.uk

P. Campisi (ed.), *Security and Privacy in Biometrics*,
DOI 10.1007/978-1-4471-5230-9_13, © Springer-Verlag London 2013

This chapter will examine first contradictions in public policy making that multiply as biometric applications are more widely adopted, often in the name of either enhancing territorial and personal security, or boosting access to services at a time and place that are personally convenient and independent of physical location. It will then illustrate how quantum (in)security and public (un)accountability arise. It concludes with reflections on new questions and limits arising from new technological applications of biometrics for our understanding of responsibility, consent, trust and control.

13.1 Introduction

There are at least five underlying problems in over-optimistic and unwarranted 'trust' in biometric technologies (ICTs) especially in relation to scalability issues when an application developed for small group use is applied at large scale. The first problem is that reliance on assumed technological 'certainty' encourages groupthink and reliance on automated decisionmaking that potentially exacerbate rather than cut risks. The second is that what I call 'quantum surveillance' is inevitable given the tendency to interpret all manner of things—behaviour, movement, online activity, relations, associational links and emotion, as a 'biometric': and, as such, *a signifier of intent*. The third is that baked-in privacy by design and smart data functionalities to ensure that the ICTs themselves safeguard and only reveal what the data subject permits on the basis of 'informed consent' are not being introduced swiftly or securely enough, and may even be too little too late. The fourth is that cost and efficiency criteria coupled with ignorance of the potential and limits of ICTs leads those responsible for public procurement to rely on private industry and vested interests sometimes to the detriment of society, the public purse and democratic accountability. Finally, the transformational impact of biometrics on society and governance proceeds without sufficient ethical, socio-legal or political control and public accountability.

13.2 Contradictory Trajectories

The starting point is the assumption traditionally made regarding relationships of trust between the governed and governors in polities: governors are expected to deliver security (historically conceived of as territorial security) in exchange for the loyalty of their citizens. This has been regulated by different political systems over time. Our concern is with trust and security mechanisms that evade traditional political oversight, escaping democratic controls that we take for granted and which require us to reconsider the 'democratic bargain' we take for granted. New technological advances may inspire and encourage us to trust science to deliver a better society and improved well-being. How they are applied, however, may equally demand a reappraisal of our understanding of trust, accountability and the credibility of the legitimate exercise of control by political rulers. This will be examined through the prism of biometrics.

Biometrics have a strong transformative potential precisely because technological applications (i) allow them to be used in ways that permit machines to 'decide' in place of human beings, albeit taking decisions based on algorithms devised by human beings according to the prevailing arbitrary and contextually contingent requirements of the day, (ii) illustrate the power of a digital token of identity to challenge the meaning of 'identity' and all policy decisions derived from a particular sorting of a given digitised biometric 'pseudo-identity' that can be linked with a variable degree of accuracy to a source physical being, and to both the 'real' me and the 'virtual' me(s) (as in key-stroke dynamics); and, more disturbingly, (iii) provide a means of removing responsibility for individual action (as in the case of mal-functioning implants or deep brain stimulation) and (iv) qualify, segment and erode accountability. The questions: 'who's in control' and 'what is a biometric' have never been more contingent than they are now. Why?

Innovative technologies and scientific invention are not only ubiquitous and embedded but increasingly so is the human-machine interface. The ability of robots to mimic, determine, substitute for aspects of human intervention grow. Genomics, deep brain stimulation and implants open new vistas for human achievement, both therapeutic and arguably arbitrary. As the 'border' between man and machine becomes increasingly invisible, the locus of decisionmaking becomes increasingly fuzzy, imperceptible: sub-optimum decisionmaking is inevitable and, this chapter argues, the unintended consequences are quantum (in)security and (un)accountability.

These consequences are all the more likely, the more automated decisionmaking becomes the norm. Automation in specific settings, such as border controls, access to services and goods and so on is necessarily based on discrimination and profiling derived from either an 'old' hard' or 'new soft' biometric and rests on technical means to permit or prohibit access. The easy assumption made is that machines 'decide' on a neutral basis. Insufficient regard is had to the underlying premises that informed the kind of algorithm behind the 'decision' to sort and discriminate. Real-time decisionmaking, informed by contemporary, carefully evaluated accurate information is within the reach of robots (witness their complementary use in surgery). If this is transferable in principle to other settings, do the new biometrics help to lever greater efficiency, convenience, and accuracy, and do they simultaneously lower risk? How can appropriate levels of accountability be ensured or is accountability an obsolete concept today?

13.3 Risky New Biometrics

This chapter focuses on the expanding conceptualisation of a biometric and the mission creep associated with redefining biometrics beyond the algorithmic representation of a more or less static and unique physical feature of a person (a fingerprint, vein image or iris print 'identity'). The EU originally defined a biometric as a mathematical digitised characteristic unique to an individual: something that could be used to increase the probability of a genuine link between the 'biometric' and the individual. The US Homeland Security agenda, however, went beyond this to include the notion of individual 'behaviour'. Behaviour is a loose and socio-politically contingent concept.

Defining a certain type of 'behaviour' as deviant or indicative of 'risky intent' (which is the purpose of including it within the umbrella of a 'biometric') leaves all behaviour subject to arbitrary interpretation, political vagaries, and politico-ideological preferences and goals of those in power (whether they are legitimate, elected and accountable governments or automated machines). This is highly risky. Riskiness is heightened moreover by the more recent trend to include within the term 'biometric' any 'behaviour' or 'emotion' that can be captured and digitised—from brain imaging to hypertension, 'liveness tests', face dynamics, psychological states, level of arousal (fear, anxiety, intent), and body cells, fluid or traces (such as DNA, and brain imaging for forensics in crime detection), eye movement in crowds and 'abnormal' body temperature.

A possibly false sense of security in a biometric identity is inferred from the claim that biometrics provide the most reliable document authenticating mechanism and most reliable means of verifying identity and facilitating automated profiling. Combined in MRTDs, and used against watch lists and other data bases, they are seen to be the most reliable means of detecting links between a person and a claimed identity (a concept that is contingent, context dependent and varies over time), and combat fraudulent multiple IDs. The notion of the infallibility of a biometric is risky, over-simplistic and compromises individual and collective security primarily because a biometric is used as a tool for realising other purposes. Simplistic claims jeopardise legitimate use for the primary purpose.[1]

The relatively high spoof potential of first generation biometrics partly accounts for interest among border security agencies in multi-modal biometrics, including anticipatory gestures, para-linguistics and thermal imaging. But the EU's requirement is for travel documents by 2019 to hold two first generation biometrics. So the biometric key to quantum surveillance is embedded in compulsory enrolment of a given biometric in a machine readable travel document to allow people to cross borders: passports, visas, and travel documents.

The biometric has the potential to facilitate quantum surveillance not because of its intrinsic quality but because of how it can be used or abused in systems that are inter-operable (once of the major drivers behind biometric e-identity cards), where automated exchange of information can proceed across agencies and borders, and where data can be remotely accessed and linked up in ways that are invisible to the data subject, not under his control, commodified, mined, sold and mashed without his consent. The primary purpose for the use of biometrics in territorial border

---

[1] See Agreement between the European Union and the United States of America on the processing and transfer of Financial Messaging Data from the European Union to the United States for purposes of the Terrorist Finance Tracking Programme, OJ L8 13 January 2010, p. 9.

controls is to identify and apprehend false documents and authenticate a traveller as genuine; in ecommerce and other e-card uses, the aim is broadly the same—to permit entry and access to goods and services. Biometrics have a role in reducing fraud and identity theft, but they are not a panacea.

13.3.1 Flexible Biometrics

A flexible definition of 'biometric' is a way to legitimising greater intrusion on private life, reducing the space where private human dignity can be preserved by the data subject, because a security rationale is prioritised over everything else. This is exemplified in airports where old and new biometrics and automated decision making can be portrayed as boosting traveller convenience and improving efficient travel experiences but equally intrude on human dignity (as in the case of the variably calibrated body scanner protecting male sensitivities more than female ones). The Pope before his 2010 visit to the UK[2] stressed the need to balance the dignity of the person and security imperatives. In October 2008, the first comprehensive Privacy Impact Assessment for Whole Body Imaging was published by the US Department of Homeland Security, and the UK Department of transport followed in late 2010.[3] Biometric scanners can be set to different levels of resolution for matching the biometric presented (for example fingerprint, or fingerprints for multiple applications or those for highly secure applications, either alone or with cryptology) to that stored on a travel document or data base. Different 'match levels' can be set for arbitrary reasons thereby subordinating a security rationale to a bureaucratic management imperative regardless of threat levels. Automated border controls are not infallible: a virus left 2,000 people stranded at the Sino-Russian border in April 2010. Risk can be aggravated by incompatibilities and by different quality and functional requirements.

The therapeutic uses of medical technology (such as magnetic resonance and brain imaging and scanning) are now presented as a 'biometric' that can be reapplied for use in 'security' arenas. Whole body imaging—body scanners (first developed in 1992)[4] provide a 'biometric measurement' of a person's physique. Body scanners are not universally used at EU entry and exit points: this results in discrim-

---

[2]Papal audience on 23 Feb 2010 to representatives of Ente Nazionale per l'Aviazione Civile Italiana (www.enac-italia.it) and Ente Nazionale per l'Assistenza al Volo (http://www.enav.it/portal/page/portal/PortaleENAV/Home) responsible for airport workers. http://212.77.1.245/news_services/bulletin/news/25164.php?index=25164&po_date=20.02.2010&lang=en.

[3]UK Department for Transport, *Interim Code of Practice for the Acceptable Use of Advanced Imaging Technology* (*Body Scanners*) *in an Aviation Security Environment*, London, 2010. http://www.dft.gov.uk/pgr/security/aviation/airport/.

[4]X-ray security screening system (The Secure 1000) was developed in 1992 and commercialised by RAPISCAN, http://www.dspguide.com/secure.htm.

ination within a state and across the EU. Moreover, the UK 2010 Code of Practice[5] prohibits the selection of passengers for security checks based on gender, race etc but this does not meet the generic criticism of discriminatory intent and impact. Profiling is the intent: technology and quantum surveillance the tool.

Rejected by the 2004-9 European Parliament as excessively intrusive on personal privacy, criticised as such by the British Information Commissioner, the body scanner discriminates among EU citizens from different states because each state decides locally on the type of equipment used at border posts. Refusal to use a scanner resulted in travellers not being allowed to travel, contrary to EU policy,[6] views from the Commission's consultation of the EDPS, Article 29 Working Party,[7] and Fundamental Rights Agency on their use. In October 2008, the first comprehensive Privacy Impact Assessment for Whole Body Imaging was published by the US Department of Homeland Security. In 2011, the EU Information Commissioner[8] belatedly underlined growing concern about the intrusive impact of biometric border controls, like scanners. Marking Data Protection Day, she said:

> In our external relations we should firmly promote fundamental rights including the right to privacy and protection of personal data. *The right to data protection should also be respected when performing simple operations like transferring money, booking a flight ticket or passing a security check at the airport.* Why should citizens have to reveal their personal information in order to prove that they have nothing to hide?

This illustrated that compartmentalised policymaking by governments inhibits cross-sectoral learning about biometrics and their pervasive applications; and this in turn aggravates arbitrary uses and justifications for using sometimes disproportionate tools. The arbitrariness surrounding biometric border controls, whether automated or manned, were exemplified by the epassport reader problems that led to long entry delays at a British airport: match-rates were lowered to accelerate processing even though this cut their reliability. Waiting times at automated border gates can be manipulated to 'encourage' passengers to use them instead of manned posts. Arbitrariness abounds, as does, therefore, the local perception of acceptable security risks. It would be unrealistic to suppose that similar arbitrariness would not be present in other e-card applications using very basic biometrics or multi-modal biometrics depending on the purpose and what the vendor might arbitrarily consider adequate security architectures and data handling procedures to protect data. If cctv

---

[5]UK Dept. for Transport, *Interim Code of Practice for the Acceptable Use of Advanced Imaging Technology (Body Scanners) in an Aviation Security Environment*, http://www.dft.gov.uk/pgr/security/aviation/airport/.

[6]TRAN/D/2008/57605, 26.09.2008. http://ec.europa.eu/transport/air/consultations/2009_02_19_body_scanners_en.htm; EP Hearings, Summary of hearing of Viviane Reding—Justice, fundamental rights and citizenship; Commission's Green Paper on detection technologies in the work of law enforcement, customs and other security authorities, COM(2006)474 final.

[7]http://ec.europa.eu/justicehome/fsj/privacy/indexen.htm;   http://ec.europa.eu/justice_home/fsj/privacy/workinggroup/wpdocs/2009-others_en.htm.

[8]http://europa.eu/rapid/pressReleasesAction.do?reference=SPEECH/10/16&format=HTML&aged=0&language=EN&guiLanguage=en.

footage is considered a biometric, especially for crime detection and prosecution, who mans and analyses the footage is a legitimate question: outsourcing this to private firms (many of whom are known to employ convicted criminals) raises serious ethical and politico-legal concerns.

There are legion questions and ethical concerns around accepting broad interpretations of the term 'biometric'. Above all, broad definitions of what constitutes a 'biometric' open the door to the remote and automated monitoring of all the activity of a person. Where legislation does not narrowly define a 'biometric', the temptation exists to include new biometrics without further regulation. This does not stop at intrusive monitoring of Internet use, key strokes, CCTV use in public spaces, Google Earth, the metaverse of avatars, voice patterns or crowd behaviour. Rather it facilitates and acclimatises publics to pervasive unaccountable surveillance by stealth that ultimately insecuritises individuals and society: quantum surveillance. This happens regardless of the safeguards of Article 8 ECHR, court rulings (as in the Marper case[9]) and data protection authorities' interventions.

Equally troubling is the associated discourse about the potential privatisation of online security: those who can afford to pay for higher levels would therefore be offered greater protection; and everyone should be reminded of a personal responsibility for protecting their data. Such an argument is disingenuous. The divisive implications for society are well-known. However, once more automated decision-making facilitated by the use of biometric e-tokens become more widespread across a range of activities, an additional consequence is de-responsibilisation of the individual for protecting data, using data responsibly, minimising and limiting the purpose of data collection and use, and securing consent for the proportionate enrolment, disclosure, time-limited storage of data. The more automated decisions occur by machines, in front of an individual data subject, or somewhere in the cloud, the more it is plausible to argue that blame for 'errors' lies with the ICTs rather than with a visible, identifiable person or authority who can be held accountable for mistakes and abuses. The therapeutic benefits are not at issue for the disabled and infirm of relying on a machine—which they may allow to act for them by supplying their biometric key, assuming they are physically able to do so. But responsibility for what happens next is highly problematic, especially in the event of machine error, failure or deliberate distortion.

The locus of accountability shifts not only in relation to context but also in relation to who or what acts and on the basis of whose instruction. Is a biometric freely enrolled and used for authentication, or used under duress (as in criminals forcing an owner to use his biometric for access controls to something they wish to appropriate), or without explicit consent, or without the subject's knowledge (as

---

[9]European Court of Human Rights (EctHR) *Case of S. and Marper versus the United Kingdom* Application nos. 30562/04, Strasbourg, 4 December 2008. See Equality and Human rights Commission (2009) The Equality and Human Rights Commission's response to the government's consultation on: Keeping the right people on the DNA database, London. Electronic Privacy Information Center (EPIC) (2003) *Biometric Identifiers* (EPIC: Washington, DC). www.epic.org/privacy/biometrics/.

in the case of multi-modal biometrics, ubiquitous data mining of web browsing, or cctv scanning of public and private spaces)? Identifying *who is responsible for what happens next* to the data subject (or his digital self) is far from easy, especially where data handling is outsourced, off-shored, privatised and re-outsourced in fuzzy public-private arrangements.

The problem is that this compounds anxiety over whether a biometric delivers the security gain—certainty in minimising risk—promised for it or denudes it of the unique capabilities initially attributed to it. Is the biometric risky or its deployment? Accepting a broad definition of biometrics to include behaviour and emotion opens the door to, and is the pre-condition, of a quantum surveillance state of commodified citizens. Biometrics per se are not problematic: their naïve use for diverse purposes is and raises serious ethical issues about their impact on society. Naive use of biometrics compromises claimed security objectives, inadvertently imperils citizens' rights, and does not necessarily boost either interoperability at the technical level, or politico-security goals at member state and EU level. Well-thought out ethical use of ubiquitous ICTs is imperative. Ubiquitous ICTs make governments, businesses and citizens more vulnerable than they realise to intrusion on their privacy, their data, and their 'identity' and compromise their ability to demonstrate their public accountability.

13.4 Eborders: The Door to Quantum Surveillance States of Commodified Citizens?

The epassport chip may or may not be readable remotely, and the biometric may be stored within it or separately in data bases that can be interrogated for other purposes—as in the case of the Netherlands where there was deep concern over its enrolment for the Dutch passport but its storage separately from passport data. The Dignotar row illustrated deep flaws. Similarly, Britain's 'shared secrets' National Identity Register is separate from the passport data but links to other data. Home Secretary Alan Johnson confirmed in January 2010 that the National Identity Register contains National Insurance numbers and answers to 'shared secrets' to 'aid identity verification checks for identity cards and, in time, passports' and welfare and tax databases.

Online tracking provides multi-purpose commercially valuable data not simply allowing RFID asset tracking and association (e.g. of laptops and persons, location data, permits to access them and so on) but about individuals that can be mined for indeterminate, sometimes, questionable and disproportionate purposes anywhere in the world. Identity matching software allows governments and organisations to search and match identity data from over sixty countries simultaneously in batch and real time in ways helpful to law enforcement and to commerce. However, the attendant growth of public-private partnerships and dependencies, near field communication and innovation create ever more difficult questions regarding the acceptability, legitimacy, reliability, safety and responsiveness of responsibility and accountability mechanisms, and of the enforceability of legal protection for citizens.

Mission creep is inevitable and unavoidable if the broad definition of a biometric is accepted and if the data subject has been obliged both to enrol a biometric (or not travel) and has lost (as we generally seem to have) the capacity and the right to retain control over data, and give informed consent for others to access 'biometric' data for whatever purposes. Informational self-determination may be a right under the EU data protection directive 95/46 but it is one that is not well-appreciated or invoked or usable by the majority of citizens. Similarly insufficient attention is paid to assessing and planning for strategic risks to multiple e-ID systems.

The quality of a biometric, how biometrics are enrolled, costs, technical equipment and local practices vary within and across the EU27. A fragmented approach to testing biometric components and systems compromises quality, and the predictive ability and reliability of given biometrics. Local practices vary greatly and undermine citizen equality. Enrolment practices differ and exacerbate problems of (un)reliability: imperfect enrolment and mistakes are notoriously hard to correct. Deterioration impairs verification. Fingerprint tampering has commercial potential, and the use of fake or altered fingerprints by people seeking entry to states occurs. Newer, less intrusive and/ or more mobile means of capturing biometrics, identity management and verifying identity include latest generation mobile phones. Ubiquitous computing, multi modal biometrics, smart and ambient intelligence applications will be become ever more invisible and a fact of life in metropolitan areas especially.

Technical problems still remain for interoperability and for individual devices. Mobile biometric scanners cannot (yet) be used effectively on biometric data enrolled in stationary environments. Pre-enrolled registered/trusted/frequent traveller arrangements to allow automated fast-track border crossing (such as the Privium iris recognition system at Schiphol airport and Gatwick's iris system) are not interoperable. However, cards using biometrics permit surveillance and sorting of various sorts and with varying degrees of potential intrusion on the privacy of the card holder even if his identity per se is not breached and even in the face of attempts to uphold the requirements of data protection authorities.[10] Balancing privacy and as secure as possible 'identities' remains problematic and contingent.

13.5 The Problem of Invisible Data Handlers and Undetectable Loci of Accountability

Biometrics are associated with surveillance not simply for legitimate reasons related to information exchange for improving integrated border management (e.g. Eurosur and Frontex),[11] but also with disproportionate, imprecise and invisible use. Indiscriminate deployment of biometrics aggravates anxiety as to their disproportion-

---

[10] See Italy's case: GARANTE PER LA PROTEZIONE DEI DATI PERSONALI Provvedimento generale sulla biometria.

[11] Stockholm Programme p. 18.

ate use, mission creep, the associated potential intrusiveness and potential infringe-
ments of citizens' privacy and rules on data protection, and possibilities for redress.
Their discriminatory potential is misused by public and private sector applications
in ways that compromise the creation and protection of a European civic identity
based on common values and the Charter of Fundamental Rights.[12] Possibilities for
judicial redress are compromised by cross border information exchange arrangements within the EU and bilateral accords with third states (such as the US)[13] not
subject to approval by the European Parliament. Private bodies' practices, values,
norms and concepts of criminal offences deviate from those of individual EU states:
intra-EU differences can be exploited for bilateral gain.

Public liability and intellectual property rights lawyers have considered these
issues in connection with data protection and privacy rules, industry audit codes
and best practice guides. While important benchmarks and laws can be established
and revised as technology advances, accountability remains problematic. Individual
data subjects are not generally aware of who accesses their data, handles it, stores
it, when, where, how and for what purpose with or without their explicit consent
or with their implicit (sometimes uncomprehending) consent when they fail to opt
out of commercial online tracking. The loci of accountability may be undetectable,
invisible, outside the territorial scope of EU law, not subject to EU laws or hard to
find for the individual data subject. This is one reason why interest has grown among
data protection and privacy regulators in supplementing existing legal protection and
updating laws by introducing a new principle or right for a data subject to have their
privately or publicly held data erased after a given period of time.

The Article 29 Committee repeatedly stressed data subjects' rights to oblivion,
freedom and dignity over the past decade.[14] Delayed adoption and fragmented practice leads to the erosion of citizen equality, dignity, privacy and security, and fragmented leaky borders. Legal opinion is divided over whether EU rules should inform UN conventions on associated cyber crime, human rights, copyright and cy-
berspace.[15]

13.6 Disproportionate Biometrics: A Problem of Mission Creep?

Mission creep arises from the multifaceted, multidimensionality and inseparability
of internal and external security. It is entrenched by privatising security, by vested

---

[12]Communication from the Commission, Compliance with the Charter of Fundamental Rights in
Commission legislative Proposals, 27.04.2005. COM(2005)172 final.

[13]Council of the EU, Presidency to Delegations, *Reports by the High Level Contact Group (HLGG)
on information sharing and privacy and personal data protection*, JAI 822, DATAPROTECT
74,USA102, 15851/09, 23 Nov 2009.

[14]www.europa.eu.int/comm/indernal_market/en/dataprot/wpdocs/index/htm.

[15]In April 2010 Irish Judge Peter Charleton argued that the Internet is merely one communication tool of many, and not 'an amorphous extraterrestrial body with an entitlement to norms
that run counter to the fundamental principles of human rights' http://courts.ie/Judgments.nsf/
09859e7a3f34669680256ef3004a27de/7e52f4a2660d8840802577070035082f?OpenDocument.

commercial and industrial interests looking to boost their market share, by scattered outsourcing, public and private partnerships not amenable to sufficient parliamentary control, and by semi-privatising and outsourcing public administration. Mission creep is endemic in the application of biometrics, as *Trends in Biometrics* confirmed in 2005.[16] Specious, misleading, implausible, unclear and contradictory approaches abound in their advocacy and use by the public and private sectors. The argument that biometric data is not personal data is implausible because unless linked to the person, biometric data is not that useful. That is why its primary use was initially for territorial border controls, for identifying potential suspects likely to endanger collective security.

Mission creep in deploying biometrics is matched by mission creep in policies on exchanging information across and among agencies within and beyond the EU 27, in the type and range of biometric information to be taken directly (by intrusive) technologies, or indirectly (by 'remote' or non-invasive technologies not requiring direct physical contact with the data subject, such as cctv, temperature monitoring, gait analysis). Mission creep insufficiently and inadequately respects the principles of necessity and proportionality and legitimacy of processing that form the basis for the relevant Community regulatory instruments for the information society which are linked to the principles of being the *minimum* necessary to meet specified objectives; enhance legal certainty; and be technologically neutral. These principles mean that instruments should not exceed what is necessary to achieve the objective in question.

The problem with how biometrics are used relates to the imprecise and infinitely expanding objectives that ICTs implicitly allow. Major problems for accountable and legitimate regulation arise because governments and the private sector evade scrutiny and control, leaving parliaments to catch-up. Amending legislation later is difficult as they know. Soft law abounds with weak controls and inadequate levels of knowledge about the respective technologies and the possibilities opened by them. National parliaments, with a strong European Parliament and EDPS, must ensure accountability and legitimacy. There is an urgent need to re-assess the scope of a framework directive on data protection for law enforcement purposes before realising the principle of availability and widespread inter-operability of 'biometric' data, and to set out an EU model on biometricised egovernance.

13.7 Disproportionate Use of Biometric eIDs?

Biometricised e-IDs rest on diverse reliability requirements, technical specifications and standards,[17] and sometimes incompatible security architectures and suffer from sub-optimal management. EU member states differ over whether an eID should be compulsory or not, who is responsible for securing it, and over what precise form

---

[16]IP/C/LIBE/FWC/2005-08/SC3 PE 378.262.

[17]BioTesting Europe, PASR 2006 Action report 2008.

it should take. In the case of epassports, differences remain regarding processing, handling in respect of lost or stolen passports and visas, and enrolling biometrics. The biometric eID is portrayed as something that boosts certainty and hence 'security'; and biometric evaluation methodologies have been around for many years. Unauthorised traceability attacks, however, facilitate tracking and invade privacy.

e-IDs are used for tracking cross border entry and exit, smart ticketing,[18] automated gate recognition, mobile financial transactions, payment for goods, tracking persons and goods. They are also used for logging onto to smart phones and computers, verifying and authenticating a person's identity as they seek access to information, such as in law enforcement or health care. Their use in smart environments to boost the competitiveness of the EU's knowledge and information society is regularly applauded by governments. Increasingly, used for mundane purposes, biometric eIDs can be developed by anyone and used for any purpose. R&D to advance the e-health agenda is welcomed as an example of beneficial public-private cooperation, improved service delivery, effective and efficient governance and convenience and security gains to citizens. Problems, including insider and outsider fraud and theft, are downplayed or full disclosure delayed.[19] Poor data handling practices compromise the security of data subjects, as in the case of UK banks using customer data during software trials. Data mining and data integration can be vital cost management tools for organisations. This is not at issue. The problem resides in disproportionate data storage on cards or elsewhere accessible by unknown 'others'.

Disproportionate data, for example, is typically held on eID biometric cards used to prove age as a condition of legal entitlement to purchase alcohol, for example in the UK.[20] Some supermarkets' check-out desks demand a passport instead. The previous Labour government's identity card (subsequently withdrawn) targeted and charged young people for identity cards claiming they would make their lives more convenient. Varying data retention practices exist. Sites for data handling expand, e.g. biometrics for visas and passports (fingerprints and photographs in the UK can be enrolled at designated Home Office bureaux or at 17 registered Post Offices on payment of an extra fee); checks are outsourced or privatised, to agencies outside the EU.

13.8 Biometrics and Risks to (In)securitising Individuals

Arguments around using biometrics for public policy purposes arise from the discourse on securitisation, migration and border control. Weak appreciation of the

---

[18]Department for Transport and Detica report (2009) The benefits and costs of a national smart ticketing infrastructure, London.

[19]As in the case of bank data, e.g. HSBC Private bank in Switzerland (like many others) in 2010 revealed the true extent of data theft to be three times higher than originally disclosed. See too the reports by data integrator Informatica, March 2011.

[20]UK shops can be prosecuted for selling alcohol to people under 18.

riskiness of privatised and semi-privatised security remains. Over-optimistic 'trust' in biometrics as a panacea to separate safe from unsafe bodies—thereby eliminating risk—is unwarranted. Individual and collective security are at risk, and an already ambiguous locus of accountability muddied. Over 30 different agencies are already involved in border controls in the EU and data is accessed and exchanged with many others outside the EU.

Biometric specifications[21] and standards change overtime and quality and functionalities vary among vendors and equipment.[22] Common standards across identity management systems would assist interoperability—a general goal of governments and ICT vendors.[23] Biometric measures differ and are not equally reliable or appropriate. Technical specifications, quality standards, functionalities and technological legacies, obsolescence, cost, ageing and adjustments significantly affect deployment, and compromise reliability. How and where fingerprints are taken differ enough to allow the source of a passport to be deduced from them. Exception handling for fingerprints that are hard to record (from the very young, older and disabled people) varies. RFIDs in passports allow remote tracing of whether the passport is in range or not (as was shown to be the case with French epassports in 2008). Encryption in basic access controls is inadequate—making it possible to detect the origin/nationality of the passports of some ten EU states remotely.[24] Unique digital identifiers in next generation US epassports and driving licences are reputedly clonable,[25] and, according to a British team of researchers, 30 million epassports in 50 countries are vulnerable. Traceability attacks and tracking in real time can therefore be carried out for all manner of purposes by criminals, illegitimate and legitimate agencies.

Technological innovation, and EU Member governments' acceptance of a definition of biometrics originating in the USA and homeland security agenda, has led to implicit acceptance of surveillance based on a loose definition of 'biometrics'.[26] The EU's recent commitment to intelligence-led internal security rests on this broad interpretation of 'biometrics', and moreover on automated systems and their capacity to trigger action. It is disingenuous to separate consideration of biometrics from any ICT process involving the transaction of any information that can be linked to

---

[21] Council Regulation (EC) No. 2252/2004 on standards for security features and biometrics in passports.

[22] Bundesamt fur Sicherheit in der Informationstechnik (2010), Technische Richtlinie TR-03127: Architektur elektronischer Personalausweis und elektronischer Aufenthaltstitel, Version 1.10, 31. März, Bonn.

[23] ISO/IEC 247 13-1.

[24] ePassports from Austria, Belgium, Greece, Italy, France, Germany, Poland, Spain, Sweden and the Netherlands inter alia fall into this category.

[25] The theft of British citizens' identity in the Dubai case raised numerous concerns about the security against breaches of chips in epassports.

[26] US VISIT Smart Border Alliance RFID Feasibility Study, Final Report, www.dhs.gov/xlibrary/assets/foia/US-VISIT_RFIDattachB.pdf.

an individual. Biometrics are designed to enable that. Artificial distinctions in purpose specification between electronic identity tokens (eIDs) for internal market or AFSJ purposes—illustrated by e-services, eIDs and ejudicial cooperation—lead to unintended insecuritisation of citizens and society.

In the UK, opposition to identity cards has been ignored by softening the young public up to 'identity cards for entitlements' (such as entry to bars), and by the passport service developing an ID card function within it. Some governments, moreover, use biometrics (and EU requirements for them in travel documents) as an excuse to create centralised data bases—as the Dutch government did—using biometrics as the key to do so.

Biometric tools were originally intended to boost security and minimise risk for legitimate, operational security reasons. In an ambient, 'smart' intelligent, interoperable world, they potentially inadvertently add to risk and insecurity.

13.9 Biometric Problematisation of Accountability

At EU level the introduction of biometric identity documents (not an EU responsibility) have been semi-legitimised by soft law measures such as European Council conclusions. Their implementation eludes sufficient control and scrutiny by national parliaments or by the European Parliament. It is not acceptable to abdicate responsibility to private or semi-private-public partnerships when government and parliament should require their measured legitimate use. *Data protection bodies and ombudsmen are essential but insufficiently influential at the stage before draft rules are finalised.* It is too easy for governments and commerce to proceed in defiance of them. Updating the 1995 Data Privacy Directive is long overdue.

Individuals are insufficiently aware of and unable to use adequately their right to information self-determination. The legal concept of an electronic identity has yet to be sufficiently defined and regulated.[27] If ICTs produce a problem, can ICTs also be constrained by ethical requirements in order to ensure that they provide an acceptable 'solution'?

The enrolment of biometric data for mundane transactions' tracking (e.g. library books or school registers) makes biometric enrolment ubiquitous, more risky, intrusive, and compromises privacy and the integrity of the primary use biometric card—the epassport. In 2009, the European Data Protection Supervisor Peter Hustinx[28] criticised the insufficiencies in the EU Commission's June 2009 proposal to create an agency responsible for the long-term management of the second-generation of the EU's three major data bases associated with border controls: EURODAC,[29] SIS

---

[27]P. McCarthy, Report on Individual Identity, Rise, 2009.riseproject.eu.

[28]http://www.edps.europa.eu.

[29]COUNCIL REGULATION (EC) No. 2725/2000 of 11 December 2000 concerning the establishment of 'Eurodac' for the comparison of fingerprints for the effective application of the Dublin Convention, OJL316/1 15 December 2000.

II (the Schengen Information System) and VIS (the Visa Information System). He stressed the imperative to ensure it was completely independent, especially given the likelihood of mission and function creep and underlined the need for unambiguous legislation about the agency's scope, conduct and competences.

The need for a more robust approach effecting accountability among those systems relying on biometric tools as part of a security strategy is confirmed in the more recent proposals on EU information exchange and internal security.

The Stockholm programme envisages a new agency developing entry/exit alongside existing registered traveller programmes by 2015, a European Schengen visa,[30] and common visa centres. The *Internal Security Strategy* affirms 'anticipation and prevention' through cross-agency cooperation involving not just policing and judicial authorities and civil emergency response and planning but also domestic services, including health and welfare and an integrated, comprehensive model of information exchange based on the principle of availability. 'Intelligence sharing' 'in time to prevent crime. . . .[31] advocates increasing 'substantially the current levels of information exchange. . . and use the Information Management Strategy to develop a secure and structured European Information Exchange Model. . . so that there can be interaction between them, as far as it is needed and permitted, for the purpose of providing effective information exchange across the whole of the EU and maximising the opportunities presented by biometric and other technologies for improving our citizens' security within a clear framework that also protects their privacy.' It goes on to affirm that this information exchange model must be proportionate and always fully respect the right to privacy and protection of personal data.'

There are echoes of the view of the European Data Protection Supervisor that the interoperability of large-scale IT systems should *only* be made possible with full respect for data protection principles and in particular with full respect to the purpose limitation principle.[32] Is this a pious hope when so many measures implicitly imply the retention and processing of 'biometrics' in a raft of bilateral agreements as

---

[30]European Commission (2006) Document de travail des services de la Commission, Accompagnant le Projet de proposition de Reglement du Parlement Européen et du Conseil établissant un Code Communautaire des Visas RESUME DE L'ANALYSE D'IMPACT {COM(2006)403 final} {SEC(2006)957} C6-0254/06, SEC(2006)958, Bruxelles, 19.7.2006. See too Draft Report by the European Parliament's LIBE committee 9 July 2007 on the proposal for a regulation of the European Parliament and of the Council establishing a Community Code on Visas (COM(2006)0403— C6-0254/2006—2006/0142(COD)) 2006/0142(COD).

[31]http://register.consilium.europa.eu/pdf/en/10/st05/st05842-re02.en10.pdf. Council of the EU to: Delegations Subject: Draft Internal Security Strategy for the European Union: "Towards a European Security Model", 5842/2/10 REV 2 JAI 90, 23 Feb 2010.; and on criminal records sharing see ECRIS Council Decision 2009/316/JHA of 6 April 2009 on the establishment of the European Criminal Records Information System (ECRIS) (OJ 2009, L 93/33) and the Opinion of the EDPS of 16 September 2008 (OJ 2009, C 42/1).

[32]See Opinion of the EDPS of 7 December 2009 on the proposal for a Regulation of the European Parliament and of the Council establishing an Agency for the operational management of large-scale IT systems in the area of freedom, security and justice, and on the proposal for a Council Decision conferring upon the Agency established by Regulation XX tasks regarding the operational management of SIS II and VIS in application of Title VI of the EU Treaty.

well as in Eurodac, SIS II, VIS, Prüm, US_VISIT programme and the SWIFT bulk data sharing with the US, for instance.[33] While the European Parliament had some success in blocking the latter in 2010, delayed implementation, partial opt-outs, soft law instruments and bilateral arrangements undermine attempts to achieve EU coherence.[34] *This is unacceptable, insecuritises citizens and weakens accountability.*

Ambitious European goals, legal requirements and values become meaningless if division among the EU27 and delay result in the agenda being set by third states. Growing outsourcing/off-shoring mean that the intention to ensure uniform practice will be readily evaded: variable and weak accountability is inevitable. The EU and its agencies have roles to play but local implementation within member states, for example with respect to airport security, remains a member state prerogative open to influence by outside commercial and government interests. Different branches of government retain responsibility for the systems: Home Office in the UK, Bundespolizeiamt in Germany, Schiphol group in the Netherlands, for instance. Controls are fragmented and variable around the external border and 'exported' to posts outside the EU (e.g. in North Africa) or at the domestic border controls extended from one member states to inside other member states (such as at Eurostar terminals) and at sea.[35] Technical and financial arrangements differ (sometimes led by airlines). Large scale cooperation within the EU is in its infancy.[36] Consequently, fragmented ICTs for border controls mean that overall leaky borders around the EU persist.

One attractive way around the problem of politico-legal harmonisation is to encourage the technologies to produce compatible, interoperable and mutually interrogative systems. Even so, whereas the Article 29 Data Protection Working Party supports the principle of privacy by design[37] and uniform application and interpretation of relevant rules, inevitably national divergence persists.[38] This is exacerbated

---

[33] DG Internal Policies of the Union, Citizens' Rights and Constitutional Affairs, *Data Protection in the Area of Freedom, Security and Justice: A system still to be fully developed?* PE 410.692, March 2009.

[34] Council of the European Union, Council Decision on the conclusion of an Agreement between the European Union and the United States of America on the processing and transfer of Financing Messaging Data from the European Union to the United States for the purposes of the Terrorist Finance Tracking Programme, 2010/0178(MLE) 24 June 2010.

[35] European Commission Communication on the creation of a European border surveillance system (EUROSUR), COM(2008)68, 13.2.08.

[36] See for the Prüm-system Council Decision 2008/615/JHA and 2008/616/JHA of 23 June 2008 on boosting cross-border cooperation in combating terrorism and crime (OJ 2008, L 210/01) and the Opinions of the EDPS of 4 April 2007 (OJ 2007 C 169/2) and 19 December 2007 (OJ 2008, C 89/1).

[37] See on this the Article 20 Data Protection Working Party Work Programme for 2010–2011. http://www.ec.europa.eu/justice_home?fsj/privacy/docs/wpdocs/2010/wp170_en.pdf, 3 March 2010.

[38] The Article 29 Working Party on the Protection of Individuals with regard to the Processing of Personal data is an independent advisory body on data protection and privacy, set up under Article 29 of the Data Protection Directive 95/46/EC. Comprising member states' national data protection authorities, the EDPS and the European Commission, it examines the application of national measures adopted under data protection directives in order to contribute to their uniform

by legacy ICTs, bilateral agreements on border matters with third states, loopholes and discrepancies in data protection, the increasing number of international conventions, and patchy international and EU instruments, ad hoc provisions and relevant case law.[39] The EU's Internal Security Strategy paid scant attention to known problems of data loss and data leakage in domestic public and private systems. Improving data protection and accountability to the European Parliament under the Lisbon treaty are but steps in the right direction. Especially where security is concerned, the concepts of 'essential national security interests and specific intelligence activities in the field of national security' (article 14)[40] are so loose as to mean anything an authority wants them to mean: exceptionalism used to provide a modicum of a safeguard. There is much rhetoric around forensic readiness, data handling cultures, e-disclosure and risk management approaches to data management, much is made of an intention. Yet, other branches of government boost data mash-ups (and associated income generation) and bilateral accords.

Accountability becomes obscured by the alternative approach advocating technical specification standards. The EU-US joint declaration on aviation security accepted 'enhanced technologies'. Support grew in the EU and elsewhere for privacy by design, privacy enhancing technologies, baked-in security and privacy to guide against disproportionality.[41] But a security rationale undercuts what the public infers about them, compared to what technical 'filters' ICT developers produce that permit private and public sector purchasers to continue using them. The Commission's public-private consultation on this ducked the issue pending an EU health and safety impact assessment.[42] In January 2010, some wanted common rules and a single Regulation on the use of ICTs, others responsible for the AFSJ supported rolling out ICTs, biometric border controls and greater information exchange among a growing web of agencies. Citizens are generally clueless about where their data is held.[43] This means that they are equally uninformed about how they might hold data handlers—including EU agencies—accountable

Acknowledging citizens' calls in responses to the *public consultation* on the reform of the General Data Protection Directive for stronger and more consistent data

---

application. Its tasks are set out in Article 30 of Directive 95/46/EC and Article 15 of Directive 2002/58/EC. It issues recommendations, opinions and working documents.

[39] LIBE *Data Protection in the Area of Freedom, Security and Justice: A System still to be developed?* PE 410.692, March 2009:3.

[40] EDPS (2008) EDPS sees adoption of Data Protection Framework for police and judicial co-operation only as a first step, Press release, Brussels 28 Nov 2008. Council Framework Decision 2008/877/JHA of 27 November 2008 on the protection of personal data processed in the framework of police and judicial cooperation in criminal matters, OJ L350/60, 13 Dec 2008.

[41] Ann Cavoukian, Information and Privacy Commissioner of Ontario, "Whole Body Imaging in Airport Scanners: Activate Privacy Filters to Achieve Security and Privacy", March 2009.

[42] http://ec.europa.eu/transport/air/consultations/doc/2009_02_19_body_scanners_questionnaire.pdf, October 2008, the first comprehensive Privacy Impact Assessment for Whole Body Imaging was published by the *US Department of Homeland Security*.

[43] http://ec.europa.eu/information_society/eyouguide/navigation/index_en.htm.

protection legislation across the EU will be meaningless unless robust and consistent legislation follows swiftly. *Technological advance and mission creep suggest that it is already (almost) too late.* The problem is not so much using biometrics for border controls as the disproportionate way in which biometrics are used in a context of ubiquitous data amassing and automated exchange by public and private agencies here and abroad that flout the intent of existing legal provisions designed to protect individuals.[44]

Cross border exchange of information, whether automated or not, geared to combating serious international crime and illegal movement of goods, services, capital and persons is essential in sustaining the EU's goals and area of freedom, security and justice within the common external border. Entry and exit to and from that bordered space is regulated differently and so fragments the border.[45] The security rationale and administration-gain rationale and logic of e-cooperation and data linkage are compelling for law enforcement, border controls, judicial and police cooperation, combating Internet crime, paedophile networks and avatar crime.

Dispersed and obscure accountability, coupled with inconsistent practice on biometric information (both in its narrowest and in its widest senses) mean that data subject integrity, privacy and identity are open to being compromised: security and privacy become not merely arbitrary but contingent. As the locus of accountability dissipates, the space for an abuse of power grows.

13.10 Dispersed and Obscure Accountability: DNA and Arbitrary Security and Privacy

The use of DNA illustrates generic problems of inconsistent practices, incompatible and quickly obsolete (but expensive) ICT systems which magnify discrepancies among those able to afford 'state of the art' systems and robust security architectures, and those unable to do so. Privacy and security against intrusion should not be hijacked by capacity to pay. In the case of DNA (now seen as a biometric, previously rejected as such) discrimination arises from differing technological capabilities, costs and practices regarding access to, retrieval, retention and use of 'new'

---

[44]These include Article 8 of the 1950 Council of Europe Convention for the Protection of Human Rights and Fundamental Freedoms; the 2007 Charter of Fundamental Rights of the European Union, the 1891 Council of Europe Convention for the Protection of Individuals with regard to Automatic Processing of Personal Data (known as Convention 108 and vital to the AFSJ and police cooperation transactions) and the variety of ad hoc data protection provisions under Europol, the partial application of the EU Directive (pre-Lisbon) to pillar I issues and hence to Eurodac and partially to Schengen II and the Visa Information Systems. LIBE PE 410.692, p. 7.

[45]Communication from the Commission to the European Parliament, the Council, the European Economic and Social Committee and the Committee of the Regions, Examining the creation of a European Border Surveillance System (EUROSUR) Brussels, 13.2.2008, COM(2008)68 final Commission Communication, on an entry/exit system at the external borders of the European Union, facilitation of border crossings for bona fide travellers, and an electronic travel authorisation system, COM(2008)69 final, Brussels, 13.2.2008.

biometrics such as DNA samples (which can be accessed under Schengen rules and under the Prüm treaty by different agencies exchanging information). DNA samples are taken and stored for different purposes and according to different definitions of 'offence' for different periods of time in the EU27. In the UK, the EU state with the largest DNA database and a weak record of erasing DNA samples, using mobile biometric technology, a DNA sample can be taken from anyone suspected of an 'offence', including at the roadside for a traffic infringement.[46]

Outsourcing and even off-shoring forensics to the private sector and third states is expensive, risky and potentially counter-productive for security and privacy. It may lead to disproportionate (in)securitisation.

13.11   (Un)ethical Discrimination, Insecuritisation and Arbitrary Intent: Is This Dystopia?

Biometric surveillance is everywhere in some member states. It erodes citizen equality and goes beyond the informatisation or algorithmatisation of the body. The implicit purpose of 'invisible control' is facilitated by unthinking or naive adoption and commissioning of technological applications that, because used for generic rather than specific purposes, pose risks to citizens' personal privacy and security. The contribution 'new biometrics' make to collective security has yet to be adequately proven.

Soft biometrics raise serious ethical questions about the nature of society being created. Understanding of discrimination is blinkered by a focus on racial and gender issues. The socio-political element and detrimental implications for all sectors of society—whether handicapped, ageing, socially excluded, young, ill, political dissidents or simply 'different'—can be manipulated by authorities in line with arbitrary intent. How and why biometrics are used to discriminate opens the door to pervasive insecuritisation of individuals and society at the very time that a privatisation of security is expanding and an 'all-government departments' approach to intelligence-led internal security is advanced by the EU.

There is an unthinking adoption of technologies designed for one purpose when it is obvious that they can be used for others. The principles of data minimisation, purpose limitation, proportionality, purpose minimisation and the principle of moderation in the justifiable use of personal data are laudable but too easily disregarded by the vendors of the technologies concerned with market share and commercial gain.

---

[46]M.J. Beloff QC in August 2009, when asked to advise the Equality and Human Rights Commission whether the [British] Government's proposals for a National DNA database set out in a consultation document from the Home Office on "Keeping the Right People on the DNA Database" comply with the European Convention on Human Rights stated that 'if the proposals were enacted into law they are likely to breach the Convention and lead to findings of violations by the European Court of Human Rights. In practice, it is unclear whether much has changed as a result.'

Automating profiling or verification on the basis of 'biometric' matches breaches chains of duty and trust. Risks are compounded by ICTs and how they are used notably in disproportionate, unethical and potentially illegitimate ways. Disparate practices undermine the rhetoric of biometric certainty, yet law enforcement bodies, notably in the UK, want blanket tracking. This involves an invisible 'authority'; skews choice; commodifies citizens and results in a quantum surveillance state.

Moral ambivalence in the consumption and selling of security grows in parallel with ICT advances, smart devices, ambient intelligence environments, ubiquitous robots, and nano technologies that not only enable but depend on biometric enabled tracking, intrusion and the erosion of public accountability. The biometric paradox lies in both the presentation of a de-personalised token of 'identity' with a re-personalisation facilitated by tracking. Is citizenship to be redefined by an ability to enrol and retain that token? Are those unable to do so, non-citizens?

13.12 The Biometric Diversion of Dystopian Quantum Surveillance

Is the focus of concern over biometrics a misplaced diversion from the bigger picture of personal data being collected by public and private agencies here and abroad in ways that are neither proportionate to the goal to be achieved nor necessary nor in conformity with the intention of lawful use? Creeping 'off-shoring' of data handling is gathering pace in the UK where the government department responsible for tax and customs (HMRC) is 'off-shoring' data handling via its commercial partner to India. Some UK law firms are 'concentrating' services outside their territorial jurisdiction, yet progress on a European criminal records system is insufficiently coordinated. Is this ethical when internet crime and identity fraud are escalating? Is it fair and just that citizens whose security is thereby potentially compromised are kept in ignorance of the consequences of such practices and in many cases are denied the right to opt out of providing the kind of personal data that is central to fraudsters being able to commit fraud in their name? EU citizens are not only increasingly unequal as a result but, should they wish to participate in the Citizens Initiatives allowed by the Lisbon Treaty, are required to provide the very same data, minus a biometric but often embedded in a biometric document?

At issue here is not who sets the agenda but who ensures that it is democratically legitimated, subject to easily understood and enforceable controls, vigilance and justiciability? It is neither ethical nor democratic to berate the lag between legislative measures to protect and safeguard data and privacy when simultaneously data escapes everywhere, permitting tracking (for altogether disproportionate purposes), reconfiguration, splicing, mashing, re-selling and automated access by all manner of people for legitimate and illegitimate purposes.

Just because technology (ICTs) allows one to do something with data does not make it legitimate, desirable, sensible or ethical to do so. For ICT companies to suggest that they can sell privacy enhancing technologies to bake in security, privacy by design or to write programmes that better respect or protect data by minimising the opportunities for re-use or misuse is disingenuous and unethical. Why was security not baked in from the start? The profit-motive is not a legitimate or ethical excuse for manipulating personal data or endangering it by making it susceptible to growing insider fraud and theft. Nor is any claim of ignorance. There is an urgent need to reconsider what legitimate strategic purposes might justify the enrolment, distribution, outsourcing, off-shoring (usually in conjunction with the private IT provider) and sharing of personal data for government and *commercial* purposes. Promised efficiency gains rarely materialise. Therefore a review is needed to determine whether and under what conditions outsourcing and off-shoring data handling beyond the territory of the EU27 might be in the public interest.

Biometrics are big business[47] and integral to identity management across increasing spheres of life. The biometrics industry expects strong growth in demand in 2010 despite public sector cuts owing to the recession. Can regulators and parliaments sufficiently impede those who defy rules on purpose limitation, data minimisation and purpose specification in the use of biometrics sometimes embedded in systems for other purposes? Fines for data breaches may have a deterrent effect but are insufficient. Vigilance is needed regarding the implications of biometrics for compliance with data protection and privacy regulations and law, and the kind of regulatory measures needed in view of the vulnerability of identity management systems to degradation, malevolent intrusion and cyber-attacks inter alia. These in turn raise in the minds of citizens growing concerns about (i) the potentially greater insecurity biometric IDs imply for the citizen and his means of proving his identity, and (ii) government demands that access to public services depend on the enrolment of biometric data in identity documents used for identity management purposes that may, or may not, relate specifically to border controls and 'security' but be infinitely linkable and used for imprecise purposes. The European Parliament should carefully scrutinise COSI and hold it accountable for action under the European Information Exchange Model and associated measures linked to enhancing border control capacity (also in third states).

The rationale behind *stringent safeguards in the use* of biometric IDs has so far been primarily located within the discourse about their potential intrusiveness on the physical body of the individual and their potential for boosting identity certainty. Stronger laws, and scrutiny by national parliaments and the European Parliament under the AFSJ, good practice and *independent* auditing, and more robust architectures and technical specifications, are vital. Compliance is often sub-optimal. The pace of technological advance outstrips the ability of parliaments to legislate and introduce measures to safeguard citizens, deter malpractice and e-crime.

---

[47]http://www.spiegel.de/international/business/0,1518,682790,00.html.

13.13 Too Little Too Late? ICT Innovation Outstripping Naive Legislators?

There is contradiction and tension in what some EU governments seek (more auto-mated exchange of information under the Stockholm Programme, often for legiti-mate operational purposes) and what regulators, parliaments and the European Parliament want. The latter's legitimate demands for proper consultation, transparency and accountability remains fraught, and a battle ground which tests parliamentary capacity for effective scrutiny and vigilance of the executives, and also of techno-logical innovation. Once an issue is voiced by parliament, it is often too late to repair or overturn government approval for actions parliaments wish to question or reject. This is especially likely to be the case regarding matters of 'security'. The AFSJ is no longer the responsibility only of the EU's and member states' public authori-ties. As long ago as 2001, the Spanish Presidency pushed the idea and in 2007, then FSJ Commissioner Frattini noted the co-responsibility, too, of the private security sector.[48] This is about more than freedom to establish services and goods and com-petition policy.[49] The European Parliament must redress this and develop its role to control their operation, and any formal status for such run-for-profit bodies.

Should citizens be able to opt out of e-IDs? Linking ehealth systems with pre-scribing systems, social welfare and fiscal systems) is pushed by the EU27 govern-ments, EU Commission[50] and industry alike. Potential technical, procedural, legal, managerial and security weaknesses in realising interoperability compromise citi-zen privacy, individual and collective security. Specious claims are made by gov-ernments and industry to justify prioritising interoperability over data protection, privacy and individual security.

While governments increasingly demand and embrace biometric identity man-agement systems (naively arguing that these will modernise, boost efficiency and effective service delivery within and across state borders), they have not yet suffi-ciently understood:

---

[48]"Security by design", Homeland Security Europe, speech by Commissioner Frattini to the EU Security Research Conference, Berlin, 26 March 2007: http://www.homelandsecurityeu.com/currentissue/article.asp?art=271247&issue=219.

[49]http://ec.europa.eu/internal_market/smn/smn21/s21mn11.htm summarises findings in Single Market News No 21 (2000). C *OUNCIL OF THE EUROPEAN UNION Brussels, 13 December 2001 (20.12) (OR. es) 15206/01; ENFOPOL 156 NOTE* from: the future Spanish Presidency to: Police Cooperation Working PartyNo. prev. doc.: OJ C 340, 10.11.1997, p. 1 Subject: Network of contact points of national authorities with responsibility for private security. *Brussels, 29 January 2002 (OR. es) 5135/02 ENFOPOL 5 LEGISLATIVE ACTS AND OTHER INSTRUMENTS* Subject: Initiative of the Kingdom of Spain on the setting up of a Network of contact points of national au-thorities responsible for private security http://www.statewatch.org/news/2002/apr/priv07245.pdf As under *29 April 2004 Case C-171/02: Commission of the European Communities v Portuguese Republic based on Articles 39 EC, 43 EC and 49 EC—Directive 92/51/EEC.*

[50]http://ec.europa.eu/information_society/activities/health/index_en.htm.

(i) their relevance for robust e-security, complete with understanding the need to treat e-identity management systems as part of a state's critical infrastructures requiring appropriate contingency and crisis response plans

(ii) the possibility that citizens' trust in governments and parliaments will weaken and decline the more they are seen to be lax in terms of their own data handling arrangements

(iii) the possibility that citizens' trust in law enforcement and policing authorities will fall and be compromised as (a) cross-border automated information exchange and cross-border mutual access to information by 'foreign' and/or private agencies grows; and (b) civil-criminal law distinctions become fuzzy, less visible and so less openly accountable

(iv) the possibility that citizens' belief in the trustworthiness of government authorities' claims to uphold law and justice will be compromised by their apparent failure to prevent 'corrupt' agencies accessing information, harvesting data, using web analytics (such as Phorm), stealing personal data and personal identity documents

(v) the possibility that the assumed bonds of trust and accountability between citizens and governments and parliaments will be severely challenged and tested

Wide definitions of 'biometrics' facilitate mission creep and quantum surveillance that potentially erode privacy and compromise civil liberties in the absence of sufficient publicly legitimated accountability. It is no longer sensible to regard a biometric or technology as having neutral socio-economic, or legal and political impacts. Newer biometrics are fluid, include behavioural and emotional data that can be combined with other data. Therefore, a range of issues needs to be reviewed *together* in view of the increasing privatisation of 'security' that escapes effective, democratic parliamentary and regulatory control and over-sight at national, international and EU levels.

The intertwining of internal (AFSJ and internal market, including sustainable economy, environment and knowledge society) policies with external security presents significant challenges to innovative thinking. Disjointed policymaking insecuritises citizens and states and erodes the capacity of democratically legitimated bodies to credibly act in and safeguard the public interest.

Intelligence led internal security rests on a broad interpretation of 'biometrics', and on automated systems. For civil liberties and democratic values to be upheld, public accountability through parliamentary cooperation between national and the European parliaments is vital and must urgently be strengthened to ensure consistency and to insist on robust encryption and data and purpose minimisation. The European Parliament and national parliaments themselves should:

1. insist on encryption and systems that cannot interrogate all the information held on a biometric token (such as an ID card) to minimise data disclosure
2. enforce purpose limitation
3. set high level *mandatory* standards to complement voluntary codes of practice
4. Monitor system performance, compliance annually with major simultaneous public debate in the EP, national parliaments and regional bodies at levels closest to citizens

5. Clarify informational privacy for multiple identity tokens and documents
6. Legislate on the quality and accreditation of forensic and law enforcement communicators
7. Set up rules on disclosure and unlawful disclosure to and by humans and other machines with the subject's explicit knowledge and consent by reconsidering data encryption, device controls and infrastructure requirements and management in view of pervasive ambient intelligence
8. Re-regulate redress in view of its inaccessibility and infeasibility to most citizens and set up a meaningful ethical swift redress against identity theft and review chains of duty and trust in cyber space.

13.14 Conclusion

It is vital to clarify the benefits *to the citizen and society* of interoperable biometric e-IDs: just because industry claims a convenience gain to citizens of onetime data enrolment does not mean that duplicate identity data does not exist elsewhere about the same citizen, nor that duplicate data standards and formats in different systems are compatible when interoperability is compromised by legacy standards and systems, as well as technical capacity and the standards for and kind(s) of biometric associated with given data. The principle of the data subject in control of his data is an ideal, probably unattainable but should be the norm not the exception. As private space shrinks and those immersed in creating virtual identities and existences for themselves grow, the biometric tokenised identity might become the preferred way of linking all these identities to one physical person. The random and disproportionate use of biometrics is dangerous, unnecessary and ill-thought out. It shows weak regard for ethical understanding, ethical norms or determined debate as to the impact on and implications for the principles of respect for privacy and the right to private family life. A review of the use and accountability of ICTs in a society where automated decisionmaking, both at territorial border posts and more generally, is growing is long overdue to avoid creeping arbitrariness, erosion of democracy, and a state of quantum surveillance—enabled by exciting technological advances and quantum computing—falling prey to those who would abuse their power. The risks of not remedying deficiencies lie in compounding public disaffection and distrust in political authority and facilitating a privatised surveillance state with all that implies for a loss of public accountability, openness and transparency, and greater insecuritisation of citizens. This opens the door to irrational forces opposed to the common good.

References

1. Agreement between the European Union and the United States of America on the processing and transfer of passenger name record (PNR) data by air carriers to the United States Department of Homeland Security, OJ L 204, 4 August 2007, p 16

2. Agreement between the European Union and the United States of America on the processing and transfer of financial messaging data from the European Union to the United States for purposes of the terrorist finance tracking programme. OJ L8 13 January 2010, p 9
3. Article 29 Data Protection Working Party. Opinion 4/2004 on the processing of personal data by means of video surveillance, adopted 11 February 2004, 11750/02/EN WP89
4. Bigo D, Jeandesboz J (2009) Border security, technology and the Stockholm programme, INEX Policy Brief, CEPs
5. Bundesamt fur Sicherheit in der Informationstechnik (2010) Technische Richtlinie TR-03127: Architektur elektronischer Personalausweis und elektronischer Aufenthaltstitel, version 1.10, 31. März, Bonn
6. Carrera S, Wiesbrock A (2009) Civic integration of third-country nationals nationalism versus Europeanisation in the common EU immigration policy, CEPs, October 2009
7. Commission of the European Communities (2004) Proposal for a Council Regulation on standards for security features and biometrics in EU citizens' passports. COM(2004)116 final, 2004/0039 (CNS), 18 Feb 2004
8. Commission of the European Communities (2005) Proposal for a Council Decision concerning access for consultation of the visa information system (VIS) by the authorities of member states responsible for internal security and by europol for the purposes of the prevention, detection and investigation of terrorist offences and of other serious criminal offences. COM(2005)600 final, 24 Nov 2005
9. Commission of the European Communities (2005) Proposal for a council framework decision on the exchange of information under the principle of availability. SEC(2005)1270, COM(2005)490 final, 12 October 2005
10. Commission of the European Communities (2006) Communication from the Commission to the Council and the European Parliament. Report on the implementation of the Hague. Programme for 2005. SEC(2006)813, SEC(2006)814, COM(2006)333 final, 28 June 2006
11. Commission of the European Communities (2007) Communication from the commission to the European Parliament and the Council on public-private dialogue in security research and innovation. SEC(2007) 1138, SEC(2007)1139, COM(2007)511 final, Sept 2007
12. Commission of the European Communities (2008) Communication from the Commission to the European Parliament, the Council, the European Economic and Social Committee and the Committee of the Regions. Preparing the next steps in border management in the European Union. SEC(2008) 153, SEC(2008)154, COM(2008)69 final, Brussels, 13 Feb 2008
13. Commission of the European Communities (2009) Amended proposal for a regulation of the European Parliament and of the Council concerning the establishment of 'EURODAC' for the comparison of fingerprints for the effective application of regulation (EC) No[.../...]. COM(2009)342 final, 10 September 2009
14. Commission of the European Communities (2009) Communication from the Commission to the European Parliament and the Council. An area of freedom, security and justice serving the citizen. COM(2009)262/4, 25 Nov 2009
15. Commission of the European Communities (2009) SEC(2009)837 Commission staff working document accompanying documents to the proposal for a regulation of the European Parliament and of the Council establishing an agency for the operational management of large-scale IT systems in the area of freedom, security and justice and proposal for a council decision conferring upon the agency established by regulation XX tasks regarding the operational management of SIS II and VIS in application of title VI of the EU treaty impact assessment. COM(2009)292 final, COM(2009)293 final, COM(2009)294 final, SEC(2009)836 Brussels, 24.06.2009
16. Council of the European Union to: delegations subject: draft internal security strategy for the European Union: towards a European security model. 5842/2/10 REV 2 JAI 90, 23 Feb 2010. http://register.consilium.europa.eu/pdf/en/10/st05/st05842-re02.en10.pdf
17. Council of the European Union (2009) Proposal for a council framework decision on the use of passenger name record (PNR) for law enforcement purposes. Doc 5618/09, 23 January 2009

18. Council of the European Union. Council decision on the conclusion of an agreement between the European Union and the United States of America on the processing and transfer of financing messaging data from the European Union to the United States for the purposes of the terrorist finance tracking programme. 2010/0178(MLE), 24 June 2010

19. Council Regulation (EC) no 2725/2000 concerning the establishment of eurodac for the comparison of fingerprints for the effective application of the Dublin Convention, 15 Dec 2000

20. de Hert PJA (2005) Biometrics: legal issues and implications. European Commission, January 2005. http://cybersecurity.jrc.es/docs/LIBE%20Biometrics%20March%2005/LegalImplications_Paul_de_Hert.pdf

21. Department for Transport and Detica Report (2009) The benefits and costs of a national smart ticketing infrastructure, London

22. EDPS (2007) Third opinion of the European data protection supervisor on the proposal for a council framework decision on the protection of personal data processed in the framework of police and judicial cooperation in criminal matters. OJ C 139/1, 23 June 2007

23. EDPS (2008) Opinion of the European data protection supervisor on the draft proposal for a council framework decision on the use of passenger name record (PNR) data for law enforcement purposes. OJ C 110/1, 1 May 2008

24. EDPS (2008) Opinion of the European data protection supervisor on the final report by the EU-US high level contact group on information sharing and privacy and personal data protection, 11 November 2008

25. ENISA. ENISA REPORT on the state of pan-European eID initiatives, January 2009

26. Eurojust. US-Eurojust agreement. http://www.eurojust.europa.eu/official_documents/Agreements/061106_EJ-US_cooperation_agreement.pdf

27. European Commission, Joint Research Centre (2005) Biometrics at the frontiers: assessing the impact on society. EUR21585

28. European Court of Human Rights (EctHR) (2008) Case of S and Marper versus the United Kingdom. Application nos 30562/04, Strasbourg, 4 December 2008

29. European Data Protection Supervisor (EDPS) (2009) Press release on ePrivacy Directive close to enactment: improvements on security breach, cookies and enforcement, and more to come, 9 Nov 2009

30. European Parliament (2007) Draft report on the proposal for a regulation of the European Parliament and of the council amending regulation (EC) no 562/2006 establishing a community code on the rules governing the movement of persons across borders (Schengen borders code), as regards the implementing powers conferred on the Commission. COM(2006)0904—C6-0015/2007—2006/0279(COD)

31. Europol (2007) US-Europol cooperation agreements. http://www.europol.europa.eu/legal/agreements/Agreements/16268-2.pdf; http://www.europol.europa.eu/legal/agreements/Agreements/16268-1.pdf

32. Group of Experts on Information and Communication Policy (1993) Reflection on information and communication policy of the European community. Report by the group of experts chaired by Willy De Clercq, Brussels, March 1993

33. Hayes B Homeland security comes to Europe. http://www.statewatch.org/analyses/no-90-homeland-security-comes-to-europe.pdf

34. House of Commons, Justice Committee (2010) Justice issues in Europe. Seventh report of session 2009-10, vols I and II, HC162-1, HC 162-II. The Stationery Office, London, 6 April 2010

35. House of Lords, European Union Committee (2010) Protecting Europe against large-scale cyber-attacks. Report with evidence, 5th report of session 2009-10, HL paper 68. The Stationery Office, London, 18 March 2010

36. Liberatore A (2007) Challenging liberty. In: Lodge J (ed) Are You Who You Say You Are? The EU and Biometric Borders. Wolf Legal Publishers, Nijmegen

37. Lodge J (2010) Biometrics in Europe: inventory on politico-legal priorities in EU27, Del 7.1 for biometrics stakeholder network (BEST) Brussels

38. Lodge J (2012) Dark side of the moon: accountability, ethics and new biometrics. In: Mordini E, Tzovaras D (eds) Second Generation Biometrics. Springer, New York
39. Lodge J (2011) Transformative biometrics and the exercise of arbitrary power. In: BIOSIG, Darmstadt
40. Monahan T, Wall T (2007) Somatic surveillance: corporeal control through information networks. Surveillance & Society 1:154–173
41. Mordini E, Wright D, de Hert P, Mantovani E, Wadhwa KR, Thestrup J, Van Steendam G (2009) Ethics, e-inclusion and ageing. Studies in Ethics, Law, and Technology 3(1):5
42. Pawlak P (2009) Made in the USA? CEPS
43. Privacy International (2009) Statement on proposed deployments of body scanners in airports, 31/12/2009. www.privacyinternational.org/article.shtml?cmd%5B347%5D=x-347-565802
44. The EU/US Passenger Name Record (PNR) agreement, 5 June 2007
45. The Passenger Name Record (PNR) Framework decision—report with evidence, London, 11 June 2008
46. UK Department for Transport. Interim code of practice for the acceptable use of advanced Imaging technology (body scanners) in an aviation security environment, London, 2010. http://www.dft.gov.uk/pgr/security/aviation/airport/
47. US VISIT Smart Border Alliance. RFID feasibility study, final report. http://www.dhs.gov/xlibrary/assets/foia/US-VISIT_REFIDattachD.pdf
48. Van Steendam G et al (2006) The Budapest meeting 2005, the case of reproductive cloning, germ line gene therapy and human dignity. Science and Engineering Ethics 12:731–793

Chapter 14
Best Practices for Privacy and Data Protection for the Processing of Biometric Data

Els Kindt

Abstract Self-regulatory initiatives by data controllers can contribute to a better enforcement of data protection rules. This is especially important for the use of biometric data in identity management systems, because of risks of use as unique identifiers and identification. This chapter explains the Best Practices which were developed in the Turbine project. These Best Practices recommend inter alia the creation of multiple trusted revocable protected biometric identities, which are irreversible and unlinkable.

14.1 Introduction

Biometric characteristics are increasingly used in Identity Management (IdM) systems in the private sector as means to provide a more secure solution for authenticating individuals. The deployment of biometric data, however, could have serious life long implications for these data subjects. The reason is that the biometric characteristics provide a unique link which is in principle persistent and unchangeable with the person concerned. This is highly problematic in the case of misuse, such as identity theft or the re-use of biometric data for purposes which were not initially envisaged at the data collection. Because of the unique link, biometric data can also be used as a universal identifier for linking information about the same data subject within or across various information sources. Furthermore, biometric data allow to identify a person. Last, but not least, biometric data may also reveal sensitive information. This chapter discusses best practices which have been suggested for the processing of biometric data, taking privacy and data protection into account, in particular for the private sector. The European Commission recently recalled in a Communication on personal data protection that self-regulatory initiatives by data controllers can contribute to a better enforcement of data protection rules.[1] After a brief discussion of some initiatives taken in the past, we focus on

---

[1]European Commission, *Communication from the Commission to the European Parliament, the Council, the Economic and Social Committee and the Committee of the Regions. A comprehensive*

E. Kindt (✉)
Law Faculty, ICRI-iMinds, K Leuven, Leuven, Belgium
e-mail: els.kindt@law.kuleuven.be

P. Campisi (ed.), *Security and Privacy in Biometrics*,
DOI 10.1007/978-1-4471-5230-9_14, © Springer-Verlag London 2013

the Best Practices which were developed in the Turbine project. The Turbine Best Practices recommend the creation of multiple trusted revocable protected biometric identities, which are irreversible and unlikeable, and may present a response to the challenges of the deployment of biometric data.

In discussions about biometric data processing systems, it is important to use a clear vocabulary. We discerned with relief that such harmonized vocabulary has been suggested by the Working Group 1 of Subcommittee 37 of the Joint Technical Committee 1 of the International Standardisation Organisation (ISO) and was adopted in 2012.[2] We reiterate that a clear and common understanding of terms in relation with highly technical systems—which biometric systems are—is a prerequisite for an interdisciplinary discussion and debate about biometric systems among experts with differing backgrounds, i.e. technical, societal, ethical, legal, commercial and governmental backgrounds.[3] We will use the terminology proposed by this Group as much as possible in this chapter. We also inform that this chapter is based on research in the 7th Framework Programme Turbine (2008–2011) supported and funded by the EU Commission.[4]

14.2 The Formulation of Best Practices: Rationale and Some Initiatives for Biometric Systems in the Past

14.2.1 Rationale of the Formulation and Use of Best Practices

Best practices are a list of recommendations formulated in a particular domain and are suggested to stakeholders to apply in their practice. Such recommendations, for example in the domain of personal data processing, are sometimes also presented in the form of a code of conduct. Best practices and codes of conduct are examples of a *self and/or co-regulatory approach* and are typically drafted for *a particular sector* in which the data protection controllers experience similar difficulties.

---

approach on personal data protection in the European Union, 4.11.2010, COM(2010) 609 final, p. 12, available at http://ec.europa.eu/justice/news/consulting_public/0006/com_2010_609_en.pdf ('Commission, Communication. Personal Data Protection, 2010'). All links in this chapter have been last visited in February 2011.

[2] ISO/IEC 2382-37:2012 Information technology—Vocabulary—Part 37: Biometrics, 13.12.2012, 28 p.

[3] About the importance of such common vocabulary, see also E. Kindt, 'Biometric applications and the data protection legislation. The legal review and the proportionality test' in *Datenschutz und Datensicherheit* 2007, p. 167.

[4] The contribution in this chapter is representing however only the author's view and is binding Turbine partners, the European Commission nor the EDPS.

The general Data Protection Directive 95/46/EC contains a special chapter and several provisions on codes of conduct. Article 27 of the Directive 95/46/EC encourages drawing up codes of conduct which are intended *to contribute to the proper implementation* of the provisions of the data protection legislation. These codes of conducts can be established on the national level or on the European Union level. In the first case, they need to be submitted to the national the Data Protection Authorities (DPAs) for their opinion,[5] in the latter to the Article 29 Data Protection Working Party.[6] In both cases, the views of the data subjects may be asked. A similar provision is maintained in the Reform proposal for a General Data Protection Regulation of January 2012.

There are various *reasons* for best practices or the use of codes of conduct. First of all, the matter or the sector for which the recommendation are used may be very complex and subject to rules which may be presented or interpreted in different ways. Few countries issued specific legislation for the processing of biometric data.[7] Biometric data processing remains in such case subject to the general privacy and data protection legislation and to (varying) interpretation by the DPAs. The best practices or codes of conduct would in such case typically contain *more precise or additional practical rules and guidelines* which are in practice easier to follow than the more general data protection legislation. Codes of conduct could therefore be considered in some cases as an efficient means to have the legislation applied.

Furthermore, the adoption of codes of conduct and best practices could in some cases also be an indication that *there is the intention* of the sector and its members to comply with data protection and privacy regulation. Additional legislation could in such case be no longer a priority for the government or the parliament.

Finally, codes of conduct established by a sector may also be used *as a commercial argument* towards the data subjects as an indication that data protection is taken seriously by the sector and, if certified, guaranteed.

In the field of data protection, the use and the implementation of codes of conduct vary from member state to member state and were in Europe not a wide success.[8] Reasons which were mentioned include lack of interest of the DPAs and insufficient means and resources to promote and validate codes of conduct.[9] The Commission therefore announced in 2010 that it will examine means for and the active promotion of codes of conduct.[10]

---

[5] Article 27, 2 Directive 95/46/EC.

[6] Article 27, 3 Directive 95/46/EC.

[7] Exceptions exist, e.g., France.

[8] For example, on the European level, in 2009 only two organizations representing a sector have drawn up with success codes which were validated by the Article 29 Data Protection Working Party: the International Air Transportation Association (IATA) and the Federation of European Direct and Interactive Marketing (FEDMA). See N. Robinson, H. Graux, M. Botterman, L. Valeri, *Review of the European Data Protection Directive*, Cambridge, Rand, 2009, pp. 9-10 and p. 37, available at http://www.ico.gov.uk/upload/documents/library/data_protection/detailed_specialist_guides/review_of_eu_dp_directive.pdf ('Rand, 2009').

[9] Rand, 2009, p. 37.

[10] Commission, Communication. Personal Data Protection, 2010, pp. 12–13.

We hereunder discuss some initiatives of best practices for data protection compliance[11] from the past, followed by an overview of the Turbine Best Practices relevant for biometric data processing in the private sector.

14.2.2 Some Initiatives of Best Practices for Biometric Data Processing Systems in the Past

In the last decade, several initiatives have been taken promulgating best practices for biometric data processing. These initiatives include the Best Practices developed in the framework of the 'BioPrivay initiative' by the International Biometric Group around 2001, the formulation in the BioVision project of the Privacy Best Practices in Deployment of Biometric Systems of 2003 and the Privacy Code of the Biometrics Institute in Australia.

The International Biometric Group (IBG) is a biometric integration and consulting firm, with offices in the United Kingdom and the United States, providing advice to government and commercial clients. IBG announced in 2001 the so-called 'Bio-Privacy Application Impact Framework'. The suggested framework was meant to provide a tool in *assessing the privacy risks* of a biometric application. The idea behind the initiative was that not all biometric deployments bear the same privacy risks, but that specific features of biometric deployment increase or decrease privacy. IBG described and analyzed the relationship between biometric data processing and privacy. IBG hereby stated that biometric data processing poses a lower or higher risk of privacy invasiveness depending on the answer to ten questions relating to the characteristics and the functioning of the biometric system, the ownership of the biometric data and the type of biometric technology used. To reduce the risks and the potentially harmful impact of the deployment, several Best Practices recommendations were formulated and published on the BioPrivacy Initiative website.[12]

The BioPrivay Best Practices are addressed to the full range of biometric systems, 'from small-scale physical access to nationwide identification programs'. The suggested practices are divided in four categories, in particular (1) Scope and Capabilities, (2) Data Protection, (3) User Control and Personal Data, and (4) Disclosure, Auditing, Accountability, Oversight. The recommendations are in fact a combination of data protection principles, including the purpose limitation and transparency principles, with recommendations for an impact assessment and independent audit. Interesting is the firm position that biometric information should not be used as a universal unique identifier.

---

[11] Best practices initiatives in relation with biometric data in domains other than data protection have been taken as well, such as for testing methodologies or for particular (large-scale) applications. These initiatives are however not discussed in this chapter.

[12] International Biometric Group, *Best Practices for Privacy-Sympathetic Biometric Deployment*, available at http://www.bioprivacy.org/best_practices_main.htm.

Another initiative are the Best Practices formulated in the BioVision project (IST-2001-38236) (2002–2003) funded by the European Commission.[13] The document refers to the European legal framework, in particular Directive 95/46/EC and its core is *directly based upon the legal requirements* set forth therein. The aim was to develop it further to become a practical code of conduct relevant to all stakeholders dealing with biometric data.

These BioVision Best Practices, aiming to provide *inter alia* 'guidance for system integrators, guidance for suppliers (i.e. manufacturers, middle ware developers, system architectures) in order to develop privacy compliant and even privacy enhancing biometrics from the beginning of a development of a biometric system'[14] in fact also contained principles (e.g., 'Give users control over their personal data ("identity protector")) which can be considered as principles of 'Privacy by Design' (PbD).[15]

A third and last initiative of self-regulation for the processing of biometric data which we would like to mention and which was taken outside Europe, is the Privacy Code of the Biometrics Institute in Australia. The Code was expected to positively promote the importance of individuals' privacy across the biometric and related industries and to help educate consumers in their privacy rights. After an independent review, the Code *was approved by the Office of the Privacy Commissioner* and took effect as from September 2006.[16] One of the drivers of the Code was the need to build assurance 'to encourage informed and voluntary participation in biometrics programs'.[17] The Code contained a full set of obligations equivalent to those set out in the Australian general privacy and data protection legislation and some additional principles, intended to provide additional privacy protection to data subjects. Interesting is for example the principle that '[w]herever it is lawful and practicable, individuals must have the option of not identifying themselves when entering transactions with a Code Subscriber' (Principle 8). The supplementary principles include the auditing of compliance with the Code by a third party (Provision 13.2) and compliance with international standards as specified. In 2008, the Biometrics Institute started a review process of the Code.[18] The major obstacle found was the inadequate nature of the general Australian Privacy Act 1988 on which the Code

---

[13] A. Albrecht, *BioVision. Privacy Best Practices in Deployment of Biometric Systems*, BioVision, 28 August 2003, 49 p. ('BioVision, Best Practices, 2003'); see also A. Albrecht, 'Privacy best practices', in *Biometric Technology Today*, November/December 2003, pp. 8–9.

[14] BioVision, Best Practices, 2003, pp. 5 and 13.

[15] We discuss the meaning of this principle further *below* in Sect. 14.4.2.

[16] Office of the Privacy Commissioner, *Approval of the Biometrics Institute Privacy Code*, Australia, 19 July 2006, 24 p., also available at www.Biometricsinstitute.org.

[17] See Preamble of the Biometrics Institute Privacy Code, second consideration.

[18] The review started with the establishment of a Privacy Committee and surveys to its members. The results were presented later in 2008 and 2009.

relied.[19] The Code was further (only) binding for the organizations that had agreed and signed the Code. According to the public register maintained on the site, only four companies had subscribed the Code (status of January 2011). Further to the Institute and the review, however, a significant number used the Code as a start and reference. In April 2012, the Code was nevertheless revoked.[20]

Because the progress in the adoption of legislation containing detailed rules on the use of biometric data processing remained limited, attention is given to the formulation of best practices for the privacy friendly processing of biometric data in the more recent EU-funded project Turbine project as well.[21] These Best Practices *took the fore-mentioned initiatives into account* and were based in part on the common and useful elements thereof. In addition, the Turbine Best Practices reflect several *recommendations and opinions* of various DPAs, the Article 29 Working Group and the European Data Protection Supervisor (EDPS) on biometric data processing. They also make use of the *privacy-enhancing technical developments* in relation with the use of biometric technologies. Some of these technologies, in particular relating to template protection of fingerprint, have been researched, tested and implemented in demonstrators in Turbine. We will take hereunder a more detailed look at the suggested Turbine Best Practices.

14.3 The Best Practices Developed in Turbine

The Best Practices developed in Turbine aim at formulating practical guidelines for the design, the development and the implementation of biometric identity management systems in the private sector.[22] The *focus* of these Best Practices is on *specific issues* with which the controllers and processors have to cope upon the processing of biometric data in IdM systems. The aim was *not* to give a new overview on how the legal requirements, in particular the requirements resulting from the Directive 95/46/EC which apply to all personal data processing systems, should be implemented. Such overview on how the general data protection principles should be interpreted and implemented for biometric data systems was given before, such

---

[19]The inadequacies found included making a separation of government and non-government privacy principles, the exemption from the Act of small businesses, media and other, the variation of jurisdictions, the exemption of employee records from the act and the fact that Privacy Impact Assessments and Audits were not mandatory while this was the case in the Code.

[20]See Revocation of the Biometrics Institute Privacy Code, available at http://www.comlaw.gov.au/Details/F2012L00869.

[21]TrUsted Revocable Biometric IdeNtitiEs project (TURBINE) (IST-2007-216339) (2008–2011) (7th Framework Programme), with homepage at www.turbine-project.eu ('Turbine'). About the technology developed in Turbine, see also the contribution of J. Binger and H. Chabanne in Chap. 11 in this book.

[22]For the full text of the Best Practices, see Turbine, D.1.4.3 Practical Guidelines for the privacy friendly processing of biometric data for identity verification, available at http://www.turbine-project.eu/index.php.

as by the Article 29 Data Protection Working Party in the Working Document on Biometrics of 1 August 2003, the Council of Europe in its Progress report relating to biometric data of 2005,[23] and for example also in the Privacy Best Practices document of BioVision of 2003 discussed above. These documents contain all highly relevant attempts to solve the difficulties in the interpretation and the compliance issues upon the processing of biometric data, but do not solve issues very specific to biometric data, such as the need for revocability and to restrict linkability. The approach to limit the content of the Turbine Best Practices was chosen deliberately to have a focused discussion on those best practices and principles which are *specifically required* for the processing of biometric data. The Best Practices have further been discussed with the advisory board to the project and have been presented during conferences in order to receive further input of the community. The EDPS has also commented on the suggested practices as we will explain.

14.3.1 Overview

The Turbine Best Practices are structured along the various steps when deciding, designing and implementing a biometric IdM system: the specification of the controller's need (and the definition of the purposes), followed by the design, the enrollment and the actual deployment of the system. The identity provider and/or the service provider will in principle take the decisions relating to each of these steps.[24] System designers, integrators and suppliers will give advice which is important as well, but they will usually not take the final decisions over the 'means and purposes' of the application and hence not be considered data processing controllers. One important decision will relate to the functionality to be deployed in the system. This is addressed in Best Practice N° 1. Another important layer to be kept in mind during all phases, are the organizational and security measures and certification, represented in Best Practice N° 10. It was also an aim to present the recommendations in a concise way easy to retain. This should allow stakeholders to keep at all times an overview of the various actions needed. A visual overview of the structure and the subjects of the Best Practices discussed, is shown in Fig. 14.1.

We hereunder briefly comment the suggested Turbine Best Practices and include in our description a short motivation as well. To clarify the Turbine Best Practices, we will apply the principles in two particular use cases, i.e. use of biometric data (a) for authentication of the owner of a banking account before engaging remotely

---

[23]Consultative Committee of the Convention for the Protection of Individuals with regards to Automatic Processing of Personal Data [CETS No. 108] (T-PD), *Progress report on the application of the principles of convention 108 to the collection and processing of biometric data*, Strasbourg, Council of Europe, CM(2005)43, March 2005, 22 p.

[24]In some cases, the identity provider and the service provider may be one and the same entity.

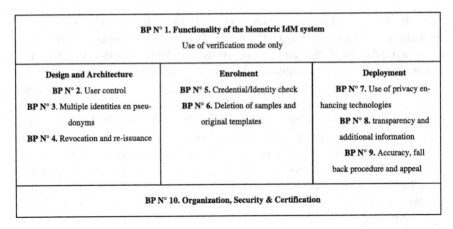

BP N° 1. Functionality of the biometric IdM system Use of verification mode only			
Design and Architecture BP N° 2. User control BP N° 3. Multiple identities en pseudonyms BP N° 4. Revocation and re-issuance	**Enrolment** BP N° 5. Credential/Identity check BP N° 6. Deletion of samples and original templates	**Deployment** BP N° 7. Use of privacy enhancing technologies BP N° 8. transparency and additional information BP N° 9. Accuracy, fall back procedure and appeal
BP N° 10. Organization, Security & Certification		

Fig. 14.1 Overview of the suggested Turbine Best Practices for a biometric IdM system, including the suggestion of the EDPS about accuracy in BP N° 9

on a banking transaction ('ebanking') and (b) for access control to stored ehealth data[25] ('ehealth').

14.3.2 Discussion

Best Practice N° 1: Biometric Data Shall in Principle Only Be Used for Verification and Stored Locally   Probably the most important decision about the use and the implementation of a biometric system is the description of the needs and the purposes that the biometric IdM system has to fulfill. Available technologies or systems should not make that decision. Instead, the controller of a biometric IdM system shall clearly and carefully define the *specific, explicit, and legitimate purposes* of the system and shall not use the data for incompatible purposes. At that moment, the controller shall also determine the *functionality* to be used in the system.

Biometric systems can perform two functions and use biometric data in two different ways. The *verification function* compares the submitted biometric data with one particular usually previously submitted and already stored set of biometric data of the same person.[26] It gives an answer on whether both characteristics belong to the same person. If the 1:1 comparison is positive, the system will render a positive decision. The *identification function* recognizes an individual by comparing the

---

[25] See and compare also, e.g., with the U.S. federal privacy requirement in the Health Insurance Portability and Accountability Act of 1996 (HIPAA) and its regulations to implement technical policies and procedures that allow only authorized persons to access electronic protected health information.

[26] Verification is therefore also referred to as a 'one to one comparison' (1:1 comparison).

submitted biometric characteristic with all previously submitted and stored biometric characteristic in a database through a search.[27] The identification functionality tells upon comparison whether the data subject is registered (or not), and/or (ii) if names or other personal details are mentioned with the stored characteristics in that central database (or which can be linked with these characteristics) to whom the submitted biometric characteristic belongs. The identification functionality allows to check whether or not someone is on a particular list or database (this list may also be a so-called 'watch list' or a black list) and the identification functionality can be used by the controller to identify persons.

The verification functionality allows to *tie a person* and his or her presence to a particular access procedure and *offers increased security* to the data controller because of the use of biometric data.

Identification, which is sometimes regarded as less cumbersome for the data subject (no token is required), is for security purposes of an access system in principle not required and the required central storage of the biometric data from a privacy point of view *excessive*. The security is for most IdM systems guaranteed if the (verification) comparison can confirm that the person is enrolled. Only in exceptional cases, and upon duly legislative motivation, identification could be required.[28] Besides such very specific cases, the use of the identification functionality is interfering with fundamental rights and generally not proportional with the purposes and the interests of the identity and service provider controllers of IdM systems in the private sector. Identification also implies and requires the storage of biometric data in a database. Precisely this database allows to use the identification functionality. The *storage of the biometric data in a central place* which permits identification, seriously enhances the risks for the data subject (such as, e.g., re-use, unauthorized access or theft) over which the data subject has no further control, and will for these reasons equally be regarded as interfering with the fundamental rights of the data subject, excessive and *not proportional*. The choice as to whether the verification over the identification functionality has to be used, is hence more than a proportionality issue. Identification requires an explicit legal basis. Many countries have adopted legislations which specify when citizens are under an obligation to identify themselves or may be identified including in the private sector. The use of the verification functionality is therefore also a matter of legality of the processing.

The use of the verification functionality in addition *permits to reduce the error rates*. Systematic and statistical errors of the measurement by the algorithms increase if the comparison is made in the identification mode. Best Practice N° 1 hence provides for a clear guideline to use the biometric characteristics in the biometric system for verification purposes only.

---

[27] This is also referred to as a 'one to many comparison' (1:n comparison).

[28] For example, if a sector would be entitled by law and under specific conditions to keep 'black lists' (e.g., the insurance sector). 'Black lists' excluding individuals from access rights or practical services, requires in several countries explicit legal provisions authorizing the use of such lists, in particular because such lists may imply some form of discrimination.

For the ebanking use case, BP N° 1 implies that the system requires the submission of the biometric characteristic(s) for comparison with biometric data stored on a badge, card or token, aiming at ensuring that the person is a customer of the bank as having previously been registered and is actually the same person as the owner of the account and is authorized to perform the transaction. For the ehealth scenario, the biometric data stored on an access control card or token, enables to verify whether the person authorized to access the ehealth data is actually present when the card is used. In both scenarios, the use of the verification functionality for the biometric data system increases the security considerably.

Best Practice N° 2: User Control over Biometric Data by Default   For the *design and architecture*, important decisions will have to be made again. In order to minimize privacy and data protection issues, additional criteria should be adopted including that the user *has control* over the use of his or her biometric characteristics. The data subject does not obtain more control if he or she is merely informed of the use of his or her data, even if the data subject would retain the right to consent or not. The data subject may only retain control if he or she *has to cooperate* for the release and/or the use of the biometric data, for example by handing over the smartcard, the token or the document on which the biometric reference is stored, after which the comparison process can start.

It is for this reason strongly recommended that the collected biometric data are stored *locally on an object under the control* of the individual. The fact that only the data subject holds the biometric data, increases in addition the transparency of the use of the biometric data. In exceptional cases, the controller may motive the central storage of the reference biometric data which should then only be used for verification purposes.[29]

The concept of user control over personal information is not established in the data protection legislation of most countries as such.[30] Nevertheless, several DPAs are suggesting the local storage of biometric data since some time and advise to store biometric data not centrally.[31] Local storage is also considered important by

---

[29]For example, because the central storage would be more convenient for the user and the biometric characteristic does not allow the use of the identification functionality (e.g., hand geometry). Compare, e.g., with the Unique Authorization N° AU-007 of 27 April 2006 by the French DPA, the CNIL, for biometric systems based on hand geometry verification for access control, management of time and attendance and of the canteen in the workplace in France.

[30]Presently, the data subjects have information, access and correction rights, and the right to object under specific conditions. They also have the right to freely refuse consent.

[31]For example, the French DPA, the CNIL, has warned since 2000 for the central storage of biometric data, especially fingerprint, and thereupon developed a position on the use of biometric identifiers which shall in principle not be stored centrally but locally. See also for a similar position the DPAs of Greece and Belgium. See also the report R. Hes, T. Hooghiemstra and J. Borking, *At Face Value. On Biometrical Identification and Privacy*, Achtergrond Studies en Verkenningen 15, The Hague, Registratiekamer, September 1999, p. 52, issued by the Dutch DPA. Compare, however, with CNIL, *Communication de la CNIL relative à la mise en œuvre de dispositifs de reconnaissance par empreinte digitale avec stockage dans une base de données*, 28 December 2007, 12 p.

the Article 29 Working Party. In its contribution to the consultation of the Commission on the future of privacy and data protection rights, it stated that '[b]iometric identifiers *should be stored in devices under control of the data subjects (i.e. smart cards) rather than in external data bases*' (emphasis added).[32]

However, a mere local storage requirement is not sufficient and additional guarantees for the processing of biometric data locally stored will remain required, for example, that no copies are kept in the enrollment database or after comparison and that the data cannot be used in contexts different from those originally intended. This could be done by the transformation of the biometric data, whereby the data are linked to particular services for use by the IdM service provider (see *below*).

The implementation of this BP N° 2 for the ebanking and the ehealth use cases is linked to implementation of BP N° 1. It would imply that the biometric data are stored on the object held by the customer, respectively, authorized person entitled to access the ehealth information.

Best Practice N° 3: Multiple Identities and Pseudonymity   Best available technologies chosen at the design phase can contribute to strengthen privacy and security. The decision to use techniques for the creation and use of one or multiple identities in combination with pseudonyms based on the same biometric characteristics but which are different for each application or the service suppliers considerably limit the risks of the use of the biometric characteristics as unique identifiers and re-use of the personal data.

Because unique identifiers present privacy risks, for example due to the possibility of linking various (trans)actions, sometimes across databases, it is best practice to avoid the use of biometric data as single unique identifier if there is no legal basis for the use of biometric data as identifier. The Article 29 Working Party has clearly warned for the privacy and data protection risks of identifiers: 'The use of identifiers, whatever form they take, entails data protection risks. Full consideration should be given to all possible alternatives. If user identifiers are indispensable, the possibility of allowing the user to refresh the identifier should be considered'. Multiple identities and accountability is also a requirement mentioned in the Prime White paper for identity management systems in general.[33] The use of multiple biometric identities for one person implies that privacy enhancing technologies shall be used to transform for each (type of) application the original biometric data and to create one or more multiple identities. It is therefore recommended for biometric IdM systems to use technology that allows the creation of *multiple* identities and identifiers. A clear and easy to use interface for choosing the appropriate identity for a particular service will in that case be very important. Another aspect is that the identifiers for

---

[32] Article 29 Data Protection Working Party and the Working Party on Police and Justice, *The Future of Privacy. Joint contribution to the Consultation of the European Commission on the legal framework for the fundamental right to protection of privacy*, WP 168, 1 December 2009, p. 14.

[33] Prime, *Prime White paper*, 2008, v.3.0, 19 p., available at https://www.prime-project.eu/prime_products/whitepaper/PRIME-Whitepaper-V3.pdf.

each of the multiple identities should preferably, depending on the application, be a pseudonym.[34]

The term 'pseudonym' is in general used in IdM systems as a term to explain that not the real, 'civil identity' name is used, but another name or another identifier. Pseudonyms allow data subjects to choose and to use a different name with each organization and allow service providers to create accounts for individual users, while they cannot determine the real identity of the data subjects.

Some data protection legislations explicitly refer to the use of pseudonyms. The German Federal Data Protection Act, for example, states that *use is to be made* of the possibilities *for aliasing* ['*Pseudonymisierung*'] and *rendering persons anonymous*, insofar as this is possible and the effort involved is reasonable in relation to the desired level of protection' (stress added).[35] The need for the possibility to connect to a network with a pseudonym has been made explicit by the Article 29 Working Party as well: '*All possible efforts should be made to allow anonymous or pseudonymous use of online authentication systems*'.[36]

The implementation of multiple identities and pseudonyms as set for in this BP N° 3 will depend, as stated, upon the application. For the ebanking use case, for example, it may not be desirable to deploy *within* a particular application more than one biometric identity (e.g., for accounts belonging to the same banking customer). However, multiple identities may remain useful to disable the linking of customer information for different activities (e.g., banking as opposed to insurance transactions). In any case, the use of technology to create multiple identities would imply that even in case a single biometric identity would be created and used, this identity would differ from other biometric identities used by the data subject *for other service suppliers*. For the ehealth application, the use of different identities could be linked to different levels of authorization for accessing particular (highly sensitive) personal information of others. The use of pseudonyms in both use cases may be less relevant, as the disclosure of the 'real' (civil) identity of the bank customer, respectively, of the person authorized to access the ehealth records may be mandated by law and/or (trans)actions logged.

Best Practice N° 4: Revocability of Biometric Identities and Re-issuance   The fore mentioned technology making it possible to issue various identities based on the same characteristics, should also allow the revocation of the biometric identities

---

[34] Additional aspects of the multiple identities are set forth in Best Practice N° 4 (revocability) and Best Practice N° 7 (irreversible and unlinkable across contexts) discussed *below*. About the architecture using pseudo identities in the project, see J. Breebaart, C. Bush, J. Grave and E. Kindt, 'A reference architecture for biometric template protection based on pseudo identities', in A. Brömme (ed.), *Proceedings of the Special Interest Group on Biometrics and Electronic Signatures*, Bonn, Gesellschaft für Informatik, 2008, pp. 25–37.

[35] See Sect. 3(a) German Federal Data Protection Act.

[36] Article 29 Working Party, *Working Document on on-line authentication services*, WP 68, 29 January 2003, p. 15, available at http://ec.europa.eu/justice_home/fsj/privacy/docs/wpdocs/2003/wp68_en.pdf.

in case of misuse or theft or in case of termination of the access to the services. Turbine has developed, tested and demonstrated a mechanism to issue such revocable biometric identities.

The revocation may also prove to be useful in case a biometric identity leads to too many failures. The revocation could be at the demand of the data subject or of the identity/service provider. A revocation policy, which should be fully transparent for the data subject, shall be agreed upon and contain the specifications of the procedure.

The use of revocable biometric identities is an important privacy-enhancing aspect of biometric IdM systems. As long as there are no mechanisms used to permit a data subject to revoke a biometric identity, the use of biometric data in an IdM system endangers the rights of data subjects whose characteristics have been (mis)used or stolen for ever.

For the use cases of ebanking and ehealth, existing revocation procedures will to some extent already be in place and should be extended to include revocation of the biometric identifiers for the implementation of this BP N° 4.

Best Practice N° 5: Credential and/or Identity Check   Biometric systems which attempt to increase security will in most cases involve an enrollment phase. Specific guidelines which address this phase are therefore needed as well. A biometric IdM system which provides security at a given point is just a link in a security chain. Credentials or identity documents to be provided at enrollment are often less secured and therefore more likely to be subject to forgery and counterfeiting. For this reason, it is of crucial importance that the control of the credentials or of the identity of the individuals who enroll in biometric IdM systems is thorough and reliable. If the wrong person becomes enrolled, all later use of the biometric system is compromised. The security of biometric IdM system is hence only trustworthy as long as the credential or identity check is reliable.

This check is not only important for IdM systems in the public sector,[37] but also for biometric IdM systems in the private sector for which the credentials or identity of the individuals before enrollment are important (e.g., biometric payment scheme). Therefore, the *procedure(s)* for such credential check or identification, and in particular *which* documents shall be submitted and the *way* such documents shall be provided (in original, copy, etc.), shall be agreed between the identity providers and the service providers and shall be documented.

For biometric IdM systems in which the identity is not relevant or necessary, but rather whether an individual is able to submit a credential in combination with a biometric identifier, the *procedure(s)* for linking the biometric identifiers with the credentials (for example, a minimum age, the belonging to a particular profession, etc.) shall be agreed and documented.

---

[37] See, e.g., for the importance of this aspect for the issuance of biometric passports, EDPS, *Opinion of 26 March 2008 on the proposal for a Regulation of the European Parliament and of the Council amending Council Regulation No. 2252/2004*, O.J. C 200, 6.08.2008.

The implementation of this BP N° 5 requires for the ebanking use case appropriate procedures for verification of the identity of the customer, which may be influenced by legislation requiring identity evidence of customers. For the ehealth use case, the identity and/or credentials check of persons or entities entitled to having access to health information shall be set out and documented and may be determined by legislation concerning ehealth records as well.

Best Practice N° 6: Deletion of the Samples and of the Original Templates
The conditions under which the local storage of biometric data enhances the privacy and data protection include that (i) the original image of the biometric characteristic, (ii) all the forms of the image in between the extraction steps and (iii) the unprotected template shall not be stored but *always deleted* after the extraction process for enrollment or comparison. This should not only happen on the local device level (such as, e.g., on the biometric scanner or sensor) but also *from all other components* of the biometric system.

The protected templates should also be deleted if there is no need anymore for processing thereof in compliance with existing data protection requirements.[38]

The EDPS and DPAs require in general that the controllers shall have a policy about the deletion of personal data after the processing. The term for which the data are kept is also often requested in notification forms. Such deletion strategy is even more important for biometric data.

The implementation of this BP N° 6 for the ebanking use case and the ehealth use case should not entail particular difficulties, especially if the biometric comparison remains according to Best Practice N° 2 local. Automatic deletion procedures and mechanisms could assist in this task.

Best Practice N° 7: The Use of Privacy-Enhancing Technologies   The operation and deployment of the biometric system is another phase which requires attention as well. Specific privacy enhancing technologies should make the identities unlinkable and irreversible. Anonymous verification procedures are hereby recommended as well.

First of all, because of the various risks of the use of biometric samples and of templates (e.g., the possibility that they contain information about the data subject's health[39]) it is best practice to transform the original biometric data (both biometric samples and the template) and to destroy the biometric samples and templates afterwards.

The transformed information, however, will still refer to a given person—which is after all the goal of the use of the biometric IdM system—and the transformed information will hence still function as identifiers. For this reason, it is important

---

[38] See and compare, e.g., Biometrics Institute Privacy Code, 2006, Sect. F.11.4.

[39] See on this risk, e.g., M. Meints & M. Hansen, 'Additional and in some cases health related information in biometrics', in E. Kindt and L. Müller (eds.), *D.3.10. Biometrics in identity management*, Frankfurt, FIDIS, 2007, pp. 83–86, available at http://www.fidis.net/resources/deliverables/hightechid/#c2057.

that additional privacy-enhancing technologies are implemented in order to render these identifiers irreversible and unlinkable.

Irreversible Biometric Identities   Captured biometric characteristics, especially the biometric samples (previously referred to as the 'raw biometric data') may include more information than what is needed for the comparison, in particular information which reveals racial or ethnic origin or concerning health. The transformation of the captured and processed information, especially of the biometric templates, in transformed templates limit the chances that such additional information is still contained therein and is advised. This requires, however, that it is *not possible to reverse engineer* the samples and the original templates from the transformed templates.

Unlinkable Biometric Identities   It is further best practice that the digital representations of the biometric characteristics are processed with mathematical manipulations (encryption, etc.) *with different parameters for every biometric product, system or service* and *specific techniques* which guarantee low mutual information between templates derived from equal or very similar biometric data. This should avoid the combination of personal information of the data subjects through the comparison of templates across databases and applications. The unlinkability also prevents that databases would be searched. These manipulations have as a result that the use of biometric data is limited to a specified context (context-specific use).[40]

The use of the fore-mentioned kinds of privacy-enhancing techniques is sometimes referred to as the deployment of 'protected templates'.[41] There were standardization efforts in Subcommittee 27 of the Joint Technical Committee 1 of ISO/IEC in relation with protected templates, leading to the adoption of a standard for the protection of biometric information.[42] The concept of protected templates of biometric characteristics refers essentially to protecting the biometric data and related identity by (1) the transformation and the generation of a secure reference to the biometric data by means of a robust one-way- function from which it is impossible to retrieve the original biometric information (transformation and irreversibility), (2) which reference does not permit cross matching between different databases (unlinkability), and (3) which is revocable and renewable (renewability).

---

[40] See and compare also with earlier recommendations of the Committee of experts on data protection (CJ-DP), *The introduction and use of personal identification numbers: the data protection issues*, Council of Europe, 1991, pp. 15–17, available at http://www.coe.int/t/dghl/standardsetting/dataprotection/Reports/Pins_1991_en.pdf.

[41] See J. Breebaart, C. Bush, J. Grave and E. Kindt, 'A reference architecture for biometric template protection based on pseudo identities', in A. Brömme (ed.), *Proceedings of the Special Interest Group on Biometrics and Electronic Signatures*, Bonn, Gesellschaft für Informatik, 2008, pp. 25–37.

[42] See J. Breebaart, B. Yang, I. Buhan-Dulman, Ch. Busch, 'Biometric Template Protection. The need for open standards' in *Datenschutz und Datensicherheit* 2009, pp. 299–304.

A recommendation nor a requirement of unlinkability of personal data is in many data protection legislations set forth in explicit terms.[43] General data protection legislation principles, however, require purpose specification and purpose binding for the collection and processing of personal data. It has been advocated to interprete these principles *as an obligation to prepare personal data for context-specific usage.* This could imply that it should be prevented that data could be linked for different purposes. Because of the increasing availability of biometric data over networks, it will become moreover difficult to enforce the purpose binding of personal data, unless technical measures are adopted.

The Article 29 Data Protection Working Party has stressed the technical possibility of linking data as a risk factor.[44] In the context of biometric data processing, it expressed its concern that biometric data is used as a unique identifier and recommended that the use of biometric data for linking should be avoided as much as possible.[45]

In very specific cases, (unprecedented) legislation referred to the irreversibility and the requirement that encrypted biometric data cannot be used as a unique identifier, capable of facilitating linking with other information, combined with deletion of the original information.[46]

The unlinkability and irreversibility techniques shall be applied and could be recognized as 'best available techniques'[47] which render the use of biometric data more proportional with the risks for the data subjects.

Tunable Trust   In function of the application, different trust levels may be required. By varying the amount of biometric information exposed by each individual, the concept of tunable trust allows to control better the uncertainty and reliability of a biometric system.

Anonymous Verification   While biometric characteristics enable in essence that an individual is identified or that his or her identity is verified, it is also possible to use biometric data without the identity of the data subject being revealed. If there is no need for identification or verification of the identity, semi-anonymous or fully anonymous access control mechanisms should be put in place to manage and to verify the authorization of a given person to an area or place. These could be combined

---

[43]The data protection legislation of only a few countries contain specific provisions relating to the linking of information, e.g., Slovenia.

[44]See, e.g., Article 29 Working Party, *Working Document on on-line authentication services*, WP 68, 29 January 2003, p. 12.

[45]Article 29 Working Party, *Working Document on Biometrics*, WP 80, 1 August 2003, p. 10.

[46]In particular, in Ontario, Canada, the Social Assistance Reform Act of 1997 (later revoked) and the Ontario Works Act of 1997 (Article 75).

[47]See also about the use of 'best available techniques' as one of the recommendations for privacy and data protection in the Union, ENISA Ad Hoc Working Group on Privacy & Technology, *Technology-Induced challenges in Privacy & Data Protection in Europe*, M. Langheinrich and M. Roussopoulos (eds.), October 2008, pp. 9 and 35–36 available at http://www.enisa.europa.eu/doc/pdf/deliverables/enisa_privacy_wg_report.pdf.

with the use of biometric characteristics if the controller has a legitimate interest to deploy biometric data to enhance the security. A protocol for anonymous verification was implemented and demonstrated in Turbine by using a group signature protocol in the General Application Demonstrator ('GADM'), a mock up demonstrator representing specific applications for pharmacists.

The anonymous use of biometric data[48] is in compliance with the data minimization principle of Directive 95/46/EC. This principle is maintained in the Reform proposal for a General Data Protection Regulation of January 2012. All data protection legislations of Member States require that no 'excessive data' shall be processed, while some legislations are very specific on this point.[49] Some DPAs have explicitly stated that anonymous group verification is preferred when using biometric data.[50] This is also important in the evaluation of the proportionality of a system.

For the ebanking and ehealth scenarios, this Best Practice N° 7 recommending the use of specific privacy enhancing technologies shall be evaluated and implemented according to the (legitimate) need for that particular application to make the identities (un)linkable. Even in case only one biometric identity or pseudonym would be used, as a result whereof the transactions performed with the same biometric identity could be linked (e.g., for auditing the access to ehealth information), the use of the technology would render the linking of biometric identities across several service suppliers impossible. In both scenarios, the biometric identities deployed should also be irreversible to the original data.

Best Practice N° 8: Transparency and Additional Information for the Data Subjects   The data subject shall receive clear and sufficient information about the biometric comparison process.

In addition to the legal information which shall be provided according to current data protection legislation,[51] it is for this reason recommended to inform the data subjects, of (i) the functioning of the system, in particular whether the verification or identification *functionality* is pursued and effectively deployed and where the biometric data are *stored*, (ii) the *error rates* of the particular system at the threshold set, and (iii) the procedure in case of failure of the system (fall back procedure) or

---

[48]This should not be confused with to what some refer to as 'anonymous biometric data'. The latter is in our view strictly speaking *a contradictio in terminis*, since all biometric data refer and relate to an individual, whether directly identifiable or not.

[49]For example, the German Federal Data Protection Act explicitly states as a general principle that 'data processing systems are to be designed and selected in accordance with the aim of collecting, processing or using *no* personal data *or as little* personal data *as possible* (. . .)' (Sect. 3a).

[50]For example, the Belgian DPA. See CBPL, *Advice N° 17/2008 of 9 April 2008 upon own initiative relating to the processing of biometric data for the authentication of persons*, N° 77 ('CBPL, Advice N° 17/2008'). See and compare also with the Biometrics Institute Privacy Code which promotes anonymity (Article 8).

[51]The current information obligation includes *inter alia* the obligation to inform about the identity of the controller, the purposes, the recipients of the information and the access and correction right of the data subject as specified in the applicable national data protection legislations.

of appeal by the data subject against the result of the comparison.[52] The notice could also inform the data subject about the deletion of copies of the biometric characteristics and of any specific security measures taken. It is also recommended to inform the data subject of the name and contact details and the role of the identity provider and of the service provider.

The additional information could take advantage of the possibility to be incorporated into a so-called 'multi-layered information notice'. Such notice essentially allows controllers to employ a simplified short notice in their user interface, as long as the latter is integrated in a multi-layered information structure, where more detailed information is available, and the total sum of the layers meets national requirements.

This Best Practice N° 8 also includes that biometric data shall *not be collected* from an individual *without his or her knowledge*.

For the ebanking and ehealth use cases, this Best Practice N° 8 requires the inclusion of more precise information for the data subjects in the interface. This Best Practice has also been implemented in the Turbine GADM. Simple icons guiding the data subject to the topics of the (additional) information can be used as well.

Best Practice N° 9: Accuracy, Specification of Fall Back Procedures and of the Procedure to Appeal a Comparison Decision   Last, but not least, the controller(s) shall need to specify alternative procedures ('fall back procedure') in case the data subject cannot be enrolled (FTE), the biometric data cannot be acquired for further processing (FTA)[53] and/or if the data subject does not consent with the biometric data processing. These alternative procedures can be *different protocols* (e.g., the use of other fingers in a fingerprint access control system), but can also be *alternative access* procedures (e.g., the use of non-biometric access control means). A fall back procedure will also be required to control and review alleged false rejections (e.g., by determining the additional checks to be done by human intervention).

Such alternative procedure shall provide to the data subjects the *same* access rights, *without significant delay* and *at no (extra) cost* for the data subject. In general, one shall take care that such alternative procedures shall in no way result in any discriminatory treatment of the data subjects.

The need to establish alternative procedures could be compare with the need for a back up solution of a failing IT system in general. This is a general security measure, also mentioned in international IT standards (see ISO/IEC 27000 standards) and therefore qualified as 'good practice'. This 'good practice' is less straightforward from these standards in case of specific individual failure. The EDPS and the national DPAs have repeatedly stressed the need of fall back procedures for biometric systems.

---

[52]See also CBPL, Advice N° 17/2008, N° 79. The need for transparency and agreement on FTE and FRR has also been recognized repeatedly in public sector applications, such as for the use of biometric passports.

[53]Increasing the number of attempts may already address various failures in a simple way. However, this will affect the security provided by the system. Moreover, it may not always solve the issue and additional fall back procedures will remain required.

The EDPS stressed with regard to the Turbine Best Practices, which he reviewed, that the guidelines should also include a requirement to set the precise level of accuracy expected from a biometric system and to review this level on a regular basis. This accuracy requirement is therefore now included in this Best Practice N° 9 as this will also impact the fall back procedures which have to be set based on the level of accuracy as well. We discuss the opinion of the EDPS further *below*.

For the ebanking use case, the fall back procedures could be inspired by existing scenario's (e.g., in case of remote banking, use of a helpline by which the bank requires additional information to authenticate the customer). For ehealth, additional checks should be set up as well. For both cases, the accuracy level shall be set in accordance with the need to secure the (sensitive) data.

Additional Best Practice N° 10: On the Organization, the Security and the Certification of a Biometric IdM System   In addition to the Best Practices for the design, the enrollment and the implementation which enhance the privacy and data protection rights of the data subjects, organization and security measures need to be specified and implemented.

First of all, appropriate organizational measures are needed to back up the recommended practices. For example, in addition to the technology to revoke biometric identities, revocation schemes will have to be defined, organized and be set up for the revocation. In order to address the privacy concerns at the stage of the design of a biometric IdM system, it shall be organized that these concerns are discussed right from the start. The organizational measures shall in principle address the various steps of a biometric system. For enrollment, sufficiently *trained and qualified* staff shall assist in this procedure.[54] Clear agreements have to be made about the identity credentials that the data subject shall submit for the enrollment in the IdM system and any exemptions for enrollment, for example for children under a certain age or for elderly people. Access to any data in the system shall be *restricted* and reserved for duly *authorized* persons authenticated by one or multiple factors. A list of such persons has to be made and kept up-to-data.

Furthermore, the biometric data processing controller shall assess, analyze and address the specific *risks* of each component of the biometric system. This includes risks associated with the support medium of the data (e.g., a smart card), the biometric sensor(s) and any other processing unit and the communication links between the various components. The data protection legislation imposes upon the data controllers the obligation to implement appropriate technical and organizational measures to protect personal data against (i) accidental or unlawful *destruction*, (ii) accidental *loss*, (iii) *alteration*, (iv) unauthorized *disclosure or access*, in particular where the processing involves the transmission of data over a network, and against (v) all *other unlawful forms* of processing.[55] General measures for protecting bio-

---

[54] See and compare, e.g., with the new Article 1 a introduced by Regulation (EC) No 444/2009 of the European Parliament and of the Council of 28 May 2009 amending Council Regulation (EC) No 2252/2004 on biometric passports and travel documents.

[55] See also Art. 17 (1) of the Directive 95/46/EC.

metric data are, however, not sufficient.[56] The level of security needs to be *appropriate* to the risks presented by the biometric system. The controller shall hereby take *the state of the art in account*, as well as the *cost* of implementation of such state of the art measures.[57] The general data protection legislation mandates the data controllers to take *the risks represented by the biometric processing* and *the specific nature of the biometric data into account*. Some DPAs have issued guidelines for the controllers with more recommendations for the implementation of security measures, but these general guidelines do not sufficiently address the specific risks of biometric systems.[58] The risks of processing biometric data (e.g., identity theft, re-use,... but also the spoofing of the sensors and other attacks,...) shall hence be *defined, documented* and appropriate security measures *implemented*. If the controller relies on one or more processors, the controller shall choose a processor which provides sufficient guarantees that such measures shall be implemented and shall ensure the compliance with these measures. The controller shall therefore enter into a *written or equivalent contract with the processor*.

Certification should also contribute to the privacy friendly development of biometric systems. Various DPAs and the EDPS have stressed the opportunities that certification may offer.[59] Certification schemes, including for example the use of privacy seals for compliant products, are relevant for the data subjects and the users of the biometric system as an indication that the system is compliant and/or privacy enhancing. Moreover, the use of certified systems and products could be an element in the review of the liability and responsibility of the data controllers.[60] Because the technical operation and effects of biometric products and systems are difficult to evaluate, such biometric products and systems should be reviewed by experts, both IT-experts and legal experts and the certification should address the security aspects and data protection aspects.

The implementation of the fore mentioned Best Practices N° 10 for the use cases would—besides the experts mentioned—benefit from the involvement of professional organizations of the banking and health sector who could assist the sector and the controllers in the definition of the organizational measures specific for biometric systems and the security risks to be covered. Their involvement could also be significant for the trustworthy set up of certification programs, such as privacy seals.

---

[56] See, e.g., ISO19092: 2008 for a concise overview of infrastructure requirements.

[57] See also Art. 17 (1) §2 of the Directive 95/46/EC.

[58] See, e.g., for Belgium, CBPL, *Reference measures for the security for every processing of personal data*, 4 p., available at http://www.privacycommission.be/nl/static/pdf/referenciemaatregelen-vs-01.pdf.

[59] See, for example, the Independent Centre for Privacy Protection Schleswig-Holstein (ICCP/ULD), Germany, which leads the EuroPriSeconsortium. See also the CNIL, which joined the French governmental institute AFNOR, with the goal to be heard in domains such as biometrics (CNIL, *30 ans au service des libertés. 29e rapport d'activité*, p. 52); the ENISA Ad Hoc Working Group on Privacy & Technology also reiterated the benefits of certification in its report on '*Technology-Induced challenges in Privacy & Data Protection in Europe*'.

[60] Commission, Communication. Personal Data Protection, 2010, pp. 12–13.

14.3.3 Opinion of the EDPS

On February 1, 2011, the EDPS issued an opinion in relation to the Turbine project, including on the fore mentioned Best Practices.[61] It was the very first time that the EDPS issued an opinion on a European research project, hereby giving effect to the EDPS's 2008 policy paper entitled "The EDPS and EU Research and Technological Development", in which the possible roles of the EDPS for research and development (RTD) projects in the context of the 7th Framework Programme for Research and Technological development (FP7) are described.

The EDPS listed the Best Practices identified by the Turbine project. He also referred to a list of common basic requirements proposed by the EDPS, taking into account the specific characteristics of biometric data. These common requirements are (i) targeted impact assessment, (ii) emphasis on the enrollment process, ensuring for a majority of individuals to enroll and taking into account the level of false rejection rate or false acceptance rate, (iii) readily available fallback procedures, and (iv) highlighting the level of accuracy of the system.

The EDPS agreed that developing the best practices listed '*will help* to implement appropriate measures for *any* biometric Identity Management System conducted *in compliance* with the EU regulatory framework' and stated that 'such a check list could indeed allow development of *more privacy friendly systems*, if they are taken into account *from the start* of projects' (emphasis added).

With regard to the fallback procedures and the level of accuracy, the EDPS clarified that they have to be defined according to the precision of the system and monitored constantly in relation to the population using the system. The investment which needs to be made in the fallback procedures will be defined by the level of those rates. The EDPS stated that setting the precise level of accuracy expected from a biometric system is of great importance and recommended that this should be established early in the system and be integral part of the Best Practices as well.[62] This additional aspect will therefore be mentioned in an Annex to the Best Practices as developed in Turbine, reflecting the EDPS's opinion.

In addition to the review of the Best Practices, the EDPS analyzed several other aspects of the project, including in particular the features of irreversibility and revocability of the biometric identification technology developed in Turbine. The implementation of these two features contributes according to the EDPS significantly to legal compliance by providing acceptable privacy compliant solutions.[63]

According to the EDPS, the overall objective of his opinion was to promote and reinforce the application of the principle of '*Privacy by Design*'. The EDPS ex-

---

[61] EDPS, *Opinion 1.02. 2011 on a research project funded by the European Union under the 7th Framework Programme (FP 7) for Research and Technology Development (Turbine (TrUsted Revocable Biometric IdeNtitiEs)*, available at http://www.edps.europa.eu/EDPSWEB/edps/cache/off/ Consultation/OpinionsC/OC2011 ('EDPS, Turbine Opinion, 2011').

[62] See EDPS, Turbine opinion, 2011, §34–37.

[63] EDPS, Turbine opinion, 2011, §67 and §69.

plained that 'Privacy by Design' extends 'not only to the design and technical solutions of ICT systems, but comprises the various steps in the set up of the project and its organizational practices'. This can be achieved by 'ensuring legal compliance, implementing the required data protection principles, and by implementing procedures and training developed to ensure correct information and training of all the parties involved'. The intent of stakeholders to implement this principle could *inter alia* be deduced from documentation in with legal, functional and technical requirements are being prepared at an early stage of a project.[64]

14.4 Evaluation

We described above some examples of the development of best practices for respecting privacy and data protection rights for the processing of biometric data of the last years and the Best Practices developed in the Turbine project. We make hereunder a brief evaluation and discuss the concept of 'Privacy by Design'.

14.4.1 Relevance of the Fore Mentioned Best Practices Initiatives

The BioPrivacy Best Practices contain many useful recommendations of which several, although developed a decade ago, are presently still very relevant. For example, the rejection of biometric data's use as 'universal unique identifier' in these Practices remains important. The recommendation with regard to 'anonymous enrollment' such as in a web environment, stating that 'where individuals can assume alternate identities through email addresses or usernames, there may be no need for a biometric system to know with whom it is interacting' is in our view also very valuable. The Practices, however, do not address the functionality or place of storage. These aspects are only taken into account in IBG's 'BioPrivacy Technology Risk Ratings' in order to measure the 'impact on privacy' of the technology.[65] We regret that the criteria for privacy preserving biometric systems are split up in two different documents, in particular the 'BioPrivacy Technology Risk Ratings' and the BioPrivacy Best Practices, rather than being set out in one set of best practices. We further believe that it is not possible for best practices or a code of conduct to address the wide range of biometric applications, both in the public or the private sector. The needs are obviously very different and choices need to be made. If a code intends to have directive value, these choices should in our view not be left to the actors involved. Therefore, the BioPrivacy Best Practices covering all possible types of biometric systems lose for this reason strength. It is indirectly admitted as the BioPrivacy Best

---

[64] See EDPS, Turbine opinion, 2011, §16.

[65] International Biometric Group, *BioPrivacy Technology Risk Rating*, available at www.bioprivacy.org.

Practices state that 'it is not expected that any deployment will be compliant with all Best Practices, and non-compliance with one or more Best Practices does not necessarily make a deployment privacy-invasive'. In this way, companies and data controllers soon lose view which suggestions remain crucial. We have further no information about the adoption of the BioPrivacy Best Practices.

The BioVision Best Practices envisioned to provide guidance to developers and suppliers in order to develop privacy compliant biometric systems, giving users control over their data. This approach to embed and to implement privacy and data protection from the early design stage, also referred to as 'Privacy by Design' is as by the EDPS in his Opinion in relation with the Turbine project approved the way to go forward. It is now also explicitly mentioned in Article 23 of the Reform proposal for a General Data Protection Regulation. We will evaluate this concept further below. The BioVision Best Practices provide overall useful guidance for developers and controllers for biometric systems, including for data protection compliance. Although it was the intention of BioVision Best Practices to become a code of conduct, we have not found evidence of further discussions that could have led to its adoption as a code of conduct.

The Privacy Code of the Biometrics Institute in Australia of 2006 could be considered as one of the (very) few codes of conduct in the strict sense in the field of data protection and biometric data processing, i.e. approved by the Australian Privacy Commissioner. It provides detailed guidelines on how to apply the general data protection principles, as well as some supplementary principles, such as restriction to access biometric data to those with a specific need. The low adoption of the Code and its later revocation are however discouraging.

The Turbine Best Practices intend to give a comprehensive overview of guidelines for identity and service provider controllers of biometric systems in the private sector. Examples of biometric IdM system for which the Best Practices are relevant can be found in for example the banking sector to authenticate customers or are ehealth applications intended to authenticate ehealth professionals or to verify their professional qualification. As such, the Best Practices are *not a mere set of legal compliance guidelines* but provide guidelines which are recommended in addition to compliance with existing legal data protection obligations for the privacy-enhancing processing of biometric data. The use of the verification functionality in combination with the local storage of the biometric data under the control of the data subject are hereby considered important. In addition, the use of Privacy-Enhancing Technologies ('PETs'),[66] in particular the deployment of protected templates of biometric data for the irreversibility, the unlinkability and the renewability and revocation

---

[66]PETs have been considered since some time as necessary in preserving privacy of individuals in networks (see, e.g., EU Commission, *Communication from the Commission to the European Parliament and the Council on Promoting Data Protection by Privacy Enhancing Technologies (PETs)*, COM(2007) 228 final, 10 p.), and as having an important role in biometric systems (see also R. Hes, T.F.M. Hooghiemstra and J.J. Borking, *At Face Value. On Biometrical Identification and Privacy*, The Hague, Registratiekamer, September 1999, 74 p.). We will elaborate this some more below.

of biometric identities, and anonymous verification, have been given a clear role in these Best Practices (see BP N° 3, 4 and 7). The use of the irreversible unlinkable biometric (pseudo) identities is in our view of particular importance for biometric IdM systems in order to counter the risks for individuals. Template protection for various biometric characteristics has been researched by the biometric (research) community and is being presented as a solution for particular privacy threats for the data subjects.[67] The EDPS describing that in the project 'the proposed biometric system uses a method which "pseudonymizes" biometric data (fingerprint), replacing them with encrypted irrevocable derivatives (biometric identities) arising through one-way cryptography techniques with the application of hash functions', stated that 'the use of a biometric identity, instead of the raw biometric fingerprint, enhances the protection of the latter, since it is considered impossible, in technical terms, to extract the fingerprint information directly from the biometric identity as proposed (...)' and that this irreversibility 'is welcomed from a data protection and security point of view'.[68] While particular methods or technology will further develop, the *irreversibility, unlinkability and revocability of biometric identities remain essential aspects* for the privacy-enhanced processing of biometric identities and should become required. Independent testing and review in the Turbine project demonstrated that these technologies were in the project performing well and preserving privacy without decrease in performance targets as compared to the use of other technologies.[69] The use of protected templates is also subject of a new standard ISO/IEC 24745 developed in SC 27 WG 5 of ISO/JCT 1, dealing with identity management and privacy technologies.[70]

The use of PETS is, however, not sufficient. Other guidelines are set forth in the Turbine Best Practices as well as described. It is further important to retain that the suggested Best Practices are not a check list for compliance and that a review of

---

[67]See, for an overview of the 'state of the art' in template protection, several presentations given by experts internal and external to the Turbine project of research institutions and companies during the Turbine final public workshop on 17–18 January 2011, available at http://www.turbine-project.eu/workshop_presentations.php; also on these new techniques, see C. Busch and H. Reimer, 'Biometrie in neuem Licht ?', *Datenschutz und Datensicherheit*, 2009, p. 271 and the several contributions in this number on template protection, and Grijpink, J., 'Trend report on biometrics: Some new insights, experiences and developments', *Computer Law & Security Report* 2008, pp. 261–264.

[68]EDPS, Turbine opinion, 2011, §20 and §25.

[69]In the Turbine project, a FRR of less than 1 % was aimed at with a FAR of 0.1 %. According to several project reports, this goal has been met. For the specific results, see C. Bush, D. Gafurov, B. Yang and P. Bours, *Turbine performance evaluation. From Benchmarks to Airport Deployment*, 17 Jan. 2011, available at http://www.turbine-project.eu/workshop_presentations.php and the various publications of Turbine partners about the technology listed on the Turbine website.

[70]See in detail about this standard which is in the meantime adopted, J. Breebaart, B. Yang, I. Buhan-Dulman, Ch. Busch, 'Biometric Template Protection. The need for open standards' in *Datenschutz und Datensicherheit* 2009, pp. 299–304. It is clear however that additional work is required for determining the benchmarks and metrics for these technologies to be able to test and compare several solutions incorporating these aspects of template protection.

any given biometric IdM system with the *applicable national data protection legislation(s)* remains required. Various DPAs have by now also issued opinions on the interpretation of the local data protection legislation with regard to the processing of biometric data. For the compliance of each biometric IdM system all of the data protection requirements as set out in the provisions of the applicable legislation, in particular the special legal requirements for biometric data processing, such as, if applicable, prior notification or authorization by the DPA, and as set forth in these opinions should therefore be checked.

The Turbine Best Practices were also reviewed and commented by the EDPS. An additional aspect which should be taken into account for the deployment of the system and the definition of the fall back procedures is the setting of a specific level of accuracy.

The suggested Turbine Best Practices will be further disseminated and may receive additional feedback. They could be used as a framework for a discussion of the principles, and application, subject to further details, in particular sectors. They could hereby be used as a first step towards a code of conduct. They may also be relevant for a debate about the further regulation of biometric data processing in the private sector. In the meantime, several elements of the Best Practices have also been mentioned in the Article 29 Working Party's Opinion 3/2012 of 27 April 2012 on developments in biometric technologies, in particular in relation to the use of renewable multiple and independent biometric protected templates.

For these reasons, the best practices initiatives should be considered—if followed up—as a further step towards privacy compliant and privacy enhanced processing of biometric data. They also contribute to the Privacy by Design for biometric IdM systems.

14.4.2 The Importance of 'Privacy by Design' for Biometric Systems

The 'Privacy by Design' concept has been mentioned several times already. A basic assumption of the concept is that regulation is only one aspect of privacy and data protection. Legal measures alone will not be able to ensure compliance with the regulatory framework. For this reason, there is rather an approach of 'Privacy by Design' ('PbD') needed. The concept of PbD refers to the principle that at *an early stage* of the design of a system, thought shall be given to *the necessity* to collect and process personal data and to the protection of personal data. PbD principles hence includes, for example, that no more data than those *strictly necessary* shall be collected and processed and that the data shall be processed for the *purposes for which they have been collected.*[71] If privacy is built in the *design and the architecture* of

---

[71] See, e.g., CBP, *Uitgangspunten voor Privacy by Design*, available at the webpages of the theme 'privacy by design' of the Dutch DPA, at http://www.cbpweb.nl/themadossiers/th_pbd_uitgangspunten.shtml.

processing systems, the chances that privacy and data protection legislation are respected, are positively influenced. PbD means that 'privacy and data protection are embedded throughout the entire life cycle of technologies, from the early design stage to their deployment, use and ultimate disposal'.[72] The aim hereby is that privacy protection compliance becomes an integral part of the system and processes, and not just something that is afterwards imposed and reviewed for compliance. PbD understands privacy as a functionality that belongs to the core of the system to be developed. For that reason, PbD could *prevent* that privacy invasive events occur, rather than just offering remedies for resolving privacy breaches.

Some DPAs, in particular the DPA of the Netherlands, the CBP, and outside Europe, the DPA of Ontario, Canada, have stressed since some time the concept of PbD. The CBP hereby included in the concept the approach to review the necessity to identify persons as compared with the possibility to process data anonymously. The CBP also stresses the principle 'less is more' for data protection purposes and recommends to review and refine the authorization procedures for accessing personal data within an organization.[73] The DPA of Ontario, Canada, is of the opinion that PbD can achieve not only *privacy but also security*. It is referred to as the 'positive sum' approach of the DPA of Ontario. The DPA stresses that the concept implies protection from the first step where information is being collected, throughout the *whole lifecycle* of the data, until the deletion of the data. The business practices which comply with a set of rules should be further *transparent*, subject to verification and control. Finally, the data subject should be offered strong privacy protection by default, appropriate notice and empowering user-friendly options.[74] Both DPAs also carefully outline that privacy compliant data processing is also an issue for the whole organization. '[P]rivacy assurance must ideally become *an organization's default mode of operation*' (stress added).[75]

PbD implies in many cases the use and requires the support of technological elements and technical measures, also referred to as—mentioned above—Privacy-Enhancing Technologies or PETs. These PETs could be seen as the *tools* for reaching PbD and in some cases compliance with some specific obligations. The forementioned DPAs refer to the deployment of PETs as a way to cope with privacy and data protection issues. PETS has been described by the EU Commission in its

---

[72]European Commission, *Communication on 'A Digital Agenda for Europe'*, COM(2010) 245, p. 17, footnote 21.

[73]See CBP, *Privacy by Design zelf toepassen*, available at the webpages of the theme 'privacy by design' of the Dutch DPA, at http://www.cbpweb.nl/themadossiers/th_pbd_praktijk.shtml.

[74]See Information and Privacy Commissioner of Ontario, *Privacy by Design. The 7 Foundational Principles*, available at http://www.privacybydesign.ca/background.htm.

[75]*Ibid.* See, e.g., for a detailed description of the implementation of the concept in combination with the use of protected templates for face recognition in a real life environment (for limiting 'self-excluded' problem gambler access to gaming venues) in combination with a watch list, see A. Cavoukian and T. Marinelli, *Privacy-Protective Facial Recognition: Biometric Encryption. Proof of Concept*, Information and Privacy Commissioner Ontario, Ontario Lottery and Gaming Corporation, November 2010, 16 p., available at www.ipc.on.ca. See also Chap. 9 in this book.

Communication on PETs of 2007 as 'a coherent system of ICT measures that protects privacy by *eliminating* or *reducing* personal data or by *preventing unnecessary* and/or *undesired processing* of personal data, all without losing the functionality of the information system'.[76] While the European Commission's objective was and still is to promote the use of PETs, its fore mentioned Communication in 2007 was by some considered as disappointing.[77]

The importance of PbD and of PETs in relation to the use of biometric systems is, however, increasingly recognized and obvious, as we indicated above. The specific nature and the risks relating to the processing of biometric data may be reduced by deploying the appropriate PbD and PETs for preserving privacy without giving in on performance targets.[78]

At the same time, the relation between PbD, PETs and existing legislation is in our view at least muddled. Some principles in the present data protection legislation, such as the data minimization principle, may lead some to belief that the adoption of PbD is mandatory. As mentioned, PbD is now also mentioned as an obligation of the controller in the Reform proposal in Article 23. While the data minimization principle implies that controllers shall carefully review whether the personal data they collect (such as biometric information) is necessary, the present legislation does not impose upon controllers particular PbD technologies or methods to be used. While the use of PbD is recommended by many DPAs, the EDPS and also the European Commission, specific measures which are part of PbD are not imposed.[79] Some of the examples on PbD for biometric systems and put forward by the Article 29 Working Party in its Opinion 3/2012, such as automated data erasure mechanisms, are however in this regard very useful. The importance of PbD, PETS and data minimization will in our view only increase in view of the expected future massive collection of personal data in general. Presently, it remains up to the personal data controllers, including the controllers of biometric data, to decide upon the deployment of practical PbD measures and methods.

The question may further raise whether PbD may replace compliance measures by the controller in general. PbD will remain, however, in principle *complementary*

---

[76]European Commission, *Communication from the Commission to the European Parliament and the Council on Promoting Data Protection by Privacy Enhancing Technologies (PETs)*, COM(2007) 228 final, p. 3. The research in PETs often relates to identity management systems.

[77]See J.-M. Dinant, 'Chap. 5. The Concepts of Identity and Identifiability: Legal and Technical Deadlocks for Protecting Human Beings in the Information Society', *Reinventing Data Protection?* in S. Gutwirth, Y. Poullet, P. De Hert, C. de Terwange, S. Nouwt (eds.), Springer, 2009, (111), pp. 118–119.

[78]See also E. Kindt, 'The use of privacy enhancing technologies for biometric systems analyzed from a legal perspective', in M. Bezzi et al. (eds.), *Privacy and Identity*, IFIP International Federation for Information Processing AICT 320, 2010, pp. 134–145.

[79]The Commission stated it in its Communication on PETs of 2007 as follows: 'The use of PETs can *help* to design information and communication systems and services in a way that minimizes the collection and use of personal data and facilitate compliance with data protection rules' (emphasis added).

to appropriate legislation and the legal enforcement thereof. Technology may be useful to solve various privacy and data protection issues and to improve the privacy-compliance of systems,[80] but cannot replace the legislative framework. PdB may be fit to mitigate particular risks, but shall not be relied upon as the only approach which makes legislation superfluous. Notwithstanding this, PbD is sometimes promoted by some as the (only) way to ensure privacy and data protection compliance.

14.5 Conclusion

Best Practices are at irregular intervals suggested and discussed as a way to solve the many outstanding issues and risks for biometric data processing systems. We have discussed above a few examples of the past as well the suggested Best Practices developed in Turbine, which takes new developments of technology into account. Such best practices are also often intended to implement PbD. These initiatives are valuable and should be more relied upon. At the same time, one should not omit to question whether a code of conduct or recommendations formulated in the form of best practices are the best way to go forward. It is true that industry has most often favored self-regulation above legislation. This position can be followed to the extent legislation would prove to be unbalanced, too detailed or in the worst case remain silent or is of bad quality. A list of best practices is also very helpful if the technology is being developed and several uncertainties remain. Best Practise, to the extent formalized in a code which can be formally adopted, such as in the example of Australia, could in this case be a valuable alternative, provided the code *is* widely adopted. This is often the weak point. Incentives for the adoption are therefore needed. In Europe, a code of conduct in the domain of biometric data processing approved by the data protection authorities which can be formally adopted by a particular sector, does to our knowledge not yet exist. A code of conduct for the processing of biometric data by a particular sector, approved by the national DPA or the Article 29 Working Party would certainly be a step forward in the regulation of biometric systems. The formal adoption of such code—subject to an independent audit and certification—could also be a requirement for particular contracts.

Some aspects, however, should not be left too long to best practices alone. For example, the use of biometric data as a universal unique identifier, should in our view be strictly regulated and possibly forbidden by law, unless legislation details the specific purposes, access and other sufficient guarantees for the data subjects.[81] Member States have in fact the obligation under the Directive 95/46/EC to determine more precisely the conditions under which any identifier of general application may be processed[82] but very few Member States have enacted specific legislation for biometric data processing so far.

---

[80] See and compare also, e.g., with recital 46 and Article 14(3) of Directive 2002/58/EC.

[81] See and compare, e.g., with the use of biometric data as identifier in legislation setting up large-scale systems on Union level such as Eurodac.

[82] Article 8.7 Directive 95/46/EC.

Finally, technology does have an important role in protecting privacy and data protection rights of individuals in biometric IdM systems. In particular the revocability, the irreversibility and unlinkability of biometric (pseudo)identities guaranteed by specific methods and technologies are essential for the use of biometric data in the private sector from a privacy and data protection point. The EDPS has underlined the importance of these aspects in his opinion on the Turbine project as well. Incentives to adopt the appropriate technologies should be given. Including them in a list of best practices for biometric data processing is only a first step.

Chapter 15
Biometrics and the Challenge to Human Rights in Europe. Need for Regulation and Regulatory Distinctions

Paul De Hert

Abstract This report calls for regulation. With biometric applications gradually rolling out in the public and private sector, legislation, even detailed legislation, on the use of biometrics might make compliance to general data protection principles more likely than it is today. A regulatory distinction needs to be made between large scale information systems at EU level and others. The former are in need of tailor made data protection solutions and require (with every new system added or altered) a separate parliamentary and democratic debate. The latter are in need of guidance and best practices, which once found, should be better enforced. Today codification of best practices as developed by DPA's and other regulatory or supervisory authorities becomes a possibility. We see no good reason *not* to affirm that public or private controllers of data should *not* store raw data (because it is unique and therefore dangerous), *not* collect fingerprints (because fingerprints leave traces and are not accepted by many), *not* store biometrics in a central database (there are alternatives), or *should* encrypt biometric data used for processing, *should* use *multiple authentications*, *should* offer alternative schemes of authentication when biometrics are asked on basis of consent, *should* in case of a rejection, as a result of a biometric system, be obliged to re-examine the case and *should*, where necessary, offer appropriate alternative solutions. It is true that the technical possibilities of biometrics make *its* assessment complex, but by making the right regulatory distinctions this can be overcome.

"The application of biometrics raises important human rights questions. The integrity of the human body and the way it is used with regard to biometrics constitute a branch of so called "human dignity". Therefore, in considering whether or not to apply biometrics as a solution to a specific problem, controllers should exhibit special ethical responsibility. Biometrics is in its infancy and there is still little knowl-

P. De Hert (✉)
Vrije Universiteit Brussels (VUB- LSTS), Pleinlaan 2, 1050 Brussels, Belgium
e-mail: paul.de.hert@vub.ac.be

P. De Hert
Tilburg University (TILT), Tilburg, The Netherlands

P. Campisi (ed.), *Security and Privacy in Biometrics*,
DOI 10.1007/978-1-4471-5230-9_15, © Springer-Verlag London 2013

edge about possible draw-backs. Once the technique is chosen on a larger scale, an irreversible development is started with unforeseeable effects. The precautionary principle requires a certain reticence under these circumstances" (Committee [21, sub 10]).

"Very few countries have enacted general legislation regulating the processing of biometric data. Some countries have (more recently) enacted legislation regulating the use of camera surveillance. Article 5 of the Directive 95/46/EC states as a general rule that Member States shall determine 'more precisely the conditions under which the processing of personal data is lawful'. In the absence of such legislation and conditions laid down therein for biometric systems, which exist in a large variety and modalities, this principle of 'fair and lawful' processing remains for biometric systems therefore vague and in our view difficult to enforce" (Kindt [61, p. 23]).

15.1 Introduction

Biometric data are unique and individual physical characteristics that differ from one human being to the next and that remain unaltered for life (e.g. DNA samples, fingerprint images, pictures of the iris or the retina and voice-recording). Biometric data are very reliable means of authentication because they allow one to prove a very strong connection between an individual and his alleged identity through the verification of an individual's unique physical biometric data.

In comparison with other means of authentication, such as badges or passwords, biometric data reduce the chance of abuse because they cannot be transferred to third parties. Therefore, biometric technologies that use biometric data to confirm an individual's claimed identity can both improve overall safety and reduce risk of fraud.

In 2005 the Council of Europe issued a "Progress report on the application of the principles of convention 108 to the collection and processing of biometric data". This report has been prepared by the Consultative Committee of the Convention for the Protection of Individuals with regard to automatic processing of personal data (T-PD) of the Council of Europe. It was made public in February 2005 by the Council of Europe in order to contribute to the debates and projects on biometrics that are currently under way in many member states of the Council of Europe and in other international fora, such as the OECD and the ICAO (International Civil Aviation Organization). It contains an analysis of the specificities of biometrics, a discussion on the criteria for choosing a system architecture and guidance for the application of the Council of Europe Convention for the Protection of Individuals with regard to Automatic Processing of Personal Data (Convention 108) to the use of biometrics. Acknowledging the fact that many aspects of biometrics are not yet fully known, the report does not state any final conclusions and leaves them open to future revision or addition by the Council of Europe.

Five years later it is time to look at biometrics again, but it is still doubtful whether more clarity can be reached. Technological progress in the development of biometric techniques is unmistakable. The technological functionality of available systems is maturing and showing improved capability. With biometric techniques, we refer to the identification or authentication of individuals based on a physical or behavioral characteristic through the use of mathematical and statistical methods. It is obvious that without information technology (especially ever improving network capabilities) and the availability and advances made in new sensor technology, the world of biometrics would not show such rapid development. Proliferation of sensor technology has had immediate implications for biometric technologies, it will extend their range and heighten their accuracy and intrusiveness. It is the emerging intelligent distributed sensor networks that are paving the way for second generation biometrics.

The average minister, official or parliamentarian involved in law making will already face difficulties in assessing the efficiency and implications of the first generation biometric techniques as used in commercial applications currently available on the market. The main reason for this is that the information available is often contradictory. An additional complication is the blurring of boundaries between potential (future) and current capacity of biometric applications [72]. This is, and will remain, a source of technical and political confusion [85]. Even more complex (even for experts), is an assessment of the societal impact of the use of biometrics [4, 6, 10, 49, 50, 58, 74, 76]. A systematic, constantly updated and forward looking analysis and assessment of the societal, economic and legal impact of increased application biometrics is needed to inform the political process.

In this report we will mainly restrict ourselves to an analysis of the legal implications of first and second generation biometric applications.

The handling of first generation biometric data—such as finger- and iris-scans—already creates fundamental discussions about the scope of data protection and human rights law. The introduction of soft biometrics, i.e. the use of general traits such as gender, weight, height, age, or ethnicity for automated classification, is even more contested [86]. It has attracted the criticism of indiscriminate social sorting, as automated decisions are created that divide people into categories for further processing. What are the legal implications of automated sorting of people on the basis of their behavior (and/or general traits) into classifications such as for example, Asians and non-Asians, young and old, gay and hetero, and so forth? On the one hand, as machines are taking the decisions, the act of sorting takes on a seemingly neutral dimension. On the other hand, the embedded systems, ambient intelligence, distant sensing and passive biometrics involved require no conscious cooperation from subjects and thus pose a challenge to the traditional concepts used in the fields of data protection and human rights. In short, the problematic legal aspects of these developments are covert data capture, lack of transparency and consent. Some second generation biometrics used for authentication or multiple factor assessments such as heart rate, body temperature, brain activity patterns, and pupil dilation even question the validity of current consensus on what constitutes personal data. These new body data, often collected in an embedded and passive fashion, need to be assessed from a legal viewpoint. So where does the traditional approach become problematic? At first sight this is the issue of transparent collection of biometric data by consent.

Many second generation biometrics are collected whilst the data subject is unaware. Data is collected from a distance and the collection does not need to be apparent. The paradigm change here is that tracking and tracing becomes the norm. This is the fundamental change that insidiously installs a surveillance society. The question then becomes: where does this leave the law [80]?

This report calls for regulation. With biometric applications gradually rolling out in the public and private sector, legislation, even detailed legislation, on the use of biometrics might make compliance to general data protection principles more likely than it is today. A regulatory distinction needs to be made between large scale information systems at EU level and others. The former are in need of tailor made data protection solutions and require (with every new system added or altered) a separate parliamentary and democratic debate. The latter are in need of guidance and best practices, which once found, should be better enforced. Today codification of best practices as developed by DPA's and other regulatory or supervisory authorities becomes a possibility. We see no good reason *not* to affirm that public or private controllers of data should *not* store raw data (because it is unique and therefore dangerous), *not* collect fingerprints (because fingerprints leave traces and are not accepted by many), *not* store biometrics in a central database (there are alternatives), or *should* encrypt biometric data used for processing, *should* use *multiple authentications*, *should* offer alternative schemes of authentication when biometrics are asked on basis of consent, *should* in case of a rejection, as a result of a biometric system, be obliged to re-examine the case and *should*, where necessary, offer appropriate alternative solutions. It is true that the technical possibilities of biometrics make *its* assessment complex, but by making the right regulatory distinctions this can be overcome.

15.2 Legal Principles Governing Personal Data

Since the 1960s, and especially during the 1970s, it had been felt that, for the right to respect of one's private life, to offer sufficient guarantees for the individual in front of such developments, special attention needed to be granted to the automated processing of personal data. This perception notably lead to the adoption of the Convention for the Protection of Individuals with regard to Automatic Processing of Personal Data of 1981 (Convention 108),[1] as well as of many other legal instruments focusing on the regulation of the processing of personal data.[2] As a starting point for this report, we assume that all biometric data are personal data protected

---

[1]Convention for the Protection of Individuals with regard to Automatic Processing of Personal Data, Strasbourg, 28/1/1981 (Convention N° 108), and Additional Protocol to the Convention for the Protection of Individuals with regard to Automatic Processing of Personal Data regarding supervisory authorities and transborder data flows, Strasbourg, 8/12/2001.

[2]See, notably: OECD-Guidelines on the Transborder Flows of Personal Data, Paris, 23 Sept 1980 (via www.oecd.org) and the Directive 95/46/EC of the European Parliament and Council of 24 October 1995 on the protection of individuals with regard to the processing of personal data and on the free movement of such data, *OJ* L281, 23.11.1995, pp. 31–50.

by European data protection legislation [29, 30, 59, 60] (see also *below*). Before going into detailed analysis of these regulations, we will first extract some basic principles behind data protection law and formulate some questions that show how these principles might affect the choice or even admissibility of the use of certain types of biometrics.

The Convention and the Directive aim to protect the rights and freedoms of persons with respect to the processing of personal data. It does so by laying down rights for the person whose data is processed, and setting guidelines and duties for the controller, or processor thus determining when this processing is lawful. The rights, duties and guidelines relate to: data quality; making data processing legitimate; special categories of processing; information to be given to the data subject; the data subject's right of access to data; the data subject's right to object to data processing; confidentiality and security of processing; and notification of processing to a supervisory authority.

In accordance with Article 5 of the Convention and with Article 6 of the 95/46/EC Directive (which has been implemented in all EU member states), personal data must be collected for specified, explicit and legitimate purposes only and may not be further processed in a way that is incompatible with those purposes. In addition, the data themselves must be adequate, relevant and not excessive in relation to the purpose for which they are collected (principle of purpose). Once the purpose for which data are collected has been established, an assessment of the proportionality of collecting and processing these data can be made. Hence, some data protection principles relevant in the context of this report are confidentiality, purpose specification, proportionality and individual participation. If we translate these principles into day-to-day biometrics they can lead to questions such as:

- *Confidentiality*: Has the biometric system concerned been sufficiently tested to warrant a minimum level of confidentiality protection?
- *Purpose specification*: Is there sufficient protection against unauthorized use of the biometric data for purposes beyond the original goal. Can purposes keep being added? To what extent does the collection of biometric data aim discriminate?
- *Proportionality*: Are the biometric data adequate, relevant and proportional in relation to the purpose for which they are collected? More specifically, is verification used, when there is no need for identification? Is one biometric measure more proportional than another?
- *Individual participation*: Are fallback procedures put into place in cases where biometric data, be it raw images or templates, become unreadable? Can individuals opt not to provide their biometric or not to have their biometrics read?

15.3 The European Data Protection Framework and Biometrics

15.3.1 General

The abovementioned Convention 108 and Directive 95/46/EC [33] constitute the main and general legal framework for the processing of personal data. The Convention applies to the automatic processing of personal data (Article 1). Personal data are defined as data that contain information about an identified or identifiable natural person (Article 2, Paragraph a). The Directive came afterwards and brings electronic visual and auditory processing systems explicitly within its remit.[3] The preamble says *"Whereas, given the importance of the developments under way, in the framework of the information society, of the techniques uses to capture, transmit, manipulate, record, store or communicate sound and image data relating to natural persons, this Directive should be applicable to processing involving such data".*[4] Processing of sound and visual data is thus considered as an action to which the Directive applies. Processing is very broad: it can be automatic or manual and can consist of one of the following operations: collection, recording, organization, storage, adaptation, alteration, retrieval, consultation, use, disclosure by transmission and so forth. The sheer fact of collecting visual (for example face scan) or sound data can therefore already be considered as processing. Without going into too much detail, we will make a quick scan of the provisions of the Directive in relation to biometrics [52, 77].

15.3.2 The Notion of Personal Data

Article 2(a) of that Directive defines personal data as 'any information relating to an identified or identifiable natural person', in a similar way to Convention 108 (see above). Although neither text mentions biometric data as such, its legal provisions and principles also apply to the processing of biometric data since they meet the requirements laid down in Article 2(a) of the Directive and Article 2, Paragraph a of the Convention.[5] In a generic biometric system, processes can be broken down into five stages: data collection, transmission, signal or image processing, matching decision, storage [2, p. 13]. In the sense of the Convention and the Directive, all

---

[3]We note in passing that the EU Directive has some limitations to its scope unknown to the Convention. The Directive does not apply to the processing of personal data by a natural person in the course of a purely personal or household activity and to the processing of personal data in the course of an activity that falls outside the scope of European law, such as operations concerning public security, defense or State security.

[4]Directive 95/46/EC, Preamble, §14.

[5]The four key elements to the definition of personal data are "any information", "relating to", "identified or identifiable" and "natural person". According to the *Biovision Best Practice Report* [2]: personal data that relate to the implementation of a biometric at least include: the image or record captured from a censor; any transmitted form of the image or record between sensor and processing systems; the processed data, whether completely transformed to a template or only partially processed by an algorithm; the stored image or record or template; any accompanying data collected at the time of the enrollment; the image or record captured from the sensor during normal operation of the biometric; any transmitted form or image or record at verification or identification; the template obtained from the storage device; any accompanying data obtained at the time of verification or identification; the result of the matching process when linked to particular actions or transmissions; and any updating of the template in response to the identification or verification.

these five processes in biometric systems should be considered as processing of data unless they take place in a personal or household context such as data handling in a family home biometric entry system.[6]

15.3.3 Who Is in Control of Biometrical Data?

Article 2, Paragraph d of the Convention and Article 2(e) of the Directive define the controller and the processor of data. In most cases, under this definition, the data controller or processor of biometric data will be the operator who runs the system. The controller is the person who establishes the purpose of the data, the categories of data to be collected and their use (Article 2, Paragraph d Convention). In the Consultative Committee report [21, sub 54–56] attention is drawn to the complex arrangements behind biometrical schemes with either controllers or sub-contractors who process biometric data on behalf of the controller. These arrangements do not diminish the controller's full responsibility in law, but can render it less clear in practice. The Committee rightly recommends that in all these complex situations it is necessary to make explicit who the controller is and to make this transparent for the data subject.[7]

15.3.4 Consent

In theory the first collection of biometric data (to be enrolled) will be either compulsory, on the basis of a law, or voluntary. Outside the realm of public law, most biometric schemes are based on consent. Article 7(a) of the Directive requires consent to be 'unambiguously' given. The Convention is almost silent on the issue of consent but states that personal data should be obtained and processed fairly and lawfully (Article 5, Paragraph a). Fairness is a broad concept that can be understood as implying consent and/or (at least) information. With regard to biometric data, it

---

[6]It has been claimed that the Convention and the Directive do not apply to biometric data in specific processing circumstances, that is to say when the data can no longer be traced back to a specific identifiable person [60]. Nevertheless, one has to acknowledge that the essence of all biometric systems per se is that the data processed relate to identified or identifiable persons. These systems use personal characteristics to either identify the person to whom these characteristics belong or to verify that the characteristics belong to a person that has been authorized to use the system. In most cases where biometric data are concerned, there is a link to the person at least for the data controller, who must be able to check the final proper functionality of the biometric system and cases of false rejects or false matches. See [21, sub 51–52].

[7]"The data subject has the right to know, without elaborate research, whom to address in case of alleged contraventions to the rules of data protection. It is not up to him or her in such complex cases to find out who is willing to or—after being sued—is compelled to assume responsibility" [21, sub 56].

implies in particular that the data subject is informed of the collection of data on him or her. The data subject must be aware of the purpose of the collection and of the identity of the controller. The inclusion of consent in the Directive was controversial from the start. In a 2009 study on *The Future of Privacy* the Article 29 Working Party notes that there are many cases in which consent cannot be given freely, especially when there is a clear unbalance between the data subject and the data controller (for example in the employment context or when personal data must be provided to public authorities). 'In addition, the requirement that consent has to be informed starts from the assumption that it needs to be fully understandable to the data subject what will happen if he decides to consent to the processing of his data. However, the complexity of data collection practices, business models, vendor relationships and technological applications in many cases outstrips the individual's ability or willingness to make decisions to control the use and sharing of information through active choice' [90, p. 17]. In 2005 the Council of Europe's Consultative Committee voiced similar concerns: "It is said that the data subject has a free choice, for instance to get a bank card for withdrawing money. The Committee notices that similar systems started in the past with a free choice for the client but evolved through a mass application and the acceptance of nonnegotiable standard contracts or clauses into a situation where de facto there is no longer a choice for data subjects that want to take part in ordinary life. Although there is no law obliging citizens, technology has become so pervasive that for individuals that want to take part in daily life a real choice is no longer available" [21, sub 58].

The solution to this is partly to enforce the data subject's standing by enhancing transparency as a pre-condition for valid consent, impose opt-in rather than op-out mechanisms, and, where appropriate, facilitating the data subjects' right to revoke consent, with subsequent data deletion in all servers involved (including proxies and mirroring) [90, pp. 8 & 14].[8] However, and this is also acknowledged by the Working Party, the other half of the approach, is attained by simply excluding consent in situations where it is not the appropriate legal basis [90, p. 8]. The observation is more than relevant for biometrics and we will therefore come back to it. It means in the current state of affairs that regulatory intervention is needed, either by regulating biometrics at the level of European and Member State's law or through regulatory intervention by the National Data Protection Authorities.

15.3.5 Biometrical Data and the Prohibition of Processing Sensitive Data

Article 8(2) of the Directive states a general prohibition on the processing of sensitive data to which some exemptions apply. Sensitive data in terms of biometrics can

---

[8]Compare "When biometric systems are introduced based on consent as a general rule a non-biometric back up procedure is required as users may opt out at any time" [68, p. 147].

include medical, ethnic/racial, behavioral information, or data concerning sex life. In general, processing of sensitive biometric information (relating to ethnic origin for example) will need the explicit consent of the data subject. This requirement sits uncomfortably with the automatic sorting into categories of people on the basis of their bodily traits that characterizes some second generation biometric applications.

Article 6 of the Convention ('Special categories of data') is far more concise than Article 8(2) of the Directive, but its message is of great value. The Article states that the processing of sensitive data is prohibited 'unless domestic law provides appropriate safeguards'. Again we find a regulatory incentive, which clearly favors legislative intervention (see paragraph *above*). We will come back to this *below* in Sect. 15.7.3.

15.3.6 Data Accuracy

Article 6(d) of the Directive states that data must be accurate and, where necessary, kept up to date. In terms of biometrics, this imposes the obligation to use only such biometric systems that have low false match rates so that there is only a small probability of processing incorrect data.

15.3.7 Prior Checking

With regard to the regulatory options it is useful to discuss Article 20 of the Directive stating that the Member states shall determine processing operations likely to present specific risks to the freedoms of data subjects and shall check that these processing operations are examined prior to the start thereof. An assessment of risks created by biometrics is subject to interpretation by member states. The margin of interpretation regarding this provision has turned out to be wide. Whilst the French authorities regard every biometric system as presenting potential risks, other national data protection authorities have come to different conclusions. The Dutch Data Protection Authority has so far not used the power of *prior checking* as granted by this provision.

This situation, so we believe, has less to do with biometrics. There are big differences regarding the position of the DPAs in the Member States. This is due to the differences in history, case law, culture and the internal organization of the Member States, but also because Article 28 of Directive, Article 13 of the Convention *and* the Additional Protocol to the Convention 'regarding supervisory authorities and transborder data flows'[9] lack precision in several aspects. On top of that, the Directive, supposedly more up to date and more specific then the Convention, has, to a certain

---

[9]*CETS* No. 181. The Protocol entered into force (only) in 2004.

extent, been poorly implemented in some jurisdictions. This has resulted in large
divergences between the Member States regarding, amongst others, the position, resources and powers of DPAs [90, pp. 21–22]. The instrument of prior checking as
contained in Article 20 of the Directive seems to be a suitable instrument to regulate biometrical applications with critical or non mature features. The regulatory
framework needs to be enriched with a provision allowing a more harmonized approach, for instance by giving WP 29 the power to make prior checking operational.
A similar instrument could be introduced and developed at the Council of Europe
level.

15.3.8 Rules on Automated Decisions on Individuals

Finally, Article 15(1) of the Directive lays down the rules on automated decisions
on individuals subjected to biometric processing. Central here is the notion of human intervention before a final decision is taken. Examples of an automated decision using biometrics could include border crossing and immigration processes in
the public sector, and biometric processes at the workplace in the private sector. In
cases where the biometric application is only used to support an authentication process and the legal decision is not based solely on the biometric process, Article 15
ought not to apply. In all other cases it does. We will come back to this provision
when discussing second generation biometrics below, but here we want to highlight
a paragraph in the Council of Europe's Committee on fair processing and profiling.
Although the Convention does not contain a prohibition on machine decisions comparable to Article 15 of the Directive, a similar prohibition (and a corresponding
duty to process and profile in a transparent way) is instated by the principle of fair
processing enshrined in the Convention operates in a similar fashion.[10]

15.4 The Article 29 Data Protection Working Party on Biometrics

The above mentioned Council of Europe "Progress report on the application of the
principles of Convention 108 to the collection and processing of biometric data"

---

[10]"A legitimate purpose for the processing of associated data is to secure the good functioning of
the biometric system. As a side-effect somebody's behavior may be profiled. Each time the data
subject submits his or her biometric features he or she may leave more or less exact traces of
where he or she was, when, for how long, with whom, etc. The principle of fair processing would
entail the data subject being able to know of each collection of associated data. Often it will be
evident to the data subject as he or she has to submit his or her biometric data deliberately. In
other cases, it is because he or she will need to be informed by the controller. Depending on the
circumstances, it might be sufficient to give the information in general terms. In cases where it is
not self-evident that in a concrete manner associated data are collected, the principle of 'fairness'
implies that information is given to the data subject on each occasion the data are collected. The
associated data should not be used for purposes incompatible with those for which they have been
collected" [21, sub 60].

(2005) written by the Consultative Committee of the Convention for the Protection of Individuals with regard to automatic processing of personal data (T-PD) of the Council of Europe makes a footnote reference to the 2003 guidelines drafted by the Article 29 Data Protection Working Party (hereinafter the WP29). This is an EU independent European advisory body established by the above mentioned EU Directive, whose membership consists of representatives of national supervisory bodies. The statements and opinions of WP29 not only have an impact on national judiciaries but also on the national supervisory bodies themselves [31, pp. 23–24]. In fact, one of the core objectives of WP29 has been to help Europe's data protection practices move and evolve together instead of moving apart. As part of this mission they have undertaken a review of the interpretation of personal data across member states and adopted guidance to help clarify their position.

In August 2003, the WP29 provided specific guidelines for the processing of biometric data in a working document on biometrics [61, 69, 88]. These guidelines are highly relevant for biometric identity management systems in general, whether used in the public sphere or for private commercial purposes. The Working Party considers that biometric data will, due to its content, be covered by the EU Data Privacy Directive (95/46/EC) as it is transposed into national legislation of the Member States. Biometric systems serve two main purposes, on the one hand identification on the other hand authentication/verification of a person. Depending on the objective of the system, different types of storage can/should be used. For identification purposes a centralized database can be used. In such a case, as the Working Party considers this to present certain special risks, it calls for regular checks by the competent national data protection authority. In other cases of authentication/verification, decentralized storage is to be preferred, e.g. in a smart card under the control of the relevant data subject.

Additionally, the Working Paper also highlights the need to heed the following:

- collecting biometric data can be a particularly dangerous endeavor, if it is done without the subject's knowledge (e.g. distance face or voice recognition);
- the (re)use of the biometric data for a purpose other than that for which it was collected (e.g. shift from access control purpose to surveillance in the workplace);
- the necessity and proportionality principles (e.g. access to a school restaurant with the use of school children's fingerprints, has been found to be disproportional);
- automated decisions making admission based on biometric data (e.g. access control to airports); and
- specific safeguards should be enacted to protect biometric data that contain sensitive personal data (e.g. face recognition systems that reveal racial or ethnic origin or health status).

Lastly, the Working Party recommends that the industry develop codes of conduct to implement data privacy principles with regard to the use of biometric identifiers.

The 2003 Working Paper was the first of its kind. It was well received, but the general feeling was that the document did not say 'it all', especially with regard to the principle of proportionality and the purpose limitation principles, both of which are regarded as decisive principles guiding authorities and controllers in their choice of biometrics [59, 66]. In the years after, the Working Paper would focus its efforts on the use of biometrics in applications controlled by governments, such as in passports, travel documents and ID cards and in large scale databases such as a Visa Information System (VIS) and the Schengen Information System (SIS II). In its opinions on these initiatives, the Working Party highlights the risks of the implementation of biometrics in these applications in its current form.

WP29 has further reflected on the meaning of biometric data in an opinion on the concept of personal data [89]. In this opinion, the function of biometric data to establish a link with an individual and to function as an identifier was stressed. The working party therefore pulled up just short of regarding all biometric data as sensitive data under the directive. The advantages offered by using biometrics as a key identifier are contested. As all biometric applications and especially large scale systems are still in the roll out phase, the WP29, followed by many technical experts, finds it a dangerous strategy to place complete reliance on the security and reliability of biometrics as a key identifier (see also [51, 60, 77]).

In the already mentioned 2009 study on *The Future of Privacy* from the Article 29 Working Party, biometrics is touched upon several times, but not in a systematic way [90, p. 17]. We will come back to these remarks made in the sections on user empowerment, privacy enhancing technologies and on proportionality. Of interest here is the closing section of the study 'Conditions for law and policy making' in which the Working Party insists on guarantees with regard to governmental use of data, especially in the context of law enforcement:

"109. The need for evaluation of the existing legal instruments and their application is of utmost importance and should take into account the costs for privacy. Evaluation of existing measures should take place before taking new measures. Additionally, a periodic review of existing measures should take place.

110. Transparency is an essential element. Clear information should be available to data subjects on the use of the information collected and the logic underlying the processing and should only be limited if necessary in individual cases to not jeopardize investigations and for a limited period of time. Access and rectification rights of the data subject should be addressed in a cross border context to avoid that the data subject loses control.

111. Special attention is needed for transparency and democratic control in the legislative process. Privacy impact assessments, appropriate forms of consultation of data protection authorities and an effective parliamentary debate, at national and EU level, should play an important role.

112. The architecture of any system for storage and exchange of personal data should be well elaborated. Some general considerations are:

- Privacy by design and PETS (certification scheme) should determine the architecture. In the area of freedom, security and justice where public authorities are the main actors and every initiative aimed at increasing surveillance of individuals and increasing the collection and use of personal information could have a direct impact their fundamental right to privacy and data protection, those requirements could be made compulsory.
- Purpose limitation and data minimization should remain guiding principles.
- Access to large databases must be configured in such a way that in general no direct access on line to data stored allowed, and a hit/no hit system or an index system is in general considered preferable.
- The choice between models with central storage, meaning systems with a central database on EU-level and decentralized storage should be made on transparent criteria and in any

event ensure a solid arrangement providing for a clear definition of the role and responsibilities of the controller/s and ensuring the appropriate supervision by the competent data protection authorities.
- Biometric data should only be used if the use of other less intrusive material does not present the same effect.
(...)

114. Special attention—including where necessary tailor made safeguards for data protection—is needed for large scale information systems within the EU.
(...)
116. Cooperation between DPAs in charge of ensuring lawfulness of data processing should be strengthened in all matters and integrated in the legal framework, also by envisaging stable mechanisms similar to those currently applying to first pillar matters, in order to foster a harmonized approach across the EU and beyond" [90, pp. 26–27].

All these recommendations are worth discussing in detail and it strikes the reader that biometrics is referred to in several of them. If 'government teaches by example' is the credo, then there is reason for concern. In the following we would like to elaborate on the last recommendation. In the current framework, national DPA's play an important role when assessing new technologies that are being introduced on the market. The biometrics experience allows us to investigate the strength of that system.

15.5 Data Protection Agencies

15.5.1 General

The national Data Protection Agencies (the DPAs) have all embarked on the task of the interpretation of the data protection legislation applied to biometrics for use in the private sector. In most countries national data protection legislation based on the Directive does not explicitly mention biometrics. In the majority of cases, DPAs have reviewed the processing of biometric data upon request for a preliminary opinion by the data controller or upon notification of the processing. In France, it has become mandatory, since 2004, for controllers to request such an opinion. The controller needs this opinion, in fact an authorization, before the start of the processing of biometric data.[11] France is therefore one of the few countries that has acted proactively in response to the emerging trend of the use of biometric data by imposing such prior authorization. This has created an enormous workload for the CNIL, resulting in the creation of the concept of 'unique authorizations' to help ease the task in 2006. The CNIL is not alone in being too understaffed a data protection authority to be able to carry out its tasks [82].

The DPAs have many more competences to exercise. These competences include, according to the Directive, endowment with investigative powers, such as access to

---

[11]Later on, in 2006, the CNIL issued some 'unique authorizations' which permit controllers, if they comply with all requirements, to file a declaration of conformity.

the (biometric) data processed by a controller and powers to collect all the information necessary. In addition, powers of intervention, including the competence to order the erasure of data or to impose temporary or definitive bans on the use of (biometric) data, and the power to engage in legal proceedings against controllers if they do not respect data protection provisions. The DPAs can also hear claims of individuals who state that their rights and freedoms with regard to the processing of personal data have been infringed or hear claims of organizations representing such individuals. Appeals against the decisions of the DPAs are in principle possible before the national courts of the country where the DPA is established. Appeals should conform to the existing procedure for appeal against such (administrative) decisions. In the United Kingdom, for example, the 'Information Tribunal' has been set up (formerly the 'Data Protection Tribunal') to determine appeals against notices and decisions served by the Information Commissioner [83].

15.5.2 The Dutch Data Protection Authority

In the Netherlands, the general data protection law of 2000, as modified, (hereinafter the 'Data Protection Act') is in principle applicable to the collection and processing of biometric data. The Data Protection Act, however, does not contain specific provisions that mention biometric data as such.

In contrast to France (see above), in the Netherlands it is not mandatory to request an opinion on the processing of biometric data. Normally, except for an administrative check, the DPA does not take further steps after it receives a notification of the processing of biometric data.[12] A notification of the use of a biometric application with the DPA is thus all that is required to get a new biometric application going. Formally, a notification to the data protection authority does not imply a formal 'go'. On the contrary, the notification allows the authority to react on whether this is needed or not. In practice, and due to staff constraints, this seldom happens. It is also not required that the processor or controller wait for a 'green light'. The controller can start the processing straight after notification.

The DPA has been very active on the issue of biometrics. In 1999, it already proactively published an extensive report on the privacy aspects of biometrics [52]. It was the result of a study performed jointly by the DPA and the Netherlands Organization for Applied Research-Physics and Electronics Laboratory (TNO-FEL). The report concluded that designers, developers, suppliers and users of products using biometrics for identification, authentication, or exposure of emotions needed to consider ways to protect the privacy of users. The report also provided a checklist with practical directions, for those who want to build a privacy-enhanced product that processes biometrical data. It stated that personal data should be pro-

---

[12]The Dutch Data Protection Authority is the CBP (College Bescherming Persoonsgegevens). See also [28].

tected with proper PET[13] and referred to crucial decisions in the design phase. In particular, to decisions concerning the question whether to protect data by decentralization of the template storage and/or verification, or encryption.[14] In the next section of this report, the options for using biometrics as a privacy enhancing technology will be discussed. Here it suffices to observe that the Dutch DPA produced a detailed report at a very early stage, a report that was authoritative and contained conclusions, practical directions and recommendations. To date, it has not been followed up by more detailed guidelines or descriptions of best practice.

The role of the DPA in practice has been to receive notifications, conduct administrative checks on them and place all notifications on a register accessible through its website (see www.cbp.nl). A few organizations have asked the DPA to issue a preliminary opinion, and it has done so. Whilst the 1999 report was very proactive, since then the Dutch DPA activities have been of a more responsive nature. Concerning the semi public or private use of biometric applications, the main supervisory activity of the DPA has been the publication of three preliminary opinions. The first we will discuss is the opinion relating to an access control system through a biometric disco pass. The second is the DPA opinion given on the bill changing the passport legislation in order to introduce biometrics in 2001.[15] The third is a 2003 opinion on the use of facial recognition and the use of biometrics for access control to public events, combined with use for police investigations which will not be further discussed here.[16]

In 2001, a producer requested an opinion from the DPA on an access control system named 'VIS 2000' with biometrics intended for use by restaurant owners, sport centers, and similar clubs or establishments.[17] The system allowed access control, served marketing and management purposes and keeping a 'blacklist' of customers who had violated the rules. The VIS 2000 stored fingerprint and face templates. The templates of the face were stored in a central database, combined with the membership card number and a code for the 'violation of club rules'. The card number would be linked to the personal details of the visitor/members communicated upon the issuance of the card. The biometric data would also be stored on a smart card, and used for membership verification when entering the club. Whilst a person entered the premises, the system performed a check against the black list of banned persons, one of the main purposes of VIS 2000. The biometrics were hence used for the purposes of verification (1:1 check, comparing whether the holders of the membership cards were the owners of the card) and

---

[13]The report identifies PETs as: different technological elements that can help to improve privacy compliance of systems [52, p. 49].

[14]See pp. 58–59 of the report [52].

[15]CBP, Wijziging Paspoortwet z2001-1368 (invoering biometrie), 16 October 2001.

[16]CBP, Vragen over de inzet gezichtsherkenning z2003-1529, 3 February 2004.

[17]Registratiekamer, Biometrische toegangscontrole systeem (discopas), 19 March 2001, www.cpbweb.nl (last accessed 28 September 2008).

of identification (1:N check, comparing whether the holders were registered on the blacklist of VIS 2000). In case of incidents, violators could be identified by their biometric characteristics. This involved reverse engineering of the stored templates of the face to images, comparing the images with the images of the violators taken by surveillance cameras, and connecting the templates with the name, address and domicile data if a membership card had been issued. The purposes of VIS 2000 were named as to increase the security of the other visitors and employees at the clubs, to maintain order and to refuse access to unwanted visitors.

The DPA stated in its opinion that the use of biometric data for access control purposes is far-reaching and that it should be evaluated whether the use of biometric data is *in proportion with this purpose*. To this end, the DPA checked the collection and use of the biometric data against several obligations of the Data Protection Act. However, it did not report on investigating whether there were other, less intrusive means to maintain order and to refuse black listed individuals to the club at their next visit without storing biometrics in a central database.[18] In this opinion, the DPA explicitly recognizes the possibility of the algorithm used to reconstruct the face of the original scanned facial image from the template. This reverse engineering of the templates was one of the main functionalities of VIS 2000 to identify violators of the rules of the establishments using the system. This technical feature, however, has important consequences. First, it should be noted that the face scan might well contain information about race, which should not be processed in principle. The Dutch Data Protection Act contains an explicit exception to this prohibition of processing of this information, in particular, when such processing is used for the identification of the person and to the extent as it is necessary for this purpose. The DPA considered the use made of templates of the face (containing information about race) for the identification of troublemakers to be inevitable.[19] The DPA continued that the use of personal data for marketing purposes should not include biometric data and that the processing for this purpose should be separated from the other purposes. The DPA concludes its opinion with several recommendations, including with regard to the term of storage and security (requirement for encryption of the templates and membership card numbers) and for the operation of the biometric system. The DPA also requested that any systems already installed be made compliant with these requirements.

---

[18]For example, the simple confiscation of the membership card of the person concerned in combination with checking new applications against a central list of suspended individuals. See also, FIDIS deliverable *D3.10 Biometrics in Identity Management*, E. Kindt and L. Müller (eds.), www.fidis.net (last accessed on 28 September 2008) [61].

[19]As stated above, the DPA *did not make a proportionality test about the use of biometric data*, and the opinion therefore indicates that a necessity test to use information about race should be regarded as sufficient for the purpose of determining.

15.5.3   Towards a Harmonized Approach?

The divergence of the outcome of this opinion of the Dutch DPA is interesting as compared with the evaluation, comments and conclusion of the Belgian DPA with regard to a similar system. The Belgian DPA reported in its annual report of 2005 that it rendered a negative opinion on a similar system. It considered the use of biometric characteristics for access control for a dancing club not proportionate with such purpose. In particular, the Belgian DPA found the use of biometrics for identification purposes disproportionate and that it entailed risks for the privacy of the visitors. There are other examples of different national DPAs coming to contradictory decisions or positions for similar biometric systems. Kindt gives the example of the use of biometrics for air travel: on 5 November 2003, the DPA of the Hellenic Republic rendered a negative decision on the use of iris and fingerprint biometrics on a smart card for air passengers, while the 'Privium' program, using iris on card for frequent travelers, has been operational at the Schiphol airport in the Netherlands for about five years now [59].

The principle of proportionality is a decisive factor in the legal review of biometric systems by the Data Protection Authorities (DPA) in EU member states. However, in the working document on biometrics the Data Protection Working Party gives little guidance. There remain uncertainties as to how the proportionality principle must be applied to biometrics. Below we will propose a strict interpretation of the necessity criterion or proportionality criterion contained in Article 8 of the European Convention on Human Rights, but analysis of the work of the national DPA's points at a lack of uniformity when applying the criterion and guiding the data controllers [59, 66]. Above (sub 3.6.) we noted that the Dutch data protection authority has so far not used the power of *prior checking* as granted by the Directive, whereas the French DPA has done so. If the biometrics example teaches us one thing, then it is that effective mechanisms fostering a more harmonized approach across the EU are lacking. Although there will be inevitable differences in the application of principles, more harmonization is needed to prevent the European data protection community from voicing contradictory signals to the world of technology vendors. This conclusion was reached in a detailed comparative study carried out within the FIDIS network of academics. The study showed that neither case law nor the existing legal framework *provide clear answers* to the issues which are raised by the use of biometric data.[20]

A much better solution was adopted with regard to Radio Frequency Identification (RFID). On 15 May 2009, the European Commission adopted a Recommendation on the implementation of privacy and data protection principles in applications supporting radiofrequency identification (RFID). The Recommendation pro-

---

[20]"Present legal provisions stipulate that personal data which are 'adequate, relevant and not excessive' shall be processed 'fairly and lawfully', 'for specified, explicit and legitimate purposes' and shall not be 'processed in a way incompatible with those purposes' (see Article 6 Directive 95/46/EC). It is not clarified what these notions mean for the applications which process biometric data. As a result, interpretations vary, resulting in sometimes opposing opinions or advices from national data protection authorities on similar data processing applications" [63, p. 115].

vides some guiding principles to companies and public authorities ('Operators') on privacy related aspects of the design and operation of RFID applications.[21] The Recommendation gives EU Member States two years to inform the European Commission of the actions that they have taken in order to achieve the Recommendation's objectives. Thereafter, the Commission will draft a report on the implementation, the effectiveness and the impact of the Recommendation. We note that the Recommendation saw the light after broad public consultations and stakeholder consultation. For us it is obvious that a similar document with regard to biometrics, whatever its status (soft or hard law), and whatever the institutional context (Council of Europe or EU) is more than needed on the condition that (a) it contains regulatory choices that (b) allow for assessment and evaluation after some time.

15.6 Understanding the Privacy and Data Protection Challenges of Biometric Data Processing

So far we have said nothing about the threats biometrics create for human rights and values. We have limited ourselves to the observation that the European data protection law applies and we have discussed some of the implications and applications of this set of rules and principles made by the WP29 and DPAs. But what is really the issue with biometrics?

A brief description of some general trends in relation to new technologies helps to prepare the answer to this question. The increased use of biometrics in all kind of settings clearly does not develop in a vacuum. Technological advances in biometric technology open up possibilities, and these are taken up based on a supply and demand that is the result of political and societal developments. The latter affect the introduction of the technology in a range of different settings. Some of the current and relevant trends that can be identified are:

- The increasing volume of data that is gathered, processed and exchanged;
- Linking of data banks and data sets, both by government agencies and by commercial parties;

---

[21]The Recommendation lays down the following general principles:

- When implementing RFID technology, Operators should assess the implications of the RFID application on the protection of personal data and privacy. Moreover, they should take appropriate technical and organizational measures to ensure the protection of personal data and privacy;
- Operators should develop and publish an information policy for each of their RFID applications which provides information regarding the type of data that are processed, the purpose of the application, the identity concerned and an assessment of the privacy risks resulting from the use of the RFID application. A clear label indicating the identity and contact data using the RFID application should also be provided on the devices that read RFID information;
- Consumers should also be informed of the presence of RFID tags (such as smart chips) embedded in consumer products. When consumer products containing RFID tags are sold, the seller should automatically deactivate or remove the RFID tag at the point of sale, unless the consumer explicitly consents to keeping the RFID tag operational.

- Function creep (as a process by which data are used for different purposes than originally collected);
- Increased tendency to keep data on file for possible future use (rather than discard data);
- Mounting pressure on individuals to disclose personal information and to allow data linkage both by government agencies and by business organizations (the latter mainly through the Internet);
- Proliferation of types of hardware that hold large data sets (CD ROMs, USB sticks, small gadgets and portable computers, data holding phones and so forth) that pose new security risks.

The growth in network capabilities offered by information technology and the availability and advances of new sensor technology combined, create the technical possibilities for these trends to re-enforce each other. New possibilities in the information exchange between new technologies and ICT have an attraction difficult to resist. The tendency to use data for other purposes than originally collected can thus be observed in the private—but is even more striking in the public domain. The opening up of the EURODAC site to police and other law enforcement agencies is the most quoted European example of this. The bulk of the literature on the European wide introduction of biometric technologies in the public sector identifies the core problem as the government demand to focus on surveillance, control and fraud detection more than on data collection minimization, and security- and risk-mitigation. The consensus is that in the public sector, function creep is a logical development when the emphasis is on surveillance and control and therefore on tracking, identifying and controlling individuals.

Biometric applications are seen as useful tools that can play a role in the new systems of data management that result from these trends. In general, expectations placed on biometrics in the short term seem to be high. On the contrary, the expectations of the impact and precise role of biometrics in the long term appear rather vague and not very well documented. In this light, it is important to keep in mind the technical imperfection of biometrics, which has also been underlined by the European Data Protection Supervisor (EDPS) in its opinion on the proposal for VIS [44]. First, 5 % of individuals are estimated not to be able to enroll because of having no readable fingerprints or no fingerprints at all. This would mean with regard to the use of VIS, which was expected to include data on 20 million applicants in 2007 that 1 million persons cannot be checked by the normal procedure. Secondly the opinion also states that, with regard to biometrics being a statistical process, a False Rejection error rate of 0.5 to 1 % is considered normal (although the False Acceptance is considerably lower at 0.1 % or less), which would mean a False Rejection Rate of 0.5 to 1 % with regard to measures and checks based on VIS [44].

The expectations in connection with biometrics are overestimated. Indeed, biometrics could lead to too much trust in the effectiveness of electronic solutions. Biometrics is based on probabilities: false positives and—negatives are unavoidable. If only one percent of a targeted group of 100,000 people a day suffers from a false negative, this would cause 1000 people every day to be incorrectly processed. The specific process error (i.e. False Rejection or False Acceptance) would then define how those people were further handled. In this case, those with a False Rejection error would be 'automatically' (but wrongfully) stopped. Current studies on the longer term reliability of biometrical data show that, for example, finger scans change throughout time, illustrating this risk [87, p. 14].

Furthermore, the information relating to the reliability, accuracy and efficiency of biometrics, provided by the vendors of biometrics, is considered by certain parties to be inflated and unreliable. Over the past decade a number of independent tests have been done which have yielded a more reliable and objective picture, however, considering the lack coherence in guidelines and testing by independent organizations, there is still a concern that vendors' claims are being overly relied on [34]. The 'Biometric summary table' in a 2004 report from the Organization for Economic Cooperation and Development [71] shows that the biometric technology—as it is—shows varying rates of reliability. Moreover, no biometric technology seems to be in line with all data protection principles and user acceptance at the same time (data quality principle, transparency principle, data security principle). Whereas the reliability of fingerprint scanning is only 'possibly' very high, the user acceptance is medium to low. Whereas the accuracy of facial recognition is medium to high, the stability and the transparency are low.

The use of biometrics will not exclude identity theft or forgery. The possibility of falsification will be discussed *below* (Sect. 15.7.3). Here we note that although biometrics prevent so-called 'identity substitution' to a certain degree, the fraudulent issuance of a genuine passport cannot be excluded. This lack of security of the new e-passports, currently introduced in a number of EU Member States was first illustrated by a German computer security expert. He demonstrated how personal information stored into the documents could be copied and transferred to another device, including fake passports. According to experts, despite several improvements since, the German passport is still lacking security, particularly with respect to confidentiality [7, p. 55]. Recent works have verified in a formal manner that security leaks exist in basic access control (BAC) and even in extended access control (EAC). Most of these leaks have been known about for years and have been demonstrated in experiments. It is likely that new weaknesses appear in the data handling implementation of electronic passports [79]. The trend that can be noted in other EU policies on biometrics too is that expectations of near perfect reliability are gradually reduced over time [47, 56]. As biometric technology is in the roll out phase [32, 34, 67], this means that the high expectations in the short term will probably be adjusted sooner rather than later [12].

15.7 The Human Right to Data Protection and Privacy

15.7.1 Article 8 of the European Convention on Human Rights

Let us now turn to the values of privacy and data protection enshrined in European legal texts. The human right to data protection is explicitly recognized in Article 8 of the Charter of Fundamental Rights of the European Union. Whereas the right to data protection is covered in Article 8 of the Charter, the right to privacy is covered in Article 7. This highlights the difference between privacy and data protection, and underlines the need for both rights to coexist. There are, after all, circumstances when the right to privacy applies while the right to data protection does not (and vice versa) [25, 26].

Article 7 of the Charter of Fundamental Rights of the European Union *and* Article 8 of the European Convention on Human Rights (ECHR) provide for the fundamental right to privacy. Article 8 ECHR states: '1. Everyone has the right to respect for his private and family life, his home and his correspondence. 2. There shall be no interference by a public authority with the exercise of this right except such as is in accordance with the law and is necessary in a democratic society in the interests of national security, public safety or the economic well-being of the country, for the prevention of disorder or crime, for the protection of health or morals, or for the protection of the rights and freedoms of others'. In Article 7 of the Charter of Fundamental Rights of the EU, it is stated: 'Everybody has the right to respect for his or her family life, home and communications'.

In different judgments, the European Court of Human Rights (ECtHR) has applied Article 8 of the ECHR on the basis that it provides protection against the systematic collection and storage of personal data. Article 8 was invoked in the *Rotaru vs. Romania* [39] and in June 2006, the ECtHR ruled that the continued storage of personal data (in this case, for a period of more than 30 years) by Swedish security and intelligence agencies was disproportional, and represented a breach of the applicants' right to privacy [40].

In a judgment on the interpretation of Directive 95/46/EC on the protection of individuals with regard to the processing of personal data and on the free movement of such data the European Court of Justice (ECJ) has confirmed that the criteria and limitations set out in Article 8 apply when assessing whether the processing of personal data conforms to Community law [35].

Article 8 imposes strict limitations on interference in an individual's private life by public authorities—any law that interferes with the private lives of EU citizens requires further justification. The 'necessity criterion' is of considerable importance here. The second paragraph of Article 8 stipulates that state interference must be 'necessary in a democratic society:

- in the interests of national security, public safety or the economic well-being of the country,
- for the prevention of disorder or crime,
- for the protection of health or morals, or
- for the protection of the rights and freedoms of others'.

The necessity criterion relates to the proportionality principle applied under data protection law. In other words, 'personal data must be adequate, relevant and not excessive in relation to the purposes for which they are collected and/or further processed'. Non-compliance with the proportionality principle implies the simultaneous infringement of the necessity criterion (assuming the right to privacy under

Article 8 of the ECHR applies of course). This is confirmed by the European Court of Human Rights: "the notion of necessity implies a 'pressing social need'. To be more specific, the measure(s) employed must be *proportionate to the legitimate aim pursued*" [38]. If too much or irrelevant data are processed in relation to the processing purpose, the processing can be considered illegitimate.

15.7.2 The Necessity Criterion

The 'necessity' criterion—indispensable to interfere with an individual's private sphere—plays a prime role in the discussions on the legitimacy of biometrics. Critics point at the technical imperfections of biometrics discussed above and cast doubts on the reliability, accuracy and efficiency of biometrics. In principle, biometrics make the processing of data easier. Biometrics are stronger identifiers as they identify individuals and link them to existing data. Since they are unique identifiers they can potentially be used as a key to link data in several databases. The privacy argument then goes that the use of such a powerful tool is not (always) warranted and that the danger of function creep and identity theft is of such a nature that it would make the choice for biometrics disproportional. The proliferation of biometrics makes individual biometric data more accessible. It also makes the biometric data more linkable to other personal data, thus making the technology privacy invasive per se. Instances of function creep, such as the use of biometric data collected for immigration purposes used in the context of unrelated criminal investigations [37], might occur in the private sector also. To give an example: biometric applications first introduced with the purpose of fast and efficient entry of employees or customers can be used for time registration or customer profiling at a later stage. Here the information given to customers and legal rights to be informed and the right to correct come into play.

The foregoing can be summarized as follows: because biometrics are powerful, they cannot be deployed in all cases and because they are still imperfect, deployment should be limited. A similar position is defended in the EU WP 29 study where it is recommended that biometric data should only be used if the use of other less intrusive material does not present the same effect and where special attention—including where necessary, tailor made safeguards for data protection—is needed for large scale information systems within the EU [90, p. 27]. This cautious 'precautionary' approach towards the use of biometrics is fueled by two questions that remain unanswered: Are biometrics sensitive data in the sense of data protection law and does the obligation to be subjected to biometrical identification not conflict with people's feelings of (bodily) dignity?

15.7.3 Factor 1: Are Biometrical Data Sensitive Data?

First, there is the issue whether biometrical data are to be considered sensitive data. Article 8 of the EC Directive 95/46 on Data Protection principally prohibits the processing of sensitive data. Sensitive data are "personal data revealing racial or ethnic origin, political opinions, religious or philosophical beliefs, trade-union membership, and data concerning health or sex life". The use of biometrics can involve the processing of sensitive data in the sense of Article 8. Biometrical data of disabled people may relate to their medical condition and correlations could for example be made between papillary patterns and diseases such as leukemia and breast cancer The WP29 opinion on Council Regulation 2252/2004 [88, p. 68] states: "In the case of storing fingerprints attention will have to be paid in so far as various correlations between certain papillary patterns and corresponding diseases are discussed. As for instance certain papillary patterns are said to depend on the nutrition of the mother (and thus of the fetus) during the 3rd month of the pregnancy. Leukemia and breast cancer seem to be statistically correlated with certain papillary patterns. Any direct or precise correlations in these cases are not known...". Face recognition can reveal racial or ethnic origin [88]. The processing of biometrical data may thus reveal—more or less immediately—sensitive information about an individual. This possibility goes far beyond the purpose for which biometrical identification is supposed to be used.

The foregoing teaches us that the *taking* of fingerprints and photos may involve the processing of sensitive data. Above (Sect. 15.3.4) we highlighted the requirement set out by Article 6 of the Convention ('Special categories of data') allowing the processing of sensitive data only when 'domestic law provides appropriate safeguards', a requirement that we considered to be a legal push factor in favor of regulatory intervention. To fine tune this endeavor some distinctions can be made (or need to be looked at), e.g. between different biometrics (e.g. non-sensitive fingerprint vs. sensitive facial image or non-sensitive fingerprint schemes vs. sensitive fingerprint schemes). A useful starting point for this can be found amongst others in the case law of the European Court of Human Rights protecting (quasi) all bodily data but insisting on the special status of some.

> In the Marper Judgement the Court concluded that the retention of both cellular samples and DNA profiles amounted to an interference with the applicants' right to respect for their private lives, within the meaning of Article 8 §1 of the European Convention on Human Rights. The applicants' fingerprints were taken in the context of criminal proceedings and subsequently recorded on a nationwide database with the aim of being permanently kept and regularly processed by automated means for criminal-identification purposes. It was accepted that, because of the information they contain, the retention of cellular samples and DNA profiles had a more important impact on private life than the retention of fingerprints. However, the Court considered that fingerprints contain unique information about the individual concerned and their retention without his or her consent cannot be regarded as neutral or insignificant. The retention of fingerprints may thus in itself give rise to important private-life concerns and accordingly constituted an interference with the right to respect for private life [41].

In the past we have been critical about the case law of the European Court on data protection rights issues, finding data protection law more complete in its approach to personal data then the more traditional human rights approach of the European Court. Up until today the Court has distinguished between private data and non private data, whereas data protection law protects all personal data with almost no distinction. Throughout the years the European Court has begun to understand better and better the concerns and the approach contained in data protection law, but the exercise is still far from complete [23, 27]. The Marper paragraph *above* suggests that fingerprints need to be protected, but are less delicate then other body samples. However, as was clearly understood by the French DPA, fingerprints are very delicate biometrics in that they are easily traceable. Falsifications are possible. Fingerprints taken from a glass can be used to create in wax a similar fingerprint on a storage medium. Other biometrics create a similar risk.[22] Regulating personal data is not only a function of the nature of the data, but also of its use and other interests. This does not go to say that the nature of the biometrical data is *not* a starting point for regulation. It is one of them.

A second starting point is the processing of biometrical data itself. Further, it is not clear if the algorithms and machine-readable templates that contain the information are always to be considered as sensitive personal data. Several stages in the processing of biometrical data can be identified and the risk for processing medical data perhaps only surfaces in certain of them.[23] (We will see other regulatory distinctions *below*.) It would be erring however to concentrate all the energy on cases where the biometrical data *is* the direct source of health data. With the second generation biometrics the danger for health and other privacy sensitive issues resides not *in* the data, but in the *use* made of data (automatic sorting into categories of people on the basis of their bodily traits).

15.7.4 Factor 2: The Human Dignity Argument

Second, there is the question about human dignity. Taking, measuring, and processing of biometrical data may also harm a person's personal feeling or experience of dignity. The fact that people feel uncomfortable with close observation and bodily scrutiny (they are obliged to look into a lens, they are obliged to put fingers on holders used by other people etc.) has already been observed as a possible feeling of intrusion upon one's dignity [87, p. 15]. That taking facial images is related to this observance, may also be derived from the fact that for example the Quality

---

[22]"More cumbersome is the programming of computers in order to artificially produce pictures as long as is necessary to match the template on a stolen data storage medium. That picture (e.g. imprinted in wax) can be falsely used as belonging to the stolen medium. This form of identity theft is insensitive to any encryption of the template stored on the stolen storage medium" [21, sub 35].

[23]The first stage is the capture or measurement of the human characteristic and the creation of a template. In this stage the 'raw' or unprocessed template sometimes contains information which can directly be interpreted in terms of e.g. race or state of health. Examples are facial images showing skin color or certain signs of illnesses. These initial templates can in those cases be classified as sensitive data. Subsequent steps often follow in the processing, in which the original data are being manipulated. Whether these processed data still classify as sensitive data is questionable but very relevant for the application of data protection law to second generation biometrics [52].

Assurance (QA) software—used to examine the properties of the applicant's photo for a passport or travel document—can reject a photo without explaining *why* [46, p. 5]. Exceptions to the photo requirements are possible for handicapped citizens and for certain religious reasons, but this may at the same time confront people with themselves as being an exception; and force them to reveal their religion.

The use of 'your' body as an identification tool for others might likewise infringe what is called our informational privacy. In other words, as stated by Anton Alterman: "The degree to which the body is objectified by the process, suggest[s] that biometric identification alienates a part of the embodied self. *The body becomes an object whose identity is instantly determinable by purely mechanical means, and subject to external controls on that basis; while those means themselves are removed from the control of the subject. The representations are infinitely reproducible by their owner, but are not even accessible to the subject whose body they represent.* The embodied person now bears, more or less, a label with a bar code, and is in this respect alienated from her own body as well as from the technology used to recognize it. If having an iris scan on file is not quite like being incarcerated in the world at large, being made known to mechanical systems wherever they may be is still a tangible loss of privacy that is not precisely paralleled by any other kind of information technology." [Emphasis added] [3, p. 146].

Alterman, in line with a strict Kantian understanding of human dignity prohibiting every de-humanizing action towards humans-, takes a very negative stand towards biometrics. In literature and policy circles this view has not been followed, as far as we can see. In the Council of Europe report the integrity of the body is marked as an aspect of human dignity, which 'forces controllers to exhibit special ethical responsibility' in considering whether or not to apply biometrics as a solution to a specific problem [21, sub 10]. The Committee, seemingly, attaches two consequences to the human dignity analysis

- *Precaution*: Biometrics is in its infancy and there is yet little knowledge about possible draw-backs. Once the technique is chosen on a larger scale, an irreversible development might have been started with unforeseeable effects. The precautionary principle requires a certain reticence under these circumstances [21, sub 10]. Simple convenience is insufficient justification for choosing biometrics. The purpose for which this instrument is called upon should justify its use [21, sub 27].
- *Inclusion*: Questions about handicapped people or people whose physical characteristics do not fit technical standards need to be answered. Fallback procedures should be available in case of failure of the system if anyone's physical characteristics do not fit the technical standards. On the other hand the collection of personal data in view of their automatic processing raises specific questions of data protection, in particular as biometric data might reveal unnecessary but sometimes unavoidable sensitive data e.g. information about certain illnesses or physical handicaps [21, sub 10].

The key words are not 'rejection' but 'slowing down' and 'respect for human dignity while processing biometrics' ('During the process of collection and use of bodily features, human dignity should be fully respected'). Compared to Alterman this is certainly not an absolute position, but neither is it a laissez-faire position.[24] Data protection law is seemingly misleading in the way that it treats all processing of personal data alike. This general approach is only a starting basis for further regulation tackling issues with more appropriate means, including criminal and administrative law instruments for non appropriate use of biometrics [25].

15.7.5 Other Human Rights at Stake

One of the particularities of data protection law is that it protects interests beyond the realm of privacy. Other protected interests are fair trial, equality, freedom of expression and the need for checks and balances [24]. This explains, for instance, why the Eurodac Regulation, opens with the statement that '...the procedure for taking fingerprints shall be determined in accordance with the safeguards laid down in the European Convention on Human Rights and in the United Nations Convention on the Rights of the Child'.[25] In the following we briefly discuss rights and interests such as the freedom of movement of persons and the human right to a fair trial.

Freedom of Movement   The use of the databases discussed above can cause people to be stopped (at border controls) on illegitimate grounds. It is not unimaginable that applications for visa or travel documents are refused without the applicant being informed of the underlying reasons. Likewise, people may not be informed of the reasons why they are stopped at a border (or that they are stopped solely on the grounds of personal data such as criminal convictions). A situation where agents act solely on the outcome of a database query can also arise, preventing the free movement of people.

In a recent case involving the use of the SIS (the Schengen Information System), the European Court of Justice declared that the Spanish authorities had—by refusing an EU citizen entry into the Schengen area—infringed the right to freedom of movement of (family members of) EU citizens. The person in question and his spouse were refused an entry visa *on the sole ground that they were persons for whom alerts were entered in the Schengen Information System for the purposes of refusing them entry, without first verifying whether the presence of those persons constituted a genuine, present and sufficiently serious threat affecting one of the fundamental interests of society* [36]. The Council Directive infringed by the

---

[24]The Committee's view on human dignity is clearly inspired by a certain amount of relativism towards the broad concepts of human dignity. Its content varies in function depending on the subject and the time [21, sub 26]. This conditional approach to human dignity (it 'might be affected by the use of biometrics') does not imply that we have to reject the analysis. On the contrary: "Sociocultural aspects and possible reluctance towards the instrumental use of the human body, should be taken into account" [21, sub 107].

[25]Articles 4 and 8 of the Eurodac Regulation.

Spanish authorities (64/221—Article 3) states that "measures taken on grounds of public policy or of public security shall be based exclusively on the personal conduct of the individual concerned" and that "Previous criminal convictions shall not in themselves constitute grounds for the taking of such measures".[26]

The Human Right to a Fair Trial   Article 6 of the ECHR guarantees the right to a fair trial, which constitutes a basic right of a democratic society governed by the rule of law. Specific guarantees exist under the second paragraph of Article 6: *'Everyone charged with a criminal offence shall be presumed innocent until proved guilty according to law'*.[27] Reference to the values behind this provision was made by the European Court on Human Rights in the Marper judgment expressing a particular concern over the risk of stigmatization, stemming from the fact that persons in the position of the applicants, who had not been convicted of any offence and were entitled to the presumption of innocence, were treated in the same way as convicted persons. It was true that the retention of the applicants' private data could not be equated with the voicing of suspicions. Nonetheless, the Court continued, their perception that they were not being treated as innocent was heightened by the fact that their data were retained indefinitely in the same way as the data of convicted persons, while the data of those who had never been suspected of an offence were required to be destroyed [41]. On 21 December 2004, the French Data Protection Authority, CNIL published a report on the proposals of the French government to register the biometric data of those aliens whose visa had been refused.[28] CNIL considered this national measure neither justified nor necessary. According to CNIL, this measure would entail the risk of stigmatization of those persons being refused a visa, as every renewed application for a visa could be refused again, only on the basis of the information stored in this central database.

Equality and Non Discrimination   Everybody has a right to be treated equally and without discrimination. We discussed the possibilities to exempt certain groups of people from biometrical controls because of religious and other reasons (*above* Sect. 15.7.4). People rejecting the idea of passing through a body scan should be offered appropriate alternative solutions to prove their 'innocence', without being categorized negatively for the simple reason of choosing the alternative solution. The example shows how equality will often be the core value at stake in disputes about biometrical data collection and storage. In the Marper judgment, the Court considered that it was not necessary to examine separately the complaint under Article 14 of the European Convention on Human Rights, but it is clear from the facts of the case that fear of discrimination is the main driver behind Maper's decision to find his way to the Court.

---

[26]On 30 April 2006, Directive 64/221 was replaced by a new Directive (2004/38), which sets out the right of citizens and their family to move and reside freely within the European Union. (Adopted on 29 April 2004. *OJ* L 229/35, 29.06.2004.)

[27]This right is also included in Article 48 of the EU Charter of Fundamental Rights.

[28]See *L'expérimentation de visas biometrique: la position de CNIL*, 21/12/2004, on www.cnil.fr, visited in December 2004.

15.8 Some Useful Distinctions for the Regulatory Debate

15.8.1 General

With unanswered questions like those regarding human dignity and the use of biometrical data for sensitive (health analysis) purposes, it can come as a surprise to note that the human rights debate around biometrics is in some regards deadlocked. We believe that one way out is to look more closely at the technology itself. Technical developments and shifts in the way the technology is used are of such a nature that they impact on the proportionality question at the core of both the privacy and the data protection debate. In that context one can point at new exciting technologies that have been developed both to improve the possibilities created by encryption and in overcoming the problems of false positives due to noise [16, 84]. More fundamental for the discussion are the following distinctions regarding the use of biometrics.

15.8.2 The Distinction Between Identification and Verification

The most important distinction always made is that between the goals of identification and verification. This distinction separates biometric systems aimed at bringing about automated identification of a particular person and those aimed at verification of a claim made by a person who presents him or herself. Verification is not a process that investigates the identity of a person, it only determines if two data belong to the same person. As the identification function requires a one to many-comparison whilst the verification function requires a one to one-comparison, privacy risks involved in the use of the biometric technology vary considerably from application to application. In principle, the verification function permits the biometric characteristic to be stored locally, even under the full control of the individual, so that the risk that the biometric data are used for other purposes is limited (although it should be pointed out that this comes with its own set of issues as the specific device runs the risk of being lost, stolen, shared or forged). This does not mean that all biometric systems that could be restricted to serving the verification function have actually been designed to maximize the control of the individual over his or her biological data. Most biometric applications used in the semi private domain in the Netherlands, for example, have been introduced for verification purposes [78]. In most instances the objective is to grant authorized persons access to physical or digital spaces. Control over personal data in these situations needs to be clarified, and the legal conditions determining the handling of data as well as the enforcement of applicable law are issues that need scrutiny.

The usefulness of the notion of control over biometric data when assessing privacy will be discussed below. What suffices here is to establish that the identification function cannot be performed without the use of a (central or decentralized) database. Whilst it is true that certain situations lend themselves to, or even require one-to-many systems (watch lists for example), in the case of biometric identification procedures, biometric data are never under the strict and full control of the individual. Privacy guarantees can still be built in but are far inferior in terms of control compared to the privacy options that can be devised for biometrical verification schemes.[29]

15.8.3 Difference in System Architecture

The above shows that the difference between identification and verification is a starting point for regulation. The choice between central data storage and decentralized or smart card data storage partly depends upon it. Central data storage is less privacy friendly because it diminishes user control by the data subject. This is not to say that the way in which data are stored centrally does not matter in terms of privacy protection, quite the contrary.[30]

The Council of Europe Committee report on biometrics starts becoming a bit technical when it observes, rightly so, that the distinction between an individual storage medium and a database does not run parallel to the distinction between the functionalities of verification and identification [21, sub 48]. It should, so we believe, but it does not. It is indeed possible, *and this much against privacy reflexes*, to base verification systems *not* on the mere storage on an individual storage medium or on a database. Often this is the easy, privacy unfriendly way out, and the report therefore rightly stresses that implementing a database for the functionality of verification requires special justification [21, sub 48].

As seen *above* a system for identification implies *necessarily* a database in order to check the submitted data with the enrolled biometric data of more than one individual, but the Council of Europe report is keen to stress that here again important

---

[29]PETs or privacy friendly options are another distinctive category of products that already exist on the market [79]. When verification is the goal of the system, the processor can opt for decentralization of the template storage and verification. By decentralization of both the template storage and verification process, the biometrical data are processed in an environment controlled by the individual or an environment from which no connection to a central database can be made. When identification is the goal these options do not exist. This makes these systems more dangerous in terms of loss of control. Privacy options do however exist with regard to another privacy aspect, viz. security. In case of central template storage and verification, mathematical manipulation (encryption algorithms or hash-function) can ensure encryption of databases so that it is not possible to relate the biometric data to other data stored in different databases, at different locations. In the case of EURODAC, the PET aspect is the HIT-No HIT facility in the first instance, but of course in the case of a HIT, biometrics are de-encrypted so that they can lead back to the other personal details of the person involved.

[30]The use of biometric encryption in combination with the use of a "protected safe" that is only accessible to a small number of people, greatly enhances the privacy protection of individuals enrolled in a system with central storage. The biometric applications using these techniques are still in development or in the early phases of roll out [15, 84]. It is also important to make a distinction between the protection of biometric data stored within systems and the use of biometrics by operators to safeguard authorized access to other type of data stored in a system.

architectural choices can be made: "Another way to shape the architecture of a biometric system is to store the enrolled data in a local or regional database, for instance under the sole control of the municipal authorities responsible for the issuance of a passport. The data can also be additionally stored on an individual storage medium for the data subject. Through his or her database the controller can check whether the biometric data of an applicant already exist in the system. Taking as an example the passport, the municipal authorities can check whether a local resident has perhaps already applied for a passport under another name. If there are other guarantees, this (sole municipal control) might be regarded as sufficient to prevent the acquisition of a double identity. Thus, the German law on passports does not allow the creation of a federal database filled with biometric data originating from local passport issuing authorities. Neither can the data be automatically searched by federal authorities" [21, sub 47].

The example nicely illustrates the amount of political choices that technology allows us to make. Regulation of technology is seldom an all or nothing issue.

The same report, being very inspired on the distinction between central, decentralized and smart card data storage, also warns that sensor technology is threatening old understandings of the privacy safety of smart card storage giving full control to the owner of the card.[31] System architecture constantly evolves, which calls for regulatory scheme updates. The example of the second generation biometrics *below* illustrates this point. Biometrical issues are moving far beyond the old storage question that nevertheless remains of importance depending on the biometrical scheme.

15.8.4 The Distinction Between Compulsory and Voluntary Enrollment

Equally relevant is the distinction between biometric applications used in the private or semi-public domain and those used in the public domain. Often this boils

---

[31]"The architecture of a biometric system can be shaped in different ways. The first possibility is that the enrolled data can be stored solely on a secured individual storage medium, for example a smart card. For verification purposes this might suffice. The necessary data are available only on the card. If the data subject looses his or her card, all the data are gone. The card is comparable with a key. Until recently it was assumed that the data subject thus keeps control over the use of the data relating to him or her. It was thought that when he or she does not use his or her card, the data cannot be accessed. The controller who established the purpose of the system, its means and the categories of data to be processed, would have no access to the data unless the data subject himself or herself submitted them to the system knowingly and willingly. A new technology makes it possible to equip a smart card to allow the contact less reading of the enrolled data stored on it. Thus the data subject loses the exclusive control over the use of his or her data. This could be compensated by additional security measures. For instance, the principle of fair processing could be given effect by informing the card holder each time that the data are read from his card. Surreptitious reading of data, if necessary, should be specifically provided for by law including adequate guarantees against abuse. Even so, if the data subject is not within the ambit of a reader, the controller does not have access to the data" [21, sub 45].

down to whether providing biometric samples is obligatory or voluntary for the individual concerned. With first generation biometrics, applications in the private or semi-public domain are used on a voluntary basis. This means that the individuals asked to provide their characteristic could refuse this and use another facility, for example another swimming pool not using a biometric entry system or the individual can make use of a similar service without the biometric at the same institution (for example voice recognition when managing your bank account). When there is an alternative way to obtain the services offered then the element of choice, consent and control is in the hand of the individual. Here information is a key factor. The users of biometric systems often fail to realize the implications of offering their characteristics for storage on a database, and the loss of individual control over their characteristics once this has happened. Rights, such as the right to correct, are seldom exercised and other ex ante measures remain unused.

Our analysis *above* was both critical of consent based biometrical schemes and government schemes. The former often lack true consent or should not be established at all, not even with consent (*above* Sect. 15.3.3); the latter have often been introduced too boldly without proper assessments and democratic scrutiny [30].

When there is no alternative available, and this is the case with most public sector introductions of biometrics such as the biometric passport, a risk that then arises is that biometric based systems are hacked or are used by other persons and for other purposes than foreseen [46, 57]. In 2005, the 27th International Conference of Data Protection and Privacy Commissioners adopted a Resolution in which it expressed its awareness '*of the fact that the private sector is also increasingly processing biometric data mostly on a voluntary basis*'. The Conference called for '1. Effective safeguards to be implemented *at an early stage* to limit the risks inherent to the nature of biometrics; 2. the *strict distinction* between biometric data collected and stored for public purposes (e.g. border control) on the basis of legal obligations and for *contractual purposes* on the basis of consent; 3. the *technical restriction* of the use of biometrics in passports and identity cards to verification purposes comparing the data in the document with the data provided by the holder when presenting the document' (emphases added) [22]. In the Council of Europe Committee report, the problem of function creep is looked at from the reverse side: governments asking database controllers to incorporate the technical facility to collect more biometric or associated data or a more detailed template than is necessary for the purpose of the system, into the overall architecture. The Committee states that it is not in a position to answer this question, but that at any rate all the requirements of Article 8 Paragraph 2 of the European Convention on Human Rights and the case-law of the European Court of Human Rights relating thereto, in particular as regards the requirement of proportionality, need to be respected [21, sub 49]. At one other place in the report the Committee is much more straightforward and plainly rejects every demand from controllers to collect more biometrics for the sake of the government.[32]

---

[32]"Questions may arise about accurateness with regard to a possible secondary purpose that is incompatible with the purpose of the system. It would be contrary to the principle of proportionality

15.8.5 The Distinction Between Raw Data and Templates

Also there is the importance in the legal implications of storing raw data for the use of templates. Under raw data we understand the unmodified output of the sensor device. This can be the image of a fingerprint, a face, an iris, or a sound from a microphone. Some pre-processing is allowed in the definition, provided that neither information nor redundancy is added or dropped. Raw data can serve particular processes or aims which templates cannot, such as providing the possibility for human intervention on the final stage as opposed to automated decisions on individuals, making a court case or for backup purposes. The raw data should be stored in a secure "vault" with limited access, while templates are used for a normal mode of operation.

Template data are shadows made from raw data. A template can be compared to a list of key words extracted from a text where the text itself is not retained [21, sub 65]. Template data are those data which are compared in the matcher unit. Normally, templates will only contain information necessary for comparison [11].

From a privacy perspective working with templates offers the distinct advantage that if they get stolen or hacked you do not lose your digital fingerprint. There is the possibility of making a new template based on other algorithms. However, when raw data gets stolen, the subject cannot produce other and distinct raw data. Identity theft of raw data is therefore a more serious problem. Some hold that storage of the raw template only occurs in very basic biometric systems handling raw data and will soon become a relic of the past. However, these systems are still on the market and they are in European passports.

From a data protection point of view, working with templates has, so far, the additional advantage that the original picture of the biometric feature cannot be reconstructed as no text can be reconstructed from a list of key words [21, sub 65].

Templates will not resolve all human rights issues. There are many choices to be made in light of human rights and the choice for templates is only one of them. Furthermore, there is strong evidence (at least in the case of fingerprints and faces) that raw data can be reconstructed from template data (at least partially). Furthermore, misuse of templates does not necessarily need a reconstruction of raw data [11, 14, 45].

---

to demand that a system using biometric data be more accurate than necessary for the original purpose of the system for the sole reason that in exceptional cases the data could be requested in accordance with Article 9 of the Convention for a secondary, incompatible purpose, e.g. for law enforcement. For instance, in the case of a biometric system for a specific purpose it might be sufficient to enroll a template consisting of 12 elements extracted from the original biometric sample. For the secondary, incompatible purpose a template consisting of at least 50 elements would be desirable. This exceptional incompatible use cannot justify the storage of these 50 elements. If in exceptional cases the data might be used for such secondary purposes, their limited trustworthiness should be taken into account" [21, sub 34].

15.8.6 Differences Between Biometrics

A last set of differences touches upon the kind of biometrics that a controller chooses. Some biometrics have 'better' false acceptance rates and false rejections rates: it is clear that the controller takes these technicalities into account. Human dignity and differences in culture also account for certain choices pro and contra. One relevant criterion is that of the choice between biometric technologies that leave traces (e.g. DNA samples and fingerprint images) and those that do not (e.g. pictures of the iris). Seen from one angle, the latter are less intrusive and constitute a smaller risk for invasion of the privacy of the individual, although it must be noted that in the specifics of use of each technology risks can grow or diminish (pictures of the iris, for example, can be taken without the individual's permission, thereby raising its associated risk considerably depending on the context of its use).

An issue that needs to be mentioned in this context is the choice to combine biometrics. Data protection is also about security and accuracy. In the name of these principles some hold that controllers should take no risk and collect as much data as possible to lower the error rate. That option has been taken in Regulation 2252/2004 on EU passports requiring both fingerprinting and iris-scans. This introduction of two biometric identifiers in EU passports and travel documents is questionable. The impact of these choices can be great. The US and the ICAO only require one, and this only involves a digital photograph. The inclusion of a fingerprint biometric is unprecedented. The US has no intention to implement fingerprints in their passports. In the Regulation it is said that these choices are 'in accordance with the principle of proportionality' and do 'not go beyond what is necessary in order to achieve the objectives pursued, in accordance with the third paragraph of Article 5 of the Treaty'.[33] This Article of the EC Treaty contains the proportionality principle of the EC law.[34] It should be noted that, exactly based on this same principle of proportionality, some members of the European Parliament proposed to limit the passports to only one identifier.[35] Referring to the fact that all EU citizens will have to be

---

[33] Council Regulation 2252/2004 of 10 December 2004, Recital 9.

[34] EU legislation must conform to the principle of proportionality (Article 5 EC, third paragraph) to be valid. Article 5 of the EC Treaty provides that "action by the Community shall not go beyond what is necessary to achieve the objectives of this Treaty". The form taken by Community action must be *the simplest form* allowing the proposal *to attain its objective* and to be implemented as efficiently as possible.

[35] "The respect of the principle of proportionality requires proof that there are no other means to achieve the objective of increasing document security. The Commission has not provided yet the Parliament with the requested information on:—the scope and the seriousness of the problem of false documents;—the results of the former improvements (integration of a photograph on visas and residence permits;—the cost of biometrics, the error rate of the various biometric options, the risk of misuse; the principle of proportionality, the confidential requirement.... Only a detailed knowledge of the above mentioned questions will allow the Parliament to give a balanced opinion on the introduction of any other biometric data in visas, residence permits and passports" (Justification to Amendment 18 proposed by Tatjana Ždanoka in Committee on Civil Liberties, Justice and Home Affairs, 14 October 2004, Doc PE 349.798v01-00/15-30).

fingerprinted and to the costs this will involve for both citizens and Member States, Steve Peers reaches a similar conclusion.[36]

15.8.7 Bringing the Different Choices Together

The above list of differences partly explains why regulating biometrics is a challenge. First the controller needs to determine the purpose of the systems. The purposes that the system should serve are relevant to the choice of whether or not to install a system of identification or verification. Only then can it be determined whether the system needs to be centralized or not, how many biometrics are needed, whether consent is the appropriate ground and whether raw data is needed. One can find in these issues, reasons to believe that a lawmaker or a DPA could not generally recommend choosing one or the other system (compare [21, sub 62]) or that regulation of biometrics is not far short of being impossible.

This position creates an undesirable situation. Our fieldwork shows that especially external supervision on the use of biometrics in the Netherlands is lacking. Due to staff shortage and lack of powers, the Dutch DPA has not been able to develop an active policy on the stimulation of good practice in the use of biometrics. At the same time, the DPA cannot possibly be expected to provide informed steering of the approach to biometrics alone. So far, the introduction of biometrics in the private sector seems to have escaped the attention of government, parliament and the data protection community [78]. We doubt whether the picture in other Member States is brighter.

Today there is enough regulatory experience with biometrics. It is only a question of crystallizing the outcome and establishing a more solid legal framework to articulate it at the national and European level. A nice illustration of this is the opinion (No. 17/2008) on biometrics issued by the Belgian DPA.[37] In this document the DPA praises the qualities of biometrics as a verification tool, but notes that certain biometric data are very intrusive as regards privacy because they can reveal information about the state of health or the racial background of an individual. Therefore,

[36]"It might be argued that the Commission's initial proposal conformed to the proportionality principle, but there are far greater doubts that the latest version of the legislation (Council document 15139/04) conforms to the principle. The key change is the decision to fingerprint all EU citizens who need a passport. This will entail considerable costs for citizens and Member States' administrations and considerably alter the process of obtaining a passport in most Member States. The doubts about the proportionality principle are particularly cogent in light of the position of the US government and the ICAO standards related to document security, which do not require fingerprinting for the purposes of travel document security. The Commission's initial proposal expressly accepted that the security and identity checking objectives and objectives of meeting US and ICAO standards could be achieved without making fingerprint data mandatory. In light of this position it is difficult to justify the validity of mandatory fingerprinting in light of the proportionality principle" (Steve Peers, 'The Legality of the Regulation on EU Citizens' Passports', http://www.statewatch.org/news/2004/nov/legal-analy-bio-passports.pdf, 3).

[37]The advice can be found on http://www.privacycommission.be. See also [62, 75].

the Commission emphasizes the importance of a careful evaluation of the benefit, use, desirability and justification of the use of biometric data in order to confirm an individual's claimed identity. In its advice, the Commission distinguishes between biometric technologies that leave traces or do not and clearly expresses a preference for the latter (e.g. pictures of the iris or of the retina).

In general, the Commission considers the processing of biometric data to be in compliance with the Data Protection Act if:

- the biometric data are not stored in a central database but on a secure removable carrier that can be kept by the individual him/herself (e.g. a chip card) in order for him/her to keep control over his/her own data;
- the biometric data are stored in template form (numbers) and not in a picture form;
- the individuals are at all times informed about the use of their biometric data for the purposes of their authentication;
- only biometric technologies with a very high degree of security are used and these technologies are kept up to date at all times and can be adapted in view of new technological evolutions and new safety risks.

Similar 'findings' can be found in the 2009 study of the Working Party on the *Future of Privacy*. We have already discussed its findings regarding consent and announced that a short discussion of other relevant paragraphs would follow (see *above* Sect. 15.3.3). The basic recommendation of the Working Party seems to be that large scale information systems within the EU needs to be set apart and looked at separately.[38] I think this proposal is of a nature to simplify considerably the regulatory debate on biometrics. These large scale systems are strongly linked with law enforcement; they are top down fabrics of an unparalleled scale with international aspects. It is useful to look at these large scales separately and look for tailor made regulation. This leaves us with the bulk of biometrical schemes used by governments in less sensitive areas and by private actors. As said before, the 2009 study of the Working Party does not contain a systematic analysis of biometrics. It does contain a recommendation that biometric identifiers should be stored in devices under the control of the data subjects (i.e. smart cards) rather than in external data bases and that video surveillance in public transportation systems should be designed in a way that the faces of traced individuals are not recognizable or other measures are taken to minimize the risk for the data subject [90, p. 14]. Furthermore the study

---

[38] "Access to large databases must be configured in such a way that in general no direct access on line to data stored is allowed, and a hit/no hit system or an index system is in general considered preferable. The choice between models with central storage, meaning systems with a central database on EU-level and decentralized storage should be made on transparent criteria and in any event ensure a solid arrangement providing for a clear definition of the role and responsibilities of the controller/s and ensuring the appropriate supervision by the competent data protection authorities (...) *Special attention—including where necessary tailor made safeguards for data protection—is needed for large scale information systems within the EU*" [90, p. 27] [Emphasis added].

contains recommendations to create a legal framework allowing governments to impose Privacy by design (PbD) and privacy enhancing technologies (PETs) that will have, so we believe, in the end, the effect of clearing the market of 'bad' or privacy unfriendly biometrical technology [90, p. 12].

If these distinctions, nuances and developments are taken into account, the privacy balancing might well produce different outcomes in every concrete case. It might even be the case that the use of biometrics in a privacy enhancing way turns out to be the better option.[39]

---

[39]Although there is an abundance of literature on privacy enhancing technology, much of it does not pay any attention to biometric technology [1, 8, 9, 42, 53, 64, 65, 73, 81]. Based on the small body of literature that deals with biometrics [5, 49, 52, 78, 91] we can detail the following illustrations of what constitute privacy enhancing and potential privacy invasive features of biometric applications. The one-off use of fingerprints in medical screening, for example, is a biometric application that enhances privacy (PET or privacy enhancing technology). This makes having to use patient names to match with their diagnostic results unnecessary. There is a double advantage to the one off use of biometrics in this instance: patients can remain anonymous and there is greater reassurance that data are released to the correct person. Another obvious example is the ex post measure already mentioned in *biometric* authentication to restrict operator use in a database. This use of biometrics makes operators more accountable for any use/misuse of data. A more generic example is the match on card-sensor: biometric authentication without the biometric characteristics left on devices owned by the individual [70]. Biometric encryption is a privacy enhancing technical solution that integrates an individual's biometric characteristics in a revocable or non-revocable cryptographic key. This method now forms an integral part of all but the cheapest biometric applications on the commercial market. When the transformation is reversible,, this introduces issues relating to function creep and law enforcement. At the same time, there are possibilities for a three-way check to come to an architectural design that restricts the number of people having access to the data. In addition, there are applications that offer two-way verification and therefore integrate the "trust and verify" security principle. Another privacy enhancing possibility would lie in the certification of the privacy compliance of biometrical identification products; this is therefore not a PET but a certification of the biometric application as a PET. When we concentrate on biometrics as a privacy invasive technology an obvious example would be the storage of information in a manner where medical or racial information can be inferred. Equally intrusive is the use of an individual's biometric data to link their pseudonimity/identity between different applications/databases. Another example is the use of biometrics for surveillance or sorting, where no permission is asked to take (moving) images of people, for example of face recognition systems (although there have been examples of the positive use of this possibility, for example a gamblers' self exclusion program at casinos). Most second generation biometrics fall under this category (see below). Then there is central storage of raw biometric data, central storage of biometric templates and so forth aimed at identification. Then there are biometric systems aiming at interoperability, maybe even using a biometric as a unique identifiable key (instead of another personal detail such as the name (alphabetical identifier) or a number (numerical identifier)). These systems are built on as much identification as possible and link data that would otherwise go unconnected. Also very privacy intrusive is the use of a biometric choice for biometric identification. To be more precise: the use of a biometric system for identification, where verification would already have met the objectives of the application. (Although once again, the invasiveness of the system will depend on the context of its use. There are access control identification systems that are convenient and, at the same time, not privacy intrusive. For example, biometric locks where several family members and guests are enrolled. People would not have to carry a token/card or memorize a PIN for one-to-one verification; the door could be opened with a fingerprint.)

It is time to complement the legal framework with some basic rules that are of a nature which catches the attention of the private sector, governments, and the data protection community that so far have not acted in a convincing way, exhibiting the 'special ethical responsibility' required when dealing with biometrics. We see no good argument against clear cut, enforceable rules that might for example consist of an explicit legal prohibition to process raw images, an obligation to encrypt biometric data used for processing and an obligation to use multiple authentications and a prohibition on the use biometric technologies that leave traces. The guidelines as discussed *above* and as contained in many other documents such as those issued in the UK[40] exist, and making them more explicit and enforceable would be one way of providing a lead and improving the information position of data subjects. Also increased powers for the DPA, more in line with the French approach, for example a system whereby prior approval of a certain biometric application is needed, needs to be considered. Many Member States have created a separate legal framework for CCTV, including procedures of certification, monitoring and control by independent bodies.[41] A separate framework for biometrics would allow tackling its specific characteristics. In particular we refer to its probabilistic nature creating the possibility of a false recognition or a false non-recognition, sometimes with serious consequences for the data subject. New rights, respectful of fair trial and equality, need to be introduced guaranteeing that if, as a result of a biometric system, a data subject is rejected, the controller should, on his or her request, re-examine the case and should, where necessary, offer appropriate alternative solutions. Procedures should be in place and made known to the data subject in the case of an allegedly false system result [21, sub 107], [62].

The question as to whether in practice these regulatory goals cannot be achieved with other means such as information provision, broadening of administrative powers, extensive use of opinions and effective enforcement through increased consultation is, so we believe, unfair. These traditional responses have had their time and did not succeed. Human rights logic requires governments to act and to protect human rights through the elaboration of an adequate legal framework. That framework needs to be foreseeable and acceptable. General data protection laws are a starting point, but do not offer the amount of foreseeability that is capable of taking into account all the differences regarding biometrics identified *above*.

15.9 Biometrics and the Second Generation

So to conclude, what are the important elements of second generation biometrics and will they give rise to a new set of legal issues to be analyzed and discussed? We

---

[40]www.ico.co.uk.

[41]Compare with [21, sub 107]: "A procedure of certification and monitoring and control, if appropriate by an independent body, should be promoted, particularly in the case of mass applications, with regard to the quality standards for the software, the hardware and the training of the staff in charge of enrollment and matching. A periodic audit of the system's performance is recommendable".

identify two developments in biometrics that together form the main step away from the first generation applications of the technology. The first is the emergence of new biometric traits, the so-called soft biometrics and physiological biometrics, and the second is the shift to embedded biometric systems, with elements such as distant sensing and 'passive' biometrics. These distinct developments are the basic changes that might catapult us into the world of ambient intelligence and ubiquitous computing. Then, the already complex legal assessment of biometric data handling will be taken to a different level altogether and pose serious challenges to existing legal approaches (basically based on data protection law). The dream of second generation of biometrics is a person's identification on the basis of that person's dynamic behavior. In this respect second generation biometrics play a role in the wider field of behavioral surveillance. In fact, the attempt is not made to identify a person, no: the objective is to read the person's mind. So instead of enrolling and identifying or verifying a person, second generation biometrics is aimed at a categorization of individuals. The threats caused by this de-personalization are many fold. Of course unjustified selection according to profile will result in discrimination. Stigmatization will occur and will involve allocation to a group on the basis of relatively random profiles which will impact the persons' future. Confrontation of individuals with unwanted information is another side effect that is very likely to occur. Profiling may result in a limited information supply: according to perceived but incomplete profiles. Similarity in profiles will cause de-individualization. Finally, there will be unknown effects as a result of the linking of dispersed information.

15.10 Concerns About Second Generation Biometrics

One of the most fundamental challenges in the protection of personal biometric data are related to the incremental change from visible to invisible data collection. So, let us assume first that the individual subject knows that he is subject to biometric processing of the second generation. There is then mainly a tension between the processing of second generation biometric data and the individual participation principle. How to check and verify if the biometrical data are still accurate? The obvious risk that the systems (and not only personal data) may be used by other persons and for other purposes than foreseen is difficult to minimize, without the traditional possibilities for individual participation. How to exercise the right to have the data corrected or the right to object to certain types of data processing? Does an individual for example know that the biometrical identifiers are still working? Here a number of transparency tools can be developed that give the individual more insight into who is taking which decisions on the basis of data collected. The current lack of possibilities to enforce individual participation is paltry, if not insignificant, when it comes to assessing the applicability of data protection law in situations where the subject is unaware of the invisible data collection. Therefore, our main and immediate legal concern regarding second generation biometrics is the applicability of data protection regulation in those situations and the specific use of the data for profiling.

First, there is the applicability of data protection regulation. If no attempt is made to identify a person, can we define the data concerned as personal data? If not, what guarantees remain against unwarranted and unfit social categorization?

Secondly, there is the issue of profiling. It is not clear whether and when profiling falls directly under the rights and obligations of the EC Directive 95/46 [54, 55]. The Directive may allow statistical processing or profiling of personal data, once the data are made anonymous. Recital 26 states *"whereas the principles of protection shall not apply to data rendered anonymous in such a way that the data subject is no longer identifiable"*. Article 6.1.b is very specific: *"further processing of the data for historical, statistical or scientific purposes is not considered as incompatible provided that appropriate safeguards are provided by the Member States whereas these safeguards must in particular rule out the use of the data in support of measures or decisions regarding any particular individual"*. Article 15 of the Data Protection Directive principally prohibits that a person is subject to automated decisions which produce legal effects concerning him, or significantly affects him, and which are based solely on automated processing of data intended to evaluate certain personal aspects relating to him. This Article thus gives individuals the right to object to decisions affecting them when decisions are made solely on their profiles [26, p. 283]. This provision however, is accompanied by numerous exceptions that do not set strong and clear-cut limits to targeted profiling actions. The results of data profiling can be applied afterwards to data subjects without them knowing that the profiles are applied to them, for example: people can be individually stopped or checked at a border control because they fall under a certain profile. How is it guaranteed that the data subject is informed that such automated individual decisions are applied to him? Are there any guarantees that the data subject can exercise the right to obtain from the controller knowledge of the logic involved in such automatic processing operations? Will all authorized agents acting upon these automated decisions 'know' this logic involved and be able to communicate this logic to the data subject?

In conclusion, the use of second generation biometrics will have to lead to a reassessment of the traditional data protection approach that only data relating to identified or identifiable persons have to be protected. In fact, existing European legal mechanisms cannot guarantee effective protection against profiling. This has already led to a call for widening the protection currently granted through the regulation of 'unsolicited communications' via the new notion of 'unsolicited adjustments'. The notion of unsolicited adjustments' would close a legal loophole allowing a situation in which objects that seemingly have a neutral guiding function, in practice secretly track individuals to surreptitiously adapt their performance based on undisclosed criteria [48]. Similarly, gaps in current data protection, in the case of second generation biometrics applied in real life situations, can lead to forms of profiling that leave some of the rights of the individual, such as the right to have data corrected, or the right of access to the data, unprotected.

Recommendations

- Because biometrics are powerful tools to identify, verify and interconnect, they cannot be deployed in all cases and because they are still imperfect, deployment should be limited. Biometric data should only be used if the use of other less intrusive options does not present the same effect. Special attention—including where necessary tailor made safeguards for data protection—is needed for large scale information systems within the EU (cf. 15.7.2 of the report).

- Data protection law misleads when it suggests that all processing of personal data is one. This general approach is only a starting basis for further regulation tackling issues with more appropriate means, including criminal and administrative law instruments for non appropriate use of biometrics (cf. 15.7.4 of the report).
- To clarify the regulatory debate about biometrics large scale information systems within the EU needs to be set apart and be subjected to tailor made data protection rules following democratic scrutiny. The regulatory focus can then turn to biometrical schemes used by governments in less sensitive areas and by private actors (cf. 15.8.2 of the report).
- It is necessary to make explicit who the controller is and to make this transparent for the data subject (cf. 15.3.2 of the report).
- Consent is often an inappropriate ground for processing biometrical data. Transparency needs to be enhanced as a pre-condition for valid consent. Other solutions are to impose opt-in rather than op-out mechanisms, and, where appropriate, facilitating the data subjects' right to revoke consent, with subsequent data deletion in all servers involved. Important is to exclude consent in situations where it is not the appropriate legal basis. (cf. 15.3.3 of the report).
- The instrument of prior checking as contained in Article 20 of the Directive seems to be a suitable instrument to regulate biometrical applications with critical or non mature features. The regulatory framework needs to be enriched with a provision allowing a more harmonized approach, for instance by giving WP 29 the power to make the instrument operational. A similar instrument could be introduced and developed at the level of the Council of Europe (cf. 15.3.6 of the report).
- Profiling practices based on biometrics need to be based on transparency and will have to respect the right of the individual not to be subject to a decision which produces legal effects concerning him or significantly affects him and which is based solely on automated processing of data intended to evaluate certain personal aspects relating to him (cf. 15.3.7 of the report).
- All biometric systems that could be restricted to serving the verification function should be designed to maximize the control of the individual over his or her biological data (cf. 15.8.2 of the report).
- Human rights logic requires governments to act and to protect human rights through the elaboration of an adequate legal framework. That framework needs to be foreseeable and acceptable. General data protection laws are a starting point, but do not offer the amount of foreseeability that is capable of taking into account all the differences regarding biometrics identified in this report (cf. 15.8.7 of the report).
- A separate framework for biometrics would allow tackling its specific characteristics. In particular we refer to its probabilistic nature creating the possibility of a false recognition or a false non-recognition, sometimes with serious consequences for the data subject. New rights, respectful of fair trial and equality, need to be introduced (cf. 15.8.7 of the report).

References

1. Adams C (2006) A classification for privacy technologies. University of Ottawa Law and Technology Journal (UOLTJ) 3(1):35–52
2. Albrecht A (2003) BIOVISION: deliverable 7.4 privacy best practices in deployment of biometric systems
3. Alterman A (2003) A piece of yourself: ethical issues in biometric identification. Ethics and Information Technology 5(3):139–150
4. Androunikou V, Demetis D, Varvarigou T (2005) Biometric implementations and the implications for security and privacy. Journal of the Future of Identity in the Information Society 1(1):20–35
5. Andronikou V, Demetis D, Varvarigou Th (2007) Biometric implementations and the implications for security and privacy, 1st in-house FIDIS journal issue, 2007-1. http://www.fidis.net/fileadmin/journal/issues/1-2007/Biometric_Implementations_and_the_Implications_for_Security_and_Privacy.pdf
6. Ashbourn J (2005) The social implications of the wide scale implementation of biometric and related technologies. Background paper for the Euroscience open forum ESOF (2006) in Munich. http://www.statewatch.org/news/2006/jul/biometrics-and-identity-management.pdf. Accessed 25 January 2010
7. Berthold S (2009) Epass 5.3. In: Sprokkereef A, Koops BJ (eds) D3.16: Biometrics PET or PIT? FIDIS, Brussels
8. Borking J (2008) Organizational motives for adopting privacy enhancing technologies. Data protection review. DPA, Madrid
9. Borking J (2008) The business case for PET and the EuroPrise seal. Europrise deliverable
10. Bray E (2004) Ethical aspects of facial recognition systems in public places. Journal of Information, Communication & Ethics in Society 2(2):97–109
11. Bromba M (2006) On the reconstruction of biometric raw data from template data. http://www.bromba.com/knowhow/temppriv.htm. Accessed 25 January 2010
12. Brussee R, Heerink L, Leenes RE, Nouwt J, Pekárek ME, Sprokkereef ACJ, Teeuw W (2008) Persoonsinformatie of Identiteit? Identiteitsvaststelling en Elektronische Dossiers in het Licht van Maatschappelijke en Technologische Ontwikkelingen. Telematica Instituut. Report TI/RS/2008/034, pp 1–98
13. Camenish J, Leenes R, Sommer D (2008) PRIME deliverable the PRIME architecture, Brussels, February 2008
14. Cappelli R, Lumini A, Maio D, Maltoni D (2007) Fingerprint image reconstruction from standard templates. IEEE Transactions on Pattern Analysis and Machine Intelligence 29(9):1489–1503
15. Cavoukian A, Stoianov A (2007) Biometric Encryption: a Positive-Sum Technology that Achieves Strong Authentication, Security and Privacy. Information and Privacy Commissioner's Office, Ontario
16. Cavoukian A, Stoianov A (2009) Biometric encryption: the new breed of untraceable biometrics. In: Boulgouris NV, Plataniotis KN, Micheli-Tzanakou E (eds) Biometrics: Fundamentals, Theory, and Systems. Wiley/IEEE Press, London, pp 655–718
17. Cehajij S, Sprokkereef A (2009) Case study Germany. In: Kindt E, Müller L (eds) D13.4. The Privacy Legal Framework for Biometrics. FIDIS, Brussels, pp 67–78. http://www.fidis.net/fileadmin/fidis/deliverables/new_deliverables3/fidis_deliverable13_4_v_1.1.pdf
18. Cehajij S, Sprokkereef A (2009) Case study United Kingdom. In: Kindt E, Müller L (eds) D13.4. The Privacy Legal Framework for Biometrics. FIDIS, Brussels, pp 100–114. http://www.fidis.net/fileadmin/fidis/deliverables/new_deliverables3/fidis_deliverable13_4_v_1.1.pdf
19. Charter of Fundamental Rights of the European Union (2000) Official journal C 364 of 18 December 2000
20. Cho A (2008) University hackers test the right to expose security concerns. Science Magazine 322(5906):1322–1323

21. Consultative Committee of the Convention for the Protection of Individuals with Regard to Automatic Processing of Personal Data (T-PD) of the Council of Europe (2005) Progress report on the application of the principles of convention 108 to the collection and processing of biometric data. http://www.coe.int/t/e/legal_affairs/legal_co-operation/data_protection/documents/reports_and_studies_of_data_protection_committees/2Biometrics_2005_en.pdf. Accessed 25 January 2010

22. Data Protection Commissioners 27th International Conference of Data Protection and Privacy Commissioners (2005) Resolution on the use of biometrics in passports, identity cards and travel documents. http://www.edps.eu.int/legislation/05-09-16_resolution_biometrics_EN.pdf. Accessed 25 January 2010

23. De Beer D, De Hert P, González Fuster G, Gutwirth S (2010) Nouveaux éclairages de la notion de «donnée personnelle» et application audacieuse du critère de proportionnalité. Cour européenne des droits de l'homme, Grande Chambre, S et Marper C Royaume-Uni, 4 décembre 2008. Revue Trimesterielle des Droits de l'Homme (RTDH) 19(81):141–162

24. De Hert P (2009) Citizens' Data and Technology. An Optimist Perspective. Dutch Data Protection Authority, The Hague, p 51

25. De Hert P, Gutwirth S (2006) Privacy, data protection and law enforcement. Opacity of the individual and transparency of the power. In: Claes E, Duff A, Gutwirth S (eds) Privacy and the Criminal Law. Intersentia, Antwerp/Oxford, pp 61–104

26. De Hert P, Gutwirth S (2008) Regulating profiling in a democratic constitutional state. In: Hildebrandt M, Gutwirth S (eds) Profiling the European Citizen. Cross-Disciplinary Perspectives. Springer, Berlin, pp 271–292

27. De Hert P, Gutwirth S (2009) Data protection in the case law of Strasbourg and Luxembourg: constitutionalisation in action. In: Gutwirth S, Poullet Y, De Hert P, Nouwt S, De Terwangne C (eds) Reinventing Data Protection? Springer, Berlin, pp 3–45

28. De Hert P, Sprokkereef ACJ (2008) Biometrie en recht in Nederland. Computerrecht 25(6):299–300

29. De Hert P, Scheurs W, Brouwer E (2007) Machine-readable identity documents with biometric data in the EU—part III—overview of the legal framework. Keesing Journal of Documents & Identity 22:23–26

30. De Hert P, Scheurs W, Brouwer E (2007) Machine-readable identity documents with biometric data in the EU. Critical observations. Part IV. Keesing Journal of Documents & Identity 24:29–35

31. De Hert P, Gutwirth S, Moscibroda A, Wright D, González Fuster G (2008) Legal safeguards for privacy and data protection. Working paper series REFGOV-FR-19. http://refgov.cpdr.ucl.ac.be/?go=publications. Accessed 25 January 2010

32. de Leeuw E (2007) Biometrie en nationaal identiteitsmanagement. Privacy & Informatie 2(10):50–56

33. Directive 95/46/EC of the European Parliament and of the Council of 24 October 1995 on the protection of individuals with regard to the processing of personal data and on the free movement of such data. OJ, L 281

34. EBF (European Biometrics Forum) (2007) Security and privacy in large scale biometric systems. Seville: JRC/ITPS. http://is.jrc.es/documents/SecurityPrivacyFinalReport.pdf. Accessed 25 January 2010

35. ECJ (2003) 20 May 2003, Österreichischer Rundfunk and others, Joint cases, C-138-01, C-139/01 and C-465/00

36. ECJ (2006) 31 January 2006, Commission v Spain, Case C-503/03

37. ECJ (2008) 16 December 2008, Heinz Huber V FRG, Case 524/06, OJ C44/5 of 21.2.2009

38. ECtHR (1986) Gillow vs the United Kingdom, 24 November 1986. Series A, vol 109

39. ECtHR (2000) Rotaru vs Romania, 4 May 2000, Appl no 28341/95 reports 2000-V

40. ECtHR (2006) Segerstedt-Wiberg and others v Sweden, 6 June 2006, Appl no 62332/00

41. ECtHR (2008) S and Marper v the United Kingdom, 4 December 2008, Appl nos 30562/04 and 30566/04

42. European Commission (2007) A fine balance 2007: privacy enhancing technologies; How to create a trusted information society. Conference summary. ftp://ftp.cordis.europa.eu/pub/fp7/ict/docs/security/20080228-pet-final-report_en.pdf. Accessed 25 January 2010

43. European Commission (2009) Recommendation on the implementation of privacy and data protection principles in applications supported by radio-frequency identification. SEC(2009) 585, C(2009) 3200 final. http://ec.europa.eu/information_society/policy/rfid/documents/recommendationonrfid2009.pdf

44. European Data Protection Supervisor (EDPS) (2005) Opinion on VIS, Brussels. http://www.edps.europa.eu/12_en_opinions.htm. Accessed 25 January 2010

45. Feng J, Jain AK (2011) Fingerprint reconstruction: from minutiae to phase. IEEE Transactions on Pattern Analysis and Machine Intelligence 33(2):209–223

46. Friedrich E, Seidel U (2006) The introduction of the German e-passport. Biometric passport offers first-class balance between security and privacy. Keesing Journal of Documents & Identity 16:3–6

47. Gasson M et al (eds) (2007) FIDIS deliverable D.3.2.: a study on PKI and biometrics. www.fidis.net. Accessed 25 January 2010

48. González Fuster G, Gutwirth S, de Hert P (2010) From unsolicited communications to unsolicited adjustments. Redefining a key mechanism for privacy protection. In: Gutwirth S, Poullet Y, de Hert P (eds) Data Protection in a Profiled World. Springer, Berlin, pp 105–118

49. Grijpink J (2001) Biometrics and privacy. Computer Law & Security Report 17(3):154–160

50. Grijpink J (2005) Two barriers to realizing the benefits of biometrics. Computer Law & Security Report 21(3):249–256

51. Grijpink J (2008) Biometrie, veiligheid en privacy. Privacy & Informatie 11:10–14

52. Hes R, Hooghiemstra TFM, Borking JJ (1999) At face value, on biometrical identification and privacy. Registratiekamer Achtergrond Studies en Verkenningen 15:1–70

53. Hes R et al (2000) Privacy-enhancing technologies: the path to anonymity. Registratiekamer Achtergrond Studies en Verkenningen 11:1–60. Revised edition

54. Hildebrandt M, Backhouse J (eds) (2008) FIDIS deliverable D7.2: descriptive analysis and inventory of profiling practices. http://www.fidis.net/resources/deliverables/profiling/int-d72000/. Accessed 25 January 2010

55. Hildebrandt M, Gutwirth S (eds) (2008) FIDIS deliverable D7.4: implications of profiling on democracy and the rule of law. http://www.fidis.net/resources/deliverables/profiling/int-d74000/. Accessed 25 January 2010

56. Hornung G (2005) Die digitale Identität. Rechtsprobleme von Chipkartenausweisen: Digitaler Personalausweis, elektronische Gesundheitskarte, JobCard-Verfahren. Nomos Verlagsgesellschaft, Baden-Baden

57. Hornung G (2007) The European regulation on biometric passports: legislative procedures, political interactions, legal framework and technical safeguards. SCRIPT ED 4(3):246–262

58. JRC (Joint Research Centre) (2005) Biometrics at the frontiers: assessing the impact on society. Technical report series, Institute for Prospective Technological Studies (IPTS), Seville

59. Kindt E (2007) Biometric applications and the data protection legislation (the legal review and the proportionality test). Datenschutz and Datensicherheit (DuD) 31:166–170

60. Kindt E (2007) FIDIS (Future of Identity in the Information Society). Deliverable 3.10: biometrics in identity management

61. Kindt E (2009) The privacy legal framework. In: Kindt E, Müller L (eds) D13.4. The privacy legal framework for biometrics, Fidis, pp 12–28. http://www.fidis.net/fileadmin/fidis/deliverables/new_deliverables3/fidis_deliverable13_4_v_1.1.pdf

62. Kindt E, Dumortier J (2008) Biometrie als herkenning- of identificatiemiddel? Enkele juridische beschouwingen. Computerrecht 25(6):202–298

63. Kindt E, Müller L (eds) (2009) FIDIS deliverable D13.4: the privacy legal framework for biometrics. 134 p. http://www.fidis.net/fileadmin/fidis/deliverables/new_deliverables3/fidis_deliverable13_4_v_1.1.pdf

64. Koorn R et al (2004) Privacy Enhancing Technologies. Witboek voor Beslissers. Ministerie van Binnenlandse Zaken, The Hague

65. Levi M et al (2004) Technologies, security, and privacy in the post-9/11 European information society. Journal of Law and Society 31(2):194–200
66. Liu Y (2009) The principle of proportionality in biometrics: case studies from Norway. Computer Law & Security Review 25(3):237–250
67. Lodge J, Sprokkereef A (2009) Accountable and transparent e-security- the case of British (in) security, borders and biometrics. Challenge. http://www.libertysecurity.org/article2488.html. Accessed 25 January 2009
68. Meints M, Gasson M (2009) High-tech ID and emerging technologies. In: Rannenberg K et al (eds) The Future of Identity in the Information Society. Challenges and Opportunities. Springer, Dordrecht, pp 129–185
69. Michielsen P (2003) EU—working paper on legal protection of biometric data. Stibbe ICTlaw Newsletter 12:3
70. Neuwirt K (2001) Report on the Protection of Personal Data with Regard to the Use of Smart Cards. Council of Europe, Strasbourg
71. OECD (2004) Background material on biometrics and enhanced network systems for the security of international travel working party on information security and privacy. http://www.oecd.org/dataoecd/16/18/34661198.pdf. Accessed 25 January 2010
72. Petermann Th, Sauter A (2002) Biometrische Identifikationssysteme Sachstandsbericht. TAB working report nr 76. http://www.tab.fzk.de/de/projekt/zusammenfassung/ab76.pdf. Accessed 25 January 2010
73. Philips D (2004) Privacy policy and PETs. New Media & Society 6(6):691–706
74. Rundle M, Chris C (2007) Ethical implications of emerging technologies: a survey (UNESCO, Information for All—IFAP). UNESCO, Communication and Information Sector, Paris
75. Schuit St (2008) Belgian commission issues advice on biometric data. Stibbe ICT Law Newsletter 31:5
76. Sprokkereef A (2008) Data protection and the use of biometric data in the EU. In: Fischer Huebner S, Duquenoy P, Zaccato A, Martucci L (eds) The Future of Identity in the Information Society. IFIP International Federation for Information Processing, vol 262. Springer, Boston, pp 277–284
77. Sprokkereef ACJ, De Hert P (2007) Ethical practice in the use of biometric identifiers within the EU. Law, Science and Policy 3(2):177–201
78. Sprokkereef ACJ, De Hert P (2009) The use of privacy enhancing aspects of biometrics: biometrics as PET (privacy enhancing technology) in the Dutch private and semi-public domain. Tilburg Institute for Law, Technology and Society, Tilburg. http://arno.uvt.nl/show.cgi?fid=93109. Accessed 25 January 2010
79. Sprokkereef A, Koops BJ (eds) (2009) FIDIS deliverable D3.16: biometrics: PET or PIT? http://www.fidis.net/fileadmin/fidis/deliverables/new_deliverables2/fidis-WP3-del3.16-biometrics-PET-or-PIT.PDF. Accessed 25 January 2009
80. SSN (Surveillance Studies Network) (2006) A report on the surveillance society—for the information commissioner by the surveillance studies network. Information commissioner, London (full report). http://www.ico.gov.uk/upload/documents/library/data_protection/practical_application/surveillance_society_full_report_2006.pdf
81. Tavani H, Moor J (2001) Privacy protection, control of information, and privacy-enhancing technologies. Computers & Society 31(1):6–11
82. Thomas R (2008) The UK information commissioner: on funding in evidence to the house of commons Justice Committee on the protection of personal data report, H of C Justice Committee report: protection of private data, HC 154
83. Turle M (2007) Freedom of information and data protection law: a conflict or a reconciliation? Computer Law & Security Report 23(6):514–522
84. Tuyls P et al (eds) (2007) On Private Biometrics, Secure Key Storage and Anti-counterfeiting. Springer, Boston
85. van der Ploeg I (1999) The illegal body: 'Eurodac' and the politics of biometric identification. Ethics and Information Technology 1(4):295–302

86. van der Ploeg I (2002) Biometrics and the body as information, normative issues of the socio-technical coding of the body. In: Lyon D (ed) Surveillance as Social Sorting: Privacy, Risk, and Digital Discrimination. Routledge, New York, pp 57–73
87. Wayman J (2006) Linking persons to documents with biometrics. Biometric systems from the 1970s to date. Keesing Journal of Documents & Identity 16:14–19
88. WP29 (Article 29 Working Party) (2003) Working document on biometrics 12168/02, 1 August 2003
89. WP29 (Article 29 Working Party) (2007) Opinion 4/2007 on the concept of personal data, 20 June 2007
90. WP29 (Article 29 Working Party) (2009) Working party on police and justice. The future of privacy, joint contribution to the consultation of the European commission on the legal framework for the fundamental right to protection of personal data (WP 168), 1 December 2009
91. Zorkadis V, Donos P (2004) On biometrics-based authentication from a privacy-protection perspective—deriving privacy-enhancing requirements. Information Management & Computer Security 12(1):125–137

Chapter 16
Recommendation on the Use of Biometric Technology

Niels Christian Juul

Abstract Biometric technology is based on the use of information linked to individuals. Hence, privacy and security in biometric applications becomes a concern and the need to assess such applications thoroughly becomes equally important. Guidelines for application of biometric technology must ensure a positive impact on both security and privacy. Based on two cases of biometric application, which have been assessed by the Danish Data Protecting Agency, this chapter present a set of recommendations to legislators, regulators, corporations and individuals on the appropriate use of biometric technologies put forward by the Danish Board of Technology. The recommendations are discussed and compared to the similar proposal put forward by the European Article 29 Data Protection Working Party.

16.1 Introduction

Biometric technologies promise to enhance many systems with more convenience and have the potential to also provide better privacy and higher security. While the field is developing rapidly, it can be difficult to identify the real advantages and disadvantages associated with the use of biometry [2]. At the European level, biometry is already in use, not only in passports, identity cards and visa applications, but also in every day access control as well as the long tradition of forensic usage in criminal investigations. The same is the case internationally. The issues regarding privacy and security in more recent usage of biometrics has been addressed in EU by both the European Data Protection Supervisor [6] and the Article 29 Data Protection Working Party [1]. In Scandinavia including Denmark, the use of biometry is also growing [10] and [11]. Biometry is indeed applied for a large variety of purposes. In this chapter we focus on the challenges to privacy when applying biometry to security solutions.

N.C. Juul (✉)
Computer Science, Roskilde University, Roskilde, Denmark
e-mail: ncjuul@acm.org

P. Campisi (ed.), *Security and Privacy in Biometrics*,
DOI 10.1007/978-1-4471-5230-9_16, © Springer-Verlag London 2013

16.1.1 Challenges

There is a broad range of challenges that must be addressed when biometric technology is used for security purposes. Our focus is on the additional challenges imposed by adding biometry to security solutions. Some of the questions to be answered are:

1. Does the added biometry make the final solution more or less reliable and trustworthy?
2. Are the biometric data processed and stored securely?
3. Are the collected biometric data protected against being reused for additional purposes (function creep)?
4. Does the biometric solution prevent unfair discrimination of groups or individuals?

The first question challenges not only the technical solution of the biometric security system provided, but also the socio-technical implementation of the system. The reliability must be evaluated with regards to the matching process, the storage procedures, and the enrollment process. The second and third question involves legal challenges related to the EU data protection directive [7] and the national implementation of the directive. The fourth question challenges whether biometry introduces any discriminatory effects, e.g. due to age, culture or handicaps.

16.1.2 The Danish Recommendations

This chapter reports on the work done together by a multidisciplinary working group[1] established by the Danish Board of Technology to address a number of themes relevant to an overall evaluation of biometric technologies. In beginning of 2010 the Board of Technology issued a report in Danish of the findings including recommendations of the working group on use of biometric technology in the Danish society [9]. The report contains:

- A set of recommendations to legislators, regulators, corporations and individuals on the appropriate use of biometric technologies.
- A final discussion section, where opportunities and challenges are sketched.
- A descriptive part where the characteristics of the various technologies are reviewed.

Although the report addresses the challenges in a national (Danish) context, the results may be generalized. As Danish legislation on privacy protection is based on European legislation, the application to the European scene is straightforward.

---

[1]The members of the working group are presented in the Acknowledgements.

16.1.3 Chapter Outline

The aim of this chapter is to present and discuss these recommendations. The chapter begins with two examples showing how biometry can be applied. The two cases present some of the dilemmas to be addressed in accessing the biometric technology. Based on the lessons learned from the cases, the recommendations of the working group are presented. They are discussed and contrasted to the work of the EU Article 29 Working Party, and finally the results and the need for further investigations are summarized.

16.2 Biometric Application for Access Control

There are many implementations of biometry in daily use. In the following we look at biometry usage for access control with two different purposes. The first is to give access to know customers, whereas the second is to reject access to know (former) customers. Both require enrollment of at least one group of customers either those given access or those rejected access. The two cases were both presented to the public by the companies, who both wanted to make access control more reliable and more smoothly for their (paying) customers. The first case concerns access control to facilities across the country of a nationwide fitness club using fingerprints; whereas the second concerns unwanted guests across a chain of nightclubs.

The two cases are presented and discussed in the following.

16.2.1 Access Control to Fitness Clubs

Authenticated access to Fitness Clubs across the country using fingerprints would make the membership personal and prevent members from lending their membership card to friends giving them unauthorized access. The company found the alternative too expensive and error prone, i.e. adding pictures of cardholder on membership cards and doing matchmaking between cardholder and picture manually. Both solutions utilize biometry, but the fingerprint would allow a more correct and automate access control.

The company wanted to enroll all customers in a central database of templates of fingerprints and utilize access control to the Fitness Clubs by means of an unsupervised fingerprint scanner at all entrances.

With supervised enrollment and a reliable technical solution for template creation and matching such a system seems reliable and trustworthy for the purpose of access control to enrolled guests only. The company may add supervision to the access control scanners to ensure that falsely rejected customers can get access by manual intervention and to ensure that the customer providing the fingerprint is also the customer allowed access.

For security reason, the template creation after each scanning should be made in the confinement of the scanner before match making against the central database to limit the risk of leaking the fingerprint. If template protection (from the enrollment) is hard and compact enough, the database of templates might even be replicated to each scanner to provide matching in the confinement of the scanner. In this case, the scanner must also be tamperproof to protect the templates. This will constitute a logically centralized database with massive replication of customer templates. The actual implementation must be investigated further before the protection of user sensitive data can be evaluated.

Initially one may observe that biometry is well suited to maintain the link between the personal membership and the physical person by maintaining a biometric sample unique to the physical person along the notification of the membership (or at least the membership class). However, the collection of fingerprints and saving of fingerprint templates in central databases both might threaten the customers' right to privacy.

Additionally, if the company maintains a register of attendance, logging the usage of the provided fitness services for each customer; such register is a surveillance track attacking the privacy of the customer also without the usage of biometric technology. Biometry only adds to the trustworthiness of the tracking.

When looking at the request from the company from a privacy perspective, their wish to check that an individual customer is the same as the one subscribing to the service might actually be performed without identifying the customer personally. What they need is to ensure that the customer paying a monthly fee is actually the same person at each visit during the payment period. Thus customers wanting privacy must be provided with a service to register a non-revertible and anonymous fingerprint template (allowing them access for the payment period by providing the same fingerprint) along with an anonymous payment, e.g. cash. Such a biometric solution could be provided with a central database of templates or even more privacy friendly by utilizing access cards with build-in fingerprint scanner, template and matchmaking software communicating pseudonyms or completely anonymous access ids with the access points.

The Danish DPA [3] found the collection of personal data too invasive for this purpose as the solution implied a central database of customer fingerprint templates and such a database was not acceptable without further justification. During private communication with the Danish DPA we have learned that the decision was primarily based on a very brief (and broad) application. Thus, the DPA might accept such centralized fingerprint-based biometric access control system if both the purpose is thoroughly explained and the purpose justifies the collection of the personal data (the templates of fingerprints of all customers). From other rulings of the DPA only the lack of a thoroughly explained purpose seems to have been the problem in this case. As the suggested solution might easily be extended for additional purposes, the risk of *function creep* must also be addressed and limited before the solution is approvable.

16.2.2 Blacklisting Trouble Makers from Nightclubs, Bars etc.

A chain of nightclubs asked the DPA permission to maintain a shared list of trouble makers to enable on site rejection of people known for unacceptable behavior from entering their nightclub. They further asked to be allowed to maintain the list across different chains of bars, nightclubs, restaurants, etc. Their implementation was based on a shared database of all customers' fingerprint template where they could mark those customers, whom they decide to reject entrance in the future (presumably after they have made themselves know for causing troubles).

The solution requires enrollment of all customers during their first visit to any of the facilities sharing the system. This implies that enrollments will be distributed among the facilities which will all have to ensure a high quality of the data-collection mostly done in the dark hours while the customers are in a good (partying, maybe even under influence) mood. Thus quality insurance of the enrollment procedures might be hard to control and the degree of voluntary and informed consent by the customer to the collection of their personal data might not be that high (to say the least).

During their enrollment additional data regarding the customers might be entered, e.g. name, contact information (email, mobile phone, address, etc.), sex, age/birthday or even their national citizen id-no. As nightclubs might not allow minors' entrance, the age-verification at enrollment will further easy the entrance during future visits. The trade-off between the benefits and loss of privacy by maintaining these additional data is, however, not evaluated here as we focus on the biometry part of the system.

Storing fingerprints of all customers or more preferably templates generated from fingerprints in a central database shared by hundreds of individually owned access point requires high security measures around the entire system (both the central part and the scanners distributed across the nightlife sector). One might ask if this is at all achievable. Moreover, whenever a blacklisting takes place, special precautions must be taken to ensure the correct linking between fingerprint templates and the blacklisted person. There must be added some rights for the blacklisted persons to challenge the blacklisting by taking the case to court (legal rights).

We can, however, observe that for the purpose of being able to reject entrance to the nightclubs of a rather limited group of people, all legitimate customers have to enroll their fingerprints into the system. It seems disproportionate to register *all* with the purpose of discriminating the *few* and thus, the system should be considered unfair and customer unfriendly.

During the public discussion of this, a solution maintaining a blacklist only was proposed. Such a biometric solution was, however, not pursuit, and one of the reasons given was that it would be hard to enforce the unwanted guests to enroll with their fingerprints. This implies that it would be easier to enroll all guests and then later tag the records of unwanted guests after their misbehavior has been observed. We note that the issues of security and privacy of a biometric system as mentioned above still remains if the system contains the blacklisted people only. The group of people at risk could, however, be limited to those who had misbehaved if the matching is implemented inside the scanners at the entrance and all non-matching customer fingerprints from legitimate customers are discarded immediately.

Despite these security and privacy issues, the DPA [4, 5] accepted the proposed solution registering all customers in the "nightlife sector" instead of requiring the application of biometry in the least invasive way to customer privacy.

16.2.3 Case Observations

The two cases are both concerned with access control of customers entering closed buildings of companies providing paid services inside the building. Both cases had privacy issues even before adding biometry to the access control solution.

When looking at the privacy issues introduced by the proposed biometric solution the reliability and trustworthiness does not seem to change in either of the cases. One of the weak points are the enrollment phase, especially when enrollment has to be done at the door to the nightclub in the second case. Errors in enrollment jeopardize the reliability of all future usage of the system. One might also ask whether consumer consent to the enrollment is done completely voluntarily and based on fully enlightened information in these situations.

Both cases rely on a central database where personal (privacy sensitive) information is being linked to biometric samples. At least the biometric samples stored should be templates from which the original samples cannot be reestablished. Moreover, to protect the biometric templates they must be encrypted, the communication lines between the database and the sensors and the sensors themselves must also be secured. Both solutions might benefit if the central databases of biometric templates are removed and the biometric solution is limited to personal access cards with biometric scanner, on-card template storage and matching (so called "system on card technology").

The central databases make it possible to add new usage of the collected templates, e.g., as access cards to other facilities with leakage of the collected data into the new usage context. To prevent function creep regulatory measures must be taken regarding extended usage of the collected data. Deployment of "match on card technology" would also help to prevent function creep, as the user must be engaged before the biometry is used for new purposes.

We note that the usage of fingerprints in both cases does discriminate against people unable to provide usable fingerprints.

In conclusion, biometric based systems are challenging privacy and security.

16.3 The Danish Recommendations

The working group has made the following recommendations regarding the use of biometric technology in the Danish society. These recommendations are based on the investigation of state-of-the-art biometric technology and current and planned usage of the technology.

The recommendations include the need for guidelines, assessments and clarification of legislation. Biometric systems shall be used to gain higher privacy protection and to ensure that citizens are in control of their own data. Privacy Enhancing Technologies (PET) and Privacy Impact Assessment (PIA) shall be used. "System on card technologies" shall be favored over "match on card technologies" and databases of templates or biometric features shall be avoided whenever possible, especially central databases.

A holistic approach shall be used when assessing the security of systems utilizing biometric technologies. Procedures for capturing, collecting, saving and deleting biometric data need standardization for interoperability and fair use policies. Fallback procedures must be in place, both to cope with uncertainties (no system will be 100 % secure) and to prevent discrimination towards people not capable of providing their biometric data. Standardized test and performance measures of biometric systems are needed to compare and evaluate before deployment.

These recommendations are listed here and detailed in the following sections:

1. A set of guidelines for the use of biometric systems must be developed

    1.1. The Danish Data Protection Agency must be assigned more resources especially more technological expertise to be able to carry out inspections and assessments of biometric systems both before and after deployment.
    1.2. Deployment of biometric systems in practice must be offered advice and opportunity for prior approval
    1.3. Clarification of the interpretation of the Privacy Act

2. Biometrics can be used to achieve greater privacy and to ensure that users have control over their own data

    2.1. Biometric systems must be designed in such a way that they take the utmost account to privacy protection
    2.2. Registration of citizens and customers must be done while offering as much privacy protection as possible

        • Nightclubs, bars and restaurants should use "match on card technology"
        • Fitness Clubs should use "match on card technology"
        • Industry must work together on a common solution in which users retain control over own data

3. A future biometric citizen cards will be based on "System on Card technology", or similar technologies
4. Start by defining the purpose of the biometric solution
5. The security of a biometric system depends on the security of the entire system
6. Procedures for enrollment of biometric data must be standardized
7. Procedures for storage and matching of biometric data must be standardized
8. There must always be safe alternatives and "fall-back procedures"
9. There is a need for more testing of biometric systems

10. Touch-free devices should be used in environments where the interests of hygiene is important

16.3.1 The Detailed Recommendations 1–4

1. *A set of guidelines for the use of biometric systems must be developed.* In light of technological development and digitization in general, the current procedures for assessment and verification of biometric systems are not adequate. The rapid development of new technologies requires not only the necessary legal expertise but also the technological expertise to assess whether a biometric system is appropriately designed or not. The working group recommends involving people with technological knowledge in the assessment of biometric systems and their usage guidelines, and the establishment of a continuously monitoring process to verify that the systems are used in accordance with these guidelines. Secondly, the working group recommends that individuals and companies wishing to use systems in which biometry is included, to have much better access to both public advice and prior approval in early stage than they have today. Thirdly, the working group calls for a more precise interpretation of the Danish Privacy Act applied to the extensive development of biometric technologies and other technologies that have taken place. In this context, the working group recommends that:

   1.1. *The Danish Data Protection Agency must be assigned more resources especially more technological expertise to be able to carry out inspections and assessments of biometric systems both before and after deployment.* Assessment of new technological solutions demands more and more skilled technical expertise. The working group recommends modifying the procedures for legislation on the use of biometric solutions, to involve people with technological insight in the assessment. The working group recommends looking to the practice in Norway for inspiration in this respect. A change of practice in Denmark will require more resources, but the working group believes that it is absolutely necessary actions, given that this would ensure a more qualified assessment of individual cases.

   1.2. *Deployment of biometric systems in practice must be offered advice and opportunity for prior approval.* A growing number of companies and organizations wish to deploy biometric systems. Currently, they cannot get their solutions pre-approved or obtain initial technical advice to ensure correct implementation. Due to the complexity of biometric systems, it is far from easy to foresee how a solution that meets the requirements for efficiency and privacy can be most appropriate constructed. The option for getting both advices and pre-approval will first of all make it more likely that deployment of a biometric system will have less risk of being directed to changes later in the process. Secondly, it will help to ensure that solutions achieve a higher quality.

1.3. *Clarification of the interpretation of the Privacy Act.* A number of technologies have developed significantly over the last decade and many are facing a massive breakthrough. Biometrics is one of those technologies, but also Radio Frequency Identification (RFID) and video surveillance could be mentioned in this context. Due to their impact on privacy, the Personal Data Act—and at least its interpretation—must be clarified with respect to these technologies. The working group suggests that a guide that interprets the Privacy Act is developed and authorized. The guide should also show how these technologies shall be applied in practice and how privacy-enhancing concerns, such as Privacy Impact Assessment (PIA), Privacy Enhancing Technologies (PET) and Privacy by Design (PbD), should be taken into consideration in the implementation of the new technologies.

2. *Biometrics can be used to achieve greater privacy and to ensure that users have control over their own data.* Biometry enables enhanced privacy protection because the technologies can be deployed as secure authentication (confirmation of access rights) without revealing one's full identity. Moreover, a range of sensitive personal data can be protected through various forms of biometrics combined with passwords. The working group recommends avoiding creating biometric systems, where for example a fingerprint alone gives access to sensitive personal information. Furthermore, the working group recommends the development of a privacy impact assessment (PIA) before any new biometric systems is planned. The PIA ensures a reasonable balance between the purpose of the system, the level of identification possible, the stored personal data, and the risk of data misuse and theft. Privacy issues and transparency must be part of the system design, and the use of "Privacy Enhancing Technologies (PET)"—the technologies that support the protection of individual privacy—must be considered. At the same time ethical considerations regarding the risks of social stigma, social inclusion and social exclusion must be reflected from the very start. The working group also points out that a legislative focus on strengthening privacy protection by using biometrics will enhance the general acceptance of biometrics as the risk of abuse is hereby minimized.

2.1. *Biometric systems must be designed in such a way that they take the utmost account to privacy protection.* It is always important that the objective of a biometric solution is reached with the least possible violation of the privacy of users. An initial assessment of this objective may be addressed by answering these questions:

- Does the design of the system avoid storing of sensitive personal information if at all possible (use of PbD)?
- Is it possible, in order to avoid central storage of sensitive personal data, to store data decentralized and ensuring that users have control over their own data—e.g. by using "system on card" or "match on card" solutions?
- Is it possible to achieve the objective of the system without linking the user's identity, e.g. the name of the user, with the biometric data?

- Are there alternative solutions for users who cannot or do not want to use biometry?
- Is it possible to use a pseudonym-based centralized database, e.g. a database where people's real names are replaced by pseudonyms?
- Is the biometric system isolated from networks?
- Is encryption used?
- Are there established procedures regulating the access to biometric templates or data associated with the templates?
- Are templates and associated data that are no longer used deleted?

2.2. *Registration of citizens and customers must be done while offering as much privacy protection as possible.* Recently a number of nightclubs, fitness clubs, etc. have asked the Data Protection Agency permission to use biometry. These requests have led to differing responses to which the working group makes the following comments:

- *Nightclubs, bars and restaurants should use "match on card technology".* The working group considers the wish to use biometry by the nightlife industry inappropriate. The industry's goals could be achieved in less privacy invading ways where the customers retain their biometry. One alternative would be to issue biometry based smart cards to guests and thus avoiding the current bundling of name, image and biometry. The working group estimates that storing both biometric data such as name and image in a central database represents an unnecessary interference with individual privacy. Instead the goal may be achieved by "match on card technology", i.e. a solution where the biometric data is stored in encrypted form on a plastic card with a chip that does the matching with the outcome of a scan of the guest's fingerprint. Another alternative would be the use of negative lists, where only the unwanted guests are registered. Such solutions might be challenged by blacklisted guests trying to fool the scanners by misplacing or "twisting" their fingers to avoid matching and gain access. Any solution based on negative lists or self-service requires scanners and matching technology that cannot be fooled by falsified fingerprints. In general, it is necessary to establish robust systems of readers that cannot be cheated, and continually monitor technological developments and continuously upgrade the security.
- *Fitness Clubs should use "match on card technology".* Several fitness clubs have applied for permission to use biometrics in order to avoid cheating while providing easier access to the clubs for members. The Data Protection Agency has refused to allow those gyms to use a system with an associated database where member's biometry would be stored in encrypted form. The working group believes that the gyms should be able to issue membership cards based on "match on card technology"—a solution where the biometric data in encrypted form is stored on the card's chip and access to the fitness club will be based on a match with the result of a scan of the user's fingerprint. This solution implies an additional cost

for the fitness clubs; but the system will also reduce the problem due to cheating with membership cards. The working group recommends that such a system must be voluntary and based on consent from users, and it should be possible to choose an alternative that does not reduce the service to the users compared to the biometric solution.

- Industry must work together on a common solution in which users retain control over own data. In light of the above-mentioned requests from private companies opportunities for private companies to jointly design a system—that enhances security, enables the use of services more convenient, and lets users retain control over their own data—should be explore. A suitable business case to explore in this context is biometric "match on card technology"—possibly combined with a pin code—as a replacement for access cards, membership cards, debit cards, etc.

3. A future biometric citizen cards will be based on "System on Card technology", or similar technologies. The working group believes that a citizen card with encrypted biometric data, which is based on "System on Card technology" or similar technologies, is a desirable solution from a safety point of view. "System on Card" means that the user by means of biometric identification has access to a personal card that contains a series of electronic keys for different purposes—including exchanging information with public authorities. Users utilizing this technology will have full control over their own data, and the system will be more privacy protective than for example the current digital signature. The working group recommends that a citizen card is based on decentralized data storage and that the citizen via the card can activate a variety of keys. In cases of theft or loss of card it must be possible to block the card and create a new without significant costs to neither the public nor the user. The price for such a system is currently relatively high, and hence, it is worthwhile to consider alternatives to a citizen card issued and funded by the state. The working group estimates that it will soon be possible to use biometry in mobile phones, PDAs and similar mobile devices where access to the stored information, codes and keys are controlled by the users themselves. The working group notices that use of mobile phone rather than a citizen card will have several advantages:

- The users are already accustomed to use mobile phone
- Users (always) carry their mobile phone
- Users pay for it themselves
- The mobile phone has built-in processor and can therefore generate codes and keys
- An increasing number of mobile phones have camera, microphone and touch-sensitive display, which potentially allows the use of the following biometric technologies: Dynamics of typing, iris scanning, facial recognition, signature analysis and voice recognition, and more will follow soon.

4. *Start by defining the purpose of the biometric solution.* If the purpose of the biometric solution is clearly defined in advance it is possible to avoid unrealistic expectations of the solution's capabilities. Experiences from other countries

show that lack of purpose specification may result in biometric solutions that do not meet the expectations of neither the companies nor the customers. Hence, the working group recommends creating maximum clarity on the biometric solution's real purpose and performance from the beginning of the development of the solution. This will also highlight potential pitfalls, e.g. the risk of so-called "function creep", which means that data is used for anything other than the original purpose. The working group recommends that a staff handbook or similar states the purpose of the biometric system and also defines exactly what the data collected will be used for. It will give employees the assurance that data is not used for purposes other than those intended. The working group considers that a clear and objective specification will provide reassurance about the biometric solution among employees/users. Simultaneously it limits the risk of misuse of data.

The working group emphasizes that the possible consequences of misuse of data collected in a biometric solution depends on the solution's size and scope.

16.3.2 The Broader Recommendations 5–10

The following recommendations are primarily aimed at larger biometric installations:

5. *The security of a biometric system depends on the security of the entire system.* The security of a biometric system will always depend on the security of the entire system enclosing it including—but not limited to—the enclosing IT solution. The working group emphasizes the importance of assessing the security of a system holistically. The risk in any given system of hacking and spoofing[2] must be assessed in all the phases of usage, both in relation to enrollment and other usages of the system. The working group points out that the enrollment process in a biometric system is a particularly vulnerable stage. It requires only one inattentive employee in the enrollment to create a legally issued passport where the biometric data fits with someone else's identity.

6. *Procedures for enrollment of biometric data must be standardized.* To ensure interoperability across borders—the interoperability of products, systems and business processes to work together on solving a common task—the working group recommends standardization of the enrollment of biometric data. Preferably by global standards, but at least by European. The working group recommends that a person before being enrolled in a biometric solution is informed of the purpose and extent of registration. It should also be possible for the user to see and check whether the registered information is correct. The enrollment procedure shall also contain a clear, standardized procedure on how to remove

---

[2]Spoofing is when a person pretends to be someone else, for example by using a fake fingerprint.

data about a user from the system. Trained staff and transparent procedures must ensure full transparency for the users enrolled. Standardized procedures for deleting data must also be in place.

7. *Procedures for storage and matching of biometric data must be standardized.* The working group recommends avoiding central databases for biometric solutions whenever possible. If a biometric solution is based on a central database anyhow then the quality of data must be maximized and examined by certified personnel. At the same time it must be possible for users to retract or edit their own data, if users find that there are deficiencies in the data recorded. There also has to be standard procedures to handle complaints which fully respects the individual's sovereignty and supports the procedures in a democratic society. The working group recommends further never storing the biometric data in raw format as with a digital image of a fingerprint. Instead data must be stored as encrypted templates. This will reduce the risk of identity theft and misuse of personal data significantly. The working group disrecommends outsourcing data processing to third parties as this reduces the ability to ensure safety control of the stored information. Finally, the working group recommends greater standardization at the technical level in terms of common algorithms, calibration and interface and in relation to the training of certified personnel. Standardization in these areas should be global, at least at EU level. The working group recommends that biometric matching only matches the biometric data without requesting the personal data linked to the biometric data. This reduces the risk of sensitive personal information falling into the wrong hands significantly.

8. *There must always be safe alternatives and "fall-back procedures".* The working group notes that biometric identification also has its weaknesses: Biometry will never be 100 percent accurate and biometric systems will always both reject and accept a share of "wrong" persons. Additionally some people cannot provide usable biometric features, e.g. a fingerprint might be damaged in a way that makes it impossible to register correctly. These circumstances make it impossible to create a secure system based solely on biometry. There will always be a need for one or more clearly defined alternatives—so-called "fall-back procedure." The operators, e.g. in automated border control, must be trained to treat both correctly and incorrectly dismissed the people in a decent way to prevent social stigma and the like.

9. *There is a need for more testing of biometric systems.* It is currently very difficult to compare the performance of different biometric systems. Most of the available tests have been carried out by the producers themselves in laboratories and not exposed to the errors in real environments where systems are applied. An extensive testing of biometric systems by the British government has shown a very large real error rate for systems based on fingerprint scanning, iris recognition or facial recognition. The working group recommends introducing more standardized tests thereby creating more openness about the true capabilities of biometric systems.

10. *Touch-free devices should be used in environments where the interest of hygiene is important.* The working group recommends non-contact scanners or remote

sensors in applications needing a high degree of hygiene. E.g., scanning the hand a few centimeters above the scanner would be useful in hospitals. The working group suggests scanning of iris or vein in these contexts as an alternative to fingerprint scanning.

16.4 Discussion and Comparison to European Recommendations

In [1] the EU Article 29 Data Protection Working Party has applied the EU Data Protection Directive [7] to biometry. It contains similar recommendations as the Danish working group presented here. We will comment on the Danish recommendations and a few differences to the European in the following.

The need for guidance, pre-approval, and more resources for the Danish DPA in the first recommendation are targeting the Danish parliament and government. It reflects in part the wishes from industry to limit losses due to investment in the wrong technology; but it is certainly also a strong statement regarding the lack of technically qualified inspections by the Danish DPA in comparison to other DPAs in Europe.

The entire report from the working group embraces biometric technology positively while raising privacy concerns. The privacy concerns in the report are reaching beyond the biometric issues (the scope of this chapter) which also reflect that the working group wants to raise awareness on privacy issues due to the minor role played by privacy in the Danish public debate on security measures etc.

The recommendations in the two case stories to use "match on card technology" does address the concerns about central databases with potential sensitive personal data derived from biometric samples. To prevent leakage of biometric data "system on card technology" would have been even better. In the case of blacklisting we find the collection of non-blacklisted customers out of proportion and thus a database of the blacklisted would be more suitable—even if it is centralized. The enrolled individuals should however have the right to challenge their enrollment by taking the issue to a court to ensure fair practice. The rule of proportionality and fair usage seems more prominent in the Article 29 document.

There seams to be consensus regarding the observation that the collected biometric data must be considered *sensitive personal data* and specifically protected in accordance with article 8 [7].

The 10th recommendation suggests using non-contact scanners or remote sensors for hygienic purposes. While this certainly serves the purpose, it also exposes another risk in biometric systems: the collection of biometric data while the target is unaware of the scanning. We envision that some versions of such systems could allow us to pass through a protected gate without doing anything special and while potentially being unaware of the collection of our personal biometric data. The event might also be recorded without the knowledge and explicit consent of the user and this might later be utilized for additional surveillance purposes.

In the following we present our findings regarding the questions focusing on the privacy issues imposed by applying biometry to the security solutions:

1. Does the added biometry make the final solution more or less reliable and trustworthy?
2. Are the biometric data processed and stored securely?
3. Are the collected biometric data protected against being reused for additional purposes (function creep)?
4. Does the biometric solution prevent unfair discrimination of groups or individuals?

16.4.1 Reliability

Though promising in many application areas, biometry is not the silver bullet solving security issues completely. Biometry, like other security solutions, will never be able to create 100 percent security as they are based on probability. This does not imply that biometry should not be used at all; instead any security solution based on biometrics must also be assessed with respect to the likelihood of providing wrong answers. Even though biometric solutions are usually published with probability figures for false matches (FAR = False Acceptance Rate) and for not matching where it should (FRR = False Rejection Rate), these figures are usually made with the assumption that both the enrollment and all provisions of a biometric sample for test are error-free. Hence, additionally the probability of false enrollment and the probability of providing a false biometric sample must also be assessed. Resent research [8] tries to address the latter by also testing "aliveness" of the biometric sample with a certain (high) probability.

To compare biometric security solutions with each other and with other security solutions, one has to make a full probability model including all these factors and add it to the security and risk assessment of the system/assets to be protected.

16.4.2 Protection of Biometric Data

Biometric solutions must always address the privacy issues involved in utilizing personal data about an individual. Whether data is original or derived from biometric features of a person (as in biometric templates), the whole idea of using biometry, is to link these data to an entity (very often a specific individual). Thus when biometric data is collected, the EU data protection directive [7] demands special care about the processing and storage of the data (article 6 [7]). If the biometric data is also linked to other personal data, the EU data protection directive demands an even higher degree of protection (article 8 [7]). Moreover, the rule of proportionality applies (article 6–8 [7]), i.e., the privacy invasion must be weighted against alternative measures to the achieved the same goal.

The maintenance and use of the enrollment data for match-processing impose a risk of privacy exposure. We describe this risk from high to low risk by focusing on how a biometric system depends on protection and control over the sensor, the processing, and the maintenance of the enrollment data. The sensor introduces a risk of falsification, listed from high to low risk:

1. Public unsupervised sensors (might even be tampered with at the uplink to the system).
2. Tamperproof and supervised sensors with uplink protection.
3. Tamperproof and supervised sensors with build-in template generators.
4. Tamperproof and supervised sensors with build-in template generators and match-processing.
5. Tamperproof and supervised sensors with build-in template generators and match-processing towards a build-in database of templates.

Though unlinking the biometric templates from the physical person by one-way function encoding (e.g. hash-functions) does prevent leakage of private information when the template is leaked, the use of biometry for identity management creates other links between the encoded template and other identification data linked to the user.

16.4.3 Function Creep

Any unintended usage of collected data must in general be prohibited to protect against function creep. Moreover, the collected data should be maintained in a way that prevents an imposter from creating a (false) matching sample.

As biometry might include data which could potentially be used to derive other characteristics of the individual, like race, sex, age, religious believe, and health, it is specifically important to ensure that such characteristics cannot be derived from the stored data, e.g. the templates.

According to article 8 [7] such data is classified as personal data. They must be protected and only collected when specifically necessary.

16.4.4 Discrimination

The use of biometry might also lead to discrimination when it excludes users with certain limitations on biometric features. Some people might not be enrolled, and some might not be able to use the biometric systems, e.g. due to mental or physical handicaps. So providers of solutions using biometric technologies must at least pay attention to and limit any discriminatory effects.

We have found it hard to ensure inclusive—non-discriminative—biometric solutions when deploying sensors recording physical or behavioral characteristics as such characteristics might be missing for at least a minor part of the users. The combination of multiple characteristics with allowance to omit some for each user (where the user is not able to provide the characteristics) is one way to pursuit further. Usually multi-modal biometry is used to enhance security by requiring multiple classes of characteristics, so the usage of multi-modal biometry for inclusiveness challenge this enhanced security.

For multi-modal biometry it is important to know whether the different derived templates from each biometric feature of the same individual can be considered dependent or independent variables. If we can ensure a large independence between different types of biometric samples from the same individual, e.g., between the ten different fingerprints, or between finger, iris or hand geometry of the same person, the multi-modal biometrics enhance security. However, to include individuals missing a few features (e.g. a pair of fingers), the interdependency among the templates does not matter. Ultimately, we might create template at enrollment using on set of biometric features and later match these templates against collection of other sets of biometric features.

16.4.5 Conclusion

Biometric technology can be used and misused, and its application might have both positive and negative implication. Especially when concerned with privacy, the use of personal information inherently present in biometry must be assessed thoroughly. Hence, it is important that guidelines for application of biometric technology ensure a positive impact on both security and privacy.

During the year 2009, the Danish Board of Technology instantiated a working group on the use of biometric technology in the Danish society. The report from the working group contains a set of recommendations to legislators, regulators, corporations and individuals on the appropriate use of biometric technologies as well as different usage scenarios and an overview of the current state of biometric technologies.

The Danish recommendations falls in line with those of the EU Article 29 working party, but the Danish recommendations also addresses specific deficiencies in the enforcing of data protection in Denmark.

Acknowledgements   Each year the Danish Board of Technology carries out a debate-creating IT security project for the Ministry of Science, Technology and Innovation. The Directors of the Board of Technology have in conjunction with the Danish IT and Telecom Agency decided to implement a technology assessment of biometry as the 2009 project. The project aims to assess the benefits and challenges introduced by the proliferation of biometric technologies.

To illustrate this, the Board of Technology has established a multidisciplinary working group. The working group was lead by Project Manager, Jacob Skjødt Nielsen and Project Officer, Peter Lemcke Frederiksen from the Danish Board of Technology and included experts from civil society (Anette Høyrup, Danish Consumer Council), law (Charlotte Bagger Tranberg, Aalborg University), industry (Henning Mortensen, Confederation of Danish Industry and Lars Kornbek, Vitani A/S), computer science (Niels Christian Juul, Roskilde University), and ethics (Thomas Laursen, Secretariat of the Danish Council of Ethics).

On September, 30, 2009 the Board of Technology held a workshop where a wide range of selected stakeholders debated a discussion paper from the working group and provided input to the project.

Its content is also presented in Danish on the website www.biometri.info. The website is open to the public and enables the Danes to seek information about biometry and to express their views in an attitude survey.·

COST Action 2101   EU COST action 2101, Biometry for IDentification and Smart cards (BIDS) has been collaborating for four years on biometrics research and industrial applications. In May 2010, the action hosted a workshop on Security and Privacy in Biometrics at University of Las Palmas.

Contributions   Both the collaboration and discussions in the working group hosted by the Danish board of Technology and within the COST action 2101 has influenced this chapter. The contributions of both are hereby acknowledged.

This work was also presented and discussed in a preliminary form at the COST action 2101 Workshop on Security and Privacy in Biometrics at University of Las Palmas, Grand Canarias, May 2010.

References

1. Article 29 Data Protection Working Party. Working document on biometrics, WP 80, 12168/02/EN, 1 August 2003. http://ec.europa.eu/justice_home/fsj/privacy/docs/wpdocs/2003/wp80_en.pdf
2. Chandra A, Calderon T (2005) Challenges and constraints to the diffusion of biometrics in information systems. Communications of the ACM 48(12):101–106
3. Datatilsynet. Adgangssystem til motionscenter baseret på fingeraftryk. A decision in Danish from the Danish Data Protection Agency on an access control system for a fitness center based on finger prints, date: 2004.11.26, journo 2004-219-0208. http://www.datatilsynet.dk/afgoerelser/arkiv-over-afgoerelser/artikel/adgangssystem-til-motionscenter-baseret-paa-fingeraftryk/
4. Datatilsynet. Adgangskontrol på diskoteker og førelse af intern karantæneliste. A decision in Danish from the Danish Data Protection Agency on access control at discothèques and maintence of an internal list of quarantined persons, date: 2008.06.20, journo 2008-42-0742. http://www.datatilsynet.dk/afgoerelser/arkiv-over-afgoerelser/artikel/adgangskontrol-paa-diskoteker/
5. Datatilsynet. Afslag på tilladelse til advarselsregister for diskoteker. A decision in Danish from the Danish Data Protection Agency refusing permission to maintain a warning register for discothèques, date: 2008.08.02, journo 2008-43-0011. http://www.datatilsynet.dk/afgoerelser/arkiv-over-afgoerelser/artikel/afslag-paa-tilladelse-til-advarselsregister-for-diskoteker/
6. European Data Protection Supervisor, Peter Hustinx. The case for responsible use of biometrics from the perspective of the European Data Protection Supervisor. Third joint parliamentary meeting on security: "Which technologies and for what security? The new instruments of internal and civil security", Maison de la Chimie, Paris, 23 March 2010. http://www.edps.europa.eu/EDPSWEB/webdav/site/mySite/shared/Documents/EDPS/Publications/Speeches/2010/10-03-23_Speech_Paris_EN.pdf
7. European Union. Directive 95/46/Ec of the European Parliament and of the council on the protection of individuals with regard to the processing of personal data and on the free movement of such data (EU data protection directive), 23 November 1995. http://www.edps.europa.eu/EDPSWEB/webdav/site/mySite/shared/Documents/EDPS/DataProt/Legislation/Dir_1995_46_EN.pdf

8. Qureshi MK (2011) Liveness detection of biometric traits. International Journal of Information Technology and Knowledge Management 4(1):293–295
9. Teknologirådet. Biometri—brug af biometriske teknologier I det danske samfund. Anbefalinger fra en arbejdsgruppe under Teknologirådet. A report in Danish from the board of technology on the use of biometric technologies in the Danish society. Teknologirådets rapporter 2010/2, ISBN 978-87-91614-55-2, March 2010
10. Tranberg CB (2008) Biometric data in Scandinavia. European Business Lawe Review 19(2):387–403
11. Tranberg CB (2010) Tommelen opp for biometri? In: Schartum DW (ed) Overvåkning i en rettsstat. Fakbokforlaget, Oslo, pp 262–280

Index

Index

Printed in the United States
By Bookmasters